LIVES OF THE GEORGIAN AGE

LIVES BEFORE THE TUDORS

in preparation

LIVES OF THE TUDOR AGE

1485–1603

by Ann Hoffmann

LIVES OF THE STÜART AGE

1603–1714

by Laurence Urdang Associates

LIVES OF THE GEORGIAN AGE

1714–1837

by Laurence Urdang Associates

LIVES OF THE VICTORIAN AGE

1837–1901

in preparation

★

Series Editor: ROGER CLEEVE

The biographies presented in these books are of
those who, during the period covered, attained
their peak of achievement. Cross-references are
given to the relevant volume where this distinction
is not obvious.

LIVES

OF THE

GEORGIAN AGE

1714–1837

Compiled by Laurence Urdang Associates
Editor: William Gould
Managing Editor: Patrick Hanks

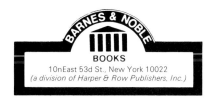

BARNES & NOBLE
BOOKS
10nEast 53d St., New York 10022
(a division of Harper & Row Publishers, Inc.)

Published in the U.S.A. 1978 by Harper & Row Publishers, Inc.
Barnes & Noble Import Division

Designed by Frederick Price

Library of Congress Cataloging in Publication Data

Laurence Urdang Associates.
Lives of the Georgian age.

Includes bibliographies.
1. Great Britain—Biography. 2. Great Britain
—History—1714–1837—Biography. I. Gould,
William. II. Title.
CT781.L35 1978   920'.041   77-2684
ISBN 0-06-494332-1

Filmset and printed in Great Britain by
BAS Printers Limited, Over Wallop, Hampshire

PREFACE

The present volume contains approximately 300 short biographies of eminent men and women of the Georgian or Hanoverian period from 1714 to 1837.

As with other volumes in this series, selection has proved difficult and what some may consider serious omissions are unfortunately inevitable. In general, entries have been confined to those people who made a real impact on the age. A few influential foreigners who lived and worked in Britain have been included, and a careful selection has been made from among those colonial Americans who flourished before the final break with Great Britain. The men of 1776, however – Washington, Jefferson, and the other leaders of the American Revolution – have been omitted. Their lives are part of the history of an independent America.

The full articles, arranged alphabetically, appear under the surnames of the persons concerned, while a cross-reference appears under a title. In the case of married women, it has been decided to place the article under the surname by which the subject is best known. Thus, the article on Fanny Burney has been placed at BURNEY, FRANCES, with a cross-reference under ARBLAY, whereas the article on Mrs. Thrale appears under THRALE, MRS. HESTER, with a cross-reference at PIOZZI.

A highly selective bibliography is given at the end of most entries. This includes the standard biography and definitive editions of works where applicable. Books of a more general nature have usually been omitted from individual articles for lack of space, but a small number of works having general relevance for the period is provided below. Locations of publication have been provided only for books originating outside the United Kingdom.

In addition to the bibliographies, many articles also carry a selective iconography, listing the principal portraits and their locations, with special regard to the accessibility of the paintings to the interested viewer.

Sources

The *Dictionary of National Biography* is still a major source of information, although in many respects it has been superseded by more recent research involving modern interpretations of historical facts and events. Information on the lives of the colonial Americans included here may be found in Allan Johnson (ed.), *Dictionary of American Biography* (20 vols.; New York, 1927: reissued with supplements in 16 vols.; New York, 1972).

No entirely satisfactory modern bibliographical volume exists for the Hanoverian period. The excellent *Bibliography of British History: the Eighteenth Century, 1714–1789*, edited by Stanley Pargellis and D. J. Medley, was published in 1951 and is now dated. G. R. Elton, *Modern Historians on British History, 1485–1945* (1970) goes some way to filling the gap. Papers relating to the period are to be found in *English Historical Documents* (vol. 10 edited by D. B. Horn and Mary Ransome, 1957, and vol. 11 edited by A. A. Aspinall and E. A. Smith, 1959). Further important sources, including some general histories, are given below.

J. R. Alden, *The American Revolution 1775–1783* (1954).

R. J. Allen, *Life in Eighteenth-Century England* (Boston, Mass., 1941).

T. S. Ashton, *An Economic History of England: The Eighteenth Century* (1972, rev. ed.).

T. S. Ashton, *The Industrial Revolution* (1969, rev. ed.).

G. Beard, *Georgian Craftsmen and their Work* (1966).

J. D. Bernal, *Science and Industry in the Nineteenth Century* (1953).

Sir C. M. Bowra, *The Romantic Imagination* (1950).

Sir Arthur Bryant, *The Years of Endurance* (1942).

Sir Arthur Bryant, *Years of Victory* (1944).

C. W. Chalklin, *The Provincial Towns of Georgian England* (1975).

Sir G. N. Clark, *The Idea of the Industrial Revolution* (1953).

Sir R. Coupland, *The British Anti-Slavery Movement* (1933).

J. M. Creed and J. S. B. Smith (ed.), *Religious Thought in the Eighteenth Century* (1934).

Bonamy Dobrée (ed.), *From Anne to Victoria* (1937).

Sir Keith Feiling, *The Second Tory Party, 1714–1832* (1938).

D. Fitz-Gerald (ed.), *Georgian Furniture* (1969, rev. ed.).

R. Hart, *English Life in the Eighteenth Century* (1970).

A. R. Humphreys, *The Augustan World* (1954).

D. Jorret, *Britain, 1688–1815* (1965).

M. Jourdain and F. Rose, *English Furniture: the Georgian Period, 1750–1830* (1953).

W. E. H. Lecky and L. P. Curtis, *A History of Ireland in the Eighteenth Century* (reissued Chicago 1972).

D. Marshall, *Eighteenth-Century England* (1962).

Sir L. B. Namier, *England in the Age of the American Revolution* (1962, rev. ed.).

Sir L. B. Namier, *The Structure of Politics at the Accession of George III* (2 vols.; 1929, 1957).

A. Nicoll, *A History of Early Eighteenth Century Drama* (1952, rev. ed.).

A. Nicoll, *A History of Late Eighteenth Century Drama* (1952, rev. ed.).

A. Nicoll, *A History of Early Nineteenth Century Drama* (1955, rev. ed.).

Gearold O'Tuthaigh, *Ireland Before the Famine, 1799–1848* (1972).

Sir Charles Petrie, *The Jacobite Movement* (1959, rev. ed.).

J. Piper, *English Romantic Artists* (1946).

J. H. Plumb, *England in the Eighteenth Century* (1963, rev. ed.).

J. H. Plumb, *The First Four Georges* (1956).

K. T. Rowland, *Eighteenth Century Inventions* (1974).

C. Sinclair-Stevenson, *Inglorious Rebellion: the Jacobite Risings of 1708, 1715 and 1719* (1971).

J. Summerson, *Architecture in Britain, 1530–1830* (1953).

N. Sykes, *Church and State in England in the XVIIIth Century* (1934).

P. D. G. Thomas, *The House of Commons in the Eighteenth Century* (1971).

D. Thomson, *England in the Nineteenth Century* (1950).

G. Tillotson, *Eighteenth Century English Literature* (1969).

A. S. Turberville, *The House of Lords in the Eighteenth Century* (1927).

E. K. Waterhouse, *Painting in Britain, 1530–1790* (1962).

J. Steven Watson, *The Reign of George III, 1760–1815* (1960).

B. Willey, *The Eighteenth Century Background* (1940: reissued 1972).

Basil Williams, *The Whig Supremacy, 1714–1760* (1962, rev. ed.).

E. N. Williams, *The Eighteenth Century Constitution, 1688–1815* (1960).

E. N. Williams, *Life in Georgian England* (1962).

A. Wolf, *A History of Science, Technology and Philosophy in the 18th Century* (1952, rev. ed. by D. McKie).

E. L. Woodward, *The Age of Reform, 1815–1870* (1962, rev. ed.).

Iconographies

Information on portraits is derived largely from O. Millar, *Tudor, Stuart, and Early Georgian Portraits in the Royal Collection* (1963) and *Later Georgian Portraits in the Collection of Her Majesty the Queen* (1969; 2 vols.), and from Maureen Hill, *National Portrait Gallery: Concise Catalogue, 1856–1969* (1969). These authorities have been supplemented by other research.

Abbreviations

The few abbreviations used appear mainly in the bibliographies and iconographies. The principal ones are:

N.P.G.	National Portrait Gallery, London
R.T.H.	Radio Times Hulton Picture Library
Scottish N.P.G.	Scottish National Portrait Gallery, Edinburgh
V. & A.	Victoria and Albert Museum, London

Dates

Until September 1752, England employed the Julian or Old Style calendar, which by the time of its abandonment was eleven days behind the Gregorian or New Style calendar in use in the rest of Europe. The changeover from Old Style to New Style dating in Britain has been disregarded in this volume and following the custom of most historians, dates before 2 September 1752 may be assumed to be given according to the Julian system and the rest according to the Gregorian.

For those persons who do not fit neatly into the Georgian period, the practice followed has again been to cross-refer individuals to an earlier or later volume in the series. Thus the entry for John Churchill, for example, directs the reader to an article in *Lives of the Stuart Age*, while Sir Robert Peel is cross-referred to *Lives of the Victorian Age*. A diligent attempt has been made to determine whether individuals should be entered in this or another volume by establishing the period of their peak of achievement.

CONTRIBUTORS

Charles Boyle
Edward R. Brace
Susan Brown
Alan Dingle
Sue Gaisford
William Gould
Francesca Greenoak
Patrick Hanks

Sarah Hayes
Catharine Hutton
Alan Isaacs
Thomas Hill Long
Catharine Limm
John Marsh
Lila Pennant
Lois Powell

Joan Ratcliffe
Edwin Riddell
Kenneth Scholes
Arthur Taylor
John Hugh Thomas
Alexandra Urdang
Eileen Williams

ILLUSTRATIONS

WITH ACKNOWLEDGEMENTS

A

Adam, Robert (1728–92), architect and designer.

Robert Adam was born at Kirkcaldy, the second son of a prosperous architect. He was educated at Edinburgh University, where he soon began to make architectural sketches, as yet heavily indebted to William Kent (q.v.) and the Palladians. In 1754, accompanied by the aristocratic Charles Hope and with £5,000 in his pocket, he set off for the Grand Tour. Using his wealth and status to open doors, Adam stayed at, and studied, many of the great houses of France.

In Florence he met Clerisseau, one of Europe's finest architectural draughtsmen, and immediately employed him as his tutor. Adam then spent two years in Rome, studying antique statues, visiting Roman archaeological sites, and making many architectural sketches, whose extravagance and fantasy reveal a debt to his friend Piranesi. Perhaps Adam's most fruitful experience was a five-week visit to Diocletian's palace at Spalato; it was the first such study ever made of a Roman domestic building, and it finally freed Adam from the constricting 'rules' of classical architecture by demonstrating that the Romans had used a much freer hand in their buildings than later generations had cared to admit.

On his return to England Adam set up in practice with his brother James, and from then on they received numerous commissions from the famous and influential. In 1758 the brothers designed the Admiralty screen in Whitehall, and in 1762 Robert was appointed royal architect. However, during the first decade of his career he seldom worked on public buildings; indeed he did not design anything from scratch, being instead employed by the aristocracy to remodel existing houses or to complete half-finished ones. Amongst his earliest efforts were Hatchlands in Surrey and Shardeloes in Buckinghamshire. Later, in such houses as Syon Park and Osterley Park in Middlesex, Kedleston Hall in Derbyshire, and Harewood in Yorkshire, Adam's style matured. Syon Park (1762) typically involved recasting the interior of an original Jacobean structure. Adam's solution was to create an impeccably neoclassical succession of staterooms arranged around the central quadrangle.

At Kedleston Hall, left unfinished by James Paine, Adam built a grand domed

salon and fronted it with a façade in the shape of a triumphal arch, a neoclassical flourish new to domestic architecture. Not that Adam was particularly attached to neoclassicism – its immobility was alien to him; his method was to select the best features of the many available styles and blend them together in an intensely personal way, which went beyond mere eclecticism. His chief limitation was an inability to plan on a large scale – his essentially decorative style produced far better interiors than exteriors.

In 1768 the Adam brothers embarked upon their grandiose private venture, the Adelphi, noted for its 'palace' treatment of the terrace. An enormous Thames-side block with protruding wings, it incorporated wharves, warehouses, and an advanced system of multilevel traffic circulation; but owing to legal difficulties, it became a financial liability to the brothers and they disposed of it by lottery in 1773.

In 1773 Adam published the first folio volume of his *Works of Architecture*, which was a best-seller, and the following year, at Derby House in Grosvenor Square, he brilliantly contrived to fit a grand sequence of rooms of contrasting shapes within the constricted space of a terraced house. Here the interior decoration showed a new restraint, even austerity.

By 1775, however, the enormous cost of the War of American Independence was severely restricting house-building, and the fortunes of the Adam brothers declined accordingly. Although Horace Walpole dismissed the Adam style as 'gingerbread', in 1777 Robert adopted Walpole's beloved Gothic style for Culzean Castle, in Ayrshire. This fantastically shaped fortress with Georgian detail and entirely classical interiors was perhaps a result of the many romantic drawings of moonlit mock-Gothic edifices that Adam was producing at that time. His last buildings, however, reverted to a more classical style: Edinburgh University (1789) was obviously inspired by Adam's Italian experience, while Charlotte Square, Edinburgh (1791) and Fitzroy Square, London (1790) were magnificent examples of his 'palace' street designs.

Robert Adam was an ambitious man, and for much of his working life he was a famous one. However, this was only achieved by utter dedication; he not only designed houses, but their entire contents as well, from bookcases and sedan chairs to salt cellars. Though he took part in public life, becoming M.P. for Kinross in 1768, he was not a particularly well-loved person. He died at his house in Albemarle Street on 3 March 1792, and was buried in Westminster Abbey.

A. T. Bolton, *The Architecture of Robert and James Adam* (1922).

J. Fleming, *Robert Adam and his Circle in Edinburgh and Rome* (1962).

E. Kauffman, *Architecture in the Age of Reason* (Cambridge, Mass., 1955).

J. Lees-Milne, *The Age of Adam* (1948).

Portraits: oil, three-quarter length, attributed to George Willison, *c.* 1770: N.P.G.; plaque, miniature, by James Tassie, *c.* 1792: Scottish N.P.G.

Addington, Henry (1757–1844), 1st Viscount Sidmouth; statesman; Speaker of the House of Commons (1789–1801), First Lord of the Treasury (1801–4), and Home Secretary (1812–22).

Henry Addington was born on 30 May 1757 in London, the son of Dr. Anthony Addington, a prominent physician and the personal doctor and friend of the Earl of Chatham (see Pitt, William, the Elder). Educated at Cheam, at Winchester College, and at Brasenose College, Oxford, Addington embarked on a legal career, but his friendship with William Pitt the Younger, a friend from childhood, led him to abandon the law for politics. He was elected M.P. for Devizes, Wiltshire, in 1784, and when Pitt formed his first administration at the end of that year Addington was one of his most ardent supporters. He became Speaker of the House of Commons in 1789.

Addington's father died in 1790 and he came into the family property. His financial circumstances were now secure and he purchased a small estate at Woodley, near Reading. When war broke out with revolutionary France in 1793, Addington became a firm supporter of Pitt's war effort: he suggested the raising of a voluntary subscription (1797–8), donating £2,000 of his own to the fund, and he also organized and commanded a troop of volunteers at Woodley.

In 1801 Pitt carried the Act of Union with Ireland and promised the Irish Catholics emancipation as the price of their acquiescence. However, George III disapproved of Catholic emancipation and his fears were shared by Addington, who favoured the union for reasons of national security but preferred to coerce rather than to conciliate the Catholics into acceptance. The King wrote to the Speaker asking him to persuade Pitt not to press the point, and when Pitt proved unwilling to break his promise to the Irish, George invited Addington to form a ministry. Addington took office as First Lord of the Treasury in 1801.

Since the outbreak of war with France Britain's major role had been that of paymaster to her continental allies. The Treaty of Luneville (1801) had marked the military collapse of these allies and Britain's own ability to subsidize European armies was shaken if not exhausted. Addington recognized the war-weariness of the country and concluded the Peace of Amiens with France on 27 March 1802. The peace was highly popular and Addington immediately put the armed forces on a peace footing, much to the unease of Pitt and his friends. He seems to have been convinced of Bonaparte's sincerity, but before the end of the year it became apparent that the peace was no more than a temporary truce to enable the First Consul to consolidate his position in France. European expansion was still Napoleon's goal and war resumed in 1803 over Britain's refusal to return Malta to the Knights of St. John.

Addington, totally unsuitable as a war minister, planned a purely defensive effort based on British control of the seas. He was mercilessly attacked over the hasty rundown of the armed forces. Canning ridiculed Addington's stature as a leader in the cruel rhyme,

> Pitt is to Addington
> As London is to Paddington.

Addington, whose popularity quickly waned and whose authority was challenged by Pitt, resigned on 30 April 1804. In May Pitt formed his last administration and Addington, who was now raised to the peerage as Viscount Sidmouth, joined it in January 1805 as Lord President of the Council. However, the reconciliation was short-lived, for Pitt's and Sidmouth's supporters were openly hostile to one another and as a result Sidmouth resigned in June.

After Pitt's death in 1806 Sidmouth joined the coalition government of Lord Grenville and Charles James Fox (qq.v.), first as Lord Privy Seal and then as Lord President of the Council. He was out of sympathy with many of his new associates but felt it his duty to serve and hoped to exercise a moderating influence on their policies. He was not offered office by Perceval in 1809 but was taken into the government in 1812 again as Lord President of the Council. When Lord Liverpool (see Jenkinson, Robert) reconstructed the administration later that year after Perceval's assassination, Sidmouth became Home Secretary.

He continued in this post for ten years and had to contend with the agricultural and industrial depression caused by the war and with the social unrest and agitation that followed from this. Although a kindly man in personal relationships, Sidmouth reacted with unwavering sternness and severity to any civil disturbances such as the Luddite riots fearing that political unrest, if unrestrained, might lead to the excesses of the French Revolution. As popular discontent took on an increasingly political form he used all the methods of repression at his disposal. In 1817 he proposed the suspension of Habeas Corpus and the revival of laws against seditious meetings. He also tried to limit the freedom of the press and after the Peterloo massacre of 1819 it was Sidmouth who, with unseemly haste and provocative lack of tact, proceeded to thank publicly the magistrates and troops concerned. Soon afterwards he was responsible for introducing four of the repressive 'Six Acts' passed by the government.

Sidmouth retired from office in 1822, although he remained in the cabinet until 1824. In parliament he opposed Catholic emancipation in his last speech in 1829 and voted against the Reform Bill in 1832. He died on 15 February 1844.

F. O. Darvall, *Popular Disturbances and Public Order in Regency England* (1934).

G. Pellew, *The Life and Correspondence . . . of Viscount Sidmouth* (3 vols.; 1847).

P. Ziegler, *A Life of Henry Addington, First Viscount Sidmouth* (1965).

Portrait: water-colour, full-length, by G. Richmond, 1833: N.P.G.

Addison, Joseph (1672–1719), essayist, critic, and poet.

Joseph Addison was born on 1 May 1672 at Milston, Wiltshire, the eldest son of Lancelot Addison, who later became Dean of Lichfield. He was educated privately by his father and at Lichfield grammar school before spending a year at Charterhouse, where he became a friend of Richard Steele (q.v.), his future collaborator on the *Tatler* and the *Spectator*. He attended The Queen's College, Oxford, at the age of fifteen, and then held a demyship at Magdalen. He received his M.A. in 1693 and was a fellow of Magdalen from 1698 to 1711. As a student Addison distinguished himself as a writer of Latin verse that won praise from Dryden. He subsequently met Dryden, to whom he addressed his first poem in English, published in Dryden's miscellany *Examen Poeticum* (1693).

Addison's literary reputation grew rapidly. He became acquainted with Congreve and other prominent writers and his work was soon noticed by Sir John Somers and Charles Montagu, later 1st Earl of Halifax, the Chancellor of the Exchequer and leader of the Whigs (see *Lives of the Stuart Age*). At the request of these patrons, Addison wrote 'Poem to his Majesty' (1695). About this time he also published some verse translations of Ovid, the Latin poem '*Pax Gulielmi*', and an essay on Virgil's *Georgics*, which was printed in Dryden's translation of Virgil. Although he had early entertained a notion of taking holy orders – indeed, the moralizing tone of the lay preacher is a conspicuous feature of his prose style – he now decided in favour of a more active life. His Whig sponsors procured for him a pension of £300 from the government and from 1699 to 1703 he travelled in France and Italy, where he continued his literary work, prepared himself for diplomatic service, and, during much of his stay, acted as tutor to Edward Wortley Montagu. While abroad he wrote one of his best poems, 'Letter from Italy' (published in 1704), addressed to Halifax, and a topographical poem, 'Remarks on

Several Parts of Italy' (1705).

When Addison returned to England the Whigs were out of office, his patron Halifax having fallen from power on the death of William III. Addison's own fortunes were not long affected by this, however. He came to know a number of leading Whigs and became a member of the Kit-Cat Club. On the recommendation of Halifax, Addison was chosen to eulogize the Duke of Marlborough's victory at Blenheim. 'The Campaign' (1705) was instantly popular in London and well pleased his political patrons. As a result, Addison was appointed a commissioner of excise. During the next few years he led a full life, both politically and in the field of literature. He assisted Steele in completing his comedy *The Tender Husband* (1705). The following year he served as Under-Secretary of State to Sir Charles Hedges and to his successor, the Duke of Sunderland, and then acted as secretary to Halifax on a diplomatic mission to the Elector of Hanover. The opera *Rosamund*, with text by Addison, was produced in 1707 but was not a success. In 1708 Addison was elected to parliament, briefly holding a seat for Lostwithiel, Cornwall, and then, from 1709 until his death, for Malmesbury. Although he never spoke in the House of Commons and was never as interested in politics as was Steele, for example, Addison could be an effective political pamphleteer when he chose and this talent was obviously appreciated by the political leaders who had supported him from the first. *The Present State of the War* (1708) was an able defence of the government and led to his being made chief secretary to the Earl of Wharton, whom he accompanied to Ireland when Wharton became Lord Lieutenant (1708–10).

In Ireland Addison kept in friendly contact with Swift, whom he had known in London. He also learned that the pseudonymous Isaac Bickerstaff who had founded the *Tatler* in April 1709 was Richard Steele. To this thrice-weekly periodical Addison sent contributions, writing forty-six complete numbers and, when he returned to England, collaborating with Steele on thirty-six more. The *Tatler* was typical of the increased journalistic activity that occurred because the Licensing Act had not been renewed by parliament in 1695. It was still not possible, however, to make outspoken political comment in print. Addison's contributions to the *Tatler* have no political content, but Steele's readiness to write political essays inevitably brought on conflict with the Tory government then in power and as a result the *Tatler* ceased publication in 1711. In March of that year, two months after the last number of the *Tatler* appeared, Addison and Steele founded the *Spectator*, which appeared until December 1712, after which it was briefly revived by Addison alone in 1714. It is difficult enough to discern any political matter in

the *Tatler*; the *Spectator* is completely devoid of politics and in this it reflects the dominance of Addison, who from the start took the leading part in the second periodical. He wrote 274 numbers (signed C., L., I., and O.) and twenty-four further numbers after its revival in 1714. The importance of Addison's essays in the *Spectator* lies in the skill with which he popularized the ideals of Augustan culture. With an unerring instinct, Addison treated in restrained and lucid prose the topics that appealed to the intellectual interests of the middle class. Science, philosophy, and social behaviour were covered; the most original of his contributions, however, are the notion of taste, which he developed in some literary essays, the attention paid to the interests of female readers, and the genius with which he drew the character of Sir Roger de Coverley, who was created by Steele but raised to literary immortality by Addison. In general the civilized spirit of impartiality and common sense that informs Addison's work is summed up in the motto of the *Spectator*, 'Honour the gods according to the established modes.'

Addison contributed to several other periodicals, such as *The Whig Examiner* (1710) and Steele's *The Guardian* (1713), and reached the height of his literary career with the staging of *Cato* (1713), a tragedy most of which had been written while he was in Italy. With the death of Queen Anne, Addison once more entered the service of the Whigs and held a number of public offices, eventually becoming Secretary of State in 1717, a post he held for only a year, being forced to resign because of bad health. Addison married the Dowager Countess of Warwick in 1716. His comedy *The Drummer*, staged anonymously the same year, was a failure. The last few years of his life were marked by two unfortunate personal incidents. Of the first and lesser of

these little is clearly known. Pope, annoyed that Addison preferred another translation of the *Iliad* to his, satirized him as Atticus, the literary man 'Willing to wound, and yet afraid to strike'. Addison apparently was not angered by the attack, which he saw in manuscript; he made no reply and Pope did not publish the verses until long after Addison's death, when he incorporated them in a section of the 'Epistle to Dr. Arbuthnot'. The second, a serious quarrel, arose with Steele because of a political disagreement over the Peerage Bill, which Addison publicly supported and Steele attacked. The argument grew bitter as the two old friends exchanged personal remarks in print, and Addison died before a reconciliation could be effected.

In 1718 Addison retired from public life, having been given a pension of £1,500. He died at his wife's home, Holland House, on 17 June 1719 at the age of forty-seven. He is buried in Westminster Abbey.

George A. Aitken (ed.), *The Tatler* (4 vols.; 1898–9).
D. F. Bond (ed.), *The Spectator* (5 vols.; 1965).
D. F. Bond (ed.), *Critical Essays from the Spectator* (1970).
W. Graham (ed.), *Letters of Joseph Addison* (1941).
R. Hurd (ed.), *The Works of the Right Honourable Joseph Addison Esq.* (6 vols.; 1811: reprinted 1854–6).
P. Smithers, *The Life of Joseph Addison* (1968, rev. ed.).

Portraits: oil, half-length, by Kneller, 1703–10: N.P.G.; oil, three-quarter length, by Dahl, 1719: N.P.G.; oil, unknown artist: Ickworth, Suffolk.

Althorp, Viscount (1782–1845), see Spencer, John Charles.

Amherst, Jeffrey (1717–97), 1st Baron Amherst; field marshal and commander in chief of the army; leader of the campaign against the French in North America (1758–60).

Jeffrey Amherst was born on 29 January

1717 at Riverhead, Kent. His parents were neighbours of the Duke of Dorset, who took the boy into his service as a page. Recognizing his ability, the Duke obtained an ensigncy for him in the Foot Guards in 1731 and also brought him to the attention of General Ligonier, who was then commander of the army in Germany. Ligonier appointed him to his staff as aide-de-camp, a post which Amherst filled with distinction. He subsequently served on the Duke of Cumberland's staff, and by 1756 had been promoted to Lieutenant Colonel of the 15th Regiment.

In 1758 Pitt, on the advice of Ligonier, chose Amherst to lead an expedition of 14,000 men against the French in Canada. Pitt's object was to frustrate French plans to link the colonies of Canada and Louisiana, which would prevent further English expansion to the west. He also hoped to seize Montreal, the centre of French strength, and thus bring all of North America under British rule. To this end, he had selected a number of brilliant officers for the expedition, chief among them Wolfe (q.v.). Known for his prudent judgment, Amherst was put in command with the rank of major general. In May 1758 the army sailed from Portsmouth in 151 ships, landing first at Louisbourg, a strategic French island fortress at the mouth of the St. Lawrence. Wolfe and the grenadiers led a successful assault against the fort, which surrendered to the English forces on 26 July.

Amherst was then made commander in chief and assumed his command in Albany in September. He soon defeated the French at Fort Duquesne and then set about realizing Pitt's plan for the offensive against Montreal, a campaign that was to prove to be the main achievement of his career. Since Montreal seemed impregnable to direct attack, the English forces were divided into three for a converging advance on the city. Wolfe was assigned to lead one column westward up the St. Lawrence in order to capture Quebec. Another column, under General Prideaux, was to take Fort Niagara, thus severing French communication with Louisiana. Amherst accepted the task of taking Ticonderoga and other French forts on Lake Champlain, thus removing the danger of French attacks against the New England colonies. In July 1759 Niagara and Ticonderoga were captured; in August, Amherst took Crown Point; and in September Quebec fell and was occupied by Wolfe. The three forces then advanced on Montreal, which surrendered without resistance in September 1760. Canada became British.

Amherst was immediately rewarded with the appointment of Governor General of North America, received the thanks of parliament for the victory, and was made a Knight of the Bath. He remained in America for three years, chiefly involved in an unsuccessful attempt to suppress an Indian rebellion led by Pontiac. He returned to England a popular hero, however, since his failure to quell the Indians went unreported. He was made Governor of Virginia in 1768, an office he resigned shortly afterwards because of a quarrel with George III. He was soon on good terms with the King again, however, for George became aware of his great popularity and, somewhat later, welcomed the firm support that Amherst gave to him during the War of American Independence.

For the rest of his life Amherst held numerous offices and commands. He was successively made Governor of Guernsey (1770); a Privy Councillor (1772); officiating commander in chief of the forces (from 1772; made commander in chief in 1793); and was promoted to general (1778), and to field marshal (1796). He was raised to the peerage in

1776, and recreated Lord Amherst in 1787 with remainder to his nephew. He loyally acted as adviser on the War of American Independence to George III, and in 1780 had a part in suppressing the Gordon Riots. Unfortunately he permitted abuses in the army during his long tenure of office. Nothing in his later career equalled his central role in the conquest of Canada. He died at his house at Sevenoaks, Kent, on 3 August 1797.

I. R. Christie, *Crisis of Empire: Great Britain and the American Colonies, 1754–1783* (1966).
J. C. Long, *Lord Jeffrey Amherst* (1933).
J. C. Webster (ed.), *Journal* (1931).

Portrait: oil, half-length, by Gainsborough: N.P.G.

Arblay, Madame d' (1752–1840), see Burney, Frances.

Arbuthnot, John (1667–1735), wit and doctor of medicine, noted chiefly as a member of the Scriblerus Club and as a friend of Pope and Swift (qq.v.).

John Arbuthnot was born in April 1667, the son of a Scottish clergyman in Kincardineshire. After acquiring the degree of M.D. at St. Andrews University in 1696, he moved to London, where he supported himself by giving lessons in mathematics. He published several learned papers and in 1704 was elected a Fellow of the Royal Society. It is not clear when he took up the practice of medicine, the subject in which he acquired his degree, but having the good fortune to be in the right place at the right time, he attended Prince George of Denmark when the latter was suddenly taken ill at Epsom. As a result he was appointed, on 30 October 1705, as a physician to Queen Anne, and in 1709 he became her chief medical adviser. In 1710 he became a Fellow of the Royal College of Physicians, in which society he played an active part, becoming Censor in 1723 and Harveian Orator in 1727. He continued to practise medicine until his death, attending many of the great and powerful in the land during their illnesses; he attended Queen Anne during her last illness in 1714.

In 1712–13 Arbuthnot wrote a celebrated series of pamphlets, which appeared under various titles but is now best known as *The History of John Bull*. This is a political allegory dealing with the events leading up to the Treaty of Utrecht (1713), in which the Englishman John Bull, 'an honest plain-dealing fellow, choleric, bold, and of a very unconstant temper', is very nearly duped by Lewis Baboon (Louis XIV of France), Lord Strutt (Charles II of Spain), and Nicholas Frog (the Dutch). It is not certain that Arbuthnot invented John Bull as the typical Englishman, but he certainly popularized the character.

During the last years of Queen Anne's reign, Arbuthnot became acquainted with the leading Tories of the day, among whom he acquired the reputation of a wit. He also met Pope and Swift, with both of whom he formed a lifelong friendship. It was at about this time that Pope, Swift, Arbuthnot, and others banded together to form the Scriblerus Club, the intention of which was to satirize 'the abuses of human learning in every branch' in the form of the supposed writing of an imaginary pedant, Martinus Scriblerus. Although *The Memoirs of Martinus Scriblerus* were not published until 1741 (in an edition of Pope's works), the activities of the club were widely known at the time and manuscripts and fragments were widely circulated. *The Memoirs* are thought to be chiefly the work of Arbuthnot, although it is generally not possible to identify individual contributions.

Arbuthnot was quite unconcerned about his literary reputation. He was content to publish some of his best pieces anonymously, and it is reported that he let his children make kites out of his manuscripts. All who knew him acknowledged his great charm, warmth, and humanity; Pope, in his 'Epistle to Dr. Arbuthnot' (1735), addressed him as:

> Friend to my life! (which did not you prolong,
> The world had wanted many an idle song).

Swift, with whom Arbuthnot carried on a frequent correspondence after the Dean's retirement to Ireland, wrote of him: 'Our doctor hath every quality in the world that can make a man amiable and useful; but alas! he hath a sort of slouch in his walk.'

The remainder of Arbuthnot's life was uneventful. In the early 1730s his health began to fail, and in 1734 he moved to Hampstead in the hope that the air would improve it. He continued to decline. In October 1734 he wrote to Swift: 'A recovery in my case and at my age is impossible; the kindest wish of my friends is euthanasia.' He died on 27 February 1735.

George A. Aitken (ed.), *The Life and Works of Arbuthnot* (1892).

L. M. Beattie, *Arbuthnot: Mathematician and Satirist* (Cambridge, Mass., 1935).

M. Teerink (ed.), *The History of John Bull* (Amsterdam, 1925).

Portrait: oil, by W. Robinson: Scottish N.P.G.

Argyll, 2nd Duke of (1678–1743), see Campbell, John.

Arkwright, Sir Richard (1732–92), industrialist and inventor of spinning machinery.

Arkwright was born on 23 December 1732 in Preston, Lancashire, the youngest of seven children, and managed to make the best of a fairly rudimentary education. He was brought up to be a barber and wigmaker. As an apprentice he travelled about England buying hair for wigs, which he prepared and dyed himself by a special process. The country was alive with innovations in spinning and weaving and in the course of his travels Arkwright developed a keen interest in the new processes of manufacture. The flying shuttle had speeded up the method of weaving to such an extent that there was a huge demand for yarn which, until the invention by James Hargreaves (q.v.) of the spinning jenny in 1767, was made by hand. Hargreaves's invention, however, produced thread only suitable for the weft. The rove or warp thread still had to be made by hand.

In 1750 Arkwright moved to Bolton, and over a period of years experimented with machines that would produce a fine thread. He moved to Nottingham with John Kay (q.v.) of Bury, inventor of the flying shuttle, and was later joined by Jedediah Strutt and Samuel Need, who provided the capital for his work. In 1769 he took out a patent for a spinning frame.

Arkwright's spinning frame was at first powered by horses, but later water power was substituted and from then on it was known as the water frame. It worked on a tooth-and-pinion mechanism and made use of four pairs of rollers to produce a rove of considerable fineness and strength. The use of rollers was not Arkwright's idea but Lewis Paul's. Arkwright, however, improved on them and put them into operation more successfully. The frame has not yet been superseded or substantially modified; it is in use to this day with only minor improvements.

The invention of the water frame enabled a cloth made purely of cotton to be manufactured for the first time. Previously cotton had been used for the weft and linen for the warp. In spite of its proven excellence, however, the big Lancashire manufacturers declined to use the machine and in its early days it was operated solely to produce stockings and calicoes. In 1736 Arkwright's progress was further impeded by an act of parliament that placed a double duty on cotton cloth 'to protect the woollen manufacturers of England'. By this time Arkwright had invested about £1,200 in the development of his machine and seen scarcely any return on his money.

In 1774, however, the tide turned, when an act exempting 'stuffs made wholly of raw cotton wool' was passed, and from this time Arkwright's affairs prospered. He improved and modified his machine, introducing a carding process so that the whole work of spinning was now fully mechanized. He sold grants of his patent and in 1775 acquired a new patent for the whole process of yarn manufacture. Cotton manufacture grew to be the leading industry in Northern England, and by 1782 Arkwright had a capital of £200,000 and employed 5,000 workers.

He interested himself in the planning of factories as well as of machines and put into practice involved plans for the large-scale organization of labour. He introduced a system of division of labour in his works and put much emphasis on cleanliness, thus laying the foundations for the planning of the New Lanark mills and the work of Robert Owen (q.v.).

In 1785 wrangles over the originality of his ideas resulted in the cancellation of his patents, but by this time Arkwright was so well established that his finances were not seriously affected by this reversal.

Arkwright married twice. He was knighted in 1786, and was chosen High Sheriff of Derbyshire in 1787. He died a very rich man at Willersley Castle on 3 August 1792, and was buried at Cromford church: he had built both.

R. S. Fitton and A. P. Wadsworth, *The Strutts and the Arkwrights, 1758–1830* (1959).

Portraits: oil, half-length, by J. Wright: Nottingham Castle Art Gallery; marble sculpture, J. Nollekens: Guildhall, Hull.

Arne, Thomas Augustine (1710–78), composer of operas and other theatre music.

Arne was born on 12 March 1710 in London, the son of an upholsterer. He was educated at Eton. His father planned a legal career for him, and upon leaving school he entered a solicitor's office for three years. However, he found law an uncongenial discipline, preferring instead the pleasures of music. He soon involved himself in formal music-making, leading a chamber orchestra in a series of private concerts; after initial parental disapproval he was finally given permission to devote himself to music, abandoning all plans for law.

Arne's younger sister, Susanna Maria, possessed a singularly lovely singing voice and, helped by her brother's training, she appeared with great success in Lampe's opera *Amelia* in 1732 when only eighteen years of age. Excited by her success, Thomas reset Addison's opera *Rosamund* as a vehicle for Susanna's talents and she performed the role of the heroine in a well-received production at Lincoln's Inn Fields in March 1733.

Arne's reputation was established in 1738 when he was commissioned to compose music for Milton's *Comus*, adapted by Dalton. The masque was performed at Drury Lane Theatre with great success. Arne's style, so Burney informs us, was found to be so 'easy, natural and agreeable' to the English taste that it became the standard of perfection at all theatres and public gardens until it was overtaken by a more modern Italian style.

In 1737 Arne married Cecilia Young, daughter of Charles Young, organist of All Hallows, Barking. Cecilia was a particularly fine soprano. With a talented wife to perform his songs, Arne continued composing almost exclusively for the theatre, notably for Drury Lane, where he became resident composer in 1744.

In 1742 Arne and his wife made the first of three visits to Ireland, remaining there for two years. Here he composed his first oratio, *The Death of Abel*, based on Metastasio's poem *La Morte d'Abele*. It received its first performance in 1744. On his return to London in the same year, he took up a permanent post at Drury Lane. In the following year, 1745, he enlarged his sphere of activity by becoming composer at Vauxhall Gardens. The pastoral dialogue *Colin and Phoebe* was the first of many successes there, and he also had music performed at Ranelagh and Marylebone.

The decade 1745–55 was a time of great activity and increasing acclaim, and the summit of Arne's career was reached in 1759, when the degree of Doctor of Music was conferred upon him by Oxford University. His personal affairs during this period were less successful, however. His marriage to Cecilia came to grief on a second Irish visit in 1755, when he abandoned her in Dublin. Arne seems to have been faithless and even cruel as a husband. Indeed, Burney suggests that the only child of the marriage, Michael Arne (born in 1740 or 1741), was in fact an illegitimate son of Arne's. Despite the long estrangement, however, Cecilia and Arne were eventually reconciled a year before the composer's death.

In 1760, probably after a disagreement with Garrick (q.v.), Arne's centre of activities moved from Drury Lane to Covent Garden. He had written a number of works for Covent Garden theatre since 1749, and in 1760 he became its resident composer, with his successful opera *Thomas and Sally*. His subsequent setting of Metastasio's *Artaserse* (1760) in his own translation was in a radically different style, being much more florid, and sung throughout. Yet it still triumphed.

Next, wishing to write a work for the newly-arrived Italian castrato, Manzuoli, he chose for his libretto Metastasio's *Olimpiade*. The work was a failure: it received only two performances at the King's Theatre in the Haymarket before being withdrawn. Arne never again composed music for an Italian text. He continued to compose and present music at Covent Garden up to November 1777, though he also had works produced at the Haymarket and Drury Lane. He died on 5 March 1778 and was buried at St. Paul's, Covent Garden.

Throughout his working career Arne composed largely though by no means exclusively for the theatre. His overtures, concertos, keyboard pieces, and chamber works are relatively few in number and not very significant. The charm and ease of his style is best seen in his Shakespeare settings for the revivals of *As You Like It*, *Twelfth Night*, *The Merchant of Venice*, and other plays. But for those who know nothing else of his music, Arne's fame rests on the patriotic air 'Rule, Britannia' from the masque *Alfred* (1740). This song, made timeless by its constant popularity, has attained something of the status of a national anthem, yet it is very much in the style of the eighteenth century.

E. R. Dibdin, 'The Bi-Centenary of "Rule Britannia"', *Music and Letters*, xxi (1940).

B. H. Horner, *Life and Works of Dr. Arne* (1893).

H. Langley, *Dr. Arne* (1938).

J. A. Parkinson, *An Index to the Vocal Works of Thomas Arne and Michael Arne* (Detroit, 1972).

Portrait: coloured etching, three-quarter length, after Bartolozzi: N.P.G.

Arnold, Thomas (1795–1842), head-master, see *Lives of the Victorian Age*.

Austen, Jane (1775–1817), novelist noted for her witty and astute, usually ironic, depiction of human nature and character.

Jane Austen was born on 16 December 1775, the second daughter and the

youngest of seven children of the rector of Steventon and Deane, Hampshire, the Rev. George Austen, and his wife Cassandra Leigh.

Jane Austen appears to have led the typically quiet life of an unmarried country gentlewoman, spending the first twenty-five years of her life largely at Steventon. In 1801 her father decided to retire, and transferred the living to his son James, following which the family moved to Bath. After George Austen's death in 1805 they had no settled residence, lodging first in Bath and then in Southampton, until Jane's brother Edward gave them a home on his estate at Chawton, near Winchester, where Jane Austen spent the rest of her life. Although there is a story that she once became deeply involved with an officer in the navy who died soon afterwards, she never married, and apart from visits to friends and relatives, including a few trips to London, her life was outwardly uneventful. By her family's account, however, she was lively and witty, and it is possible that reasons of finance or ill health contributed to her essentially domestic life.

Little is known about Jane Austen's own character, since her beloved sister Cassandra destroyed the more intimate parts of their correspondence. From family recollection we are told that she was 'tall, slender, and remarkably graceful . . . a clear brunette with a rich colour, hazel eyes, fine features, and curling brown hair'. It is said that 'her domestic relations were delightful' and that she was especially attractive to children.

Jane Austen started her literary career by way of mimicry, writing burlesques of some of the contemporary vogues in the novel. It is partly this impulse that lies behind *Northanger Abbey* and *Pride and Prejudice*, which are in some measure satiric thrusts at the Gothic novels of Mrs. Radcliffe (q.v.) on the one hand and the domestic romances of Fanny Burney (q.v.) on the other, while *Sense and Sensibility* was first cast as an epistolary novel in the tradition of Richardson's *Clarissa* and *Pamela*.

It is difficult to match the order of composition of her first three novels with their actual appearance in print, since she published them only after much revision. The novel in letter form called 'Elinor and Marianne' was completed in 1795. This formed the basis of *Sense and Sensibility*, being revised in 1797 and again in 1809–10 after rejection by the publisher Thomas Cadell; it finally appeared in 1811. During 1796–7 she appears to have been working on 'First Impressions', the forerunner of *Pride and Prejudice*. She was working in 1798–9 on *Northanger Abbey*, then called 'Susan' from the name she first gave to its heroine, Catherine Morland. The manuscript of this work was sold to the publisher Richard Crosby in 1803, but he did not publish it and it was bought back by the Austens in 1816, possibly revised by the author, and published posthumously in 1818. *Northanger Abbey* is the first of her completed works in order of composition. The somewhat confusing history of her early novels corresponds to an unsettled period of her life in Bath and Southampton, where she seems also to have written the fragment known as *The Watsons* and a short epistolary novel, *Lady Susan*, both being unconsidered works conceived before she wrote for a public.

On her arrival at Chawton in 1809 she had in her possession the manuscripts of three unpublished novels. Before the first of these, *Sense and Sensibility*, was brought out in November 1811, she had already commenced work on *Mansfield Park* (published 1814). The revised 'First Impressions' appeared as *Pride and Prejudice* in January 1813, and in the following year (January 1814) she began *Emma*, which was published in December 1815, the year of Waterloo. Her last completed novel, *Persuasion*, was started that summer and finished in 1816, being published together with *Northanger Abbey* in 1818, six months after her death. Early in 1817 she began the fragment *Sanditon*, which she was working on at the time of her death.

Her reputation, based on six novels, is due to her consummate skill in using her country families, with their ordinary concerns of marriage and fortune, as the basis of a close and accurate observation of human nature. If her characters do not run to the extremes of spiritual and social crisis, of the romantic jeopardy of the Gothic novels she delighted to satirize, it is because these experiences were not the stuff of everyday life and therefore not her concern; in so far as they existed at all, she chose to ignore them. Her characters and conflicts exist away from the tide of history, which touches only the margins of her world, as when the Napoleonic Wars inconveniently remove the object of Anne Elliot's romantic interest in *Persuasion*. Jane Austen herself had two brothers who became admirals, but the military men in her novels are always in civilian dress and are never heard to discuss their professional affairs.

The position of women in society is a paramount consideration in her novels, and one of the basic conflicts they present is that between romantic love and the need – or rather the requirement – of the heroine (who in all her novels is a young woman of marriageable age) to make the right match. Marriage therefore becomes, as in *Emma*, the supreme exercise of the values of choice, discrimination, and morality, since it concerns two factors of crucial dramatic interest. One is the ability of the heroine to distinguish true worth from that which is flawed, as in Emma's choice between Mr. Knightley and Frank Churchill. The other is the degree to which the woman of merit but unpromising fortune – Elizabeth Bennet, Fanny Price, Jane Fairfax, and Anne Elliot – can triumph over adversity and be recognized by the worthy man as worth the loss of a fortune. Into this central conflict is poured the whole ethical and emotional substance of Jane Austen's art: together with the moral conflict between true and apparent merit, its concomitant dramatic reversals of fortune, and its necessary end in the right or the wrong marriage partner, goes the emotional structure of family or social tyranny over the individual heart, as in the situations of Fanny Price and Elizabeth Bennet.

In the autumn of 1816 Jane Austen's family began to be seriously concerned over her health. She seemed to have lost both strength and appetite, and her skin had developed dark brown patches. Her doctor was unable to diagnose the trouble, and in May 1817 she moved from Chawton to lodgings in Winchester, in order to be near her doctor and in the hope that constant medical surveillance would lead to a successful diagnosis. She was by now very weak and emaciated; the doctors could do nothing, and on 18 July she died. She is buried in the cathedral. Subsequent research suggests that her final illness was almost certainly Addison's disease.

W. and R. A. Austen, *Jane Austen, Her Life and Letters* (1913).

J. E. Austen-Leigh, *A Memoir of Jane Austen* (1817, 2nd ed.).

H. S. Babb, *Jane Austen's Novels: The Fabric of Dialogue* (Hamden, Conn., 1967).

F. Bradbrook, *Jane Austen and Her Predecessors* (1966).

R. W. Chapman, *Jane Austen, Facts and Problems* (1950, rev. ed.).

R. W. Chapman (ed.), *The Oxford Illustrated Jane Austen* (6 vols.; 1923–54; vol. 6 rev. by B. C. Southam, 1968).

R. W. Chapman (ed.), *Jane Austen's Letters* (1952, 2nd ed.).

R. W. Chapman (ed.), *Selected Letters of Jane Austen 1796–1817* (1955).

Margaret Drabble (ed.), *Lady Susan, The Watsons, and Sanditon* (1974).

E. Jenkins, *Jane Austen* (1938).

M. Lascelles, *Jane Austen and Her Art* (1939).

M. Laski, *Jane Austen and Her World* (1969).

M. Mudrick, *Jane Austen: Irony as Defense and Discovery* (Princeton, 1952).

B. C. Southam, *Jane Austen's Literary Manuscripts* (1964).

I. P. Watt, *Jane Austen: A Collection of Critical Essays* (1963).

A. H. Wright, *Jane Austen's Novels: A Study in Structure* (London and Toronto, 1964, rev. ed.).

Portrait: pencil and water-colour, half-length, by Cassandra Austen, *c.* 1810: N.P.G.

B

Bach, John Christian (1735–82), original name Johann Christian Bach; composer and impresario, known as the 'London Bach'; an influential architect of musical taste in eighteenth-century London.

John Christian Bach was born on 5 September 1735 at Leipzig, the youngest son of Johann Sebastian Bach and his second wife, Anna Magdalena Wilken. He was educated at St. Thomas's School in Leipzig, where his father was musical director, and received his earliest musical training from the great Johann Sebastian himself. After Johann Sebastian's death in 1750, when John Christian was only fifteen years old, the financial circumstances of the family made it necessary for him to be taken into the home of his elder brother, Carl Philipp Emanuel, who was then at Berlin.

John Christian inherited a little of his father's prodigious talent for music, and at nineteen, no doubt to perfect his musical ability, he left his brother's home for Italy. Here he tasted success in Naples and Turin, where his earliest operas were enthusiastically received. His reputation spread abroad, and he was invited to come and arrange performances at the King's Theatre, London. Bach arrived in England late in 1762.

Bach initially continued in the tradition of his predecessor, Gioacchino Cocchi, by arranging pasticcios and directing productions. For these works, however, he did compose his own overtures, as, for example, with the production of Galuppi's opera, *La Calamita de Cuori*, in 1763. He did not present a complete opera of his own until 19 February 1763, when his *Orione* was staged.

It was probably in 1764 that Bach started his duties as music master to Queen Charlotte and her children. He also embarked on a new venture with the composer Carl Friedrich Abel, now also resident in London. They announced their intention of presenting a public concert, which was to be held for their mutual benefit at the Great Room in Spring Gardens, near St. James's Park. This venture succeeded and they next offered the public a series of subscription concerts, the first in this country. Although no programmes survive, we know that Bach's earliest set of published symphonies (Op. 3, 1–6) was included.

During his stay in England, the young Mozart met Bach and a close friendship developed, despite the great difference in their ages. J. C. Bach certainly had some influence on Mozart, notably by introducing him to the Italian style of composition.

For more than twenty years J. C. Bach exercised a decisive influence over music-making in London, particularly through the Bach–Abel concerts. From the very first series in 1765 they were an unequivocal success both financially and musically, and often featured Bach's own symphonies, concertos, arias, and songs. Following the six concerts in the first series, Bach and Abel offered fifteen in a second and a third series in 1766 and 1767. Audiences continued to increase and by 1774 the concerts had become weekly affairs running from January to May. Also in 1774 Bach, Abel, and Sir John Gallini, manager of the King's Theatre, planned to build a new concert hall, the Hanover Square Rooms, to provide a permanent home for the Bach–Abel concerts. It was finished in 1775.

Ironically, however, the year 1774 also witnessed the start of a decline in Bach's prosperity. The public, whose ever-increasing support had encouraged him to build his new concert hall for their greater pleasure, began to desert him. His capital steadily decreased, and on 1 January 1782, the very day that the *Public Advertiser* announced the eighteenth season of subscription concerts, John Christian Bach died, leaving debts amounting to £4,000.

Besides his work as teacher and impresario, John Christian Bach had been first and foremost a composer. He produced about a dozen operas of his own, more than sixty symphonies, concertos, and countless other works. His work reflects his personality, possessing elegance, charm, wit, refinement, and grace.

C. S. Terry, *J. C. Bach* (1929; 2nd ed. 1967, with foreword by H. C. Robbins Landon).

Banks, Sir Joseph (1743–1820), botanist, explorer, and patron of science.

Joseph Banks was born in London on 13 February 1743, son of William Banks, a wealthy Lincolnshire landowner, and educated at Harrow, Eton, and Christ Church, Oxford. He became intensely interested in natural science, especially botany, at an early age. When his father died (1761), he was left a small fortune, which he used to obtain private tuition in botany and finance several scientific expeditions of great value. The first of these took place in the summer of 1766, just after young Banks's election as a Fellow of the Royal Society. He set out with a friend, a naval lieutenant, to explore the coasts of Newfoundland and Labrador. They returned with many

valuable plant and insect specimens, which formed the beginning of a vast collection that Banks freely shared with other scientists in the promotion of the study of natural history.

In 1768 Banks joined Captain Cook's expedition aboard the *Endeavour*. He persuaded Daniel Carl Solander, a young Swedish medical botanist and former student of Linnaeus, to join him. At each landfall – in Tierra del Fuego, New Zealand, and Australia – they added extensively to a growing collection of specimens. In Botany Bay Banks collected the first specimen of a shrub that now commemorates his name – Banksia. On his return to England in 1771 he was warmly greeted by his colleagues, and honoured by George III, who granted him a private interview. This was the start of a politically useful royal interest, which no doubt had much to do with Banks's election as President of the Royal Society (1778). He remained in this appointment, exercising a somewhat despotic control, until his death forty-two years later.

In July 1772 Banks financed an

expedition to Iceland, again accompanied by Solander, who was by now his secretary. During the expedition he not only collected specimens but purchased a large number of Icelandic books and manuscripts which he incorporated into his vast library. This unrivalled collection of books and periodicals on natural history is now housed in the British Museum, together with Banks's herbarium.

Banks was a man of wide interests. He belonged to several learned societies, including the Society of Arts, and he was also one of the founders of the Royal Institution. But he is best remembered for his scientific patronage. He had a particular interest in the development of agriculturally economic plants and their acclimatization in areas where they could be beneficial. The breadfruit expedition of the ill-fated *Bounty* is a famous example of the kind of work Banks tried to undertake in this field.

Banks did much to improve the Royal Botanical Gardens at Kew, of which he was honorary director, by organizing several expeditions to increase its stock. His personal and financial contributions to botanical research permitted significant advances in the subject and made him one of botany's most important patrons. He received many honours in his lifetime, culminating in a knighthood (1795) and an appointment to the Privy Council (1797). He died on 19 June 1820 at Isleworth, Middlesex.

J. C. Beaglehole (ed.), *The Endeavour Journal of Joseph Banks, 1768–1771* (2 vols.; Sydney, 1962).

H. C. Cameron, *Sir Joseph Banks, K.B., P.R.S., The Autocrat of the Philosophers* (1952).

W. R. Dawson, *The Banks Letters: A Calendar of the Manuscript Correspondence of Sir Joseph Banks* (1958).

J. H. Maiden, *Sir Joseph Banks* (1909).

Portraits: pencil, half-length, by T. Lawrence: N.P.G.; oil, half-length, by T. Phillips, 1810: N.P.G.

Barry, Sir Charles (1795–1860), architect, see *Lives of the Victorian Age*.

Bath, 1st Earl of (1684–1764), see Pulteney, William.

Beckford, William (1759–1844), novelist, dilettante, and eccentric.

William Beckford was born on 29 September 1759 at Fonthill Gifford, Wiltshire, the only son of William Beckford, a millionaire sugar planter who was twice Lord Mayor of London. The course of his life was conditioned by the almost inconceivable wealth inherited from his father. He was a headstrong but brilliant child. Chatham said he was 'all air and fire'. At the age of seventeen, he wrote a *History of Extraordinary Painters* in order to mislead the gullible old housekeeper at Fonthill, by attributing the family portraits to such unlikely artists as Og of Bashan. Beckford's mother disapproved of universities, so during the period 1777–82 she sent her son on frequent long trips to Europe, particularly Geneva, to round off his education. Beckford candidly described his European experiences in *Dreams, Waking Thoughts, and Incidents*, completed in 1783 but long suppressed.

It was probably in 1781 that Beckford wrote his masterpiece, *Vathek*, in 'three days and two nights'. Characteristically, he wrote in French; the idiomatic English translation, which caused a stir when it was published in 1784, was the unauthorized effort of a country vicar. *Vathek* is a Voltairean moral tale in extravagant Oriental fancy dress; typical of its acidulous mixture of fantasy and tragedy is the Hall of Eblis, inhabited by those guilty of 'unrestrained passions', who must for ever clutch their flaming hearts. Eblis himself, whose face mirrored both 'pride and despair', is the prototype of Byron's anti-heroes. Indeed, it was precisely Beckford's exaggeration, his lack of literary 'taste', which made his book so appealing to an audience possibly tired of Augustan good sense.

In 1783 Beckford married Lady Margaret Gordon. The couple went to live in Switzerland, where two daughters were born to them, but tragically Margaret died in 1786. The disconsolate Beckford wandered around Europe for the next ten years. He was on good terms with the Portuguese court, but greatly enjoyed poking fun at it in his many letters home. While in Paris in 1789 Beckford witnessed the storming of the Bastille. In 1792 at Lausanne he purchased Edward Gibbon's library and shut himself up hermit-like for a whole year to read through it. Beckford returned to Portugal in 1794, to live in beautiful surroundings at Cintra.

Beckford returned home in about 1795 and wrote two cruel burlesques of the 'sentimental' novel, *The Elegant Enthusiast* (1796) and *Amezia* (1797), his last published works. From now on he exercised his colourful imagination on the family home, Fonthill. He built a huge wall around the estate, pulled down the old house, and spent £250,000 on building a gigantic caricature of a Gothic abbey. Its central feature was a 300-foot tower, built by teams of labourers working day and night; unfortunately, owing to practically non-existent foundations, it fell down, so Beckford promptly ordered another to be built (which also fell down, but not immediately). Beckford now shut himself up in this monstrous folly, and spent twenty years amassing an enormous and bizarre collection of *objets d'art* of every conceivable description. Far from being an effete dreamer, Beckford was in fact a shrewd and argumentative collector; nor was he a misanthrope, since he was unfailingly courteous to visitors and had a healthy appetite for flattery.

Unfortunately, he had over the years irresponsibly neglected his West Indian sugar estates, and in 1822 he was forced to sell Fonthill. In 1823 Beckford's collection was disposed of in a famous thirty-seven-day sale, described by Hazlitt as 'a desert of magnificence, a glittering waste of laborious idleness'. Beckford took the best items and his library with him and created a miniature Fonthill at Lansdowne Terrace, Bath. He died on 2 May 1844 and was buried under a huge tower that he had had built on Lansdowne Hill, overlooking Bath.

B. Alexander (ed.), *William Beckford: Journal* (1954).
B. Alexander (ed.), *William Beckford: Life at Fonthill 1807–22* (1957).
B. Alexander (ed.), *England's Wealthiest Son* (1962).
G. Chapman (ed.), *The Episodes of Vathek* (2 vols.; 1929).
G. Chapman (ed.), *The Vision; Liber Veritatis* (1930).
G. Chapman (ed.), *The Travel Diaries* (2 vols.; 1928).
G. Chapman, *Beckford* (1952, rev. ed.).
J. W. Oliver, *The Life of William Beckford* (1932).
A. Parreaux, *Beckford: Auteur de Vathek* (Paris, 1960).

Portrait: oil, by John Hoppner, *c.* 1800: Salford Museum and Art Gallery.

Bell, Sir Charles (1774–1842), Scottish anatomist and physiologist, known for his pioneering investigation of the central nervous system.

Charles Bell was born in November 1774 at Edinburgh, the youngest son of William Bell, a clergyman. When his father died, his education was entrusted to his older brothers, John and George. Although Charles managed to attend school and university in Edinburgh, he maintained in later life that 'my education was the example set me by my brothers'. Indeed, it was his brother John – a distinguished Edinburgh surgeon and anatomist – who decided Charles's choice of a career.

When he left university, Charles began his study of anatomy under John's supervision. At the age of twenty-four, while still a student, he published his first work, *A System of Dissections, Explaining the Anatomy of the Human Body, the Manner of Displaying the Parts, and Their Varieties in Disease* (1798).

In 1799 Bell was admitted to the Royal College of Surgeons of Edinburgh. Not long afterwards he was appointed to the local Royal Infirmary, where he soon acquired a reputation as a competent surgeon. Bell continued to be fascinated by the structure and function of the central nervous system. In 1802 he published a series of engravings of the brain and spinal cord. Two years later he collaborated with his brother John in publishing *The Anatomy of the Human Body*, in which Charles was responsible for writing the account of the nervous system.

In November 1804 he decided to move to London. By 1811 he had become associated with a thriving and prestigious school of anatomy in Great Windmill Street.

In 1806 Bell had published a book with a curious title, but one which had a great effect on both his reputation and his further research on the nervous system. In this book, *The Anatomy of Expression*, Bell set the groundwork for his future discoveries in neurophysiology. He attempted to show how the physician or surgeon could gain valuable information on the extent of serious diseases by observing facial and bodily displays of pain, muscular tension, depth of breathing, and so on. The book was richly illustrated by the author, who by now was considered one of the best medical artists of the day.

During the next few years Bell devoted himself to the study of the physiology of the nervous system. In 1811 his *New Idea of the Anatomy of the Brain* appeared, and in the following year he was appointed surgeon at the Middlesex Hospital. He frequently contributed papers to the Royal Society, the first of which was on the functions of the fifth and sixth pairs of cranial nerves.

Bell always maintained a realistic balance between theory and practice, and his skill as a surgeon was continually improving. His care of the wounded after the Battle of Waterloo gave him much valuable experience. In 1824 he was appointed senior professor of anatomy and surgery at the Royal College of Surgeons, and two years later was elected a Fellow of the Royal Society.

The greatest contribution Bell made to the understanding of the body was his discovery that the anterior and posterior roots of spinal nerves have separate and distinct functions. His experiments demonstrated two types of nerve, those that cause muscular movements (motor nerves) and those that convey sensations (sensory nerves). He also showed that some nerve bundles contain elements of both types (sensorimotor). This discovery formed the basis of all subsequent research in neurology.

Bell returned to Scotland in 1836, where he accepted the post of professor of surgery at the University of Edinburgh. He died on 28 April 1842 at Hallow Park, Worcestershire, during a journey to London.

G. Gordon-Taylor and E. W. Walls, *Sir Charles Bell, His Life and Times* (1958).

Portrait: oil, three-quarter length, by J. Stephens: N.P.G.

Bentham, Jeremy (1748–1832), philosopher and jurist; the leading proponent of Utilitarianism.

Bentham was born in London on 15 February 1748, the son of an ambitious and wealthy attorney. He was a restless and precocious child – at the age of four he was already familiar with the Latin and Greek languages, and two years later he was beginning to learn French. Up to the year 1755, when he was sent to Westminster School, he spent much of his time at the peaceful but stimulating homes of his grandmothers at Reading and Barking.

His independence was thus an early characteristic, and it is not surprising that he could not adapt easily to the more formal institutions of school and university. At The Queen's College, Oxford, which he entered in 1760, he found that his tutors had little that was interesting to teach him, and he was later to write that 'mendacity and insincerity' were the chief characteristics of a university education. Bentham left Oxford with his M.A. degree in 1766 and was called to the bar at Lincoln's Inn in 1772. But his pursuit of the law was short-lived.

At the age of twenty, Bentham was greatly impressed by 'the Greatest Happiness Principle' as defined in the writings of Helvetius, and from this time onward he devoted his life to the building of a scientific foundation for legislation and jurisdiction. The *Fragment on Government*, published anonymously in 1776, marked the first stage of this project: in a vigorous and lucid style he attacked the platitudes and contradictions of contemporary jurisdiction, and repudiated the basis of Natural Law and historic precedent upon which Sir William Blackstone, his former teacher, had based his defence of the British constitution. One of the consequences of this work was Bentham's meeting with Lord Shelburne, at whose house at Bowood he then began to write his *Introduction to the Principles of Morals and Legislation* (published in 1789), the work in which the central doctrines of Utilitarianism find their first and clearest expression. Bentham argues that what moves a man to action is always a desire to secure his own pleasure or avoid

his own pain, and from this psychological principle he deduces the moral principle that actions are to be approved or disapproved according to their tendency to increase or diminish the general happiness of a society.

In 1785 Bentham travelled to Russia to visit his brother, Samuel, who was employed as a government engineer. One of the features of the industrial works being built by Samuel was a circular inspection house, termed a Panopticon, and after his return to England Bentham attempted to put into practice his own adaptation of this Panopticon for use in prisons. Land near Millbank in London was acquired for this purpose, but the idea was not an immediate success.

The patronage of Lord Shelburne afforded Bentham both time and opportunity to develop his ideas; the letters that he wrote from Bowood are relaxed, confident, and witty in tone, and his works of this period include the *Critical Elements of Jurisprudence* (1789) and the *Rationale of Punishments and Rewards* (Paris, 1811; England, 1825). After his father died in 1792 he inherited a large amount of money, enabling him to increase even further the pace of his work: many letters, pamphlets, and essays were now written, on the poor laws, the English libel law, and the reform of the Scottish constitution. An admirer whom he met at Bowood, a citizen of Geneva called Dumont, offered to edit and interpret the mass of disorganized manuscript material that Bentham was now producing, and his work consequently acquired a reputation that spread to much of Europe.

After his meeting with James Mill (q.v.) in 1808, Bentham's intellectual development was strongly influenced in the direction of philosophic radicalism. His own family background was sturdily Tory, but Bentham now came to believe that democratic government was the system through which 'the greatest happiness of the greatest number' could most effectively be realized. In 1814 he moved from London to Ford Abbey, near Chard in Somerset, where he wrote the controversial papers on education entitled *Chrestomathia*; these were revolutionary in their emphasis on the role of science and their attack on the traditional pre-dominance of Latin and Greek, and led indirectly to the foundation of London University in 1825. In 1823 Bentham contributed much of his own money to the initial publication of the *Westminster Review*, the journal in which James Mill and his son John Stuart Mill helped to promulgate the ideas of Utilitarianism and apply them to the contemporary political scene.

Much of Bentham's time at Ford Abbey was now being spent in the codification of laws, leading to the publication of the first volume of the *Constitutional Code* in 1827 and a further volume in 1830. His interests in law and education were both determined by what he saw as their potential for developing the doctrines of Utilitarianism and mak-ing them practically effective. In private conduct Bentham saw no need for rules at all, as a man should choose the action which maximizes pleasure rather than one prescribed by rule, but in terms of social practice he was realistically aware that an effective ethical system must be based on a strict and rational constitution. Of all Bentham's varied interests it is probably his contribution to jurisprudence that has had the most enduring effect.

Those who visited him at Ford Abbey have described Bentham's physical ap-pearance in memorable terms: a robust vigorous personality, his clothes loose and untidy, his long hair straggling in the wind beneath a grotesque straw hat. His correspondents in later years included the

Duke of Wellington, Simon Bolivar, and the Emperor Alexander of Russia. He died peacefully on 6 June 1832; his body, according to the best Utilitarian prin-ciples, he left to be dissected, and it now lies embalmed at London University.

J. H. Burns *et al.* (eds.), *The Collected Works of Jeremy Bentham* (1968–   ).

C. W. Everett, *The Education of Bentham* (New York, 1931).

F. R. Leavis (ed.), *Mill on Bentham and Coleridge* (1950).

S. R. Letwin, *The Pursuit of Certainty* (1965).

Mary Mack, *Jeremy Bentham: An Odyssey of Ideas* (New York, 1963).

L. Stephen, *The English Utilitarians*, i (1900; reprinted 1968).

Portraits: oil, full-length, by T. Fryre, *c.*1761: N.P.G.; oil, full-length, by H. W. Pickersgill, 1829: N.P.G.; silhouette, quarter-length, by J. Field: N.P.G.; medallion, attributed to J. Wilson: Scottish N.P.G.

Bentinck, Lord William George Frederick Cavendish (1802–48), Pro-tectionist politician, see *Lives of the Victorian Age*.

Bentinck, William Henry Cavendish (1738–1809), 3rd Duke of Portland; statesman, First Lord of the Treasury in 1783 and 1807–9.

Bentinck was born on 14 April 1738 at Bulstrode, Buckinghamshire, the eldest son of William Bentinck, 2nd Duke of Portland. He was educated at Westmin-ster and Christ Church, Oxford, and succeeded his father as Duke of Portland in 1762. He was possessed of enormous wealth and an honest, likeable character, and soon entered into a political alliance with the Marquis of Rockingham (see Watson-Wentworth, Charles), and when Rockingham formed his first cabinet in July 1765, Portland was appointed Lord Chamberlain of the Household and sworn into the Privy Council. He retired with the Rockingham Whigs in December 1766.

In Rockingham's second ministry, Portland was appointed Lord Lieutenant of Ireland (April 1782). The King's decision to appoint Lord Shelburne to head the government, however, brought to the surface certain irreconcilable elements in the Whig party. Charles James Fox (q.v.) combined with Lord John Cavendish to ask the King to make Portland Prime Minister instead of Lord Shelburne. In August 1782, when their request was refused, Fox and Cavendish resigned, along with Burke, Sheridan, and Portland himself. Eventually even Lord North joined the active opponents of Shelburne, with the result that in April 1783 he finally resigned. Portland now became nominal head of the government, with Fox and North, the real men of power, as Secretaries of State. The administration fell in December 1783, when Fox's India Bill was, as a result of the King's influence, thrown out by the House of Lords.

After the collapse of this cabinet, although Portland was generally acknowledged as leader of the Rockingham Whigs, he left all party tactics to Fox and Burke. Meanwhile he devoted himself to country life and to the study of music, of which he was extremely fond. The progress of the French Revolution eventually compelled him to relinquish this peaceful existence. The stand against 'French principles' was led by Pitt, who seized this opportunity to gain the support of the great Whig families, and the Duke, after some hesitation, publicly declared his alliance with Pitt. The latter, in gratitude, made him Secretary of State for the Home Department in his new ministry (1793).

The seven years from 1794 to 1801, during which he was Home Secretary, were the most significant in Portland's political career. The repressive acts, such as the Alien Act, the Treason Act, and the Sedition Act, had placed immense arbitrary power in the Home Secretary's hands. Although not a great man, Portland was tolerant and well enough experienced in human affairs, and there was little public dissent during his tenure of office.

The suppression of the Irish insurrection was followed by the passage of the Act of Union (1800) in circumstances of degrading corruption. Portland gave steady support to the negotiations being carried out by Cornwallis (q.v.) and Castlereagh (see Stewart, Robert), but he was very reluctant to countenance the bargaining in honours which arose when the Irish peers, seizing upon the government's need for their support in passing the Act of Union, used their advantage to obtain peerages for themselves. He was prepared also to be statesmanlike over the Roman Catholic question, and supported Castlereagh's plans for subsidizing the Roman Catholic church in Ireland and making it a state church.

Under Addington Portland remained in office in the purely nominal capacity of Lord President of the Council. The weakness of Addington and his friends and the need to form a capable and energetic administration after the renewed outbreak of war with Napoleon in 1803 were both soon apparent to him. Pitt was called on to form a new government although hostility on the part of George III hampered him in his choice of ministers. Portland continued as Lord President of the Council but eventually relinquished this office, although not his cabinet status, in January 1805. On Pitt's death in 1806, he retired.

It was to be a short retirement, however, since the failures of the Ministry of All the Talents brought Pitt's friends back to power again. In March 1807 Portland, now an old man suffering from gout, accepted the office of Prime Minister out of a sense of duty. By this time he was unequal to the task. It needed a far stronger man to control the disparate and opposing personalities of Castlereagh and Canning (q.v.) who at this time dominated the cabinet. After their celebrated duel on Wimbledon Common, both statesmen resigned. This shock was too much for the old Duke, whose health had for months been failing. In October 1809 he insisted on resigning, and shortly afterwards, on 30 October, he died at Bulstrode.

A. Aspinall (ed.), *Later Correspondence of George III*, iv (1962–70).

J. Carron, *The Fox-North Coalition* (1969).

D. Gray, *Spencer Perceval: the Evangelical Prime Minister, 1762–1812* (1963).

A. S. Turberville, *A History of Welbeck Abbey and its Owners*, ii (1939).

Portraits: engraving, by J. Murphy after a painting by J. Reynolds: British Museum; plaque, miniature, artist unknown: R.T.H.

Bentinck, Lord William Henry Cavendish

Bentinck, Lord William Henry Cavendish (1774–1839), soldier and colonial administrator, whose many radical innovations during his governor-generalship in India (1828–35) helped to found the modern state.

Bentinck was born on 14 September 1774, the second son of the 3rd Duke of Portland. Entering the army in 1791, he saw action in the Peninsular War, commanding a division under the Duke of Wellington, who disapproved of him and thought him headstrong. Appointed Governor of Madras in 1803, at the early age of twenty-nine, Bentinck performed his duties satisfactorily enough, but his administration was clouded by disagreement with his council and was abruptly terminated by a mutiny at Vellore in July 1806, which was accompanied by attacks on officers and British troops. The outbreak was suppressed with heavy loss of life, and Bentinck was held responsible and recalled. Believing he had been treated unjustly, he pressed for the next twenty years for a chance to vindicate his name by further service in India.

In 1811, as the Napoleonic Wars wore on, he was sent to Sicily as envoy to the court of Sicily and as commander in chief of the British forces on that island. Assuming virtual governorship of the island, he followed a very independent line and engineered the deposition of the Bourbon king in favour of the heir apparent, while insisting on a liberal Sicilian constitution with a legislative body modelled on the English parliament. In 1814 Bentinck commanded a successful expedition against Genoa. He was recalled to England in 1815 and was elected to the House of Commons.

Bentinck was appointed Governor General of Bengal in 1827, and arrived in India in 1828. After a difficult two years with Wellington as Prime Minister, he was supported by the reform ministry of Lord Grey (1830–4) as well as by the directors of the British East India Company. In these circumstances he was able to carry through a series of measures that introduced a new era into Indian government.

Bentinck's immediate instructions were to rescue India from its financial difficulties. By economies and good management he soon succeeded in turning the government's deficit into a surplus. The economies included some measures unpopular among military circles, but the fruit of all this work was the renewal of the Company's government by the Charter Act of 1833, whereby Bentinck became the first Governor General of all India.

Bentinck next dealt with judicial and revenue reform. In the judicial department he admitted Indians to two grades of judgeships, as the first stage in the admission of Indians to important branches of the government. Land and revenue administration, however, remained utterly confused. A settlement of the land revenue in the north-western provinces was achieved, but a great deal of work was still left to be done in spite of Bentinck's efforts.

Bentinck's administration scored its most notable successes in the field of social and intellectual reform. In effect he introduced the West to India, not only in its personnel but in its institutions and spirit. He prohibited *suttee*, the Hindu custom of the burning of widows on the funeral pyres of their husbands, and suppressed *thuggee*, the practice of ritual murder by robber gangs. With T. B. Macaulay's support he made English the language of government business and the higher courts, instead of Persian. Government-aided education was to be on Western lines and the medium of instruction English. These measures had profound effects. Flogging in the Indian Army was also abolished, long before it ended in the British Army.

In foreign policy Bentinck was cautious, and in his relations with the Indian states he followed the traditional policy of non-intervention. As a result of ignoring the internal condition of Indian states while there was still time for improvement, the British were later forced to take drastic action, and Bentinck himself had to take over the administration of Mysore in 1831.

During the latter part of his government Bentinck's health was seriously impaired, and he resigned his post and embarked for England on 20 March 1835. He left behind many admirers, both European and native, who respected him for his high moral courage, his earnestness of approach, and his irreproachable private life. Having refused a peerage, he entered the House of Commons in 1836 as liberal member for Glasgow. Re-elected in 1837, he retained the seat until a few days before his death in Paris on 17 June 1839.

D. C. Boulger, *Lord William Bentinck*, volume 17 in the series Rulers of India (1892).

C. H. Philips (ed.), *The Correspondence of Lord William Henry Cavendish Bentinck* (in preparation).

John Rosselli, *Lord William Bentinck and the British Occupation of Sicily 1811–14* (1956).

Portraits: pen and ink head sketches, by J. Atkinson: N.P.G.

Bentley, Richard (1662–1742), classical scholar and critic.

Richard Bentley was born on 27 January 1662 at Oulton, Yorkshire, the son by a second marriage of Thomas Bentley, a minor landowner impoverished by the Civil War. In 1676 he entered St. John's College, Cambridge and in 1680 he obtained an excellent B.A. Two years later he came to London under the patronage of Dr. Edward Stillingfleet, Dean of St. Paul's and later Bishop of Worcester. Installed at Stillingfleet's London home, Bentley acted as tutor to the Dean's son, James. Here he gained access to Stillingfleet's vast personal library. From this Bentley profited enormously. By the end of six years he had compiled a glossary of Biblical Hebrew, and had attained great erudition in the classics.

In 1689 Bentley accompanied his pupil to Oxford. Fascinated by the Bodleian Library, he now also made the acquaintance of some leading Oxford scholars, including in particular John Mill, the principal of St. Edmund Hall. In 1690 Mill undertook an edition of the *Chronographia* of the Syrian chronicler, John Malalas (?491–?578). Before the book went to press, Mill agreed that Bentley should look over the manuscript. The letter, written in Latin, that Bentley sent to Mill after making his examination amounted to a startlingly brilliant commentary on the work, pointing out inaccuracies and possible emendations and even showing where Malalas himself had gone wrong. In June 1691 Mill's edition was published with Bentley's *Epistola ad Joannem Millium* as an appendix.

In 1692 Bentley was elected a Fellow of the Royal Society and became librarian to King William III. Having already taken holy orders in 1690, he became Chaplain in Ordinary to William in 1695.

Bentley now became involved in violent controversy – something for which in future years he would have to develop a taste. The aristocratic scholar Charles Boyle had in 1694 begun work on an edition of a work supposedly dating from the sixth century B.C., the *Epistles of Phalaris*. In 1697 Bentley denounced this work as an early Christian forgery. An acrimonious debate followed, and in 1699 Bentley published his *Dissertation on the Epistles of Phalaris*. This dissertation not only demonstrated the truth of his case, but also founded a whole new tradition of classical scholarship, based on the comparative analysis of sources in order to arrive at an accurate form (and dating) of the original text – a technique requiring not only great patience but also great erudition. Bentley had conclusively proved his hypothesis, but the controversy continued to simmer for another five years; in 1704 Boyle's friend, Jonathan Swift, made further mockery of Bentley in *The Battle of the Books*.

In 1700 Bentley was made Master of Trinity College, Cambridge, where he remained for the rest of his life. His tenure of the office was characterized by a continuous battle between himself and the fellows of the college. Bentley was not only an aggressive controversialist, but also a reformer with high academic ideals. He introduced written scholarship examinations and laid down more open rules for entrants for scholarships and prizes; he improved teaching and research facilities; and he brought in foreign lecturers of international repute.

However, he also showed a total lack of tact and a cavalier disregard for the rights and privileges of the fellows of the college. Several times between 1710 and 1738 they tried to have him removed, but each time a political crisis or some loophole in the college statutes saved him. He even succeeded in regaining his degrees in 1724 after losing them six years earlier over a theological controversy involving his flagrant flouting of college regulations. The fellows eventually gave up the struggle and, apart from suffering a mild stroke in 1739, Bentley passed his closing years relatively free from worries. He died on 14 July 1742, aged eighty.

In addition to his controversial involvements, Bentley found time at Cambridge for much writing and critical commentary. Among his works must be mentioned his editions of Horace (1711) and of Terence (1726). In his old age he also published an appalling 'corrected' edition of Milton's *Paradise Lost* (1733). His work on Homer is legendary, not so much because he supported the view that the Homeric poems represent the coalition of several earlier traditions, but rather for something much more abstruse. Perhaps it is fitting that this pedantic scholar is remembered as the first person to realize the former existence of the Greek letter digamma.

A. Dyce (ed.), *Works of Richard Bentley* (3 vols.; 1836–8).

A. Fox, *John Mill and Bentley: a Study of the Textual Criticism of the New Testament* (1954).

J. H. Monk, *Life of Richard Bentley* (2 vols.; 1833).

R. J. White, *Dr. Bentley: a Study in Academic Scarlet* (1965).

C. Wordsworth (ed.), *Correspondence of Bentley* (2 vols.; 1842).

Portrait: oil, by James Thornhill, 1710: Trinity College, Cambridge.

Berkeley, George (1685–1753), Bishop of Cloyne, Ireland; one of the most influential philosophers of the eighteenth century.

George Berkeley was born on 12 March 1685 at Kilkenny, the eldest son of William Berkeley, a commissioned officer of the dragoons, who was distantly related to Lord Berkeley of Stratton, Lord Lieutenant of Ireland from 1670 to 1672. He spent his childhood at Dysart Castle, near Thomastown. Precocious as a boy, he was entered at Kilkenny school at the age of eleven, and four years later matriculated at Trinity College, Dublin, where he received a B.A. degree in 1704. In 1707 he received his M.A., was elected to a fellowship, and became a tutor. He had in the meantime been influenced by the empirical philosophy of John Locke (see *Lives of the Stuart Age*) and the sceptical thought of Nicolas Malebranche. Under these influences he had undertaken a study of vision and time while waiting for a fellowship, and had at this time already conceived a theory of immaterialism, which he was soon to revise and refine. His first published work was mathematical and perhaps written as an academic thesis: *Arithmetica* and *Miscellanea Mathematica* (1707, published as one volume).

In 1710 Berkeley was ordained as a priest. He led a very active academic life, and at the same time published three books that formed the basis of his philosophy of immaterialism: *An Essay Towards a New Theory of Vision* (1709), an investigation of sight and touch, which arrived at the conclusion that 'the proper (or real) objects of sight' are within the mind even though 'the contrary be supposed true of tangible objects'; the *Treatise Concerning the Principles of Human Knowledge*, Part I (1710), in which the argument was further developed and all objects perceived by the senses are held to be within the mind and material substance

is denied; and *Three Dialogues between Hylas and Philonous* (1713), in which the theory is restated in a less technical dialogue argument, probably the best example of this literary form in English. Berkeley's ideas did not immediately receive widespread serious discussion and were for a time subject to trivial misunderstanding; the basis of his reputation, however, was solidly established in these books. He published one other volume, *Passive Obedience* (1712), in which he collected three sermons that deal with his political views, those of a Tory committed to the support of the Hanoverians.

In 1713 Berkeley went to London, where he enjoyed great personal success among men of letters such as Swift, Addison, Steele, and Arbuthnot (qq.v.). Swift presented him at court and recommended him to Lord Peterborough (see Mordaunt, Charles, in *Lives of the Stuart Age*), who took Berkeley as his chaplain on a diplomatic mission to Sicily in November 1713. Berkeley returned to England the next year.

After the death of Queen Anne, many of his friends were no longer in favour at court. He was himself suspected of Jacobite sympathies because of views that he had expressed earlier in *Passive Obedience* and consequently could not find an appointment in London. In 1716 he left on a second journey to Italy, acting as tutor to the son of the Bishop of Clogher. While abroad, he wrote four diaries of his travels in Rome and southern Italy, and after returning to England published a Latin treatise, *De Motu* (1721), in which he took issue with Newtonian theories of motion, space, and time. In the same year he returned to Dublin, taking up his post at Trinity College, where he remained until 1724.

When Berkeley returned from Italy in 1720, England was undergoing the speculative madness of the South Sea scheme. Berkeley saw the affair as a disastrous corruption and responded to it by publishing *Essays Towards Preventing the Ruine of Great-Britain* (1721), in which he made economic and moral proposals for restoring society to its senses. His well-known verse, 'Westward the Course of Empire Takes its Way', appeared shortly thereafter. Having small hope that the reformation of society that he sought was possible in Britain or Europe, he turned his attention to the New World and conceived a plan for founding a college in Bermuda. Its purpose was to be the education of native American Indians and the sons of planters in order to ensure the Christian civilization of the New World. In 1724 Berkeley ended his long association with Trinity College, becoming Dean of Derry with an income of £1,100 a year. In May of the preceding year he had been left half of her estate by Esther Vanhomrigh, Swift's 'Vanessa', whom he had probably never met. In these easy circumstances, Berkeley selflessly began to pursue his plan for a college at Bermuda. He was initially successful. He went to London and was introduced to George I, who granted a charter for the college. Berkeley worked tirelessly for three years in London arousing interest in the project. There were generous public subscriptions, and the Archbishop of Canterbury agreed to act as trustee. The House of Commons finally voted a sum of £20,000 for the endowment of the college despite some opposition and some wavering on the part of Walpole. On the strength of this promised grant, Berkeley, who had recently taken a wife, Anne Forster, departed for America on 4 September 1728, settling temporarily (as he thought) at Newport, Rhode Island, to prepare himself for his new role. There he bought land and built a house, preached in local

churches, and carried on philosophical discussion with a number of people. He found a prominent disciple in Dr. Samuel Johnson, who later became President of King's College (Columbia University) and who propagated his philosophy in America. His first son, Henry, was born in Rhode Island.

Berkeley never reached Bermuda. He was eventually told that the parliamentary grant had been withdrawn. In the autumn of 1731, having signed over his property in order to found scholarships at Yale University, Berkeley returned with his family to England.

In 1732 he published *Alciphron: or, The Minute Philosopher*. Written in Rhode Island, these philosophical dialogues, which resemble Plato's, defended Christianity against agnostics and mixed scenic descriptions with the arguments. He answered criticisms of the book in *The Theory of Vision ... Vindicated and Explained* (1733). This was followed by *The Analyst, or, a Discourse Addressed to an Infidel Mathematician* (1734), in which he argued, in defence of religion, that some

27

mathematical assumptions cannot be definitely and fully known any more than religious beliefs. In the same year he was consecrated Bishop of Cloyne in Southern Ireland, and for the next eighteen years he spent most of his time there, devoting himself more and more to the social problems of Ireland. His concern for the poverty of the Irish inspired *The Querist* (1735–7, in three instalments), a work composed of maxims on economic matters cast in the form of questions. His last and perhaps most popular major work was *Siris, A Chain of Philosophical Reflexions and Inquiries on the Virtues of Tar-Water* (1744).

In 1751 Berkeley's favourite son, William, died. With the King's consent, he appointed his brother as vicar general at Cloyne and with his wife and two surviving children went to Oxford in August 1752. He died there suddenly on 14 January 1753, and was buried in the cathedral of Christ Church.

D. M. Armstrong, *Berkeley's Theory of Vision* (Melbourne, 1960).

G. W. Engle and G. Taylor (eds.), *Berkeley's Principle of Human Knowledge: Critical Studies* (1968).

G. A. Johnston, *The Development of Berkeley's Philosophy* (1923: reprinted 1965).

J. Johnston, *Bishop Berkeley's Quest in Historical Perspective* (Dundalgan, 1970).

A. A. Luce, *The Life of George Berkeley, Bishop of Cloyne* (1949; reprinted 1968).

A. A. Luce (ed.), *Philosophical Commentaries, Generally Called the Commonplace Book* (1944).

A. A. Luce and T. E. Jessop (eds.), *The Works of George Berkeley, Bishop of Cloyne* (9 vols.; 1948–57).

W. E. Steinkraus (ed.), *New Studies in Berkeley's Philosophy* (New York, 1966).

G. J. Warnock, *Berkeley* (1969).

G. J. Warnock (ed.), *The Principles of Human Knowledge and Three Dialogues Between Hylas and Philonous* (1962).

Portraits: oil, half-length, by J. Smibert, *c.* 1732: N.P.G.; oil, by James Latham: Trinity College, Dublin.

Beverley, Robert (?1673–1722), historian of Virginia.

Robert Beverley was born in Middlesex County, Virginia, about 1673, the second son of Robert Beverley, a representative of a 'cavalier' family of minor gentry from Yorkshire who had emigrated to Virginia in 1663. After being educated in England he returned to Virginia, taking on administrative posts in local government. After becoming a freeholder in Jamestown, he entered politics and sat as the Burgess for the Capital in the Assemblies of 1699, 1700–2, and 1705–6. While on a visit to England in early 1705 he read Oldmixon's *British Empire in America*. He found the account of Virginia so tedious that he determined to put together his own *History and Present State of Virginia*, which appeared in 1705. This little book has survived over the centuries because of its lovely prose style and its shrewd observations on the contemporary political scene in Virginia, and seems to foreshadow an independent American approach to the writing of history free from English attitudes.

In 1706 Beverley retired from politics to live at Beverley Park, his estate in King and Queen County, where he remained for the rest of his life, experimenting with vine-growing and serving as a magistrate in the county court. The latter experience inspired him to publish in 1722 *The Abridgment of the Public Laws of Virginia*. In the same year there was a new revised edition of the *History*, but with few improvements. Beverley died the same year.

L. B. Wright (ed.), *History of Virginia in Four Parts* (Chapel Hill, 1947).

Bewick, Thomas (1753–1828), wood-engraver, noted as having virtually revived the art of wood-engraving in England.

Bewick was born on 12 August 1753 at Cherryburn in the parish of Ovingham, Northumberland, the eldest son of a local farmer. His early education was conducted by the local vicar, and it was during his childhood that his twin interests in drawing and in the countryside were both developed. The conviction and accuracy of his later engravings owe much to his early love of nature, and he was unhappy at leaving the farm when he was apprenticed to a Newcastle metal-engraver, Ralph Beilby, in 1767.

During his early years of apprenticeship, Bewick worked mainly with metal rather than wood, but when in the early 1770s a series of educational books for children was commissioned from Beilby, it was Bewick who produced most of the illustrative woodcuts. The art of wood-engraving was effectively almost non-existent at this stage of Bewick's career, having declined during the eighteenth century into a process of mere reproduction, and his early exercises were usually limited to letter heads and bill heads.

The future with Beilby was uncertain, and on completion of his apprenticeship in 1776, Bewick went to London. He soon returned to Newcastle, however, to work in partnership with Beilby, and in 1779 he completed a series of engravings for Gay's *Fables* which he had begun as an apprentice, and for which he was awarded a prize by the recently founded Society of Arts. Another book, *Select Fables*, followed in 1784: most of the engravings were still copies of earlier illustrations, but in his detailed naturalistic improvements and in his command of the overall design Bewick's originality was beginning to declare itself. *The Chillingham Bull* (1789), a single large engraving that was his most ambitious work so far, was evidence of Bewick's growing confidence in his own talents, and in his engravings for the *General History of Quadrupeds* (1790), these talents were fully developed.

The next project of this productive partnership between Bewick and Beilby (who wrote the texts) was a *History of British Birds*, published in two volumes in 1797 and 1804. Recognizing that the least successful of his illustrations for the *Quadrupeds* had been those of animals he had never seen, Bewick now confined himself to subjects with which he was wholly familiar. He used a personal graver instead of a knife, and by working on the end grain of the wood rather than the plank he was able to achieve a wide range of tone and texture. The *History of British Birds* went into several editions in Bewick's lifetime, evidence of the extent to which he had restored the art of wood-engraving almost single-handed.

The *Fables of Aesop*, published in 1818, was one of the very few works that Bewick produced after the age of fifty. His reputation spread widely, but he was content to live out his old age in unhurried tranquillity. At his shop in Gateshead he now had several pupils, and his wood-carving techniques were carried on, though with less artistic talent, by his younger brother John and his son Robert Eliot. Bewick is remembered as an industrious, methodical, and independent craftsman, with an enduring love of the countryside. He died on 8 November 1828, in a room above his shop in Gateshead.

Jane Bewick (ed.), *Memoirs of Thomas Bewick Written by Himself, 1822–28* (1862).

G. Reynolds, *Thomas Bewick: A Resumé of His Life and Work* (1949).

S. Roscoe, *Thomas Bewick* (1953).

Portrait: oil, half-length, by J. Ramsay, 1823: N.P.G.

Black, Joseph (1728–99), Scottish chemist, known for his pioneering work in the chemistry of gases and for originating the concepts of specific heat and latent heat.

Joseph Black was born on 16 April 1728 in Bordeaux, France, the son of a Scots-Irish wine merchant. He was educated at

Glasgow University, where he studied chemistry under William Cullen (1712–90), in addition to medicine, anatomy, and languages. In 1751 he transferred to the University of Edinburgh to complete his medical training. His M.D. dissertation, 'On the Acid Humour Arising from Food, and on Magnesia Alba', was important for its description of the effects of heating magnesium carbonate ('magnesia alba') and for its rediscovery of carbon dioxide (which Black called 'fixed air'). He was the first to show that a gas distinct from common atmospheric air could be detected by means of its weight.

In 1756 Black published an extended version of this dissertation under the title *Experiments Upon Magnesia Alba, Quicklime, and Some Other Alcaline Substances.* The principles inherent in this work helped lay the foundation for modern quantitative chemistry. His experiments on calorimetry enabled him to distinguish between heat and temperature. This led

him to realize that each substance required a different quantity of heat to raise its temperature by the same amount. The amount of heat required to raise unit mass of a substance by one degree he called the specific heat of the substance (now called specific heat capacity). At the same time he realized that an extra quantity of heat was required to convert a solid to a liquid and a liquid to a gas. This he called latent heat.

Black succeeded Cullen as lecturer in chemistry in 1756, and was later appointed professor of medicine. For a short time he established a medical practice, although his main interests were in basic chemical research. Three years after demonstrating the phenomenon of latent heat (1763) he became professor of chemistry at the University of Edinburgh. James Watt (q.v.), a friend and student of Black's, undoubtedly benefited from observing Black's studies on the latent heat of steam, and was to make practical use of the results of these experiments in constructing his steam engine.

In 1775 Black published 'The Supposed Effect of Boiling on Water, in Disposing It to Freeze more Readily'. His final scientific contribution appeared in 1794, in the *Transactions of the Royal Society of Edinburgh*: 'An Analysis of the Water of the Hot Springs in Iceland'. Black died in Edinburgh on 10 November 1799, at the age of seventy-one.

J. G. Crowther, *Scientists of the Industrial Revolution: Joseph Black, James Watt, Joseph Priestley, Henry Cavendish* (1962).

W. Ramsay, *Life and Letters of Joseph Black* (1918).

Portraits: oil, by David Martin: Scottish N.P.G.; paste medallion, quarter-length, by James Tassie, 1788: N.P.G.

Blake, William (1757–1827), poet, painter, and visionary.

William Blake was born on 28 November 1757 at Golden Square,

London, the son of a prosperous hosier of Irish descent. His father encouraged his son's talents by sending him at the age of ten to Par's drawing school, the best in London. He also gave him money to buy prints, so that the boy soon became known to auctioneers as 'the little connoisseur'. However, Mr. Blake was less sympathetic to childhood visions; young William once claimed to have seen a tree full of angels in Dulwich and was only saved from a severe beating by his mother's intervention. Paradoxically, it was from his family that Blake early on absorbed Swedenborg's teaching that the only true world is the world of the spirit, a concept which was absolutely fundamental to everything he later painted, engraved, or wrote.

Blake began writing poetry when he was twelve, and some of these accomplished early lyrics were published in *Poetical Sketches* (1783). At fourteen he was apprenticed to James Basire, official engraver to the Society of Antiquaries, whose hard linear style of engraving, the antithesis of the fashionable 'fuzziness' of Bartolozzi, profoundly influenced the young Blake. Blake spent a happy apprenticeship gradually developing the sympathy with medieval sculpture that is so plainly evident in his later 'visionary' engravings. In his spare time he began drawing incidents from English history and the Bible, and also did much reading, rejecting rationalism in favour of bold, imaginative writings.

In 1778 Blake became a student at the newly-formed Royal Academy. At a time when public taste favoured the urbanity of Guido Reni and the Carracci, he strongly preferred the vigour of High Renaissance painting, and soon quarrelled bitterly with Moser, the Academy's keeper. Blake became convinced that a painting should be 'a vision of eternity', and finding that such conventional

exercises as life drawing 'smelt of mortality', he soon left the Academy.

From 1780 Blake earned his living by making engravings after other artists' original drawings, for inclusion in illustrated editions of such classics as *Don Quixote* and *A Sentimental Journey*. His original painting was still fairly conventional, and in 1780 he exhibited his *Death of Earl Godwin* at the Royal Academy's first exhibition. However, the mysterious engraving *Glad Day* gives a foretaste of his later style; thought to represent the giant Albion, it is typical in that it owes its inspiration to a classical original.

In 1782 Blake married Catherine Boucher, a Battersea market gardener's daughter, who turned out to be a truly devoted wife. Two years later, in partnership with the engraver Parker, he opened a print shop in Broad Street, and brought his beloved brother Robert to live with them. Blake here engraved John Flaxman's austerely beautiful illustrations for the *Iliad*, and exhibited even more apocalyptic paintings at the Royal

Academy. It became increasingly obvious, however, that he had reached an impasse; his powerful creative urge needed a more satisfying outlet than other men's visions.

Robert's untimely death in 1787 provided an eerie catalyst. The grief-stricken Blake sold his shop, moved to Poland Street, and tried in vain to get his beautiful *Songs of Innocence* published. His dead brother appeared to him in a dream and told him to combine painting and poetry on the same page. Expending his meagre resources on materials, he proceeded to engrave the text of his lyrics on copper plates, adding complementary illustrations in the margins. He laboriously coloured the printed pages by hand, whilst the loyal Catherine worked the press and bound the finished copies. Though it was hardly commercially viable, this new technique seemed to unfetter Blake's imagination, and he used it for all his subsequent masterpieces.

Blake felt strongly that the human spirit was being stifled by conventional morality, rationalist philosophy, and established religion, and in 1791, at the house of Johnson the bookseller, he met others who shared these 'subversive' opinions. Inspired by the French Revolution, men such as Priestley the scientist, Godwin the philosopher, and Tom Paine the writer openly criticized the social order, and Blake was the most radical of them all, audaciously wearing a cap of liberty in the streets. With the onset of the Terror, an anxious British government began persecuting unorthodox thinkers, and by 1793 Johnson's group had been dispersed. Disillusioned and desperately poor, Blake went to ground at Hercules Buildings, Lambeth.

During the next six years he suffered a severe spiritual crisis. He became obsessed with the problem of evil, to which he now sought a personal solution by 'spiritual strife'. This gave rise to the first group of 'prophetic books', from *The Book of Thel* (1789) through *The Marriage of Heaven and Hell* (1793) to *The Book of Urizen* (1794), all on etched plates with integral illustrations. They employ throughout an intensely personal mythology wherein Christ the redeemer represents good and the oppressive Jehovah of the Old Testament evil. Around these fundamentals Blake weaves a dense texture of symbolism, but this is redeemed from obscurity by his expressive (if somewhat leisurely) verse, a combination of simple lyricism and stately rhetoric, and a vigorous cast of characters who signify elemental forces. These very long, apparently abstruse poems dealt with real-life political issues, such as the spread of industrialization or the excessive power of the state. The illustrations complement this sombre mood; menacingly distorted nudes increasingly take the place of physical beauty.

Blake's disillusionment found more conventional expression in *Songs of Experience* (1794). In place of the fresh and direct optimism of *Songs of Innocence*, a sadder and wiser Blake now drew harshly expressive cameos of society's selfishness and repressiveness. Typical of this new clear-sightedness is 'The Tyger', an ambiguous symbol of both beauty and destruction. Blake also had other work during this period. He drew and engraved over 500 plates for an edition of Young's poem *Night Thoughts*.

In 1800 the poet William Hayley, a friend of Southey and Romney (qq.v.), invited Blake to settle in a little cottage at Felpham, on the Sussex coast, and collaborate on illustrated books. Blake was charmed by his rural surroundings, and manfully struggled to illustrate his employer's bizarre *Anecdotes of Animals*, but he found the 'polite ignorance' of Hayley and his shallow social set exasperating, and a pointless incident in which he ejected from his cottage garden a troublesome drunken soldier, who promptly told the authorities that Blake had uttered seditious statements, led to his trial at Chichester assizes; fortunately he was acquitted.

The stay at Felpham, however, inspired the prophetic poem 'Milton' (1804), which marks Blake's cautious return to optimism. He disliked the overt Puritanism of Milton, but praised his apparently half-conscious delight in depicting Satan the anti-hero and the lush Garden of Eden. Blake found that by extolling man's honest sensual impulses, he could effect a partial reconciliation between the material and spiritual worlds.

Blake now returned to London and drew a set of superb illustrations to Blair's *The Grave* for the publisher Cromek. The engraving, however, was entrusted to another artist, and as if this was not enough, Cromek, who had noticed some drawings for the *Canterbury Tales* in Blake's studio, promptly commissioned yet a third artist to do a set of Chaucer illustrations without telling Blake.

Heartily sick of this erosion of his reputation, Blake in 1809 mounted a one-man exhibition of his own work. The *Descriptive Catalogue* to this contains a fascinating commentary by Blake on each of his paintings, as well as a defiant Prologue in which he claims to have rescued 'real art', as practised by Michelangelo and Raphael, from the 'ignorances' of such as Titian, Rubens, and Rembrandt. But this was not enough; Blake exhibited for the last time at the Royal Academy in 1808, sending such masterpieces as *Jacob's Dream* and *The Last Judgment*, and thereafter went into the wilderness for ten years.

A chance meeting in 1818 with a twenty-six-year-old painter, John Linnell, ushered in the period of Blake's finest achievements. Around the elderly visionary there soon gathered a circle of young and brilliant disciples, who encouraged Blake to do a series of *Spiritual Portraits*, astonishing pencil sketches of such subjects as *The Ghost of a Flea* and *The Man who Built the Pyramids*.

In 1820 Blake engraved perhaps his most influential illustrations, for Thornton's translation of Virgil's *Eclogues*. They were his first and only woodcuts and his first and only landscapes, but despite a crude technique they breathe a serenely poetic feeling. Samuel Palmer saw in them 'visions of little dells and nooks and corners of Paradise' and so, through Palmer, Blake became the ultimate inspiration of the 'visionary' school of English landscape painting.

Blake moved to Fountain Court in the Strand, where, amid increasing poverty, he completed his last masterpieces. The illustrations to the *Book of Job*, commissioned by Linnell, are Blake's final pictorial statement on the conflict between good and evil. In a style refined to a monumental simplicity, he recommends fortitude as the solution by depicting the ineffectiveness of Jehovah's cruelty in the face of Job's patience. Soon afterwards Blake finished his greatest prophetic poem, 'Jerusalem', which had been twenty years in the writing. After the turbulent questionings of his earlier poetry, he now accepted something like the conventional Christian answer to evil; just as Christ's sufferings redeemed a sinful Creation, so Christ-like behaviour by each individual will save a corrupt society. In accordance with this sense of reconciliation, the illustrations to 'Jerusalem' return to the flowing forms and tranquil colours of Blake's earliest days.

Although he was only a struggling artist himself, the devoted Linnell saved the aged Blake from starvation by giving him £3 a week regularly, in return for illustrations to Dante's *Divine Comedy*. Blake set to work joyously and had completed over a hundred drawings, expressing a new and tender lyricism, before his health began to fail. On the morning of 12 August 1827 William Blake 'sang loudly and with true ecstatic energy, and seemed so happy that he had finished his course', and at six o'clock that evening he died.

J. Beer, *Blake's Humanism* (1968).

Sir A. F. Blunt, *The Art of William Blake* (1959).

J. Bronowski, *William Blake and the Age of Revolution* (1965, rev. ed.).

D. V. Erdman, *Blake, Prophet Against Empire: A Poet's Interpretation of the History of His Own Times* (Princeton, 1969, rev. ed.).

D. V. Erdman and H. Bloom (ed.), *The Poetry and Prose of William Blake* (Garden City, N.Y., 1965).

N. Frye, *Fearful Symmetry: A Study of William Blake* (Princeton, 1947).

Geoffrey Keynes (ed.), *The Complete Writings of William Blake* (1957).

Geoffrey Keynes (ed.), *The Note-Book of William Blake, Called the Rossetti Manuscript* (1935).

K. J. Raine, *Blake and Tradition* (2 vols.; Princeton, 1969).

A. C. Swinburne, *William Blake: A Critical Essay* (1868; reprinted 1967).

M. Wilson, *The Life of William Blake* (1969).

Portraits: oil, half-length, by T. Phillips, 1807: N.P.G.; water-colour, quarter-length, by J. Linnell, 1821: N.P.G.; pencil, by J. Linnell: Fitzwilliam Museum, Cambridge.

Bligh, William (1754–1817), naval commander; captain during the famous mutiny on H.M.S. *Bounty*.

William Bligh was born in Plymouth on 9 September 1754. At the age of eighteen he was chosen to accompany James Cook on the latter's second voyage of circumnavigation (1772–4), during which he made the significant discovery of breadfruit on the island of Tahiti. In 1787, having reached the rank of lieutenant, Bligh was given the command of H.M.S. *Bounty* with instructions to collect breadfruit plants from Tahiti and to transport them to the British West Indies, where it was hoped that they might be acclimatized. After a long voyage under a strict captain, the crew of the *Bounty* spent six lazy months gathering breadfruit on Tahiti; the sunlight and freedom of these days, as well as the warm welcome given to them by the natives, combined with the promptings of Fletcher Christian, their ringleader, to provide reason enough for an overthrow of authority, and on 28 April 1789, in the vicinity of the Friendly Isles, the crew mutinied and Bligh and eighteen others were cast adrift in a longboat.

In this 23-foot-long craft, equipped with little food and no map, Bligh accomplished one of the most skilful and courageous voyages of history. After sailing more than 3,500 miles he landed at Timor, an island off the coast of Java, on 14 June 1789, and early the following year he arrived back in England with his twelve surviving companions. A ship sent to Tahiti to search for the mutineers came back with only three, all of whom were hanged at Portsmouth; the others, under the leadership of Christian, had moved to Pitcairn Island, where they remained undiscovered till 1808.

Bligh received promotion and a new command from the admiralty, and in 1792 he successfully fulfilled a commission almost identical to that of the *Bounty*. He fought at the battles of Camperdown (1797) and Copenhagen (1801), and in 1801 he was elected a Fellow of the Royal Society in recognition of his navigating abilities and his services to botany. In 1805 he was appointed Governor of New South Wales; the members of this colony, many of them transported convicts, reacted against his 'oppressive' rule in a manner for which the precedent had been set, and in 1808 Bligh was arrested and imprisoned by his deputy. Released after two years, he returned to England, and the deputy was cashiered.

The victim of two successful mutinies, Bligh has inevitably been portrayed as a tyrannical and intolerant commander. According to the evidence, however, Bligh was no more authoritarian than his duties demanded, and the chief defect of his character was probably his inability to conduct human relationships in a tactful and sympathetic manner; certainly he was no more punitive or severe than the great majority of his contemporary officers. He was promoted Rear Admiral in 1811 and Vice Admiral three years later, and he lived during his later years with his wife and six daughters at Farningham in Kent. He died in London on 7 December 1817.

Sir John Barrow, *The Eventful History of the Mutiny and piratical seizure of H.M.S.* Bounty, ed. S. W. Roskill (1976).

A. Hawkey, *Bligh's Other Mutiny* (1976).

G. Mackaness, *The Life of Vice-Admiral William Bligh* (1951).

O. Rutter, *Turbulent Journey: A Life of William Bligh* (1936).

Portraits: pencil, half-length, by G. Dance, 1794: N.P.G.; pencil and water-colour, half-length, by J. Smart: N.P.G.

Bolingbroke, 1st Viscount (1678–1751), politician and political philosopher, see St. John, Henry, in *Lives of the Stuart Age*.

Boscawen, Edward (1711–61), British admiral in the War of the Austrian Succession and the Seven Years War.

Edward Boscawen was born on 19 August 1711, the third son of Hugh Boscawen, 3rd Viscount Falmouth. He entered the navy in 1726, and in the war that broke out in 1739 against Spain he served with credit, seeing action in the West Indies, the Mediterranean, and in home waters.

In 1742 he returned to England, married and took his seat in parliament as M.P. for Truro. Two years later the French entered the war, and Boscawen passed through several commands at home. As captain of the 74-gun *Namur* he took part in the rout of La Jonquière's 38 ships at the first Battle of Cape Finisterre (3 May 1747). Here he was wounded, but for his actions he was promoted Rear Admiral of the Blue.

In the same year he led a small expedition to the East Indies, and after arriving in India tried to take Pondicherry by siege. But the stoutness of the French defence and the incompetence of his own forces rendered the attack a failure. The end of the conflict followed hard on these events and Boscawen returned to England in 1749. In June 1751 he was nominated one of the Lords Commissioners of the Admiralty, retaining the appointment until his death.

In 1755 he was promoted Vice Admiral and sailed for North America with a squadron of eleven ships of the line with specific orders to attack French ships wherever he found them in those waters. An effective state of war already existed between the two nations in the colonies, although nominally there was peace. Boscawen encountered two transports and a 64-gun warship on 10 June, but one of the transports escaped into the fog that shielded the remainder of the French convoy as it passed safely into the St. Lawrence. The first shots of the Seven Years War were fired when Richard Howe, one of Boscawen's subordinates, aboard his vessel *Dunkirk*, overwhelmed the French ship *Alcide* (11 June 1755). The English squadron entered Halifax, but the outbreak of a virulent epidemic of fever, which killed over 2,000 of his men, forced Boscawen to return home.

His time was now divided between administrative duties and sea-going commands in the Channel and its approaches. He was involved in the dismal episode of the court martial of Admiral Byng (see Byng, John), and as Commander in Chief, Portsmouth, signed

Byng's execution order. On 8 February 1758 he was promoted Admiral of the Blue and placed in charge of a fleet of forty-one ships which gave naval support to General Amherst (q.v.) in his expedition against Cape Breton Island. The siege and capture of Louisbourg (June–July 1758) by army forces could not have been accomplished without the powerful presence and energetic support of Boscawen's command. When he returned home in December, he was formally thanked by the House of Commons.

In April 1759 Boscawen took a squadron out to the Mediterranean, flying his flag in the new 90-gun *Namur*. His purpose was to watch the French squadron in Toulon, which was under orders to come out to cover projected landings in western Scotland and the mouth of the Thames. La Clue, commanding the French fleet, eluded Boscawen and passed through the Straits late on 17 August; Boscawen, many of his ships still unready for sea, nevertheless gave chase immediately. Losing most of his ships in the ensuing action at Cadiz, La Clue took the last four under his command into the neutral waters of Lagos Bay on the Portuguese coast, where Boscawen followed him on 19 August, risking the diplomatic uproar which would probably ensue. La Clue died in the subsequent combat and two of his ships were captured.

Boscawen returned to England, and was rewarded with the lucrative appointment of General of Marines, based chiefly at Quiberon Bay. However, in the winter of 1760 he contracted a virulent fever, and died on 10 January 1761 at his estate in Surrey.

C. Aspinall-Oglander (ed.), *Admiral's Wife: Life and Letters of the Hon. Mrs. E. Boscawen, 1719–61* (1940).

P. K. Kemp (ed.), 'Boscawen's Letters to His Wife, 1755–56', *Naval Miscellany* (Navy Records Society, vol. 4; 1952).

Portrait: oil, half-length, after Sir J. Reynolds, *c.* 1755: National Maritime Museum, Greenwich.

Boswell, James (1740–95), biographer of Dr. Samuel Johnson (q.v.).

James Boswell was born in Edinburgh on 29 October 1740, son of the judge Lord Auchinleck, who came from an old and dignified Scottish family. Educated privately and at Edinburgh High School and Edinburgh University, Boswell progressed to Glasgow University to study civil law in 1759.

In 1760 he ran away to London, was received into the communion of the Church of Rome (but kept this fact secret all his life), played with the notion of entering a monastery, and enjoyed a social whirl, but after three months obeyed his father's instruction to return to resume his legal studies. After coming of age he returned to London in 1762. Greatly impressed by the social and cultural atmosphere of the capital, he was determined to make a name for himself. He tried vainly for a commission in the Guards, and contributed to various journals, both much against his father's wish. He assiduously sought acquaintanceship with eminent persons, especially politicians and writers, and met John Wilkes and the great Dr. Johnson. From the start he kept notes of Johnson's conversation and followed his suggestion that he should keep a full journal. Recalled to Scotland by a threat of disinheritance, Boswell dutifully agreed to study law at Utrecht, departing thither in August 1763.

After nearly a year of dull study he set out on the Grand Tour. By the time he returned to England (escorting Rousseau's mistress, Thérèse Levasseur) in 1766, he had visited the German courts,

Switzerland (where he had called on Voltaire), Italy, and Corsica. Back in Scotland again, he set up a fairly successful legal practice, and began to make a name for himself as a man of letters with the publication in 1768 of his *Account of Corsica*. This ran to three editions and was much admired.

Boswell married his cousin Margaret Montgomerie in November 1769. They settled in Edinburgh, but Boswell greatly missed London, which he could visit only during the spring recesses of the Scottish law courts. During the recess of 1772 he met Johnson again and began a correspondence with him that lasted until the latter's death in 1784. Besides these spring visits, Boswell proudly accompanied Johnson on a tour of the Hebrides from August to November 1773, which prompted books by both travellers. The two also met on several other occasions, all away from London. Johnson engineered Boswell's election to the *élite* Literary Club in 1773, despite several objectors, including Burke, although the latter subsequently became fond of Boswell.

Boswell's home life was becoming less happy. He spent money that he could ill afford on mistresses, and had, by 1780, five children to support. He did not impress clients with his capacity as a lawyer; moreover neither his wife nor his father could sympathize at all with his admiration for Johnson.

In 1782 Boswell achieved financial independence on the death of his father, an event that, as Johnson remarked, 'had every circumstance that could enable you to bear it' – and he became, rather surprisingly, a very efficient laird. With various pamphlets and open letters he attempted to gain political status but was unsuccessful. His last meeting with Johnson was at dinner at Sir Joshua Reynolds's house, where he tried to obtain the money for Johnson to winter in Italy.

Johnson, however, died of dropsy and asthma before this plan could be put into effect.

In spring 1786 Boswell published his *Journal of a Tour to the Hebrides*, and began work on his life of Johnson, continuing still to press for some kind of public office, and denouncing Pitt in 1789 for his 'utter folly' in not rewarding a man of 'my popular and pleasant talents'. He took a house in London but only managed to 'keep hovering as an English lawyer' and got very little business. His wife's health was deteriorating and in 1789, to his deep grief and remorse, she died at Auchinleck. After a humiliating quarrel (involving a stolen wig) with Lord Lonsdale, the only patron who ever gave him employment, Boswell resigned the recordership of Carlisle and decided to leave Scotland and take chambers in the Temple, where he got very few briefs. He settled his children at expensive boarding schools and found himself very short of money, until at last the publication in 1791 of *The Life of Samuel Johnson, LL.D.* proved an immediate success. Arguably the best biography in the language, it is remarkable as much for its candour as for its vivid and detailed picture of the London both men enjoyed so much. Johnson is shown in every mood, for Boswell refused to 'cut off his claws and make my tiger a cat to please anyone'.

Though the reception of his great work must have cheered him, Boswell was still subject to deep depressions, increased by his intemperate drinking habits. In June 1793 he was knocked down and robbed when drunk and vowed for the hundredth time to be 'a sober regular man'. In spring 1795 he came home 'weak and languid' from a meeting of the Literary Club, fell seriously ill, and died of uraemia and a tumour on the bladder on 19 May 1795. He was buried at Auchinleck.

Boswell was a man of many eccentricities. His vanity was relieved by a touching confidence in and love of his fellow man. His great contemporaries loved him; as the writer of an obituary put it: 'It does not seem to me that he ever did, or could, injure any human being intentionally.'

C. H. Bennett and F. A. Pottle (eds.), *The Journal of a Tour to the Hebrides with Samuel Johnson* (1963).

F. Brady, *Boswell's Political Career* (New Haven, 1965).

F. Brady and F. A. Pottle (eds.), *Boswell on the Grand Tour: Italy, Corsica, and France* (1955).

David Daiches, *James Boswell and his World* (1976).

G. B. Hill (ed.), *The Life of Samuel Johnson* (6 vols.; 1887, rev. L. F. Powell, 1934–50 and 1964).

F. A. Pottle, *Boswell: The Earlier Years* (1966).

F. A. Pottle, *The Literary Career of James Boswell, Esq.* (1929).

F. A. Pottle (ed.), *Boswell's London Journal, 1762–1763* (1966).

F. A. Pottle et al. (eds.), *The Yale Editions of the Private Papers of James Boswell* (1950–   ).

G. Scott and F. A. Pottle (eds.), *The Private Papers of James Boswell from Malchide Castle* (18 vols.; New York, 1928–34).

C. B. Tinker, *Young Boswell* (1929).

Portraits: pencil, half-length, by G. Dance, 1793: N.P.G.; oil, quarter-length, studio of Reynolds, 1785: N.P.G.; pencil, half-length, by T. Lawrence:

N.P.G.; oil, quarter-length, by J. Reynolds, 1785: N.P.G.; oil, three-quarter length, by George Willison: Scottish N.P.G.; oil, by G. Langton: Gunby Hall, Lincolnshire.

Boulton, Matthew (1728–1809), industrialist and engineer.

Matthew Boulton was born on 3 September 1728 in Birmingham. His father was a silver stamper and piercer, and Matthew entered this business young and devoted considerable energy to developing and expanding it. His father died in 1759, and the following year Matthew married Anne Robinson of Lichfield, who brought him a considerable dowry. He founded the famous Soho factory, which opened in 1762, and very soon established a reputation for the high standard of workmanship and artistry of its wares. Boulton employed agents to search for the finest objects in metalwork, pottery, and other materials for use as models.

As the Soho factory expanded, Boulton started investigations into the possibilities of steam engines to power the pumps. He made several experiments himself, and came into contact with James Watt (q.v.), who was at this time struggling to develop his engines. In 1775 they set up in partnership. Watt's powers of mechanical inventiveness allied to Boulton's energy, vision, and astute business sense were eventually to make a rewarding union. Prosperity was slow in coming, however, and Boulton was verging on bankruptcy before the tide turned financially.

In 1775 Boulton had succeeded in extending the steam engine patent for another twenty-five years by act of parliament. Assisted by the engineer and inventor William Murdock, the partnership of Boulton and Watt laid the foundations of the steam engine industry, erecting engines to drain the Cornish tin mines and to fan air into factories. Boulton urged Watt to design a double-acting rotative engine, and this was patented in 1782. 1788 saw the patenting of the 'Watt engine' for powering the lapping mach-ines in the cotton industry. At last all difficulties were vanquished and by 1800 there were about 500 working engines installed in the British Isles and abroad.

Boulton was also involved in the reform of copper coinage. He set up steam-powered coining presses in Soho in 1788 (patent dated 1790), and produced quantities of coins for the East India Company, the colonies, and foreign governments. In 1797 he was appointed to produce a new copper coinage for Great Britain. He also supplied the machinery for the new mint on Tower Hill in 1805.

Matthew Boulton had a well-earned place in the scientific society of the day. Among his friends were Benjamin Franklin, Joseph Priestley, Erasmus Darwin, and Josiah Wedgwood. He was made a Fellow of the Royal Society in 1785 and was also a member of that thriving Birmingham group, the Lunar Society, whose meetings were held at his house. He died on 18 August 1809, aged eighty.

H. W. Dickinson, *Matthew Boulton* (1937).

Portraits: oil, quarter-length, by unknown artist: N.P.G.; miniature, quarter-length, after W. Beechey: N.P.G.

Bowring, Sir John (1792–1872), linguist and traveller; editor of the *Westminster Review*, see *Lives of the Victorian Age*.

Boyce, William (?1710–79), organist, composer, and musical antiquarian.

William Boyce was born about 1710 in London, where his father, John Boyce, was a joiner and carpenter. One of four children, he received his earliest musical training as a chorister at St. Paul's Cathedral. Even before the ending of his apprenticeship his hearing had shown signs of deterioration, and soon he became all but deaf. This misfortune, however, seemed to have little effect on Boyce and in no way diverted him in his chosen career.

Boyce's first post, taken up in 1734, was that of organist at Oxford Chapel, Vere Street, Cavendish Square. He also began teaching the harpsichord, chiefly in boarding schools, at the same time undertaking a further course of study himself, under John Christopher Pepusch (q.v.).

Boyce's earliest compositions, pro-duced under Pepusch's guidance, were single songs. His first large-scale work, a masque for Lord Lansdowne, *Peleus and Thetis*, was composed around 1734. In the following year he accepted the con-ductorship of the Annual Festival of the Sons of the Clergy.

In 1736 Boyce became organist at St. Michael's, Cornhill, and in the same year he also became Composer to the Chapel Royal, in which capacity he wrote a great deal of sacred music. In 1737 he further extended his activities by becoming conductor of the Three Choirs Festival, a post that he held for some years.

Before he was thirty, in addition to a quantity of church compositions and smaller pieces he had a number of large-scale works to his credit, including his *Lamentation over Saul and Jonathan*, and two Odes for St. Cecilia's Day. Other major projects soon followed, including the splendidly colourful and evocative serenata, *Solomon* (1743), his Twelve Sonatas for Two Violins and a Bass (1745), and a collection of songs and cantatas (published together in 1747).

In July 1749 Cambridge University conferred on him the degrees of Bachelor and Doctor of Music, and in the wake of his academic honours, he was asked to become organist of All Hallows the Great and the Less, Thames Street, London, where a new organ had just been built. About this time Boyce married. Nothing is known of the marriage except that his wife's name was Hannah and there were two children, Elizabeth (born in 1749) and William (born in 1764).

Boyce entered the field of theatre music in 1749 with the revival of *Peleus and Thetis*. In the same year he provided songs to Garrick's farce *Lethe* for Drury Lane, and set to music Moses Mendez's drama, *The Chaplet*. With Thomas Arne (q.v.) Boyce was to create an indigenous style of theatre music which challenged the supremacy of the Italian masters in London.

In 1755 the death of Boyce's early teacher and subsequent close friend, Maurice Greene, led to his appointment as Master of the King's Musick. He also took up a project that Greene had started in his last years, namely the collection and publication of 'the most esteemed services and anthems composed for the use of the reformed church' during the previous two centuries. The result was Boyce's epoch-making *Cathedral Music* published in three volumes 1760–78. Its influence was decisive and, despite gaps and editorial discrepancies, the selection formed the basis of the choice of church service music sung by choirs throughout the succeeding 150 years.

Already extremely busy, Boyce accepted a post as one of the three Organists to the Chapel Royal in 1758. He went on playing until his deafness finally made his playing objectionable, and forced him to retire in 1768. His last years, plagued by his worsening hearing and the onset of gout, were spent in teaching, composing, and completing his *Cathedral Music*. Boyce died on 7 February 1779, and was buried with great honour and ceremony at St. Paul's Cathedral.

The music by which Boyce is best known today is that of the Eight Symphonies in Eight Parts (1760). These tiny overtures show an exquisite mastery that is but one facet of a many-sided talent. His best-known song, 'Heart of Oak', appeared in the music for Garrick's pantomime *Harlequin's Invasion* (1759) and is still popular.

G. Beechey, 'Memoirs of Dr. William Boyce', *The Musical Quarterly* (January 1971).

D. Dawe, 'New Light on William Boyce', *The Musical Times* (September 1968).

Portraits: pastel, quarter-length, by J. Russell, 1776: N.P.G.; oil, by Thomas Hudson: Bodleian Library, Oxford University.

Bradley, James (1693–1762), astronomer whose refined observations did much to confirm the theories of Copernicus and Newton; succeeded Edmond Halley (see *Lives of the Stuart Age*) as Astronomer Royal.

James Bradley was born at Sherborne, Gloucestershire, in March 1693. He was educated at Balliol College, Oxford, and obtained his M.A. in 1717. Intended originally for the church, he had also shown tremendous interest in astronomy and was encouraged in this pursuit by his uncle, the Rev. James Pound, through whom he met Halley, at this time Secretary to the Royal Society. On Halley's recommendation, the young astronomer was elected a Fellow of the Royal Society on 6 November 1718.

In 1719 Bradley was presented to the vicarage of Bridstow. Later, through the good offices of his friend and subsequent colleague, Samuel Molyneux, he became absentee rector of a parish in Pembrokeshire. 1719 also saw his first astronomical publication, embodying the results of some recent observations of the satellite system of Jupiter.

In 1721 Bradley abandoned his career as a clergyman. In the ensuing period, working first at Molyneux's house at Kew

Green and then with improved instruments at Wanstead rectory, he and Molyneux made numerous observations in order to detect stellar parallax. This change in the apparent position of a star over a six-month period was felt to be the deciding factor as to whether or not the earth orbited the sun. Though accepted by many astronomers, it had failed, even at this late date, to be satisfactorily observed. Selecting the star Gamma Draconis, Bradley observed a displacement during 1725 but found it to be too great for a parallactic displacement. The cause of this was the aberration of light from the star. This aberration was deduced to be the quantity represented by the resultant of the velocity of light from the star, and the velocity of the *moving* earth in its solar orbit. Having discovered this phenomenon, Bradley was in a position to give support not only to the theory of Copernicus, but also to that of Newton. He published his findings on the subject in a paper delivered to the Royal Society in 1729.

Bradley had, however, kept back a supplementary discovery. Gamma Draconis, as it happens, is a star lying close to the north celestial pole. Bradley discovered over the period 1727–32 an annual change in the declination (angular distance above the equator) of this and other stars. The change was greater for polar than for equatorial stars. It was brought about by the phenomenon of nutation (a periodic 'nodding' or oscillation of the earth's axis associated with its precession and caused mainly by the gravitational force of the moon, which exerts a stronger influence at the poles than at the equator). The oscillation occupies a period of about nineteen years, during which time the node of the moon's orbit appears to move westwards along the ecliptic, the path of the earth's orbit. Bradley was understandably cautious; despite the fact that

Halley had been involved in work on the saros (cycle of solar and lunar eclipses), an allied phenomenon, Bradley nevertheless waited for another nineteen-year cycle before presenting his results before the Royal Society in February 1748.

In 1729 Bradley became reader in experimental philosophy at Oxford, holding the post until 1760. The pinnacle of his career, however, was reached in 1742 when, after Halley's death, he was appointed Astronomer Royal at Greenwich Observatory. In the same year, Oxford granted him the degree of Doctor of Divinity.

At a cost of £1,000 – a very great sum for that time – Bradley then obtained new astronomical instruments and during ten years as Astronomer Royal, he made many general improvements in the equipment at Greenwich. Under his aegis the observatory continued to advance its reputation for accurate measurements. He continued his observation of the Jovian system and made from Greenwich most precise assessments of the longitude of both Lisbon and New York.

In 1752 Bradley retired from his post at the Observatory and continued lecturing at Oxford. In 1761, having suffered a deterioration in health, he withdrew to Chalford, Gloucestershire, and died there on 13 July 1762.

James Bradley is recognized by many as one of the founding fathers of modern astronomy. He developed new observational techniques and fostered increased precision in the construction of scientific instruments. His writings, after a long quarrel over their rightful ownership between his heirs and the Admiralty, were finally published by the Oxford University Press in 1798–1805.

G. Abetti, *The History of Astronomy* (1954).
S. P. Rigaud (ed.), *Miscellaneous Works and Correspondence of James Bradley, D.D.* (1832).

H. Spencer Jones, *The Royal Observatory, Greenwich* (1948).

Portrait: oil on panel, half-length, after Thomas Hudson, about 1742–7: N.P.G.

Bridgewater, 3rd Duke of (1736–1803), see Egerton, Francis.

Brindley, James (1716–72), engineer and canal-builder.

James Brindley was born at Thornsett, Derbyshire, in 1716, the son of a careful and clever mother and an idle and dissolute small farmer who neglected his family. Having received very little education, Brindley was apprenticed, at the age of seventeen, to Abraham Bennett, a millwright of Sutton, near Macclesfield. He was a poor workman but was kept on because of his remarkable talent for repairing machinery. These mechanical skills eventually led to his being put in charge of Bennett's shop. Brindley, his apprenticeship complete, moved to Leek in 1742, after Bennett's death. He obtained a good living and, as a result of his advancing reputation, was employed by the Wedgwoods to construct flint mills. In 1752 he set up an engine of his own design for draining some coal pits at Clifton, Lancashire, while in 1755 he completed the machinery for a silk mill at Congleton.

Brindley's fame spread and in 1759 the Duke of Bridgewater (see Egerton, Francis) asked for his advice on the building of a canal in Lancashire by which coal from the Worsley mines could be cheaply and efficiently moved to Manchester. The difficulties were great, but his plan was ingenious, including a design for an aqueduct by which the canal was to be carried at a height of 39 feet over the river Irwell at Barton. This was the first important canal built in England and was the basis of the future system of inland waterways.

Brindley superintended the building of numerous other canals, probably well over 360 miles in all, including the Bridgewater canal connecting Manchester and Liverpool and the Trent and Mersey or 'Grand Trunk' canal, which connected Humberside with the Mersey.

Brindley was almost totally illiterate and did all his calculations in his head; yet his rough, untrained genius played no small part in early English engineering. He died at Turnhurst, Staffordshire, on 30 September 1772.

C. Hadfield, *British Canals* (1959).

Portrait: engraving, miniature, by Pierre Condé: British Museum.

Brougham, Henry Peter (1778–1868), 1st Baron Brougham and Vaux; radical Whig politician who was Lord Chancellor from 1830 to 1834.

Brougham was born on 19 September 1778, the son of middle-class parents in Edinburgh. In later life he invented an aristocratic genealogy for himself, but he was in fact an impoverished Scot.

Brougham took a degree at Edinburgh University when he was thirteen. A precocious scientist and mathematician, he also began studying the law, and was called to the Scottish bar in 1800. In addition he contributed articles to the *Edinburgh Review*, and wrote a full-length study of European colonialism.

Brougham's law practice in Scotland was not profitable. He soon became restive and in 1803 moved to London where he eventually made the acquaintance of Charles James Fox (q.v.), and became the leading polemical journalist of the radical Whigs. In 1810 the Duke of Bedford secured his election to parliament for the pocket borough of Camelford.

He had been called to the English bar in 1808 and already had a lucrative practice and a reputation as an incisive and emotive court-room orator. In parliament, his power of oratory was such that members flocked to the House to hear him, though they rarely acted on his pleas. In 1812, however, he managed to persuade Castlereagh's government to revoke the Orders in Council which, by banning exports to continental Europe, had caused more harm to English industry than to Napoleon, against whom they had been directed. At the election later that year Brougham lost his influence with Bedford and was consequently to be out of parliament for the next four years.

Brougham, as a lawyer, now became involved in the case of George IV's attempted divorce of Caroline of Brunswick (q.v.) on the hypocritical ground of adultery. Brougham had become legal adviser to Caroline in 1812, and eventually when the bill for the annulment of the royal marriage and the deposition of the Queen was brought into the House of Lords in July 1820, he defended her. He entirely discredited the crown's witnesses and his enthusiastic summing-up lasted two days. The bill was thrown out, and Brougham became the most popular lawyer in England, with a practice worth £7,000 a year.

Having returned to parliament in 1816, Brougham found himself frustrated. The Whigs were hopelessly divided, and Brougham's malicious personality ensured that he would never lead or unite them. He saw only too clearly the need for radical reforms, but he was powerless to bring about such changes. Nevertheless, he was the driving force and spokesman for the reformers in the country. His ideas did not always produce immediate action, but often they formed the platform on which later reforms were based. In February 1828 he delivered a magnificent speech on civil law reform which, like his bankruptcy bill and his proposed re-organization of local courts, took effect

years later – in some cases the reforms came after he had retired from public life. Throughout his career he lost no opportunity to press for the abolition of slavery. In the field of education he was a founder of the Society for the Diffusion of Useful Knowledge, a founder of the non-sectarian University of London, and a promoter of the early Education Acts.

In 1830 the Whigs returned to power after nearly fifty years, and Brougham was elected for the county of Yorkshire. The new Prime Minister, Earl Grey (q.v.), considered him too able and too powerful to be left out of the government. Yet there was some difficulty over what post he should have, since Lord Althorp (see Spencer, John Charles) refused to have him as a cabinet minister in the House of Commons, and his mercurial and vitriolic personality frightened the Lords, Whig and Tory alike. Eventually, however, he was offered and accepted the office of Lord Chancellor.

He carried out his duties vigorously, played a major role in promoting the great Reform Act of 1832, and incidentally created the Central Criminal Court in London, stamping out some of the worst inefficiencies and confusions in the legal system. He also reorganized the Privy Council. However, cabinet and opposition members were hostile to him, and his familiar, contemptuous, and voluminous correspondence with William IV gave offence to the latter.

After Grey's resignation, Brougham continued to serve in the short-lived first administration of Lord Melbourne (see Lamb, William). However, on 10 November 1834 Melbourne was summoned to Brighton to hear the King call for the resignation of his government. On his return to London the next evening Melbourne met Brougham and told him, in confidence, of the events of the day. Brougham ignored the confidentiality and rushed off to place a paragraph in *The Times*, blaming the Queen (of all people) for his dismissal.

For Melbourne, since he disliked Brougham personally, this was the last straw. When he returned to power five months later, he was determined to keep Brougham out of office. During 1835 Brougham assiduously attacked the government's weak points, until the appointment early in 1836 of Lord Cottenham as Lord Chancellor finally shocked him into silence.

It was not until the accession of Queen Victoria that he spoke again – to sneer at the court, at the Queen's affection for 'Lord M.', and at his fellow Whigs in general. His most furious invective, brought against his former friend 'Radical Jack' Durham (see Lambton, John George) for his conduct in quelling a Canadian rebellion, caused the latter's resignation. The government survived, however, and Brougham at last seemed to realize that his career was over.

Henry Brougham lived on for over thirty years. He became increasingly eccentric and given to excessive high living. From 1838 onwards he spent much time at Cannes, then a Mediterranean fishing village. He bought a villa there and devoted himself to writing his autobiography (published in 1871). Over the years he popularized Cannes as a tourist resort, and died there on 7 May 1868.

A. Aspinall, *Lord Brougham and the Whig Party* (1927).
Henry Brougham, *Life and Times of Henry, Lord Brougham* (3 vols., 1871).
G. T. Garratt, *Lord Brougham* (1935).
F. Hawes, *Henry Brougham* (1957).
C. W. New, *The Life of Henry Brougham to 1830* (1961).

Portraits: oil, half-length, by T. Lawrence: N.P.G.; oil, half-length, by J. Lonsdale: N.P.G.; marble bust, by J. A. Acton, 1867: N.P.G.

Brown, Lancelot (1716–83), known as 'Capability' Brown; landscape gardener and architect.

Brown was born in 1716 of humble parentage in the village of Kirkharle, Northumberland. Despite the poverty of his upbringing, he received a good local education. His gardening career started with employment on an estate near his native village, but in 1739 he moved south, to Wotton in Buckinghamshire, and by 1742 was in the employ of Lord Cobham at Stowe, near Buckingham. Here he was put in charge of the kitchen gardens, but it was also one of his duties to show visiting guests the entire gardens. It was thus that he first came to the notice of his future clientele.

At this time William Kent (q.v.) was carrying out extensive alterations to the gardens at Stowe over a period of several years. Through careful study and observation Brown was eventually to absorb the details of Kent's technique as well as his general approach. By the time of Kent's death in 1748, Brown had attained supervisory status and was able successfully to complete his predecessor's plans for the grounds of Stowe, which were to become one of the most celebrated gardens in England.

In 1751 Brown moved to London in order to set up an independent practice as a landscape gardener. He was immediately successful and soon earned his nickname, 'Capability', for he developed the habit of telling his clients that their gardens had 'capabilities of improvement, great capabilities'. One of his earliest patrons was the Duke of Grafton, and from there he went on to redesign and 'improve' more than 140 estates throughout England. It was fairly early in his independent career that Walpole, having seen the garden at Warwick Castle, spoke of it as being 'well laid out by one Brown, who has set up on a few ideas of Kent. . . .'

Although Brown's best works were the envy of his professional successors and although his skill brought him great wealth, he has also at various periods suffered severe criticism for his work and its methods. He has been accused not only of destroying the time-honoured concept of a formal garden with his ideas, but also of reducing the beauty of nature to a hackneyed repetition of a set of regular features. His general aim was to accentuate the natural undulations of the land, and this he achieved by surrounding the sweeping and rolling turf with thick belts of woodland, generally beech. In the middle distance would be a lake of serpentine outline and scattered clumps of oaks and chestnuts positioned on the house approach. The whole effect is one of serene grandeur, of 'nature ordered' rather than of human endeavour. Among his finest works are the grounds of Longleat in Wiltshire, Harewood in Yorkshire, Heveningham in Suffolk, Burghley in Northamptonshire, and Petworth in Sussex. His masterpiece of landscaping, however, is at Blenheim Palace in Oxfordshire, undertaken comparatively early in his career. Of special interest here are the clumps of trees along the Grand Avenue, sited to represent the positions of the opposing armies at the Battle of Blenheim. One of the best and most characteristic features is the lake in front of the house, made by damming the tiny River Glyme. This large and characteristic serpentine lake is crossed by a magnificent bridge designed by Blenheim Palace's original architect, Sir John Vanbrugh (see *Lives of the Stuart Age*).

Brown reached the peak of his professional career with his appointment in 1764 as Royal Gardener to George III at Hampton Court. His talents were, however, not limited to gardening alone. In 1751 Brown had begun architectural work on Croome for the Earl of Coventry, mainly, it seems, in order to ensure that the house and buildings should harmonize with the landscape that he was designing. In the 1770s, no doubt with the assistance of his architect son-in-law Henry Holland, he completed Claremont for Robert Clive. Both were fine buildings in the Palladian style, and perhaps the best examples of his large architectural practice.

By the end of his life Brown had progressed from being a kitchen gardener to being a member of the landed gentry; an architect of imposing confidence and the leading 'improver' of the country, he returned in his last years to a country house in Huntingdonshire, where he had been appointed High Sheriff, and died on 6 February 1783.

Dorothy Stroud, *Capability Brown* (1950).

Portraits: oil, quarter-length, by Nathaniel Dance: N.P.G.; oil, half-length, by Nathaniel Dance: N.P.G.

Bruce, Thomas (1766–1841), 7th Earl of Elgin and 11th Earl of Kincardine; Scottish diplomat who assembled the Elgin Marbles.

Thomas Bruce was born on 20 July 1766 in London, and succeeded to the earldoms of Elgin and Kincardine on the death of his elder brother, William Robert Bruce, in 1771. After attending Harrow and Westminster, he went on to St. Andrews University and Paris to complete his studies before entering the army at the age of nineteen. A special mission to the Emperor Leopold in 1790 marked the beginning of his career in the diplomatic service. In 1799, after holding successive appointments as envoy in Brussels and Berlin, Elgin was sent to Constantinople as envoy to the Porte.

Elgin was keenly interested in the Parthenon and the other ancient Greek remains which then lay within the Turkish empire, and he was anxious to use the opportunity afforded by his position to have them closely studied and documented. His enthusiasm was such that in 1800, at his own expense, he engaged the services of the Italian painter Lusieri and of various draughtsmen and modellers and sent them to Athens to start work on drawing and documentation. At first, hampered by restrictions imposed by the authorities, the men could do little more than make drawings of the ancient buildings, but in 1801 Elgin was granted permission to erect scaffolding round the Parthenon, to make plaster casts and moulds of the friezes and figures and, moreover, to take them away. Although it had not been part of Elgin's original plan to remove any of the sculptures, he eventually decided to do so in order, he claimed, to save them from the danger of wilful damage and destruction that threatened them. The first consignment was ready to be sent to England in 1803. Elgin himself left Turkey at this time and withdrew from Athens all the craftsmen except Lusieri, who stayed behind to direct further investigations. The first shipment, meanwhile, was lost at sea near Cythera, and it was not until three years later that the marbles could be retrieved by divers.

When Elgin finally reached England, having been detained in France in 1806 following the breach of the Peace of Amiens, he was greeted by a storm of criticism. He was accused of vandalism, notably by Byron in his 'Curse of Minerva'; nevertheless further additions to the collection continued to arrive in England even as late as 1812. Partly in an attempt to mollify his critics, Elgin decided to open his collection to the public. In 1816 the House of Commons allocated £35,000 to purchase the marbles for the nation. Elgin himself, it has been estimated, must have spent in the order of £74,000 to assemble the collection.

The marbles were gradually moved to their present home, the British Museum, and Elgin retired from public life. He died in Paris on 14 November 1841.

E. Edwards, *Lives of the Founders of the British Museum; with Notices of Its Chief Augmentors and Other Benefactors, 1570–1870* (2 vols.; 1870).
W. St. Clair, *Lord Elgin and the Marbles* (1967).

Brummell, George Bryan (1778–1840), known as 'Beau' Brummell; Regency man of fashion.

George Brummell was born on 7 June 1778, the youngest of the three children of the private secretary to Lord North.

In 1790 George Brummell was sent to Eton. He took well to the life there and enjoyed considerable popularity. At this stage in his life he was nicknamed 'Buck' Brummell, and already he was displaying those qualities which were to earn him the enduring title of 'Beau': a fastidious elegance of dress, a prompt wit and flamboyant social graces.

In 1794 he entered Oriel College, Oxford, but, finding he had no disposition whatsoever towards study, he left in the same year, at about the time of his father's death. While at Eton he had been noticed by the Prince of Wales, who on 17 May 1794 engaged him as a cornet in his own regiment, the 10th Hussars. However, in 1798 on coming into an inheritance, he retired from the service. It has been wryly recorded that there were three memorable aspects of 'Beau' Brummell's time in the army: his inability on parade to remember which troop he commanded; his role as escort to Princess Caroline when she first arrived in England; and his resignation from the army when his regiment was posted to Manchester.

Part of his wealth went towards an establishment in Mayfair, at 4 Chesterfield Street. Brummell had the art of making friends, and he made them in important places. He was also able to keep them. Companions from Eton and Oxford maintained contact with him, and the leaders of society were among his personal acquaintance. However, it was his close friendship with the Prince of Wales that assured his social success. Brummell's influence was such that the Prince is said to have 'begun to blubber when told that Brummell did not like the cut of his coat'. 'Prinny' was a frequent visitor at 4 Chesterfield Street; he came to see the 'Beau' dress, and as often as not 'staid on to a dinner, prolonged to orgie far into the night'. Brummell introduced and popularized the fashion of wearing trousers instead of breeches.

The Prince is said to have admired the way in which Brummell straightened his cravat and mixed his snuff, but there was clearly more to the 'Beau' than mere dandyism. He was not a fop; his dress was characterized by studied moderation, rather than extravagance. However, in 1813 Brummell quarrelled with his friend and patron, now Prince Regent. The Prince was displeased with the 'Beau' on account of slights to Mrs. Fitzherbert (whom the Prince had married secretly in defiance of the King his father and of the Royal Marriage Act). Arriving with this lady at a ball, the Prince cut Brummell; whereupon Brummell asked the host in clearly audible tones who his 'fat friend' was. For a time Brummell managed to keep his position in society, but in 1816 gambling losses forced him to flee abroad. He settled in Calais, where he resumed his habitual way of life. Friends, including the Duke of Wellington, visited him in his new abode. Soon, however, he fell into debt again and found himself in severe financial difficulties. In 1821 his former friend, now King, stayed in Calais on a rare trip abroad to Hanover, but there was no meeting and no offer of aid of any kind.

On 10 September 1830, Brummell was

appointed British Consul at Caen; this was a sinecure which, at his own recommendation, was abolished in 1832. His creditors began to close in on him and in May 1835 he was thrown into prison. He was soon released but the degradation seemed to have broken his spirit, which a small income supplied by his friends failed to restore. By 1837 his mind was failing and he relived the past in imaginary gatherings for former celebrities. The antithesis of his old self, he neglected personal cleanliness, becoming slovenly and diseased to the extent that it was found difficult to engage an attendant for him. Eventually, a place was found for him at the asylum of the Bon Sauveur at Caen, where he died on 30 March 1840.

K. Campbell, *Beau Brummell* (1948).
C. M. Franzero, *The Life and Times of Beau Brummell* (1958).

Portraits: oil, by Sir J. Reynolds: Iveagh Bequest, Kenwood House, London; engraving, by John Cook (1844) after a miniature, *c.* 1800–10: British Museum.

Brunel, Marc Isambard (1769–1849), engineer and inventor; designer of the

Rotherhithe tunnel; father of Isambard Kingdom Brunel (see *Lives of the Victorian Age*).

Brunel was born in the village of Hacqueville, near Gisors in Normandy, on 25 April 1769. He came of a moderately prosperous family of farmers who had held the 'ferme Brunel' in unbroken succession for three hundred years.

Marc, a younger son, was educated for the priesthood. He showed remarkable talent in drawing and mathematics, but thoroughly disliked the classics, and at length, despite some harsh castigation from his father, he contrived to qualify for the navy. He sailed to the West Indies as a *volontaire d'honneur* in 1786 on the corvette *Le Maréchal de Castries*. In 1792 he returned to a revolutionary Paris, where his royalist sympathies put him in considerable danger. Forced to flee his native country, he boarded a ship for New York in 1793.

During his six years' stay in America, Brunel acquired a considerable reputation as an architect and engineer. He was appointed chief engineer and architect of New York, in which capacity he designed a new cannon foundry and devised ingenious machinery for the arsenal.

He had for some time been experimenting with a mechanical means of manufacturing ships' blocks (pulleys), a particularly costly item in the shipbuilding of the day, and in 1799 he sailed to England with his designs. In November of that year he married Sophia Kingdom, whom he had met and begun courting in Paris before his flight to America. Frenchmen were generally regarded with suspicion in England, but with his reputation and the help of Earl Spencer, Brunel got his drawings for block-making machinery accepted by the navy. It was arranged that the craftsman-mechanic Henry Maudslay should make the machines and that Brunel should superintend their installation at Portsmouth docks. The work took six years and for it the Admiralty paid him £17,000, a fraction of the savings made by his machines. The Portsmouth installation became a showpiece, the first example of fully mechanized production in the world. There were forty-three machines which, it was calculated, enabled the work of a hundred men to be done with precision by ten.

A government contract was next given him to install timber machinery at Chatham dockyard, and he also erected his own sawmills at Battersea. Becoming interested in steam power, he planned a steam relay system for towing ships up the Thames, which was, after considerable delay, rejected by the government. He also patented an improved printing process, but *The Times* broke the agreement they had made with him for this. In neither case was Brunel indemnified.

Unlike his son, Marc Brunel was not a shrewd businessman, and in the post-war depression after 1815 he suffered severe financial loss when the government declined to honour its commitment on a boot-manufacturing project that he had begun after seeing the state of troops returning from Corunna. In 1814 fire destroyed most of his machinery at Battersea, but with typical resilience, Brunel set about re-equipping the mills. However, his personal finances were in complete disarray and in May 1821 he was sent to the King's Bench Prison for debt. He appealed to friends for help, but it was only after six months that he was able to obtain his release.

Brunel was a man of extraordinary versatility. He introduced the skill of mechanical drawing to England and also designed a drawing aid something like a pantograph. He invented a knitting machine, an air engine, and machines for sawing, bending, and cutting timber, submitted plans for swing bridges for Liverpool, and in 1826 introduced the famous floating landing piers there. In 1824 a subscription was raised to begin financing his most ambitious project, the tunnel under the Thames between Rotherhithe and Wapping. It was made feasible by his invention of a special tunnelling shield propelled by screw power, which made it possible to bore through water-bearing strata. The work began in 1825, and against great physical and financial odds, was completed in 1842. The river broke in from above five times, and work was frequently halted for lack of funds. Brunel finally received recognition for his work in the form of a knighthood in 1841. The strain of the enterprise had taken its toll, however, and he suffered a stroke, although this did not prevent his attendance at the official opening of his tunnel in March 1843.

Another stroke in 1845 left Marc Brunel partially paralysed, and he lived very quietly after that until his death on 12 December 1849. He was buried at Kensal Green Cemetery.

R. Beamish, *Memoir of the Life of Sir Marc Isambard Brunel* (1862).

Lady Celia Brunel Noble, *The Brunels, Father and Son* (1938).

Portraits: oil, threequarter-length, by S. Drummond: N.P.G.; oil, threequarter-length, by J. Northcote, 1813: N.P.G.; engraving, threequarter-length, by D. J. Pound, after photo by Mayall: Science Museum.

Burgoyne, John (1722–92), British general in the Seven Years War and the War of American Independence, now remembered primarily for his defeat at Saratoga.

John Burgoyne was born in 1722 at Sutton, Bedfordshire, the only son of Captain John Burgoyne, who died in a debtors' prison. He was educated at Westminster School, where he formed a lasting friendship with Lord Strange, eldest son of the Earl of Derby.

Burgoyne's military career began in 1740 when he purchased a cornetcy in the 13th Dragoons, becoming a lieutenant in 1741 and a captain after his elopement with and marriage to Lord Strange's sister, Lady Charlotte Stanley (1743). In 1746 debts forced him to sell out, and because of the hostility of his father-in-law, Lord Derby, he and his wife had to leave for a period of exile in France. In 1756, thanks to a softening in Derby's attitude and a consequent restoration of influence, Burgoyne obtained a captaincy in the 11th Dragoons, which he exchanged two years later for a captaincy and lieutenant-colonelcy in the Coldstream Guards. The Seven Years War was in progress, and he saw active service on Pitt's diversionary raids against Cherbourg and St. Malo.

In 1759 it was decided to raise two whole regiments of light cavalry, following the experimental introduction of troops of light horsemen into the British dragoon regiments for scouting and outpost duties. Well established by now,

with good looks and social graces to match his Derby connection, Burgoyne was directed to raise one of the proposed regiments, designated the 16th Light Dragoons, recruiting around Northampton. He proved an excellent trainer of men, and his official code of instructions discloses a radical and humane mind.

In 1762 Burgoyne and his regiment formed part of a British force sent to support Portugal against the Bourbon powers. In July, having by now been promoted to Brigadier General, Burgoyne led his brigade of British and Portuguese infantry on a night march that culminated in the storming of Valencia de Alcantara and the capture of the Spanish commander. Later a similar night attack against a Spanish position in the mountains across the Tagus brought the campaign to a close.

Burgoyne now returned home and began a long spell as an M.P. In 1772 he served as chairman of a House of Commons select committee set up to investigate allegations of corruption against the East India Company's servants

in Bengal, notably Robert Clive (q.v.). Although Burgoyne's committee endeavoured to fasten specific charges on Clive and others, the House merely registered a general complaint.

Meanwhile Burgoyne continued to move in the most fashionable circles. He was a friend of Sir Joshua Reynolds, gambled, and dabbled in amateur theatricals. In 1774 he wrote a play, *Maid of the Oaks*, performed first at his country house at Epsom and in the following years under Garrick's auspices at Drury Lane. His court standing brought him military sinecures and promotion to Major General (1772), which together yielded an annual income of £3,500.

But the American rebellion changed things. In September 1774 Burgoyne was sent with two fellow Major Generals, Howe (see Howe, William) and Clinton, and reinforcements to support Gage in Boston. Inactivity under Gage suited him ill, and after some imprudent indulgence in correspondence in which he complained about his superior, Burgoyne returned to England in 1775.

He went back to North America in June 1776 as second in command to Sir Guy Carleton (q.v.) in Canada. There was some action on Lake Champlain and a half-hearted foray down the Hudson Valley, but once again Burgoyne took himself back to England in disgust. At Lord North's request he then drew up a plan of campaign to isolate New England by a three-pronged drive. 12,000 troops, accompanied by 2,000 Canadian pioneers and 1,000 Indian scouts, were to thrust down the Hudson Valley to Albany, where they would be joined by a section of Howe's force striking north from New Jersey and a subsidiary advance from Oswego on Lake Ontario. Unfortunately, Howe submitted his own version, which allowed him to make the capture of Philadelphia his first priority, and this was approved by Lord George Germain, Secretary of State for the American Colonies.

On arrival in Canada to command the northern drive, Burgoyne found only half the number of troops that he had been promised, and those not properly equipped. Nevertheless in May 1777 his small force marched out in fulfilment of his task under the plan. On 6 July, after a six-day siege, he took Ticonderoga. On receipt of the news, George III promoted him to Lieutenant General.

However, Burgoyne now found his force threatened by the Americans under Benedict Arnold, while Howe remained absorbed in the campaign against Philadelphia. Burgoyne therefore attempted to cut his way to safety to the south. On 19 September he encountered the Americans, now commanded by Gates, firmly entrenched on Bemis Heights, and determined to stand. He attacked but, with reduced forces, could not make any impression on the American position. He made another sortie on 7 October, before retreating to a prepared camp near Saratoga, after an American assault led by Arnold breached his own lines. Ten days later he surrendered, his total losses in the campaign amounting to 4,689. It was the turning point in the war.

Washington allowed Burgoyne to return to England, where he faced considerable public criticism for the surrender, as well as more private criticism for his failure to share the captivity of his men. The opposition Whigs supported him, however, and thereafter he associated with them politically. He was deprived of his colonelcy and governorship, but when Lord North fell in 1782 and the Rockingham coalition took office Burgoyne was appointed commander in chief in Ireland and made colonel of the 4th Foot. The former post he lost when Pitt

took office in December 1783. His last significant political act was to participate in the impeachment of Warren Hastings.

In his last years, he turned more to social and literary pursuits, and his comedy *The Heiress* (1786) proved very successful. His wife had died in 1776, but he found consolation with Susan Caulfield, a singer who bore him four illegitimate children between 1782 and 1788. Burgoyne died on 3 June 1792 and was buried in Westminster Abbey.

F. J. Hudleston, *Gentleman Johnny Burgoyne* (Garden City, N.Y., 1927).

James Lunt, *John Burgoyne of Saratoga* (1976).

Portrait: oil, three-quarter length, by unknown artist, *c*.1755: N.P.G.

Burke, Edmund (1729–97), politician and writer; one of the greatest political philosophers of the eighteenth century.

Burke was born on 12 January 1729 in Dublin. His father was a Protestant solicitor, his mother a Roman Catholic. His lifelong religious tolerance was rooted in his parents' happy though mixed marriage and in his own education. His school was the excellent Quaker school at Ballitore, which he left for Trinity College, Dublin, in 1744. At Trinity he shone in the debating society, studied Latin, founded a college periodical, and indulged in omnivorous reading.

In 1750 Burke arrived in London, ostensibly to study law at the Middle Temple, though he never qualified. He spent the next six years wandering through England and France, alone or with friends, reading and observing, until the cessation of his allowance forced him to earn a living by writing. In 1756 he published *A Vindication of Natural Society in a Letter to Lord —— by a Late Noble Writer*. The popularity of Bolingbroke (see St. John, Henry, in *Lives of the Stuart Age*), who had died five years before, prompted this clever satire.

Bolingbroke's style was widely held to be inimitable: Burke imitated it so well that many refused to believe that it was he who had in fact written it. The letter was a brilliant refutation of Bolingbroke's creed. For the first time, Burke showed his profound belief in improving the established order of things by careful change when necessary, but never by violent revolution.

In 1757 Burke published a work he had been writing for some years, entitled *A Philosophical Enquiry into the Origin of our Ideas of the Sublime and Beautiful*. This treatise became famous in its day. Johnson held it to be 'an example of true criticism', and it attracted the attention of Diderot, Kant, and Lessing.

In 1758 Burke collaborated with the publisher Dodsley on the first edition of *The Annual Register*, a survey of contemporary world affairs, with which he was anonymously connected for thirty years. About this time he was offered the post of private secretary to William 'Single Speech' Hamilton, a minor public figure. With Hamilton, Burke worked at the Board of Trade, and later in Ireland. For six years he endured 'formal, direct and undisguised slavery' in Hamilton's service, but though he loathed it, he had at least been given a taste of life in parliament. In addition he had made many valuable and lifelong friends, including Goldsmith, Garrick, Reynolds, and Johnson.

On leaving Hamilton in 1765, Burke was employed by Lord Rockingham (see Watson-Wentworth, Charles), an altogether different patron, who was at the head of a new Whig government. Until Rockingham's death in 1782 Burke stayed with him, profiting from his kindly wisdom as much as from his financial generosity. Elected M.P. for the pocket borough of Wendover in Buckinghamshire, Burke's first speeches in the Commons, on the Stamp Act, 'filled the House with wonder'. Borrowing money from Rockingham, he bought a large estate near Beaconsfield, to which he returned for peace and relaxation all his life.

Thoughts on the Causes of the Present Discontents was published in 1770. In this pamphlet Burke attacked George III for seeking to interpret the Settlement of 1689 as giving more executive power to the King than to parliament. He argued in favour of a more active role for the electorate, not through democracy as such – 'a perfect democracy is the most shameless thing in the world' – but through the party system and through parliament. This publication, asserting that a party was a body of men united on public principles, giving consistency to government and opposition alike, can justly be said to have started the regeneration of the Whigs.

In 1774 Burke was elected M.P. for Bristol, the second most important city in England. He held the seat for six years, until his liberal attitude to the American problem lost it for him in 1780; on this occasion he made his famous speech on the duties of an M.P. An M.P. should be representative, not delegate: electors were entitled to expect his integrity but must trust him to work for the public good using his own judgment, rather than being burdened with mandates and instructions; 'He owes you not his industry only but his judgment.'

Burke was in parliament for twenty-nine years. He was internationally famous and his integrity could not be faulted, yet he was never in a cabinet and his highest office was that of Paymaster. His fame as a parliamentarian rests on his clear-sighted consistency of thinking and his profound speeches and writings on all the major issues of his time. His failure to reach high office can be ascribed to three facts: first, as an Irishman he was automatically suspect, and rumours were always rife that he was a secret Catholic. Second, his name was (almost certainly unfairly) linked with those of his brother and a cousin, who indulged in shady speculation in the East India Company. Third, he was a strong-minded, often obstinate, man, of whom it was said that he would vote for no Bill unless he had drafted it himself.

Burke took little interest in parliamentary reform, busying himself with curbing the corrupt practices of the court, pressing for parliamentary control of royal patronage and regulation of the civil list expenditure, and incidentally cutting his own salary in the process.

On the question of the American colonies, Burke was clear-sighted. In famous speeches of 1774 and 1775, he argued that British policy was unwise and oppressive. The revolt of a whole people could not be counted a crime but pointed strongly to misgovernment. He called for 'legislative reason', temporizing, and giving due weight to prevalent conditions, not merely to precedent. His was a policy of reconciliation and co-operation, and he opposed vehemently the bill to close the port of Boston (1774), urging instead the repeal of tea duty.

He felt even more passionately about the Irish problem. He had seen at first hand the crippling effects of the harsh Penal Laws, under which no Catholic was allowed either to own or inherit land or to hold office. Burke constantly advocated relaxing these laws and also the commercial restrictions imposed by jealous English merchants. To the end of his life he wrote papers drawing attention to the appalling poverty of the Irish and advocating the introduction of legislative independence. 'If laws are their enemies', he wrote, 'they will be enemies to law.'

Burke was also deeply interested in India. In 1783 he drafted the East India Bill, proposing that corruption should be halted by the appointment of an independent board of commissioners. After the defeat of the Bill, Burke's anger settled on Warren Hastings. Hastings was impeached and after an eight-year trial was acquitted. Burke refused to accept that Western standards of authority could not prevail in the East. He appealed to the 'Law of Nature', to moral principles rooted in the universal order of things: 'Never, no never, did Nature say one thing and Wisdom another.' It is now widely accepted that his opinion of Hastings was ill-conceived and an error of judgment, though accusations of a personal financial interest have never been proved and would seem to be quite out of character.

In 1790 he published *Reflections on the Revolution in France*. 'Read it,' said the King to his friends, 'It will do you good.' Burke was alarmed by the favourable attitude of some Englishmen to the revolutionaries: he again argued against the principle of abstract democracy and the rule of sheer numbers, unless tempered with tradition, leadership, and inherited values. The revolutionaries wanted to destroy the hard-earned material and spiritual resources of society, which Burke thought a highly dangerous motive. His criticism is telling and acute but he was insensitive to the positive ideals of the revolutionaries. Until his death he remained hostile to the French state, and his long and close friendship with Fox ended in a dramatic parliamentary debate on France in May 1791.

In 1794, at the end of the Hastings impeachment, Burke retired to Buckinghamshire, having broken with the Whig party, whose interests he had served so long. His last years were clouded by the death from consumption of his son Richard, and he himself died, probably of stomach cancer, on 9 July 1797.

Burke was a powerful speaker, though it is said that the length and erudition of his speeches never quite caught the tone of the House of Commons, and that his delivery failed to hold the attention of his auditors. He was not witty, but very knowledgeable and a profound moderate political thinker. Dr. Johnson said of his conversation, 'He does not talk from a desire of distinction, but because his mind is full.' His was a kind and generous character – he saved the poet Crabbe from debtors' prison, and treated him as an honoured guest in his house, though he was never rich himself and was often forced to borrow, from Garrick among others. He had a deep respect for history and for established customs, though he was not blindly conservative – 'You can never plan the future by the past.' His hope, in the tradition of Aristotle, Aquinas, and Hooker, was to intensify and reconcile all the elements for good in society. When he died, Canning wrote: 'Here there is but one event, but that is an event for the world – Burke is dead.'

G. W. Chapman, *Edmund Burke: the Practical Imagination* (Cambridge, Mass., 1967).

A. Cobban, *Edmund Burke and the Revolt against the Eighteenth Century* (1960, 2nd ed.).

C. B. Cone, *Burke and the Nature of Politics* (2 vols.; Lexington, Kentucky, 1957–64).

T. Copeland *et al.* (eds.), *The Correspondence of Edmund Burke* (1958–   ).

R. R. Fennessy, *Burke, Paine and the Rights of Man: a Difference of Political Opinion* (The Hague, 1963).

C. C. O'Brien (ed.), *Reflections on the Revolution in France* (1969).

C. W. Parkin, *The Moral Basis of Burke's Political Thought* (1956).

Portraits: oil, quarter-length, studio of Reynolds, 1771: N.P.G.; miniature, after J. Barry: N.P.G.

Burney, Charles (1726–1814), musician, traveller, and writer.

Burney was born on 7 April 1726 at Shrewsbury, the son of James Burney, a portrait-painter. He was educated at Shrewsbury and Chester. His musical talents were encouraged at home and by his early teens he was able to deputize for the organist at Chester Cathedral.

An accomplished keyboard-player and violinist, Burney attracted the attention of Thomas Arne (q.v.), who took him to London as his assistant in 1744. Not long afterwards, however, Burney entered Handel's orchestra as a string-player. Some two years after his arrival in London, he became music teacher to a young aristocrat, Fulke Greville, descendant of the Tudor poet and statesman. Burney now moved in the most elegant London society. His first published music appeared in 1748, the Six Sonatas for Two Violins with Bass, and he married Esther Sleepe, described by Burney as 'a gifted young creature, one of the most pleasing, well-mannered, well-read, elegant, and even cultivated of her sex'.

Burney's patron, also newly married, now left London and went abroad. The young musician and his wife remained behind, however, to set up house in the city. Burney worked in various musical capacities, acting as church organist, playing the harpsichord in subscription concerts at the King's Arms, Cornhill, and elsewhere, and also providing theatre music for his new acquaintance, David Garrick (q.v.). In 1750 Garrick produced *Robin Hood* and *Queen Mab* at Drury Lane, both with music by Burney.

In 1752 Burney fell seriously ill, and in an effort to restore him to health the family repaired to King's Lynn, Norfolk. After a successful convalescence, Burney stayed on to take part in local music-making, acting as organist at St. Margaret's Church and composing concertos and sonatas. In 1760 he returned to London, where he was immediately in very heavy demand as a teacher: 'pupils of rank, wealth and talents were continually proposed to him, and in a very short time he had hardly an hour unappropriated to some fair disciple.' He was in demand as a conversationalist too, and his parties, to which most men of letters came, were famous.

All this came to an end with the sudden death of his wife in 1761. Burney, deeply affected by the loss, was suddenly burdened by the responsibility of looking after a young family. In 1763 he took two of his daughters, Esther and Susan, to a convent in France, leaving a third, Fanny (see Burney, Frances) in London.

He visited Paris and was impressed, interested, and cheered by everything he saw. On his return to England he collaborated with new heart with Garrick on two more Drury Lane productions, *A Midsummer Night's Dream* (1763) and Rousseau's *Le Devin du Village* (1766), produced at the Lane as *The Cunning Man* (1769). In 1768 his anthem 'I will Love thee, O Lord my Strength' won him a Doctorate of Music from Oxford University. In 1767 he married again; his new wife, Elizabeth Allen, became the chief object of his affections, but her re-

lationship with his children was not always happy.

Burney now turned with enthusiasm to his most famous project. His visit to France in 1763 had prompted him to commence translations of first one, and then another French book on music. But by 1770 he had decided that he wanted to write an original work. In that year he undertook his first tour, through France, Switzerland, and Italy, writing up a narrative of his journeys in *The Present State of Music in France and Italy, or the Journal of a Tour through those Countries* (1771).

A second tour followed in 1772, written up in *The Present State of Music in Germany, the Netherlands, and the United Provinces, etc.* (1773). The tour took Burney to Mannheim, Munich, Leipzig, and Prague, and also to Berlin, where he met C. P. E. Bach and Frederick the Great.

On his return to London, Burney became organist of Oxford Chapel, Vere Street. In 1776 there appeared the first volume of his *History of Music from the Earliest Ages to the Present Day*. This monumental study, for which Burney is justly famous, was completed in four volumes in 1789. Despite its weaknesses, especially its failure to recognize the merits of J. S. Bach, it superseded all contemporary histories and remains a thorough and reliable source even today.

After 1780 Burney confined himself to completing his history, writing hymn tunes, and contributing articles and reviews to various journals. He edited the *Memoirs and Letters of Metastasio*, and wrote an account of the first Handel Centenary Commemoration (1784; the wrong year, in fact, Handel's birth having occurred in 1685). His last years were saddened by his failure to receive a court appointment, and the death in 1785 of his second wife. In 1806 Fox granted him a pension and subsequently (1810) he became a member of the Institut de France. Burney died on 13 April 1814, shortly after his eighty-eighth birthday.

Roger Lonsdale, *Charles Burney: A Literary Biography* (1965).

Percy Scholes, *The Great Dr. Burney* (2 vols.; 1948).

Portrait: oil, half-length, by Sir J. Reynolds, 1781: National Gallery of Ireland, Dublin.

Burney, Frances (1752–1840), Madame d'Arblay, novelist and diarist.

Fanny Burney, as she is chiefly known, was born on 13 June 1752 at King's Lynn, Norfolk. She was a copious writer from an early age until her death. Her writing up to the publication of her first and best novel, *Evelina*, was a secret activity shared with her brothers and sisters and concealed from her parents for fear of disapproval. Her father, Dr. Charles Burney (q.v.), noticed that Fanny had

> a great deal of invention and humour in her childish sports; and used, after having seen a play . . . to take the actors off and compose speeches for their characters. . . . But in company she was silent, backward and timid, even to sheepishness: and from her shyness, had such profound gravity and composure of features that . . . friends . . . never called Fanny by any other name . . . than The Old Lady.

After the death of their mother in 1761, Fanny's sisters were sent to school in France, but she herself was kept in England, as it was feared that she might be susceptible to Catholicism. In London she met Samuel Crisp, a man much older than herself who was a failed playwright, but whose character and understanding she valued greatly and who encouraged her writing with constructive criticism.

In 1767 Dr. Burney's second marriage took place, his new wife becoming a major topic in the long journals and letters that the young Burneys wrote. Fanny, her earlier scribblings having been burnt on her fifteenth birthday, began her own private diary in 1768, in which she recorded 'my private opinion of my nearest relations . . . my hopes, fears, reflections and dislikes'. Later in her life, she scrupulously edited out critical references to her relations, but a few survive to show the bitter feelings which existed between the young Burneys and their stepmother; Fanny wrote, for example, that her later superior at court was her stepmother's 'exactest fellow – gloomy, dark, suspicious, rude, reproachful'. Dr. Burney, although often away from home, was adored by his children.

By 1776 Fanny was thoroughly absorbed in writing what was to be her first published novel. She had been working on *Evelina* for several years but was hampered by lack of opportunity and her need for secrecy. When a fair portion of the novel had been neatly copied one publisher, Dodsley, and then another, Thomas Lowndes, was approached; Lowndes agreed to read the anonymous manuscript and promptly accepted it for publication on condition that she completed the work first. At last, after much work, in November 1777 the third and final volume was ready for the press. *Evelina*, a realistic, humorous, and charming account of a young girl's entrance into society, ending happily in marriage, was a great success. Mrs. Thrale (q.v.) and Dr. Johnson were both impressed by the book and curious to know who the author was. Dr. Burney, having discovered the fact from one of Fanny's sisters, soon revealed that his daughter was the author, and the news immediately spread. Fanny found this publicity wholly unwelcome. She wrote: 'I part with this, my dear, long loved, long cherished snugship with more regret than any body will believe.'

From this time she became a close

friend of Mrs. Thrale. Dr. Johnson, when staying with the latter at Streatham, paid much attention to her. She was encouraged by Sheridan, among others, to write a comedy, but her attempt, called *The Witlings*, was criticized and discouraged by Mr. Crisp. She then wrote her second novel, *Cecilia*, which was in great demand from its publication in 1782. This was rather more moralistic than *Evelina*.

Her friendship with Mrs. Thrale came to an end when the latter was remarried to Piozzi, a match of which Miss Burney, like Dr. Johnson, disapproved. After this she often stayed at Windsor, where she was introduced to the royal family, and in 1786 she was offered the position of Second Keeper of the Robes in the royal household. She was very unwilling to accept this offer, but was persuaded by the enthusiasm of her father and friends. Her fears proved to be justified; her supervisor, Mrs. Schwellenberg, treated her with autocratic rudeness and cruelty and her duties and companions left her exhausted and miserably lonely. She was finally allowed to resign in 1791 after five years' service. At Mickleham she met General Alexandre d'Arblay, a French émigré, whom she married in 1793, at the age of forty. The marriage appears to have been very happy. But they had very little means of support, and so she turned again to writing to earn money. She wrote a tragedy and her third novel, *Camilla*, in which her moral and didactic intentions are much more conspicuous than before.

In 1801 General d'Arblay returned to France, where she joined him in 1802 and stayed for the next ten years. He was seriously injured fighting against Napoleon in the Waterloo campaign, after which they returned to England, settling at Bath, where he died in 1818. Madame d'Arblay devoted her last years to editing her father's *Memoirs* (published 1832) and

died at the age of eighty-seven on 6 January 1840. She was buried at Walcot Church, Bath.

For much of her life Fanny Burney had kept a detailed journal and written long letters to her family and friends. In her diaries she describes the events and scenes of her life with wit and perceptive accuracy. Thackeray very probably used her account of life behind the English lines during Waterloo in *Vanity Fair*.

E. A. Bloom (ed.), *Evelina* (1968).
A. Dobson (ed.), *Diary and Letters of Madame d'Arblay* (6 vols. from the edition prepared by Charlotte Barrett in 1842–6; 1904–9).
A. R. Ellis (ed.), *Cecilia* (2 vols.; 1882).
A. R. Ellis (ed.), *The Early Diary of Frances Burney* (2 vols.; 1889).
J. Hemlow, *The History of Fanny Burney* (1958).
R. B. Johnson, *Fanny Burney and the Burneys* (1926).

Portrait: oil, half-length, by E. F. Burney, 1782: N.P.G.

Burns, Robert (1759–96), Scottish poet, the national 'bard' of Scotland.

Robert Burns was born on 25 January 1759 at Alloway, Ayrshire, the eldest son of a struggling tenant-farmer. Despite extreme poverty and the concentration of all his physical energy in the working of his farm, Burns's father was concerned about his son's intellectual development to the extent that he joined with some neighbouring farmers in employing a university-trained tutor to teach the children. Robert Burns was thus a privileged child, for though his education was sporadic – the learning had to be fitted in when work on the farm permitted – he did at least possess at an early age an awareness of the written word that few other country children could have acquired in a lifetime. Burns's reading included the Bible, most major contemporary English writers, a little French and Latin and, later, the poems of Robert Fergusson, the Scottish poet whose achievement gave Burns himself the confidence to write his own first poems.

Following the failure of the farm at Mount Oliphant the Burns family moved in 1777 to another farm at Lochlea, near Tarbolton. As well as developing his tastes for drink and sports, the young Burns was already writing poetry, and in 1780 he formed a 'Bachelors Club' for intellectual discussions with his friends. For a brief period in 1781 he was sent to Irvine to learn the trade of flax-dressing from a relation of his mother's, but when the house in which he was lodged was burnt to the ground after New Year's Eve celebrations, Burns returned home. In 1784 his father died, bankrupt and exhausted by unceasing work. Memories of this event were to echo throughout Burns's life in his satirical attacks on the blindness of social and religious hierarchies to the suffering of the poor.

With what little money he could save from his father's creditors Burns started to work his own farm at Mossgiel, near Mauchline. He established a firm friendship with Gavin Hamilton, a neighbouring tenant farmer who also enjoyed

literature, and when Hamilton was prosecuted in 1784 for neglect of the Sabbath, Burns wrote an angry satire on the Calvinist Church. This and other poems circulated widely in the local communities but in July 1786 the Church avenged itself by demanding public penance from Burns and Jean Armour, the daughter of a local mason who was pregnant with Burns's child. When Jean was persuaded by her father not to marry him, Burns turned to another local girl, Mary Campbell, and began to plan for their emigration to Jamaica. In September Jean Armour gave birth to twins, Burns's children, and in October Mary Campbell died from a fever. Burns was oppressed by the failure of his farm as well as by these emotional involvements, but during the summer of this tumultuous year he engaged a printer in Kilmarnock to publish his *Poems Chiefly in the Scottish Dialect*. It was an immediate success and as a result, on 27 November, he set out for Edinburgh.

The poems in this Kilmarnock volume were selected with care: Burns omitted the Church satires, included many poems about nature and idealized family life, and wrote a calculated preface in which he exaggerated his homely background and lack of education. Several of the purely Scottish poems – such as 'The Holy Fair', 'To a house', and 'An Address to the Deil' – were vibrantly original and completely successful, but the tone of this volume as a whole varied uncertainly between sharp realism and trivial sentimentality. Even in 'The Cotter's Saturday Night', which contains some of his finest early writing, some of the verses are hesitant or insincere, as though Burns was uncertain of his audience and felt that he had to dress his local subject matter in an imposed morality to make it acceptable to educated readers.

The immediate acclaim awarded to

Burns by his Edinburgh readers was in fact another handicap: lacking an accepted category for a writer of such originality, Burns's contemporary admirers both abused him and tried to influence his gifts. Burns himself at first took a delight in playing the role of the child of innocent nature: during the winters of 1786–7 and 1787–8 he mingled in the society of Lord Monboddo, the Duchess of Gordon, and Adam Ferguson, and was continually feted. At times, however, he sought relief in the more familiar milieu of the Edinburgh taverns, and on his tours through Scotland in the summers of these years his desire to return to the simple life of farming was reawakened. In 1787 a new edition of his poems was published, but this included very few additions to the original Kilmarnock selection. In 1788 Burns finally married Jean Armour and settled on a farm at Ellisland in Dumfriesshire leased to him by an admirer.

Before leaving Edinburgh Burns arranged with James Johnson, an engraver and publisher, to produce a series of Scottish songs for Johnson's *Scots Musical Museum*, and this continued literary activity, together with his correspondence with many new literary and social acquaintances, meant that he could not devote the whole of his energies to the farm. To supplement his income Burns in 1789 obtained a post in the excise service, and two years later he sold the farm and moved to Dumfries to work full-time for the excise. The many songs that he wrote during this period are Burns's greatest achievement: though the melodies of many of these songs were already part of Scottish culture, the words were new; what Burns was attempting was virtually the re-creation of the tradition of Scottish folk song.

Burns's first son, Francis Wallace, was born in August 1788, and a large family

soon followed. In December 1792 Burns found it necessary to recant his declared sympathy for the revolutionary movement in France in order to keep his job; it was only the timely intervention of influential admirers that enabled him to retain a sufficient income to support his family. A new commission in 1792 to produce songs for George Thomson's *Select Scottish Airs* ensured a continued market for his verse, but for patriotic reasons Burns consistently refused to accept any payment for his literary work: in 1794 he even refused a generous contract to write for the *Morning Chronicle* in London.

Poetry was his natural expression: he wrote 'The Whistle' in October 1789 during the course of a drinking contest, and 'Tam o' Shanter' was written in a single day while out walking in the fields. The Edinburgh public, however, now tired of Burns's dishevelled appearance and appetite for drink. Mrs. Maclehose, an Edinburgh widow to whom Burns had addressed some lyrics, switched easily from admiration to hostility after his marriage to Jean Armour, and when in 1793 Burns was brutally rude to a Mrs. Riddell all the gentry of Dumfries took this as an excuse to snub him.

In 1795 one of his daughters died and Burns himself, weakened by overwork, was ill throughout the ensuing winter. According to one account, Burns succumbed to his last fever after sleeping in the open on his way home from a drinking party, but this is probably legend. He died in Dumfries of a rheumatic heart disease on 21 July 1796. His funeral was attended by large crowds, and some of his closest friends immediately started a subscription fund for the welfare of his family. His posthumous reputation provides an interesting case history in the manufacture of legends: he was considered by the Victorians as the archetypal child of nature, treated by exiled Scots as the object of their nostalgia, and is even now regarded in Russia as a symbolic spokesman for the working classes. Fortunately, those who read Burns's poems can still hear the voice of the man himself.

David Daiches, *Robert Burns* (1966, rev. ed.).

J. W. Egerer, *A Bibliography of Burns* (1964).

J. De L. Ferguson (ed.), *The Letters of Robert Burns* (2 vols.; 1931).

R. T. Fitzhugh, *Robert Burns: The Man and the Poet* (1970).

W. E. Henley and T. F. Henderson (eds.), *Poems* (4 vols.; 1896-7).

J. Kinsey (ed.), *The Poems and Songs of Robert Burns* (3 vols.; 1968).

F. B. Snyder, *The Life of Robert Burns* (New York, 1932).

Portraits: oil, full-length, by Alexander Nasmyth: Scottish N.P.G.; drawing, quarter-length, by Skirving after Nasmyth, 1796-7: Scottish N.P.G.; statue, by John Flaxman: Scottish N.P.G.

Bute, 3rd Earl of (1713-92), see Stuart, John.

Butler, James (1665-1745), 2nd Duke of Ormonde; Anglo-Irish politician and general, see *Lives of the Stuart Age*.

Byng, George (1663-1733), Viscount Torrington; naval commander.

George Byng was born on 27 January 1663 at Wrotham, Kent, the eldest son of an improvident landowner. He entered the navy at the age of fifteen as a volunteer-per-order, the official title of young aspirants to commissioned service, popularly known as 'king's letter boys'. In 1681, having gained experience in a number of ships, and chafing under an unpleasant captain, he took his discharge at Tangier and accepted a military cadetship under Governor Kirke, which quickly blossomed into an ensign's commission, followed in 1683 by a lieutenancy. The obvious patronage of Kirke caused some resentment, and the

Governor found it expedient to employ Byng afloat in command of a ketch, the *Deptford*. This irregularity was terminated by the arrival in 1683 of Lord Dartmouth and, among others, Samuel Pepys to consider the future of the garrison. At Kirke's request, Dartmouth gave Byng a lieutenant's commission in the navy and in due course he sailed home to England. From there, in 1684, he sailed to the East Indies.

Until 1687 Byng served in various operations to defend the East India Company's lodgment at Bombay, on one occasion being seriously wounded. He was offered a command in the Company's fleet, but declined to leave the King's service and returned to England in 1688.

At this point in his career, the conflicts of the Glorious Revolution (1688), which was then in the making, forced him to make a political choice. Following the lead of Kirke, now a brigadier general, he supported William of Orange, and acted as the Prince's agent in the fleet.

Byng profited by his choice, for following the establishment of William as King, a captain's commission was the first of a series of naval appointments over the next decade which eventually raised him to flag rank. He took part in the inglorious action against the French off Beachy Head (30 June 1690) and spent two years (1694-6) as First Captain to the Commander in Chief, Mediterranean.

In 1701 Byng's steady, if undistinguished, progress received a temporary setback with the death of William III. He was faced with a choice between accepting command of a private ship and resigning his commission. Lacking the means for the latter, he pocketed his pride and in July 1702 joined Sir Cloudesley Shovell's fleet in command of the *Nassau*.

His promotion to Rear-Admiral of the Red came on 1 March 1703, when he was appointed Shovell's second in command in the Mediterranean. In the following year he commanded a squadron under Rooke and took part in the surprise attack on Gibraltar (July), being in charge of the twenty-two ships that bombarded the fortress while marines went ashore to take it. In the ensuing battle of Malaga (24 August 1704) Byng played a prominent part. A joint French and Spanish threat to retake Gibraltar was averted without loss. However, for some reason (presumably the results of political intrigue) Byng's commander, Rooke, was dismissed from the service for alleged over-caution, while Byng was knighted and promoted to Vice-Admiral. In 1705 he also became M.P. for Plymouth, holding the seat until 1721.

For the remainder of the War of the Spanish Succession he discharged a series of appointments competently. He commanded a Channel squadron (1705), served under Leake and Shovell in the western Mediterranean (1706–7), and repelled an invasion attempt on behalf of the Old Pretender in the North Sea (1708). In 1708 he had been promoted to full Admiral and during 1709 he was Commander in Chief in the Mediterranean.

The establishment of the Hanoverian dynasty in 1714 did not disturb Byng's position, and in the next year he was placed in command of the seaborne defence of the Channel during a Jacobite rising. His close watch on the French ports made a significant contribution to the collapse of the rising, and he was rewarded with a baronetcy and a diamond ring by George I. The English succession was a matter of continental politics, however, and in 1717 Byng led a strong squadron into the Baltic to deter Charles XII of Sweden from involving himself in the Jacobite cause.

Byng was promoted to Admiral of the Fleet on 14 March 1718 and was sent out to

the Mediterranean again three months later. The Spanish king, Philip V, was attempting to recover lost dominions in southern Italy, and a European alliance was formed to prevent him. The strongest Spanish fleet since the Armada was already in Sicilian waters, and Messina was under siege when Byng's fleet anchored off Naples in July 1718.

On 26 July Byng sailed for Messina. His attempt to obtain an extended cease-fire to allow a negotiated settlement failed, and on 30 July he took his fleet into the Straits, giving chase to the Spanish ships. The ensuing action off Cape Passaro on 31 July was decisive; although he was outnumbered and sustained heavy losses himself, he succeeded in defeating the Spaniards.

Byng continued to operate in the area for a further two years, but the Spaniards did not attempt to recover the command of the sea which was essential to their success, and were finally compelled to evacuate Sicily in 1720. Byng also acted as the English plenipotentiary in negotiations for the surrender of Sardinia.

His return to England was marked by appropriate honours. In October 1720 he was made Treasurer of the Navy and he became a Privy Councillor in the following January. He became Baron Southill and Viscount Torrington in 1721, and in 1725 was made a Knight of the Bath. On 2 August 1727 he became First Lord of the Admiralty, an office that he held until his death on 17 January 1733.

Sir J. K. Laughton (ed.), *Memoirs relating to Lord Torrington, 1678–1705* (1889).

W. C. B. Tunstall (ed.), *The Byng Papers* (3 vols.; 1930–3).

Portrait: oil, full-length, by Jeremiah Davison, *c.*1725: N.P.G.

Byng, John (1704–57), British admiral executed for his failure to relieve the garrison of Minorca in 1756.

John Byng was born at Southill, Bedfordshire, in 1704, the fourth son of Viscount Torrington (see Byng, George). By virtue of his parentage he was assured of a career in the navy, which he entered in March 1718. He served in several ships as midshipman, as able seaman (not an unusual practice at the time), and, after he had passed the qualifying examination in December 1722, as lieutenant. He was given his first command in August 1727, and a succession of other commands which carried him without any kind of professional distinction to the rank of rear admiral in 1745.

At this point in the War of the Austrian Succession, only one fleet action had taken place, the Battle of Toulon (11 February 1744). In this drawn battle against a French and Spanish fleet, the tactical confusion that inhibited the British revealed both a poverty of naval leadership and a rigidity of fighting method that were the outcome of excessive political interference. The ministry of the day decided to make a scapegoat of the commander, Admiral Matthews. In the thirteen courts martial

which ensued, eight men were convicted, including Matthews, who was charged with neglecting the official Fighting Instructions by failing to 'dress his line' and with engaging the enemy in a half-hearted manner, for which he was cashiered. His second-in-command, Vice Admiral Lestock, who had been a principal cause of the débâcle through his personal animosity to Matthews, had political friends and was acquitted. Byng sat on both courts.

In 1747 he was appointed second in command of the Mediterranean fleet, attaining vice admiral's rank on 15 July and succeeding to the command when Vice Admiral Medley died on 5 August. There was no fighting, however, and the war ended in 1748 with Byng notable only for his seniority. In 1751 he became M.P. for Rochester.

The war against France was revived in 1755, and Byng's first command was of a squadron in the Channel. In March 1756 he was promoted to admiral and sent with a squadron of ten ships-of-line to join the three already in the Mediterranean, with instructions to guard Minorca and its British garrison, which was in fact already besieged by a French army.

Byng's misfortunes began at Gibraltar, where the Governor refused to deplete his own garrison to supplement Byng's marines, in defiance of the Admiralty's instructions. Nevertheless, Byng sailed for Minorca, arriving off Port Mahon on 19 May. Before he could communicate with the garrison, a French squadron of equal number to his own appeared, which could not be engaged until late on the following day because of light winds. Byng attacked downwind, while the French waited on the defensive, but the approach was confused as Byng backed in order to dress his line, as the Fighting Instructions insisted he must. His vanguard consequently went into action unsupported and suffered severe damage. Following their usual practice, the French drew off, content with minimal gains, and Byng was unable to regain contact with them.

Remaining on station for four days to refit, Byng held a council of war, which decided that, since his squadron lacked the troops to act effectively ashore, nothing could be done for the garrison. The squadron returned to Gibralter, and the garrison subsequently surrendered. Before news of this reached the government, the reports of the naval engagement had already caused the supersession of Byng by Hawke (July 1756). He was arrested on his return, and it was clear that the Newcastle ministry, already under attack for its general conduct of the war, intended to fasten the blame for its own shortcomings on the fallen admiral.

The court martial opened at Portsmouth on 28 December 1756 and concluded on 27 January of the following year. Byng was charged with failing to do his utmost to relieve the garrison in Minorca and failing in his duty to engage enemy ships. The latter came under Article 12 of the Articles of War, which carried a sentence of death and which until 1749 had contained a saving clause allowing lesser punishment at discretion. The clause had been deleted, and since Byng was technically guilty, the death sentence was unavoidable.

The Admiralty evaded its own responsibility by advising the King to consult with the judges on the point of law, on which the judges upheld the verdict. George II refused to exercise his prerogative of mercy, and Byng was shot by a firing squad of marines on the quarterdeck of *Monarque* on 14 March 1757. His fate prompted the well-known remark by Voltaire, 'The English occasionally shoot an admiral to encourage the others.'

D. Pope, *Mr. Byng Was Shot At Dawn* (1957).
W. C. B. Tunstall, *Admiral Byng* (1928).

Portrait: oil, by Thomas Hudson: National Maritime Museum, Greenwich.

Byrd, William (1674–1744), colonial planter, see *Lives of the Stuart Age*.

Byron, George Gordon (1788–1824), 6th Baron Byron of Rochdale; romantic poet.

Byron was born on 22 January 1788 in London, the son of Captain John Byron by his second wife, Catherine Gordon. Violence, promiscuity, and extravagance were characteristic traits of his ancestors on both sides of his family, and his father, 'mad Jack Byron', was no exception; his first marriage, to the divorced Marchioness of Carmarthen, whom he had seduced, began with scandal and he gambled away the entire fortune of his second wife within the space of a few months. Byron himself was born with a deformed right foot (the heel was raised and the sole turned inward), and he was to interpret this as a physical confirmation of his own inner evil nature. Captain Byron died in France in 1791 and Byron reacted against his mother's harsh criticisms of her deceased husband by idealizing him. Until 1798 Byron was cared for in lodgings in Aberdeen by his mother, whom he hated, and by his nurse May Gray, whose character was a peculiar mixture of Calvinism and profligacy. Writing of this nurse in 1821, Byron remarked, 'My passions were developed early, and from this and other hints it seems that May Gray seduced the child.

In 1798 Byron unexpectedly inherited the family title and estates on the death of his great-uncle and he thereupon moved with his mother to the family seat of Newstead Abbey in Nottinghamshire.

Three years later, after a brief preparation under a private tutor in Nottingham, Byron was sent to Harrow
school. By this time, at the age of
thirteen, he was corresponding with his
half-sister, Augusta (the only surviving
child of his father's first marriage) and
courting a distant cousin, Mary Chaw-
orth. The poetry that he wrote to the
latter and his grief over her engagement
to a rival distracted him from the
schoolboy passions and preoccupations
of Harrow. In 1805 Byron entered
Trinity College, Cambridge; an allowance of £500 a year proved insufficient
to support his extravagant tastes, and it
was partly to pay off the debts incurred
both at university and in London that he
arranged for the private printing of his
first volume of poems, *Fugitive Pieces*, in
November 1806. (On the objection of a
certain Rev. Thomas Becher to the
eroticism of certain verses Byron himself
destroyed all the remaining copies of this
volume.) In addition to keeping a tame
bear and exercising it on a lead, Byron
formed close friendships during these
early years with John Edleston, a chorister, and with John Cam Hobhouse (see
Lives of the Victorian Age).

In 1809 Byron took his seat in the House
of Lords and published anonymously a
lively verse satire entitled 'English Bards
and Scots Reviewers'. The immediate
provocation of this work was a sarcastic
review of his book of poems, *Hours of
Idleness* (1807), in the *Edinburgh Review*,
but Byron's anger is directed not merely at
individual critics but at cant and hypocrisy
in general.

On 2 July 1809 Byron sailed from
England in company with Hobhouse;
after travelling through Spain and Malta –
where Byron's affair with a Mrs. Spencer
Smith culminated in his being challenged
to a duel – they continued to Greece, and it
was here that Byron began to compose the

first cantos of *Childe Harold's Pilgrimage*.

Byron was profoundly impressed by
Greece; on 3 May 1811, he swam across
the Hellespont in imitation of the classical
Leander. Financial problems continued
to beset him and his mother. On his
return to England in July 1811 news of
her illness was brought to him and she
died at Newstead before he could reach
her.

It was on the publication of the first two
cantos of *Childe Harold's Pilgrimage* in
March 1812 that Byron 'awoke to find
himself famous'. Its greatest appeal
resided in the character of Harold, a
gloomy misanthrope burdened by a
hopeless sorrow and unnamed sins. Byron
capitalized on the popularity of this hero-
villain in 'The Giaour' (1813), 'The
Corsair' and 'Lara' (1814), all of which
sold well, and he did little to discourage
rumours that these Oriental tales, with
their dark hints of fatal love and inexpiable
crime, were really veiled autobiography.
In 1813 he wrote in his journal,

> To withdraw *myself* from *myself* (oh
> that accursed selfishness!) has ever been
> my sole, my entire, my sincere motive
> in scribbling at all; and publishing is
> also the continuance of the same object,
> by the action it affords to the mind,
> which else recoils upon itself.

Byron was now in his early twenties. In
the autumn of 1811 he met Thomas
Moore, Samuel Rogers, and other
leading figures of the literary establishment; in February 1812 he made his first
speech in the House of Lords, and in
March came the publication of *Childe
Harold* and immediate fame. All of London society now yielded before him. It is
difficult to disentangle from the web of
rumour and scandal an accurate record of
Byron's relationships with women during these years. His most notorious liaison
was with Lady Caroline Lamb (q.v.), the

daughter-in-law of his friend Lady Melbourne, while his most lasting and secret was that with Augusta Leigh, his own half-sister. 'There is something in me', Byron wrote, 'very softening in the presence of woman – some strange influence, even if one is not in love with them – which I cannot at all account for, having no very high opinion of the sex.'

Lady Melbourne attempted to save him from the consequences of his passions. In 1813 she encouraged his flirtation with Lady Frances Webster, with the objective, apparently, of diverting his attentions from both his half-sister, Augusta, and her own son's wife, and in January 1815, after a scandalous scene at a ball with the unstable Caroline Lamb, Lady Melbourne succeeded in promoting Byron's marriage to Annabella Milbanke, her own niece. This marriage was a failure: Byron drank heavily, continued his correspondence with Augusta, and spent nearly all his time in London with his publisher John Murray (q.v.) and other literary friends. On 10 December Annabella gave birth to a child, Augusta Ada, and in the following January Byron dispatched both mother and child to her parents in Durham. Annabella sought a medical statement concerning her husband's sanity, and after much acrimony a legal separation was signed. On 15 April 1816, he sailed from England for the last time.

He spent the summer of 1816 at the Villa Diodati on the shores of Lac Leman in the company of Shelley (q.v.), Mary Godwin, and Claire Clairmont (Mary's half-sister). Here he composed a third canto of *Childe Harold*, largely inspired by his visit to the battlefield of Waterloo, and *The Prisoner of Chillon*, a dramatic monologue in which the hero-narrator recounts the ordeal of his long imprisonment in a castle dungeon. In *Manfred* (1817) Byron treated the subject of

incestuous love with an honesty that reflected his own feelings, and in the short poem entitled 'Darkness', also written in 1816, he gave concise expression to images of despair:

> I had a dream, which was not all a
>   dream.
> The bright sun was extinguish'd, and
>   the stars
> Did wander darkling in the eternal
>   space,
> Rayless, and pathless, and the icy
>   earth
> Swung blind and blackening in the
>   moonless air. . . .

At the end of this summer of 1816 Shelley and the two women left for England, Claire Clairmont being pregnant with Byron's child (Byron himself remained silent when Mary Godwin wrote to inform him of the birth of his daughter in January 1817). In November 1816 Byron arrived at Venice, travelling with his loyal companion Hobhouse, and immediately made passionate advances to the wife of the man in whose house he found lodgings. In May 1817 he continued to Rome, wrote a fourth canto of *Childe Harold*, and transferred his affections to Margarita Cogni, the wife of a baker. In Venice in 1817 he wrote the poem that marks the beginning of his final poetic phase. In 'Beppo', a mock-heroic satire on Italian manners, Byron developed a new colloquial style in *ottava rima*, a form that allowed free rein to his genius for irreverent mockery.

In the summer of 1818 he began his masterpiece, *Don Juan*, which is also in *ottava rima*. The narrative that provides the skeleton of *Don Juan* concerns the adventures of a mild young gentleman who experiences love, shipwreck, harem life, war, court diplomacy, and much else besides; in the telling of this tale Byron deliberately flouted the romantic illusions and pretensions that he himself had helped to create. He continued the writing of *Don Juan* undeterred by the hostile reception of the first two cantos in July 1819, and the wary advice of his friends and his publisher. The tone of *Don Juan* is one of sardonic detachment, and with supreme confidence Byron transforms despair into self-knowledge:

> There's no such thing as certainty,
>   that's plain
> As any of Mortality's conditions;
> So little do we know what we're
>   about in
> This world, I doubt if doubt itself be
>   doubting.

There was, however, a consistency in Byron's behaviour that belied his change of poetic style, and when Shelley visited Venice in 1818 he found Byron still both promiscuous and intemperate. In April 1819 he fell in love with the nineteen-year-old Countess Teresa Guiccioli and, with her brother and father, he involved himself dangerously in radical Italian politics. Teresa was already married – her

husband was aged fifty-eight – but her devotion to Byron was perhaps more constant than that of any of his former lovers, and it was while living with her in Ravenna that Byron wrote some of his finest poetry: his work of this period comprises three more cantos of *Don Juan*, several verse dramas, and a parody of Robert Southey's 'A Vision of Judgment', including a vicious lampoon on George III.

Conscious that he was under the surveillance of government spies, in the summer of 1822 he moved with Teresa to a villa near Leghorn. Together with Shelley and Leigh Hunt (q.v.), Byron then made plans for the publication in London of a new radical journal, but after Shelley's death on 8 July his interest in this project waned. Later that year he quarrelled with John Murray about the latest cantos of *Don Juan* and though his domestic life with Teresa was superficially serene, it is evident from his journals that Byron was still distressed at his rejection by English society. In April 1823 he was asked by the London Greek Committee to act as its agent in support of the Greek fight for independence from Turkish rule, and accepted.

On 2 July 1823, therefore, he sailed from Genoa with Teresa's brother as one of his companions, and in early August they arrived at the island of Cephalonia. They remained here until after Christmas, delayed by dissension among the Greek forces on the mainland and Byron's own uncertainty about where to land and how he should make use of the financial aid he brought. In late December Byron sailed for Missolonghi; for a few brief weeks he worked hard to unite the Greek forces, but on 15 February he succumbed to a fever and was further weakened by the remedy of bleeding. In early April a drenching in a sudden rainstorm caused the fever to recur, and after a painful illness that lasted ten days, Byron died on 19 April 1824.

Viewed from afar, this was a heroic death: the romantic lord had died in the cause of liberty, and the legend was complete. In reality the man who made the final voyage to Greece was a bored lover and an exhausted poet. Byron was courageous and generous, but self-hatred made him also cruel and dangerous; his complex personality was characterized by simultaneous high idealism and clear perception of hypocrisy. His influence on European literature has been greater than that of any English writer except Shakespeare, and the poetry was but the man himself: 'It comes over me in a kind of rage every now and then, and then, if I don't write to empty my mind, I go mad.'

In 1969 a memorial tablet to Byron was placed in the floor of Westminster Abbey, his body having been refused burial there when it was brought back from Greece in 1824. Byron himself would have appreciated the irony of the fact that it took English critical opinion nearly 150 years to accept him.

S. C. Chew, *Byron in England: His Fame and After-Fame* (1924).

S. C. Chew (ed.), *Childe Harold's Pilgrimage and Other Romantic Poems* (New York, 1936).

E. H. Coleridge (ed.), *Poetry* (7 vols.; 1898–1904).

Elizabeth Longford, *Byron* (1976).

L. A. Marchand, *Byron: A Biography* (3 vols.; New York, 1958).

L. A. Marchand, *Byron: A Portrait* (1970).

L. A. Marchand, *Byron's Poetry: A Critical Introduction* (Boston, 1965).

L. A. Marchand (ed.), *Don Juan* (1958).

L. A. Marchand (ed.), *Letters and Journals* (1973–   ).

E. C. Mayne, *Byron* (1924, rev. ed.).

H. Nicholson, *Byron: The Last Journey* (1924; rev. ed. 1940).

I. Origo, *The Last Attachment* (1949).

G. Pocock (ed.), *Poems* (1963, rev. ed.).

R. E. Prothero (ed.), *Letters and Journals* (6 vols.; 1898–1901).

P. Quennell (ed.), *Byron: Selected Letters and Journals* (1949).

A. Rutherford, *Byron: A Critical Study* (1962).

A. Rutherford (ed.), *Byron: The Critical Heritage* (1970).

T. G. Steffan and W. W. Pratt (eds.), *Don Juan* (4 vols.; 1957).

P. West (ed.), *Byron: A Collection of Critical Essays* (Englewood Cliffs, N.J., 1963).

Portraits: oil, half-length, by T. Phillips: N.P.G.; oil, half-length, after R. Westall, 1825: N.P.G.; miniature, half-length, by J. Holmes, 1818: N.P.G.; oil, three-quarter length, by R. Westall, 1813: N.P.G.; oil, full-length, by George Sanders: Royal Collection; drawing, half-length, by Count d'Orsay: British Museum; miniature, artist unknown, V. & A.; oil, half-length, by Sir Thomas Lawrence: Newstead Abbey Collection; oil, half-length, by Thomas Phillips: Newstead Abbey Collection.

C

Campbell, John (1678–1743), 2nd Duke of Argyll; soldier and politician.

John Campbell was born at Petersham, Surrey, on 10 October 1678, the eldest son of the 1st Duke of Argyll (see Campbell, Archibald, 1st Duke, in *Lives of the Stuart Age*). As a boy he harboured early ambitions for a military career. These were realized in 1702, when he was given command of the 10th Regiment of Foot. On succeeding his father as Duke in 1703 he was sworn in as a Privy Councillor, invested with the Order of the Thistle, and made a colonel in the Scottish Horse Guards.

His political career began in 1705, when he was made Lord High Commissioner of the Scottish parliament. His opening speech recommended the union with England, and it was largely through his influence that the appointment of Scottish commissioners to negotiate the union was left in the hands of the Queen. In return for his services in furthering the union Argyll was created a peer of England with the titles of Earl of Greenwich and Baron of Chatham.

In the War of the Spanish Succession he served under the Duke of Marlborough (see Churchill, John, in *Lives of the Stuart Age*) and as a brigadier general was noted for his valour at the Battle of Ramillies in 1706. Raised to the rank of lieutenant general in 1709, he took part in the Battle of Malplaquet, showing considerable ability and personal bravery.

During the campaign Marlborough suggested to the Queen that he be made captain general for life. Argyll's opposition to this proposal can best be explained as a consequence of his own personal ambition rather than of any particular hostility to Marlborough. However, from this point on he worked for Marlborough's overthrow, and so commended himself to Harley and the Tories that in 1711 he was made commander in chief of English forces in Spain. He did not particularly distinguish himself in this position, but nevertheless on the conclusion of the Peace of Utrecht in 1713 he was appointed commander in chief of English forces in Scotland.

He now supported the movement for the dissolution of the union with England on the grounds that the union had not worked out in the best interests of Scotland – or England either, for that matter. A motion to this effect was defeated in parliament by four votes, but agitation continued in the country.

In the following year (1714), as Queen Anne fell into her last illness, Argyll, along with the Duke of Somerset, intervened at the last council, proposing the Duke of Shrewsbury as Lord High Treasurer. This appointment ensured the failure of Jacobite plans to gain the throne for James, the Old Pretender, so that the Hanoverian succession was assured. In consequence, Argyll was one of those who stood in high favour at court in the early years of George I. He was appointed commander in chief of the King's forces in Scotland, and in this position was given the task of crushing the Jacobite rising of 1715.

Having initially foiled the rebels in Edinburgh, he watched their every move for several months before finally confronting a force three times the size of his own at Sheriffmuir on 13 November 1715. The ground formation was such that the two armies were hidden from each other for a time, so that when they first joined battle it was found that the two forces were not directly opposed. The outcome was a victory claimed by both sides on the right wing, but Argyll achieved the overall advantage in that the rebel leader, the Earl of Mar, was among the defeated insurgents.

Argyll's subsequent march northwards was attended by few difficulties in the task of dispersing the rebels. The Pretender abandoned his artillery at Perth and the leaders embarked at Montrose for France, so that the rebellion was successfully crushed with very little bloodshed.

Despite this success the Duke was suddenly deprived of his offices for no discernible reason and at this point the Jacobites tried unsuccessfully to win him to their cause. He was soon restored to favour, however, and made Lord Steward of the Household in 1718. Thereafter he held several sinecures and other posts, including Master General of Ordnance (1725–30) and Governor of Portsmouth (1730–7).

His political career was always regulated by his relationship to the parties in power. As he never set himself to pursue one purpose he never won a position commensurate with his abilities and oratorical gifts. It was said that his ambition was to have sole command of the army, and he achieved the rank of field marshal in 1736.

His popularity in Scotland was increased by his defence of Edinburgh against the Porteous mob in 1737. However, in England an intemperate speech against the government after the bad harvests of 1740 led to his dismissal from office. His opposition to Walpole's administration contributed to its fall in 1742, but from this point on Argyll ceased

active participation in politics. Incapacitated by paralysis, he died at Petersham on 4 October 1743; an elaborate marble monument was erected to him in Westminster Abbey.

Portraits: oil, half-length, by W. Aikman: N.P.G.; oil, full-length, by W. Aikman, *c*.1715–20: Holyrood House.

Campbell, Robert (1671–1734), Highland chieftain, commonly called 'Rob Roy', see Macgregor, Robert, in *Lives of the Stuart Age*.

Campbell, Thomas (1777–1844), poet and critic.

Thomas Campbell was born on 27 July 1777 in Glasgow, youngest son of Alexander Campbell, a Virginia merchant ruined by the American wars. Influenced by the Scots songs and legends that his Highland-born mother had taught him, Campbell began writing verse when still a schoolboy at Glasgow Grammar School. In 1791 he went on to Glasgow University, where he was a fine classical scholar and became a lifelong upholder of libertarian politics. Campbell's ambition to be a clergyman was shattered in 1795 by his father's bankruptcy, and he took up a private tutorship for a time, first on Mull and later in Argyllshire.

Campbell next became a solicitor's clerk in Edinburgh, but before long was spending his time producing freelance copy for Mundell the publisher – hack writing was to be his chief means of financial support for the rest of his life. His first serious literary achievement was *The Pleasures of Hope*, a long poem published by Mundell in April 1799. Its melodious descriptive passages and heartfelt appeals for Polish freedom and the abolition of slavery made the work very popular. However, it is full of generalizations and borrowings from other writers (Rogers's 'Pleasures of Memory' had been a starting point); in this he already exhibited the fatal diffidence that would prevent him becoming a major poet.

In June 1800 Campbell went to Germany, where he had inconclusive conversations with Klopstock and tried unsuccessfully to understand Kant. His most memorable experiences in Germany were meeting the French garrison at Ratisbon, witnessing the Battle of Hohenlinden, and being chased home to Yarmouth by a Danish privateer in the spring of 1801. His father's death temporarily recalled him to Edinburgh, where he published *Lochiel's Warning and Other Poems*. Back in London, he became the protégé of Lords Minto and Holland, who introduced him into literary society. Campbell then drew on his German experiences to write poems on contemporary events, in particular 'The Battle of Hohenlinden' and 'The Battle of the Baltic', which reveal a talent for the lucid expression of public sentiments.

In 1803 Campbell married his cousin, Matilda Sinclair, and settled in Sydenham. His initial difficulty in making a living from his writing was alleviated by a £200 crown pension awarded him in 1805, and by the profitable publication of his collected poems. But Campbell's timidity persisted; although 'Gertrude of Wyoming' (1809), an account of an attack by Indians made upon a Pennsylvania settlement, was praised for its pathos, Walter Scott said of its author, 'He is afraid of the shadow that his own fame casts before him.' Campbell was also a hopelessly unmethodical man; despite a promising start, the series of lectures on the history of poetry that he began in 1810 at the Royal Institution soon ground to a halt. However, in 1819, after at least fifteen years' preparation, he did manage to publish his major critical work, *Specimens of the British Poets*; its biographies and commentaries reveal a perceptive literary taste (although he writes enthusiastically of Pope and Milton, he is harsh on the Metaphysical poets).

After 1820 a combination of poverty and personal tragedy – his first son had died in 1810, and his second went mad – caused Campbell to write little more of value. Attracted by the salary of £500 he reluctantly became editor of the *New Monthly Magazine*, but did not distinguish himself. In 1824 he began to campaign publicly for the founding of a non-sectarian university in London; when London University became an actuality, he called it 'the only important event of my life's little history'.

After the death of his wife in 1828 Campbell was a broken man. In 1832, however, he roused himself to found the Polish Association, devoting his slender resources to aiding Polish refugees. His last years were spent writing hack biographies, the subjects including Mrs. Siddons (1834) and Petrarch (1841). His health began to fail and he went to France in pursuit of rest and quiet. Campbell died at Calais on 15 June 1844 and was buried in Westminster Abbey; earth from the grave of the Polish hero Kosciuszko was scattered on his coffin.

W. Beattie, *Life and Letters of Thomas Campbell* (1849).

J. L. Robertson (ed.), *Complete Poetical Works* (1907).

Portraits: oil, half-length, by T. Lawrence: N.P.G.; pencil, quarter-length, by J. Henning, 1813: N.P.G.

Canning, George (1770–1827), statesman; Prime Minister for a short time during 1827, but chiefly remembered for his liberal policy as Foreign Secretary from 1822 to 1827.

George Canning was born on 11 April 1770 in London, son of a gentleman of County Londonderry in Ireland, who died in 1771. Left destitute with a year-old son, his mother became an actress in order to support herself and him, but compounded her problems by becoming the mistress of an actor, Samuel Reddish, by whom she had five sons. The young George was eventually taken under the care of a wealthy uncle, Stratford Canning, who financed his education at Eton and Christ Church, Oxford. After graduating in 1791 he entered Lincoln's Inn, but soon decided on a political career. At Oxford his ideas had been decidedly radical, but there could be little political future for a young man of his talents if he followed that course. The Whigs were out of the question because he was born outside the great Whig families like the Cavendishes, the Russells, and the Bentincks. So it was that a combination of enlightened self-interest and respect for Pitt led him into the Tory party. As with many of his contemporaries, his early radicalism faded away as the French Revolution lurched into anarchy and violence.

In July 1793 Canning was elected for the pocket borough of Newtown, Isle of Wight, and it soon became apparent that his oratory would be a great asset to the Tories in the House. The spring of 1796 saw him appointed an Under-Secretary in the Foreign Office, and the same year he was elected for another pocket borough, Wendover in Buckinghamshire.

Between 20 November 1797 and 9 July 1798 he contributed to the *Anti-Jacobin*, a weekly journal devoted to the ridicule of both French and English republicans. Canning was the wittiest of its writers. In 1799 he left the Foreign Office and was named one of the twelve commissioners for India. In May 1800 he was promoted to the office of Joint Paymaster of the Forces and made a Privy Councillor, posts that he held till the retirement of Pitt the Younger in 1801. A few months later he married Miss Joan Scott (who brought with her a fortune of £100,000), by whom he had four children. The marriage was not only a wealthy but also a happy one.

Canning's reputation up to this point had rested more on his oratory than on any political achievement. However, the Tory aristocracy never allowed him to forget that he was the son of an actress. Politically he had more in common with liberal Whigs such as Melbourne (see Lamb, William) than with the Tories.

On the formation of Pitt's second ministry (May 1804–January 1806) Canning became Treasurer of the Navy, although his humble origins kept him out of the cabinet. Pitt's death forced him to resign along with his colleagues, but the failure of the 'Ministry of All the Talents' left the King with no choice but to recall 'the friends of Mr. Pitt' to form a government in March 1807. Under the Duke of Portland (see Bentinck, William Henry Cavendish) Canning became Secretary of State for Foreign Affairs (1807–9).

Canning's first tenure of office as Foreign Secretary coincided with the beginning of the Peninsular War. He was anxious to prosecute the war and planned the successful seizure of the Dutch fleet. Defeats in Spain (at Corunna) and Holland (at Flushing), however, upset his irritable temperament and he bestowed the full blame upon the Secretary for War, Viscount Castlereagh (see Stewart, Robert), and demanded his instant dismissal. Portland was too old and indecisive to take such radical action and in the event both men resigned. On 21 September 1809 a duel was fought between Canning and Castlereagh on Wimbledon Common, in which Canning was wounded in the thigh.

On the death of Portland, Canning offered to form a new government but he was distrusted and was passed over in favour of Spencer Perceval (q.v.). The former Foreign Secretary was now to spend seven years in the political wilderness.

However, he was still the ablest and most effective speaker on the Tory side, and in 1816 he was recalled to a minor post as President of the Board of Control. He had earlier refused the opportunity to be Foreign Secretary during the peace negotiation at Vienna, because of his hostility to Castlereagh. In 1812, after moving from constituency to constituency, he was elected for Liverpool and formed a common bond of interest with the men of commerce there. Canning had a far better grasp of economics than most of his Tory colleagues and was able to compose highly technical speeches on such subjects as the regulation of gold bullion.

Resigning his office at the time of Queen Caroline's trial (December 1820), Canning thought badly of his political future at home and accepted the governor-generalship of India. Viscount Castlereagh's suicide in 1822, however, deterred him from leaving to take up the appointment and Liverpool and Wellington sought his support as being so vital that they were prepared to take him on his own terms. He succeeded to the 'whole inheritance' – the post of Foreign Secretary and the leadership of the House of Commons – in September 1822. In the next year he resigned his Liverpool seat and was elected for Harwich, which he left for Newport in 1826.

In domestic politics Canning maintained Tory principles. He supported the repressive domestic policy of the cabinet and opposed the movement for parliamentary reform. On the other hand he favoured Catholic emancipation and realized that the Tory party could check the reform movement only by adopting progressive policies itself. He took care to explain his foreign policy in terms that Englishmen understood and of which they approved. To this may also be added his support of Huskisson at the Board of Trade. The general effect of his policies was a lull in the clamour for parliamentary reform.

Canning's foreign policy was one of non-intervention and the patronage, if not actual support, of liberal movements in Europe. In essence his policy differed little from the guidelines laid down by Castlereagh before the Congress of Verona in 1822. The matter on which the two men did differ was the style of their administrations. Canning did not attend Verona as Castlereagh had planned to do, but allowed England to be represented by Wellington instead. He cut England off from the Holy Alliance of Eastern powers in 1823; prevented, by the supremacy of the British navy, European intervention in South America on behalf of Ferdinand VII in Spain; recognized the independence of the rebellious Spanish American colonies (and so 'called the

New World into existence to redress the balance of the Old'); and gave diplomatic support to the Greeks in their struggle for freedom from Turkish rule. This ebullient foreign policy struck a chord of national pride and was especially popular with the middle classes. Canning did not profess or desire to be a European – he had no personal knowledge of Metternich and the other European leaders. 'For Alliance read England and you have the clue to my policy,' he said; 'Every country for itself and God for us all.'

Canning's methods, and Canning himself, were less popular with the old Tories than with the country. In February 1827, Liverpool (see Jenkinson, Robert Banks) had a paralytic stroke; at once the unity of the Tory party was broken. Canning had every right to claim Liverpool's place. The leading Tories in the Commons, with the exception of Peel, wanted him; but the Lords, distrusting Canning's support for Catholic emancipation and his liberal foreign policy, refused to have him. The King acted astutely; he knew that a Tory cabinet without Canning and his friends was impossible. Canning therefore became Prime Minister and Wellington, Peel, and others resigned from the cabinet. However a number of Whigs came to his assistance, and most of the independent M.P.s supported him with their votes. His ministry, however, lasted only four months; his health broke down under the strain, and he died on 8 August 1827 at Chiswick, in the house of the Duke of Devonshire.

Having proved himself to be one of the ablest of the liberal Tories, despite the opposition of his own party, Canning was soon accorded his place in the political history of the nineteenth century. His speeches appeared in six volumes in 1828, and his private secretary, Augustus Granville Stapleton, has provided us with two valuable assessments of him in *Political Life of George Canning, 1822–1827* (3 vols.; 1831, 2nd ed.) and *Canning and His Times* (1859).

Peter Dixon, *Canning: Politician and Statesman* (1976).

Wendy Hinde, *George Canning* (1973).

Sir Charles Petrie, *George Canning* (1946, 2nd ed.).

P. J. V. Rolo, *George Canning: Three Biographical Studies* (1965).

E. J. Stapleton (ed.), *Some Official Correspondences of George Canning* (2 vols.; 1909).

H. V. W. Temperley, *The Foreign Policy of Canning, 1822–27* (1925).

Portraits: oil, full-length, by T. Lawrence and R. Evans: N.P.G.; oil, full-length, by T. Lawrence, 1828: Buckingham Palace; marble bust, by J. Nollekens: Apsley House, London; marble bust, by William Spence, Walker Art Gallery, Liverpool.

Carleton, Sir Guy (1724–1808), 1st Baron Dorchester; Irish-born military commander who became Governor of Quebec.

Guy Carleton was born at Strabane on 3 September 1724. His father died when he was fourteen and it was to his stepfather, the Rev. Thomas Skelton of Newry, that he was obliged for his education.

Carleton's military career began in 1742 when he joined the Earl of Rothes's regiment as an ensign; by 1757 he had risen to the rank of lieutenant colonel, and on his embarkation for America in the following year he was made quartermaster general and an acting colonel. He took part in the sieges of Louisbourg, Quebec, Belle Isle, and Havana, and in 1762 he became a full colonel. Four years later he was serving as Deputy Governor of Quebec when the Governor himself had to return to England, and in 1768 Carleton began his first term as official Governor of the city with which his whole subsequent career came to be linked.

After a quiet but efficient first term, during which he did much to conciliate the French-Canadian landowners, Carleton returned to England in 1770, where, two years later, he was promoted to the rank of major general. In the same year (1772) he married Lady Maria, the daughter of the 2nd Earl of Effingham, by whom he was to have eleven children. He helped to draft a bill concerning the administration of Quebec that was passed by parliament in June 1774, and the following year he sailed from England to resume his post as Governor of Quebec and take up a further appointment as commander in chief of the British forces in Canada.

On his arrival Carleton faced an army advancing from America under Benedict Arnold and Richard Montgomery. The British forces in Canada at this time were below strength, and while attempting to save the beleaguered town of St. John's, Carleton's army was defeated and he himself narrowly escaped capture. Disguised as a fisherman, he managed to return to Quebec, where for several desperate months he held the city with only a small garrison against the American forces. In May 1776 the arrival of a British relief squadron enabled Carleton to take the offensive, and after defeating Arnold at the Battle of Lake Champlain and recapturing Crown Point he was able to drive the Americans completely out of Canada.

In 1777, feeling that he had been unjustly deprived of command of the British forces in Canada and America, Carleton returned to England. He was made a Knight of the Bath in 1776, and awarded the governorship of Charlemont in Ireland, but his semi-retirement ended in 1782, when he was made commander in chief of the British forces in America. Although he held this difficult post for only a year, Carleton's conciliatory policies gained him the respect of the Americans and eased the way for the

treaty of 1783 that marked the official conclusion to the War of American Independence.

In 1786 Carleton was created Baron Dorchester and was again appointed Governor of Quebec. After the division of Canada into two administrative provinces by an act of parliament in 1791, he briefly returned to England, but two years later he was back in Quebec: this city was by now his true home, and by the time he retired in July 1796 its citizens had come to treat their Governor with affection as well as admiration. Carleton himself seemed to lose all interest in public affairs after this, and his final years were spent in quiet retirement at his homes at Kempshot near Basingstoke, Hampshire, and at Stubbings near Maidenhead, Berkshire. Sir Guy Carleton died on 10 November 1808, completing at the age of eighty-four a life that was both publicly successful and privately serene.

A. L. Burt, *The Old Province of Quebec* (1933).
A. L. Burt, *The United States, Great Britain and British North America* (1940).
A. L. Burt, *Guy Carleton, Lord Dorchester 1724–1808* (1955, rev. ed.).

Caroline Amelia Elizabeth of Brunswick-Wolfenbüttel (1768–1821), known as 'Caroline of Brunswick'; legally recognized wife of George IV.

Caroline was born on 17 May 1768, the second daughter of Duke Karl Wilhelm Ferdinand of Brunswick-Wolfenbüttel and Princess Augusta of England. As a child, she showed herself to be kind-hearted and affectionate. Caroline was the niece of George III, and it was his will that she should marry her first cousin, the Princes of Wales. The Prince, however, was violently hostile to this proposition, being already involved with Maria Fitzherbert (q.v.), whom he had secretly and illegally married in 1785. He never regarded the Princess as other than 'fat, ugly, garish, and vulgar in manner, dress, and language', but observing the King to be adamant, he acquiesced in the match as a means of bargaining for extra funds from the Treasury. He fulfilled his part of the arrangement grudgingly and with bad grace from the day of his wedding, which he spent in a state of extreme drunkenness.

Caroline's arrival in England was not propitious; she left Brunswick on 30 December 1794, but owing to the Prince's 'difficulties' in meeting her, she remained at Cuxhaven until March 1795, when Beau Brummell was prominent in her escort to London. She was married in the Chapel Royal at St. James's on 8 April 1795, after which she lived at Carlton House, in a state of some unhappiness, disliked by her mother-in-law Queen Charlotte and mocked by the ladies of the court.

Three months after the birth of her daughter Charlotte, on 7 January 1796, the Princess of Wales was deserted by her husband. She lived at Shooters Hill for a period, moving in 1802 to Blackheath. It was only thanks to the intervention of her father-in-law the King that she was allowed access to her child. Worse was to follow. As a result, apparently, of unguarded conversation on the subject of children with Lady Douglas, Caroline became the object of unfounded allegations that William Ellis, a young man in her entourage, was her illegitimate son. A commission of the House of Commons in 1806 repudiated this charge, accused Lady Douglas of perjury, and cleared Caroline of misdemeanour.

In 1811 the Prince of Wales became Regent, but Caroline was ignored. In fact her situation deteriorated further when the Prince re-opened the charge of immorality against her, and denied her access to her daughter. She protested against this decision to the House of Commons, but the House ruled that 'the Regent's will should prevail' and that he should be 'sole judge of the conduct to be observed in the education of his daughter', even to the exclusion of the company of her mother.

Prohibited from attending court and worn out by ill treatment, the Princess obtained permission to travel abroad, and at the end of 1813 left England. Her conduct continued to be the subject of rumour and scandal, involving in particular her companion, Bartolomeo Bergami, on whom she piled a number of honours, including the order of St. Caroline, instituted by herself. The Princess and her party travelled throughout the Levant, and reports flowed back to the English court of her 'constant levity'.

In 1820, when the Prince of Wales became King, Caroline's name was omitted from the state prayers. She rejected an offer of settlement with the conditions that she lived abroad and did not claim the title of Queen. Public feeling swayed strongly in her favour, and on her return to England in June people marched in the streets with banners bearing the words, 'The Queen's guards are the people'. A bill was now brought against her for divorce on the grounds of immoral conduct with Bergami, but popular support for her coupled with the oratory of Henry Brougham (q.v.) caused the case to be dropped. The persecution continued, however; Caroline was refused a palace and was forcibly excluded from the coronation on 29 July 1821. She died only a few days after this event, on 7 August.

There was yet another stormy incident before Caroline was laid to rest. The King refused to allow her body to be carried through the streets of London, but the populace felt otherwise and there was a bloody encounter at Hyde Park Corner, in which the Life Guards fired on the crowd. However, Caroline's body went through the city and was conveyed out of the country. She was buried beside her father at Brunswick on 26 August 1821.

E. A. Parry, *Queen Caroline* (1930).
E. E. P. Tisdale, *The Wanton Queen* (1939).

Portraits: oil, three-quarter length, by T. Lawrence, 1804: N.P.G.; oil, half-length, by J. Lonsdale: N.P.G.; oil, full-length, by Gainsborough Dupont, 1804: Buckingham Palace; pen and ink sketch, by Sir George Hayter: British Museum; oil, by T. Lawrence: V. & A.

Caroline Wilhelmina of Ansbach

(1683–1737), wife of George II and Queen of England (1727–37).

Caroline was born on 1 March 1683, the daughter of Johann Friedrich, Margrave of Brandenburg-Ansbach. Her father died when she was four years old. Her mother remarried, and until her death in 1696 kept the daughter of her first marriage with her at Dresden, where her second husband, the Elector of Saxony, resided. When her mother died Caroline went to Berlin to live under the tutelage of Frederick, King of Prussia, and his consort, Sophia Charlotte. A warm friendship grew up between the two women and they welcomed several talented young men into their circle, among them Leibnitz. Caroline was greatly upset by Sophia's death in 1704.

Several matches were discussed for her, but it was not until 1705 that she married George Augustus, Prince of Hanover. He was 'captivated by her charm and manners' and throughout her life she continued to retain his respect and affection. Although there was little personal joy for Caroline in the relationship, she had the satisfaction of knowing that her husband had come to rely on her good sense and judgment. During the intrigue for the British succession, she made herself acquainted with the political situation and began to learn English. In spite of her efforts, she never became proficient in speaking it, but she did understand it, whereas her father-in-law, George I, was able neither to speak or understand the language of his new people.

In 1714 Caroline, as Princess of Wales, accompanied her husband to England. At this time there was a widening rift between George I and his son, culminating in the banishment of the Prince of Wales from court in 1717. Caroline shared in the disapprobation; George I had been heard to refer to her as 'cette diablesse, madame la princesse [that devil, the princess]'. Caroline and the Prince of Wales retired to Richmond Lodge near Kew, a place that became her favourite residence. The three years of disfavour were far from sombre. A group of friends drawn mainly from Whig nobility gathered around them. Stanhope, Carr, Bathurst, Scarborough, Churchill, and Lord Hervey (the last-named becoming a capable and honest adviser to Caroline), were in regular attendance, and Lady Mary Wortley Montagu, Pope, Bolingbroke, and Gay were occasional visitors.

Caroline renewed her patronage of Leibnitz.

In about 1718 the Prince started an affair with one of Caroline's ladies in waiting, Mrs. Howard, afterwards Countess of Suffolk. Caroline, exerting considerable patience and tact, reached a *modus vivendi*, and although she lost the Prince's fidelity she kept his confidence, for it was still to her that he came for discussion and advice. George Augustus succeeded as George II in 1727, and Caroline continued to give unwavering support to his chief minister, Walpole, who (as he crudely put it) had 'got the right sow by the ear' for political influence.

Caroline supported the Low Church party, adhering to her creed to the point of refusing the sacrament at her death. She succeeded in changing George II's mind on the subject of the Polish succession, bringing him round to Walpole's anti-war strategies of mediation, instead of military support for Charles VI. Her influence was considerable, and in her husband's absence she several times acted as regent.

She bore eight children. Her favourite, William Augustus, Duke of Cumberland, was born in 1721. Towards her first-born, Frederick, Prince of Wales, she felt a strong and permanent antipathy. She was capable rather than learned, but well disposed to recognize and appreciate talent. She encouraged not only Leibnitz, but Newton, Halley, and Handel, as well as a number of poets. There was genuine grief at her death, on 20 November 1737, both from her husband and friends and also on the part of the populace. Although her Low Church affiliations were regarded with suspicion, she was known popularly as 'Good Queen Caroline'. For her funeral, Handel wrote one of his most powerful anthems. She was buried in the Henry VII chapel in Westminster Abbey, where her husband later joined her.

R. K. Arkell, *Caroline of Ansbach* (1939).
Peter Quennell, *Caroline of England* (1939).

Portraits: oil, three-quarter length, by T. Lawrence: N.P.G.; oil, half-length, by J. Lonsdale: N.P.G.; oil, full-length, by Enoch Seeman: Kensington Palace; oil, by J. Highmore: Hampton Court; oil, by C. Jervas: Guildhall Art Gallery, London; bust, by J. M. Rysbrack, Wallace Collection.

Carteret, John (1690–1763), 1st Earl Granville; diplomat and statesman.

John Carteret was born at Bath on 22 April 1690, the eldest surviving son of George, 1st Baron Carteret. During his education at Westminster school and Christ Church, Oxford, Carteret was an able scholar, not only in the classics but also several European languages. Lord Chesterfield testified that Carteret possessed 'a most uncommon share of learning for a man of quality'; Jonathan Swift wrote that he had more learning 'than properly became a person of his rank'.

Carteret took his seat in the House of Lords in 1711, having succeeded to his father's barony in 1695. During the latter years of Queen Anne's reign he supported the Hanoverian succession, and on the accession of George I in 1714 was made a Gentleman of the King's Bedchamber among other sinecures. In 1719 Carteret received his first important political post as Ambassador to Sweden; in this capacity he secured the right of trade and navigation in the Baltic for British ships, and his skill in conducting peace negotiations between Russia and Sweden was admired by George I.

Carteret had declared his allegiance to the faction opposing Walpole at the very beginning of the schism in the Whig party in 1712, and on his return to England he continued to ingratiate himself with the King – with the assistance of one of George's mistresses, the Countess of Darlington – and even attempted to form his own party to oust Walpole from office. The animosity between Carteret and

Walpole was and remained more personal than political: Carteret, an ambitious and arrogant man, was jealous of Walpole's power, and the latter was deeply suspicious of his talented subordinate whose knowledge of German gave him a unique influence over the King. In 1721 Carteret was appointed Secretary of State for the Southern Department, a promotion that was engineered by the Earl of Sunderland (see Spencer, Charles), the leader of Walpole's opponents in the Whig party, but after Sunderland's death (1722) Walpole and Townshend secured Carteret's dismissal from this post and had him appointed in 1724 as Lord Lieutenant of Ireland in order to remove him from London. There was much unrest in Ireland at this time at the granting of a patent to mint coins without consultation with the proper authorities (the crisis known to history as 'Wood's Ha'pence'); ironically, Carteret himself had helped to secure this patent in order to cause annoyance to Walpole; he now had to cope with the consequences of his own action. During the long periods when the Irish parliament was not in session Carteret continued his opposition to Walpole in the English House of Lords, but during the six years of his appointment he managed to solve some of the immediate problems of Ireland, gaining the grudging respect of Jonathan Swift.

On his return to England in 1730 Carteret refused to serve under Walpole and succeeded in gaining the confidence of the new King, George II. In 1741 his resolution in the House of Lords that the King should be requested to dismiss Walpole from office was defeated, but in the following year Walpole was forced to resign because of his declining majority in the Commons. Carteret was appointed Secretary of State for the Northern Department in the new administration of Earl Wilmington (see Compton, Spen-

cer). As Carteret's power increased, however, so did his disregard for public opinion; his close collaboration with George II in foreign policy aroused accusations that he was sacrificing the interests of England to those of Hanover, and in 1744 his personal and political opponents (among whom Walpole was still active) had become strong enough to force him to resign.

In the same year Carteret succeeded to the title of Earl Granville on the death of his mother. In 1746, the King, on Carteret's advice, refused to admit William Pitt the Elder (q.v.) to office, and Carteret and Lord Bath (see Pulteney, William) were together invited to form an administration; they proved incapable of doing so, however, and after obtaining and then resigning the seals of office within four days, Carteret's political ambition declined. He remained in the King's favour and served as President of the Council from 1751 until his death, but his undoubted talents were chiefly employed during these years in making long speeches on small matters in the House of Lords. Happily for Carteret, his elaborate rhetoric was very much in fashion, and his reputation remained greater than his actual power. He died at Bath on 2 January 1763.

A. Ballantyne, *Lord Carteret, A Political Biography, 1690–1763* (1887).

N. W. B. Pemberton, *Carteret, The Brilliant Failure of the Eighteenth Century* (1936).

Basil Williams, *Cartaret and Newcastle* (1943).

Portraits: oil, three-quarter length, studio of W. Hoare, 1750–2: N.P.G.; oil, three-quarter length, by T. Hudson: N.P.G.

Cartwright, Edmund (1743–1823), inventor.

Edmund Cartwright was born on 24 April 1743, at Marnham in Nottinghamshire. His early education was at Wakefield Grammar School. At fourteen he went to University College,

Oxford, where he graduated in 1764 and was elected a fellow; an M.A. followed in 1766. From his early youth Cartwright had written verses, and in 1772 he published *Armine and Elvira, a Legendary Poem*, which went into several editions and was described by Sir Walter Scott as 'a beautiful piece'.

Cartwright took holy orders, married a lady who, it is thought, owned property in Doncaster, and was presented to the perpetual curacy of Brampton, near Wakefield. In 1779 he was made rector of Goadby Marwood, Leicestershire, and he published an ode deploring the American war. At Goadby Marwood, Cartwright conducted agricultural experiments, contributed to the *Monthly Review*, and made a firm friendship with Crabbe, who in 1782 moved into the neighbourhood as chaplain to the Duke of Rutland.

A visit that Cartwright paid to Matlock in 1784 was to change the course of his life. Richard Arkwright's cotton-spinning mills were situated at Cromford, not far from Matlock, and the two men met. Cartwright is reported to have said in conversation that he 'Would have to set his wits to work, to invent a weaving mill.' On his return home he constructed a 'power loom' without even having seen the working of a hand loom. The machine was rough and inadequate, but Cartwright took out a patent for it in April 1785. In the same year the family moved to Doncaster, probably in order to take possession of his wife's property. During 1786 Cartwright made a study of the hand loom. He continued to experiment, and took out two more patents for loom improvements, in October 1786 and August 1787. He set up a factory in Doncaster for weaving and spinning, making use there of his patent power loom, which was the forerunner of modern looms. Although Cartwright's was not the first power

loom, it was the first to make the weaving of wide cloth, such as calico, a practical proposition.

A more original invention of Cartwright's was a wool-combing machine. He took out the first patent for this in 1789 and, continuing to modify and develop his original model, he subsequently took out three more patents. Even in its early form, one such machine could do the work of twenty hand-combers, representing a saving for the manufacturers of at least £1,000 a year. Naturally the wool-combers were greatly alarmed by the implications of this and 50,000 of them signed a petition to the House of Commons. Cartwright sent in a counter-petition, offering to limit the number of his machines. In the event a committee of the House of Commons decided against taking up the wool-combers' case and no aid was given them.

Cartwright's own Doncaster factory had a fairly modest output until the introduction of a steam engine in 1788 or 1789. In 1791 a Manchester firm contracted with him for some 400 power looms. A mill was built in which some looms were run by steam, thereby saving roughly half the wages than would have been paid to hand-loom workers. The Manchester mill was, however, burned to the ground and the owners were disinclined to take the risk of re-erecting it. Cartwright's progress was continually obstructed by hostility and by the high cost of development. By 1793 he had spent £30,000 of his own money and was deeply in debt. He transferred his property to his creditors, and the patent rights to his brothers – composing a sonnet about the frustration of his hopes – and moved to London.

He built a house on what is now the site of the Coliseum, out of inordinately expensive patent geometric bricks. In 1797 he patented a new kind of steam engine, substituting alcohol for water. He also formed a friendship at this time with Robert Fulton, working with him in experiments on steam navigation. When Fulton was forced to pay compensation to the government for suppressing his invention of a secret submarine weapon, Cartwright was on the committee which assessed the amount.

By 1800, Cartwright's wool-combing machine was beginning to come into general use but the patent had only a few more years to run. There were constant infringements that were difficult and expensive to counter. He petitioned parliament and a bill was passed prolonging the patent for fourteen years. (When this extension expired, he had still made a financial loss.) He renewed his interest in agriculture; in 1793 he patented a reaping machine and in 1801 his 'Essay on Husbandry' received a prize.

In 1800 the Duke of Bedford entrusted Cartwright with the management of his experimental farm at Woburn, and his efforts there earned him recognition from the Society of Arts and the Board of Agriculture. He also acted as domestic chaplain to the Duke.

His patent for the power loom expired in 1804 at a time when it was at last coming into favour, to the considerable benefit of the Lancashire manufacturers. About fifty Manchester manufacturers in 1807 signed a petition to the Prime Minister, requesting that Cartwright's services to the country by the invention of the power loom be duly acknowledged; in 1809 the House of Commons voted him £10,000.

Cartwright bought a farm in Kent and devoted himself to agricultural inventions. He was described at this time as 'a portly dignified old gentleman, grave and polite, but full of humour and spirit'. He died at Hastings on 30 October 1823 and was buried at Battle.

T. S. Ashton, *The Industrial Revolution, 1760 to 1830* (1948).

P. Mantoux, *The Industrial Revolution in the Eighteenth Century* (1928).

Portrait: engraving, quarter-length, by J. Thomson: Science Museum, London.

Castlereagh, Viscount (1769–1822), see Stewart, Robert.

Cavendish, Henry (1731–1810), chemist and physicist, who carried out pioneering research in gases, electricity, and geophysics.

Henry Cavendish was born on 10 October 1731 at Nice in the south of France, where his mother had gone for the sake of her health. He was the elder son of Lord Charles Cavendish by the Duke of Kent's daughter, Lady Anne Grey, who died when the boy was two years old in giving birth to his brother Frederick. Henry was sent in 1742 to Hackney seminary, and from 1749 to 1753 he was at Peterhouse, Cambridge, which he left without a degree, possibly because of reluctance to swear allegiance to the Church of England.

After touring Europe, he lived quietly in London with his father with whom, until the latter's death in 1783, he did much of his research on electricity and chemistry. At the age of forty he had inherited a fortune amounting to about a million pounds, and was described as 'the richest of all learned men, and very likely the most learned of the rich'. He continued, however, to live in modest style, spending money on little except scientific books and equipment. He was rarely seen in public except at scientific meetings, and was a confirmed misogynist, ordering all female household staff to remain out of his sight and communicating with his housekeeper only through daily notes. He seems never to have formed an attachment for anyone outside his family.

In 1760 he had been elected a Fellow of the Royal Society and he also became one of the only eight foreign associates of the Institut de France. Cavendish published some of his findings, starting with a paper on the preparation of gases in 1766, but much of his work lay in manuscript form, unknown until after his death. His influence was therefore largely posthumous, and it was not until 1879, when his unpublished works began to appear in print, that his full stature as a scientist could be realized. In his experiments with gases, or 'factitious airs' as he called them, he was among the first to recognize hydrogen, and made findings crucial to the discovery of argon a hundred years later. He studied the properties of 'fixed air' (carbon dioxide), preparing it by the action of an acid on marble, and also discovered the existence of calcium bicarbonate. Cavendish's study of the composition of the atmosphere led to the discovery that water was not an element but a compound, and that it could be synthesized by exploding hydrogen in air. Analogous conclusions were reached at the same time by James Watt (q.v.). The chemical researches of Cavendish, like those of Priestley and other contemporaries, were based on the traditional concept of phlogiston, the intangible substance thought to be released from an object or gas in the form of fire. But Cavendish was apparently well aware that his results could equally well be explained in terms of the new anti-phlogiston theories of the French chemist, Antoine Lavoisier.

Cavendish's researches into electricity would have brought him contemporary renown if he had published them. He discovered that the force between a pair of electrical charges is proportional to the inverse of the square of the distance between them, a basic law of electrostatics, later established by the French scientist C. A. Coulomb. He also anticipated Faraday's discovery that the amount of electrical energy that a capacitor is able to store depends on the substance inserted between its plates. The 'concept of potential', first made explicit by Cavendish, represented a considerable advance in electrical theory. He also discovered independently what later became known as Ohm's Law, a remarkable feat since he had no means of measuring the strength of the current except by grasping the ends of the electrodes with his hands and noting whether he could feel the shock in his fingers, up to his wrists, or all the way up to his elbows.

His work on heat, likewise largely unpublished, ran along the same lines as research being undertaken by Joseph Black (q.v.). The last major piece of research that he undertook was the experiment to which he gave his name, whereby a highly sensitive torsion balance was used to deduce the density of the earth. J. H. Poynting, who developed a similar experiment, wrote in 1913 that Cavendish carried out his experiments 'in a manner so admirable that it marks the beginning of a new era in the measurement of small forces'.

Cavendish died on 24 February 1810, from what appears to have been the first illness he had ever had in his life. His grave is in what is now Derby Cathedral, and his fortune was left to his relatives, who commemorated his name by building the Cavendish Physical Laboratory in the University of Cambridge.

A. J. Berry, *Henry Cavendish: His Life and Scientific Work* (1960).

J. G. Crowther, *Scientists of the Industrial Revolution: Joseph Black, James Watt, Joseph Priestley, Henry Cavendish* (1962).

Sir J. Larmor, Sir T. E. Thorpe, *et al.* (eds.), *The Scientific Papers of the Honourable Henry Cavendish, F.R.S.*, vol. i, *The Electrical Researches*; vol. ii, *Chemical and Dynamical Researches* (1921).

George Wilson, *The Life of the Honourable Henry Cavendish* (1851).

Portrait: drawing, full-length, by William Alexander: British Museum.

Cavendish, William (1720–64), 4th Duke of Devonshire and Marquis of Hartington; Whig statesman; First Lord of the Treasury from November 1756 to July 1757.

Cavendish was born in 1720, the eldest son of William Cavendish, 3rd Duke of Devonshire. On coming of age in 1741 the young Cavendish was elected to the House of Commons as member for Derbyshire. In 1748 he married Charlotte, the daughter and heiress of Richard Boyle, Earl of Burlington and Cork, who brought Lismore Castle and Irish estates into the Cavendish family. This marriage put him at the head of a great Whig association and considerably enhanced his political standing.

In March 1754 Cavendish's Irish connection and his loyal service to the Whig group recommended him to the post of Lord Lieutenant of Ireland. A sound if unimaginative administrator, he proved popular with all parties and his personal conduct was beyond reproach. He succeeded his father as 4th Duke of Devonshire in December 1755.

The outbreak of the Seven Years War in 1756 led to so great a dissatisfaction with the Duke of Newcastle's handling of affairs that Devonshire was summoned from Ireland as a possible successor. Popular opinion demanded that William Pitt the Elder (q.v.) should be made chief minister, but he rendered himself ineligible by offending George II. Devonshire, the leader of the Whigs and a less controversial figure, was therefore asked to form an administration. He agreed, appointing Pitt as Secretary of State to manage the war. In practice it was Pitt who dictated the policies of the new government, while Devonshire used his influence to manage parliament. Their partnership was never very secure, however, and in April 1757 Pitt resigned over the court-martial and execution of Admiral Byng. His departure left the ministry a 'mutilated, enfeebled, half-formed system' and in July 1757 Devonshire himself resigned, having perceived that Pitt and Newcastle had settled their differences and were ready to form an administration to prosecute the war.

Devonshire was appointed Lord Chamberlain of the Household and remained a fairly influential figure in politics until in 1762 he was dismissed by George III because of the latter's pathological suspicion, no doubt fostered by Bute, of the activities of the great Whig families. His health began to suffer, and he died at Spa in Belgium on 3 October 1764 at the age of forty-four.

Chambers, Sir William (1726–96), architect; designer of Somerset House in London.

William Chambers was born in Stockholm, Sweden, in 1726. His grandfather, a prominent Scottish merchant, had once supplied the Swedish King with money and military equipment, and it was because of his father's persistent efforts to extract payment for these goods that Chambers was born in Sweden.

In 1728 the family returned to England and most of Chambers's childhood years were spent on the family estates near Ripon in Yorkshire. At sixteen he joined the Swedish East India Company, in whose service he made at least one voyage to China; in 1749, however, he resolved to devote his career entirely to architecture. As a means of educating himself in the first principles of this profession he travelled extensively in Italy and France, not returning to England to begin his own work until 1755.

He now married, set up house in Poland Street, London, and quickly made the necessary contacts for commissions among the nobility. In 1757 he won a contract to provide architectural adornments for Kew Gardens; for five years he worked happily on the pagoda and the mock temples, freely indulging his tastes for both Chinese and classical designs, and by the end of this contract his name was established. In 1759 he published a *Treatise of Civil Architecture*, an influential volume that was reprinted twice in his lifetime. Only Robert Adam (q.v.) offered any serious competition to Chambers's commanding position as an architect, and the royal favour that continued after he became architectural tutor to the future George III was a firm foundation for his personal fame.

Chambers exhibited some of his own drawings with the Society of Artists from 1761 onwards, and when the Royal Academy was established in 1768 he was appointed its first treasurer. A gift of some more of his drawings to the King of Sweden in 1771 was rewarded by a Swedish knighthood, and George III immediately allowed him to assume the rank and title of an English knight also. In 1772 the inflated style and naïve opinions of Chambers's *Dissertation on Oriental Gardening* attracted considerable criticism, but Chambers himself, in his position as Comptroller of His Majesty's Works, was serenely immune.

After a brief visit to Paris in 1774 Chambers was awarded his most important commission, that of designing Somerset House. As befitted a building that was to house government offices as well as those of the Royal Society and the Royal Academy, the plans that Chambers now produced were both more conservative and more mature than most of his earlier work: Somerset House, a solid and unoriginal building that yet has its

own individual character, is an impressive demonstration of the competence that lay beneath Chambers's more extravagant exercises.

During his later years Chambers applied less of his energies to architecture and more to the social life of the London clubs. His friends included Johnson, Goldsmith, Reynolds, and Garrick, and his commissions – which included work at Blenheim Palace for the Duke of Marlborough and in Bloomsbury for the Duke of Bedford – enabled him to sustain his life-style in the manner to which he had become accustomed. Towards the end of his life Chambers suffered from attacks of asthma; he died, after a long illness, on 8 March 1796 and was buried in Westminster Abbey.

T. Hardwick, *A Memoir of the Life of Sir William Chambers* (1825).

Portraits: oil, half-length, by J. Reynolds: N.P.G.; wash, quarter-length, after Reynolds: N.P.G.; oil, half-length, by J. Reynolds: Royal Academy of Arts, London.

Chantrey, Sir Francis (1781–1841), sculptor.

Francis Chantrey was born in Norton, Derbyshire, on 7 April 1781, the son of a small farmer and carpenter. After attending the village school, he worked as an errand boy for a grocer in near-by Sheffield. In 1797, however, impressed by the shop window of Mr. Ramsey, a local wood-carver, he became his apprentice. While at Ramsey's, Chantrey met an engraver, John Raphael Smith, who encouraged him to take lessons in oil painting. In 1802 Chantrey gave up his apprenticeship, rented a studio, and began painting portraits of the local worthies at five guineas a time. The following year he went to try his luck in London, and after brief studies at the Royal Academy he was fortunate enough to become a protégé of the poet Samuel Rogers. In 1804 his first painting, a portrait of his uncle, was exhibited at the Academy.

By late 1804, however, Chantrey was practising almost exclusively as a sculptor, and his work was soon noticed by London's leading portrait sculptor, Nollekens, who provided him with many useful introductions. In 1807 Chantrey received the first of many official commissions, a series of colossal busts of British admirals for Greenwich Hospital. That same year he married his cousin Miss Wale, who had £10,000, and in 1808 they bought a house in Eccleston Street, with a studio attached.

Despite his humble origins, Chantrey was already becoming well-known in London society; he had competed successfully for the Guildhall statue of George III in 1808, and of the six busts he exhibited at the 1809 Royal Academy exhibition, most were of prominent politicians. Before long he had gathered commissions to the value of £12,000, and was charging each sitter 150 guineas. Perhaps his best work of this period is the 1812 monument to Marianne Johnes at Hafod church; the figures of the recumbent girl and her mourning parents are carved with a warmth and directness far removed from neo-classical practice, though not without a strong vein of sentimentality.

In 1814 Chantrey visited Paris, where he bought dozens of casts of classical statues, and also met Antonio Canova, Europe's most celebrated sculptor. Over the next five years he visited Italy and Holland, keeping records of his journeys in his sketchbooks. From this time on Chantrey was asked to sculpt the most famous Britons of his day; he did busts of Wordsworth, James Watt, and Walter Scott (1820). The example of classical sculpture led him to carve impressive standing figures of Canning swathed in a toga and Pitt in a flowing cloak. In contrast, his equestrian statues, particularly those of Wellington and George IV, are strangely tame – Chantrey seems to have had little taste for outright heroics. His gentler gifts are evident in the memorial to the two Robinson daughters (1817) in Lichfield Cathedral.

By now Chantrey was Britain's most celebrated sculptor. In 1818 he became a full Royal Academician, and in 1822 George IV paid him an unprecedented 300 guineas for a bust. Despite being a frequent guest at such great houses as Petworth, Chantrey remained unselfconscious about his lack of 'polish'; his language was as colourful as ever, and his favourite pursuits were still drinking and hunting. His later sculptures are uneven, since pressure of work led him to employ assistants, but the best of them still exhibited a typical serenity of expression and cleanness of modelling.

In 1835 Francis Chantrey was knighted by William IV; other honours included a doctorate of Civil Law from Oxford, an M.A. from Cambridge, and his election as a Fellow of the Royal Society and the Royal Society of Arts. On 25 November 1841, Chantrey died of heart failure. He was buried in his native village, with a tombstone of his own design, and in his will he left £150,000 – the Chantrey Bequest – to be used to buy art for the nation. The international paintings and sculptures purchased with this money are now housed in the Tate Gallery.

G. Jones, *Sir Francis Chantrey* (1849).

Works in:
Royal Collection.
N.P.G.
Scottish N.P.G.
V. & A.
Soane Museum, London.
Royal Academy.
Westminster Abbey.
St. Paul's Cathedral.

Portraits: oil on panel, half-length, by T. Phillips: N.P.G.; self-portrait, chalk, half-length: N.P.G.

Charles Edward Louis Philip Casimir Stuart (1720–88), commonly called 'The Young Pretender' and 'Bonnie Prince Charlie', leader of the final, unsuccessful Stuart bid for the English throne.

Charles Edward Stuart was born on 31 December 1720 in Rome, the eldest son of the Stuart pretender James III (see James Francis Edward Stuart). His childhood was perturbed and his education desultory largely because of parental differences. His instructors ranged from Jesuit priests through Protestant tutors to Jacobite soldiers. The Duke of Liria testified to his resolution as a young man during the siege of Gaeta (1734), and his charm so captivated everyone that the government's spy in Rome (Baron Philip von Stosch, alias John Walton) wrote to London saying, 'Everybody says that he will be in time a far more dangerous enemy to the present establishment . . . than ever his father was.'

In 1744, at the invitation of Louis XV, Charles made a secret journey to Paris, via Florence, where Sir Horace Mann described him as 'above middle height and very thin . . . his face is rather long . . . the forehead very broad, the eyes fairly large – blue, but without sparkle; the mouth large, with the lips slightly curled.' The eyes were in fact brown. Charles assured his father, whom he was never to see again, that he was going 'in search of three crowns, which I doubt not but to have the honour and happiness of laying at Your Majesty's feet'.

Louis had summoned Charles to be used when opportunity occurred; war had not yet broken out between France and England, and an attempt in March 1744 to take Charles across the Channel as Regent for his father was foiled when a storm shattered the ships in harbour at Gravelines. Charles was subsequently informed that no further aid from Versailles was forthcoming, so he could only continue negotiations with the Jacobites in Scotland, the sole source from which he received definite encouragement at this time.

By early summer 1745 Charles had decided to depart secretly for Scotland, informing both Louis and his father by letters sent on his departure. He sought aid by every means possible: he ordered his jewels to be pawned, accumulated a small quantity of arms, and secured a frigate named *Du Teillay* (or *Doutelle*) with the *Elizabeth* to escort her. He set sail on 12 July from Belle Ile with 'The Seven Men of Moidart': the Duke of Atholl, Aeneas Macdonald, Francis Strickland, Sir Thomas Sheriden, the Rev. George Kelly, Sir John Macdonnell, and John William O'Sullivan. Four or five days later they encountered an English man-of-war, H.M.S. *Lion*, which, having engaged the *Elizabeth*, forced her to put back with all the ammunition, while Charles went on alone, to land on the Isle of Eriskay in the Hebrides late in July.

Charles was immediately advised by Macdonald of Boisdale to go home, but replied, 'I am come home.' He refused to be dispirited, despite widespread prediction of failure without French aid. After gaining the support of Cameron of Lochiel, Charles's adherents grew to 600 by 19 August 1745, when the royal standard was raised at Glenfinnan. The government in London put a price of £30,000 on Charles's head and ordered Sir John Cope to assemble his scattered forces. By 26 August Charles was at Invergarry Castle, and Cope, uncertain of the Jacobite numbers and hampered by the government's reluctance to arm even the Whig clans, decided to retreat, even though in so doing he left open the way south.

In Perth Lord George Murray (q.v.) joined the Jacobites, now numbering 2,000, and on 17 September the Old Pretender was proclaimed as James VIII of Scotland at Edinburgh Cross. On 21 September Charles routed Cope's troops at Prestonpans.

Alarmed, the Whig government placed several regiments recalled from Flanders under the Duke of Cumberland (see William Augustus); and it ordered Marshal Wade at Newcastle to prevent the Jacobites from marching south. Charles stayed at Holyrood House in Edinburgh for five weeks, denounced the Act of Union, and gave pledges of religious tolerance.

Then, marching on England, Charles laid siege to Carlisle on 8 November. Wade failed to relieve Carlisle, and soon the rebels (now numbering about seven or eight thousand) were between Wade and London. They reached Preston on 27 November, and then Manchester. Cumberland, expecting the rebels to march into Wales, left open the route to Derby, which Charles reached on 4 December. There was panic in London: shops shut; business was suspended; there was a run on the banks; and guards were marched to Finchley.

Yet at this moment of strength the Jacobites were discussing retreat. Desertions had reduced them to 4,500, two large armies were pursuing them, the English Jacobites had failed to rise, and the French had not arrived. Charles reportedly told his council, 'You ruin, abandon, and betray me if you don't march on', but could not overrule the vehement opposition of his officers to a continued advance. The clans began a rapid retreat north on 6 December, defeating Hawley (Wade's successor) at Falkirk in January 1746, but followed doggedly by Cumberland. On 16 April about 7,000 Jacobites, hungry and low in morale, met nearly 9,000 government troops at Culloden, and suffered a severe defeat, which effectively ended Charles's hopes.

Charles fled to Invergarry and thence in search of a safe retreat to the Hebrides. His hiding places were never revealed, although he spent five months as a fugitive in the Highlands with a huge price on his head. Eventually escaping to Brittany on 10 October 1746 and seeking French assistance, Charles received only the conditional offer of a pension from Louis. He angrily rejected the suggestion, as he did the opinion of his father and brother Henry that their cause was now lost. Additional bitterness mounted in the Prince when Henry became a cardinal in 1747 and when Charles was forcibly removed to Avignon by Louis in 1748 after the treaty of Aix-la-Chapelle. The British government objected to his stay here, and on 28 February 1749 Charles voluntarily left the city for an unknown destination.

For several years following this his movements are not certain. He lived secretly in Paris with a certain Clementina Walkenshaw for some time, much censured by Charles's supporters because she was held to be a spy. Charles adopted the Protestant faith during a secret visit to London in 1750, vainly trying to revive the cause. However, bitterness, drink, and jealousy caused preparations during 1752–3 for another rising to come to nothing. In 1760 Clementina left Charles, taking with her their daughter Charlotte (born 1753); their public drunken quarrels had long been common gossip.

In 1766 his father died, and Charles was bitterly disappointed when the Pope failed to acknowledge him. On 17 April 1772 he married Princess Louise of Stolberg but, to the disappointment of Jacobite hopes, the marriage was childless and eventually, in 1780, Louise ran off with a lover, Vittorio Alfieri. In his last years Charles acknowledged his daughter Charlotte. She joined him in Florence in 1784 in spite of her own ill health, and nursed him through the asthma and dropsy that beset his final years. He died on 31 January 1788 and was buried in St. Peter's, Rome.

Charles's brother Henry never made a formal claim to the English throne, and with his death in 1807 the last of the Jacobite hopes died too. Andrew Lang summarized Charles as a youth thus: 'Misfortune was to sour and not to strengthen a character which was never strong: [rather, it was] always self-centred and petulant, though adorned with certain attractions of audacity and of bearing.' Popular memory has preserved these latter qualities.

David Daiches, *Charles Edward Stuart* (1973).
A. C. Ewald, *Life and Times of Prince Charles Stuart* (1883).
Andrew Lang, *Prince Charles Edward Stuart* (1903).
Compton Mackenzie, *Prince Charlie* (1932).
A. and H. Tayler, *1745 and After* (1938).

Portraits: oil, half-length, attributed to H. D. Hamilton, *c.* 1785: N.P.G.; oil, half-length, by A. David, *c.* 1729: N.P.G.; pastel, quarter-length, after Q. de la Tour, 1748: N.P.G.

Chatham, 1st Earl of (1708–78), see Pitt, William, 'the Elder'.

Chatterton, Thomas (1752–70), poet and literary forger, who was a central figure in the Gothic revival.

Thomas Chatterton was born on 20 November 1752, three months after the death of his father. He was brought up in poverty by his mother, a needlewoman, who did not appreciate her son's exceptional gifts; when he was eight, she spoke of him as being 'little better than a fool'. He possessed a sensitive imagination and an inquiring mind that encouraged him to study a black-letter Bible and spend a great deal of his time at the church of St. Mary Redcliffe in Bristol, where manuscripts found in the neglected muniment room and supposedly dating back to the Wars of the Roses fascinated him. His formal education, however, at Colston charity school from 1760 to 1765 was probably no more than rudimentary. In 1762 he produced his first poem, 'On the Last Epiphany', published a year later in Felix Farley's *Bristol Chronicle*. In 1764 he wrote a satirical poem, 'The Churchwarden and the Apparition', which lampooned a churchwarden named Joseph Thomas for destroying a medieval cross. In the same year he presented his first forgery, 'Elinoure and Juga', claiming that it came from the Canynges coffer. Because of his efforts consistently to maintain obsolete calligraphy, spelling, and vocabulary, its authenticity went unquestioned, though there were tell-tale linguistic inaccuracies. Encouraged, he next conceived the fifteenth-century 'Rowley Romance', supposedly by Thomas Rowley, a fictitious secular priest at St. John's Church and supposed friend and confessor of William Canynges, an actual mayor of Bristol.

At fifteen he found employment as a

clerk under an attorney named Lambert. He continued his self-education, trading poems for books with Bristol businessmen. Using the pseudonym of Dunelmus Bristoliensis, he contributed to *Town and Country*, hoaxing all of Bristol in 1768 with his description 'from an old manuscript' of the opening of Bristol Bridge in 1248. A year previously, in 1767, he had concocted an impressive pedigree for a pewterer embarrassed by his humble origins, again using 'original records'.

In 1769 Chatterton sent Horace Walpole (q.v.) some 'Rowley' poems and the 'Rise of Painting in England', also supposedly by Rowley. Walpole was at first impressed by 'so masterly a genius' but later ignored Chatterton when he learned that the works were forgeries. Embittered, Chatterton began to satirize former patrons. His employer Lambert burnt his work, pronouncing it 'stuff'. However, when in the spring of 1770 Lambert discovered Chatterton's 'last will and testament' written 'in the utmost distress of mind', he released Chatterton from his indenture and the poet set out for London with only £5.

At the outset prospects seemed good, since editors gave him great encouragement, but the death of Mayor Beckford, father of William Beckford (q.v.) and a possible patron, together with a political clamp-down on the press, caused his work to be generally unpaid or rejected, apart from the successful production of his burlesque opera, *The Revenge*, in 1770. He moved into a garret in Brooke Street, Holborn: an application for a post as ship's surgeon failed. Penniless, his 'damn'd, native, unconquerable pride' allowed him to accept no assistance.

Chatterton was seventeen when he died. His suicide by arsenic on 24 August 1770 (apparently through distress at his poverty), his room littered with torn scraps of his poetry, and his burial in a pauper's grave were to excite the imaginations of later Romantic poets. 'The marvellous boy,' Wordsworth called him, 'the sleepless soul that perished in his pride.'

Chatterton's forgeries have a music all their own, despite their inaccuracies. But his later attempts to write poetry in contemporary idiom are disappointing. Editions of the poems of 'Thomas Rowley' appeared in 1778 and 1782. Chatterton's collected works were published in 1803 and a 'modernized' or 'rationalized' edition of them was made by W. W. Skeat in 1871.

E. P. Ellinger, *Thomas Chatterton, the Marvellous Boy* (1930).

W. S. Lewis et al. (eds.), *Walpole's Correspondence with Chatterton* (in vol. 16 of the Yale edition of Horace Walpole's correspondence, New Haven, 1952).

E. H. W. Meyerstein, *A Life of Thomas Chatterton* (1930).

E. H. W. Meyerstein, 'Chatterton: his Significance Today', *Transactions of the Royal Society of Literature*, xvi (1937).

D. S. Taylor and B. B. Hoover (eds.), *The Complete Works of Thomas Chatterton* (2 vols.; 1971).

Chesterfield, 4th Earl of (1694–1773), see Stanhope, Philip Dormer.

Chippendale, Thomas (1718–79), cabinet-maker and designer.

Thomas Chippendale was born at Otley, Yorkshire, and baptized there on 5 June 1718. Both his father and his grandfather were local joiners and woodcarvers. In 1727 he moved with his father to London, and in 1749, a year after his first marriage, he opened a shop in partnership with James Rannie in Long Acre. Here he employed a modest twenty-two workmen. These premises were destroyed by fire, and in 1753 the firm moved into larger premises in St. Martin's Lane. The first edition of his book, *The Gentleman and Cabinet Maker's Director* was published in 1754, reprinted in 1755, and finally produced as the third enlarged edition in 1762. The year 1760 saw Chippendale elected to the Society of Arts. The first partnership with James Rannie was terminated in 1766, and in 1771 Chippendale entered into association with Thomas Haigh, his book-keeper.

The Gentleman and Cabinet Maker's Director was not the first publication of its type, but it was the first to be devoted entirely to cataloguing and illustrating most types of furniture known. The work was enthusiastically received, and its influence soon spread to the Continent and the colonies, causing Chippendale's reputation to eclipse that of any other English contemporary cabinet-maker.

Few of the designs in the *Director* were Chippendale's own – although many are by his employed designers H. Copeland and M. Lock.

The designs can be divided into four main groups: first, the Chinese manner exhibiting fretted railings, pagodas, and so on; second, the Gothic style (a romanticized version of medieval tracery work); third, the anglicized rococo manner illustrated in the discreet use of C-scroll carving; and last, the neo-classical manner deriving from a later association with Robert Adam (q.v.). Chippendale's achievement was to integrate these diverse elements into an artistic and structural unity.

In its time, Chippendale's small shop developed into a large and successful business, to which his eldest son Thomas later succeeded. Chippendale possessed fine business acumen and devoted most of his career to its organization. Because of the wide sales of the *Director*, almost all the English furniture made in the middle Georgian period has been loosely termed 'Chippendale'.

From 1760 onwards, the firm was responsible for furnishing and decorating many English houses of note. There are several interesting examples of his work throughout England. The table from Harewood House is at Temple Newsam, Leeds. Nostell Priory has important furniture in the Adam manner and the Chippendale archives there form the largest single collection of source material. In the Victoria and Albert Museum, London, is the furniture from Garrick's house at Hampton, as well as other examples of Chippendale's style.

Chippendale died of tuberculosis on 13 November 1779, two years after his second marriage, and was buried in St. Martin's-in-the-Fields, London.

O. Brackett, *Thomas Chippendale* (1925).
A. Coleridge, *Chippendale's Furniture* (1968).
R. Edwards and M. Jourdain, *Georgian Cabinet Makers, c.1700–1800* (1955).
F. Kimball and E. Donnell, *Creators of the Chippendale Style* (1929).

Churchill, John (1650–1722), 1st Duke of Marlborough; general, see *Lives of the Stuart Age*.

Cibber, Colley (1671–1757), actor, dramatist, and poet laureate (1730).

Colley Cibber was born on 6 November 1671 in Bloomsbury. His father was Caius Gabriel Cibber, the Danish-born sculptor (see *Lives of the Stuart Age*).

Cibber was educated at Grantham, Lincolnshire, where, according to his own report, he displayed a precocious intelligence and skill at poetry. In 1690 he started working with Thomas Betterton (see *Lives of the Stuart Age*) at Drury Lane, after serving briefly with a group of volunteers in support of William of Orange during the Revolution of 1688. He married in 1693. In 1696 his first play, *Love's Last Shift, or the Fool in Fashion,* established him as both playwright and actor. In Vanbrugh's sequel to this play, *The Relapse*, Cibber acted the leading role of Lord Foppington. *Love's Last Shift* had a remarkable reception from the public and an equally remarkable effect on the English theatre. The sentimental comedy had been born and was to dominate the stage for the next century.

1700 saw one of his most famous – or notorious – plays, an adaptation of Shakespeare's *Richard III*. Although now recognized as a travesty of the original – it was pilloried by some contemporary critics too – it was extremely popular in its day and was even preferred to Shakespeare's own version, which was not revived until Henry Irving staged it in 1871. Other plays followed quickly, including the comedies *She Would and She Would Not* (1702) and *The Careless Husband* (1704).

In 1706 Cibber left Drury Lane and in 1707 wrote and produced *The Double Gallant* at the Haymarket which he also managed. In 1708 he became a shareholder of Drury Lane where, with his partners Robert Wilks and Thomas Doggett, he obtained control of the patents.

Throughout his career, Cibber acted, produced, and wrote prodigiously; in all he wrote or adapted nearly thirty plays. His tragedies, such as *Xerxes* (1699), were never well received but his comedies were brilliant successes. In 1717 his play *The Nonjurors* won general acclaim among the Whigs; he became the friend of Steele and Horace Walpole (qq.v.) and the King liked his work enough to make him poet laureate in 1730.

However, Cibber also acquired many enemies. Pope elevated Cibber to the throne of Dulness in the 1741 edition of *The Dunciad*, substituting him for the scholar Lewis Theobald, the original butt of the attack. Cibber's practice in dealing with his enemies was usually to treat them

with indifference. On this occasion, however, he was moved to write three open letters to Pope on the subject. Sadly, they do little to redeem him.

Fielding also attacked him on his appointment as poet laureate, but Cibber found eloquent advocates in favour of his work, and his plays were undeniably popular. Long after Cibber's death, Hazlitt paid tribute to him as 'a man of wit and pleasantry, a diverting mimic, an excellent actor, an admirable critic, and one of the best comic writers of the age'.

In his plays and adaptations, Cibber borrowed freely. For *The Comical Lovers, or Marriage à la Mode* (1704), he used two plays by Dryden; *Love Makes the Man, or The Fop's Fortune* (1701) had been based on a piece by Beaumont; and he also turned to Molière for material: *Tartuffe* supplied the substance for *The Nonjuror* (1717) and *Les Femmes savantes* for *The Refusal, or Ladies' Philosophising* (1721). One of Cibber's last efforts for the stage was his completion of *The Provok'd Husband* (1728), a play begun by Vanbrugh. In 1734 he declared that he was retiring from the stage, though he did not in fact make his final appearance until ten years later, at the age of seventy-three, when he took part in his own adaptation of Shakespeare's *King John*.

In his old age he wrote an autobiography, *Apology for the Life of Mr. Colley Cibber, Comedian* (1740). It contains possibly the best description of the English theatre at the beginning of the eighteenth century that we have, as well as some excellent portraits of Thomas Betterton and Mrs. Anne Bracegirdle among others.

In appearance Cibber was 'unheroic', and he had a rather weak voice. His personality was lively and his business sense was astute. Congreve's comment on his first play is probably the best summary of his whole career: 'It has in it a great many things that were like wit, that in reality were not wit.'

Cibber outlived most of his enemies, and died peacefully on 11 December 1757. He was buried in the Danish Church, Wellclose Square, East London.

The Dramatic Works of Colley Cibber (5 vols.; 1777).

L. R. N. Ashley, *Cibber* (New York, 1965).

R. H. Barker, *Mr. Cibber of Drury Lane* (New York, 1939).

B. R. S. Fone (ed.), *An Apology for the Life of Mr. Colley Cibber, Comedian* (Michigan, 1968).

D. M. E. Habbema, *Appreciation of Colley Cibber* (1928).

F. D. Senior, *The Life and Times of Colley Cibber* (1928).

Portraits: coloured plaster bust, attributed to L. F. Roubillac, *c.*1750: N.P.G.; engraving, three-quarter length, by E. Fisher, 1758, after a painting by J. B. Van Loo, 1740: British Museum.

Clare, Earl of (1693–1768), see Pelham-Holles, Thomas.

Clare, John (1793–1864), poet.

John Clare was born on 13 July 1793 at Helpstone, Northamptonshire, the son of Parker Clare, an unemployed labourer living on parish relief. Although his mother was illiterate, his father 'could read a little in a Bible, and was very fond of the superstitious tales that are hawked about the street for a penny'. John Clare received a brief education at the village school, but when the boy was seven he was sent out, despite his weak constitution, to earn his keep by threshing corn or looking after sheep on the common. There Clare came to love the sights and sounds of the English countryside, and learned much traditional folklore and song from the village cowherd. He developed a 'furious' passion for reading, and on winter evenings he would walk five miles to Glinton to attend classes.

When he was thirteen Clare saved up one and sixpence, walked to Peterborough, and bought a copy of Thomson's *Seasons*. In 1808 he got a job as a servant at the Blue Bell, whose publican let him scribble down sonnets during working hours, and actively encouraged his studies. Clare now fell in love with Mary Joyce. Her father, a rich farmer, was not impressed by the boy's prospects and discouraged the liaison. Disappointed, Clare left home to work as an under-gardener at Burghley Park, but the drunkenness and brutality he found there drove him back to Helpstone.

In 1812 he enlisted with the militia for a short period, but spent most of his time at Oundle barracks reading and writing. In 1817 he found a nine-shillings-a-week job at a limekiln, which emboldened him to propose to Martha Turner, but once again the parents, this time 'cottage farmers', disapproved.

Clare next attempted to have his poetry published. A Mr. Henson of Market Deeping promised to print an edition if Clare paid him £10 and guaranteed 100 subscribers. However, although he prepared an imposing prospectus including a specimen sonnet, he could only find seven subscribers. Moreover, he was sacked from his limekiln job for 'scribbling' and had to draw parish relief. Fortunately, a Stamford bookseller named Drury came across Clare's prospectus, and offered to help get his work published. Drury contacted John Taylor, a leading London publisher, who realized that this 'peasant poet' could profit from the vogue for Burns, and so in January 1821 appeared *Poems descriptive of Rural Life and Scenery, by John Clare, a Northamptonshire peasant*. It was a huge success: the reviewers were full of praise, Rossini set one of the poems to music, and the Marquis of Exeter gave Clare a £15 pension. Later that year Clare married Martha Turner, three weeks before their first child was born.

Admirers flocked to Clare's cottage at Helpstone, and he dined in London with men of letters, painfully self-conscious about his uncouth manners. In September 1821 he published *The Village Minstrel*. Despite its autobiographical strain, this collection was a failure, partly because Clare's novelty value had worn off, and partly because his publisher had pressured him into writing more 'typical' verse, that is, to mar the freshness of his vision by portentous philosophizing about nature. In 1822, 1824, and 1828, Clare paid further visits to London, where he drank too much and met Hazlitt, Coleridge, De Quincey, and Lamb.

In 1827 appeared *The Shepherd's Calendar*, Clare's masterpiece. But this was another commercial failure. It is the most colourful and penetrating vision of rural life in English literature, but was clumsily hacked about by Taylor before publication. When Clare complained, the publisher simply handed over to him all remaining copies. Clare conscientiously hawked them around, but no money was forthcoming. He became a farm labourer once more, having made three unsuccessful attempts to start a farm. By 1833, when Clare's seventh child was born, the cottage was full of beautifully bound presentation copies, but empty of food. Lord Fitzwilliam, however, gave Clare a cottage, and one or two others did what they could to help. In 1835 Clare published *The Rural Muse*, a wretched collection of commonplace thoughts expressed in poetical clichés; it earned him £90.

Battered by conflicting demands from his publisher, his family, and his own artistic integrity, Clare's mind eventually gave way. He suffered a fit at the theatre in Peterborough, and in 1837 was lodged in Dr. Allen's private asylum in Epping Forest. Here he was well treated, being allowed to ramble in the forest and write poetry. But he gradually became obsessed by his youthful affair with Mary Joyce and in July 1841 he fled the asylum and walked back to Helpstone to try to find her, though she had been dead for some years. He was re-committed, this time to the county asylum at Northampton, where he spent the rest of his life.

Clare's finest lyrics date from the years of his supposed madness; poignant love poems inspired by the memory of Mary Joyce, profound contemplations on time and loneliness such as 'Song's eternity' and 'Now is past', and nature poetry of visionary intensity. The asylum register records his death on 20 May 1864, 'after years addicted to poetical prosing'. Clare was buried in his native village of Helpstone.

G. Grigson (ed.), *Selected Poems* (1950).

G. Grigson (ed.), *Poems of Madness* (1949).

E. Robinson and G. Summerfield (ed.), *The Shepherd's Calendar and The Later Poems* (1964).

J. W. and A. Tibble, *Clare: A Life* (1932, rev. ed. 1956).

J. W. Tibble (ed.), *Poems* (2 vols.; 1935).

J. W. and A. Tibble (eds.), *Prose* (1951).

J. W. and A. Tibble (eds.), *Letters* (1951).

Portraits: oil, half-length, by W. Hilton: N.P.G.; oil, by T. Grimshaw, 1844: Northampton Public Libraries Collection.

Clementi, Muzio (1752–1832), Italian-born pianist and composer.

Clementi was born in Rome on 23 January 1752. His father, a silversmith, was musical and, observing his son's precocious talent, enlisted a choirmaster relation named Buroni to teach him music. In 1761 Clementi won a position as organist, and at the age of twelve had his oratorio *Il Martiro de' Gloriosi* performed in Rome, followed two years later by a mass.

In 1766, Clementi's father was persuaded to let the boy continue his studies in England. Clementi lived quietly with his patron, Peter Beckford, a cousin of William Beckford (q.v.), in Wiltshire until 1773, when he began to appear publicly, much lauded as 'the young Roman'. The pianoforte had become popular in England and Clementi, having studied its special mechanical and tonal features, made brilliant and original use of the new instrument.

From 1777 to 1780 he was employed as cembalist by the Italian Opera in London, and within four years his reputation was to bring him invitations from all over Europe. In Vienna he met Haydn and, at the instigation of Joseph II, took part in a musical competition with Mozart. The victor, it appears, was left undecided, but the experience made an impression on Clementi, who conceived a lasting admiration of Mozart, and from that time began to concentrate less on his technique and more on the quality of his playing and composition. Mozart was not so impressed by Clementi's performance, disdaining his 'mechanical' brilliance.

Clementi also went into the musical instrument business which, after initial setbacks, brought him some prosperity. Among his pupils were Field (q.v.), Czerny, Klengel, Mayerbeer, and Berger. In 1802 he took Field to St. Petersburg. He returned to London in 1810 and made England his permanent home.

Clementi was a major influence in the development of music for the piano. He was the first composer fully to understand the instrument, and the first master of the piano sonata. Beethoven was an admirer of his work, and his book of études, *Gradus ad Parnassum* (1817), is still in use today.

He wrote some twenty symphonies, which were lost after his death – though two were successfully reconstructed in the early twentieth century by Alfredo Casella. He spent the latter part of his life at his country house near Evesham, where he died on 10 March 1832. His remains were buried in Westminster Abbey.

G. C. Paribeni, *Muzio Clementi, nella vita e nell' arte* (Milan, 1922).

G. de Saint-Foix, 'Muzio Clementi', *The Musical Quarterly* (1923).

Portrait: engraving, miniature, artist unknown, 1803: British Museum.

Clive, Robert (1725–74), Baron Clive; military commander and governor of India.

Robert Clive was born on 29 September 1725 at Market Drayton in Shropshire, the eldest son of Richard Clive, a local gentleman. His scant education was acquired at a series of schools; he appears to have been a troublesome boy. In 1743 he entered the East India Company and sailed for India, a course commonly adopted by misfits. Late in the following year he took up his duties in Madras, and the tedium, coupled with loneliness, drove him to an attempt at suicide.

The European War of the Austrian Succession spread to the British and French interests in India, and in September 1746 Madras was captured by the French. Most of the civilian prisoners received parole, but Clive and a colleague absconded soon afterwards, making their way 100 miles down the coast to Fort St. David, where a small garrison was holding out against the French until relieved by an English fleet.

Clive received an ensign's commission in the Company's army and participated in Admiral Boscawen's unsuccessful siege of Pondicherry in 1748. The end of the war in Europe brought a mutual exchange of conquests, and Madras was restored to Britain. During this period Clive was involved in two violent quarrels with brother officers, one of which involved a duel.

Dupleix, the French Governor of Pondicherry, was unwilling to rest content with the commercial status quo in the Carnatic; intrigues and fighting ensued, which brought Clive another taste of military service in 1749. Subsequently he participated as captain in a

few minor actions around Trichinopoly, in central Madras. Trichinopoly (now called Tirushirapalli) was besieged by a French-supported army and, on Clive's own suggestion, he was sent with a small column of 500 men, less than half of them European, to draw off the besiegers by attacking the capital of the Carnatic, Arcot. The garrison of the fort there fled at his approach; he entered it and strengthened it for a siege, making forays to provoke a response from the enemy. His provocation had the desired effect, and Clive sustained an energetic defence for fifty days until relief arrived. This was followed by a campaign that resulted in the surrender of the French army outside Trichinopoly and ultimately in the recall of Dupleix. Clive, however, returned in poor health to England in 1753.

Here he was able to rescue his father from financial difficulties and to incur some of his own by living beyond his means and running for parliament. An early return to India was thus forced upon him, this time as Lieutenant Governor of Fort St. David, where he arrived on 20

June 1756. By then, Great Britain was again at war with France.

Two months previously Siraj-ud-daula had become Nawab of Bengal in succession to his uncle Alivardi Khan. Siraj, already antagonistic to the English, determined to assert his authority, and seized Calcutta by armed force on the very day that Clive took up his appointment. The task of recovering the possession was given to Clive, who sailed for the Hugli river in October with 2,400 men and entered Calcutta on 2 January 1757, after very little fighting but much dispute with his fellow Company officials and British officers. Energetic measures for Calcutta's defence were undertaken, and Clive was fully prepared when the Nawab's army moved against him in the following month. He resolved to attack Siraj in his camp, and the confused engagement that followed was enough to induce the Nawab to accept a negotiated settlement restoring the Company's privileges in Calcutta.

Clive's next step, the elimination of the French post at Chandernagore, destroyed French influence in Bengal and increased the English Company's stock among the native princes. Clive now began to explore ways of overthrowing Siraj in favour of a more pliable ruler. Out of a labyrinth of intrigue emerged an agreement whereby the Company's support would be given to a relative of the Nawab, Mir Jafar, in return for privileges and compensations for the Company and its principal agents. On 13 June 1757 Clive marched against the Nawab with a force of 800 Europeans and 2,200 native troops through monsoon rain and flooded fields to the village of Plassey. Here he was attacked on 23 June by the Nawab's 53,000-strong host. The natives suffered heavy casualties under the fire of the British artillery and received no effective direction from their leaders. The affair became a rout. Siraj fled, and later was captured and executed. Mir Jafar claimed the throne he had done so little to deserve, and Clive's personal share of the spoils amounted to £234,000.

Clive now worked to consolidate Mir Jafar's power and thus that of the East India Company in Bengal. This involved the suppression of native revolts, military action against Dutch intervention, and continual political activity to out-manoeuvre the jealous intrigues against him. He was completely successful and on his return to England in 1760 received official acclaim. He was elected M.P. for Shrewsbury, and in 1762 was given an Irish barony. Two years later he was created a Knight of the Bath. Company politics were as virulent at home as overseas, however, and dissension be-tween Clive and Lawrence Sulivan, the chairman of the Court of Directors, resulted in the supersession of the latter.

Meanwhile in India, Mir Jafar's incompetence brought about a native reaction in favour of his son-in-law, Mir Kasim. Ferocious fighting broke out in 1763 and was only checked by a British victory at Buxar in October 1764. It was this battle, rather than Plassey, that was decisive for the future of British power in Bengal, but before it was fought alarm among the Company's shareholders had procured the return of Clive. He sailed in June 1764 but did not arrive in Calcutta until May 1765, to find that Mir Jafar's son ruled in his stead.

Clive now set about consolidating British influence by reforms in adminis-tration. The *diwani* (right of revenue-collection and administration of civil justice) in Bengal was taken over from the Mogul emperor, so that the Company became responsible for civil govern-ment. Important consequences for both India and Great Britain were to stem from this in the following century.

The reform of the Company's internal affairs proved less simple to effect, the twin roots of its problems being the inadequate salaries paid at all levels and the opportunities to remedy the deficiency by private trading at the Company's expense and by the Indian custom of making presents to those in authority. Clive's solution was to regulate the last two in the hope of improving the first. However, his success was limited. The reduction, on orders from London, of allowances paid to military officers provoked open defiance, which Clive met on the one hand by firmness and on the other by the establishment of a pension fund out of a legacy that he had personally received from Mir Jafar.

He retired in February 1767, but had made many enemies within the Com-pany, who mounted a systematic cam-paign against him in England, forcing him to defend himself in the House of Commons. A parliamentary inquiry considered the evidence over two sessions until May 1773, after which, with some mild criticisms, the House resolved that Clive had 'rendered great and meritorious service to his country'. However, Clive had always been a victim of mental depression, and he had resorted to opium. He committed suicide on 22 November 1774.

Mark Bence-Jones, *Clive of India* (1975).
A. M. Davies, *Clive of Plassey* (1939).
H. H. Dodwell, *Dupleix and Clive* (1920).
G. W. Forrest, *The Life of Lord Clive* (2 vols.; 1918).
Lucy Sutherland, *The East India Company in the Eighteenth Century* (1952).

Portraits: oil, three-quarter length, by N. Dance, *c.*1770: N.P.G.; marble statue, by Robert Scheemakers: Foreign and Commonwealth Office, London; bronze statue, by John Tweed: Tate Gallery, London.

Cobbett, William (1763–1835), politi-cal journalist.

William Cobbett was born near

Farnham, Surrey, on 9 March 1763. His grandfather had been a farm labourer, but his father owned his own land. At the age of fourteen he ran away from home to work in Kew Gardens, London; at the age of nineteen he ran away again, this time to become a solicitor's clerk; a year later he joined the army, in which he reached the rank of regimental sergeant major. During service overseas, first in Nova Scotia and then in New Brunswick, Cobbett became aware of the fraud and corruption practised by many of his officers, and when his regiment returned to England in 1791 he left the army and demanded the court martial of the officers involved. This eventually took place but by now Cobbett himself was in danger of prosecution for writing a pamphlet on army abuses and in March 1792, together with his newly-married wife, he fled to France. Later that year he sailed to Philadelphia.

For a few months Cobbett supported himself in America by giving English lessons to French immigrants, but in 1794 the arrival of Joseph Priestley led to the

start of his career as a political pamphleteer. Priestley was an English writer forced into exile because of his sympathy with the revolutionary movement in France, and was received in America with much enthusiasm. In response to this Cobbett wrote a series of pamphlets attacking the French Revolution, its sympathizers, and every other form of political radicalism including American democracy. The style of these pamphlets is direct, vigorous, and passionate. From 1797 to 1799 Cobbett produced his own newspaper, Porcupine's Gazette. He also reprinted much propaganda material from Britain. In 1797 he had to pay substantial damages for libelling the prominent doctor and politician, Benjamin Rush. Cobbett proceeded to publish personal attacks on the judge who had heard the case. In 1800, after further clashes with the authorities, Cobbett returned to England.

Having established a reputation through his American pamphlets, Cobbett was welcomed in London as a promising recruit to British political journalism. William Pitt the Younger (q.v.), offered him the editorship of an official government newspaper, but Cobbett preferred instead to establish his own journal, The Porcupine. In 1801 he established a bookshop in Pall Mall; in 1802 he reprinted his American writings under the title Porcupine's Works; in 1803 he began publication of the Parliamentary Debates (these were later bought by his printer, Hansard, by whose name they are now known); in 1806 came the first of thirty-six volumes of The Parliamentary History of England; and three years later, in 1809, there followed the first volume of Cobbett's State Trials.

The Porcupine ceased publication after only a year, but in 1802 Cobbett received financial help from William Windham, a disciple of Edmund Burke, that enabled him to start the weekly *Political Register*. This paper was edited and mostly written by Cobbett until his death in 1835, and its early numbers record Cobbett's remarkable conversion from vigorous anti-Jacobinism to vigorous radicalism. Under Pitt's government in 1804 Cobbett found himself increasingly in alliance with Windham and the Whigs, yet when his new friends came to power in 1806 he lost faith in them also. From this time, therefore, the *Political Register* began to demand parliamentary and economic reform as well as peace with France.

Cobbett's return to active farming in 1805 seems to have contributed to his new radicalism. At his farm at Botley, near Southampton, Cobbett was struck by the contrast between the contented rural life that he had known as a child and the wretched existence of the farm workers now dispossessed by enclosure and suffering from inflated wartime prices. He became increasingly critical of government apathy and again came into conflict with the authorities: in 1809, after witnessing at Ely the public flogging of soldiers who had mutinied over deductions from their pay, he wrote a pamphlet that resulted in his prosecution for sedition. He was fined £1,000 and imprisoned in Newgate for two years. On his release from prison, after having had to sell his farm at Botley and several of his publishing enterprises, Cobbett redoubled his efforts on behalf of the rural poor. During the depression that followed the ending of the Napoleonic Wars in 1815 he reduced the price of the *Political Register* to 2d and addressed his articles directly to the labouring classes. He thus became not only their most influential champion but also an obvious target for government repression, and in order to avoid arrest he again fled to America.

For two years, 1817–19, Cobbett rented a farm on Long Island, New York, and concentrated on writing; among the books he wrote here was a *Grammar of the English Language*, an educational manual for working-class students. In 1819 Cobbett returned to England, bringing with him the bones of Tom Paine, and he resumed at once his agitation for parliamentary reform. He also bought a farm at Kensington where he experimented with the cultivation of maize, locust trees, and Spanish turnips. In 1820 he publicly supported Queen Caroline in her quarrel with George IV.

Cobbett's most enduring achievement was published during the 1820s in the *Political Register* and in book form in 1830: *Rural Rides* is a series of accounts of his travels through the countryside of England. It describes country houses and slums, farms and factories, political exploitation and working-class poverty, written in an intimate style that allows innumerable digressions and political arguments. The tone of the book is both compassionate and radical:

> A labouring man, in England, with a wife and only three children, though he never lose a day's work, though he and his family be economical, frugal and industrious in the most extensive sense of these words, is not now able to procure himself by his labour a single meal of meat from one end of the year unto the other. Is this a state in which the labouring man ought to be?

In 1830 the Whig party under Lord Grey was elected to office, parliamentary reform having become the dominant political issue. Agitation increased throughout the country and in 1831 the government decided to prosecute Cobbett for sedition. Cobbett defended himself at his trial with an impressive speech, and the jury refused to convict him. In the following year (1832) the Reform Act became law, and at the consequent general election Cobbett was elected M.P. for Oldham.

Even after the Reform Act, however, parliament remained primarily an organ of the propertied classes and Cobbett's influence as a journalist remained greater than it ever was as an M.P. For the two-and-a-half years of his parliamentary career Cobbett was the leader of a tiny and largely ineffective group of extreme radicals. He fought in vain against the Poor Law of 1834; he spoke also against the Combination Acts. 'Better call for a law to prevent those inconvenient things called spring tides,' he said.

Cobbett was one of the first men in England to perceive the social consequences of the Industrial Revolution – as early as 1807 he described how a labourer, after looking upon 'his half-naked and half-famished children', comes to his door and 'surveys all around him the land teeming with the means of luxury to his opulent and overgrown master' – but he was unable to translate this awareness into terms of effective social policy. *Rural Rides* is full of references to an idealized past, and in such books as *Cottage Economy* (1822) Cobbett advocates a return to customs that have been superseded: the future, the realm of theory rather than of personal experience, is not within his vision.

Cobbett was active to the very end of his life. Almost every day he rose early and worked on the land, wrote at his desk, or attended to his parliamentary duties. He died after a severe attack of influenza on 18 June 1835 at Normandy Farm near Guildford in Surrey, the location of his last experiment in planting imported seed.

G. D. H. and M. Cole (eds.), *Rural Rides* (3 vols.; 1930).

G. D. H. and M. Cole (eds.), *The Opinions of Cobbett* (1944).

G. D. H. Cole, *The Life of William Cobbett* (1947, 3rd ed.).

J. W. Osborne, *William Cobbett: His Thought and His Times* (New Brunswick, N.J., 1966).

M. Pearl, *William Cobbett* (1953).

Portraits: oil, half-length, by unknown artist, *c.* 1831: N.P.G.; water-colour, half-length, by unknown artist: N.P.G.

Coke, Thomas William (1752–1842), Earl of Leicester of Holkham; M.P. and agriculturist.

Coke was born on 6 May 1752, the eldest son of Robert Wenman (who, in 1750, on succeeding to the estate of his maternal uncle, Thomas Coke, Earl of Leicester, had assumed the surname and arms of Coke). After an education at Eton he travelled abroad, spending a considerable time at Rome, where he acquired the nickname of 'the handsome Englishman'. In 1774 he returned to England. Upon the death of his father in 1776, Coke was elected to parliament in his place as member for Norfolk. He was the youngest member when he entered parliament and the oldest when he retired. A friend and supporter of Charles James Fox (q.v.), Coke secured a reputation as a sturdy and aggressive Whig with special agricultural interests. Having refused the offer of a peerage in 1776 and again in 1806, he was created Earl of Leicester of Holkham and Viscount Coke in 1837.

Coke is best remembered as a pioneer of agricultural techniques. Inheriting land around Holkham that was poor and neglected, he introduced many improvements and obtained the best expert advice. In a few years wheat was being grown upon his farms, and the breeds of cattle, sheep, and pigs greatly improved. The origin of the improvement of the district was the refusal in 1778 of one of Coke's tenants to accept a renewal of his lease at a rent of five shillings an acre, enabling Coke to farm the land himself. The other farmers in the district gradually followed his example, and among other things

Coke was able to boast that he had converted West Norfolk from a rye-growing into a wheat-producing area. It has been said that 'His practice is really the basis of every treatise on modern agriculture.' His success was due in part to the introduction of covenants respecting the mode of cultivation in all the leased properties on his estate. Hitherto the tenants had been at liberty to cultivate the land in any way they chose. Under Coke's direction the rental of the Holkham estate is said to have increased from £2,200 to over £20,000 a year.

Coke was a keen sportsman, and in his younger days was considered to be one of the boldest riders and best shots in England. In the game-book at Holkham it is recorded that on one November day he killed eighty-two partridges in eighty-four shots. He married twice, the first time in 1775, when he was twenty-three. After his wife's death in 1800 he did not remarry until 1822, when he was sixty-nine. In all he had nine children, six of whom were born of his second marriage.

He died at Longford Hall, Derbyshire, on 30 June 1842, in his ninety-first year, and was buried in the family mausoleum attached to Tittleshall Church, Norfolk.

J. D. Chambers and G. E. Mingay, *The Agricultural Revolution: 1750–1850* (1966).

A. N. W. Stirling, *Coke of Norfolk and His Friends* (1912).

Coleridge, Samuel Taylor

(1772–1834), Romantic poet and critic, influential in many different areas of intellectual activity.

Coleridge was born on 21 October 1772 at Ottery St. Mary in Devon, where his father was vicar and also headmaster of the local grammar school. He was the tenth child of his father's second marriage, the youngest of thirteen children in all; he later described his mother as 'an admirable economist'. Delicate in physique and sensitive in temperament, Coleridge retreated from the taunts of his school-fellows into a world of dreams and books: at the age of six he was haunted by ghosts from *The Arabian Nights*, by his early twenties he was already acquainted with all the major works of the neo-Platonist philosophers, and when he wrote to Thomas Poole in 1797 that 'I have read almost everything – a library cormorant', his remark contained as much truth as exaggeration.

In July 1782, after the death of his father, Coleridge was sent to school at Christ's Hospital in London, and did not see his home again for eight years. His education included the close study of contemporary poets, as well as Milton, Shakespeare, and the classics.

Coleridge entered Jesus College, Cambridge, in October 1791. Towards the end of 1793, heavily in debt and having been rejected in love by Mary Evans, the sister of a school friend, Coleridge left university and enlisted in the Light Dragoons under the name of Silas Tomkyn Comberbacke. His eldest brother managed to buy him out in the following April, but Coleridge was too restless now to return to university. After a chance meeting with Robert Southey (q.v.) at Oxford, Coleridge's hopes were briefly revived by their joint plans for an ideal community to be known as a Pantisocracy – a scheme by which twelve young men and their wives were to emigrate to America and live in harmony with primitive nature – but nothing came of this project. Coleridge went off to London to make a final and unsuccessful proposal to Mary Evans, Southey lost enthusiasm, and the only practical result of the scheme was the arranged marriage that took place in October 1795 between Coleridge and Sara Fricker, the sister of Southey's own fiancée.

The first few months of Coleridge's

married life were spent contentedly in a cottage at Cliveden in Somerset, but his relationship with his wife was one of duty rather than love, and was always vulnerable. The uncertain progress of Coleridge's career from this time forward was influenced by the conflicts between his intellectual ambitions, his emotional frustrations, and the constant need to provide food and money for the upkeep of his family. Between March and May of 1796 he published ten issues of *The Watchman*, a journal devoted to literature and radical politics, and he travelled to many of the larger industrial towns to canvass subscribers; he also preached in Unitarian chapels, wrote articles for various magazines, and undertook private tuition. William Hazlitt walked ten miles to hear one of Coleridge's sermons, and was profoundly impressed by the manner in which Coleridge 'launched into his subject like an eagle dallying with the wind'. The reality, however, was less sublime: Coleridge was desperately poor, even more so after the failure of *The Watchman* and the birth of his first son in

September, and was only able to continue writing because of the generosity of his friend Thomas Poole and an annuity of £150 that he was given in early 1798 by the brothers Thomas and Josiah Wedgwood.

The most significant friendship of Coleridge's career began on a June day in 1797, when he travelled to Racedown in Dorset to visit his fellow poet William Wordsworth (q.v.), whom he had met briefly two years earlier. After an exchange of visits Coleridge persuaded the Wordsworths to move to a house near his own at Alfoxden, and the intimate relationship that inspired the greatest work of both poets was thus established. Coleridge had long admired Wordsworth as 'the only man to whom at all times and in all modes of excellence I feel myself inferior', but their partnership was that of equals: Coleridge's brilliant and restless intellectual energy was the perfect complement to Wordsworth's more receptive, contemplative nature, and though the characteristics of their poetry are very different, they depended upon each other for the fulfilment of their individual talents. For the *Lyrical Ballads*, the volume of poems whose commitment to emotional sincerity and simplicity of style marked the first conscious expression of the Romantic movement in English literature, the divergence of their personal temperaments was recognized by the agreement that Wordsworth should concern himself with 'the loveliness and the wonders of the world before us', while Coleridge's own endeavours 'should be directed to persons and characters supernatural'. In the first edition of the *Lyrical Ballads*, published in late 1798, the preface and all but four of the poems were written by Wordsworth, but Coleridge's main contribution, 'The Rime of the Ancient Mariner', is certainly his most famous and perhaps also his finest achievement in the medium of poetry.

In several other poems written during 1798, including 'The Nightingale' and 'Frost at Midnight', Coleridge demonstrated his ability to write the more reflective, meditative style of verse favoured by Wordsworth, but the uniqueness of his talent lay in his ability to so describe inanimate natural objects that they vibrate with symbolic reference to human life: 'In looking at the objects of Nature,' Coleridge wrote, 'I seem rather to be seeking, as it were asking for, a symbolical language for something within me that already and forever exists.' The weakness of 'Christabel' (written 1798–1800), a Gothic romance with incidental details that would not be out of place in a modern horror film, is that its symbolic elements are made too explicit and therefore become unconvincing; the perennial fascination of 'Kubla Khan' (written 1799), on the other hand, is due to the fact that its symbolism is open to so many different interpretations.

The legend that Coleridge received inspiration for this last poem while under the influence of opium is well known, and while the details of this legend are disputed, it remains true that Coleridge's habit of taking laudanum to alleviate the pain of his toothache was already becoming addictive. On his return from Germany, where he had travelled with the Wordsworths in late 1798 to attend the lectures of several eminent German philosophers, Coleridge was introduced to Sara Hutchinson, the sister of the girl whom Wordsworth was to marry. The confused emotion that he came to feel for this second Sara were another cause of the suffering that led to the decline of his poetic powers and his estrangement from Wordsworth.

Coleridge was briefly able to supplement his income by political journalism for the Morning Post and by his translations of plays by the German dramatist Schiller, and in 1800 he moved with his family to Greta Hall near Keswick to be near the Wordsworths. Yet the true nature of his personal feelings during these years is expressed in the 'Ode to Dejection' (written in 1802 and addressed, in its original form, to Sara Hutchinson):

A grief without a pang, void, dark, and drear,
A stifled, drowsy, unimpassioned grief,
Which finds no natural outlet, no relief.

This poem marks Coleridge's effective farewell to poetic inspiration. In 1803 he joined the Wordsworths for a walking tour in Scotland but returned home early suffering from ill health and acute depression. In the following year, on the Wordsworths' advice, he decided to separate from his wife and accept a post as secretary to Sir Alexander Ball, the Governor of Malta.

The personal reappraisal that Coleridge conducted during his two years in Malta led only to an increased awareness of what he felt to be his own moral defects, and he returned to England in 1806 in no better health than when he had departed. Robert Southey had now moved into Greta Hall, and cared for Coleridge's wife while Coleridge himself joined the Wordsworths. He wrote a series of political essays for The Friend, a publication that he established in 1809, but in 1810 Sara Hutchinson, who had been assisting him with this project, went to live with her brother in Wales, and Coleridge, who suspected Wordsworth of encouraging her departure, resolved to break off all relations with the Wordsworths and to live alone in London. Despite the popularity of his lectures to the London Philosophical Society and the success of his play Osorio (which ran for twenty nights at Drury Lane in 1813) most of Coleridge's personal writings during his subsequent years in London are characterized by depression and self-criticism: opium, despite the feelings of remorse that it aroused within him, retained its hold, and Coleridge sought 'a refuge from bodily pain and mismanaged sensibility in abstruse researches, which exercised the strength and subtlety of the understanding without awakening the feelings of the heart'.

The chief product of these researches was the *Biographia Literaria*, on which Coleridge worked from 1814 to its publication in 1817. Although his grand project for an all-encompassing philosophical work was never realized, the *Biographia* contains fragments from almost all of Coleridge's literary, philosophical, and theological doctrines, ranging from a detailed critique of Wordsworth's poetry through autobiographical digressions to a summary of the underlying principles of Romanticism. The whole work is given unity by Coleridge's reverence for the faculty of imagination, 'the shaping and modifying power' of all human creative activity, and his exploration of the operative processes of this faculty anticipates the principles of modern psychology.

The same concern with fundamental principles is evident in Coleridge's religious conjectures in *Aids to Reflection* (1825) and his political theories as expressed in *On the Constitution of the Church and State* (1830). From 1811 onwards Coleridge delivered a pioneering series of lectures on Shakespeare's plays in which his psychological insight illuminated both his material and himself. Thomas De Quincey described Coleridge's idiosyncratic but powerful manner of lecturing, 'a continuous strain of eloquent dissertation'; among those present were Lamb, Hazlitt, and Lord Byron.

From 1816 until his death Coleridge lived at the residence in Highgate of James Gillman, a sympathetic surgeon under whose care he placed himself as a voluntary patient. 'Neither physically nor morally was he understood,' Gillman wrote, 'and had he been more favoured in his bodily constitution he would not have been censured for frailties that did not attach to him.' By those who knew him personally Coleridge was much loved. In 1822 he began his Thursday evening classes, and these weekly meetings at Highgate were attended by a group of young intellectuals who became his disciples. Selections from Coleridge's table talk and incidental writings were collected by his nephew, Henry Nelson Coleridge, and published in 1835. An annuity that accompanied his election as a Fellow of the Royal Society of Literature in 1824 enabled Coleridge to enjoy a degree of material comfort during his later years, even though he remained burdened by the awareness that 'My judgment was stronger than were my powers of realizing its dictates.' He died at Highgate on 25 July 1834.

Coleridge's reputation as a poet is out of all proportion to the small amount of verse that he actually published, and the authority of his philosophical and political theories stems rather from the influence they exerted than from any achieved body of work to which they contributed. His writings offer on every separate page evidence of his restless mind, continually opening up whole new areas of experience and speculation that the reader himself is challenged to explore.

J. R. Barth, Jr., *Coleridge and Christian Doctrine* (Harvard, 1969).

W. J. Bate, *Coleridge* (1968).

J. Beer (ed.), *Poems* (1963).

K. Coburn (ed.), *Philosophical Lectures* (1948).

K. Coburn (ed.), *Notebooks* (1957–).

K. Coburn (ed.), *Coleridge: A Collection of Critical Essays* (1967).

K. Coburn *et al.* (eds.), *The Collected Works of Coleridge* (1969–   ).

J. Colmer, *Coleridge: Critic of Society* (1959).

J. Cornwell, *Coleridge, Poet and Revolutionary, 1772–1804: A Critical Biography* (1973).

R. H. Fogle, *The Idea of Coleridge's Criticism* (Berkeley, 1962).

E. L. Griggs (ed.), *Collected Letters* (6 vols.; 1956–71).

H. House, *Coleridge* (1953).

J. L. Lowes, *The Road to Xanadu* (Boston, 1964, rev. ed.).

H. M. Margoliouth, *Wordsworth and Coleridge 1795–1834* (1953).

J. M. Muirhead, *Coleridge As Philosopher* (1930).

T. M. Raysor (ed.), *Shakespearean Criticism* (2 vols.; 1960, rev. ed.).

T. M. Raysor (ed.), *Miscellaneous Criticism* (1936).

E. Schneider, *Coleridge, Opium and Kubla Khan* (Chicago, 1953).

G. Watson (ed.), *Biographia Literaria: or Biographical Sketches of My Literary Life and Opinions* (1956).

Portraits: oil, half-length, by W. Allston, 1814: N.P.G.; oil, quarter-length, by P. Vandyke, 1795: N.P.G.; pencil-and-wash, quarter-length, by R. Hancock, 1796: N.P.G.; oil, by J. Northcote: Jesus College, Cambridge.

Collins, William (1721–59), poet.

William Collins was born on Christmas Day 1721 at Chichester, the third child and only son of William Collins, a prosperous hatter and haberdasher. He was sent as a scholar to Winchester in 1733. Collins started writing poetry at the age of twelve, and while still at school had verses published in the *Gentleman's Magazine*. He went to Oxford in 1741, at first to Queen's and then as a demy to Magdalen. Collins was a cheerful, easy-going student who found time to write the *Persian Eclogues* (1742), which were well received.

In 1743 he graduated and in the same year he wrote an 'Epistle' to Sir Thomas Hanmer on his edition of Shakespeare. Uncertain of what career to take up, he visited his uncle, Colonel Martin, who pronounced him 'too indolent even for the army' and suggested the church, from which Collins was dissuaded by the rich tobacconist and philanthropist, John Hardham. He went to London to try literature.

For a time Collins lived in London, a happy spendthrift, moving in literary and theatrical circles and planning tragedies; though, as Johnson said, 'He only planned them', for 'A man doubtful of his dinner . . . is not much disposed to abstracted meditation.' Johnson found him in lodgings where he was dogged by a bailiff 'prowling in the street', and arranged for him an advance from a bookseller on the strength of a proposed translation of Aristotle's *Poetics*.

In 1746 he settled in Richmond near James Thomson (q.v.). Here he wrote twelve odes – to Liberty, Evening, Mercy, Peace, Simplicity, and the Poetical Character, among other things, and also to the Passions. The collection, which was originally conceived as part of a joint publication with Joseph Warton, included the well-known 'How sleep the Brave'. In the end the two poets' contributions were published separately, in December 1746, but while Warton's poems achieved success Collins's *Odes* excited very little public interest, though their excellence is now acknowledged.

Helped by small legacies from his relatives, the poet paid off his creditors and lived on at Richmond until the death of Thomson in 1749. He stayed in London to see his ode on Thomson's death published, and then returned to his birthplace, Chichester, where, after long conversations with two formidable Scots, Alexander Carlyle and John Home, he wrote the 'Ode on the Popular Superstitions of the Highlands', his last major poem to survive.

His uncle Colonel Martin died in 1749, leaving Collins enough money to live on, though not the fortune often supposed. In 1751 he was very ill and thought he was dying. With the intention of improving his health, he travelled to France.

However, on his return he was put in an asylum in Chelsea, from which his sister Anne rescued him and took him to live with her at Chichester for the rest of his life.

His last illness has been variously attributed to severe nervous disorder, drink, and religious mania. It is certain that he was weak, though not raving. Warton, who often visited him, said that 'what he spoke wanted neither judgment nor wit, but a few minutes exhausted him'. He died on 12 June 1759 and was buried in St. Andrew's, Chichester.

Collins is often hailed as a precursor of Romanticism. His vivid imagination and the sensitivity of his language support this claim. Had his life been longer and happier, he might well have eclipsed his more prolific contemporary poets, for the few poems he left to posterity show an individual and striking talent. They are, as Southey later described them, 'the effusions of an ardent poetical spirit'.

E. G. Ainsworth, *Poor Collins: his Life, his Art and his Influence* (Ithaca, 1937).

P. L. Carver, *The Life of a Poet* (1966).

J. S. Cunningham (ed.), *Drafts and Fragments of Verse, Edited from the Manuscripts* (1956).

H. W. Garrod, *The Poetry of Collins* (1928).

R. H. Lonsdale (ed.), *Poems* (1969).

A. Lane Poole (ed.), *Gray and Collins: Poetical Works* (rev. ed.; 1966).

Combe, William (1741–1823), satirist; creator of 'Dr. Syntax'.

William Combe was born in Bristol in 1741. He was educated at Eton. In about 1760 he went up to Oxford, but spent much of his time in dissipation and left without a degree. Soon afterwards he inherited £2,000 cash and £50 a year from his supposed 'godfather', William Alexander – who was more probably his natural father.

Combe now set off on the Grand Tour, during which he met Laurence Sterne (q.v.) in Italy. On his return he nominally took up the legal profession, but in fact pursued the life of a socialite. A handsome man with charming manners, Combe lived in a grand house in St. James's and kept 'two carriages, several horses, and a large retinue of servants'. He was seen at all the best watering-places and invited to the most exclusive balls, and by the mid-1760s his flamboyant life-style had reduced him to bankruptcy. During the next few years he is reputed to have been successively a common soldier, a waiter in Swansea, a teacher of elocution, a cook at Douai College, and a private in the French army. In about 1771 he returned to England, determined to earn his living as a writer, and in 1774 published his first book, a colourful description of Patagonia based on the journal of a Jesuit, Father Falkner.

In 1775 he married the former mistress of Lord Irnham. Irnham had promised him a large sum of money to take the lady off his hands, but did not pay up. The irate Combe accordingly wrote his 'Diaboliad' (1776), mercilessly attacking 'the worst man in His Majesty's dominions'; it was such a success that he soon produced sequels, entitled 'Diabo-lady' and 'Anti-Diabo-lady'.

But these were insufficient to keep Combe from a second bankruptcy, and in 1780 he was confined within the Rules of the King's Bench Prison, where he remained until his death over forty years later. Penury and his own lack of principle soon drove him to literary forgery, and he published the spurious *Letters of Sterne to Eliza*, suggested by his meeting with Sterne years before, and the *Letters of Lord Lyttelton*, profiting from the late aristocrat's 'diabolic' reputation. Despite their disreputable origins, both works are thoughtful and well written. In 1789 Combe took up the trade of political pamphleteer. This brought him to the notice of Pitt, who gave him a £200 pension. His financial difficulties thus alleviated, Combe now churned out numerous works, including prose tales, topographical works, and editions of other writers. His facile pen led him to journalism, and in 1803 he joined the *Times* where, as a 'consulting man' in the editorial offices, he worked hard and kept long hours.

In 1809 Ackermann, publisher of the influential *Poetical Magazine*, was offered by Thomas Rowlandson a series of plates illustrating the adventures of a pedantic schoolmaster on a tour of Britain. Combe was employed to write the accompanying text, which he achieved under extraordinary conditions; each month Rowlandson, whom he had not met, sent a fresh illustration to Combe's chambers in the King's Bench Prison, whereupon the elderly writer dashed off several hundred lines of suitable doggerel, with the printer hovering at his shoulder.

The complete work, *Dr. Syntax in Search of the Picturesque*, ran to thirty plates and ten thousand lines of verse. A hilarious parody of the sentimental travel literature of the time, it was a great success. The raw-boned Dr. Syntax, clad in his ancient black suit and seated on his equally ancient mare, named Grizzle, is reminiscent of Don Quixote in his optimism in the face of adversity:

I'll *prose* it here, I'll *verse* it there,
And *picturesque* it everywhere.

Although he is for ever falling into rivers, fleeing from angry bulls, or being robbed, Syntax's good nature never falters. Despite its frequent moralizing, the poem convincingly demonstrates that Combe was a sharp-eyed journalist who knew the ways of ordinary folk.

Further collaboration with Rowlandson produced 'Dance of Death' and 'Dance of Life' which, though containing Combe's best verse, were too solemn to be popular. The public obviously still wanted Syntax, so in 1820 the good doctor rode out on his second tour, this time 'in Search of Consolation', since his wife (like Combe's) had died at the end of the first tour. Despite the addition of an eccentric Irish manservant, this poem exhibits flagging invention, although in Dr. Syntax's third tour (1823), 'in Search of a Wife', Combe returns to something like his old form.

William Combe died at Lambeth on 19 June 1823. His *Letters to Marianne*, published later that year and cast in the form of slightly preposterous *billets doux* to a young girl, provide an appealing self-portrait of the hack writer who almost accidentally created one of the most 'companionable' figures in English literature.

H. W. Hamilton, *Doctor Syntax: a Silhouette of Combe* (1969).

J. C. Hotten (ed.), *The Three Tours of Dr. Syntax* (3 vols.; 1903).

Portrait: pencil, quarter-length, by G. Dance, 1793: N.P.G.

Compton, Spencer (?1673–1743), Earl Wilmington; Whig politician, First Lord of the Treasury in 1742.

Spencer Compton was the third son of James Compton, 3rd Earl of Northampton. He was educated at Trinity College, Oxford, and subsequently entered parliament (at the second attempt) in 1698 when he was elected M.P. for Eye.

It was expected that like the rest of his family, Compton would support the Tories, which in fact he did for a time. But he soon changed allegiance and entered the ranks of the Whigs, becoming in 1705 the Chairman of the Committee of Privileges, an annually elective post that he held until 1710. He received other politically unimportant but lucrative offices in the course of the next few years, and in 1709 sat on the committee appointed to organize the impeachment of Henry Sacheverell (see *Lives of the Stuart Age*).

In the Tory landslide of 1710 Compton lost his seat, but he was back three years later, representing East Grinstead. In 1715 he sat for Sussex and was unanimously elected Speaker of the House of Commons, a position that he held for the next dozen years. In 1716 he was appointed a Privy Councillor, in 1722 he took over the lucrative office of Paymaster General, and three years later, in 1725, he was made a Knight of the Bath.

With his solemn air and resonant voice, Compton had presence, although it is reported that he could not keep order in the House. Yet of all the jobs he undertook, that of Speaker was probably the one he did best.

In 1727 the new King, George II, ordered Compton to draft the monarch's first declaration to the Commons. It was well known that Compton was a royal favourite and that George had it in his mind to appoint him as First Lord of the Treasury (virtually Prime Minister). But lacking in both competence and ability, Compton was simply not able to carry such office; because of his basic political ignorance he could not even write the King's declaration, and was compelled to solicit the aid of Walpole, who actually drew it up and gave it to Compton to give to the King. Walpole, having nothing to fear from the mediocre Compton, was well supported in his political position through the interest of Queen Caroline.

In 1728 Compton was created Baron Wilmington, and was raised to an earldom two years later. He even accepted the post of Lord Privy Seal under Walpole's administration and in the same year (1730) was made Lord President of the Council. In 1733 he was made a Knight of the Garter.

While Walpole was a real politician, Wilmington simply toed the line set by the King. Generally derided by political journalists and satirists of the day, he was completely discounted as a cipher. Yet he was not totally a cipher. In 1739 when the final split came with Walpole over the imminent war with Spain – the King supported it, so Wilmington did also – Wilmington became something of a thorn in Walpole's side, and in 1741 the Earl abstained from voting on Carteret's motion to oust Walpole.

After Walpole's subsequent resignation over the Chippenham election petition, King George called on Wilmington to form a government. Truly the most useless member of the executive, he was utterly outshone by the real policymakers, Pulteney, Carteret (qq.v.), and Newcastle (see Pelham-Holles, Thomas). A boring, tired, and by now aged time-server, he contributed little in debate or in committee and attracted as much abuse from satirists as ever. The 'old, dull, important lord', as Charles Hanbury Williams calls him, died unmarried on 2 July 1743, and was buried at Compton Wynyates, Warwickshire, leaving nothing to posterity except his name.

J. H. Plumb, *Sir Robert Walpole* (2 vols.; 1956).

Portrait: oil, half-length, by Sir Godfrey Kneller, *c.*1710: N.P.G.

Constable, John (1776–1837), landscape painter.

John Constable was born on 11 June 1776 at East Bergholt, Suffolk, the son of a wealthy miller. Before leaving Dedham Grammar school in about 1793 to work for his father, Constable had already made several paintings of the local Suffolk scenery. He was deeply impressed by the drawings of Thomas Girtin (q.v.) and the seventeenth-century French painter, Claude Lorraine. In 1795 he visited London, where he learned the art of etching and sought advice from the colonel, and was elected M.P. for Leicester (1768). He served again briefly in Madras (1769–70), but was unable to agree with the existing civil governor and came home without marring his career. He was created Knight of the Bath in August 1771, and given the colonelcies of two successive regiments. He became M.P. for Poole in 1774, and was promoted to major-general in September 1775.

The British presence in India had been placed on a different footing by Lord North's Regulating Act of 1773, and Warren Hastings (q.v.) carried out the duties of Governor General, harassed by a hostile majority of his own Council. In 1777 Coote was appointed commander-in-chief of the forces in India, with promotion to lieutenant-general on 29 August. He took up his office in March 1779 and, although he endeavoured to avoid involvement in the Council's factions, he generally supported Hastings, benefiting in return from Hastings's indulgence in the twin matters of allowances and army patronage – transactions that were later to form part of the dossier on Hastings that led to his impeachment.

In July 1780 the ruler of Mysore, Haidar Ali, invaded the Carnatic and threatened Madras. Hastings at once sent Coote to take charge of operations in the presidency, while a strike force was sent overland under Colonel Pearse. Coote arrived in Madras in November, and marched out with all available troops in the following January. Haidar was more adept in the field than Lally, however, and luring Coote as far as Cuddalore, interposed his force between Coote and his base. Fortunately, Coote was able to receive supplies by sea, but the morale of his men flagged as the period of their isolation lengthened.

Eventually, after a minor repulse at Chelambakam, he retreated to Porto Novo, close to the sea. Convinced that Coote was at his mercy, Haidar followed and began constructing a fortified camp near by. Coote resolved to hazard all in an assault, and marched out his 8,500 in the early hours of 1 July 1781. After some preliminary manoeuvres, in which he was assisted by the guns of a schooner in-shore, he made a final attack and carried the entrenchment manned by 47,000 Mysoris. Coote himself lost only 306 of his men.

A month later he linked up with Pearse, and further victories followed, notably at Pollilore and Solingar, until ill health forced Coote to hand over his command in January 1782 to Major-General Stuart and retire to Bengal. Somewhat recovered, he was returning by sea to Madras in April 1783 when his ship was chased by a French cruiser, an unlooked-for excitement that precipitated his final collapse. He died within two days of landing, on 26 April 1783. His body was taken back to England and buried in Hampshire.

E. W. Sheppard, *Coote Bahadur* (1956).

Portrait: oil, half-length, attributed to H. Morland: N.P.G.

Copley, John Singleton (1738–1815),

American painter of portraits and historical subjects, who for forty years was resident in England.

Copley was born on 3 July 1738 at Boston, Massachusetts. He was introduced to art through his stepfather, Peter Pelham, an English engraver. Studying other New England painters, such as John Smibert and John Greenwood, he also made extensive examinations of imported English engravings. He quickly developed the realistic style of painting for which he was to become renowned. Although based initially within the bounds of the existing school of colonial portraiture in America, Copley's early work, with its direct approach to its subjects, was considerably superior to that of his predecessors, and was to become the cornerstone of a flourishing new school of American portrait painting.

In 1766 he sent his *Boy with a Squirrel* to London for exhibition at The Society of Artists. It received great acclaim, not least from Joshua Reynolds, who subsequently persuaded Copley to come to England.

Copley's portraits completed during the 1760s, most of which are to be found in American galleries, are characterized by a great sense of immediacy, and although he was happy to use the conventional devices of the period, such as seeking to characterize a sitter by portraying him surrounded by the objects of his daily life, Copley's use of such conventions is never merely mechanical. The American portraits painted by him in his twenties are already assured in execution and bold in colouring.

Copley finally decided to set out for England. He arrived with his family in 1775, settling in London and embarking immediately on a career as a society portrait painter. He adapted his style to contemporary English taste, but never managed to establish himself as successfully in London as he had in Boston. His commissions remained few in number, and these few seem to lack the buoyant vitality of his earlier American period.

However, Copley now extended his ambition into historical painting, selecting large-scale historical subjects invested with as much drama, realism, and factual content as possible. His first major picture along these lines, *Watson and the Shark* (1778), was a revolutionary work, anticipating the nineteenth-century Romantic image of man struggling against a hostile world. It was well received, and Copley was encouraged to develop the new genre further. His next major historical painting was *The Death of*

Chatham, painted in 1779 and exhibited at the Royal Academy in 1783, earning him the rank of academician.

The new genre was to become immensely popular in France during Napoleonic times, but although Copley had revolutionized historical painting in Europe and still continued to receive portrait commissions, by the turn of the century he was in financial difficulties. Public taste had turned away from him, and his work had become more self-conscious, less natural and exuberant. His last years were constantly menaced by debt, and he died in London on 9 September 1815.

J. T. Flexner, *John Singleton Copley* (Boston, Mass., 1948).

B. N. Parker and A. B. Wheeler, *John Singleton Copley, American Portraits in Oil, Pastel and Miniature, with Biographical Sketches* (Boston, Mass., 1938).

J. D. Prown, *John Singleton Copley* (2 vols.; Cambridge, Mass., 1966).

Portraits: oil, quarter-length, by G. Stuart, *c.*1784: N.P.G.; oil, with his family, by himself, *c.*1776: National Gallery of Art, Washington, D.C.

Cornwallis, Charles (1738–1805), 1st Marquis Cornwallis; general and statesman.

Charles Cornwallis was born in London on 31 December 1738, the eldest son of Charles, 1st Earl Cornwallis and Elizabeth, niece of Sir Robert Walpole. On completion of his education at Eton and at Clare College, Cambridge, he joined the Grenadier Guards in 1756 and became aide-de-camp to the Marquis of Granby in 1760. Later in the same year he was elected M.P. for the family borough of Eye in Suffolk, and in the following year he was made lieutenant colonel of the 12th Regiment of Foot, serving in Germany during the Seven Years War. He returned to England in 1762 to take his seat in the House of Lords as the 2nd Earl Cornwallis, following the death of his father.

In 1765 Cornwallis was made an aide-de-camp and Gentleman of the Bedchamber to the King, and in 1770 Constable of the Tower. In 1775 he was promoted to major general. He had opposed taxation of the American colonists but, when the time came, he did not refuse to take part in the war against them.

In America, under Sir William Howe (q.v.), Cornwallis showed great military ability, taking Fort Lee in 1776 after the Battle of White Plains, and for the next five years he managed to keep the southern states in fair order, repelling the attacks of organized colonial forces in spite of difficulties in communication and manpower. In 1780 he defeated General Horatio Gates at Camden, South Carolina. But in 1781 the English troops were finally surrounded by combined French and American forces and compelled to capitulate at Yorktown. The War of American Independence was thus at an end, but through no fault of Cornwallis whose admirable schemes might have succeeded had it not been for the arrival of the French troops.

Cornwallis was so well thought of in England that he was encouraged to take the post of Governor General of India in 1786. The first three years of his Indian government were taken up with attempts at radical reforms, in both the military and the civil sphere. By raising the salaries of tax collectors he hoped to prevent peculation, but generally failed. Similarly, his plans for the consolidation of the Company's inefficient European troops and the Royal Army troops into one royal army had little success.

His reforms were interrupted by the outbreak of the Third Mysore War. In 1790, encouraged by the weakness of the Madras government, Tipu Sultan, ruler of Mysore, attacked the Raja of Travancore, a faithful ally of England. Cornwallis's political ability was shown in the manner in which he isolated Tipu by obtaining the help of both the Nizam, the ruler of the state of Hyderabad, and the Peshwa, ruler of Maratha in south and central India. The campaign of 1792 began on 25 January with a march on Seringapatam, Tipu's capital. A month later, after much discussion, a peace treaty was signed by which about half Tipu's lands were divided between the East India Company, the Nizam, and the Peshwa. This was eventually to lead to jealousy between the two native powers, resulting in another war after Cornwallis's departure. For the time being, however, Tipu's power had been broken and the way was paved for his final overthrow by Lord Wellesley (see Wellesley, Richard Colley). In recognition of his services in India Cornwallis was created a marquis in 1792.

Back in Calcutta, Cornwallis pressed on with his reforms, which culminated in the Cornwallis Code of 1793. This gave social and political stability to Bengal though it neglected the rights of lesser landowners and excluded Indians from any share in administration.

In 1793 Cornwallis resigned from the governor-generalship of India and returned home. In 1794 he set out on a special mission to bolster the coalition between England, Prussia, and Austria. In 1798 he was asked to accept the offices of Viceroy and Commander in Chief of Ireland. His period of office was marked by the suppression of the rebellion of 1798 and by the carrying of the Act of Union.

In 1798 Lord Castlereagh (see Stewart, Robert), acting secretary to the Lord Lieutenant, had been informed of a plan for rebellion and took steps to quell it. On 22 August news arrived that the French under General Humbert had landed at Killala Bay. After a surprising early victory, the French were defeated and Cornwallis was left to punish the ringleaders of the rebellion. He saw, however, that the problem was rooted in the corruption of government officials, and recognized that the only permanent solution to Ireland's problems lay in Catholic emancipation and the abolition of the unrepresentative Irish parliament.

The credit for the Act of Union, passed two years later, must rest with Lord Castlereagh, who had Cornwallis's active support. Initially defeated in January 1799, the Union Bill was finally passed, after much wholesale and open bribery by Castlereagh, on 7 June 1800. However, when Cornwallis heard that the King had refused to grant Roman Catholic emancipation he decided to resign and retire from public life.

In 1801 he was made British plenipotentiary to negotiate with the French at Amiens, but lacked the necessary diplomacy for the mission. On his return from France he again planned to live out his life peacefully, but in 1805 returned to India, where the schemes of Arthur Wellesley (q.v.) seemed doomed to failure. Cornwallis was not able to do anything to relieve the situation, however, and he died at Ghazipur, in the region of Benares, on 5 October 1805.

A. Aspinall, *Cornwallis in Bengal* (1931).

C. H. Philips, *The East India Company, 1784–1834* (1940).

W. S. Seton-Karr, *The Marquis Cornwallis*, in the series Rulers of India (1890).

Portraits: oil, half-length, by T. Gainsborough, 1783: N.P.G.; pencil and wash, quarter-length, by J. Smart, 1792: N.P.G.; oil, by J. S. Copley: Guildhall, London.

Cotman, John Sell (1782–1842), landscape painter and etcher; a leading member of the group of landscape painters known as the Norwich School.

Cotman was born on 16 May 1782 in Norwich, the son of a prosperous silk merchant. At the age of sixteen he was sent to study in London. Here he came into contact with J. M. W. Turner and Thomas Girtin (qq.v.). To a certain extent he was influenced by Girtin, and it is possible that a visit to Wales in 1800 was made by Cotman in company with Girtin. In Wales he became a member of the artistic circle surrounding the collector Sir George Beaumont. At this period he started exhibiting at the Royal Academy. His watercolour *Greta Bridge* (1805), now in the British Museum, is typical of his early and best period and is one of his best-known works. Cotman was not particularly highly regarded in his own day, but it is works like *Greta Bridge* that have contributed to his subsequent reputation, representing the technique of classic watercolour painting at its purest.

In 1806 he returned to East Anglia, settling first in Norwich and opening a drawing school. He became a leading member of the Norwich Society of Artists, founded by John Crome (q.v.); he exhibited regularly with the society and in 1811 was elected its president. The following year, 1812, he moved to Great Yarmouth, where he acted as drawing master to the family of Dawson Turner, a local antiquarian. He also undertook archaeological sketches for Turner, and after the end of the Napoleonic Wars they joined the army of English artists who overran the continent. Together they visited northern France for three short tours, in 1817, 1818, and 1820, and there Cotman collected material for a book of etchings, published in 1822 with a text by Dawson Turner under the title *Architectural Antiquities of Normandy*. These etchings are much richer in detail than the early watercolours, and much poorer in design and overall effect. In 1823 he left Yarmouth and returned to Norwich.

Cotman's last period, spanning the final decade of his life, has met with widespread disapproval among successive art historians. Although in 1834 he was appointed drawing master at King's College, London, a post he held until his death, Cotman nevertheless continued the attempt that he had started around 1818 to emulate in watercolour the richness of oil painting: in 1831 he started to use a mixture of rice paste with watercolour, with an effect that seems to have pleased nobody except himself, being generally judged vulgar and gaudy in contrast to his earlier work. His work as a teacher of drawing is summarized in a last book of etchings, *Liber Studiorum* (1838). This is an important work, done in Cotman's favourite soft-ground technique, which produces a result resembling chalk and pencil drawing.

Cotman died in London on 24 July 1842. Not fully appreciated in his lifetime, he has come to be recognized only in the twentieth century.

S. D. Kitson, *The Life of John Sell Cotman* (1937).
V. G. R. Rienaecker, *John Sell Cotman* (1953).

Works in:
British Museum.
Tate Gallery.
National Gallery.
Victoria and Albert Museum.

Portrait: pencil, half-length, by H. B. Love, 1830: N.P.G.

Cowper, William (1731–1800), poet.

William Cowper was born at Berkhampsted on 15 November 1731, the son of the Rev. John Cowper and his wife Anne Donne, a descendant of the poet. On his mother's death Cowper was sent at the age of six to a boarding school at Market Street, and from there at the age of ten to Westminster School, where one of his contemporaries was Warren Hastings.

On leaving Westminster at eighteen, Cowper was articled to a solicitor for three years. He wrote that he was not fond of the law, 'But I am very fond of the money that it produces.' He was already

beginning to suffer from severe depression, but this lifted as a result of religious devotion, the poetry of Herbert, or perhaps a sailing holiday with Sir Thomas Hesketh, husband of his cousin Harriet. About this time he fell in love with another cousin, Theodora, but her parents opposed the match. She never married and always loved Cowper, becoming herself subject to the family weakness of depression as she grew older.

Cowper was called to the bar in 1754 and took chambers in the Inner Temple. He was made a commissioner of bankrupts, but he preferred writing to the law, and he joined the Nonsense Club and began to contribute to the *Connoisseur*, Duncombe's *Translations from Horace*, and the *St. James's Chronicle*. In 1763 yet another cousin, Major Cowper, suggested that he apply for one of two available administrative posts in the House of Lords. Dreading a *viva voce* examination, he attempted to commit suicide – by poison, by drowning, and lastly by hanging himself with a garter. Fortunately, the garter broke in time to save his life. His brother John realized the severity of his condition, which was by now exaggerated by religious delusions and a conviction that he was damned. His family took him to a private asylum at St. Albans, where after eighteen months of sensitive care he recovered.

Wanting to cut all links with London, he resigned his commissionership and in 1765 went to lodgings in Huntingdon. In November 1765 he became a lodger in the house of the Rev. Morley Unwin, a retired clergyman who taught private pupils at Huntingdon. Living on a small allowance from his family, Cowper became a strict Evangelical. Intensely devout, he even considered taking holy orders, and found great comfort in the many religious exercises of the Unwin family. When Morley Unwin died Mrs.

Mary Unwin took Cowper and her children to Olney, Buckinghamshire, where Cowper acted as lay-curate to the zealous and energetic Evangelical reformer John Newton.

Newton encouraged Cowper to write hymns, to visit the sick and dying, and to attend services and prayer meetings. The strain of these activities was too much for his frail nerves. He spent a month at his brother's deathbed, succeeding in converting him to his Evangelicalism, and soon afterwards became engaged to Mary Unwin, but a new attack was approaching. One night he was persuaded to stay at Newton's house, and then could not leave for a year. During this time he wrote the well-known hymn 'God moves in a Mysterious Way His Wonders to Perform', but again suicidal tendencies and the belief that there was no hope for him reasserted themselves. Newton treated him kindly, and in May 1774 he returned home to the Unwins.

Newton left for London in 1779 after arranging for the publication of the Olney hymns, and Cowper began to take pleasure in sketching, gardening, and keeping pets. At last, with Mary's encouragement, he began writing poems: Newton asked the far-sighted publisher Joseph Johnson to read them, and they were published in 1782, with moderate success. They were not in his happiest style, being rather heavily moralistic, and the *Critical Review* thought them a 'dull sermon', but Benjamin Franklin wrote from France praising them.

Lady Austen, the widowed sister of a local clergyman, now became a friend of Cowper's. She urged him to try blank verse. The result was *The Task*, his first really popular poem. She also told him the story of John Gilpin, but in 1783 she left, and Cowper began work on a translation of Homer.

In 1785 *The Task*, a long gentle meditative rural poem, and his best-known work, 'The Diverting History of John Gilpin', were an instant and dramatic success. 'John Gilpin' was especially popular, for Cowper had turned Lady Austen's story into a charming comic ballad. Cowper was suddenly the leading poet of the day, and an anonymous benefactor settled £50 a year on him. Additional subscriptions followed, and his cousin Harriet Hesketh persuaded Cowper to move with Mrs. Unwin to the neighbouring village of Weston. The death of Mary's son William in 1786 occasioned another attack of Cowper's madness, and again he tried to hang himself, but was cut down by Mary. Though his recovery was fast, it was never complete, and he often afterwards heard voices and suffered other delusions.

Cowper's Homer appeared in 1791. In its determination to avoid the excesses of Pope's elaborate ornamentation, Cowper's style is judged too bald and halting by today's critics, but the book was very popular when first published. Cowper now began work on a new translation of Milton's Latin and Italian poems, which occupied him for several years. Meanwhile Mary's health deteriorated, and, advised to try a change of air, they moved to Norfolk and settled at East Dereham. Cowper was still capable of writing the exquisite poems 'To Mary', but in 1796 she died. Soon after this he wrote the haunting poem 'The Castaway' and then, growing weaker, lapsed into deep apathy. Convinced that he was destined for hell, he died on 25 April 1800. He and the faithful Mary Unwin are buried in Dereham church.

Cowper's poetry at best has a gentle descriptive and reflective charm, like some pieces of Collins (q.v.), but far removed from the formal meditative style of most of his contemporaries. He pleaded for a 'manly rough line' rather than 'oily smoothness' in poetry, and his own well-observed pictures of country life are reminiscent of Crabbe (q.v.), whose work to some extent he foreshadowed. His hymns have dignity, and many of them are now well-known and indispensable elements of Protestant worship: 'O for a closer walk with God' and 'Hark my soul, it is the Lord' are fine examples of his work. His letters have vivacity, his ballads humour, and his lyric verse great beauty.

David Cecil, *The Stricken Deer, or the Life of Cowper* (1929).

L. C. Hartley, *William Cowper, Humanitarian* (1938).

R. Huang, *Cowper: Nature Poet* (1957).

H. S. Milford (ed.), *The Poetical Works of William Cowper* (1934, 4th ed.).

M. J. Quinlan, *Cowper: A Critical Life* (Minneapolis, 1953).

C. Ryskamp, *William Cowper of the Inner Temple, Esq.* (1959).

T. Wright (ed.), *Correspondence of William Cowper* (1904).

T. Wright (ed.), *Unpublished and Uncollected Letters of William Cowper* (1925).

Portraits: pencil, half-length, by W. Harvey after L. F. Abbott: N.P.G.; pastel, quarter-length, by G. Romney, 1792: N.P.G.; oil, three-quarter length, by L. F. Abbott, 1792: N.P.G.; oil, by J. Jackson, Northampton City Art Gallery.

Cox, David (1783–1859), painter, noted for his watercolour landscapes.

David Cox was born on 29 April 1783 at Deritend, near Birmingham, the son of Joseph Cox, a blacksmith. He was educated at the village school, and later at Birmingham Free School. While bedridden after an accident, he was given a paintbox, and soon became proficient at copying engravings. Accordingly, his father sent him to Joseph Barber's drawing school, intending to have him trained for the lucrative 'toy trade' – the painting of snuffboxes and lockets.

At the age of fifteen, however, David was apprenticed to the Birmingham miniaturist Fielder, an apprenticeship that was cut short after eighteen months by Fielder's suicide. Cox then took a job at the Birmingham Theatre, run by the father of the notable actor William Charles Macready – he went on tour with the company and as well as painting scenery also took walk-on parts. In 1804 he went to London to paint scenery for the Surrey Theatre, and later worked at theatres in Swansea and Wolverhampton.

By 1805 Cox was making a determined attempt to earn his living by painting watercolour landscapes. He took lessons from John Varley, went on a sketching trip to North Wales (which was to prove the inspiration for his finest works), and sold views of the Thames to a Soho art dealer for two guineas a dozen. In 1808 he married the daughter of his former landlady, Ann Ragg, who was twelve years his senior, and they went to live in a tiny cottage at Dulwich.

The next few years were hard; the precarious living Cox made by giving private drawing lessons was further reduced when he went into hiding to avoid conscription, and to pay his debts he spent a miserable year (1813) as drawing master at Farnham Military Academy. His fortunes improved after 1814, when he settled in Herefordshire; he was employed as drawing master at a succession of local schools, gave private lessons, and published several painting manuals, including a *Treatise on Landscape Painting and Effect in Watercolour* (1814: reprinted 1922) and *Progressive Lessons in Landscape* (1816), illustrated with his own etchings and full of practical advice. Cox worked hard at his painting too, experimenting with various techniques, and frequently sketching in North Wales. He soon began to acquire a modest reputation – in 1824 he exhibited twenty-three landscapes at the Society of Painters in Watercolour. In 1827 he moved to London, but still followed the same arduous routine of teaching and painting, interspersed with sketching trips.

A decisive change in Cox's career occurred in 1841 when, against the advice of his friends, he took up oil-painting. Always humble and willing to learn, he watched the fashionable young artist William James Müller at work, and then settled at Harborne, in his native Midlands, and proceeded to confound the pessimists by producing the finest paintings of his lifetime, most of them oils. As always, North Wales was his inspiration. Though his work was always uneven, Cox at his best, as in *The Vale of Clwyd* or *Night Train*, demonstrated with his sombre palette and bold brushwork an intensity of vision almost the equal of Constable's. But he was not a worldly success – his paintings never fetched more than £100, and were consistently rejected by hanging committees. Nor was Cox's private life particularly happy; in 1844 his beloved wife died, and he himself suffered increasingly from ill-health, culminating in a stroke in 1849.

Despite all this, Cox patiently persevered in learning as much as he could from his fellow-artists, especially Turner and Cotman, and in his last years he began painting powerful watercolours on coarse-surfaced paper, using broad, almost expressionist brush-strokes. When censured by the Watercolour Society for the 'roughness' of these, he replied: 'These are the work of the mind, which I consider very far before portraits of places.'

David Cox died on 7 June 1859 and was buried in Harborne churchyard. Ironically, within twenty years of his death his paintings were selling for up to £3,000 apiece.

Sir G. T. Cox, *David Cox* (1947).

Portraits: pencil, quarter-length, by unknown artist: N.P.G.; oil, half-length, by W. Radcliffe, jun., 1830: N.P.G.; oil, quarter-length, by W. Boxall, 1856: N.P.G.

Crabbe, George (1754–1832), poet.

George Crabbe was born on 24 December 1754 at Aldeburgh on the Suffolk coast, the eldest son of George Crabbe.

Educated locally, Crabbe worked for a time in a warehouse on Slaughden quay until 1768, when he was sent as an apprentice to a doctor at Wickham Brook, near Bury St. Edmunds. Here he worked reluctantly as errand boy and farm labourer, before being transferred in 1771 to Mr. Page, a surgeon at Woodbridge, where he met and fell in love with Sarah Elmy, the niece of a wealthy Framlingham yeoman. This love inspired his first poetry, mainly light and spontaneous lyrics, of which some were published in Wheble's *Lady's Magazine*. He published a didactic poem, 'Inebriety', anonymously at Ipswich in 1774.

Qualified by his apprenticeship to call himself a doctor, Crabbe returned to Aldeburgh with severe doubts of his ability to practise medicine, and so elected to return to warehouse work. Eventually he was taken on as assistant to a rascally surgeon named Maskell. Still engaged to Sarah but unable to succeed as a local doctor, he borrowed £5 and set off for London.

He took lodgings in the city and began to hawk his poems. 'The Candidate', published in 1780, won cold critical comment, and the collapse of his publishers meant that he made no profit at all from it. He pawned his watch, clothes, and instruments, witnessed the horror of the Gordon riots and the burning of Newgate and, on receiving news of the death of his adored mother, began to know real despair. He applied by letter to Lord North, Lord Shelburne, and Thurlow, the Lord Chancellor. Thurlow answered coldly, the others not at all. A journal written for Sarah vividly describes his problems and, although his letters to her were more restrained, she and her mother realized his position and sent him what little they could afford. At last, in 1781, he wrote to Burke, saying that unless he could find £14 within a week he would be in a debtors' prison.

His fortunes had changed, however, for Burke read and liked his poems, persuaded Dodsley to publish *The Library* – bringing him into the public eye – and took Crabbe to his home at Beaconsfield. He met Reynolds, Johnson, and Fox, and was even invited to breakfast by Thurlow, who apologized for his earlier rudeness and gave him £100.

Burke now advised Crabbe to take orders and persuaded the Bishop of Norwich to ordain him deacon. He returned to Aldeburgh as curate but was given a hostile reception, so when in 1782 Burke got him an offer of the chaplaincy to the Duke of Rutland, he went happily to live at Belvoir. Treated kindly by the ducal family, he was able to finish *The Village*, which was published in 1783. This poem, in showing how harsh country life could be, shattered the popular myth of rural paradise exemplified by Goldsmith and Gray, but was nonetheless a great success. Thurlow now offered him the livings – to be held in absentia – of Frome St. Quentin and Evershot in Dorset, and the Archbishop of Canterbury gave him the degree of LL.B. to qualify him.

At last he felt able to marry, and in 1783 brought his patient bride Sarah to Belvoir. In 1785, when the Duke of Rutland went to Ireland, the Crabbes went too, to Stathern, where the poet became curate. Crabbe published a memoir of Robert Manners, his patron's brother; in 1785 he brought out *The Newspaper*, and then published no more for twenty-two years.

During this time he wrote a great deal, including three novels, but nearly all his manuscripts were periodically and ceremoniously burnt. In 1787, on the death of the Duke of Rutland, Crabbe moved to become the rector of Muston and Allington, settling at Muston parsonage, but in 1791 his wife's uncle died and left them his money and they went back to live at Ducking Hall, in East Anglia, later moving to Great Glemham Hall and then Rendham, leaving a curate in charge at Muston. Although Crabbe took on the curacy of neighbouring parishes his pluralism won him many enemies.

Five of the Crabbes' seven children died, driving Sarah into a deep and incurable depression, while a stomach complaint started George Crabbe's habit of taking opium. Yet despite these domestic worries, Crabbe was a good friend to the poor and his sermons drew large crowds. Official notice was now taken of the fact that he did not live in his parish and in 1805 he had to return to Muston, where he attacked the newly established Dissenters vigorously. He finished 'The Parish Register' in 1806 and dedicated it to Charles James Fox, who read, corrected, and enjoyed it just before he died. It was published with 'Eustace Grey' in 1807, and was followed by *The Borough* in 1810. All met with great success, as did *Tales in Verse*, published in 1812.

In September 1813, to Crabbe's great grief, his wife Sarah died, and he himself became ill. The young Duke of Rutland, son of his former patron, offered him the living of Trowbridge, Wiltshire, where he was inducted in June 1814. In 1819 Murray decided to publish *Tales of the Hall*, for which Crabbe was paid £3,000. Murray, however, made a loss. Crabbe's poetry could not hold its own against that of Byron, and only one edition appeared – an eight-volume one in 1834, reprinted as late as 1901.

In 1822 Crabbe visited Edinburgh, where he stayed with Scott and met local celebrities. After this trip he led a very quiet life, occasionally going back to Suffolk to see his sister or visiting his son George, now vicar of Pucklechurch, or the house of Samuel Hoare at Hampstead. His second son, John, became his curate at Trowbridge, and Crabbe lived on there taking services and, despite a painful form of neuralgia, enjoying his grandchildren. Crabbe died at Trowbridge on 3 February 1832, and his parishioners put up a statue and monument to his memory in Trowbridge church.

Crabbe's poetry has attracted favourable attention, even in the twentieth century. Benjamin Britten's 1945 opera *Peter Grimes* is based on a character in *The Borough*. His realism and the faithfulness of his descriptions of Suffolk and its people give his work a lasting quality of compelling integrity.

Neville Blackburn, *The Restless Ocean: the Story of George Crabbe* (1972).

E. Blunden (ed.), *The Life of the Rev. George Crabbe by his Son* (1947).

R. L. Brett, *George Crabbe* (1956).

A. J. and R. M. Carlyle (eds.), *Poetical Work* (1914).

E. M. Forster (ed.), *The Life of the Rev. George Crabbe by his Son* (1932).

L. Haddakin, *The Poetry of Crabbe* (1955).

R. Huchon, *Un Poète Réaliste Anglais: Crabbe* (Eng. tr. 1907).

Peter New, *George Crabbe's Poetry* (1976).

A. W. Ward (ed.), *Poems by George Crabbe* (3 vols.; 1905–7).

Portrait: oil, half-length, by H. W. Pickersgill: N.P.G.; oil, by Rolindo Sharples, *c.* 1827: City Art Gallery, Bristol.

Crome, John (1768–1821), landscape painter; known as 'Old Crome' to distinguish him from his son, John Berney Crome (1794–1842).

John Crome was born on 22 December 1768 at Norwich, the son of a weaver. At the age of twelve, having received a very humble education, Crome was employed as an errand boy in his home town of Norwich. Three years later, in 1783, he was apprenticed to Francis Whisler, a sign and coach painter, with whom he stayed for seven years, afterwards acting as journeyman for Whisler until 1803. His own love and talent for landscape painting had been gradually emerging, and he had joined his friend Robert Ladbrooke to travel the neighbouring countryside, painting and occasionally selling his work.

Crome's talent had been spotted by Thomas Harvey of Catton, a wealthy and educated man who allowed Crome to visit his own small collection and make copies of such artists as Hobbema and Gainsborough and thus become acquainted with the Dutch seventeenth-century style, which was to be his principal influence.

In order to support his large family, Crome had established himself as a drawing master to the children of the neighbouring gentry. In 1803 he became a founder member of 'the Norwich Society for the purpose of an inquiry into the Rise, Progress and Present State of Painting, Architecture, and Sculpture with a view to point out the Best Methods of Study to attain to Greater Perfection in these Arts'. This society was initially a discussion group, meeting fortnightly in a tavern; it did, however, also hold annual exhibitions of painting from 1805 to 1833. The society is now known as the Norwich School, and its most distinguished members were undoubtedly Crome and John Sell Cotman (q.v.), who joined in 1806. Five years after its founding, Crome became President, with Ladbrooke as Vice-President. The two men were, however, to differ on the question of funds – a difference which was only resolved when Ladbrooke withdrew and founded a rival society.

Crome voluntarily limited himself and his art to the Norfolk countryside, rarely visiting London or other parts of the country. His one and only trip abroad was to Paris in 1816, to see the collection of paintings seized by Napoleon.

In 1806 Crome first exhibited his landscapes at the Royal Academy and continued to do so regularly until 1818. Although principally an oil painter, he was also skilful in watercolours, though he rarely worked in this medium. Good examples of his watercolour work are *Landscape with Cottages* (more often called *The Shadowed Road*) and *The Hollow Road*, both in the British Museum. The most important of his oil paintings are *Mousehold Heath* and *Slate Quarries*, both in the Tate Gallery, and *The Poringland Oak* in the National Gallery.

Crome brought a bold simplicity of handling to the art of landscape painting. He painted just what he found just how he found it, with a complete lack of desire to romanticize or idealize situations. His work is inspired by nature and the love and respect he felt towards it. His care in the drawings of trees is especially interesting: it has been said that 'An oak as represented by Crome is a poem vibrating with life.'

Apart from his position as a landscape painter, Crome won acclaim as one of the first to take up etching for its own sake. To a great extent the Norwich School is responsible for the revival of etching as a modern medium. There are a great many examples of Crome's finely detailed work in the British Museum.

After a life in which he influenced several painters, John Crome died in his native Norwich on 22 April 1821.

C. H. C. Baker, *Crome* (1921).
Derek and Timothy Clifford, *John Crome* (1968).
H. M. Cundall, *The Norwich School* (1920).

Works in:
National Gallery.
Tate Gallery.
Kenwood House.

Portrait: water-colour, quarter-length, by D. B. Murphy: N.P.G.

Crompton, Samuel (1753–1827), inventor of the spinning mule.

Samuel Crompton was born on 3 December 1753 near Bolton. His father farmed on a small scale and also carried out domestic yarn spinning and hand-loom weaving. When his father died Crompton was five years old, and the family were at that time caretakers of the ancient mansion of Hall-in-the-Wood, at Firwood, not far from Bolton. The boy was sent to a good day school, and from an early age he practised the art of spinning. Frustrated by the inadequacy of the spinning jenny, Crompton set himself to design and construct a superior model, utilizing his time also by playing on a fiddle that he had made himself. He performed sometimes at a Bolton theatre, thereby earning a little extra money. Every spare moment and all his funds were dedicated to his invention.

After five years of labour, he produced a crude but effective machine that made a good-quality, fine, even yarn, capable of making delicate muslins, which were up to that time imported expensively from India. Crompton's 'mule' was so called because it was a cross between Arkwright's rollers and Hargreaves's spinning jenny, but it incorporated an addition peculiar to Crompton, a spindle-carriage which avoided strain on the thread before it was completed. The mule drew out a single thread, giving a final twisting to the cotton fibres which fed it, thus reproducing mechanically the actions of a hand spinner.

Crompton married the daughter of a West Indies merchant in 1780. She had attracted his attention by her skill at hand spinning, and after their marriage she assisted Crompton in his spinning work on the mule, to which he confidently devoted himself. Many people curious about the mule invaded the Hall, and although Crompton was apparently distressed by such prying, he could not afford a patent, and for some reason did not even secure the aid of a sponsor. He eventually parted with the invention, with the encouragement of a Bolton manufacturer, in return for a document that, as it transpired, had no legal validity. Eighty firms agreed to pay him a subscription, but when the invention was surrendered the subscription ceased and Crompton received only £67.

With his pitiful proceeds, Crompton moved to a small farm at Oldham, near Bolton, where he constructed a new machine. He was soured by his experiences, and refused an offer from Robert Peel (the former employer of James Hargreaves) of work in his establishment. At one time he destroyed his spinning and carding machines, crying, 'They shall not have this too.' He subsequently resumed work, and moved with his growing family to Bolton, where he had moderate success, working on his own, his sensitivity and pride impeding greater achievement.

By 1800, Crompton's mule had largely displaced Hargreaves's jenny and Arkwright's frame, and made possible a flourishing output of British muslin. A group of Manchester supporters led by John Kennedy, his first biographer, raised a subscription for the inventor. Due to the unsettled times less than £500 was collected, but with this money, Crompton enlarged his small plant. When parliament granted the sum of £10,000 to Hargreaves in 1811 for the contribution that his invention had made to British industry, Crompton set out on travels to ascertain the extent of the use of the mule, in the hope of securing similar recognition. His investigations revealed that while something under 160,000 spindles were being made on Hargreaves's jenny and just over 300,000

on Arkwright's machines, the mule accounted for well over 4,500,000 spindles. About 360 mills had the mule in use. On his return to London, he urged his claim to parliament, with support from influential friends in Manchester. In 1812 a select committee reported in his favour, and he was awarded £5,000, from which, however, he had to finance his travelling and accommodation expenses. He made two unsuccessful forays into business on what was left of this money, investing first in the bleaching trade and then going into partnership with a cotton merchant.

Again a subscription was mooted for Crompton, and Bolton friends, unbeknown to him, had raised enough to buy him an annuity that brought in £63 a year. Age did not, however, bring him repose or happiness, and amid increasing cares he died in Bolton on 26 June 1827. A £200 monument was raised in his parish churchyard. Another subscription of £2,000 was made for a statue in Bolton, the town that his invention had done so much to develop. It was unveiled in 1862 and Lord Palmerston, then Prime Minister, gave John Crompton, the inventor's only surviving son, then in his eighties, a gratuity of £50. Thus, by piecemeal subscriptions and small gratuities, did England reward the man who contributed so much to make the industrial revolution possible.

H. C. Cameron, *Samuel Crompton* (1951).

Portrait: engraving, quarter-length, by J. Morrison, after a portrait by C. Allingham: Science Museum, London.

Cruikshank, George (1792–1878), painter and caricaturist, see *Lives of the Victorian Age*.

Cumberland, Duke of (1721–65), see William Augustus.

D

Dahl, Michael (1656–1743), Swedish-born painter, see *Lives of the Stuart Age*.

Dalton, John (1766–1844), chemist and physicist, best known for his modern atomic theory explaining chemical reactions.

John Dalton was born on 6 September 1766 at Eaglesfield, Cumberland, the son of a hand-loom weaver. He was the third of six children. His early education was obtained from his father, Joseph, and at the local Quaker school under the school's headmaster, Elihu Robinson. Robinson was a meteorologist and instrument-maker, from whom Dalton gained his first interest in science. In later life Dalton was to make his own instruments and keep an extensive diary of his meteorological observations. His progress as a student was rapid, and at the age of only twelve he was permitted to teach in the school. In 1781 he and his brother moved to Kendal, where they taught in the local Quaker school. John became principal of the school in 1785, and remained there until 1793. Throughout this period he met several men who influenced his scientific pursuits, including John Gough (1751–1825), a blind mathematician and botanist of some note.

In 1793 Dalton moved to Manchester to teach natural philosophy and mathematics at the New College (Manchester Academy), where he stayed until the college was transferred to York in 1799. He remained in Manchester as a private tutor of chemistry and mathematics.

In 1794 Dalton was elected a member of the Manchester Library and Philosophical Society, to which he contributed a paper entitled 'Extraordinary Facts Relating to the Vision of Colours', setting out a new theory to account for colour blindness. His researches in this field are commemorated by the term 'daltonism', a form of colour blindness in which there is particular difficulty in distinguishing red from green.

Dalton was elected Secretary of the Manchester Literary and Philosophical Society in 1800. In 1808 he became its Vice President, and in 1819 its President. The Society purchased a house in 1799 in which Dalton was permitted to live and work for the rest of his life, keeping daily records of the local weather right up until his death. It was this early interest in the atmosphere that eventually led to his investigation of the various properties of gases. In a paper published in 1805, 'Absorption of Gases by Water and Other Liquids', Dalton formulated his law of partial pressures. It stated that in a mixture of gases the total pressure exerted is equal to the sum of the pressures that each gas would exert if occupying the same space alone.

Dalton's great contribution to chemistry was his atomic theory of the composition of matter, originally suggested in vague outline by the ancient Greek philosopher, Democritus. Dalton explained that the atoms of any one element are identical in weight, and that these atoms are able to combine with atoms of certain other elements in the formation of compounds. These combinations, he suggested, occur in simple numerical proportions. His laws of

D. S. L. Carwell (ed.), *John Dalton and the Progress of Science* (1968).

F. Greenaway, *John Dalton and the Atom* (1966).

E. Patterson, *John Dalton and the Atomic Theory* (New York, 1970).

A. L. Smyth, *John Dalton 1766–1844, A Bibliography of Works by and about Him* (1966).

Portrait: embossed paper medallion, by unknown artist, 1842: N.P.G.; engraving, three-quarter length, by W. H. Worthington after a portrait by J. Allen, 1823: Science Museum; pen and wash, by J. Jerome: Manchester City Art Gallery; marble statue, by F. Chantrey: Manchester City Art Gallery.

Darwin, Erasmus (1731–1802), scientist, writer, and poet; grandfather of Charles Darwin (see *Lives of the Victorian Age*).

Erasmus Darwin was born on 12 December 1731 at Elton, Nottinghamshire, and educated at St. John's College, Cambridge, after which he trained as a physician, studying medicine at Edinburgh and later back at Cambridge. In 1756 he started a medical practice at Nottingham but had little success. In 1757 he moved to Lichfield, where he was considerably more fortunate in his medical career. He resided at Lichfield until 1781, when he moved to Derby. Here he became a correspondent of Joseph Priestley (q.v.) and Rousseau.

In the 1790s Darwin's writings began to be published. As a poet, he could write polished occasional verse of high quality and some of his religious poems were incorporated into popular hymn-books. But his more large-scale works, such as *The Botanic Garden* (1792) and *The Temple of Nature or The Origin of Society* (published posthumously in 1803) contain pedantic and bombastic verse of negligible merit.

His prose works, however, are lucid and readable. In these he shows himself to be greatly influenced by eighteenth-century materialism. As a confirmed deist, he could believe in the existence of a

combination and multiple proportion were originally deduced and later proved with experiments. Although Dalton believed that an atom was the ultimate particle of matter, his general conceptions of atomic structure and chemical combination were of critical importance to the development of chemistry. He also produced a table of atomic weights.

Dalton continued to develop his new ideas in a series of papers published as *A New System of Chemical Philosophy* (1808–27). His two series of lectures at the Royal Institution (1804, 1809–10) were enthusiastically received and added greatly to his general reputation. In 1822 Dalton was elected a Fellow of the Royal Society, and a few years later was honoured by the French Academy of Sciences (who had appointed him a corresponding member in 1816) when they elected him one of only eight foreign associates in 1830. The British government recognized his important contributions by awarding him an annual pension in 1833. Dalton died in Manchester on 27 July 1844.

Supreme Being as a mathematical certainty but, as he once wrote, 'That He influences things by a particular providence is not so evident.' His psychological and aesthetic theories followed very much the tradition of the Enlightenment and derived in no small measure from the writings of Hume, Berkeley, and Locke. His book *Zoonomia* (1794–6) not only seems to anticipate the theories of his grandson Charles's great rival, Jean Baptiste de Lamarck, who believed that acquired characteristics could be hereditary, but even foreshadows the work of such later physiologists as Pavlov.

The canon of Erasmus Darwin's writings is completed by two prose works, *Female Education in Boarding Schools*, which appeared in 1797, and *Phytologia, or the Philosophy of Agriculture and Gardening*, published in 1799, three years before his death on 18 April 1802.

Charles Darwin, *Life of Erasmus Darwin, an Introduction to an Essay on His Works by Ernst Krause* (1879).

D. King-Hele, *Erasmus Darwin* (1963).

H. Pearson, *Doctor Darwin* (1930).

A. Seward, *Memoirs of the Life of Dr. Darwin* (1804).

Portrait: oil, quarter-length, by J. Wright, 1770: N.P.G.

Dashwood, Francis (1708–81), 15th Baron Le Despencer; Chancellor of the Exchequer and notorious rake.

Francis Dashwood was born in Great Marlborough Street, London, in December 1708, the only son of Sir Francis Dashwood, 1st Baronet, and his second wife Mary, eldest daughter of Vere Fane, Baron Le Despencer and 4th Earl of Westmorland. He was educated privately and at Charterhouse until, in 1724, the death of his father brought him the family title and estates. He subsequently set out on the Grand Tour with John Montague, Earl of Sandwich; during his tour he conducted himself in a high-spirited manner. On returning to England he became a leading member of the Dilettanti Society, a club concerned with literature and the arts, and the more bizarre Divan Club, whose members affected oriental dress at its meetings.

In these early years, Dashwood became attached in a minor capacity to Frederick Louis, Prince of Wales, and in the general election of 1741 he campaigned vigorously against Walpole's supporters to earn himself the seat for New Romney. As long as George II remained King, an associate of the Prince of Wales stood very little chance of advancement in the political world, however, and Dashwood devoted most of his time to his private interests. In about 1746 he founded a club of his own, The Knights of St. Francis, meeting initially at the George and Vulture in Cornhill. Its venue was later moved to Medmenham Abbey, situated on the banks of the Thames near Marlow, and furnished at Dashwood's expense. Dashwood acted as Grand Master of the Order, whose members included the Earl of Sandwich, William Hogarth, and a sprinkling of poets, painters, novelists, dramatists, clergymen, and politicians. John Wilkes (q.v.) joined the brotherhood in 1758 but left in 1763, when the club began to break up under the impact of political disagreements among its members. Wilkes produced a spiteful and satirical publication that 'exposed' the order and was responsible for giving it a bad reputation. A similar fate was extended to the 'Hellfire Caves' on the Dashwood property at West Wycombe (christened the 'Hellfire Club' by posterity).

In March 1761 Dashwood was appointed Treasurer of the Chamber, and in June 1762 he reluctantly accepted the office of Chancellor of the Exchequer in Bute's ministry. Since he had little competence in financial affairs or as a speaker, his appearance in that capacity was a gift to the opposition. A rash proposal to introduce a tax on cider caused fierce opposition throughout the cider counties, and when Bute fell in 1763 Dashwood resigned with him, although he did receive a sinecure, being made Keeper of the Wardrobe. In the same year he succeeded as 15th Baron Le Despencer and was made Lord Lieutenant of Buckinghamshire. As the foremost baron of England he inherited large estates, including Mereworth Castle near Maidstone, Kent.

He was made Postmaster-General in 1764, discharged the duties of the office efficiently until 1781, and through them made a lasting friendship with Benjamin Franklin. He avoided further involvement in the political manoeuvres of the day, preferring the responsibilities of the country squire at home. He died at West Wycombe after a long illness on 11 December 1781, and was buried in his own mausoleum there.

Betty Kemp, *Sir Francis Dashwood; an Eighteenth-Century Independent* (1967).

Davy, Sir Humphry (1778–1829), chemist, best known as the inventor of the miner's safety lamp.

Humphry Davy was born on 17 December 1778 in Penzance, Cornwall, the son of a woodcarver. He was the eldest of five children. His early education, in the local grammar schools, was broadly based but limited. When his father died, in 1794, the sixteen-year-old Humphry accepted the responsibility of providing for the family. The following year he was apprenticed to Bingham Borlase, a surgeon and apothecary in Penzance. During the next three years he became fascinated with the many jars containing strange powders and crystals, and began a serious study of chemistry and mathematics on his own. This interest was

further stimulated by the reading of Lavoisier's treatise *Elementaire de Chimie*, which listed the thirty-three chemical elements then known, and provided interesting ideas and speculations concerning the future of chemistry.

In 1798 Davy became an assistant to Dr. Thomas Beddoes at his Medical Pneumatic Institution in Clifton. Beddoes was then studying the effects of different gases when inhaled, and their possible therapeutic applications. Davy was given the title of chemical superintendent and placed in charge of specific projects. During experiments on the effects of inhaling laughing gas (nitrous oxide), he persuaded his friends Samuel Taylor Coleridge and Robert Southey to participate and report their findings. It was not mere fun and games, however, and on more than one occasion Davy almost lost his life from the toxic effects of various vapours.

In 1800 he published *Researches, Chemical and Philosophical, Chiefly Concerning Nitrous Oxide and its Respiration*. This scholarly work on the anaesthetic

effects of laughing gas greatly enhanced his reputation as a chemist, and he was invited to lecture at the Royal Institution, appearing there for the first time on 25 April 1801. The following year he accepted an appointment as professor, and in 1803 was elected a Fellow of the Royal Society.

Davy had become interested in research in electricity, particularly in voltaic cells. The results of these studies, combined with research in mineral analysis and a special study of methods of tanning, resulted in his being awarded the Copley Medal (1805). In 1807 his research in electrolysis led to the discovery of potassium, which he obtained from caustic potash, and the isolation of sodium. In 1808 he discovered barium, strontium, and calcium, and isolated magnesium. During 1808–9 he lectured in Dublin and was awarded an LL.D. degree by Trinity College. His interest in problems of agriculture resulted in his publishing *Elements of Agricultural Chemistry* (1813). In 1812 he received a knighthood in recognition of his services to science. His investigations of fire-damp had a practical result when, in 1815, he invented the miner's safety lamp. The design of this instrument is simple. A lighted wick is surrounded on all sides by wire gauze. In the presence of fire-damp the flame burns with a different colour, as the explosive gas passes into the lamp through the gauze. The gauze itself, however, serves to conduct away the heat and prevent the flame from spreading beyond the interior of the lamp and igniting the fire-damp outside, so causing an explosion.

In March 1813 Davy employed Michael Faraday (q.v.) as his assistant at the Royal Institution, and took him on a tour of the Continent during the next two years to help with work on investigating a new theory of volcanic action. During this period, when England and France were at war, Davy obtained written permission from Napoleon to travel freely in France, so great was his reputation as a scientist.

Davy made other significant contributions to chemistry, including his discovery of the nature and properties of iodine. In 1820 he replaced Sir Joseph Banks (q.v.) as President of the Royal Society. During the next three years he contributed many papers to the Society on his researches in the field of electromagnetism. In 1829 he was taken ill while travelling abroad, and he died on 28 May 1829 in Geneva.

J. Z. Fullmer, *Sir Humphry Davy's Published Works* (Boston, Mass., 1970).

Sir H. Hartley, *Humphry Davy* (1966).

J. Kendall, *Humphry Davy: 'Pilot' of Penzance* (1954).

A. Treneer, *The Mercurial Chemist: a Life of Sir Humphry Davy* (1963).

Portraits: oil, three-quarter length, after Lawrence: N.P.G.; water-colour, three-quarter length, attributed to J. Jackson: N.P.G.; oil, half-length, by T. Phillips: N.P.G.; oil, three-quarter length, by H. Howard, 1803: N.P.G.; engraving, threequarter-length, by Charles Turner, 1835, after H. Howard, 1803: Science Museum.

Dennis, John (1657–1734), critic, see *Lives of the Stuart Age*.

De Quincey, Thomas (1785–1859), writer, remembered chiefly for *Confessions of an English Opium Eater*.

Thomas De Quincey was born on 15 August 1785 in Manchester, the second son of Thomas De Quincey, a wealthy merchant and talented literary amateur. He was tutored at Salford by the Rev. Samuel Hall, who became his guardian after the death of his father in 1792. Thomas's elder brother, William, died of typhus at the age of sixteen, whereupon the widowed Mrs. De Quincey moved to Bath and sent Thomas, a nervous, delicate child, to the grammar school, together with his younger brother Richard.

Thomas was a brilliant classics scholar, but had to leave the school in 1798 after a prefect struck him on the head and caused permanent damage; his mother, a stern evangelical, considered this a divine judgment on his intellectual pride. Yet even at this age De Quincey's charm had won him influential friends; in 1800 he visited Lord Westport in Ireland and later Lord Carbery in Northamptonshire. Lady Carbery, then in her mid-twenties, took a liking to him, and repeatedly asked his advice in intellectual matters.

In 1801 De Quincey went to Manchester grammar school, which had a high academic reputation but was negligently run by its headmaster, Charles Lawson, an aged recluse. De Quincey soon became tired of school routine, and asked his guardians if he could leave. When they refused, he borrowed ten guineas from Lady Carbery and set out on foot for the Welsh mountains. De Quincey's uncle, Colonel Penson, soon caught up with him but found himself in sympathy with the boy's romantic notions and gave him a guinea a week allowance. Thomas then met an itinerant German scholar, De Haren, and together they tramped the hills, living under canvas, and writing love letters or business letters for farmers in exchange for bowls of bread and milk. De Quincey decided he needed £200 to continue this life until he was twenty-one and went to London to raise the money.

At first De Quincey led a rough existence, roaming the streets of London, but eventually he persuaded a titled friend to guarantee his debts, and was reconciled once more with his mother. He now went up to Worcester College, Oxford, where he was celebrated for his studiousness and his eloquent conversation; he left without a degree, however. At university he first took opium, but only to relieve toothache.

De Quincey was a great admirer of the *Lyrical Ballads* (first published in 1798) and in 1807 went to Nether Stowey to meet Coleridge, later visiting Wordsworth at Grasmere and Southey at Greta Hall. After a year of supposed legal studies, mostly in fact spent in the company of Lamb and Humphry Davy (qq.v.), De Quincey moved into Wordsworth's old cottage at Grasmere. He read much German philosophy and helped Wordsworth with his pamphlets. His chief recreation was to go on gruelling nocturnal walks with Professor Wilson.

Always prone to depression, De Quincey was by 1813 eating 340 grains of opium a day. With great effort he drastically reduced this, and in 1816 married Margaret Simpson, a local girl. Although she was an affectionate wife, De Quincey soon reverted to his old habits and by 1819 was incapable of serious literary work; his dreams were haunted by a gigantic crocodile and a curious opium-eating Malay. Moreover, what little money he had not recklessly given away he now lost when his bank was forced into liquidation.

To make a living De Quincey became editor of the *Westmorland Gazette*, but his articles were far too abstruse for a provincial newspaper and so before long he went to London to seek work. Lamb generously found him lodgings and introduced him to the owners of the *London Magazine*, which in late 1821 published his masterpiece, *Confessions of an English Opium Eater*. With its poignant account of De Quincey's youthful hardships and its vivid description of the visions opium induces, the book is a superb example of what its author casually termed 'the department of impassioned prose'. It was twice reprinted within the year. The by now famous De Quincey was invited to write for scores of magazines, on every conceivable topic. By 1828 his contributions to *Blackwood's Magazine*, which included a translation of Lessing's 'Laocöon', had become so important that he settled in Edinburgh. In 1832 he published a novel, *Klosterheim*, which was not a success, and from 1834 onwards his articles on Wordsworth and Coleridge, though well meant, upset the poets' families.

Between 1833 and 1837 De Quincey's wife and two of his children died, so he decided to lead a life independent of his surviving offspring. This was not successful; he gave all his money to beggars, began taking opium again, and allowed bills and papers to pile up so alarmingly that he frequently locked the door on them and found new lodgings. When De Quincey died he had six such paper-stores scattered around Edinburgh.

Despite these undisciplined ways, De Quincey's intellect was needle-sharp, as is demonstrated by his *Logic of Political Economy* (1844), which was greatly admired by J. S. Mill. Otherwise, he developed an intense interest in murder trials, and still went on solitary night rambles. In 1853 James Hogg persuaded him to burrow amongst his chaotic papers to put together a many-volumed collected edition. Though he was now a famous literary figure, De Quincey usually had to be dragged to attend social functions; once arrived, however, he would talk as eloquently as Coleridge. To the end he remained resolutely unworldly. He died peacefully on 8 December 1859 and was buried in Edinburgh's West Churchyard.

M. A. Eaton, *De Quincey: A Biography* (1936).
M. Elwin (ed.), *Confessions of An English Opium Eater* (1956).
L. H. and C. W. Houtchers (eds.), *The English Romantic Poets and Essayists: A Review of Research and Criticism* (New York, 1958).
J. E. Jordan, *De Quincey: Literary Critic* (Berkeley, 1952).
D. Masson (ed.), *Collected Writings* (14 vols.; 1889–90).
S. K. Proctor, *De Quincey's Theory of Literature* (Ann Arbor, Michigan, 1943).
S. M. Tave (ed.), *New Essays: His Contributions to the Edinburgh Saturday Post and the Edinburgh Evening Post 1827–28* (Princeton, 1966).

Portraits: oil, three-quarter length, by J. Watson-Gordon, 1845: N.P.G.; oil, by J. Archer: Manchester City Art Gallery; marble bust, by Sir J. Stell: Scottish N.P.G.

Despencer, 15th Baron Le (1708–81), see Dashwood, Francis.

Devonshire, 4th Duke of (1720–64), see Cavendish, William.

Dickinson, Jonathan (1688–1747), American cleric who became the first President of the College of New Jersey (now Princeton).

Jonathan Dickinson was born on 22 April 1688 in Hatfield, Massachusetts. He was the son of religious parents. On graduating from Yale College (1706) he turned to the study of theology and in September 1709 he was ordained pastor of the church at Elizabeth Town, New Jersey. A convinced Presbyterian, he was able in 1717 to persuade his congregation to join the Presbytery of Philadelphia. Dickinson took a leading part in this body, and was twice (1721 and 1742) elected Moderator of the Synod. By astute judgment he was able to balance the various factions in the Presbytery while at the same time defending Presbyterianism against external criticism. A keen participator in the religious controversies of the day, he could be both energetic and subtle in argument.

It was generally agreed that a school to train young men for the ministry was required and that the institution founded by the Rev. William Tennant was inadequate for this purpose. In 1745 the dissatisfied Presbyteries of New Brunswick and New York met at Elizabeth Town and organized the Synod of New York, with Dickinson as Moderator. On 22 October 1746 the Acting Governor of New Jersey, an Anglican, granted the first charter of the College of New Jersey. When the College was formally opened at Elizabeth Town in May 1747, Dickinson was elected its first President. Plans were already under way to remove the College to Princeton, which was more centrally situated, when Dickinson died suddenly on 7 October 1747 from an attack of pleurisy.

E. W. and C. M. Andrews (eds.), *God's Protecting Providence* (New Haven, 1945).

E. W. and C. M. Andrews (eds.), *Jonathan Dickinson's Journal* (New Haven, 1945).

H. C. Cameron, *Jonathan Dickinson and the College of New Jersey* (1880).

T. J. Wertenbaker, *Princeton 1746–1896* (New Haven, 1946).

Portrait: oil, half-length, by E. Ludlow Mooney: Nassau Hall, Princeton University.

Dinwiddie, Robert (1693–1770), British soldier; Lieutenant Governor of Virginia.

Dinwiddie was born in 1693 at Germiston near Glasgow, the son of Robert Dinwiddie, a colonial administrator. He worked as a merchant until December 1727, when he was made Collector of Customs for Bermuda. He performed his duties so well that on 11 April 1738 he was made Surveyor General for the Southern Parts of America with jurisdiction over the Carolinas, Virginia, Maryland, Pennsylvania, the Bahama Islands, and Jamaica. In his new position he revealed himself to be a stern opponent of any hint of fraud or corruption amongst his officials. He took up residence in Virginia and in October 1741 became a member of the Council of that state.

In July 1751 Dinwiddie was appointed Lieutenant Governor of Virginia; he provoked a controversy almost immediately by ordering that all landholders should take out patents at once and pay a fee for the privilege. The House of Burgesses objected to this proposal and secured its defeat in the Assembly, where the new Governor was regarded with a great deal of suspicion.

Dinwiddie was anxious to secure the Ohio region for Britain against France; consequently he supported the aims of the Ohio Company. In February 1754 he ordered a fort to be built on the site of Pittsburgh to subdue the French military presence, but his troops were beaten back by the French. In 1755 the defeat of another detachment at Great Meadows left Dinwiddie with the task of defending hundreds of miles of exposed frontier. He tackled this problem by gaining the support of friendly Indians, constructing more forts, and enticing a reluctant Assembly to grant money for the war effort. By 1757 sufficient protection had been achieved.

Dinwiddie was so disgusted with the lack of co-operation from other colonial assemblies that he recommended that the Westminster parliament should impose upon the colonies a poll tax of a shilling, and a land tax of two shillings for each hundred acres to assist in financing the war. His exertions began to tell on his health and on 22 March 1757 he wrote to William Pitt the Elder asking for leave of absence to visit Bath. He left Virginia on 12 January 1758 and went into retirement, eventually dying on 27 July 1770 at Clifton, Bristol.

R. A. Brock (ed.), *The Official Records of Robert Dinwiddie* (2 vols.; Richmond, Va., 1883–4).
L. K. Koontz, *Robert Dinwiddie: His Career in American Colonial Government and Westward Expansion* (Glendale, Calif., 1941).

Portrait: oil, half-length, artist unknown: N.P.G.

Dodington, George Bubb (1691–1762), 1st Baron Melcombe of Melcombe Regis; politician and patron of the arts.

George Bubb Dodington was born in 1691, the son of Jeremiah Bubb, an apothecary, M.P., and J.P., of Whig squire stock, and Mary Dodington, a daughter of an old and wealthy Somerset family related to the Temples.

Educated at Winchester and Exeter College, Oxford, George Bubb spent two years travelling on the Continent, acquiring a lifelong taste for Italy and the rococo style. He was elected M.P. for Winchelsea in 1715, and was soon – surprisingly – appointed envoy to Spain. Here he had the difficult task of securing a share of Spanish trade for England while preventing Philip of Spain from succeeding to the French throne. There followed the Anglo-French alliance, which guaranteed the Hanoverian and Orleans successions; he then turned his attention to trade, and soon resigned his post.

In 1720 Bubb's uncle, George Dodington, Secretary to the Treasury and a founding governor of the Bank of England, died, leaving his nephew a vast estate in Somerset, and a half-built palace designed by Vanbrugh (see *Lives of the Stuart Age*). As a result, Bubb took the name of Dodington and instructed Vanbrugh to continue the work at Eastbury.

In 1722 Dodington was elected M.P. for Bridgwater. Using his wealth, his strong connections with the City, and his political influence he paid energetic court to Robert Walpole, and in 1724 was made a Lord of the Treasury. An excellent host and fine conversationalist, Dodington entertained influential figures from the worlds of politics and letters, including Walpole, Chesterfield, the elderly Congreve, and Voltaire.

The onset of middle age, a grotesque corpulence, a taste for heavily brocaded old-fashioned coats and eccentric wigs, and also a coarse humour must have contributed to Lord Hervey's description of Dodington as 'one of those unfortunate people whom it was the fashion to abuse and ungenteel to be seen with'. Few people could have quarrelled with the gentility of Frederick Louis (q.v.), Prince of Wales, however, to whom Dodington transferred his allegiance early in the 1730s, as Walpole's power was already beginning to fade; yet despite this defection Dodington shrewdly made no open opposition to Walpole's unpopular Excise Bill (1733).

Relations between politician and patron were not always cordial: in 1734, after persuading the Prince of Wales not to press for an increase in income, Dodington retired to Eastbury in a huff when he found that his key no longer fitted the doors of Carlton House and that an enormous shrubbery had been planted between the palace and his own fine house, which had been built next door. The affair fermented until 1737 when the Prince recalled Dodington and begged him to vote for the increase in the civil list. To his credit Dodington refused, but he made considerable political capital out of his refusal by earning Walpole's gratitude and a return to his old post in the Treasury.

The last twenty years of Dodington's life were spent in continual intrigue and political toadying. The editor of his diary published in 1784 describes his career as having been 'wholly directed by the base motives of avarice, vanity and selfishness'. Though this is undoubtedly an exaggeration, it is certain that while serving under Walpole he was desperately courting the opposition. After two years out of office following Walpole's fall, overtures to Pelham, the new chief minister, were rewarded with the treasurership of the Navy. Once again seduced by the Prince of Wales, he surprised Pelham by resigning his office and allying himself firmly with Frederick.

He now revealed to an astonished London a childless marriage of seventeen years' standing to Mary Beaghan. A new London house was also revealed, a magnificent marble-pillared monstrosity not far from the present Hammersmith bridge. He called it *La Trappe* and here entertained the Princess of Wales at breakfast and felt himself to be at the height of his success.

In 1751 the Prince of Wales died, leaving Dodington in political limbo, suing for the favour first of the Princess of Wales, then of an unwilling Pelham, and finally of the Duke of Newcastle. The election of 1754, in which his support for Newcastle and the King was to secure political redemption for Dodington, saw the unexpected loss of his seat at Bridgwater.

Thoughts of retirement were abandoned with the fall of Pitt's government when Dodington returned to his post at the Navy under Newcastle. Having spoken years earlier against the death penalty for mutiny, Dodington now made a brave but futile defence of Admiral Byng. Out of office within a year, he began to cultivate the rising favourite, the Earl of Bute (see Stuart, John), but his hopes of a position of power were never realized and it was not until two years after George II's death that he achieved the ambition of a lifetime when he was created Baron Melcombe. Dodington died on 28 July 1762.

J. Carswell and L. Dralle (eds.), *The Political Journal of Bubb Dodington* (1965).

J. Carswell, *The Old Cause* (1953).

Portrait: engraving, miniature, artist unknown: British Museum.

Dorchester, 1st Baron (1724–1808), see Carleton, Sir Guy.

Durham, 1st Earl of (1792–1840), see Lambton, John.

E

Edgeworth, Maria (1767–1849), novelist; one of the earliest writers of classics for children and of regional novels.

Maria Edgeworth was born on 1 January 1767 at Black Bourton, Oxfordshire. She came from a family in which educational theory and practical science were keenly discussed. Her father, Richard Lovell Edgeworth, was the eldest surviving son of a powerful Anglo-Irish family established in County Longford. The family was almost certainly a model for the family in Miss Edgeworth's best novel, *Castle Rackrent*. During his difficult marriage to Anna Maria Elers, Maria's mother, Richard Edgeworth devoted much of his time to scientific and educational interests. Throughout her life, Maria was devoted to her father and his ideas greatly influenced her work.

Maria's mother died when she was only five and, on her father's remarriage, she accompanied him and her stepmother to Ireland. The family settled at Edgeworthstown, north-west of Dublin. Maria quickly acquired the reputation of being disobedient and insolent. Her stepmother claimed that she had been spoilt and needed to be treated with more severity. It seems more likely, however, that she longed for attention and affection, which she lacked because of her father's and stepmother's preoccupation with each other. Maria was sent to school in Derby in 1775 and later to another school in London in 1780. At school she was considered an unpromising pupil, but gained a reputation among the other girls as a story-teller.

In 1782, on account of her poor health, she was removed from school and brought back to Ireland to live with her father and his third wife, Elizabeth, the sister of his second wife, Honora, who had died in 1780. Ireland made a vivid impression on her, and her excitement and fascination upon her arrival in this new landscape recurs in her *Memoirs* and novels. She attentively and sympathetically observed the daily life at Edgeworthstown and her vigorous descriptions of the locality and its people are among the chief merits of her novels. Rather shy in public, at home she was content, and with her father's encouragement and co-operation translated a French book on education, *Adèle et Théodore*. She also wrote stories for her sisters, putting them down first on a slate and then copying them out if they were well received.

Her first published work, *Letters to Literary Ladies*, appeared in 1795. It contained many of her father's ideas on education, as did her second book, *Practical Education*, which was written collaboratively with him. Encouraged by the reception of her first two publications, she became an assiduous writer. In 1796 she produced a set of children's stories under the title of *The Parent's Assistant*, full of her father's moralizing interpolations.

Castle Rackrent, her best work, did not, however, suffer such interference. It appeared in 1800. In it she displays her great love of Ireland and keen understanding of the characters in their rural setting. The next year her collection *Moral Tales for Young People* appeared, followed by a longer novel, *Belinda* (1801). Belinda was described by Saintsbury as one of the first heroines to 'break with the tradition of fainting and blushing', and regarded by him as an influence on Jane Austen.

During the temporary truce of 1802 the Edgeworths travelled to Paris, where Maria received a proposal from Abraham Edelcrantz, an intellectual Swedish count. She rejected his offer on the grounds that she could not consider leaving her country and her family. It was under his influence that she wrote *Leonora*, which was not published until 1806. After her return to England she published a further collection of stories under the title *Popular Tales* (1804), followed in the same year by *The Modern Griselda*.

By this time she had become a literary lion, and she spent several years in London at the centre of literary society. Her prodigious output during these years included six volumes of *Tales of Fashionable Life* (1809, 1812), *Patronage* (1814, her longest novel), *Harrington* (1817), and *Ormond* (1817).

In 1817 her father died, and Maria never fully recovered from the loss. She wrote nothing at all for two years, and her first literary undertaking after this self-imposed silence was to prepare for publication her father's *Memoirs*, which appeared in 1820. Suffering from depression and poor sight, she returned to Ireland, where she lived for her last thirty years, much of her time being taken up with the management of family affairs and the estate. The last of her full-scale novels, *Helen*, appeared in 1834, but she continued to write shorter tales up to her death on 22 May 1849.

Maria Edgeworth was an important forerunner of Jane Austen and the great Victorians in the field of realistic fiction, and is notable for her realistic portrayal of character and for the liveliness of her dialogue.

Tales and Novels (18 vols.; 1832–3).

Marilyn Butler, *Maria Edgeworth* (1972).

I. C. Clarke, *Maria Edgeworth: her Family and Friends* (1950).

A. Dobson (ed.), *Tales* (1903).

E. Inglis-Jones, *The Great Maria* (1959).

P. H. Newby, *Maria Edgeworth* (1950).

J. Newcomer, *Maria Edgeworth the Novelist: a Bicentenary Study* (Fort Worth, 1967).

G. Watson (ed.), *Castle Rackrent* (1944).

Portrait: engraving, by Alonzo Chappel, 1873: British Museum.

Edwards, Jonathan (1703–58), American Congregational clergyman, theologian, and philosopher.

Jonathan Edwards was born on 5 October 1703, the son of the Rev. Timothy Edwards of East Windsor, Connecticut. A precocious child, Jonathan entered Yale College in 1716. Graduating in 1720, he spent two years of theological study in New Haven, and in 1722 he became a minister in a Presbyterian church in New York. He soon withdrew from this post, and in 1724 was appointed to the office of tutor at Yale. Illness, however, forced him to resign and instead he became assistant minister to his grandfather, Solomon Stoddard, in Northampton, Massachusetts.

The strength of Edward's brand of religion, as reflected in his diary, contrasted sharply with the conventional piety of the Northampton congregation. His life at Northampton was marked by stern discipline and devoted application to study. On the death of his grandfather, Edwards took over the ministry and commenced a religious revival in Northampton and the surrounding area that received its impetus from his fiery sermons emphasizing the power of divine judgment. *A Treatise Concerning Religious Affections* (1746) is the supreme expression of Edwards's religious psychology and expounds his belief in the beauty and joy of a personal relationship with God that transcends mere emotional fervour.

The authorities were troubled by this outbreak of religious enthusiasm and Edwards's unconventional methods led to his dismissal in 1750 – for imposing tests on his parishioners to prove their fitness for admission to his congregation. In 1751 he settled in Stockbridge, where he had been called to be a missionary to the Indians. Despite acute financial difficulties he entered keenly into religious debate with his adversaries and determined to write a critique of Arminian theology. The latter task was still unfinished when he died.

In his later years Edwards returned to the philosophical questions that had preoccupied him in his youth and in 1758 he published his great work, *The Great Christian Doctrine of Original Sin Defended*. In January 1758 he accepted the post of President of the College of Princeton, where he lectured until his death on 22 March 1758, following an inoculation against smallpox.

C. Conrad, *The Theology of Jonathan Edwards: A Reappraisal* (New York, 1966).
P. Miller, *Jonathan Edwards* (New York, 1949).
P. Miller (ed.), *The Works of Jonathan Edwards* (New York, 1957–).
Joseph Tracey, *Great Awakening: A History of the Religious Revival in the time of Edwards and Whitefield* (1969).
O. Winslow, *Jonathan Edwards* (1941).

Portraits: oil, half-length, by J. Badger: Yale University Art Gallery; oil, half-length, by H. A. Loop: Art Museum, Princeton University.

Egerton, Francis (1736–1803), 3rd Duke of Bridgewater; the founder of British inland navigation.

Francis Egerton was born on 21 May 1736, the younger son of Scroop Egerton, 1st Duke of Bridgewater, by his second wife, Lady Rachel Russell, daughter of the Duke of Bedford. On the death of his father, Francis's mother remarried and the boy was largely left to his own devices. A sickly child, he showed little intellectual promise and his parents even contemplated excluding him from the succession to the dukedom. He did become Duke, however, his elder brother having died in 1748, and accompanied his tutor on the Grand Tour in 1753.

Shortly after his twenty-first birthday he became engaged to the widowed Duchess of Hamilton, but scandal involving her sister, Lady Coventry, caused the termination of the engagement, and the Duke returned to his estate at Worsley near Manchester. There he devoted himself to his dogs, whom he had sitting at table with him, to the exploitation of the coal mines on his property, and in particular to the construction of a canal between Worsley and Manchester to cut transportation costs.

Initially he envisaged a canal on conventional lines, but finally he adopted a scheme submitted by James Brindley (q.v.). The result was the Bridgewater Canal, a gravity-flow canal, one of the first of its kind in modern Britain. Over ten miles long, it crossed the Irwell Valley at Barton near Worsley by means of an aqueduct. It was opened on 17 July 1761 and immediately the price of coal in Manchester was cut by half. Thereafter it provided an attraction for visitors from miles around.

Having been so successful in this venture, the Duke and Brindley planned the improvement of the waterway between Manchester and Liverpool. After a long struggle in parliament, which was largely due to the opposition of local landowners, the Duke finally obtained sanction for the project in 1762.

The engineering difficulties were even more formidable than those encountered in the construction of the earlier canal. The new length of waterway stretched through some twenty-eight miles of bogs, streams, and tunnels and entailed the crossing of Sale Moor Moss. The Duke had also to overcome extreme financial difficulties. The canal was finally completed in 1772 and afterwards provided a very lucrative traffic.

Throughout his life the Duke promoted the development of the Grand Trunk Navigation, spending almost £220,000 on his own canals. He also extended his own estates, buying up surrounding lands and leaving almost forty miles of underground canals for the transportation of coal from the mines.

He was a stern master but was always mindful of his employees' welfare. He was careless of his own personal appearance and became increasingly eccentric: he seldom talked about anything but canals and dogs. Nor did he often write a letter. A confirmed bachelor, he died in London, after a short illness, on 8 March 1803.

H. Malet, *The Canal Duke: a Biography of Francis, third Duke of Bridgewater* (1961).

P. Mantoux, *The Industrial Revolution in the Eighteenth Century* (1928).

Portrait: wax, quarter-length, by P. Roun, 1803: N.P.G.

Elgin, 7th Earl of (1766–1841), see Bruce, Thomas.

Elphinstone, Mountstuart (1779–1859), colonial administrator; governor of Bombay, see *Lives of the Victorian Age*.

Erskine, John (1675–1732), 6th or 11th Earl of Mar; leader of the Scottish Jacobite rebellion of 1715.

John Erskine was born in Alloa in February 1675, the eldest son of Charles, 5th or 10th Earl of Mar, and his wife, Lady Mary Maule. When he succeeded his father in 1689 he found that the debts of his estate outweighed the assets, and pressure from his creditors caused him to attach himself to the party that favoured the English government. Thus he became a commissioner for the union between Scotland and England.

In recognition of his part in bringing about the union, Mar was appointed Secretary of State for Scotland. When this position was abolished in 1707 as the union actually took effect, he was appointed Keeper of the Signet and was chosen as one of sixteen representatives of the peers of Scotland.

In spite of his work for the union, however, Mar spoke strongly in favour of the motion for its repeal in 1713. In fact he soon earned the nickname of 'Bobbing John' because of the constant shifts in his political allegiance. His marriage in 1713 to Lady Frances Pierrepoint appeared to improve his Whig connections, but that same year he also accepted the office of Secretary of State under the Tories. Similarly, upon the occasion of the Hanoverian succession, Mar wrote to assure George I of his loyalty, while secretly considering the idea of supporting the Old Pretender. He finally made his position clear when, after being deprived of office, he went in disguise to Scotland. There he placed himself at the head of the Stuart supporters, managing to convince the assembly that Scotland's ancient liberties were being undermined by the English government. The standard of James Edward Stuart was raised at Braemar on 6 September 1715, and he was proclaimed King of Scotland, England, France, and Ireland. Mar was placed at the head of the rebel forces, some 2,000 men, and they marched to Perth. There they set up their headquarters, while the Duke of Argyll (see Campbell, John) and the supporters of the English government gathered at Stirling.

Mar's plan to take Edinburgh was thwarted by Argyll, and so the rebels fell back on Perth. There Mar's elaborate preparations caused a delay that has been considered by many as contributing to the ultimate failure of the rebellion. When he was finally joined by the western clans in November 1715, it was too late to take Dunblane, and so the army formed at Sheriffmuir on 13 November. On that day an engagement took place between Mar and Argyll. Mar's force was three times as large as Argyll's but the men were ill-disciplined and the battle ended as a technical victory for Argyll.

Mar returned to Perth and soon after met the Pretender, who had recently arrived from France. A royal proclamation was issued fixing the date of James's coronation for 23 January 1716, but it was clear that there was little hope of the ceremony's ever taking place, and within a month the rebellion had completely fizzled out, due in part to Mar's lack of decisive leadership, and in part to James's inability to inspire his supporters or to generate enthusiasm among the clansmen.

Together they returned to France and Mar's intrigues continued, but now he was working for his own restoration. In 1719 he openly expressed his anxiety to come to terms with the English government, yet maintained to the Jacobites that he had no intention of keeping his side of any such bargain. He encouraged a new Jacobite plot but when this was discovered in 1722, it was suggested that Mar had himself betrayed the plot in order to ingratiate himself with the English government.

Jacobite distrust of Mar grew, particularly since his association with it brought their cause into disrepute. The plans that he put to the Regent of France for the partition of the British Empire by an adjustment of the powers of the Scottish and Irish parliaments were so blatantly unpatriotic that they finally convinced the Jacobites of Mar's betrayal. In 1725 he finally severed all connections with the Stuarts.

Mar retired from public life to busy himself with architectural designs, which included plans for the improvement of communications in Edinburgh and for a navigable canal between the Forth and the Clyde.

Mar lived in Paris until 1729, when his health demanded that he move to Aix-la-Chapelle, and it was there that he died in May 1732.

A. and H. Tayler, *1715: Story of the Rising* (1936).

Portrait: Indian ink drawing, by Sir Godfrey Kneller: Scottish N.P.G.

F

Faraday, Michael (1791–1867), physicist and chemist, known for his many discoveries in the fields of electricity and electromagnetism.

Michael Faraday was born on 22 September 1791 at Newington Butts, near London. He had little formal education. His early, extremely elementary learning was gained at various schools in Newington. At thirteen he started work as assistant to a London bookseller and bookbinder to whom he was formally apprenticed for seven years. The various scientific books that passed through his hands fascinated him, and he saved enough money to buy materials for simple chemical and electrical experiments.

In 1812 he attended four lectures by Sir Humphry Davy (q.v.) at the Royal Institution. These so impressed Faraday that he expanded the notes he had taken, prepared illustrations of the experiments, and sent the bound set to Davy with a note requesting help in entering the field of science. Davy was impressed with the young man's enthusiasm, and in March 1813 employed Faraday as his assistant. When Davy left on a tour of France, Switzerland, and Italy (1813–14) to continue research on his theory of volcanic action, Faraday went too.

During his period as Davy's assistant at the Royal Institution, Faraday was placed in charge of experiments concerned with the chemistry of chlorine, glass manufacture, and the manufacture of various alloys of steel.

In 1824 he was elected a Fellow of the Royal Society, and in 1825 made an important chemical discovery by isolating benzene (which he termed 'bicarburet of hydrogen'). Faraday's contributions to science were fully recognized by his colleagues at the Royal Institution, and in 1825 he was promoted from superintendent to director. In 1827 he accepted the chair of chemistry, which had been vacated by Davy. His lectures at the Royal Institution were received with growing interest and enthusiasm. In 1826 he initiated the now familiar series of weekly talks.

His discovery of electromagnetic rotation (1821), in which a wire carrying a current was made to rotate about a bar magnet, was the start of a continuing interest in this general field. In 1831 he conducted a series of experiments that successfully demonstrated the relationship between electricity and magnetism. By winding an iron ring with two separate coils, the first of which was connected to a voltaic battery, Faraday was able to induce an electric current in the second coil. This discovery of electromagnetic induction was one of his most important contributions to science.

Faraday was the first to conceive of magnetic lines of force, and by analogy later proposed the concept of electrical lines of force that account for the induction of electric current from one circuit to a physically isolated circuit, without the aid of an intermediate iron core. These experiments led, in 1831, to one of his most important discoveries – the dynamo. Until Faraday's discovery, electricity was no more than a plaything for scientists, depending entirely on small voltaic cells. By generating a current within a copper disc in a magnetic field, Faraday laid the foundation for the use of electricity as a source of energy. In 1834 he presented his laws of chemical affinity at the molecular level that account for the phenomenon of electrolysis. The terms that Faraday coined – 'anode', 'anion', 'cathode', 'cation', and 'electrode' – are still used today. In June 1832 Oxford University conferred upon him the degree of Doctor of Civil Law, and in December 1835 the British Government granted Faraday an annual pension of £300.

Faraday's contribution to the understanding of dielectrics was fundamental, as it was his own conception. He conducted important experiments into the specific inductive capacity (now called relative permittivity) of various materials, and coined the word 'dielectric' to indicate the nature of the resistance offered by these materials to the flow of electric current. His name is commemorated in the unit of electrical capacity – the faraday.

In 1845 Faraday made his last great discovery, the effect of magnetism on polarized light. He found that when plane-polarized light was passed through a specimen of heavy optical glass (borate of lead), it underwent a rotation of its plane of polarization. This phenomenon is known today as the 'Faraday effect'.

Among his many published works, the greatest is the collection of his various papers for the Royal Society, *Experimental Researches in Electricity* (1844–55). He also published *Chemical Manipulation, Being Instructions to Students in Chemistry* (1827; 1830; 1842), *Experimental Researches in Chemistry and Physics* (1859), and *Lectures on the Chemical History of a Candle* (1861), the last being an expansion of one of his notable scientific lectures for children.

In 1858 Faraday was given a house in

Hampton Court. His mental powers gradually declined, forcing him to abstain from further active scientific research. He died at home on 25 August 1867, and was buried in Highgate Cemetery.

J. Kendall, *Michael Faraday* (1955).

T. Martin, *Faraday* (1934).

T. Martin (ed.), *Faraday's Diary* (8 vols.; 1932–6).

S. P. Thompson, *Michael Faraday: His Life and Work* (1898).

J. Tyndall, *Faraday as a Discoverer* (1868, reprinted 1961).

L. Pearce Williams, *Michael Faraday* (London and New York, 1965).

L. Pearce Williams (ed.), *The Selected Correspondence of Michael Faraday* (2 vols.; 1971).

Portraits: oil, half-length, by T. Phillips, 1841–2: N.P.G.; marble bust, by T. Brock after J. H. Foley, 1877: N.P.G.; bust by A. L. Vago, 1882: Science Museum.

Field, John (1782–1837), pianist, teacher, and composer; creator of the nocturne.

John Field was born on 26 July 1782 in Dublin, the son of Robert Field, a violinist, and his wife Grace. He was born into a notable musical family, his grandfather having been a church organist and keyboard teacher – it was he who gave the boy his earliest musical training. His father instructed him in the piano, and after much hard work John was deemed fit to receive tuition from the Italian musician, Tommaso Giordani. He made his official début as a pianist at one of Giordani's concerts when he was only nine. Field's earliest compositions date from the same year (1792): three piano pieces based on Irish airs and popular songs by Giordani and a Hornpipe with Variations.

In 1793 the family moved to England and settled in London. On 10 August 1793 the *Norfolk Chronicle* announced that 'Master Field' would 'play a Concerto on the Grand Piano Forte at the Evening Concert, who, though only ten [*sic*] years of age, is said to be as celebrated a performer on that instrument as any now in London.' His official London début took place the following November when, in the presence of the Prince of Wales, Field played in a concert in aid of the 'Distressed Spittalfields Weavers' at the London Tavern. Another concert followed in May 1794, and then nothing for the next five years. On 7 February 1799, Field played his First Piano Concerto at the Haymarket Theatre.

In 1802, when Clementi, by now a flourishing instrument manufacturer, was embarking on his second tour of Europe, he took Field, already an established virtuoso, with him. The two men visited France, Germany, and Russia, arriving in St. Petersburg in December.

Clementi remained a few months only in Russia, but Field decided to stay, settling in St. Petersburg. He declined a court position but accepted a number of aristocratic pupils and developed a brilliant reputation as a pianist. But his enormous success greatly undermined his character and for some years he led a Bohemian existence, punctuated by love affairs that intrigued and scandalized St. Petersburg. In 1810 he married a French lady, Mlle Percheron de Monchy, one of his pupils, and they gave a number of concerts together. They separated, however, not long after the birth of a son.

During these years Field composed a large number of works including his first nocturnes. These dreamy pieces, full of beautiful melody, were published in 1814 and his first four piano concertos followed in 1815–16.

In 1822 Field moved to Moscow. His drinking and scandalous affairs were undermining his career. Though he commanded high fees as a performer he did little work. In 1832 he accepted an invitation from the Philharmonic Society to play in London and performed there in February and March. He also attended Clementi's funeral at Westminster Abbey. Later that year he met Mendelssohn and was encouraged to resurrect his career as a virtuoso pianist. He played in Paris in December 1832 and then began a concert tour, travelling to Brussels, Toulouse, Marseilles, Lyons, South Germany, Geneva, Milan, Florence, Venice, and finally to Naples, where he was taken seriously ill. Here in 1835 he was found by a noble Russian family who took him with them back to Russia. Though he seemed to be completely cured, a bronchial ailment in November 1836 severely weakened him and he died on 11 January 1837.

John Field has been called 'the only British composer of international weight in a period of two centuries or more'. Through his teaching and composition he anticipated and influenced major keyboard composers, particularly Chopin, and in his use of Russian folk melodies, Glinka and 'The Mighty Handful'. His brilliance as a pianist was legendary, though his style of playing, revolutionary in 1800, was to be regarded as old-fashioned by the time of his death.

C. Hopkinson, *Thematic Catalogue of the Works of John Field* (1961).

Patrick Piggot, *The Life and Music of John Field, 1782–1837, Creator of the Nocturne* (1974).

Nicholas Temperley, 'John Field's Life and Music', *Musical Times* (May 1974).

Portrait: engraving, quarter-length, by Carl Mayer: British Museum.

Fielding, Henry (1707–54), novelist; author of *Joseph Andrews* and *Tom Jones*, perhaps the finest comic novels of the eighteenth century.

Henry Fielding was born on 22 April 1707 at Sharpham Park, Somerset. He came of a well-connected family. His father's relations included the Earls of Desmond and of Denbigh, and his mother was the daughter of Sir Henry Gould, a High Court judge. In 1710 the Fieldings moved to East Stour in Dorset, where Henry was educated by a local parson – said to be the model for Parson Trulliber in *Joseph Andrews* – until his mother's death in 1718. Fielding was then sent to Eton. He left college at seventeen but did not go to university; instead, in 1725, after a failed elopement with a local heiress, he went to London where he took to the career of a dramatist. His first play, *Love in Several Masques*, first produced at Drury Lane in 1728, was not a success.

Fielding went abroad to study at Leiden University, but stayed less than a year, for his father could no longer keep up his allowance. Returning to London in 1730, he embarked on writing comedies, farces, and translations from Molière as a means of earning his living. In four years he wrote at least fourteen plays, none of which is significant.

In 1734 the handsome, good-natured Fielding married Charlotte Cradock, a Salisbury beauty who is supposed to have been the model for his later romantic heroines, particularly Sophia Western. In 1736 Fielding returned to London, where he became manager of the Haymarket Theatre. Here he produced two satires of his own, *Pasquin (A Dramatic Satire of the Times)* and *The Historical Register for the Year 1736.* Both were highly critical of the Walpole administration, and the government took umbrage; the Licensing Act of 1737 was passed, restricting the number of theatres and reinforcing the censorship powers of the Lord Chamberlain. The Haymarket Theatre closed and so did Fielding's career as a dramatist.

Fielding, now thirty, with a wife and daughter, had no readily available resources. He decided to become a lawyer, entered the Middle Temple in November 1737, and was called to the bar in June 1740. Meanwhile during this period he continued his literary work, contributing in particular to *The Champion*, a rather poor imitation of *The Spectator*, of twenty-five years earlier. After qualifying, Fielding started to practise as a barrister both in London and on the Western Circuit. His real interest, however, still lay in the literary world, and in 1740 his life was completely changed by the publication of *Pamela, or Virtue Rewarded* by Samuel Richardson (q.v.). Fielding, who had something of a reputation both as a libertine and a straight talker, was infuriated by Richardson's primness and his heroine's obsessive concern with her virtue and virginity. It is highly probable that Fielding wrote or had a hand in the anonymous parody *An Apology for the Life of Mrs. Shamela Andrews* that appeared in 1741, but in any event he certainly set to work on a further parody, in which Pamela's brother, Joseph, enters domestic service and is subjected to the advances of *his* employer, Lady Booby. However, Fielding soon lost interest in the satire, and most of the novel is concerned with the ridiculous adventures of Andrews and his friend Parson Abraham Adams, as they journey through the counties and inns of England.

The novel also contains several gibes at the poet laureate Colley Cibber (q.v.), whom Fielding disliked intensely.

Joseph Andrews (1742) was a great success and its author followed up his advantage with a second novel. *The Life of Jonathan Wild the Great* may have been written before *Joseph Andrews*, although it was not published until 1743. It purports to illustrate that greatness without goodness is no better than badness, by recounting the career of a 'great' rogue.

Despite his law practice and some theatrical hackwork for David Garrick, Fielding's circumstances were not always easy. His profligate habits, especially his drinking, brought on severe attacks of gout. Moreover, the death of one of his children was followed shortly afterwards by that of his wife. Fielding's grief at her death was intense, and his friends feared for his sanity. His troubles were further aggravated by debt and some conflict with the bailiffs. Yet at about the time of the publication of *Jonathan Wild*, Fielding also published *A Journey from this World to the Next*, a satirical account of his soul's journey by stagecoach to the other world, which demonstrates, if nothing else, an irrepressible liveliness even in the face of the most intolerable adversity.

By 1747, however, Fielding's fortunes were improving. Having taken up political journalism during the Jacobite rebellion of 1745, in support of the government, he was probably receiving a pension by the late 1740s. In 1747 he married his first wife's maid, Mary Daniel, and a year later an old schoolfriend and patron, Lord Lyttelton, secured for him an appointment as magistrate for Westminster. He took his duties as justice of the peace seriously, and acquired a reputation as a fair judge and in some matters a reformer. A year before his death he published 'a proposal for making an effectual provision for the poor'; in 1751, together with his friend William Hogarth (q.v.), he persuaded the government to place some restrictions on the availability of cheap gin, to the influence of which some of the excesses and crimes of the poor were traced. In May 1749 he was made chairman of quarter sessions, while his perceptiveness was so respected that difficult cases were sometimes referred to him for an opinion.

Long before his appointment as a magistrate, however, Fielding had been labouring at his finest and most richly comic novel, *Tom Jones, or the History of a Foundling*. This is the true sequel to *Joseph Andrews*, showing a great similarity to it in style and structure, but being fuller, more inventive, and certainly at least as lively. Fielding had probably started the book in 1742 or 1743, shortly after the publication of *Joseph Andrews*, and had laboured at it throughout the most troubled period of his life. Yet he did not allow his personal troubles to affect his writing; indeed, the fictional world of the novel had become a welcome refuge for the writer.

Tom Jones himself is both sufficiently complex to be real and at the same time a classic example of the naturally decent fellow whose honesty and straightforwardness constantly land him in trouble. Education is seen as little more than a training in hypocrisy, at odds with the innate goodness of a character such as Tom's. As in *Joseph Andrews*, the setting of much of the novel is the countryside, the highways, and the inns of England, with the close of the book located in London, where there is a grand reconciliation of practically the entire cast. *Tom Jones* marks a considerable advance in comic realism and in romantic characterization that is an effective contrast to the prim and dull seriousness of Richardson's novels.

The novel was finally published on 28 February 1749. It was followed in 1751 by *Amelia*, the least successful of Fielding's novels. This is altogether more sombre than his other writing, much of it being devoted to exposing some of the evils of the time. In 1752, under the pseudonym 'Sir Alexander Drawcansir', he founded *The Covent Garden Journal*, which appeared twice a week for a time. One issue was devoted to an attack on Smollett (q.v.), who replied with a scurrilous pamphlet in which Fielding was described as 'Habbakuk Hilding, Justice, Dealer, and Chapman'.

Fielding's health was now in decline. Recurrent attacks of fever and gout had broken him, and by the spring of 1754, after a severe winter, it became clear that he must move to a warmer climate. Accordingly he and his family embarked for Portugal, reaching Lisbon in August 1754. He amused himself by writing an account of the voyage (published posthumously), a good-humoured work which contained some interesting autobiographical comments. The removal proved to be of no avail, however, and within two months Henry Fielding died, aged forty-seven, on 8 October 1754.

Despite his earnings from writing, his estate proved only large enough to cover his debts. His early memorialists portray him as a hard-drinking, hard-living man with a tremendous zest for life, and although Victorian biographers tend to stress his good works as a magistrate, it is probable that these earlier writers are the most accurate. Undoubtedly Fielding was a man of justice and fairness, but the creator of Tom Jones and Joseph Andrews surely did have a zest for the pleasures of life as well as a detestation of hypocrisy and meanness. From such characteristics as these his books derive a liveliness and popularity that have not faded in more than 200 years.

R. W. Baker (ed.), *Shamela* (Berkeley, 1953).
M. C. Battestin (ed.), *Joseph Andrews* (Oxford and Middletown, Conn., 1967).

Fredson Bowers and M. C. Battestin (eds.), *Henry Fielding: Complete Works* (in prep.).
W. B. Coley *et al.* (eds.), *Complete Works of Henry Fielding* (Oxford and Middletown, Conn., 1967–).
I. Ehrenpreis, *Fielding: 'Tom Jones'* (1964).
G. E. Jenson (ed.), *The Covent Garden Journal* (2 vols.; New Haven, 1915).
M. Johnson, *Fielding's Art of Fiction* (Philadelphia, 1961).
J. MacAlpine (ed.), *Tom Jones* (1966).
C. J. Rawson (ed.), *Fielding* (1968).
H. E. Pagliaro (ed.), *The Journal of a Voyage to Lisbon* (New York, 1963).
R. Paulson (ed.), *Fielding: A Collection of Critical Essays* (New Jersey, 1962).
Andrew Wright, *Fielding: Mask and Feast* (1965).

Portrait: engraving, quarter-length, by J. Basine after a drawing by W. Hogarth: British Museum.

Finch, Daniel (1647–1730), 2nd Earl of Nottingham; Tory politician, see *Lives of the Stuart Age.*

Fitzherbert, Maria Anne (1756–1837), known as 'Mrs. Fitzherbert'; wife of George IV.

Maria Anne Smythe was born in Hampshire in 1756, the daughter of Walter Smythe of Brambridge, Hampshire. Little is known of her childhood except that she was once taken to Paris and met Louis XV. She married Edward Weld of Lulworth Castle, Dorset, in 1775, but he died the same year. In 1778 she was married again to Thomas Fitzherbert of Swynnerton, Staffordshire. After his death in 1781 she moved to Richmond.

She first met the Prince of Wales (later George IV) in 1785, and he immediately fell in love with her. She went abroad to try and escape his attentions but after a short stay in Holland and Germany she reluctantly accepted his offer of marriage. They were married on 21 December 1785 in her drawing room by a clergyman of the Church of England, though she was in fact a Roman Catholic.

From the very outset the marriage was declared invalid on two counts. First, by

the Marriage Act of 1772 no member of the royal family under twenty-five years of age could legally marry without the King's consent, and second, the Act of Settlement of 1701 declared that if the heir apparent married a Roman Catholic he forfeited his right to the crown. Yet though the marriage was thus invalidated Mrs. Fitzherbert was always accepted in the society of the time as the Prince of Wales's wife, even after his marriage to Caroline of Brunswick in 1795.

As the years passed the Prince gradually lost interest in Mrs. Fitzherbert, and in 1803 at a dinner given in honour of Louis XVIII she received the final affront. She was told that she had no fixed place at table and must sit according to her rank, that is, as plain Mrs. Fitzherbert. After this insult she retired from court on an annuity of £6,000 a year.

Mrs. Fitzherbert was probably the only woman to whom George IV was ever sincerely attached. He asked for her during his last illness and died, in 1830, with her portrait round his neck. Mrs. Fitzherbert herself died at Brighton on 29

March 1837. The true facts of her relationship with the King were for a long time kept hidden from the public.

A. Aspinall (ed.), *The Correspondence of George, Prince of Wales* (6 vols.; 1963–9).
R. Fulford, *George IV* (1949, rev. ed.).
Christopher Hibbert, *George IV, Regent and King* (1973).

Portraits: oil, half-length, by T. Gainsborough: B.P.C. Library/California Palace of the Legion of Honor; engraving, half-length, artist unknown: Mansell Collection; water-colour, miniature, by Richard Cosway: Wallace Collection.

Fitzroy, Augustus Henry (1735–1811), 3rd Duke of Grafton; statesman who led the government at the time of the Wilkes crisis and the controversy over the American tea duty.

Fitzroy was born on 1 October 1735, the grandson of Charles Fitzroy, 2nd Duke of Grafton. He was educated at Westminster School and Peterhouse, Cambridge, where he obtained an M.A. in 1753 under the title of the Earl of Euston, but declined the degree of LL.D., being unwilling to subscribe to the articles of the Church of England. In December 1756 he entered parliament as M.P. for Bury St. Edmunds, Suffolk, and ón succeeding to the dukedom in 1757 was immediately created Lord Lieutenant of Suffolk, which position he held until 1763, and again from 1769 to 1790.

Grafton was appointed a Lord of the Bedchamber in 1756 but resigned in 1758. On the accession to power of Lord Bute (see Stuart, John), he joined the opposition and by 1763 had risen to the front rank of politics. In July 1765 Grafton became Secretary of State for the Northern Department under Rockingham, but in May 1766 he resigned, stating that his party 'wanted strength, which one man only could supply'. This man was William Pitt the Elder (q.v.), and after the bulk of Rockingham's supporters resigned, Pitt reluctantly accepted the Privy

Seal. He decided to direct affairs from the Lords as Earl of Chatham, and Grafton accepted the post of First Lord of the Treasury.

At first Grafton relied heavily on Chatham, but after March 1767 the latter's illness and subsequent lack of sympathy and support caused a rift between the two men. Opposition built up within parliament – indeed, within the cabinet itself – during the spring, and by May there was a majority of only three in the Lords. Grafton was now forced to assume more responsibility for the administration.

In September 1767 Lord North (q.v.) became Chancellor of the Exchequer; Lord Gower and members of the party headed by the old politician, John Russell, 4th Duke of Bedford, were brought in in December to strengthen the government. In addition, Grafton felt a strong personal sense of loyalty toward George III, whose support he enjoyed. However, two major problems beset his ministry.

The first concerned the constitutional crisis stirred up by the radical journalist, John Wilkes (q.v.), which began in 1768 and continued until long after Grafton had resigned his position as leader of the government, a resignation probably hastened by his inability to cope with Wilkes.

The second difficulty involved the port and tea duties levied on the American colonists. Grafton thought these should be repealed, but the cabinet voted against him.

While still in power Grafton began to neglect affairs of state in favour of his country interests. As a result he became the target of considerable adverse criticism from 'Junius' (q.v.) and Horace Walpole.

Public and private difficulties often brought Grafton to the verge of resignation during his years of office but,

though a shy and politically unambitious man, he regarded it as his duty to endeavour to keep control. In October 1768 Chatham resigned the Privy Seal, but late in 1769 he re-emerged in opposition. The Cabinet was again divided. Some prominent members resigned; Yorke, the newly-appointed Chancellor, died; and Grafton eventually decided to leave office. He resigned early in 1770.

The King considered Grafton's resignation a desertion, and put pressure on him to return to public life. His reluctant acceptance of the Privy Seal in Lord North's administration (June 1771) evoked a variety of comment. Grafton later said that he had accepted this office in the hope of preventing the quarrel with America from being pushed to extremes. However, by 1775 he felt he could no longer form part of the government in view of its policy of coercion towards America, and he resigned in November of that year.

Grafton was again Lord Privy Seal in Rockingham's ministry (1782–3) but resigned on the accession of Shelburne, and finally went into retirement. He died at Euston Hall, Suffolk, on 14 March 1811, and was buried at Euston a week later.

In later life Grafton developed an interest in religious inquiry after reading some of Bishop Watson's tracts. He wrote *Hints submitted to the serious attention of the Clergy, Nobility, and Gentry, by a Layman* (1789), *The Serious Reflections of a Rational Christian from 1788 to 1797* (1797), and a *Memoir*. He also paid for the printing of 700 copies of an edition of Griesbach's Greek New Testament in 1796.

Sir W. Anson (ed.), *Autobiography of the Third Duke of Grafton* (1898).

Portrait: oil, miniature, by Pompeo Batoni: N.P.G.

Flaxman, John (1755–1826), sculptor and book-illustrator.

John Flaxman was born on 6 July 1755 at York, the son of a successful maker of plaster casts. He was a deformed and sickly child, and so had little conventional schooling; instead he spent his time making models or reading the classics in a corner of his father's Covent Garden shop. At the age of twelve he won a first prize from the Society of Arts for a medal design. By 1770 he was not only studying at the Royal Academy, but also exhibiting his drawings there. From 1775 Flaxman was employed by Josiah Wedgwood to design cameo wares, and it was at this time that he began an intensive study of classical Greek vases, which profoundly influenced his later style.

In 1780 Flaxman carved the first of the many superb funeral monuments on which his reputation chiefly rests, a memorial to Thomas Chatterton at St. Mary Redcliffe, Bristol. Despite his opinionated nature, Flaxman not only won the firm friendship of William Blake, but was also in 1782 married to the charming Ann Denman.

In 1787, subsidized by Wedgwood, Flaxman went to live in Rome, where he studied classical art, and visited many other parts of Italy to sketch everyday life. Flaxman's most important achievement in Italy was a long series of book illustrations, including seventy-three plates to an edition of Homer and 109 to one of Dante. These designs, with their strangely linear approach, flowing rhythms, and economy of means, demonstrated Flaxman's thorough mastery of classical idiom, in particular Greek vase-painting. Although their spirit was more homely than heroic, Flaxman's illustrations exerted an enormous influence on the neo-classical style, being admired and imitated by both Canova and Ingres.

Flaxman returned to England after seven years. Now a famous man, he was made a full Royal Academician in 1800. He wrote patriotic pamphlets condemning the French for looting Europe's art treasures, and he made a comfortable living out of funeral monuments – he was the obvious choice for the Nelson memorial (1808) in St. Paul's. His free-standing figures, however, such as Joshua Reynolds (1807) in St. Paul's, are stiff and awkward, probably because his early training in small-scale model-making did not fit him for the heroic mode. His best works were tightly-knit groups, such as the Lady Fitzharris monument (1815) at Christchurch Priory, which allowed him to combine classical form with intimate feeling. Flaxman's earnest nature also favoured figures engaged in reading, for example Dr. Warton (1801) at Winchester Cathedral.

In 1810 Flaxman was appointed Professor of Sculpture at the Royal Academy, but he proved a dull and confused teacher. In 1817 he drew some illustrations for Hesiod, which were engraved with dazzling virtuosity by Blake, and he designed a shield of Achilles based rather loosely on the description in Book 18 of the *Iliad* – it was elegant, but hardly Homeric.

The death of his wife in 1820 seriously affected Flaxman, although he continued working on the friezes for the new Buckingham Palace. He caught a bad cold and died on 7 December 1826. He was buried in St. Giles-in-the-Fields churchyard.

W. G. Constable, *John Flaxman, 1755–1826* (1927).
M. D. Whinney and R. Gunnis, *The Collection of Models by John Flaxman, R.A., at University College, London* (1967).

Works in:
N.P.G.
Scottish N.P.G.
V. & A.
Royal Academy.
Soane Museum, London.
University College, London.

Westminster Cathedral.
St. Paul's Cathedral.
Chichester Cathedral.

Portraits: oil, half-length, by G. Romney: N.P.G.;
oil, half-length, by H. Howard: N.P.G.; water-
colour, full-length, by J. Atkinson: N.P.G.; oil,
quarter-length, by G. Head, 1792: N.P.G.

Fox, Charles James (1749–1806), statesman, famous as a champion of liberty,
who conducted a long struggle of
constitutional significance against George
III.

Charles James Fox was born on 24
January 1749 in London, the third son of
Henry Fox, afterwards 1st Baron Holland
of Foxley, by his wife Lady Caroline
Lennox, daughter of the 2nd Duke of
Richmond. He was educated at a school in
Wandsworth, then at Eton, and finally at
Hertford College, Oxford (1764–6). His
father, having no regard for conventional
morality, interrupted his schooling in
1763 to take him on an excursion to France
and Belgium, where he was encouraged
to gamble. However, Fox studied
mathematics and acquired an extensive
knowledge of the classics.

His father's wealth enabled Fox to
travel extensively in France and Italy
before taking his seat in parliament in
November 1768 as M.P. for Midhurst in
Sussex. He joined the supporters of the
Duke of Grafton's administration and
soon won applause for his speeches,
especially those directed against the press
and in particular the radical journalist
John Wilkes (q.v.). He became one of the
foremost members of the House long
before he joined Lord North's administration in 1770 as one of the Lords of the
Admiralty.

In 1772 Fox resigned office in order to
be free to oppose the Royal Marriage Bill.
Joining Burke and Conway, he introduced his own Marriage Bill, but after
its rejection, re-entered the administration as a junior Lord of the Treasury.

George III already disliked the 'odious'
Fox not only for his recent opposition, but
also because Fox was a drinking and
gambling companion of the Prince of
Wales and George felt that he was a bad
influence on his son. The King therefore
insisted on his dismissal, which took place
on 24 February 1774.

Fox's debts after years of gambling
losses, then totalling £140,000, were paid
by his father, but in 1774 his father,
mother, and elder brother all died. As a
friend of Edmund Burke (q.v.), Fox soon
led the Rockingham Whigs (see Watson-
Wentworth, Charles) in the Commons, at
a time when the controversy over the
American colonies was becoming acute.
With unrestrained violence he opposed
North's colonial policy as unjust and
oppressive, and voiced his jealousy for the
rights of parliament on 24 March, when
he declared that it was for parliament and
not the crown to decide on the restoration
of the port of Boston.

While touring Ireland in the summer of
1777, Fox was advised in a letter from
Burke to join the Rockingham party, and

147

to lay his foundations 'deep in public opinion'. Negotiations began in March 1778 to bring Fox into the administration, but thinking that the King might be prevailed upon to sanction a change of both policy and government, Fox attached himself firmly to the Rockingham party, urging a coalition on Rockingham as an opportunity for restoring the Whigs to power.

In October Fox was returned as member for Westminster, and during 1781 continued his attacks upon North's administration and the influence of the King. North's majority dwindled in the face of Fox's assault on the maladministration of the navy, and in March 1782 Fox took office as Foreign Secretary in Rockingham's government. His appointment was very popular, but there was increasing discord with Shelburne over the peace negotiations with France. On 30 June Fox requested that the independence of America be unconditionally acknowledged, but the cabinet majority supported Shelburne's conditional view. Rockingham's death stopped Fox from resigning, but not for long. King George preferred Shelburne to Fox's suggested replacement (the Duke of Portland; see Bentinck, William Henry Cavendish), and Fox, Burke, Sheridan, and some others left the administration – and thereby broke up the Rockingham party.

Fox refused to enter any administration led by Shelburne, and the combined parties of Fox and North (following attempts to effect a coalition between them) defeated the ministry on a motion concerning peace on 21 February 1783. Fox had recently attacked North but now defended the coalition on the grounds that the cause of dissension – the war – was finished. Despite Fox's hopes that theirs would be a strong administration to resist royal intrigues, the Whigs were ruined,

for the nation was disgusted – caricature and ridicule were rife – and the King ultimately triumphed. Though Fox took office as Foreign Secretary with North under the Duke of Portland in April 1783, his policy of 'a continental alliance as a balance to the house of Bourbon' was thwarted by the indifference of King George and the unwillingness of Frederick of Prussia.

On 18 November 1783, Fox's bill for the reform of the East India Company's corrupt government in India aroused great opposition, which resented it as striking at chartered rights and the royal prerogative. But an additional and more cogent reason for the bill's failure was the fact that it vested the government of India in a set of commissioners elected by parliament, of whom it was believed Fox and North would be two. Alarmed that Fox might maintain control of India even if he was out of office in England, King George used his personal influence to secure the bill's rejection; his ministers were defeated in the Lords on 17 December and Fox and his colleagues were dismissed the next day. Fox was confident that the King would recall the late ministry, and accordingly procured the rejection of the East India Bill of Pitt's new ministry (23 January 1784), but the dissolution of parliament on 25 March put an end to his hopes.

Fox's popularity had now dissolved, although he maintained his seat in parliament, sitting for Kirkwall. He now went to live with Elizabeth Bridget Cane, known as Mrs. Armistead (whom he was to marry secretly in 1795), while leading the opposition actively but vainly for some years. In the summer of 1788 when Fox and Mrs. Armistead were touring on the Continent, King George became insane, and Fox, hoping that the Prince of Wales, upon his accession to the throne, would form a Foxite administration, hurried home, only to be thwarted again by the King's recovery in the following spring.

During 1789 Fox advocated the revolutionary cause, but his continued espousal of the cause during the Terror lost him first the support of Burke and then that of many of his followers, who during the summer of 1792 engaged in a scheme for a coalition with Pitt. Early in 1794 the more important of his former allies signified their intention of supporting the ministers, but Fox continued his opposition to the war undeterred, despite his unpopularity. This apparent want of political wisdom may serve to demonstrate his sincerity but it necessitated his temporary withdrawal from public life (1797–1802).

During 1802 Fox toured the Netherlands and France before returning to make a speech favouring peace, on 24 May 1803, which met with universal praise. He agreed to join Grenville, the opposition leader, and together they forced Addington's resignation. King George expressly excluded Fox from Pitt's planned administration, despite the latter's repeated requests, but on Pitt's death in 1806 the King allowed Fox to take office as Foreign Secretary in Grenville's Ministry of All the Talents. The two ministers agreed well, but Fox's health, having been deteriorating for some years, gave way, and he died of dropsy at the Duke of Devonshire's house in Chiswick on 13 September 1806. He is buried in Westminster Abbey.

Fox's uncalculating generosity of mind and his lifelong love of good living, drinking, and gambling brought him many friends, while his early oratory brought him considerable political influence. He hated any form of oppression, especially the excessive power of the crown (which he believed gave rise to the country's ills). Though he never held high office for long (Pitt, his only real rival, always provided a more palatable alternative for George III), Fox's significance in history did not die with him. From him came the idea that the crown must choose its chief minister from the party with the parliamentary majority, and in many respects it was Fox's posthumous influence that inspired the Reform Act of 1832.

J. Cannon, *The Fox-North Coalition: Crisis of the Constitution 1782–1784* (1969).

I. R. Christie, *The End of Lord North's Ministry, 1780–82* (1958).

F. O'Gorman, *The Whig Party and the French Revolution* (1967).

L. Reid, *Charles James Fox. A Man for the People* (1969).

G. O. Trevelyan, *The Early History of Charles James Fox* (1880).

J. Steven Watson, *The Reign of George III, 1760–1815* (1960).

Portraits: oil, three-quarter length, by K. A. Hickel, 1793: N.P.G.; chalk, head, by unknown artist: N.P.G.; oil, quarter-length, after Reynolds, 1808: Buckingham Palace; oil, by Sir Joshua Reynolds: Eton College; oil, by T. Hickey: National Gallery of Ireland, Dublin; plaster bust, by J. Nollekens: Scottish N.P.G.

Francis, Sir Philip (1740–1818), politician; now believed to have been the author of the 'Junius' letters.

Philip Francis was born on 22 October 1740 in Dublin, the only child of the Rev. Philip Francis and his wife Elizabeth Rowe. He followed his father to England about 1751 or 1752, entered St. Paul's School in 1753, and became a junior clerk in the Secretary of State's office in 1756. In 1758 he was secretary to General Edward Bligh, and was then attached to Lord Kinnoul on a special embassy to Portugal (January 1760).

In 1761, Francis was promoted to a principal clerkship in the War Office. On 27 February 1762 he married Elizabeth Macrabie, and later the same year he was appointed First Clerk at the War Office under Welbore Ellis.

Francis may have been writing in the papers, principally *The Public Advertiser*, as early as 1763, and he may well have been the author of the 'Enquiry . . . from the father of Candor' published 1764. This, together with an earlier 'Letter' signed 'Candor', dealt with the John Wilkes controversy. On the basis of this and other circumstantial evidence, Francis is regarded as the most likely author of the pseudonymous letters of 'Junius' (q.v.) which began to be published in 1769, although some had already been sent out privately in the previous year. Francis was to some extent a creature of John Calcraft, who as Deputy Commissionary General had made a great deal of money out of army contracts between 1757 and 1763. In 1763 Calcraft had joined the supporters of William Pitt, later the Earl of Chatham, and after Chatham's resignation in October 1768 Calcraft, by now an M.P., sought with others both to discredit the administration of the Duke of Grafton (see Fitzroy, Augustus Henry) by uniting with the Marquis of Rockingham's party and to effect a reconciliation between Chatham and Grenville. Francis 'concurred heartily' in these designs, regarding them as offering his only 'hope of advancement'. Whoever 'Junius' may have been, he was undoubtedly a fellow-traveller of Calcraft and Francis throughout this entire period.

Francis resigned from the War Office in 1772 and embarked on a continental tour, returning in December. In 1773 Lord North passed a Regulating Act for India, which provided that the Governor of Bengal should become Governor General of India under the control of a Council of Four. To this Council Francis was now appointed, along with George Monson and Sir John Clavering.

Soon after his arrival in Calcutta in October 1774, Francis came into conflict with the new Governor General, Warren Hastings (q.v.). The rivalry was born of bitterness and bitterness characterized it throughout; Hastings, ably supported by an Anglo-Indian, Richard Barwell, saw his decisions obstructed and his policies reversed by the antagonistic Francis, who formed with his colleagues Monson and Clavering a majority grouping opposed to what they saw as the corruption and greed of the entire Indian administration. Francis was a man of principle; he sought stricter control of the East India Company's territorial acquisitions in the subcontinent and also the prevention of British interference in Indian affairs. By 1777, however, Monson and Clavering were dead and Francis's opposition was ineffectual.

During 1778 Francis had an intrigue with the wife of a Swiss officer. In 1779 he accused Hastings of buying the support of Clavering's successor, Sir Eyre Coote (q.v.). In 1780 the rivalry finally led to a duel, in which Francis was severely wounded. He subsequently left India, reaching England in 1781.

Francis, rich but unpopular, became an M.P. in 1784 and soon joined Burke (q.v.) in attacking Hastings, assisting the prosecution at the latter's trial. In 1793 he became one of the founders of the Society of the Friends of the People, led by Grey.

After a period outside parliament, he gained the seat for Appleby in 1802. On the death of Cornwallis in 1805 he hoped for the post of Governor General of India, but had to be content with being made a Knight Commander of the Bath.

Francis retired from parliamentary life in 1807 after the death of his wife and two daughters. In 1814 he married Emma Watkins, daughter of a Yorkshire clergyman. He died on 23 December 1818. Industrious, talented and energetic, Francis was pedantic in his adherence to his Whig principles; but while he did much to vindicate the power of public opinion, he was too often inspired by selfish motives.

Beata Francis and Eliza Keary (eds.), *The Francis Letters* (2 vols.; 1901).

Joseph Parkes and Herman Merivale (eds.), *Memoirs of Sir Philip Francis* (2 vols.; 1867).

Sophia Weitzman, *Warren Hastings and Philip Francis* (1929).

See also references under 'Junius'.

Portrait: oil, half-length, by J. Lonsdale: N.P.G.

Fraser, Simon (?1667–1747), 12th Baron Lovat; Scottish Jacobite and chief of Clan Fraser.

Simon Fraser was born about 1667 and his place of birth was probably Tanich in Ross-shire. His father was Thomas, 10th Baron Lovat, the son of Hugh, the 7th Baron, and his mother was Sybilla, daughter of John Macleod of Macleod.

Fraser was educated at King's College, Aberdeen. After taking the degree of M.A. in 1683, he accepted a commission in the regiment of Lord Murray, afterwards Duke of Atholl and a supporter of James Stuart, the Old Pretender. In 1696 Fraser went to London with Murray and his cousin, Hugh Fraser, 9th Lord Lovat. Although a bequest of the Lovat estates had been granted to Simon on Hugh's death, Simon discovered that the estates had been settled on his father, Thomas, who succeeded as 10th Lord Lovat in 1696.

Thereafter Simon Fraser was determined to gain the Lovat title and estates. Part of his plan to achieve this was to marry Hugh Fraser's daughter, Amelia. When an attempt to kidnap her was thwarted he forcibly married her mother, the Dowager Lady Lovat. Lord Murray, now Earl of Tullibardine, was outraged and he brought proceedings against Fraser in the Court of Justiciary in 1698. He was found guilty of treason and sentenced to death, and as a result was obliged to take refuge on the Isle of Skye.

It was there that he illegally assumed the title of 11th Baron Lovat on the death of his father in 1699.

Outlawed for a year, he was granted a pardon by King William in 1700. However, in 1701 Lovat was summoned before the High Court when it was made known that he had paid two visits to the exiled court of James Stuart at St. Germain.

On the death of William in 1702, Lovat crossed to France for his own safety. He obtained an audience with Louis XIV of France and proposed that he and the Jacobites would raise an army of 1,200 men if the French king would lend forces in support. The Jacobites themselves were suspicious of Lovat's loyalty, however, and he was sent to Scotland in 1703 to obtain support from among the other clans.

The Highlanders were distrustful, especially when it was discovered that Lovat had betrayed his enemy, Murray, to Queensberry, the head of the Scottish ministry. Lovat denied his treachery, but when he returned to France he was nevertheless seized and imprisoned.

Meanwhile Amelia had married Alexander Mackenzie, who in 1702 gained a decree from the Court of Session settling the Lovat estate on himself and the title on his wife. The Fraser clan, incensed at such a move, plotted to free their chief, who finally managed to escape and return to Scotland in 1715.

He now considered it wise to support the English government and was instrumental in breaking the main part of the Jacobite rebellion in 1715. His services were so valuable to the government that he was granted a full pardon on 10 March 1716.

For the next fourteen years he struggled to regain his rights as Lord Lovat, aided by the eminent lawyer, Duncan Forbes of Culloden. Finally in 1730 he became the

12th Baron Lovat, but the legal bargaining continued for another three years. At the end of that time a compromise was reached by which Amelia's son, Hugh Mackenzie, was compensated with a considerable sum of money in return for a renunciation of his claims to the Lovat estates.

While Lovat continued to support the government he was given command of the Highland Regiment and also granted the position of Sheriff of Inverness. Such honours did not satisfy his ambition, however, and in 1737 he resumed communications with the Jacobites. In 1740 Lovat's efforts for the Stuart cause were rewarded when he was secretly made Duke of Fraser. Not unnaturally, the English government expressed displeasure at his change of allegiance and the honours and offices it had bestowed on him were removed.

When Prince Charles Edward landed in Scotland in 1745 with only a few troops Lovat acted cautiously, and it was not until after the victory at Prestonpans in 1745 that he openly declared for the Stuart cause. Thereupon he immediately became a hunted man. He was seized at his castle on 11 December 1745, and though he escaped within a month, all attempts to withdraw from any association with the Jacobites failed. His son stubbornly refused to withdraw his support for the Stuarts.

After the Jacobites were defeated by the English at Culloden in 1746 Lovat was forced into hiding on an island in the Lake of Morar on the western coast. There he was discovered, conveyed to London with his fellow Jacobite rebels, and lodged in the Tower. Tried before the House of Lords, he was found guilty of high treason on 18 March 1747.

During his life Lovat had become famous as a wild Highlander, and an immense crowd gathered to watch his execution at Tower Hill on 9 April 1747. Before laying his head on the block he quoted Horace: *Dulce et decorum est pro patria mori*, claiming that he died a faithful member of the Holy Catholic Apostolic Church. He had hoped to be buried in the family tomb at Kirkhill but he was interred, like his fellows, in the Tower.

W. C. Mackenzie, *Simon Fraser, Lord Lovat* (1908).
Sir C. A. Petrie, *The Jacobite Movement* (2 vols.; 1932).
A. and H. Tayler, *1715: Story of the Rising* (1936).

Portrait: engraving, after an etching by William Hogarth: Scottish N.P.G.

Frederick Louis (1707–51), Prince of Wales during the reign of his father, George II, and father of George III; a consistent opponent of Sir Robert Walpole and of George II's other ministers.

Frederick Louis was born in January 1707 in Hanover, the eldest son of George, then Electoral Prince of Hanover, and Caroline of Ansbach. George's peppery, obstinate, and humourless temperament made for poor relations between him and his son from the very beginning, though this was not to come to a head until much later. In the meantime, Frederick received honours: in 1714, upon the succession of his grandfather as George I, he became Duke of Gloucester, and in 1718 he was made a Knight of the Garter.

Upon George II's accession in 1727, Frederick was made Duke of Cornwall. He came to England in 1728 to a warm reception from the English nation and a markedly cold one from his father. In 1729 he was made Prince of Wales.

The mutual hatred grew and became the scandal of the reign. Undoubtedly part of the trouble stemmed from Frederick Louis's own mental underdevelopment. But he was an annoyance not only to his father; Queen Caroline is alleged to have said of him: 'My dear firstborn is the greatest ass, and the greatest liar . . . and the greatest beast in the whole world, and I heartily wish he were out of it.'

In 1735 Frederick retaliated by writing, or instigating the writing of, the *Histoire du Prince Titi*. The following year two English translations of this work appeared, and in it the King and Queen were grossly caricatured. Rivalry between Frederick and his father was manifested publicly over the 'Tweedledum Tweedledee' controversy, when George patronized Handel and his company and the Prince supported Buononcini.

Moreover, Frederick also entered into negotiations with the Duchess of Marlborough for the hand of her granddaughter, Lady Diana Spencer, afterwards the Duchess of Bedford, requesting that he should receive £100,000 for her portion. His motive was partly financial embarrassment, and partly a desire to pain his father. The scheme was narrowly prevented by Sir Robert Walpole.

The marriage in 1734 of his sister, the Princess Royal, was a matter of personal grievance to Frederick, since he had expected to be married first. George, however, now at last looked favourably upon a proposed marriage between the Prince and Augusta, daughter of Frederick, Duke of Saxe-Gotha. The marriage took place on 26 April 1736.

The question of Frederick's allowance was, unfortunately, not so happily worked out. Frederick had asked for at least £100,000 from the civil list. George offered him only £50,000. Goaded on by resentment and by the advice of his friends among the political opposition leaders, he appealed to parliament against the King. The appeal was turned down in both Houses.

The inevitable breach between father and son came in 1737, when Frederick concealed from his parents the fact of his

wife's pregnancy and ensured the absence of the Queen at the delivery of her grandchild by hurriedly removing Princess Augusta by night from Hampton Court at the onset of her labour pains. For this gross insult Frederick was banished from court and George put a ban on all diplomatic association with his son.

Finally settling at Leicester House, Frederick set up a rival court to that of his father and formed a close association with the anti-Walpole political faction. Frederick became the chief patron of parliamentary opposition. His associates included Carteret (q.v.), Chesterfield (see Stanhope, Philip Dormer), and Bolingbroke (see St. John, Henry, in *Lives of the Stuart Age*), whose express intention was the destruction of his old enemy, Walpole.

The death of Walpole's old ally, Queen Caroline, late in 1737 indirectly increased the Prince's power, inasmuch as it served to diminish that of Walpole. Two years later, Frederick's faction successfully forced England into war with Spain.

In 1742, just before his downfall,

Walpole advised the King to attempt a reconciliation with his son and thus detach him from the vehement parliamentary opposition of which he was the focus. Upon Walpole's resignation, a partial reconciliation was actually effected, but the King's decision to appoint not Frederick but his brother, the Duke of Cumberland, to take command against the Jacobite rebellion of 1745 was but one major cause of the revival of the longstanding quarrel.

On 20 March 1751 Frederick Louis died at Leicester House from a burst abscess resulting from a blow from a tennis ball. He was buried on 13 April, in Henry VII's chapel at Westminster Abbey 'without anthem or organ'. His unconstructive career is best summed by this anonymous epitaph:

> Here lies Fred
> Who was alive and now is dead . . .
> There's no more to be said.

His eldest son ascended the English throne in 1760 as George III.

J. H. Plumb, *The First Four Georges* (1956).

Portraits: oil, full-length, by B. Dandridge, *c.* 1732: N.P.G.; oil, three-quarter length, by P. Mercier, *c.* 1736–8: N.P.G.; oil, full-length, by Joseph Highmore, *c.* 1740–5: St. James's Palace; oil, by Charles Philips: Hampton Court.

Fry, Elizabeth (1780–1845), prison reformer, philanthropist, and minister of the Society of Friends.

Elizabeth Gurney was born on 21 May 1780 at Earlham in Norfolk, the third daughter of John Gurney, a Norwich woolstapler and banker. The Gurneys were a large and wealthy family of worldly Quakers. Elizabeth, more delicate, shyer, and less attractive than her six sisters, was given to endless self-criticism, as revealed in her diary: 'I am a bubble, without reason, without beauty of mind or person.' It was in such a state of gloomy self-obsession that she first heard the preaching of William Savery, an American Quaker, in Norwich. Elizabeth was overcome, and although she had moved to London she continued to correspond with Savery and soon began to use the 'plain' Quaker cap and dress and the 'thee' form of speech.

Elizabeth's aim in life was now to be 'a light for the blind, speech to the dumb and feet to the lame' and to this end she ran a school for between fifty and seventy poor children in the laundry at Earlham Hall. At twenty, after much deliberation, she married Joseph Fry, a Quaker importer of tea and spices, and determined to devote herself to marriage. But life at St. Mildred's Court in the City of London was difficult for the new wife and she attracted stern criticism from the insensitive Joseph. Yet he actively encouraged her interests outside the home, such as penetrating the poor districts of London and visiting the London Workhouse.

In 1809 Elizabeth defied custom by speaking at her father's Meeting for Burial, and within two years she was accepted as an approved minister of the Society of Friends. By 1811 Elizabeth was caring for six children, managing the large Fry family estate at Plashet near Epping Forest, arranging vaccinations for the poor, running a school, and preaching.

A visit to the women's quarters at Newgate Prison in 1813 shocked her into further activity. Three visits provided for the women's immediate needs, but it was not until 1817 that the real work at Newgate was begun. A Ladies' Association was formed which paid the salary of a 24-hour matron and persuaded the Governor of the prison to allow a school to be established and the laundry to be used as a workshop where prisoners could earn money by sewing patchworks for export to New South Wales. In 1818

Elizabeth was summoned to Westminster to report on conditions: she pleaded for female warders, for the complete separation of men and women prisoners, and for proper payment for prison work. This achieved, her attention was turned to the conditions of transportees to Australia who were borne in irons in open carriages to overcrowded ships, unsure of work or shelter when they arrived in New South Wales. Committees were set up to organize ship-board libraries and schools, irons were banned, barracks and a factory built at the disembarkation point, and Elizabeth herself visited 106 ships and 12,000 convicts.

It was this tremendous personal involvement in the lives of those she helped that impressed contemporaries. She was kind but distant towards her social peers but completely at home with convicts and social outcasts. Public life now made great claims on her, and she was received by English and foreign royalty, refusing, however, to curtsey to Queen Charlotte, whom she met in 1818. Never content to remain for long at home in Plashet, she found 'household cares a weighty burden', none weightier than her nine (surviving) rebellious children. Neither domestic nor public duties would weaken her reforming spirit: hearing of a boy frozen to death on a doorstep in the fierce winter of 1819–20 she set up a night shelter for the London poor; seeing a solitary coastguard pacing the Brighton cliffs, she persuaded the government to provide libraries for England's five hundred coastguard stations.

Joseph Fry's bankruptcy in 1828 – due to the failure of a South American speculation and increasing pressure on the private banks – meant a move from the estate at Plashet to a small house at Upton Lane, ten miles away. Active reform work continued throughout her last years despite increasing ill health. During

1838–41, her work having attracted attention abroad, she visited France, Germany, Switzerland, and other European countries. Her prison visits decreased with the years, but so great was her influence that it outweighed her presence.

As her health failed, Elizabeth visited numerous spas and it was during a stay in Ramsgate that she finally died, on 12 October 1845, with the words, 'I am safe.'

Katharine Fry and Rachel Cresswell (eds.), *Memoir of the Life of Elizabeth Fry* (1847).
R. B. Johnson (ed.), *Elizabeth Fry's Journeys on the Continent, 1840–41* (1931).
W. Monod, *Elizabeth Fry, 1780–1845* (1940).
J. Whitney, *Elizabeth Fry* (1937).

Portraits: miniature, half-length, by S. Drummond, *c.* 1820: N.P.G.; oil on panel, half-length, after C. R. Leslie: N.P.G.

Fuseli, Henry (1741–1825), original name Johann Heinrich Füssli; Swiss-born painter and writer working in England, who is best known for the exotic originality that he brought to his art.

Henry Fuseli was born on 7 February 1741 in Zurich, Switzerland, the son of a court painter. He grew up amid literary figures, but was compelled by his father to take up a career in the church. At the age of twenty he took holy orders, but as a result of a political publication in which he exposed a corrupt legal officer he was obliged to flee the country and never served as a priest. In 1763 he was in Berlin studying art, and several drawings of Shakespearean characters attracted the notice of the British Ambassador there, who invited him to England. In England the following year he was predominantly involved in acting as a hack translator of French, German, and Italian. One such work that he translated into English was Winckelmann's *Reflections on the Painting and Sculpture of the Greeks*, but he had time to write his own works, such as his criticism of the writings of Rousseau, and also to do occasional illustrations. Reynolds (q.v.), with whom he had come into contact, encouraged him to develop his artistic leanings and this he did by living in Italy for eight years and studying in particular Michelangelo. Staying at Rome and travelling elsewhere, he produced several paintings, notably *The Death of Cardinal Beaufort* (1774) and *The Oath of the Rütli* (1778).

After his return to England in 1779 Fuseli exhibited some of his works, such as *The Nightmare* (1781), which was his first success, and *The Witches in Macbeth*, who were both horrifying and fascinating. He began in 1786 his collaboration with Boydell on the latter's Shakespeare Gallery, from which emerged his *Titania and Bottom*, now in the National Gallery. He was elected a Royal Academician in 1790 but met with indifferent success with his exhibition of forty large paintings in the Milton Gallery in 1799. At the same time he was appointed professor of painting at the Royal Academy schools, where Etty, Haydon, Constable, and Lawrence were numbered among his pupils. He eventually (in 1804) obtained the appointment of Keeper of the Royal Academy, a post he retained until his death. In 1805 he left the professorship, returning to it in 1810.

He is remembered chiefly for his extravagantly imaginative, sometimes deliberately horrific works, which were later to appeal so strongly to the Surrealist and Expressionist movements in art. He never achieved the visionary quality of Blake (q.v.), although he admitted, 'Blake is damned good to steal from.'

Fuseli published a number of works in addition to those already cited. These include his *Lectures on Painting*, the first of which appeared in 1801, and his edited version of Matthew Pilkington's *Dictionary of Painters* (1805). One of the wittiest men in London society, Fuseli was also well known for his small stature. He died in London on 16 April 1825.

F. Antal, *Fuseli Studies* (1956).
E. C. Mason (ed.), *The Mind of Henry Fuseli* (1951).
N. Powell, *The Drawings of Henry Fuseli* (1951).

Works in:
Tate Gallery, London.
Courtauld Institute, London.
Goethe Museum, Frankfurt.

Portraits: oil, half-length, by J. Opie: N.P.G.; self-portrait, pencil, head: N.P.G.

G

Gage, Thomas (1721–87), general in the War of American Independence.

Thomas Gage was born in 1721 at Firle, Sussex, the second son of the 1st Viscount Gage. He was commissioned into the army in 1741. During 1747–8 he served in Flanders, becoming a lieutenant colonel in 1751. In 1754 he took his regiment to America as part of an expedition commanded by General Braddock, dispatched to thwart the French attempts to seal off the British colonies from the western lands. In an unsuccessful attack in 1755 upon the French outpost of Fort Duquesne on the Ohio, the British and Colonial forces were ambushed and suffered heavy losses, but Gage distinguished himself before being wounded. He was subsequently directed to raise a regiment of light infantry, and in July 1758 he was in command of the light infantry in General Abercromby's unsuccessful assault on Ticonderoga in the Hudson Valley.

A year later Gage succeeded to the command of Fort Niagara, which had been taken from the French a month previously (June 1759), but he evinced reluctance to take offensive action against another French post, La Gallette, when instructed to do so. He returned to a field command in Amherst's force, which played a large part in the reduction of the city of Montreal and thus completed the conquest of Canada. Gage was appointed the city's Governor and in 1763 was designated commander in chief of the forces in North America, with his headquarters at New York. He was promoted to major general in 1761 and

lieutenant general in 1770, relinquishing his command and returning to England in 1772.

In 1774 he returned to America as Governor-in-Chief and Captain General of Massachusetts, one of the principal storm-centres of the growing dissent. On instructions from the British government he established himself at Boston in May 1774 to implement the closure of the port of Boston and keep it closed until damages had been paid for the losses incurred by the notorious 'Tea Party'.

With his six regiments quartered compulsorily at Boston, Gage sought to pursue a cautious policy, trying to avoid undue provocation. The New Englanders, however, were as unresponsive to conciliation as they were to coercion, and the explosive situation now merely awaited a flashpoint.

Supposedly as an act of self-defence against a likely military coup, the Massachusetts militia had been armed and a store had been established at Concord, sixteen miles from Boston. On 18 April 1775 Gage sent a column of some 600 men to seize the store, the troops marching in during the early hours of the following day. The colonists' alarm organization effectively defeated the attempt at surprise; the column was challenged by armed men at Lexington. Though controversy remains as to who fired first, the colonists were overcome; thus the American extremists secured their martyrs and the rebellion was launched. The troops continued to Concord, where most of the store had already been dispersed, and had then to withdraw under continuous sniping to Boston. The Americans had lost ninety-three casualties, the British 273. More important, the Massachusetts Committee of Safety published their version of the clash first, even sending it by fast schooner to England, where it was printed in the newspaper twelve days before the government version.

Gage had been reinforced by additional troops, but he remained at Boston, limiting his action to a proclamation of martial law (12 June) and offering a free pardon to all concerned, except for Samuel Adams and John Hancock, the Massachusetts ringleaders. On 16 June a force of 1,600 Americans arrived by night on Breed's Hill above Charlestown, overlooking Boston across the river, and entrenched themselves. On the following day a Royal Navy vessel in the harbour opened fire without consulting Gage, and later, under cover of a naval bombardment, some 2,200 of Gage's men under Sir William Howe (q.v.) were ferried across to carry the heights for the loss of almost half their number in what became known as the Battle of Bunker Hill. It was an ill-planned attack, and Gage himself was dispirited by this Pyrrhic victory.

Two weeks after Bunker Hill, Washington arrived in Cambridge to take command of what was now called by the rebels the Continental Army, and in the summer of 1775 virtually besieged Boston. In August Gage was appointed commander in chief again but, with criticism mounting in military circles, he resigned, returning to England in October.

He was not the first commander whose ordinary abilities had failed to surmount the political difficulties of his situation, nor was he to be the last in this particular contest. His unfortunate experiences did not prevent his promotion to full general in April 1782, but he was not re-employed. He died on 2 April 1787.

J. R. Alden, *General Gage in America* (1948).

C. E. Carter (ed.), *The Correspondence of General Thomas Gage with the Secretaries of State, 1763–1775* (2 vols.; New Haven, Conn., 1831–4).

Portrait: miniature, quarter-length, by J. Meyer: N.P.G.

Gainsborough, Thomas (1727–88), one of the most talented landscape and portrait painters of the eighteenth century.

Gainsborough was born in 1727 at Sudbury, Suffolk, where he was baptized on 14 May. He was the youngest of nine children, his father being a prosperous cloth merchant. His interest and skill in drawing was soon apparent. In about 1740 his father sent him to London to study, and there he initially worked as an assistant to the engraver Hubert Gravelot. That he was influenced by the artist Francis Hayman is undisputed, but his principal influences were the Dutch seventeenth-century landscape painters, whose works Gainsborough copied and sometimes restored for London dealers.

In 1746 Gainsborough moved back to Suffolk, and married. His early work was comparatively artificial in composition and he produced, in his own words, 'imitations of little Dutch landscapes'. Such a work is *Cornard Wood* (now in the National Gallery), painted in 1748. In the following year Gainsborough attempted his first group portrait, and it remains one of his most outstanding. The doll-like *Mr. and Mrs. Andrews* is an unsophisticated portrait with a fresh and natural approach that he rarely recaptured. In about 1750 he set up a practice in Ipswich, where he cultivated his reputation. Here his large portraits earned him a living, and such works as the portrait of William Wollaston (1759) are evidence of his already competent and mature style. At the same time as pleasing the paying sitter, Gainsborough also painted to please himself, and his own private masterpieces, such as *The Painter's Daughters Chasing a Butterfly*, completed in 1755–6, reveal his sympathetic and tender approach.

When in 1759 he moved with his family to Bath, his success and popularity as a portrait painter were immediate. So constant was the demand for his portraits that he rarely found time to paint landscapes. Throughout the 1760s Gainsborough regularly exhibited in London, first at the Society of Artists and, subsequent to his election as a founder member, at the Royal Academy.

He attempted to popularize his informal full-length portraits, but his fashionable clientele demanded more elegant, solemn compositions. Soon after his arrival in Bath he produced his first full-length female portrait, that of Mrs. Philip Thicknesse. The portrait of Mrs. William Henry Portman (1767) is an impressive study of character interpretation. He continued to live and work in Bath until 1774, when he moved to London permanently, and set himself up in a substantial house in Pall Mall as a rival to Reynolds (q.v.).

In London, Gainsborough's landscapes became even more artificially composed than previously. He constructed small models made of moss, glass, and pebbles, which he set up in his studio, and from them he composed some of his best-known landscapes. His work impressed Horace Walpole and, according to Constable, caused 'tears in our eyes'.

By 1780 Gainsborough had become the royal favourite, and his portrait of Queen Charlotte is said to be one of his masterpieces. One of his finest male portraits of this time is that of Johann Christian Fischer, an oboe-player, and one of his most famous is *The Blue Boy*, now in California.

Gainsborough's output was massive. He executed over 700 portraits, of which

125 were full-lengths, and he produced almost 300 landscapes, besides an enormous quantity of landscape drawings. Reynolds best describes Gainsborough's style:

All those odd scratches and marks which, on a close examination, are so observable ... and which even to experienced painters appear rather the effect of accident than design; this chaos, this uncouth and shapeless appearance, by a kind of magic, a certain distance assumes form. ...

Towards the end of his career, Gainsborough experimented on 'fancy pictures' such as *A Girl with Pigs* and *The Woodman*, depicting pastoral scenes and subjects. His death came suddenly, on 2 August 1788 in London, being caused by a cancerous tumour in the neck. Reportedly, his dying words were, 'We are all going to heaven, and Van Dyck is of the party.' Reynolds devoted the fourteenth of his *Discourses* to a critical appraisal of Gainsborough's art, a tribute he never awarded anyone else.

J. Hayes, *The Drawings of Thomas Gainsborough* (2 vols.; 1970).

E. K. Waterhouse, *Gainsborough* (1958).

M. Woodall, *Thomas Gainsborough: his Life and Works* (1949).

Mary Woodall (ed.), *The Letters of Thomas Gainsborough* (1963, rev. ed.).

Works in:
National Gallery.
National Portrait Gallery.
Tate Gallery.
Wallace Collection.
Kenwood House, London.
National Gallery of Scotland.
Fitzwilliam Museum, Cambridge.
National Gallery, Washington, D.C.
Frick Collection, New York.
Boston Museum of Fine Art.
Huntington Gallery, California.

Portraits: oil, self-portrait: Courtauld Institute, London; pencil, half-length, by F. Bartolozzi after a self-portrait: N.P.G.; oil, quarter-length, by J. Zoffany, c. 1770: N.P.G.; self-portrait, half-length, c. 1759: N.P.G.

Garden, Alexander (?1730–91), Scottish naturalist and physician, who went to live in America.

Garden was born about 1730, the son of the Rev. Alexander Garden of Burse Parish, Aberdeenshire. His education at Edinburgh was science-based, and while there he was a pupil of Charles Alston, the director of the botanical gardens. In 1753 he graduated from Marischel College, Aberdeen, and emigrated to South Carolina, where he established a practice which proved both lucrative and instructive.

Garden began to widen his knowledge in 1754 when he travelled to New York state and met Cadwallader Colden, a philosopher and fellow-botanist. On his return he stopped in Philadelphia to visit the celebrated garden of John Bartran. Meanwhile he had started a correspondence with a British naturalist, John Ellis, and through him was encouraged to write to Linnaeus, the great Swedish scientist. In time he established contact with most of the great naturalists

of the day and exchanged interesting plant and animal specimens.

Among Garden's discoveries were the adverse effects of pink root upon worms and the existence of the Congo snake and the mud eel. In 1763 Linnaeus had him elected to the Royal Society of Uppsala, and ten years later he became a Fellow of the Royal Society of London. In 1775 one of his papers was read before the Society by Ellis. It was Ellis who named the gardenia in his honour.

With the outbreak of the War of American Independence, Garden supported the loyalists and was consequently banished, and his property confiscated. His last years, spent in England, were marked by ill-health caused by the onset of tuberculosis. For a short while he assumed the duties and honours of Vice President of the Royal Society, but his failing strength soon confined him to his home in London, where he died on 15 April 1791.

Garrick, David (1717–79), actor and producer, chiefly remembered for the new realism that he brought to the art.

David Garrick was born on 19 February 1717 in Hereford, where his father, Peter Garrick, was at that time stationed as a recruiting officer. Peter Garrick lacked the means to make his family independent and so Garrick was brought up at his grandparents' house in Lichfield, Staffordshire, where his grandfather, the Rev. Mr. Clough, was vicar. At the age of ten he was sent to the local grammar school where, more interested in mimicking people than in learning, he organized a group of his friends into putting on a performance of Farquhar's *The Recruiting Officer*. His family, however, opposed this acting interest, and sent him to Portugal to learn the wine trade from his uncle, but he apparently showed little aptitude and was soon returned to England.

In 1735 Samuel Johnson started an academy for classical education at Edial near Lichfield and Garrick and his brother became the first pupils there. When, two years later, Johnson decided to try his fortune in London, he set out with Garrick as his companion (Garrick's family now wanted him to study the law). The two men had practically no money between them. Gilbert Walmsley, a friend, sent a letter of recommendation for Garrick, who was entered as a student of Lincoln's Inn but had to withdraw through lack of money. Several members of his family died within a short period of time – both his parents and then his uncle. The latter left him £1,000, with which he was able to start up a wine business with his brother, but Garrick was soon taking part in private theatricals. Among others, he made the acquaintance of Charles Fleetwood, manager of Drury Lane Theatre.

In April 1740 *Lethe, or Esop in the Shades*, a classical sketch by Garrick, was put on at Drury Lane. The part of the drunken man was taken by Charles Macklin, who was Garrick's chief companion in his first years in London, and with whom he set up a *ménage à trois*, the third member being Peg Woffington (q.v.). It was from Macklin's portrayal of Shylock that Garrick first became deeply interested in the possibility of naturalistic acting in the theatre, where recitation accompanied by formal gestures was the generally accepted style of acting at this time.

In 1741, when Macklin was giving his famous performance of Shylock, Garrick was playing a small part at an unlicensed theatre at Goodman's Fields. In his first major role there he was billed as 'a gentleman who never appeared on any stage'. Making his stage début in March,

Garrick had appeared in a mask to keep his acting interests secret. Inevitably, his pretence was shortlived.

Garrick took on larger parts later in the year and gained enough confidence to approach both Drury Lane and Covent Garden for work. He was unsuccessful, however, and went back to Goodman's Fields, where in October 1741 he made a famous appearance as Richard III. The audience was awed by the variety and strength of the moods he portrayed and particularly by the feelings of foreboding and self-conviction between which Richard is torn before the Battle of Bosworth. Quin, one of the leading actors of the time, commented nervously, 'We are all wrong, if this is right.'

Garrick took other leading parts as the season progressed and his own play, *Lethe*, was put on again. Towards the end of the 1741–2 season Garrick achieved more fame for his performance of Lear. He acted out the madness he had seen in a friend who had become insane after killing his baby daughter by accident. The following summer Garrick went to act in

Dublin, where he was tremendously acclaimed. On his return to London in the autumn of 1742 he was engaged by Fleetwood to play at Drury Lane for a salary of £500 per annum, which was more than any actor had been given before.

About this time he quarrelled with both Macklin and Mrs. Woffington. Macklin was especially bitter over negotiations with Fleetwood. Owing to lack of financial resources, Fleetwood had tried to get his actors to take a cut in salary. Macklin took the lead in persuading most members of the company not to work except on their own terms, but then Garrick, faced with unemployment, succeeded in getting an improved offer from Fleetwood, which they accepted; the offer, however, specifically excluded Macklin, who was seen by Fleetwood as the troublemaker. Mutually vituperative publications followed, and performances were disrupted. Macklin's enmity as a result of these incidents subsequently contributed a good deal to the well-known legend of Garrick's vanity, although the two actors effected a reconciliation in 1747.

In January 1745 Garrick achieved another great role as Macbeth in Shakespeare's original version, which had not been performed since the Restoration. The following December Garrick went to Dublin again, where he acted at Thomas Sheridan's theatre for the next six months. When he returned he made a few appearances at Covent Garden and agreed to act there the following season. In 1747, however, having raised £8,000, he bought half of the patent of Drury Lane, and from then on was continuously associated with that theatre until his retirement. His régime there was rigorous but also reformatory. He had plans for abolishing the apron stage, for new lighting, and for controlling the audience. He presented Shakespeare 'improved' along the lines of contemporary taste but at least freed of the worst interference of the Restoration.

Garrick married the Viennese dancer, Eva Maria Violetti, in 1749. Probably as a result he lost his best actress, Mrs. Cibber, who went, as Mrs. Woffington had done, to Covent Garden. Barry, his most promising young actor, also left soon after, in spite of being allowed to play Othello, a role which had previously been Garrick's. Competition with the rival theatre of Covent Garden was keen but by determination Garrick held his own. Mrs. Cibber returned to Drury Lane in 1753, but audience riots were an incessant problem there. In 1755 a riot broke out over French dancers Garrick had employed, the war with France having just begun, and in 1763 a group of men called The Town threatened Drury Lane with more violence. After this Garrick decided to leave for a time and travel on the continent. The takings of the theatre had fallen seriously and the pit was reported to be often nearly empty.

Garrick and his wife visited France and Italy. He returned to Drury Lane in 1765 and the following year he retired from the stage but continued to put on plays at Drury Lane and write plays, prologues, and epilogues. In 1776 he gave a round of farewell performances and acted again with his former great spirit. His share of the patent of Drury Lane was sold to Richard Sheridan and two associates. From then on he travelled about, visiting the houses of friends until his death in London on 20 January 1779. He was buried in Poets' Corner, Westminster Abbey.

D. M. Little and G. M. Kahrl (eds.), *The Letters of David Garrick* (3 vols.; 1963).
Carola Oman, *David Garrick* (1958).

Portraits: oil, half-length, studio of Zoffany: N.P.G.; oil, half-length, by Reynolds, 1768: H.M. The

Queen; pencil, half-length by J. K. Sherwin: N.P.G.; engraving, full-length, after T. Gainsborough: Shakespeare's Birthplace Trust Library; oil, by Pompeo Battoni: Ashmolean Museum, Oxford; oil, by W. Hogarth: Walker Art Gallery, Liverpool.

Gay, John (1685–1732), poet and dramatist, remembered chiefly for *The Beggar's Opera*.

John Gay was born on 30 June 1685 at Barnstaple, Devon. His family appears to have been rather impoverished, although they were of some consequence in the county. After a local education he was apprenticed to a mercer in London for a short time but during the first year of his apprenticeship he sank into a decline and returned to Devon in poor health. He recovered, and in about 1707 set out for London again, apparently to pursue a literary career. In 1708 he published his first poem, 'Wine', a rather mediocre effort in blank verse suggesting that water-drinkers are incapable of literary inspiration. The poem had some success – enough for it to be pirated in a cheap edition by the notorious Henry Hills of Blackfriars. In about 1710 he made the acquaintance of Pope, Swift, and Arbuthnot (qq.v.), and in May 1711 produced a pamphlet, *The Present State of Wit*, an account of the *Tatler* and *Spectator* and other literary periodicals. He was a member of the Scriblerus Club, an association which, under the leadership of Pope and Swift, set out to satirize 'all false tastes in learning'. Other minor poems followed, including 'Rural Sports' (1713), 'The Shepherd's Week' (1714), which started as a satire on Ambrose Philips but became a series of eclogues (poems on rural life) of some interest in their own right, and 'Trivia: or, the Art of Walking the Streets of London' (1716).

In the early eighteenth century, literary success on any large scale was almost impossible to a writer who had not managed to acquire a rich and noble patron. From 1712 onwards Gay appears to have made considerable efforts to ingratiate himself with various aristocrats: in 1713 he was appointed secretary to the Duchess of Monmouth, and in 1714 became secretary to Lord Clarendon, whom he accompanied to Hanover during the negotiations for the accession of George I. In the summer of 1715 he was sent to Devon on some unspecified errand by Lord Burlington.

Burlington and other noble literati found Gay's work interesting enough to subscribe to the publication of a collection of his poems; accordingly, two volumes of ballads and occasional pieces were issued in 1720 by the booksellers Tonson and Lintot. The publication was successful and made £1,000 for Gay. He promptly invested this speculatively during the South Sea Bubble craze and made £20,000. Ignoring the advice of friends to sell, he continued to speculate wildly, lost everything, and sank into a state of morbid depression.

After this experience it was years before Gay produced anything further. In about 1723 he met the Duke and Duchess of Queensberry, who remained his patrons for the rest of his life and secured for him a sinecure as Commissioner of Lotteries, which brought him in £150 a year.

For some time now, Gay had been involved in the theatre. His first play, *What-d'ye-Call-it*, a satire on the tragedies of the day, had been produced at Drury Lane in 1714; in 1716 he collaborated with Pope and Arbuthnot in *Three Hours after Marriage*. Both plays survived the usual seven nights, but neither caused a great stir. He collaborated with Pope and others on the libretto for Handel's dramatic cantata *Acis and Galatea*, staged for the Duke of Chandos in about 1720. This had some success, but he had less luck with *The Captives*, a tragedy composed by himself

163

alone and produced at Drury Lane in January 1724. Temporarily disappointed with the stage, Gay turned to writing a series of *Fables* (1727), which became very popular and which were dedicated to the infant Prince William, later Duke of Cumberland. A second series of *Fables* was published in 1738, six years after his death.

His attention returned to the stage, and on 29 January 1728 the first performance took place at Lincoln's Inn Fields of *The Beggar's Opera*. It was instantly and enormously successful. In an age when plays rarely ran for more than seven nights, it achieved sixty-three performances in London. It was acted in almost every major city in England and performances took place as far afield as Minorca, while scenes from the play were painted by Hogarth. Intended to show the moral degradation of society, and taken by audiences as a satire on Walpole and his administration, it arose out of a remark of Swift's that a Newgate pastoral 'might make an odd pretty sort of thing'. In fact, what Gay created was the 'ballad opera', an entertainment in which spoken dialogue alternated with songs consisting of Gay's words set to popular tunes of the day. So successful was this type of production that the Italian operas proper of Handel and others suffered a serious decline in popularity.

The plot concerns the adventures of Polly Peachum, daughter of a receiver of stolen goods, who also makes an income as an informer against his clients. Polly falls in love with and marries Captain Macheath; Peachum, furious, determines to arrange the arrest and execution of his unwanted son-in-law. Macheath is duly taken off to Newgate, where he falls for Lucy Lockit, the beautiful daughter of the turnkey. Polly and Lucy battle out their claims to Macheath's affection, but all ends well as Lucy arranges Macheath's escape.

Encouraged by this success, Gay set about writing a sequel, *Polly*, in which Macheath and Polly are transported to the Virginian plantations, but the Lord Chamberlain stepped in, on Walpole's instructions, and prohibited the play's performance. Although the play could not be staged, it was published in book form and was enormously successful. The Walpole régime was seriously embarrassed; the rich and powerful in the land were divided into pro- and anti-Gay factions. Gay's patroness, the Duchess of Queensberry, was expelled from court on his account. She and her husband retired to their country house in Wiltshire, taking Gay with them.

Gay remained in Wiltshire, exercising his 'rooted laziness', for three years. He pursued a few literary schemes – or at least he wrote to Swift hinting at pursuing them – and eventually, in 1732, returned to London and the literary scene. He had written a new tragic opera, *Achilles*, and had returned apparently to supervise the staging of it. However, at the onset of winter he caught a fever and died on 4 December 1732. The production of *Achilles* continued, and Gay's last work was staged early in 1733, without any particular success. In many respects, Gay's artistic talents suffered from his indolent character, yet he was, according to his contemporaries, a man of considerable charm. *The Beggar's Opera* was adapted by Bertolt Brecht as the *Threepenny Opera* in 1928.

S. M. Armens, *Gay: Social Critic* (New York, 1954).
F. W. Bateson (ed.), *The Beggar's Opera* (1934).
C. F. Burgess (ed.), *Letters* (1966).
G. C. Faber (ed.), *The Poetical Works of John Gay* (1926).
G. C. Faber (ed.), *Plays* (2 vols.; 1923).
W. H. Irving: *Gay: Favourite of the Wits* (Durham, N.C., 1940).
Yvonne Noble (ed.), *Twentieth-Century Interpretations of the Beggar's Opera* (1975).
A. Ross (ed.), *Selected Poems* (1950).
P. M. Spacks, *John Gay* (New York, 1965).

Portraits: oil, quarter-length, by W. Aikman: Scottish N.P.G.; sketch, oil, by G. Kneller: N.P.G.

George I (1660–1727), King of Great Britain and Ireland (1714–27) and Elector of Hanover.

George Louis was born on 28 May 1660, the son of Ernest Augustus, Duke of Brunswick-Lüneburg (1629–98), better known as the first Elector of Hanover (1692–8). Through his mother, Sophia, the granddaughter of James I, and by the terms of the 1701 Act of Settlement, he was later to stand in line of succession to the English throne, but his early life was devoted to the dynastic aims in Germany of the Guelph family.

His father was concerned to enlarge the boundaries and influence of his duchy, and George Louis fully supported this ambition. In 1680 he visited England to propose marriage with the Princess Anne in order to strengthen the Hanoverian strategy by an Anglo-Hanoverian alliance, but the project failed. He was therefore married in 1682 to his cousin, Sophia Dorothea, daughter of the Duke of Celle. Their first child, the future George II, was born in 1683, and their second, the future wife of Frederick William of Prussia, in 1688. Both partners regarded the marriage impersonally and found their satisfactions elsewhere, and in 1694 George Louis disentangled himself from it by publicly arraigning Sophia for adultery, divorcing her, and confining her to the castle of Ahlden for life.

In 1698 George Louis succeeded as Elector of Hanover, and on the death of the Duke of Celle in 1705 the lands of Kalenberg also passed to him. During these years he gained military experience, serving first in the army of the Holy Roman Emperor in 1675 (taking part in Sobieski's relief of Vienna in 1683), and later joining the Hanoverian contingent that Ernest Augustus contributed to the alliance against Louis XIV of France. He particularly distinguished himself at the Battle of Neerwinden (29 July 1693).

The Act of Settlement passed by the English parliament in 1701 at first made little difference to George Louis's continental preoccupations. The outbreak of the War of the Spanish Succession in the same year saw to that, and he joined the Grand Alliance against Louis XIV in the interests of Hanover, not of England. Nevertheless, the likelihood of his ultimate succession to the English throne was now becoming a major factor in English politics. In 1706 the Regency Act made the Electress Sophia, George Louis, and his son naturalized British subjects and established a regency council which would govern the realm, in the event of the death of Queen Anne, until the Hanoverian successor was duly installed. Wisely, both George Louis and his mother refrained from any premature involvement in English politics, but in 1710 Baron Johan von Bothmar, their most trusted and discreet minister, was sent to be their ambassador in London.

At the end of 1704 Marlborough had journeyed to Hanover on behalf of the English Whig leaders to assure George Louis of their collective loyalty to the Hanoverian succession; this meeting established a personal trust, which was, however, soon forfeited by the exigencies of war. George Louis reluctantly accepted command of an Imperial army on the Upper Rhine in 1707, and was left struggling to organize it properly while Marlborough embarked upon vigorous campaigning elsewhere without the grace of prior consultation. In 1710, deprived of his chance of glory in the field, George resigned his command in disgust. However, his eminence in German affairs was signalled in 1708 by admission to the Imperial College of Electors, and in 1710 he was made Arch-Treasurer to the Empire. On 8 June 1714 his mother died; Queen Anne's death followed on 1 August.

Her passing was accompanied by frantic attempts on the part of her leading Tory ministers to preserve their endangered personal positions, with the Stuart claimant and his potential supporters hovering in the shadows. However, decisive activity by the more far-sighted of the Privy Councillors cut short the intrigues and manoeuvres before they could develop into a serious crisis and a possible invitation to rebellion. Steps were taken to secure London, Edinburgh, and the principal towns and ports, a request for a speedy arrival was sent off to Hanover, and George I was proclaimed king in the three capitals to subjects who failed to exhibit the excitement that characterized the politicians. The new monarch exhibited no excitement either – he was engrossed in the annexation of Bremen and Verden. He settled his Hanoverian affairs at leisure, and did not arrive at Greenwich until 18 September; his German entourage included his son, ministers, mistresses, and domestics.

Following the terms of the Regency Act, the regency council that had presided over the interim had been nominated by George I in advance, in a sealed list. On examination, the list was found to include those moderate Whigs and Tories who had supported the Hanoverian succession in the earlier years. It did not include the Duke of Marlborough.

On arrival, the King prepared a new list of ministers, relying on the advice of Bothmar and Jean de Robethon, previously the secretary of his Hanoverian prime minister. Robethon was a French Huguenot refugee and had been the confidential secretary of William III; he was, therefore, no stranger to English politics. His official capacity was now that of private secretary to George himself. The Hanoverian prime minister, Baron von Bernstoff, also wielded considerable influence in the new court establishment, and it was popularly supposed that the same was true of the King's principal mistresses, Ehrengarde von der Schulenburg (q.v.), later Duchess of Kendal, and Charlotte Kielmannsegge, later Countess of Darlington.

The previous principle of selection was applied to the list of ministers. Despite their majority in the Commons, only two Tories were included. Among the Whigs, Viscount Townshend (see Townshend, Charles, 2nd Viscount), his brother-in-law Robert Walpole, and General James Stanhope (qq.v.) were to prove the leading spirits in the politics of the new reign. They were quick to cement their power. The elections of 1715 yielded a strong Whig majority, for ministers had at their disposal official means to influence the polling, and with that backing they harried the Tory leaders further by impeachment. The Jacobite rising of 1715 was in the event confined to Scotland, but it served to hold the ministers together and give their exercise of power a transcendent purpose. In 1716, they guaranteed their offices by the Septennial Act, which prolonged the life of the Whig parliament beyond the customary three years.

In July of that year George felt able to return to Hanover, the government of Great Britain having reached stability. To allow him to do so, a clause in the Act of Settlement that forbade it had to be repealed, but such was the sense of security of the ministers that this was not opposed. The only practical difficulty was his relationship with the Prince of Wales, for an intense dislike, which was to be the characteristic attitude of the Hanoverian monarchs towards their heirs, made him adamant in refusing to appoint his son regent. A compromise was found by reviving the medieval title of Guardian of the Realm and Lieutenant, and severely limiting the Prince's powers, but it was clear that the King would view every official and private act of his son with suspicion and jealousy. Ministers who constitutionally depended upon the King's favour to remain in office were thus placed in a dilemma in their routine dealings with the sovereign's official representative. Furthermore, Stanhope travelled to Hanover with the King.

It was the Earl of Sunderland (see Spencer, Charles) who first sought to exploit the situation to his own advantage. Disappointed by the relatively unimportant offices he had been given in the administration, he followed the King to Hanover and deliberately stimulated his jealousy with reports of the Prince's social and political success. The latter had the advantage of knowing English; George I normally spoke French (even in preference to his native tongue) and this imposed some limitations upon political and social intercourse not encountered by the Prince. Even Stanhope fell victim to the suspicion that Townshend and

Walpole were working in his absence to supplant him and, having the King's ear, decided to strike first. In December 1716 Townshend learned that he had been removed from his secretaryship and relegated to the viceroyalty of Ireland.

The King returned to England in March 1717 and in the following month Townshend was dismissed completely, Walpole resigning in sympathy, while Stanhope went to the Treasury, forming an alliance with Sunderland, who received the coveted secretaryship. The King did not move against the Prince until November, when a private quarrel flared up between them over the protocol involved in the baptism of the Prince's second son. The King seized the opportunity to place the Prince and his wife under house arrest, and would have prolonged it had not the ministers indicated that the Habeas Corpus Act made such continental methods illegal in Great Britain. The King had to content himself with the permanent expulsion of the Prince from court and with taking the custody of the Prince's children from him.

The Prince and Princess of Wales thus of necessity set up their own establishment at Leicester House. In this way was born 'the Leicester House faction', which was to become a convention of English politics for the rest of the century. Politicians out of office found their way to the livelier rival court, in the expectation of ultimate rewards in the new reign when it inevitably came, or of trading their standing there for more immediate political gain. Townshend and Walpole were the first to avail themselves of the new device. Another result of the quarrel was the increasing absence of the King from formal cabinet councils, where he might encounter the Prince. His transactions with his chief ministers therefore took place privately in his closet, to the permanent detraction of full cabinets presided over by the monarch. This was to have important constitutional consequences in subsequent years.

Between 1717 and 1720 the two Whig factions contested for power, while the Tories were rendered progressively inactive and irrelevant. In 1720 Townshend and Walpole were able to manoeuvre their way back into office by means of a formal reconciliation staged between the King and the Prince. Apart from the prime movers, other factors in bringing about this shift of power were the desire of the ministers to secure additional assistance against the King's German advisers; the ambition of the Prince's wife, Caroline of Ansbach (q.v.), who had become a firm friend of Walpole's; a desire to strengthen her own position in the court on the part of the Duchess of Kendal (she was the principal intermediary); and the King's greed. George I's civil list had accumulated a £600,000 debt which he naturally wanted written off. Only Walpole had the necessary acumen and parliamentary standing to push through such a measure. He and his brother-in-law thus joined the administration without sacrificing the potential benefits of attendance at Leicester House, since theoretical harmony was now restored at the court.

Within a few months there was a financial crisis, when the South Sea Company's collapse (1720) ended a wave of speculation. The King himself and his mistresses had been large stockholders, and the crisis forced him to return from one of his periodic migrations to Hanover. It also brought Walpole to effective personal power. In April 1721 he became First Lord of the Treasury and Chancellor of the Exchequer. Death removed his two main rivals, Stanhope that year and Sunderland in the next. Throughout the machinery of government, supporters of the two brothers-in-law were given offices both major and minor as opportunity allowed, creating a political system which was to outlast the century, and the Tories were further loaded with the Jacobite millstone, as the result of their association with a Jacobite plot masterminded by Francis Atterbury, Bishop of Rochester (1722). In 1725, as part of his policy of increasing the scope of political patronage at his disposal, Walpole persuaded the King to revive the Order of the Bath and himself accepted a K.C.B. Whatever criticisms might be made of it, the new system assured the continuance of the new dynasty by effectively dousing the more inflammatory forms of political careerism. In 1726 George showed his gratitude to the minister who had relieved him of the tiresome burden of ordering the government of Great Britain by conferring upon Walpole the Order of the Garter.

George I had not been concerned to woo his subjects, individually or collectively. He made infrequent public appearances, toured the provinces only once, and lived simply and inactively in two rooms at St. James's Palace. One Englishwoman, Ann Brett, the daughter of the Countess of Macclesfield, was admitted to the small circle of mistresses, and in the course of time he did acquire a working understanding of the English language, but without the corresponding ability to express himself in it. After the political turmoil of the previous century, however, mutual indifference between ruler and ruled proved to be a surprisingly sound foundation on which to build a monarchy.

On 3 June 1727 George I set out for Hanover for the sixth time since his accession. He was taken ill on the journey and died at Osnabrück on 11 June. There was some uncertainty over the ultimate interment of the body, but in September it was conveyed to Hanover and given a state funeral. In England a period of formal court mourning was the only noticeable observance of the event.

J. M. Beattie, *The English Court in the Reign of George I* (1967).

J. Marlow, *George I, His Life and Times* (1973).

J. J. Murray, *George I, the Baltic and the Whig Split of 1717* (1969).

J. H. Plumb, *The First Four Georges* (1956).

J. H. Plumb, *Sir Robert Walpole* (2 vols.; 1956–61).

Basil Williams, *The Whig Supremacy* (1962, rev. ed.).

Portraits: oil, full-length, studio of Kneller, *c.*1715: Windsor Castle; oil, full-length, by unknown artist after Kneller, 1714: N.P.G.; oil, full-length, by John Vanderbank, 1726: Windsor Castle; oil, quarter-length, studio of Kneller, *c.*1714: N.P.G.; oil, three-quarter length, by G. W. Fountane: Royal Collection.

George II (1683–1760), King of Great Britain and Ireland (1727–60).

George Augustus was born on 10 November 1683, the only son of George Louis, heir to the duchy of Brunswick-Lüneburg, the future George I. In 1694 his mother was imprisoned for life by his father and their marriage was dissolved as the result of an estrangement aggravated by adultery. George Augustus was never permitted to see his mother, and afterwards came to resent the treatment she had received. In 1701 the Act of Settlement placed him in line to the English crown through his paternal grandmother; by 1705 he was naturalized and was given the Order of the Garter and appropriate English peerages. In the same year he married Caroline of Ansbach (q.v.), and their first son, Frederick Louis (q.v.), was born in 1707. As was typical among the Hanoverians, Frederick, the firstborn of seven, was almost from birth the object of his father's inexplicable hatred.

In 1708 the Electoral Prince joined the allied army campaigning against the French on the Moselle. At the Battle of Oudenarde he distinguished himself as commander of the Hanoverian cavalry

contingent under the professional guidance of General Rantzau.

Following Queen Anne's death in 1714, George Augustus accompanied his father to England, and was created Prince of Wales in September. The English were not, however, deceived about the mutual dislike that had long existed between father and son. The latter had one advantage, a better command of the English language, shared also by his wife. Their court quickly became a more attractive place than that of the King, and the more so in that they were active patrons of the arts. A centre of wit and beauty, it became also the haunt of politicians out of office who hoped to improve their long-term prospects by paying court to the heir to the throne.

Relations between King and Prince were further impaired by the existence of this rival court. The King was reluctant to leave the Prince with regent's powers when he returned to Hanover in 1716, and so revived the medieval title of Guardian of the Realm and Lieutenant with considerable restrictions upon the exercise

of the prerogative. In George I's absence, the Prince worked hard to ingratiate himself still further in his father's kingdom by assiduous attention to business and a busy programme of public appearances.

In November 1717 the baptism of the Prince's latest son provided another occasion for an outburst of mutual antagonism between him and his father. The Lord Chamberlain, the Duke of Newcastle, who had been appointed a godparent by the King, misunderstood an ill-tempered remark addressed to him by the Prince and complained to George I that he had been challenged to a duel. Without pausing to ascertain the truth, the King placed his son under house arrest, from which a group of ministers rescued him by explaining to the King the terms of the Habeas Corpus Act. The King retaliated by banishing the Prince and Princess from court, retaining their children in his own custody, and eventually – and with reluctance – rationing parental visits to one a week. The Prince took up residence at Leicester House, which became the headquarters of the opposition. He had a considerable amount of household patronage at his disposal, including safe parliamentary seats, and Townshend (see Townshend, Charles, 2nd Viscount) and Sir Robert Walpole (q.v.) were among the first to exploit the political possibilities of the situation.

An accidental result of this was that the King ceased to attend formal cabinet meetings, where he might encounter the Prince, who was a member by right and who might well communicate the business in hand to the opposition. The desire to avoid the Prince, and not the King's lack of English, was therefore the reason for this vital, if unrealized, constitutional advance.

An official reconciliation was effected in 1720, brought about by the ministers' parliamentary difficulties over the 1719 Peerage Bill, which necessitated the purchase of some opposition support, and the tactics pursued by Walpole and Caroline, who had formed a close alliance. Walpole and Townshend secured places in the ministry, the Prince recovered his proper place in court precedence, and the Princess shortly afterwards recovered her children. Thereafter, the Prince preserved a correct relationship with his father, if not a cordial one, but showed a marked coolness towards Walpole, who had made himself an indispensable minister to George I after the financial disaster known as the South Sea Bubble (1720) and had cemented his position by a judicious use of royal patronage. Walpole nevertheless still preserved his hopes for the next reign by maintaining his friendship with Princess Caroline.

Succeeding as King at his father's death on 11 June 1727, George II designated as Prime Minister Spencer Compton (q.v.), the Speaker and a Leicester House intimate. Compton declined the post, and when parliament met on 27 June Walpole proposed an increase in the civil list to support the new King's large family and make allowance for the rising cost of living. On 24 July Walpole was reappointed First Lord of the Treasury and Chancellor of the Exchequer, and Townshend Secretary of State for the North. The coronation took place on 11 October.

George II was dominated by Caroline, whom he loved sincerely, his mistresses notwithstanding, and while she lived Walpole's position was safe. For a time the opposition lacked a focus, as Frederick Louis did not arrive in England from Hanover until December 1728, when he came uninvited. The crystallization of anti-government feeling was further delayed until the new Prince of Wales was granted his own establishment. After 1737 he rented Leicester House, and devoted the rest of his life to sniping at the King from the safety of a circle of opposition friends. Princess Augusta, his wife, continued the campaign after 1751, one consequence of which was the royal suspicion and interference that was a characteristic of the reign of her son, the future George III.

Queen Caroline died in November 1737, and in the following June George installed in his household Madame von Walmoden, whom he had successfully courted in Hanover two years earlier. Walpole connived at the arrangement in the hope of preserving his influence through her, but she confined her activities to the sale of peerages; Walpole's fall, which eventually took place in 1742, was therefore now but a matter of time. Yet he maintained sufficient influence to ensure that his successors should be largely men of his own predilections, notably the Pelham brothers. Walpole's successor as First Lord of the Treasury was the King's choice, the mediocre Earl of Wilmington, formerly Sir Spencer Compton, although he remained only until August 1743. This still left out of office Walpole's most able adversary, William Pitt the Elder (q.v.).

One factor counting against Pitt was his insistence that military strategy in the War of the Austrian Succession was being directed in the interests of Hanover rather than Great Britain, and the charge was not unfounded. Willingness to share his preoccupation with Hanover was a political recommendation in George's view. Carteret (q.v.) had been brought in to 'broaden' the ministry and he certainly won that recommendation, his first success as Secretary of State being a diplomatic coup that procured a measure of security for Hanover by detaching Prussia from the Franco-Bavarian camp.

In June 1742 an allied army assembled in the Low Countries under Lord Stair. Exactly a year later, as it finally advanced into Germany, George II arrived to command it in person, accompanied by his second surviving son, William Augustus (q.v.), Duke of Cumberland. His opponent, the French Duc de Noailles, manoeuvred with greater skill and trapped George's army in front of the village of Dettingen. In a confused battle fought on 27 June, George II was in continuous personal danger as he struggled to form his troops and force his way out of the trap. Thanks to the discipline and professional skill of his men, particularly the British regiments, he succeeded and, as the last British King to command troops in battle, closed one chapter of national history with some credit for bravery if not for military skill.

Back in England, George was beset by political problems. The Pelhams now threatened to resign unless Carteret was dismissed, and in November 1744 the reluctant King was obliged to part with him in order to preserve the rest of the patchwork administration, which it had taken much effort to construct. He was in Hanover when Prince Charles Edward Stuart (q.v.) landed on the Scottish mainland in 1745, and when he returned to London in August of that year, he exercised a calming influence by his refusal to be alarmed and his intelligent participation in the hurried military preparations. The Pelhams chose that moment to resign, taking all their colleagues with them, in order to compel the King to bring in Pitt and muzzle his dangerous opposition to their rule. Failing to find successors, George was forced to accept his enemy, at first in a minor post, and then as Paymaster of the forces, which did not necessitate personal contact with him and did not embarrass the inner circle of ministers.

The Jacobite danger passed and general

peace was negotiated in 1748. George and the Pelhams had settled down in easy harmony, and the Prince of Wales's death in 1751 contributed a further measure to political stability by removing a focus of opposition. This period of political peace was brought to an end by the death in March 1754 of the effective manager of the Ministry, the First Lord of the Treasury, Henry Pelham. This marked the true end of the long period of relatively placid politics that Walpole's system had brought about, and George II was the biggest loser thereby. As he himself remarked, 'Now I shall have no more peace.'

The elder Pelham, the Duke of Newcastle (see Pelham-Holles, Thomas), took over the Treasury and the vital patronage that maintained any ministry in parliament. Other offices were also reshuffled, with the prime object of keeping Pitt away from the centre of affairs. A disappointed Pitt had even more frequent recourse to Leicester House and eventually was dismissed. Meanwhile, another war against France was in the making in America and elsewhere.

The early reverses in this war damaged the reputation of the ministers and provided Pitt with material for criticism of the administration, in the course of which he demonstrated his indispensibility to all but the King. George was adamant. As he put it, 'Mr. Pitt won't do my German business.' As in the previous war, Pitt indeed took a global view, and considered that the chance of an empire would go to France if British strategy was tied to the defence of a Continental state. He too had his condition for accepting office – nothing less than the resignation of Newcastle, with guaranteed access to the King for himself.

Inevitably, in such a tangled situation, negotiations were difficult. The King's

mistress, now anglicized as Lady Yarmouth, proved an invaluable mediator and it was through her good offices that George's objections were overcome. Newcastle resigned, and in December 1756 Pitt became Secretary of State with responsibility for the direction of the war. To his credit, George tried to work patiently with Pitt, but his prejudices remained. It did Admiral Byng (see Byng, John), for instance, no good that the chief advocate for an exercise of the royal clemency was Pitt and the final decision lay with the King. Shortly afterwards (April 1757) a pretext arose by which George could reasonably rid himself of the Secretary of State. An army was to be sent to Germany, and Cumberland refused to take command of it as long as Pitt, with his known views, remained in office. Nevertheless, a successor could not be found capable of standing up to Pitt in opposition, and negotiations began again. This time, however, it was Pitt who yielded. He came back to office in June, prepared to 'do the German business' and to work with Newcastle at the Treasury once more, in what was to be one of the most successful wartime administrations in British history.

George, however, still had his humiliations to face. Cumberland was defeated at Hastenbeck in 1757 and signed a convention at Klosterzeven, disbanding his army. It was repudiated, but Hanover had been endangered, and by none other than the King's favourite son. There were quarrels with Pitt over military appointments, and in September 1758 a dispute over the sovereign's most personal gift, the Garter. Pitt's brother-in-law, Earl Temple, asked Newcastle directly for the honour, and when he found that he was being bypassed George threatened to remove to Hanover. Pitt vowed to boycott the court, and Temple resigned. In the end, the King conferred the Order with as much bad grace as he could show.

Long expected, George II's death nevertheless came suddenly on 25 October 1760. According to his own instructions, his coffin was placed next to that of the long-dead Queen Caroline, and the sides of both removed so that the dust should mingle.

J. H. Plumb, *The First Four Georges* (1956).
C. C. Trench, *George II* (1973).
Basil Williams, *The Whig Supremacy* (1962, rev. ed.).

Portraits: oil, full-length, after Kneller, 1716: N.P.G.; oil, half-length, by T. Worlidge, *c.* 1753: N.P.G.; oil, full-length, studio of C. Jervas, *c.* 1727: N.P.G.; oil, full-length, by T. Hudson, 1744: N.P.G.; oil, full-length, by D. Morier: Royal Collection; oil, three-quarter length, artist unknown: Royal Collection; oil, by W. Hogarth: National Gallery of Ireland, Dublin; bust, by R. F. Roubillac: Wallace Collection.

George III (1738–1820), King of Great Britain and Ireland (1760–1820).

George William Frederick was born on 4 June 1738, the eldest son of Frederick Louis, Prince of Wales, and the Princess Augusta of Saxe-Gotha. Despite the laxity of the Prince's household at Leicester House, the children were subjected to a strict regimen, and following the death of the Prince in March 1751 the care of his heir became a matter of political dispute. A prominent member of the Prince of Wales's household, the 3rd Earl of Bute (see Stuart, John), established an influence over the Dowager Princess and became her son's tutor in 1755. At the hands of his mother and Bute, the new Prince developed a somewhat priggish sense of duty, a sincere religious faith, and a conviction that most of the woes of the realm were attributable to the politicians who enjoyed favour at the King's court. (It had become a convention of English politics for those out of favour to focus their flattering attentions upon the heir at Leicester House in the hope of improving their prospects when he came to his own.)

George II died on 25 October 1760, and his grandson ascended the throne determined to play a full and proper part in the business of government, but leaning heavily on Bute for advice. The latter was not without personal ambitions and in 1761 was made Secretary of State for the North, the existing holder of the office being induced to step down in return for a £4,000 pension. Politicians were willing to extend goodwill to the young monarch and for the time being the two principal ministers, Newcastle and Pitt, remained in office. However, suspicion over the royal confidant's aims quickly gathered.

An appropriate marriage for George III with a Protestant princess was speedily arranged after his accession, a proxy ceremony in August 1761 securing Charlotte of Mecklenburg-Strelitz, to whom George was thereafter completely faithful. She bore him fifteen children between 1762 and 1783. As far as possible, George kept her isolated from the unwelcome influences of the court and the aristocracy, acquiring Buckingham House in 1762 as a family retreat, into which service Kew and Richmond were also pressed.

Bute's inclusion in the administration coincided with the preliminary moves to bring to an end the Seven Years War, an unpopular development that nevertheless had the King's whole-hearted approval. In the same way, the break-up of the Newcastle ministry owed nothing to the royal initiative but was nonetheless welcome to him as the collapse of a faction that, he had been led to believe, held the legitimate functions of monarchy in thrall. In May 1762, against his own better judgment, Bute was induced by George to accept an appointment as First Lord of the Treasury; the error was compounded in October by bringing in the unpopular Henry Fox to lead the court party in the Commons as the peace proposals were pushed through. Once this had been accomplished, a purge of office-holders who had supported Newcastle followed. Politicians, well used to Walpole's system of parliamentary management through the distribution of profitable offices, were outraged that it was apparently to be used to support a parvenu against them. This was the beginning of George III's troubles and the myth of the tyrant-king under which the Whig oligarchs cloaked their battle to recover full control of the mainspring of political power.

Bute proved unwilling and unable to withstand the political assault and gave up his office in April 1763, George Grenville succeeding him at the Treasury well aware of the King's distrust. He insisted on having the vital patronage in his own hands and lasted for two years before the King was able to replace him, but during that time he managed to provide, in the Stamp Act of 1765 and in his fiscal policies in relation to the colonies in general, fuel for future rebellion in America. At home, however, the affair of the scurrilous John Wilkes (q.v.) directed political odium onto George III himself.

It was a major tactical blunder on the King's part to express his personal displeasure over the attack on the King's speech published by Wilkes in the *North Briton* (No. 45, April 1763) and to order his removal from the colonelcy of the Buckinghamshire Militia, while also dismissing the Lord Lieutenant, Lord Temple, who remonstrated with him. Grenville made enough mistakes in handling the affair officially without the added complications of a royal vendetta, which merely aided the Whig myth-makers. This coincidence of separate issues was to have a further accidental result, in that the later American rebels were the principal believers in the myth. George III became the personification of everything to which they were opposed.

In January 1765 the King suffered one of his recurring bouts of mental instability, which some modern medical authorities have diagnosed as porphyria. (There had been a mild attack three years earlier.) The lack of confidence between the King and his ministers clouded discussions over a Regency Bill, and convinced the latter that George intended to nominate Bute, who still lurked behind the throne. Bute's day was passing, however, and the King was already receiving advice from his uncle, the Duke of Cumberland. The result, in July, was the replacement of Grenville by the Marquis of Rockingham (see Watson-Wentworth, Charles) and his Whig associates, who included the formerly odious Newcastle. During the lengthy negotiations that brought this about, the lesson was rubbed in anew that the monarch's choice of ministers was governed by criteria other than the national good. Yet, obstinately, the King refused to give up his conviction that party politics were destructive of good government and that the search for a broad-based administration of talents would one day yield fruit.

The American boycott of British trade forced the repeal of the Stamp Act in 1766 and it was mendaciously put about by the Rockingham circle that the King was intriguing against his ministers to block the move. In fact, he considered the repeal necessary if regrettable and was withholding his confidence and full support simply because of their methods and personalities and in the hope that he might force their resignations and replacement.

Since his resignation in 1761, William Pitt the Elder (q.v.) had been waiting in the wings. His popularity in the country was undeniable, and George had been trying to enlist his services since the departure of Grenville. His great recommendation, but also his weakness, was his disavowal of party connections, which

174

pleased the King but made the construction of a ministry around him a difficult matter. It was accomplished in July 1766, the key figure being the young Duke of Grafton (see Fitzroy, Augustus), whom George was persuaded to bring in at the Treasury. The royal confidence in Pitt was signified by creating him Earl of Chatham. Unfortunately, this removed him from the Commons to the Lords, away from the source of his political power. Even worse, he was overtaken by mental derangement. The effective chief minister, therefore, was Grafton, who was by no means as capable as Chatham. The administration went from blunder to blunder, in America, in the affairs of the East India Company, and in a renewed contest with Wilkes. Nevertheless, George was now as dependent emotionally upon Grafton as he had formerly been upon Bute, and made every effort to keep him in office. He succeeded until 1770 by a combination of periodic tactical additions to the ministry, coupled with exploiting the disunity of the opposition groups.

During this period, George had seen his role as an essential buttress to a weak government under attack, not only in parliament but also in the press, notably in the letters of 'Junius' (q.v.) that appeared in the *Public Advertiser*, and this led him to take up inflexible attitudes on the issues involved. It was not otherwise with Grafton's successor, Lord North (q.v.), who remained at the Treasury with increasing reluctance for twelve years. A Commons man not without ability to handle its members and its business, he was even more blatantly dependent upon the successful deployment of crown patronage than any of his predecessors. Around the familiar landmarks of Wilkes, America, and the East India Company, the struggle for power raged on, inefficiencies and venialities of

the administration went unchecked, and colonial rebellion, full-scale international war, and soaring debt overtook the state.

North finally fell in 1782, by which time the loss of the American colonies was already a fact, only awaiting formal acknowledgment by treaty. The humiliated monarch drew what consolation he could from the return of Grafton as Lord Privy Seal under first Rockingham and then Shelburne (see Petty, William), but after a year the favourite was out and North came back in coalition with Charles James Fox (q.v.), a combination which offended all by its insincerity and none more than the King himself. Such was Fox's reputation for political chicanery that his India Bill of 1783, with its possibilities of placing the abundant patronage of the East India Company in Whig hands, would probably have failed anyway. George made certain of its failure by letting it be known through Earl Temple that all who voted for it would incur his enmity. After it had failed, the ministers delayed their resignations, so George dismissed them. Except for a brief period in 1806, the Whig party was now to remain out of office for almost fifty years. Earlier, the constitutional consequences of George's interference in the parliamentary process might have been serious. As it was, the public mood had turned against the domination of politics by Whig oligarchs, and an alternative now existed in William Pitt the Younger (q.v.). The 1784 election was an overwhelming success for the new partnership; Pitt had both electoral support and the royal patronage and, aided by the sense of national crisis that persisted through the economic difficulties of the peace into the wars against Revolutionary and Napoleonic France, he was able to build up a parliamentary connection, 'the party of Mr. Pitt', that relieved the King of his self-imposed duty of breaking the Whig monopoly. George III had won.

Public triumph was at once assailed by private tribulations as the wayward Prince of Wales (see George IV) reached manhood and the royal malady struck again (June 1788). The Foxite Whigs rallied to the Prince of Wales at Carlton House in the old expectant manner, and Pitt prevaricated over the regency, which would bring the Prince to effective power. The King's recovery was opportune, but his deep concern for the duties of his office slipped from him. As his association with policy in the public mind faded, his personal popularity increased. 'Farmer George', pious and blunt, in rustic retreat with his dull family, became the epitome of British virtues in the struggle against the anarchic French.

Only once did the old determination to preserve the royal prerogative and his legitimate rights burst out, in January 1801, when Pitt proposed to buy the loyalty of the Irish to the Act of Union by the ending of the penal laws against Roman Catholicism. There were reasonable political grounds for preventing the

incursion of an Irish vote into English politics, but George – in a rare moment of lucidity – preferred to take his stand upon his coronation oath to uphold the Protestant supremacy. Pitt was obliged to resign, although his parliamentary phalanx carried on under Addington (q.v.), and thereafter a plea to respect the King's state of mind became part of the armoury of every minister who wished to avoid a public commitment on the issue of Catholic emancipation.

Shortly afterwards the King succumbed again, and on this occasion recovery was slow and impeded by the ministrations of his attendants, two generations of the Willis family who had some experience of madhouse-keeping and whose presence, in his lucid moments, George feared and loathed. A further attack came in January 1804, and the Willises were replaced by Dr. Samuel Simmons in the interests of the King's life; but he, no less than they, believed in the efficacy of the straitjacket. The Prince of Wales's oafish selfishness, the Queen's reluctance to maintain anything more than the public appearance of their marriage, and failing sight all contributed to George's state of mind, added to which, in April, he had to part with Addington, whose resignation he took badly. He was, however, sufficiently in possession of his political wits to refuse Pitt's wish to bring Fox into the new administration, and in January 1805 he managed to reconcile Pitt and Addington and bring the latter temporarily into the ministry (with forty or so Commons votes in train) as Viscount Sidmouth.

Exactly a year later Pitt died. The event was not unexpected, and George had ample time to prepare for the inescapable – a predominantly Foxite Ministry of All the Talents, which presented itself as a broad coalition. The King received his new Foreign Secretary with wry courtesy; for Fox, however, the moment had come too late for rejoicing. In June he fell ill and in September he died, with the King expressing sincere regret. Without him the Grenville ministry could not survive, and in March 1807 George saw the last of the Whigs.

Family troubles there still were, however, as the parliamentary hounds sniffed out corruption in the War Office, where the King's second son, the Duke of York, was alleged to have permitted his mistress, Mrs. Clarke, too much influence in the granting of commissions to her financial advantage. Amelia, the King's youngest and favourite daughter, died in November 1810, but he could not be informed of the fact for a week because he was already in the early stages of another bout of instability.

Although a recovery was officially predicted, the Prince was sworn in as regent on 6 February 1811; this office was made permanent in February 1812. George III remained at Windsor where, with the consent of the Queen, the Willis family was able to resume its profitable custodianship until its object, blind, deranged, deaf after 1817, and unable to walk after 1818, died on 29 January 1820.

A. Aspinall (ed.), *The Later Correspondence of George III* (5 vols.; 1962–71).

S. Ayling, *George the Third* (1972).

John Brooke, *King George III* (1972).

Sir Herbert Butterfield, *George III and the Historians* (1957).

I. Macalpine and R. Hunter, *George III and the Mad Business* (1969).

Sir L. Namier, *The Structure of Politics at the Accession of George III* (1957, 2nd ed.).

R. Pares, *King George III and the Politicians* (1953).

J. H. Plumb, *The First Four Georges* (1956).

R. R. Sedgwick (ed.), *The Letters from George III to Lord Bute, 1757–66* (1939).

J. Steven Watson, *The Reign of George III* (1960).

R. J. White, *The Age of George III* (1968).

Portraits: oil, three-quarter length, studio of A. Ramsay, c. 1767: Scottish N.P.G.; oil, full-length, by R. Wilson, c. 1751: N.P.G.; oil, full-length, studio of W. Beechey: N.P.G.; oil, full-length, by Sir Joshua Reynolds, c. 1760: Royal Academy of Arts; oil, three-quarter length, by Johann Zoffany, 1771: Royal Collection; oil, full-length, by P. E. Stroehling, 1807: Royal Collection; oil, full-length, by T. Gainsborough: Royal Collection; oil, full-length, by A. Ramsay, c. 1760: H.M. The Queen.

George IV (1762–1830), King of Great Britain and Ireland (1820–30), after a nine-year regency.

George Augustus Frederick was born on 12 August 1762, the eldest of the fifteen children of King George III and Queen Charlotte. Within a few days he was created Prince of Wales, and he was baptized on 16 September.

George's parents were determined to educate their children in isolation from the profligacies of court circles, and his early years were spent chiefly at Kew or Buckingham House, with his younger brother Frederick as his principal companion. They followed a strict regimen, moral as well as academic and physical, personally controlled by their father, but it had effects opposite to those intended. The Prince's failure to live up to the high standards demanded by his father produced dislike in the one and rebellion in the other, an unhappy relationship which was aggravated by the Guelph monarchs' tendency to despise their heirs.

In 1779 the Prince gave an early intimation of his real nature by embarking upon an infatuation with the actress Mrs. Mary Robinson. It lasted two years, during which time she acquired a useful status in society and enough compromising letters to make her eventual fall from favour an expensive matter. The King instructed Lord North to recover the letters with £5,000 out of secret service funds, and the Prince was later forced to redeem his larger promises by means of an annual pension for her out of his own income. His choice of male company was

ing the services of the architect Henry Holland. During the 1784 election it was turned into an ostentatious camp for the discontented Foxite Whigs on the King's own doorstep. The Prince now plunged into another serious infatuation (there were others less serious), its object being the widowed Mrs. Fitzherbert (q.v.), a Roman Catholic. He pursued dramatic schemes to bring about a marriage in defiance of the Act of Settlement (under which a Roman Catholic partner would disqualify a claimant to the throne), and the Royal Marriages Act of 1772 (which made the King's consent a necessary preconditon). Mrs. Fitzherbert fled to France, but was induced to return in the following year, and on 15 December 1785 she was secretly married to the Prince by an Anglican priest who was released from

equally imprudent; it included Charles James Fox and Richard Sheridan, agreeable but hardly the most responsible of companions.

The Prince reached his majority in 1783 – an event marred by wrangling over the income required to support an independent establishment. Fox was enjoying a brief taste of office as Foreign Secretary and did his best for the Prince, but the main opposition to a large allowance came from the King. A compromise was eventually reached, parliament being asked to settle the Prince's existing debts of £30,000 and to provide a similar sum to fit out Carlton House as a residence. In December the Prince signalled his political ties by voting in the House of Lords for Fox's India Bill, despite the King's declaration in advance that he would not take a friendly view of any of its supporters. The Bill was beaten and the ministers were dismissed with a promptitude that exactly expressed the King's opinion of his son's circle.

Meanwhile the Prince concentrated upon refurbishing Carlton House, enlist-

the debtors' prison with the settlement of his accounts as a consideration for performing the office. Amid the other excitements of 1784, the Prince explored the delights of the seaside town of Brighton, although he did not set Holland upon converting a farmhouse into his Pavilion until 1786. By then his debts amounted to £270,000 and he was compelled to seek assistance from the King, which provoked a further bout of wrangling, public embarrassment, and an eventual parliamentary vote of adequate funds, after appropriate acts of contrition on the Prince's part.

Towards the end of 1788 the King became mentally incapacitated, and it was assumed that the Prince would exercise regency powers. The Foxites expected to be the beneficiaries of his political bounty, but the Prince and his cronies rejoiced too openly and too soon, for William Pitt the Younger (q.v.) managed to delay the Regency Bill long enough for the King to recover and render it unnecessary. As a result of his unseemly behaviour the Prince forfeited much of the public sympathy he had attracted during his financial difficulties, and this new unpopularity was to remain.

The French Revolution gave him an opportunity to play a serious part in national affairs and in mid-1792, in a maiden speech in the Lords, he supported a proclamation against seditious writing. He thus won a cheap reconciliation with the King, although this did not extend, as he had hoped, to a settlement of his new debts, now standing at £400,000; to pay them he had to negotiate a loan in Holland. The outbreak of war with France (February 1793) gave the Prince an appointment as Colonel Commandant of the 10th Light Dragoons, styled 'the Prince of Wales's Own' since 1783, and he frequently served on escort duties for the royal family. For the time being the Prince discharged his military duties enthusiastically. At his own expense he equipped his regiment's privates with tailored uniforms, and in 1795 he gave the elegant 'Beau' Brummell (q.v.) a cornetcy.

His personal interest in this regiment remained strong, but his taste for regular soldiering soon diminished. Financial embarrassment remained, and in the hope of securing an increased parliamentary allowance he professed himself willing to undertake a dynastic marriage. An eligible consort was found, Princess Caroline of Brunswick (q.v.), a cousin whom he had never met. She was brought to England, but her coarseness and personal uncleanness induced in him an intense dislike that he never overcame. On 8 April 1795 they were married in the Chapel Royal at St. James's Palace; the Prince was drunk. To add to his troubles, the settlement of his £630,000 debts was not readily undertaken by Pitt's administration, not surprisingly since the country was suffering from severe economic difficulties as well as fighting a war and was therefore in no mood to accept the

Prince's estimation of the worth to the nation of the art treasures that he was collecting beyond his ability to pay. Instead, parliament earmarked some of his existing revenues and appointed commissioners to administer his debts, leaving him with a reduced income.

On 7 January 1796 the Princess gave birth to a daughter, Charlotte. Two months later the Prince proposed the setting up of separate establishments, and the Princess retaliated by appealing direct to the King and by making her plight public knowledge. The Prince achieved his object, but at further cost to his reputation. He was forced to remain out of London to avoid public insults, while Caroline's miniature court at Blackheath flourished. For a time the Prince solaced himself with other friendships but in 1799 he began to importune Mrs. Fitzherbert to return, which she did the following year after consultation with Pope Pius VII.

The renewal of the war with France in 1803 after the brief Peace of Amiens revived the Prince's martial ambitions, and he asked for a higher military command. Addington, the Prime Minister, demurred and was supported by the King, whereupon the Prince published the entire correspondence, inviting the people to judge his zeal for the national cause. The people, however, were not noticeably moved.

It was otherwise with the 'Delicate Investigation' of 1806. Gossip about the nature of Caroline's life at Blackheath abounded, and there was a tale of an illegitimate child which the outraged Prince carried to the King. After consultation with the current Prime Minister, Lord Grenville, a Royal Commission was set up to investigate the report; in due course it completely exonerated Caroline on that count, but was critical of the general tone of her establishment. It was, however, the Prince upon whom the public fastened its disapproval, the facts of his own social life being widely known.

Meanwhile, Fox was dying. The Prince had maintained the friendship despite Fox's espousal of the revolutionary cause, and attended him closely in his last illness. After his death, however, the King forbade the Prince to attend the funeral in Westminster Abbey. With Fox dead the Prince's intimate connection with Whig politics ceased; another casualty of this period was his relationship with Mrs. Fitzherbert, who was eventually pensioned off to allow the Prince to pay court to the Marchioness of Hertford unimpeded.

Towards the end of 1810, George III's mind collapsed once more, and Spencer Perceval (q.v.), the Prime Minister and a personal friend of the Princess of Wales, rushed through a Regency Bill to prevent the Prince receiving full prerogative power until a twelve-month had elapsed. The Prince protested in vain and was seen to encourage the Whigs, while they awaited office as confidently as in 1788. On 5 February 1811 George was sworn in as regent, and on 18 February 1812 he assumed his full powers. There was no wholesale change of ministers. The war against the French was going well, and the Prince Regent discovered that he did not wish to displace Perceval after all. The most that he was prepared to offer his former Whig acquaintances was a series of minor posts in a coalition based on the existing administration. They declined and never forgave what they regarded as his betrayal.

The assassination of Perceval in May 1812 produced a ministerial crisis. George's own preference was for a broad coalition under the Marquis of Wellesley, but two months of patient negotiation failed to resolve the personal rivalries of potential members, and eventually he

invited the former Secretary of State for War, Lord Liverpool (see Jenkinson, Robert Banks) to take office with what was virtually Perceval's cabinet. The choice proved wise. Liverpool remained for fifteen years, during which the country passed without mishap from victorious war, through economic and social distress and the threat of political violence, to a period of relative stability.

The Prince Regent had cause to congratulate himself in that he had preserved an administration intent on victory, and in 1814 he was able to savour the delights of the state ceremonial attendant upon triumphant arms – the departure of the exiled Louis XVIII for his kingdom, the visits of allied monarchs – the Tsar of Russia, the King of Prussia, and Metternich representing the Emperor of Austria – and the reception of the victorious Wellington. Yet the public was still hostile to him personally, though it enthused over his guests.

He was more obviously successful in the world of the arts. From 1811 onwards, he encouraged John Nash (q.v.) in his architectural plans for London and from 1815 he employed him on the Pavilion at Brighton. In the same year he moved into the Royal Lodge at Windsor, upon which Nash had been engaged since 1812. There was a steady expenditure on furniture, paintings, and other works of art which, coupled with his lavish court entertainments, provoked much parliamentary criticism. The Hundred Days and the Battle of Waterloo gave further lustre to what afterwards was seen as a distinctive 'Regency' period in English history.

In May 1816 his daughter Charlotte was married to Prince Leopold of Saxe-Coburg. His grief when she died in childbirth in November 1817 was genuine, and his personal tragedy was heightened by the fact that the child was still-born. Ill-repute still dogged him, for while his daughter was dying he was a guest at the Marchioness of Hertford's estate and that fact was widely publicized. The Princess of Wales had left the country in 1814, touring European and Mediterranean lands in an extravagant manner. In 1818, the Prince Regent set up the informal Milan Commission to investigate reports that she was living adulterously with an Italian. The reports were confirmed, but the use made of Caroline (and also of Charlotte, when she was alive) by opposition leaders as an alleged victim of the Prince Regent's character made divorce proceedings at this point unwise.

The Prince Regent succeeded as King George IV on 31 January 1820. The immediate problem was the status of Caroline, who returned uninvited in June to claim her rights as Queen amid enthusiastic popular support, while the King absented himself from London. The government presented in parliament a bill to deprive her of her title and dissolve the marriage, the examination of evidence being wrongly described as 'The Queen's Trial'. The majority in favour of the bill in the Upper House was so low that the government preferred not to risk it in the Commons; as a result Caroline remained Queen and the King seriously considered dismissing the administration.

The coronation, which took place on 19 July 1821, was planned by the King personally and was distinguished by its pageantry and false antiquarianism, as well as by the spectacle of Caroline demanding entrance at the door of Westminster Abbey in vain. Her death on 7 August ended an increasingly embarrassing situation for the politicians on both sides, and the street riots that marked the progress of her body on its way through London to Germany were no longer significant. Cautiously, George lingered in Anglesey on his way to pay a state visit to Ireland. After a decent interval he continued to Dublin, later visited Hanover, and wintered at Brighton to recover from the strain. A proposed visit to Vienna was cancelled in 1822 on ministerial advice; a Scottish visit was suggested, and the arrangements were put in the hands of Sir Walter Scott. The display of resuscitated tribalism that was mounted for the occasion (with the King in Highland dress) proved highly agreeable to all the parties concerned, and remained to obscure the grimmer realities of Scottish history for subsequent generations.

The modernization of Windsor Castle was begun in 1824 and completed in 1828. The King had presented his father's collection of 70,000 books to the nation and had persuaded the government to purchase Sir Julius Angerstein's collection of paintings. The need to house these led to the construction of the present British Museum and the establishment of the National Gallery, although the King did not live to see either project completed. Brighton Pavilion had been finished in 1822, but the now crowded and fashionable town had lost its former attraction; so had Carleton House, which he decided to pull down. In its place Nash was commissioned to redesign Buckingham House as a palace, although the actual work fell to others after 1830.

In these last years, there was some political jealousy directed towards the King's closest companions, who were dubbed 'the Cottage Clique' and included some foreign ambassadors as well as Wellington and Lady Conyngham, whose husband, an Irish peer, was Lord Steward of the Household. It was supposed that Sir William Knighton, George's physician and secretary, exercised an influence beyond his proper office. In fact the King's interest in political affairs had declined to a few strong prejudices. His distrust of Canning in part stemmed from Canning's close friendship with Caroline, which had led him to resign from the administration in 1821. George had been very unwilling to accept him as Foreign Secretary in the following year. However, the King's misunderstanding of his foreign policy and his objection to Canning's support for the principle of Roman Catholic emancipation (which the King himself had upheld in his politically active days) was shared by many of Canning's colleagues. By 1827 Canning had sufficiently gained the King's confidence to be invited to form an administration after Liverpool's retirement, but only on the condition that the Roman Catholic issue remained dormant. It was in fact the most controversial political issue of the time, as the King well knew, and he was unable to prevent its erupting in 1828 when, in succession to Goderich (see Robinson, Frederick), the Duke of Wellington constructed a cabinet on the same principle as Canning. Circumstances in Ireland and Westminster made a measure imperative, and George's reaction to Wellington's reluctant determination in 1829 to concede emancipation became hysterical. He threatened to use the royal veto, but too much of the royal initiative in politics had been surrendered since his father's prime and there was no alternative ministry to support his stand. His acceptance of the concession was constitutionally significant.

It was also his last political act. His health deteriorated rapidly, and he died at Windsor Castle on 26 June 1830.

A. Aspinall (ed.), *The Letters of George IV* (3 vols.; 1938).
A. Aspinall (ed.), *The Letters of Princess Charlotte 1811–17* (1949).
Roger Fulford, *George the Fourth* (1949, rev. ed.).
Christopher Hibbert, *George IV, Regent and King* (1973).
Shane Leslie, *George IV* (1926).
A. Palmer, *The Life and Times of George IV* (1972).
J. H. Plumb, *The First Four Georges* (1956).
See also references under Fitzherbert, Maria Anne.

Portraits: oil, quarter-length, by T. Lawrence, c. 1820: N.P.G.; oil, full-length, studio of Lawrence: N.P.G.; miniature, by H. de Janvry, 1793: N.P.G.; oil, full-length, by G. Stubbs, 1791: Windsor Castle; oil, full-length, by T. Gainsborough: National Trust, Waddesdon Manor; oil, full-length, by D. Wilkie: Royal Collection; oil, full-length, by T. Lawrence, 1822: Wallace Collection; oil, full-length, by J. Hoppner, c. 1807: Walker Art Gallery, Liverpool.

Germain, Lord George Sackville (1716–85), 1st Viscount Sackville, see Sackville, Lord George.

Gibbon, Edward (1737–94), historian and writer; author of *The History of the Decline and Fall of the Roman Empire.*

Edward Gibbon was born on 27 April 1737 at Putney, the grandson of Edward Gibbon, an ingenious businessman who remade his fortune after losing all his original wealth in the collapse of the South Sea Company in 1720. Gibbon's parents were devoted to each other, but Gibbon himself comments that he felt little grief at the death of his mother. Her life had been almost entirely taken up with her husband and her efforts to draw him away from his gambling and extravagant style of life.

A sickly child, Gibbon remembered with much more feeling the nursing attention and encouragement of his unmarried aunt, Catherine Porten. His education was frequently interrupted by illness and he never stayed long at any education institution. His aunt, however, encouraged him to read whatever books excited his already strong curiosity, so that, he tells us, when he arrived at Oxford at the age of fourteen he had 'a stock of erudition that might have puzzled a doctor and a degree of ignorance of which a schoolboy would have been ashamed'.

Gibbon said of the fourteen months he stayed at Oxford that they were 'the most idle and unprofitable of my whole life'. Gibbon followed the diversions and extravagances of his fellow students for a time, but then abandoned them, and became thoroughly involved in Catholic tracts and ideas. Indeed, he resolved to become a Catholic and was admitted to the faith in June 1753. His father was astonished and dismayed by his conversion and Magdalen College banned him from returning. Within a fortnight Gibbon was sent off to Lausanne to the care and instruction of Monsieur Pavillard, a Calvinist minister.

At Lausanne, Gibbon was confronted with a much rougher style of life than he had been accustomed to at Oxford. In his *Memoirs*, he complains bitterly of the meanness of Mme Pavillard and her poor cooking and slovenly habits, but concludes that he gained in health and purpose from his seclusion in this uncomfortable establishment. He became fluent in French and gained freedom from English academicism; by associating with his Swiss neighbours, 'I insensibly lost the prejudices of an Englishman.' He took up reading again with his earlier enthusiasm and under the guidance of M. Pavillard learned to make systematic his knowledge in a wide variety of fields. He devoted his days to study and his evenings to social activities. In Lausanne Gibbon met Voltaire and attended his small theatrical productions. He was generally popular and was invited to many parties and entertainments. In 1757 Gibbon met and fell in love with Suzanne Curchod, a pastor's daughter, although for a time she remained less attached to him. She admired him in spite of his shortness – he was less than five feet tall – but parental disapproval was to prevent Gibbon's marriage to Suzanne.

In 1754 Gibbon had renounced his Catholicism and received the sacrament from the pastor. In 1758 he returned to

England with money obtained on the sale of some property entailed on him, and began to build up his own library. Among other studies he was re-examining the tenets of the Christian faith, and after reading *De Veritate Religionis Christianae* by Grotius, he eventually reached the conclusion that Christian faith could not be established by any reasoning.

From 1759 to 1762 Gibbon served in Pitt's new militia. He found service rather irksome but not without romantic interest. Meanwhile he read and considered what historic theme he should pursue in his future studies.

Gibbon's *Essai sur L'Étude de la Littérature* was published in 1761. He admits that he hoped to achieve a 'new and singular fame' by publishing his work in French. The English critics did not pay much attention to the work, but on the Continent one reviewer commented that it was one of the great literary works of the century.

In 1763 Gibbon set out on a tour through France and Italy. He passed through Paris and comments that he had 'heard more conversation worth re-membering, and seen more men of letters among people of fashion, than I had done in two or three winters in London'. From Paris, Gibbon proceeded to Lausanne where he spent eleven months with his former friends and companions. He led an active social life and admits to 'some riotous acts of intemperance'.

In Lausanne, Gibbon prepared for his journey to Italy reading assiduously about every aspect of Italian history and geography. In April 1764 he travelled across Savoy to Turin and from there to Bologna, Florence, Sienna, and finally Rome. He wrote later,

> My temper is not very susceptible of enthusiasm. . . . But at the distance of twenty-five years I can neither forget nor express the strong emotions which agitated my mind when I first approached and entered the Eternal City.

He searched for the scenes of the great events in Roman history and he wrote, 'It was at Rome on the fifteenth of October 1764 . . . that the idea of writing the decline and fall of the city first started to my mind.'

Gibbon spent the winter of 1764–5 at Rome and then travelled back by stages towards England, summoned by his father, who was again in financial difficulties. In England he resumed his former life but was restless. He began a history of Switzerland in collaboration with a friend, but soon abandoned it. In 1770 his father died, and he took up residence in London. In 1774 he accepted a seat in the House of Commons, where he frequently wished to express his views but fear of publicity as often restrained him, and he remained silent.

After several years spent collecting materials and devoting great attention to the style of his narrative, Gibbon sent the first volume of The Decline and Fall of the Roman Empire to the printers in the summer of 1775. The first edition was sold out well before its appearance the following year, and Gibbon received great general acclaim for the work as well as some bitter criticism for his attack on the early church in Rome. He continued work on the next volumes, but in 1782 lost the income from a sinecure on the suppressed Board of Trade and Planta-tions. Gibbon decided to use his resources more sparingly by returning to Switzerland to complete The Decline and Fall. In 1783 he settled in Lausanne again and continued with his work. Five years later he completed his great masterpiece and travelled back to England with the final volumes.

Gibbon returned to Switzerland after a year, but in 1793 he came back to England, where he died on 16 January 1794, having suffered for several years from an acute hydrocele.

Edward Gibbon was often mocked during his life for his short, stout figure, his rather pompous manner, and his habit of taking snuff even in the presence of royalty. In his writing, however, he achieved an elegant and impressive style. Writing with confidence and conviction in his history, he examines each sequence of events with insight and preserves the many elements of his vast narrative in balance through his own characteristic scepticism. Gibbon's genius as a historian was immediately recognized by his contemporaries, and it cannot be denied that The History of the Decline and Fall of the Roman Empire remains a model of style and a monument to scholarship.

H. L. Bond, The Literary Art of Edward Gibbon (1960).

G. A. Bonnard (ed.), Memoirs of My Life (1966).

J. B. Bury (ed.), The History of the Decline and Fall of the Roman Empire (7 vols.; 1926–9; an abridgment of this edition by D. M. Low appeared in one volume in 1960).

Sir G. de Beer, *Gibbon and His World* (1968).

D. M. Low, *Edward Gibbon* (1937).

D. M. Low (ed.), *Journals* (1929).

J. E. Norton (ed.), *Letters* (3 vols.; 1956).

Portraits: oil, half-length, by H. Walton, *c.* 1774: Magdalen College, Oxford; oil, quarter-length, by H. Walton, 1773: N.P.G.; water-colour, full-length, by unknown artist: N.P.G.

Gibbs, James (1682–1754), architect.

James Gibbs was born on 23 December 1682 near Aberdeen, the younger son of Peter Gibbs, a wealthy Roman Catholic merchant. He was educated at the local grammar school, and at Aberdeen's Marischal College. On the death of his parents he went to live with an aunt, but soon set off to seek his fortune in Europe. He visited France, Switzerland, and Germany, eventually entering the Pontifical Scots College at Rome in 1703. The following year young Gibbs decided against the priesthood, briefly considered becoming a painter, and finally settled for studying architecture. He became a pupil of the elderly Carlo Fontana, the Pope's Surveyor General and one of Italy's leading baroque architects.

His brother's illness caused Gibbs to return home in 1709, and he eventually settled in London, just in time to benefit from the Tory government's 1711 Act calling for the erection of fifty new churches in the city. When work began in 1714 on Gibbs's first church, St. Mary-le-Strand, it quickly became clear that a new force had entered English architecture. Eschewing the gigantic Corinthian pilasters favoured by the English baroque school, the new building exhibited two delicately-handled superimposed orders. The chief influences seemed to be Raphael's Palazzo Branconio, in the alternating curved and pointed pediments of the windows, and Wren's St. Paul's, in the semi-circular porch.

However, neither Gibbs nor his church was particularly popular. The accession of George I in 1714 had initiated the political ascendancy of the Whig aristocracy. Gibbs was both a Catholic and a Tory, his patrons including such Tory magnates as the Duke of Argyll and the Earl of Oxford, and his St. Mary-le-Strand seems to have been thought excessively Italianate, that is, 'papist'. The result was that in 1715 Gibbs lost his job as Surveyor to the Commission for New Churches. Later *Vitruvius Britannicus*, in effect the manifesto of the Palladians, though it did not attack Gibbs directly, harshly criticized both Carlo Fontana and St. Mary-le-Strand.

Henceforward Gibbs was obliged to adapt to public taste, and he never again imitated Italian architecture so closely. In his next commission, the offices of Burlington House, he adopted a more conservative style. Gibbs never actually became a Palladian, but moved closer to the style of Wren's St. Bride's, as was demonstrated in 1719 by his successful addition of a steeple to the older architect's St. Clement Danes.

Although Gibbs's Ditchley House, built 1720–2 for the Earl of Lichfield, has been described as Palladian, its unified mass with centre and end projections, its irregularly-proportioned rooms, and uniform fenestration hardly conform to Palladian canons. However, Gibbs's domestic buildings were usually less enterprising than his public ones, and indeed his next design, St. Peter's Chapel of Ease (or 'Marybone Chapel') for the Earl of Oxford, can be seen as a preliminary model for the unprecedented St. Martin-in-the-Fields.

In fact, Gibbs's initial idea for St. Martin-in-the-Fields had been a round church, modelled on a Pozzo drawing and Wren's St. Stephen Walbrook, but this had been rejected by the commissioners as being too expensive. As completed in 1726, St. Martin-in-the-Fields was in part reminiscent of Wren's St. Andrew's, Holborn. The most original feature, and the most criticized, was the steeple; totally against medieval tradition, Gibbs built it on the *inside* of the west wall, emerging through the roof. St. Martin-in-the-Fields perfected motifs which Wren had introduced in his City churches but had not had time to elaborate, and it was for long the model for new Anglican parish churches all over the world.

The Senate House, Cambridge, begun in 1722, was the only portion completed of a projected three-sided open quadrangle of buildings, and its huge Corinthian order of pilasters bears little relation to Gibbs's usual style. The great quadrangle of King's College, Cambridge, completed in 1749, was more characteristic, being in Gibbs's massively simple country-house style, but with Mannerist influence.

In 1728 Gibbs published his *Book of Architecture*. Its simplicity and moderation of style made it perhaps the most widely-used architectural pattern-book of the century. Gibbs's most individual building was his Radcliffe Library at Oxford, begun in 1737 after several preliminary designs had been rejected. Inheriting a design by Hawksmoor, Gibbs returns after many years to a Mannerist style.

In 1749 Gibbs fell ill and went to take the waters at Spa. His last commission was for St. Andrew's church in his native Aberdeen, a building that was still unfinished when he died on 5 August 1754.

James Gibbs was an architect who belonged to no particular school, but his grasp of technicalities and his impeccable taste enabled him to select the best features of all available contemporary styles, and to complete much of what Wren had set out to do.

B. Little, *The Life and Work of James Gibbs* (1955).

Portrait: oil, half-length, by J. M. Williams: N.P.G.

Gibson, John (1790–1866), sculptor, see *Lives of the Victorian Age.*

Gillray, James (1757–1815), caricaturist and satirical artist.

James Gillray was born in Chelsea in 1757, the son of a sexton. He was briefly apprenticed to a letter-engraver, but because of the monotony of the work he left this employment to join a group of strolling actors. He later studied at the schools of the Royal Academy, supporting himself by selling engravings, but appears to have been largely self-taught. The works of William Hogarth (q.v.) were the main influence upon Gillray's early development, and after the appearance in 1779 of *Paddy on Horseback*, the first work that may be definitely assigned to him, his own talent for caricature was soon widely recognized.

After 1782 Gillray devoted himself almost exclusively to political and topical subjects, and his works, popular both in England and abroad, provide a compre-

hensive record of the latter part of the reign of George III. The targets of his satire included Fox, Pitt, Napoleon, Nelson, and – most dramatically – the royal family; his *Sin, Death, and the Devil* is one of the most outrageous caricatures of a royal personality ever produced, and among his other works that exploit the same material are the famous *Farmer George and His Wife* and *The Anti-Saccharites*. Gillray's work is characterized by an imaginative inventiveness and a sense of humour that is often coarse but always relevant; his satire is more vicious than that of Hogarth precisely because it is more personal, and his influence upon many other contemporary graphic artists was considerable.

Throughout his working career Gillray lived in a room above the shop of his publisher, Miss Humphrey, at 29 St. James's Street, and his solitary life was the cause of much rumour and scandal. In 1811 Gillray was afflicted by insanity, and for the remainder of his life he was confined to his room; the causes of this madness have been variously attributed to intemperance and overwork. One day in 1815 Gillray escaped from his upper room and appeared in the shop, pale and haggard with his uncut hair flowing about his shoulders: with the aid of some passers-by he was recaptured, but he died on the following day, 1 June 1815. The number of his completed plates amounted to over 1,500, all etched and coloured by hand.

D. Hill, *Mr. Gillray the caricaturist* (1965).

Portrait: miniature, quarter-length, self-portrait, *c.*1800: N.P.G.

Girtin, Thomas (1775–1802), watercolourist and landscape painter.

Thomas Girtin was born on 18 February 1775, the son of a rope-maker in Southwark. His father died when he was eight years of age, and his mother then married a pattern-draughtsman, Mr.

Vaughan. Girtin then began his instruction under a drawing master named Fisher; he also served as apprentice to Edward Dayes, who later had him imprisoned for refusing to serve out his contract. Together with his contemporary, J. M. W. Turner, with whom he often sketched on the banks of the Thames, Girtin earned his living by making topographical drawings for London engravers, and early copies from the paintings of Canaletto and Piranesi show that he was already skilled in the use of both watercolour and pen and ink.

Girtin was employed by an amateur artist, James Moore, on a journey to Scotland, and in 1794 he exhibited his first paintings at the Royal Academy. A tour in the north of England in 1796 led to a series of paintings demonstrating his originality of tone. His landscapes of moors and downs were unprecedented in their boldness and strength of colour. The eighteenth-century watercolour tradition was one of line drawings shadowed with monochrome washes and tinted with suggestions of local colour, and the chief significance of Girtin's work is his transformation of the watercolourist's art into one of true painting, using strong colours in a naturalistic manner and greatly increasing the range of atmospheric effects.

Girtin continued to produce topographical sketches, published in *The Itinerant*. He disliked teaching and was not attracted by fashionable society, preferring to mingle with the colliers and fishermen whom he met while sketching. He married the daughter of Phineas Borrett, a respectable goldsmith, and in 1797 he moved into his own lodgings. His character, according to Edward Dayes, was vicious and self-indulgent. But Dayes's opinion is almost certainly distorted by personal malice; Girtin was actually a welcome guest at several noble establishments, and all those who knew him testified to his friendliness and generosity. His closest companions were the ten members of the sketching club which he formed in 1797, several of whom later became famous in their own right. Turner himself remained a lifelong friend, and was generous in his praise: 'Had Tom Girtin lived, I should have starved.'

At the Royal Academy Girtin exhibited watercolour paintings of places throughout England, Scotland, and Wales, as well as an enormous oil-painted panorama of London. In 1802 he travelled to Paris, suffering from a lung disease – undoubtedly tuberculosis – that was probably aggravated by the rate at which he worked, but by May he had returned to London, his disease uncured. He died at his lodgings in the Strand on 9 November 1802, having worked till within eight days of his death on his series of etchings of Paris views.

Girtin did not live long enough to exploit fully his own innovations, but his influence is clearly apparent in the later work of such painters as Turner and Cotman.

Thomas Girtin and David Loshak, *The Art of Thomas Girtin* (1954).

J. Mayne, *Thomas Girtin* (1949).

Portrait: oil, half-length, by J. Opie: National Gallery of Ireland, Dublin.

Goderich, Viscount (1782–1859), see Robinson, Frederick John.

Godwin, Mary (1759–97), see Wollstonecraft, Mary.

Godwin, William (1756–1836), English political writer, historian, and novelist.

William Godwin was born on 3 March 1756 at Wisbech, Cambridgeshire, the son of a Dissenting minister. In his early years he lived at Guestwick, Norfolk, where his father was pastor of an Independent congregation. At the age of seventeen Godwin entered the Dissenters' College, Hoxton Academy, and for five years studied for the ministry. In 1778 he was admitted a member of the Dissenting ministry and entrusted with the care of a congregation near London, subsequently moving to a similar position at Stowmarket, Suffolk.

During the next few years he became associated with the Whig extremists. He also read Helvétius, Holbach, Rousseau, and others and under the influence of Thomas Holcroft, an actor and author with revolutionary views, he became an atheist. Godwin's views on the ministry were completely transformed by the age of about twenty-six, and he abandoned the pulpit for ever. He moved to London to try his hand at literature. His first work, *Life of Lord Chatham* (1783), was published anonymously. The following year he published a series of six sermons on the lives of Aaron, Hazael, and Jesus, under the somewhat misleading title *Sketches of History*.

In 1785 Godwin began writing for the *New Annual Register* and other periodicals, and joined the Revolutionists Club, forming many friendships among leading politicians influenced by the French Revolution such as Fox and Sheridan (qq.v.). It was in this highly-charged atmosphere that Godwin published his most celebrated work, *An Enquiry Concerning the Principles of Political Justice, and its Influence on General Virtue and Happiness* (1793).

Political Justice profoundly affected the Romantic poets, including Coleridge (who did much to reconvert Godwin to theism), Wordsworth, and Byron. Godwin had been influenced by Rousseau and the French Encyclopedists, and believed that men could be convinced by reason alone of the proper actions and aspirations, and that social reform was possible by means of calm discussion. He was a firm believer in 'the perfectability of man', and argued that all existing institutions – social, political, and religious – were totally unnecessary. In theory, at least, he included the institution of marriage; but his theories were to be severely tested several years later.

In 1794 Godwin published his first novel, *The Adventures of Caleb Williams, or Things as They Are* (later dramatized as *The Iron Chest*). *Caleb Williams* attempted to show the persecution of the servant by his master and how the institutions of the day were organized to support the legal oppression of the poor by the rich. Godwin himself was more frugal than poor, although for some time he had to manage on an average income of £120 a year. With the publication of *Political Justice* his position was temporarily more secure, but money matters were nevertheless a problem for him during most of his life.

In 1796 Godwin met the feminist author Mary Wollstonecraft (q.v.). After living together for a short time, with Mary becoming pregnant, they decided to marry, despite their mutually shared views that marriage was little more than a form of female slavery. Tragically, shortly after the birth of their daughter, Mary (see Shelley, Mary Wollstonecraft), Godwin's wife died (10 September 1797). His grief at this loss is reflected in his biography of Mary Wollstonecraft, *Memoirs of the Author of the Rights of Woman* (1798).

Godwin published his second novel, *St. Leon*, in 1799. In 1801 he married Mary Jane Clairmont, and four years later set up as a bookseller and publisher. In 1814 he met Shelley, who had been greatly influenced by his *Political Justice*, and who – although already married – instantly fell in love with Godwin's first daughter, Mary. Mary's elopement with Shelley in July of that year angered Godwin, but upon the failure of a publishing venture Shelley provided him with financial aid, and Godwin grew to rely on the young poet's generosity until the latter's death in 1822 signalled Godwin's bankruptcy.

Godwin's last works include the tragedy *Faulkner* (1807), the novels *Mandeville* (1817) and *Cloudesley* (1830), and the *Treatise on Population* (1820). Still of some interest is his *History of the Commonwealth of England* (1824–8). In addition he published several children's books, including Charles and Mary Lamb's *Tales from Shakespeare*. In 1833 Godwin received a sinecure under the Grey administration, allowing him to pass his final years in reasonable comfort. He died in London on 7 April 1836.

D. McCracken (ed.), *Caleb Williams* (1970).
K. N. Cameron (ed.), *Shelley and His Circle 1773–1872* (2 vols.; Cambridge, Mass., 1961).
D. Fleischer, *William Godwin: A Study in Liberalism* (1951).
R. G. Grylls, *Godwin and His World* (1953).
D. H. Monro, *Godwin's Moral Philosophy* (1953).
F. E. L. Priestley (ed.), *An Enquiry Concerning the Principles of Political Justice, etc.* (3 vols.; Toronto, 1946).
A. E. Rodway, *Godwin and the Age of Transition* (1952).
R. M. Wardle (ed.), *Godwin and Mary: Letters of Godwin and Mary Wollstonecraft* (Lawrence, Kansas, 1966).

Portraits: oil, half-length, by H. W. Pickersgill: N.P.G.; oil, half-length, by J. Northcote, 1802: N.P.G.; oil, half-length, by J. W. Chandler, 1798: Tate Gallery, London.

Goldsmith, Oliver (1730–74), author.

Oliver Goldsmith was born on 10 November 1730 at Kilkenny West, County Westmeath, in Ireland, the son of a curate, Charles Goldsmith. He was educated locally until the age of fourteen, part of his schooling being financed by richer relations. From a very early age he had written verses and had been attracted

to Irish ballads. Although he won some respect from his seniors, he was isolated among his own age group. He lacked personal attractiveness and was often defensively brash. Throughout his life he was known for his awkwardness of manner.

When the time came in 1744 for him to go to Trinity College, Dublin, Goldsmith's father could not afford to send him as a pensioner and he was forced to attend as a sizar, with the obligation to serve the pensioners at the college. He objected to such indignity but was persuaded to accept this means of gaining a university education. At Trinity College, Goldsmith suffered from the lowliness of his rank and did not excel in his work.

In 1747 Charles Goldsmith died, and the funds available for his son's education were further restricted. In the same year, Goldsmith applied for a scholarship from the college, but was awarded an exhibition of only thirty shillings a year. He used the money for a party, which was broken up by one of the senior members

of college, whereupon Goldsmith sold his books and abandoned the place, but after living on no money and hardly any food for several days, he was persuaded to return. After five years' studies he obtained his B.A. in 1749.

His family expected Goldsmith to enter the church, and eventually he reluctantly consented to read for Orders. Goldsmith's progress towards ordination was checked when he was rejected as a candidate by the bishop. He then took up a post as a tutor, but resigned this abruptly after a year and tried to get a passage to America from Cork. Within six weeks he was home again, having sold the good horse he had and spent all his money. Goldsmith had failed again to achieve his independence and was forced to rely on his family once more.

In 1752 his relations decided to finance his studies in medicine and he was sent off to Edinburgh. He did not enrol at the medical school, but attended the lectures of Alexander Munro and dismissed the other professors as not worth going to hear. In his letters home, he claimed to be living a very solitary existence – 'I have hardly any society but a Folio book, a skeleton, my cat, and my meagre landlady' – but in fact he had attracted many friends by his wit and his lively nature. For a time he was often invited to social gatherings by the Duke of Hamilton, but he abandoned this society once he realized that 'They like me more as a jester than as a companion.'

After just over a year at Edinburgh Goldsmith announced that he was going to Leyden to complete his studies. He reached Leyden some time later, having been imprisoned with some Frenchmen at Newcastle on suspicion of having been with them collecting volunteers for the French army in Scotland. Goldsmith was delighted with Holland, its atmosphere, and its architecture, but of the university he complained again, 'Physic is by no means taught here so well as in Edinburgh.' Not speaking any Dutch, he found that he was restricted for friends to the few English students. He was, as before, often short of money; he kept himself by teaching English, borrowing, and gambling. He had gambled at Trinity and Edinburgh, and throughout his life it was probably one of the prime means by which he gained and lost money.

In 1755 he left Leyden and explained that he was going to complete his studies in Paris. He travelled thither through the Low Countries and probably supported himself there again by gambling and borrowing. From Paris he travelled through France to Switzerland and Italy. The details are uncertain; he is said to have met Voltaire, and often to have travelled on foot, playing his flute to earn money.

When he returned to England in 1756 he had no money and no resources. After trying a few occupations he set himself up as a physician at Bankside. He had a busy practice but did not earn very much by it. He entertained many schemes of earning money, including travelling to Mount Sinai to decipher ancient writing for a pension of £300 a year, until in 1757 he began to write articles and reviews for the *Monthly Review*. He was infuriated, however, at having his work thoroughly edited and stopped writing for that periodical in September. He was now also working on a translation of Bergerac, which was published by Griffiths and Dilly in February 1758. Later in the same year he wrote to friends in Ireland trying to raise subscriptions for his essay *On the Present State of Taste and Literature in Europe*. His hopes of working as a physician in the East Indies were shaken when he failed his examination in medicine at Surgeons' Hall. By this time, however, he was beginning to enjoy London life and appreciate that his own

position was not so unpleasant as it might be. He was, moreover, now on friendly terms with many literary figures, including Richardson and Smollett. In February 1759 a short life of Voltaire by Goldsmith was due to be published, but it did not appear until two years later. Goldsmith quarrelled again with Griffiths over an attack on his essay *An Enquiry into the Present State of Polite Learning* (April 1759) and they remained lifelong enemies. In this essay Goldsmith compared learning in many countries and argued that the French system of patronage for authors was much to be preferred to that of England, where authors were dependent on niggardly booksellers who demanded quantity before quality. He contributed articles to the *Critical Review* and later to the *British Magazine* and to three periodicals, *The Lady's Magazine*, *The Bee*, and the *Busybody*. He edited and wrote most if not all of *The Bee*, a thirty-two-page weekly magazine on 'The Amusements, Follies and Vices in fashion', running through a wide variety of topics in the eight issues that appeared. He edited *The Lady's Magazine* for a time and produced a series of articles on belles-lettres. In addition, Goldsmith was writing humorous sketches, at which he excelled. He had, however, signed his name only to his essay on *Polite Learning*.

In 1760 Goldsmith had also contracted with the publisher John Newbery to write two letters a week for a new daily, *The Public Ledger*. Goldsmith greatly admired the honesty and integrity of Newbery, who gave him valuable support and direction. The *Chinese Letters*, as the series was soon called, were satirical, humorous, and observant sketches of life in England, supposedly seen through the eyes of a Chinese merchant. They were highly successful.

In 1761 Goldsmith became a close friend of Dr. Johnson and Sir Joshua

Reynolds. Continuing with various commissions for John Newbery, he wrote a series of essays entitled *The Indigent Philosopher* (1762), and had his *Letters* released under a new title, *The Citizen of the World*. He also wrote a biography of Beau Nash, who had died a short time before. At this time Newbery took over the management of Goldsmith's finances with the latter's consent and arranged for Goldsmith to take up residence in a house where he himself lived in Islington. The location suited Goldsmith as it was near the fields and Highgate Hill, and he could spend the day studying and writing. He had now met Boswell, and in 1764 he became one of the original members of Johnson's Club, which met at the Turk's Head. Johnson said Goldsmith was one of the best living authors, an opinion which became general after the publication of his long poem *The Traveller* in 1764. He had achieved fame at last.

Goldsmith's novel, *The Vicar of Wakefield*, appeared in 1766, further enhancing his reputation. The following year he completed his first play, *The Good-Natur'd Man*, which was followed in 1770 by his poem on rural life and agriculture, *The Deserted Village*, a denunciation of industrialism and the rural depopulation it causes. Goldsmith suffered greatly during the delay before the production of his next play from fear of a poor reception. But *She Stoops to Conquer*, which was put on in 1774, enjoyed an enormous success.

In the last years, Goldsmith, now living in the Temple, was well known and well liked, although he was often the object of jokes concerning his behaviour, mannerisms, and speech. Yet, as Johnson observed in what we might consider to be Goldsmith's most suitable epitaph, 'No man was more foolish when he had not a pen in his hand, or more wise when he had.'

After a short illness Oliver Goldsmith died on 4 April 1774, aged only forty-three. He was buried in the Temple Church.

K. C. Balderston (ed.), *The Collected Letters of Oliver Goldsmith* (1928).

R. S. Crane (ed.), *New Essays* (Chicago, 1927).

A. Dobson (ed.), *Complete Poems* (1906).

M. Emslie, *Goldsmith: the Vicar of Wakefield* (1963).

A. Friedman (ed.), *Collected Works* (5 vols.; 1966).

A. Friedman (ed.), *She Stoops to Conquer* (1968).

F. W. Hilles (ed.), *The Vicar of Wakefield* (1951: this is also included in a larger selection edited by the same writer, 1955).

R. H. Hopkins, *The True Genius of Goldsmith* (Baltimore, 1969).

R. Quintana, *Oliver Goldsmith: A Georgian Study* (Toronto, 1967).

A. Lytton Sells, *Oliver Goldsmith: His Life and Works* (1975).

Portraits: oil, by Sir Joshua Reynolds: National Trust, Knole, Kent; oil, half-length, studio of Reynolds, c. 1770: N.P.G.; oil, quarter-length, by Reynolds: Courtauld Institute, London.

Gordon, Lord George (1751–93),

politician and demagogue; instigator of the Gordon riots of 1780.

Lord George Gordon was born on 26 December 1751, the third son of the Duke of Gordon. He joined the navy as an ensign and rose to the rank of lieutenant, but resigned his commission at the age of twenty-one, apparently because Lord Sandwich failed to promise him a ship.

Gordon entered parliament in 1774 as the member for Ludgershall, a Wiltshire borough bought for him by General Simon Fraser. Fraser's intention was to bribe Gordon not to contest the county of Inverness-shire, for which Fraser was also standing. Gordon seems to have had meagre political success and the opposition leaders in the Commons thought little of him, although he had the reputation of being rather wild and dashing. His personal ambitions were rather vague and confused in view of his dislike of Lord North and his Protestant religious fervour.

In 1778 a Relief Act removing some disabilities from Catholic military recruits had been passed in parliament. In 1779 it was proposed to extend this to Scotland, but many Scottish Presbyterians protested vigorously. An association was belatedly formed in England to call for the repeal of the act, and in December 1779 Gordon accepted the presidency of the Protestant Association. Petitions against Roman Catholicism poured into the Commons during 1780. At first these were not taken seriously, but Gordon announced that a Protestant petition would be presented to the House on 2 June 1780, backed by a procession.

London had a reputation for political independence and so not only anti-Papists but also other individuals and groups who flocked to support any protest against the executive government backed the petition. As it was presented before the House, a crowd headed by Gordon blocked the entrances to parliament. Gordon – excited and voluble – moved that the petition be considered by the House and alternately addressed the

Commons and rushed outside to harangue the crowd. The House voted to adjourn consideration of the petition, and as darkness fell, the crowd grew and became wilder. A Roman Catholic chapel in Lincoln's Inn Fields was destroyed and looting and arson began.

The Gordon riots continued until 9 June. Looting and destruction of Catholic homes and places of worship was rampant. Over the period 458 people were killed or wounded, fifty-nine rioters were sentenced to death, and twenty-one of them were hanged. Gordon was taken to the Tower, imprisoned there for eight months, and tried in 1781. He was found not guilty of high treason, since there was no proof that he deliberately incited or even approved the riots, but his career was ended.

Gordon dabbled in various matters thereafter and embraced Judaism. In 1787 he was convicted for a libel on the Queen of France, and after a fruitless attempt to take refuge in the Netherlands, he returned to England for judgment and was sentenced to five years in prison. He spent the rest of his life fairly comfortably in Newgate prison, where he had six to eight people to dine with him daily and gave a ball once a fortnight. When his sentence was completed Gordon was unable to obtain the required securities for his good behaviour and was obliged to stay in Newgate, where he soon afterwards caught jail fever, and died on 1 November 1793.

Christopher Hibbert, *King Mob* (1958).
G. Rucle, 'The Gordon Riots: a study of the Rioters and their Victims', *Transactions of the Royal Historical Society* (1956).

Portraits: glass intaglio, quarter-length, by J. Tassie, 1781: N.P.G.; engraving, from a drawing by R. Bran: British Museum.

Gough, Sir Hugh (1779–1869), general, see *Lives of the Victorian Age*.

Grafton, 3rd Duke of (1735–1811), see Fitzroy, Augustus Henry.

Granville, 1st Earl (1690–1763), see Carteret, John.

Grattan, Henry (1746–1820), Irish statesman.

Henry Grattan was baptized on 3 July 1746 in Dublin. He was the son of the Recorder of the City of Dublin, and his mother was the daughter of a chief justice of Ireland – in fact he came of a leading family of the ruling Anglo-Irish establishment. He was educated locally and then at Trinity College, Dublin, graduating in 1767.

After graduation Grattan entered chambers in the Middle Temple in London, but had little interest in legal studies, preferring to practise oratory instead. During this time he suffered the loss of his favourite sister and then his mother. Shortly afterwards he was introduced to Henry Flood, the leader of the newly-formed Irish Patriot Party pledged to free Ireland from the crippling colonial status imposed on her by England. Flood persuaded Grattan to enter politics, and as a beginning they collaborated on a series of articles for a paper called the *Freeman's Journal*, later published as a separate collection.

Grattan was called to the Irish bar in 1772, but practised only for a very short time. He heartily disliked both the corrupt legal practices of the day and many of his fellow lawyers. In 1775 he began his political career as member for the borough of Charlemont. At this time the same system of pocket and rotten boroughs prevailed in Ireland as in England, with the added injustice that the Irish parliament represented only the Episcopalian Anglo-Irish, one twelfth of the entire population. The Catholic majority and the increasing minority of northern dissenters had neither representatives nor voting rights. In practice this mattered less than one might expect, because the real power, both executive and military, lay with the Lord Lieutenant and the Privy Council in Dublin Castle, appointed direct by the English crown, and the few legislative powers that were allotted to the Irish parliament were circumscribed by a whole body of earlier restraining acts. Irish trade was also being strangled by English control, through the common eighteenth-century practice whereby all colonies were subject to trade restrictions in any area where they might threaten the market of the mother country. As a result of attempts to circumvent these restrictions, corruption was widespread.

It was this corruption that Grattan set out almost quixotically to attack, armed only with his oratorical talent and his integrity. In his maiden speech he opposed financial grants to the three Vice Treasurers of Parliament, two of whom lived permanently in England. He condemned the granting of pensions to buy support for various measures, and often vigorously attacked English trading restrictions. He opposed England's colonial policy in America. However, his opposition to the policies of successive English governments did not affect his fundamental English patriotism, and in 1778, when English troops had been withdrawn from Ireland to fight in America, he helped to raise an army of Volunteers for Ireland's defence against a possible French invasion.

In 1779 Grattan petitioned the Lord Lieutenant for free trade for Ireland, and shortly afterwards several measures were indeed passed that eased restrictions considerably. Grattan realized, however, that all measures were worthless if a British government could rescind them at will. His next move therefore was to press for Irish legislative independence. In this he had the support of the Volunteers, many of whom had refused to disband after the war, preferring to use their potential as a private army to support the campaigns for freedom of the Irish legislature and abolition of the Penal Code that had for long imposed disabilities on Catholics and later on the more radical Dissenters.

In 1782 Grattan finally achieved the repeal of Poyning's Law of 1494, under which all Irish legislation had to be approved by the English monarchy, and then of the later Declaratory Act of 1719, which allowed the English parliament to pass acts binding on Ireland. Grattan hoped thus gradually and through parliamentary democracy to achieve Irish freedom in all but name. Other Irish Patriots, however, led by Henry Flood, wanted nothing less than full independence, followed by a more widely based Protestant franchise. During the final phase, which now followed – that of 'Grattan's Parliament' – Grattan found himself gradually forced into opposition. He had refused to take cabinet office, in order to be seen to be above corruption, and trusted entirely to his own powers of persuasion to carry his arguments. He now advocated the disbanding of the Volunteers, but Flood wanted to keep them to support his Protestant reforms. The extreme radicals had hopes of enforcing the new universal suffrage. Grattan feared the enfranchisement of the illiterate but did want to see the franchise extended to all educated men.

The rift between Grattan and Flood grew, leading eventually to a duel, which both survived. Grattan continued to make eloquent speeches in the Irish parliament but they were of negligible use in taming corruption, their only real effect being to gain Grattan a reputation in England for being seditious and inflammatory.

The Irish parliament was by now drastically out of touch with affairs in the real world. From 1790 onwards, agrarian discontent grew from a rumble to a roar and many feared revolution. Though no radical, Grattan spoke out against the unfairness of the tithe system, but again to no avail. In 1797, when martial law was proclaimed in Ulster to try to prevent the 'United Irish' insurrection that was imminent, he opposed it on principle, although he too feared the United Irishmen. Eventually, unable to support repressive measures or to condone rebellion, he seceded from the House with the opposition members.

The United Irishmen's rebellion erupted in 1798. During its course Grattan was in England and in his absence was falsely accused of complicity in it. His name was stuck off the rolls of honour everywhere and as the Irish parliament came to its end in 1800 his career seemed at an end also. However, in the last session of the old House, though ill and forced to remain seated, he rose to the occasion and poured eloquent scorn on Pitt, who with his Act of Union (said to have been pushed through at a cost of two million pounds in bribes and newly created seats) proposed 'to buy . . . what cannot be sold – liberty'.

In 1805, after a seemly interval to express his protest at the dissolution of the Irish parliament, Grattan accepted a seat in London as M.P. for Malton. Later, in 1806, he became a member of the Irish Privy Council and also, more appropriately, the representative of Dublin, but he refused the post of Chancellor of the Exchequer, preferring to remain independent. His maiden speech to the English House of Commons, on behalf of the Irish Catholics, was said to have been 'one of the most brilliant and eloquent speeches ever pronounced within the walls of Parliament'. Again, however, his oratory availed him nothing.

Until his death in London on 4 June 1820, Grattan continued to fight indefatigably but unsuccessfully for Catholic emancipation, only withdrawing occasionally to relax with his hobby of translating the works of Maria Edgeworth into French. Grattan was buried in Westminster Abbey, near Chatham and Fox.

S. Gwynn, *Henry Grattan and His Times* (1939).

W. H. H. Lecky, *Leaders of Public Opinion in Ireland* (1912).

Portraits: oil on panel, quater-length, by F. Wheatley, 1782: N.P.G.; oil, after Gilbert Stuart: National Gallery of Ireland, Dublin.

Gray, Thomas (1716–71), poet and man of letters; author of 'Elegy Written in a Country Churchyard'.

Thomas Gray was born on 26 December 1716, the son of Philip Gray, a scrivener of Cornhill, London. He was the only one of twelve children to survive infancy. His father was violent and excessively jealous, given to punching and kicking his wife. She, despite seeking a legal separation from him, decided to stay with him until his death for the sake of Thomas, whom she alone supported through school and college with money from a millinery shop that she and her sister managed.

To give the rather frail child the benefit of country air and to free him from the unhappy atmosphere at home, his mother sent Gray at the age of eight to Eton, where his two uncles were masters. He showed great promise, enjoying the classics particularly, and in due time he began composing Latin verse.

On leaving Eton in 1734 Gray went to Cambridge. His letters at this time show that his life at Peterhouse was far from happy. The rough and tumble of student life pleased him as little as the obligatory study of mathematics and philosophy, and money from his mother was in short

supply. In 1736 Gray, with two former and still intimate school friends, Horace Walpole and Richard West, contributed verses to the *Hymeneals* in honour of the marriage of the Prince of Wales. In this year an aunt of Gray's left him just enough money to allow him to abandon his hated degree course, and he decided to read for the bar at the Inner Temple.

Gray's legal career was, to his joy, postponed when Walpole invited him to join him on the Grand Tour. On 29 March 1739 they sailed to Calais and started their journey through France and Italy. At first their enthusiasm for sightseeing was shared, but gradually Walpole, being on his own admission vain, insolent, and patronizing, began to disregard Gray's interests and follow his own less scholarly pursuits. They quarrelled and in September 1741 Gray returned to England alone. The tour, Gray's only journey abroad, had increased his delight in beauty and fed his appetite for history, but had temporarily lost him his close intimacy with Walpole.

Gray's father died in November 1741, leaving his family very little money. His mother went to live with her sisters at Stoke Poges, Buckinghamshire, and Gray spent a very happy winter in London, visiting the opera and theatres, and meeting the great Alexander Pope. The sad death from consumption of Richard West, however, affected Gray deeply, and inspired the last and finest of his Latin poems.

The year 1742, spent in the quiet countryside around Stoke Poges, saw a sudden burst of creative energy such as Gray never again experienced. Having written virtually no English poetry before, he began with an 'Ode on the Spring', written for West, 'not knowing he was then dead'. There followed the beautiful and moving 'Sonnet on the Death of Richard West' in August (not published in Gray's lifetime) and in the same month he finished his 'Ode on a distant prospect of Eton College' and his 'Hymn to Adversity'. It seems likely that in this summer too he began the great 'Elegy Written in a Country Churchyard', though it was not published until 1751.

In October 1742 Gray returned to Cambridge where he spent most of the rest of his life. It was cheap, had good libraries, and did not involve his making any decisions. 'I am like a cabbage,' he later wrote to Walpole; 'where I'm stuck I love to grow.' At first he maintained that his intention was to become a barrister in the Ecclesiastical and Admiralty Courts, for which he needed a degree in civil law, but this was a useful excuse to please his mother and aunts and to allow him a life among books, 'For my life is nothing but books – with different sauces.' He went back to Peterhouse as a fellow-commoner, duly became a Bachelor of Civil Law, and gave up all further interest in a legal career. His friends were at Pembroke Hall, notably James Brown, the kindly son of a Durham doctor, and Thomas Wharton, a friendly sensible man and lifelong admirer and critic of Gray, and his time was spent largely in their company and away from the communal life of his college.

In 1744 Gray revived his friendship with Walpole. In 1747 he showed him his Eton Ode, which Dodsley published in pamphlet form to little public comment. In 1748 it was republished in Dodsley's *Collection of Poems*, together with the 'Ode to the Spring' and the 'Ode on the Death of a Favourite Cat' – Walpole's cat, Selima. This poem, a witty casual gem, caught the popular fancy and achieved unexpected immortality. However, it was the only new creative work Gray produced for seven years, save for an abandoned didactic poem, 'The Alliance

of Education and Government'.

In 1750 Gray completed his best-known poem, the 'Elegy Written in a Country Churchyard'. Wolfe said that he would rather have written it than have taken Quebec; Johnson, disapproving if not openly scornful of Gray's other work, admitted, 'It abounds with images which find a mirror in every mind and with sentiments to which every bosom returns an echo.' It was an immediate popular success, and within two months of its publication, on 16 February 1751, had gone through four editions. It was reprinted in 1753, with his other works and a comic poem, 'The Long Story', in a book illustrated by Richard Bentley, and Gray's reputation was made.

At Cambridge Gray was working on two Pindaric odes, which were published in 1757, 'The Bard' and 'The Progress of Poesy'. These were a deliberate return to classical form and are highly allusive and erudite. Garrick, Goldsmith, and others voiced their admiration of the odes, but to many their remote subjects and difficult language seemed rather absurd. Gray himself always considered his odes to be his finest work.

Gray moved to Pembroke Hall in 1756, his mother having died three years before. Apart from short spells away, such as holidays in Scotland and the North, he lived quietly in Cambridge for the rest of his life. He wrote very little more poetry except for the 'Ode to Music', an occasional piece written to celebrate the installation of the Duke of Grafton as Chancellor of Cambridge University in 1769, though his journals, commonplace books, and letters show his ever-increasing erudition.

Gray was offered the laureateship on the death of Colley Cibber in 1757 and refused it, as he refused an honorary doctorate from Aberdeen in 1765. In 1768 he accepted the chair of history at

Cambridge, though he took no active part in lecturing, living privately and seeing only his friends, particularly Wharton, James Brown, Norton Nicholls, William Mason (who as his literary executor was responsible for 'preparing' and publishing Gray's journal and letters), sometimes Walpole, and later Victor Bonstetten, who wrote a memoir describing Gray's last years.

Gray was always worried about his health, and suffered frequent attacks of gout, though it appears that in fact a kidney infection caused the uraemia that resulted in his death at Pembroke Hall on 30 July 1771. He was buried with his mother at Stoke Poges, where a large monument marks the scene of his famous poem and the tomb of the poet.

Matthew Arnold, *Essays in Criticism, Second Series* (1888).

Sir Edmund Gosse (ed.), *Complete Works in Prose and Verse* (4 vols.; 1902–6, rev. ed.).

Samuel Johnson, *Lives of the Poets* (1779–81).

W. Powell Jones, *Thomas Gray, Scholar* (Cambridge, Mass., 1937).

R. W. Ketton-Cremer, *Gray: a Biography* (1955).

C. S. Northup, *A Bibliography of Thomas Gray* (New Haven, 1917).

A. Lane Poole, *Gray and Collins: Poetical Works* (rev. ed.; 1966).

H. W. Starr, *Gray as a Literary Critic* (Philadelphia, 1941).

H. W. Starr and J. R. Hendrickson (eds.), *The Complete Poems of Thomas Gray, English, Latin and Greek* (1966).

G. Tillotson, *Augustan Studies* (1961).

D. C. Tovey (ed.), *Gray's English Poems* (1922, rev. ed.).

P. Toynbee and L. Whibley (eds.), *Correspondence* (3 vols.; 1935).

L. Whibley (ed.), *Poems* (1939).

Portraits: oil, three-quarter length, by J. G. Eccardt, 1748: N.P.G.; pencil, quarter-length, by J. Basire, after W. Mason, 1771: N.P.G.

Grenville, George (1712–70), statesman, First Lord of the Treasury (1763–5).

George Grenville was born on 14 October 1712, the second son of Richard Grenville of Wotton Hall, Buckingham-shire. He was educated at Eton and at Christ Church, Oxford. He was called to the bar at the Inner Temple in 1735 but, forsaking the law for politics, was elected M.P. for the borough of Buckingham in the general election of 1741. He was appointed one of the Lords of the Admiralty in December 1744, but he temporarily opposed the government's measures during 1745 until William Pitt the Elder (q.v.) obtained preferment. Grenville became Treasurer of the Navy in the Duke of Newcastle's administration, and was sworn a member of the Privy Council in 1754.

His untiring industry had already been noted in the House by Pitt, but when in 1755 Grenville attacked the government's foreign policy, he was dismissed from his office. Twelve months later he returned under the Duke of Devonshire to his former post in the navy department, but resigned in 1757 because of the dismissal of Pitt and Temple from the government. By June, however, he was back in the same office.

After George III's accession in 1760, Grenville, under Bute's influence, began to break away from Pitt. In 1761 he was admitted to the cabinet while still Treasurer of the Navy. In the same year Pitt resigned and Grenville, refusing the post of Secretary of State, preferred to retain his navy post and take the lead in the Commons. In May 1762, however, he succeeded Bute as Secretary of State for the Northern Department and had considerable differences with him over the terms of the French peace treaty. Bute called in Fox to defend the terms of the treaty in the Commons in place of Grenville, who was forced to resign. He became First Lord of the Admiralty in autumn 1762.

In March of the following year Grenville reminded the House that the expenses of the recent war called for new taxes and 'wished gentlemen would show him *where* to lay them'. Pitt imitated the languid tone of his question in the words of an old ditty, 'Gentle Shepherd, tell me where!' and then bitterly attacked Grenville. The nickname 'Gentle Shepherd' stuck to Grenville for a long time. In the same month Fox urged Bute to remove Grenville from the government, since in his opinion the man was 'an hindrance, not a help, and sometimes a very great inconvenience to those he is joined with'.

However, on Bute's resignation (April 1763) Grenville was appointed First Lord of the Treasury and Chancellor of the Exchequer. Shortly afterwards the session ended with the King's speech, in which he mentioned 'the happy effects' of the recently concluded treaty. The speech provoked an attack by John Wilkes (q.v.) in the celebrated Number 45 of his periodical, *The North Briton*, for which he was arrested. Grenville, resenting interference from Bute, complained that his ministry did not enjoy the full confidence of the King. King George tried desperately to displace Grenville, but eventually had to ask him to remain. Grenville agreed on condition that Bute's influence with the King should cease.

On 9 March 1764 Grenville introduced his budget, followed by proposals for the imposition of duties on several articles of American commerce. These were carried without opposition. Unanimous agreement also carried his fifty-five resolutions of February 1765, which imposed on America almost the same stamp duties as those which were then established in England. After the King's first severe mental collapse, a Regency Bill was hastily introduced into the Lords, but by a blunder the name of the Princess Dowager of Wales was omitted. The King recovered while the bill was still under discussion and, weary of Grenville's

tedious manner and overbearing temper, again attempted unsuccessfully to oust him. Grenville, retaining his office, stipulated that Bute be excluded from the councils, and that his brother, James Stuart Mackenzie (Lord Privy Seal of Scotland), and Lord Holland (Paymaster General) should be dismissed. The King, reluctantly agreeing, determined to rid himself of the ministry. The Marquis of Rockingham (see Watson-Wentworth, Charles) was appointed First Lord of the Treasury on Grenville's dismissal on 10 July 1765.

When parliament met in December, Grenville immediately attacked the new administration over its American policy and opposed the repeal of the Stamp Act vigorously. During the 1767 session he and a colleague in the opposition, William Dowdeswell, defeated the ministry over its budget and carried an amendment reducing the land tax. In 1768 a pamphlet appeared that was attributed to Grenville though in fact written by William Knox with Grenville's assistance. *The Present State of the Nation; particularly with respect to its Trade, Finances etc., etc. Addressed to the King and both Houses of Parliament* contained several dreary prognostications and accused the Rockingham party of ruining the country; it elicited a reply from Burke called *Observations on a late publication intituled the Present State of the Nation*.

Though Grenville had taken a prominent part in the early measures against Wilkes, he opposed his expulsion from the Commons in 1769. Despite already failing health, he obtained leave in 1770 to introduce a bill of electoral reform, which became law on 12 April. Grenville made his last speech on 9 May and died at his house in London on 13 November 1770.

Grenville's administration had been a series of blunders: the prosecution of Wilkes discredited the executive and the legislature; his mismanagement of the Regency Bill damaged his reputation and infuriated George III; and his measures regarding America hastened the revolution. Grenville's chief gifts, however, included a considerable financial ability, unflagging industry, and an inflexible integrity in both public and private life. His speeches, though not eloquent, were fluent and impressive, but he was a tactless and obstinate man. Burke said of him: 'He took public business not as a duty which he was to fulfil, but as a pleasure he was to enjoy. . . . If he was ambitious . . . it was to win his way to power, through the laborious gradations of public service.'

Lewis M. Wiggin, *The Faction of Cousins: A Political Account of the Grenvilles* (New Haven, Conn., 1958).

Portraits: oil, by Sir Joshua Reynolds: National Trust, Petworth House, Sussex; engraving, three-quarter length, by James Watson after a portrait by William Hoare: Mansell Collection, British Museum.

Grenville, William Wyndham

(1759–1834), Baron Grenville; statesman who, as Prime Minister in 1806, was the nominal head of the so-called Ministry of All the Talents.

William Wyndham Grenville was born on 25 October 1759, the youngest son of George Grenville (q.v.). He was educated at Eton and at Christ Church College, Oxford; after graduating with a B.A. degree in 1780 he became a student at Lincoln's Inn, but two years later he abandoned his legal studies on his election as M.P. for Buckingham.

Grenville's first official appointment was as chief secretary to his brother, George Nugent Temple Grenville, then the Lord Lieutenant of Ireland; this post was not held long, however, since both men resigned in June 1783. In the first ministry of William Pitt the Younger (q.v.) Grenville was appointed Paymaster General, and he also became a member of the Privy Council. After further work as Vice President of the Committee of Trade and also as a diplomatic emissary to The Hague, Grenville was elected Speaker of the House of Commons in 1789. In a debate on the slave trade Grenville made a notable speech in support of Wilberforce's abolitionist aims, and in this and other speeches his firm principles and powerful debating abilities attracted wide notice. After only five months as Speaker, Grenville resigned in June 1789 to become Home Secretary; in the following year he became President of the Board of Control, and on the election of a new parliament he was created Baron Grenville and entrusted with the conduct of government business in the House of Lords.

As Foreign Secretary, a post to which he was appointed in 1791, Grenville's early concern for the maintenance of peace was soon replaced by a firm conviction that a policy of war against France was both necessary and right: 'in the establishment of the French republic', he declared, 'is included the overthrow of all the other governments of Europe.' This fear of the disruptive consequences of foreign revolution was complemented by a belief in the need for repressive measures at home, and the legislation with which Grenville concerned himself included the suspension of Habeas Corpus (1794) and the Seditious Meetings Act (1795).

In March 1799 Grenville moved the resolutions for political union with Ireland. Grenville and Pitt agreed completely on the need for new laws affording greater freedom to Catholics if this union was to be effective, and when Pitt resigned in 1801, following George III's refusal to countenance such measures, Grenville and several other ministers followed suit. In 1804, having worked with Pitt and Fox to bring about the collapse of Addington's administration, Grenville refused to accept office in Pitt's new ministry unless Fox also was given an appointment. George III's refusal to allow Fox to take office meant Grenville's consequent isolation, which marked the end of his friendship with Pitt.

Following Pitt's death in 1806, Grenville was asked to form a ministry. The resulting coalition administration came to be known as the Ministry of All the Talents, Grenville himself holding office as First Lord of the Treasury (chief minister); Fox was finally allowed to hold office as Foreign Secretary. The most important achievement of this ministry was the abolition of the slave trade, a measure that received the King's assent on the very day the government left office in March 1807; success in other fields was hampered by the failure of peace negotiations with France and by Grenville's own mismanagement of financial affairs. The issue that brought about the fall of his government was again that of Catholic emancipation: George III, who disliked Grenville's proposed measure for opening up careers in the armed services to Catholic entry, demanded a positive assurance from Grenville that he would never again attempt to gain concessions for Catholics, and when this was refused he began to look for other more manageable servants, appointing the Duke of Portland (see Bentinck, William Henry Cavendish) as Prime Minister.

Many of Grenville's colleagues considered that he had committed political suicide, believing that by tactful management he should have been able both to get his measures passed and also to appease the King. Grenville himself, however, held firmly to the political principles in which he believed, and at the end of Portland's administration in 1809, as well as on several later occasions, he refused to compromise these principles by accepting the offer of new ministerial appointments. In December 1809 Grenville was elected Chancellor of Oxford University. He remained an active politician, his speeches including one against the slave trade in the newly restored French colonies in 1814, and another on the need for the immediate renewal of war against France after the escape of Napoleon from Elba in 1815. In 1816 he supported a proposal for an official inquiry into the conduct of Irish affairs. His last parliamentary speech, delivered in June 1822, again concerned the issue of Catholic emancipation.

After suffering a stroke in 1823 Grenville retired from active political life to his Buckinghamshire home of Dropmore Lodge. He died there on 12 January 1834, leaving a wife, Anne Pitt, the only daughter of Thomas, Baron Camelford, whom he had married in 1792.

Correspondence of William Wyndham Grenville in the *Dropmore MSS* (Historical Manuscripts Commission, 10 vols.; 1892).

A. D. Harvey, 'The Ministry of All the Talents', *The Historical Journal*, xv, 4 (1972).

M. Roberts, *The Whig Party 1807–12* (1939).

Portrait: oil, half-length, by J. Hoppner: N.P.G.

Grey, Charles (1764–1845), 2nd Earl Grey; politician and leader of the Whig party, who was Prime Minister during the passage of the Reform Act of 1832.

Charles Grey was born on 13 March 1764 at Falloden, Northumberland, the eldest son of Sir Charles Grey, a distinguished general who was made Earl Grey in 1801. As a student at Eton and King's College, Cambridge, he was not outstanding, and he left Cambridge without a degree to undertake the Grand Tour (1784–6). In July 1786 he was elected M.P. for Northumberland. Forsaking the Tory opinions of his family, he associated himself with Charles James Fox (q.v.), the leader of the liberal Whig party and a formidable opponent of the conservative government of William Pitt. Grey was popular in London society and a member of the Whig club.

The outbreak of the French Revolution in 1789 aroused in England among certain groups of individuals a desire for greater democracy in government, but this for many seemed to pose a positive threat to the continued existence of a constitutional monarchy. Grey and a number of other young Whig aristocrats believed that radical reform could be forestalled by the introduction of moderate reform, and in 1792 they formed the Society of the Friends of the People to petition parliament in this cause. Grey became the established leader of the moderate reform movement and during the 1790s introduced a number of reform bills, all of which were heavily defeated. Pitt's administration, though repressive, was backed by public opinion, and the pro-French policies advocated by Fox and his followers not only lost them popular support but also divided the Whig party, many of whom joined forces with the Tories.

In November 1794 Grey married Mary Elizabeth Ponsonby, the daughter of a prominent Irish family. The liberal connections of this family won him over to the cause of Catholic emancipation, for which he was to remain a powerful advocate for the rest of his political life. His marriage proved so successful, however, that the delights of family life at the country house at Howick on the Northumberland coast began to take precedence over his political responsibilities, and the four-day journey to London was a sufficient obstacle to reduce his parliamentary appearances. Moreover he had lost a good deal of his radicalism and was no longer identified so closely with the anti-war stance of Fox. Grey preferred a policy of continuing to prosecute the war, yet giving due consideration to any peace initiative.

On Pitt's death in 1806 Grenville formed his so-called Ministry of All the Talents, which included the Foxite Whigs, so that Grey was appointed First Lord of the Admiralty. When Fox died in the same year Grey took his place as Foreign Secretary and leader of the Commons. He just had time to carry to a successful conclusion Fox's bill for abolishing the slave trade when, in the following year, the ministry was defeated after the King had vetoed a bill to admit Catholics to the armed forces. In 1807 his Catholic sympathies lost him the Northumberland seat in an election, and instead he represented first Appleby, and then Tavistock, before being elevated to the House of Lords after his father's death in the same year.

Grey and Grenville became the two leaders of the Whig opposition to the Tory administration of Lord Liverpool, but they were only occasionally effective. In general Grey suported Catholic claims and opposed the foreign policy of Castlereagh, especially the Vienna settlement of 1814 because it ignored the principle of national self-determination. A split in the leadership occurred when Grenville and his followers gave their support to the repressive policies of the Liverpool administration, such as the 1817 Act suspending Habeas Corpus. Many Whigs moved over to the Tories and by 1821 Grey was the sole leader of the opposition Whigs. During the 1820s many reform bills were presented to parliament, notably those of Lord John Russell, but as none of these got past a first reading in the Commons they never reached the Lords, so Grey had no opportunity to support them. He made it clear that the Whig party did not stand for universal manhood suffrage but for a conservative adjustment of the representation system that might enable the people of England to avoid the worst excesses of government by the ultra-Tories on the one hand or the democratic radicals on the other.

After the inconclusive election of July 1830, the survival of the Duke of Wellington's ministry seemed unlikely, and its fall was virtually guaranteed when Wellington replied to a question about parliamentary reform to the effect that he considered the present system of representation perfectly adequate. In November the new King, William IV, asked Grey to form an administration on the understanding that some measure of reform, for which there was by now tremendous public demand, would be introduced. The outbreak of a revolution in France, albeit a peaceful one, further worried the government. Grey found himself back in the situation of 1789; again he felt that moderate reform could prevent drastic upheaval. As Prime Minister he could now perhaps put this idea into practice. The fear of what might happen if he could not lent him boldness.

The ministry that Grey formed was composed almost exclusively of peers and persons of title, and his own family was well represented. The new reform bill was effectively drafted by a committee headed by his son-in-law, Lord Durham (see Lambton, John). Now in his old age, Grey was still a powerful orator, and it is to his credit both as a man of courage and as a delicate negotiator that he was able to carry a reform bill that, when first introduced in 1831, seemed even to his own supporters to be a little too daring. It required a fresh general election and coercion of the House of Lords before the bill ultimately passed into law. A great obstacle to its passage was King William himself, who had to be handled with great tact and patience before being convinced of its necessity.

The Reform Act finally became law, after several delays, in the summer of 1832. It was the fullest expression of the beliefs of the Old Whig party to which Grey belonged. Yet social and economic conditions were changing so fast that the act, while it abolished pocket boroughs and other corrupt practices, had the effect of enfranchising only a small number of the new property owners and industrialists. Some conditions of franchise were changed, but only 200,000 upper middle class Britons were added to the electoral roll.

Many of the Whigs who had supported reform were, in fact, less democratic than their opponents. Although a grateful public voted in 1833 for a vast liberal majority, the older Whigs did not regard this as a mandate for further reforms of church and state. Some of Grey's younger colleagues felt differently, however, and dissension grew in the ministry over the difficult problem of Ireland. Grey, now in his seventieth year, had lost his enthusiasm for leadership and he took the opportunity of a dispute over the Irish Coercion

Bill to resign with his Chancellor, Lord Althorp (see Spencer, John Charles), in 1834. He was glad to be free of the responsibilities of office and lived the rest of his life in retirement until his death at Howick on 17 July 1845.

M. Brock, *The Great Reform Act* (1973).

J. R. M. Butler, *The Passing of the Great Reform Bill* (1914).

A. Mitchell, *The Whigs in Opposition, 1815–1830* (1967).

G. M. Trevelyan, *Lord Grey of the Reform Bill* (1929, 2nd ed.).

G. Woodbridge, *The Reform Bill of 1832* (New York, 1970).

Portraits: oil, half-length, after T. Lawrence, *c.* 1828: N.P.G.; oil, three-quarter length, attributed to T. Phillips, *c.* 1820: N.P.G.; pencil, quarter-length, by B. R. Haydon, 1834: N.P.G.

Grimaldi, Joseph (1778–1837), clown.

Joseph Grimaldi was born on 18 December 1778 in Clare Market, London, the bastard son of an Italian comic dancer, Giuseppe Grimaldi, and a Mrs. Rebecca Brooker, a cockney chorus girl forty years his junior. Joe, as he was soon called, first appeared on stage at Sadler's Wells at the age of two and in 1783, when aged only four, appeared in pantomime at Drury Lane. Although sent to the boarding school of Mr. Ford at Putney, he was soon back in the theatrical world again, and in 1788 he danced at Sadler's Wells and Drury Lane on the same night, running from one theatre to the other.

In 1799 Grimaldi married Maria Hughes, the daughter of a proprietor of Sadler's Wells. He was doing well, had begun to make a name for himself as a clown, and was blissfully happy with Maria, but his life was dogged by misfortune. His investments failed and in 1800 Maria died in pregnancy. In 1802 he married again, this time an actress, Miss Bristow, who bore him a son destined to bring his parents misery by a life of drunkenness, culminating in insanity and early death.

Grimaldi was at this time acting in melodrama as well as comedy. Some said he never bettered his performance as Bob Acres in Sheridan's *The Rivals*, but already the pure clowning of the Commedia dell'Arte and its successors was his special province. One of his favourite characters was Scaramouche.

In 1806, as the clown in *Mother Goose* at Covent Garden, Grimaldi achieved his best known success. This production was revived year after year and the clown won an adoring public. However, as he approached forty he began to grow prematurely old. A friend related how, when he came off stage, his sinews were so knotted with cramp that not even violent rubbing would ease the pain. In futile efforts to protect his wife from having to work in the chorus at Covent Garden because of their poverty, he kept on clowning despite his condition, until it became impossible to continue. In 1828 Covent Garden refused him a benefit, but Sadler's Wells granted him one, to be his last performance. His weary legs could not hold him and he sang seated on a chair; yet even so his reception was rapturous. 'I have no hope,' he said, 'that I shall ever again be able to appear before you.'

Sadly he lingered on another ten years, never well, but writing his memoirs to keep his family solvent (these were later edited by the young Charles Dickens, under his pseudonym of Boz, and published in 1838). In 1837 Grimaldi sat at the back of a box at Covent Garden for a performance of *Mother Goose*. Pointed out by an actor, he was carried to the front and wildly cheered. Much moved, he could say little but 'God bless you all.' Two months later, on 31 May 1837, he died in his sleep.

Grimaldi was a small, dark man of great charm, kindness and generosity. His face and voice were wonderfully mobile and funny and he was best loved for his songs. 'Hot Codlins', a favourite, was about an old woman who felt cold,

> So to keep herself warm she thought it no sin
> To fetch for herself a quartern of . . .

'Gin!' roared the audience, and crying 'Oh! For shame!', Grimaldi would sing the next verse. Dubbed the Hogarth of the stage, he had, according to Hood, 'A free and easy body without a bone in it', but in fact he was the sad clown who punned with some truth, 'I'm Grim all-day, but I make you laugh all night.'

Charles Dickens (ed.), *Memoirs of Joseph Grimaldi* (2 vols.; 1838).

R. Findlater, *Grimaldi* (1955).

Portrait: oil, half-length, by J. Cawse: N.P.G.

Guilford, 2nd Earl of (1732–92), see North, Frederick.

Gurney, Elizabeth (1780–1845), see Fry, Elizabeth.

H

Hales, Stephen (1677–1761), chemist, botanist, and inventor.

Stephen Hales was born in September 1677 at Bekesbourne, Kent. He entered Corpus Christi College, Cambridge, in 1696, where he studied chemistry, anatomy, and mathematics. In 1702 he was elected a fellow, and in the following year graduated as B.A. During this period he also studied theology, and after taking Holy Orders he was appointed perpetual curate of Teddington, Middlesex (1709), where he became a close friend of his neighbour Alexander Pope (q.v.). In 1711 he received the degree of Bachelor of Divinity.

His casual interest in botany was greatly stimulated by reading John Ray's *Flora of Cambridge*. This early love and curiosity about plant physiology developed into a serious scientific pursuit, and in 1718 he was elected a Fellow of the Royal Society. As the result of his later contributions to the Society, Hales was twice awarded their Copley Medal (in 1718 and 1739). In 1753 he was elected a foreign associate of the French Academy of Sciences.

His research on the physiology of plants resulted in the publishing of the first volume of his *Statical Essays* in 1727. In his work, *Vegetable Staticks*, he described experiments that explained how plants receive their nourishment, how they absorb water and air, and the factors affecting their growth. He calculated the rate at which water enters roots and the rate of its rise in the stems. He measured the pressure of roots at various times during the day, and was among the first to recognize that sunlight has a crucial effect on the growth of living organisms. Many of his methods are still found useful in the teaching of experimental plant physiology and in botanical laboratories.

During the course of his experiments, Hales found that some substance in the air was vital for plant growth, although he did not realize that this was carbon dioxide. In his attempts to isolate various gases he was basically unsuccessful, and he was unaware of the potential significance of this phase of his work. His grounding in careful scientific method may be due in part to the effect of Newton, who left Cambridge in the same year that Hales arrived. Newton's influence was widely felt, and accounts indirectly for Hales's devotion to physical description and quantitative measurement.

In 1733 Hales published *Haemastatics*, the second volume of his *Statical Essays*. In this work he reported his experiments on animal physiology, in particular on the circulation of the blood. He is probably the first man ever to have measured blood pressure, by inserting hollow glass tubes directly into veins and arteries and noting the height to which the blood rose in the tube with each beat of the heart. It was from these highly original investigations that modern methods of blood-pressure measurement eventually developed.

Hales was also an inventor. He designed a ventilating device made from old organ bellows for use in enclosed spaces – such as prison cells, hospital rooms, and the holds of ships. He fully outlined his ideas and proposals in *A Description of Ventilators*, published in 1743. As a direct result of the introduction of a ventilator constructed

after his design, the death rate in the Savoy prison was greatly reduced. Similar ventilators were later successfully introduced on the Continent and were widely used throughout England. His other inventions included a mercury pressure gauge for measuring the depth of the ocean, a still that converted salt water to fresh water, a method of preserving meat, and a means of fumigating corn to protect it from weevils. He also invented special surgical forceps by means of which bladder and kidney stones could be removed. His short work on the evils of alcoholic drink, *Admonition to the Drinkers of Gin, Brandy, Etc.* (1734) was reprinted several times in the eighteenth century.

Hales was on friendly terms with Frederick Louis (q.v.), the Prince of Wales, and after his death was appointed almoner to the Princess Dowager and a canon of Windsor. He died at Teddington, Middlesex, on 4 January 1761 at the age of eighty-three.

A. E. Clark-Kennedy, *Stephen Hales: an Eighteenth Century Biography* (Cambridge and New York, 1929; reprinted Ridgewood, N.J., 1965).

C. J. Singer *et al.* (eds.), *A History of Technology*, vol. iv (1958).

Portrait: oil, quarter-length, by T. Hudson, *c.* 1759: N.P.G.

Halley, Edmond (1656–1742), astronomer and oceanographer, see *Lives of the Stuart Age.*

Hamilton, Emma, Lady (?1761–1815), celebrated mistress of Lord Nelson (q.v.).

Emma Hamilton was born perhaps as early as 1761, the daughter of Henry Lyon, a Cheshire blacksmith. She was apparently baptized as Amy Lyon on 12 May 1765 at Great Neston, Cheshire. Shortly after this her father died and her mother took her back to her own native Wales.

Emma seems to have received little or no education. At an early age she went to London to act as a nursemaid in the family of Dr. Richard Budd. Later (though this is not certain) she became the mistress of one Captain John Willet Payne, a naval officer who was probably the father of her first child, born in 1780. After various jobs, she accepted the protection of Sir Harry Featherstonehaugh, whose mistress she was until he turned her out in December 1781, by which time she was pregnant again.

With no money, Emma, at this time calling herself Emily Hart, now became attached to Sir Charles Greville. Greville kept Emma on for the next four years or so, encouraging her to learn to read and also teaching her to sing. She loved him, it seems, but by 1786 Greville was labouring under the burden of innumerable debts and his feelings for Emma had cooled considerably. He now came to an arrangement with his uncle, Sir William Hamilton, British Ambassador in Naples, by which Hamilton agreed to settle Greville's financial problems in exchange for being allowed to 'take over' his mistress.

207

Hamilton had first met Emma in 1784 on a visit to England. He had been impressed by her extraordinary beauty, which had already caught the artistic eye of one of Greville's friends, the portrait painter George Romney (q.v.). For her part, Emma was very keen to go with Hamilton to Naples, and after an initial outburst of temper when she realized that she had been in effect sold, she settled down in her new surroundings and soon became a popular and active member of English Neapolitan society. She learned to speak Italian fluently, studied music, at which her talent was not inconsiderable, and captivated everyone with her lively good looks.

In May 1791, Hamilton and Emma returned on leave to England, where they were married on 6 September. Back in Naples again after her short absence, the new Lady Hamilton got to know Queen Maria Caroline. Their association became intimate and certainly confidential intelligence concerning their respective countries passed between them. Queen Maria Caroline was undoubtedly a shrewd politician but the extent to which she used Lady Hamilton is probably overstated.

The relationship between Lady Hamilton and Nelson was prefaced by a short meeting in August 1793, when Nelson called in at Naples on his way through the Mediterranean. Their intimacy did not begin in earnest, however, until 1798, when Nelson again visited Naples on his way home from the Nile campaign. By now Nelson had lost his right eye and his right arm and Emma was starting to lose her good looks and to become stout, yet an overwhelming mutual infatuation developed between them. In 1800 Nelson accompanied Emma and Sir William Hamilton on a summer tour through Europe. Nelson remained on cordial terms with Sir William for some time, although in London during the ensuing months he and Emma were seldom apart. The attitude of London society to this liaison was to treat it as an innocent association, even in view of what subsequently transpired. For Nelson abandoned his wife, and on 30 January 1801 Emma gave birth to his illegitimate daughter, Horatia.

On 6 April 1803 Sir William Hamilton died, leaving considerable property to his nephew. To Emma he bequeathed his personal effects, furnishings and paintings worth about £1,500 from his Piccadilly house, £800 in cash, and an annuity of £800. Nelson, upon his death in 1805, was even more generous in his bequest. From him she received £200 in cash, an annuity of £500, and his Merton estate which was valued at £13,000.

Nevertheless, in spite of her wealth, Emma Hamilton's last years make a sorry tale. Even before Nelson's death she had become known for extravagance and addiction to gambling. She had already squandered her legacy from Sir William, and unsuccessfully applied for a pension to

Queen Maria Caroline. The wealth she inherited from Nelson lasted her less than three years, and despite financial assistance from her friends she continued to go downhill rapidly. In 1813 she was committed to a debtors' prison for a year, after which she was released on bail and succeeded in fleeing the country. She took refuge from her creditors in the French port of Calais where, reduced to penury and distress, she died on 15 January 1815.

O. Warner, *Emma Hamilton and Sir William* (1960). Carola Oman, *Nelson* (1947).

Portraits: oil, half-length, by G. Romney, *c.* 1785: N.P.G.; oil, by G. Romney: Iveagh Bequest, Kenwood House, London; pencil and water-colour, full-length, by R. Cosway: N.P.G.; miniature, by D. Orme, 1798: National Maritime Museum, Greenwich; pastel, quarter-length, by J. H. Schmidt: National Maritime Museum, Greenwich; enamel, by Henry Bone: Wallace Collection, London.

Hamilton, Sir William (1788–1856), metaphysician, see *Lives of the Victorian Age.*

Handel, George Frederick or Frideric (1685–1759), original name Georg Friedrich Händel; composer and musician, who is generally regarded as the supreme representative of the late baroque period in England.

Handel was born on 23 February 1685 at Halle in Lower Saxony, the son of Georg Händel, a prominent barber-surgeon in the service of the Duke of Saxony and later of the Elector of Brandenburg, and his second wife, Dorothea Taust, daughter of the Lutheran pastor of Giebichenstein. A romantic story has long been current that Handel's father was vehemently opposed to music and forbade the boy access to any musical instruments. This, along with several endearing anecdotes about Handel's boyhood, is now generally discredited. His father seems in reality to have been

friendly with several local musicians and probably encouraged his son's musical aptitude.

In 1688 Georg Händel became *Kammerdiener* to Duke Johann Adolph I of Saxe-Weissenfels and in due time he took his son to court. The Duke was very impressed by the boy's already prodigious musical abilities and prompted his father to send him to study with the eminent musician and composer, Friedrich Wilhelm Zachow, who was then organist at the Liebfrauenkirche, Halle. From Zachow Handel learned counterpoint and fugue; he became proficient on several instruments. A set of sonatas for two oboes and bass, written when he was ten, marks the already considerable magnitude of his musical talents. At the age of eleven he visited Berlin and played before the Elector of Brandenburg, the future King Frederick I of Prussia, and in 1697, the year of his father's death, the boy became Zachow's assistant.

In 1702 Handel entered the University of Halle to study law. He stayed there for a year, during which time he also became organist at the Schloss-und-Domkirche at the Moritzburg in Halle. The academically liberal and progressive atmosphere that already pervaded Halle at the outset of the eighteenth century powerfully stimulated Handel and beneficially affected his later development. He met the man of letters and musical amateur Barthold Heinrich Brockes, and the composer Telemann, on a journey through the town in 1701, became a close friend.

In 1703, having tired of his studies, Handel moved to Hamburg, where he got a job as a ripieno player among the second violins of the opera orchestra, under Reinhard Keiser. In August 1703 he journeyed with a friend to Lübeck, to hear the distinguished Danish organist Diderik Buxtehude.

In 1704, when he was only nineteen, Handel became director of the Hamburg opera orchestra. His growing reputation, however, went hand in hand with a rather arrogant bearing, which led to a heated quarrel with the musician and musicologist Johann Mattheson. The altercation, sparked off by a performance of Mattheson's opera *Cleopatra*, led to a duel, in which Handel narrowly escaped injury. A reconciliation was effected, however.

On 8 January 1705, Handel produced his first opera, *Almira*, written with the prodigious speed that was to become characteristic of his composing style. The work was a fair success and the operas *Nero* (1705) and *Florindo and Daphne* (1706), for which the music is lost, followed quickly.

By 1705 Handel's success was, according to the opinion of some current authorities, causing annoyance to the already established musician Keiser. This implies that a move may have been forced on him. It is more probable, however, that Handel wanted more experience. In any event, he took his savings and left Hamburg for Italy in 1706. He stayed for three years, visiting Florence, Rome, Venice, and Naples and making contact with Corelli and the two Scarlattis.

Handel had early and considerable successes in Italy and made a lot of money. His two operas *Rodrigo* (1707) and *Agrippina* (1709) made his name and earned him the appellation of *il Sassone*. But he also wrote a considerable amount of other music: numerous chamber cantatas, several oratorios, including *La Resurrezione* and *Il Trionfo del Tempo e del Disingano* (both 1708), a serenata, *Aci, Galatea, e Polifemo*, and some Latin church music, notably a setting of the Vespers psalm *Dixit Dominus* (1707), a remarkable merging of Germanic and Italian styles with choral writing that excellently foreshadows the glorious oratorios to come.

Towards the end of 1709 Handel, by now an operatic composer of international stature, was persuaded to accept the post of *Kapellmeister* to the Elector of Hanover. He took up his post at the Hanover court at the beginning of 1710 and, through the special relationship between Hanover and England brought about by the Act of Settlement of 1701, gained an opportunity to come to London. His first visit was made in 1711, when his opera *Rinaldo* took London by storm; the anti-Italianate vehemence of Addison and Steele in *The Spectator* represented the only significant note of dissension. After a brief return to Germany, Handel came back to London again in 1712. His extended leave of absence turned into a permanent residence. He anglicized his name and, apart from occasional visits to Germany and Italy, usually to collect singers for his operas (there were scarcely any in England of the required quality), he remained in England for the rest of his long life, becoming naturalized in 1726.

His earliest successes in London show him to have been a most astute businessman in staging his own work. He knew what the public wanted. His musical talent did the rest. His orchestrations were imaginative, and this fact was married to his ability to write the most captivating melodies. In his operas, composed along the lines of the Neapolitan school, a soloist's succession of arias built up his (or her) character for the audience in a way that Handel seemed to make his own. And when the time finally came to adapt to a different medium, he accomplished this adaptation admirably.

After his success of 1712 with the opera *Pastor Fido*, Handel brought out his *Teseo* in 1713. The same year also saw two choral pieces, a birthday ode for Queen Anne, for which he was rewarded with an annuity of £200, and the Utrecht *Te Deum* and

Jubilate, performed to celebrate the end of the War of the Spanish Succession. The deaths of the Electress Sophia and Queen Anne and the subsequent succession of Sophia's son as King George I of England did not materially affect Handel's position. The idea that he was out of favour at court because of outstaying his leave is now generally discarded by most authorities. The *Water Music*, originally thought to have been composed for a royal boat trip in August 1715 as a means of getting back into the King's good graces, is now regarded as having been produced two years later. In the meantime, in 1716 Handel visited Germany, going to Hanover and Halle. While there he produced his last work using a German text, the *Brockes-Passion*. This piece, setting rather turgid examples of Brockes's poetry, is musically competent but little else. The work lacks inspiration and belongs to a tradition of German church music for which Handel now had no aptitude.

In 1718, back in England, Handel entered the service of James Brydges, who became 1st Duke of Chandos in 1719. At his splendid country seat near Edgware Handel produced his well-known *Chandos Anthems*, his first essay in setting English words. This period also saw his earliest English oratorio *Esther* (1720) and the extended cantata *Acis and Galatea* (about 1721), completely different from his earlier Italian serenata, with words on this occasion by Gay, Pope, and others.

Handel did not remain with Chandos for long. In 1719 he gained leave to go abroad to get singers for a projected opera company backed by the King. This, the Royal Academy of Music, based at the King's Theatre, Haymarket, remained in being for nine years. Some of Handel's notable successes at this time included *Ottone* (1723), *Giulio Cesare* (1724), *Rodelinda* (1725), *Alessandro* (1726), and

Tolomeo (1728). This period was characterized by intense rivalries, principally between himself and Giovanni Buononcini. The rivalry became famous, particularly since it involved the royal family, George II supporting Handel and his son, Frederick, Prince of Wales, patronizing Buononcini. The poet John Byrom wrote a verse about it:

> Some say, compared to Buononcini,
> That Mynheer Handel's but a ninny;
> Others aver that he to Handel
> Is scarcely fit to hold a candle.
> Strange all this difference should be
> Twixt tweedle-dum and tweedle-dee.

In addition to Buononcini, Handel also had to cope with his own tempestuous singers, the redoubtable sopranos Cuzzoni and Faustina and the temperamental castrato Senesino. Factious demonstrations by gangs supporting one party or the other disrupted performances and finally led to a decline in the Italian opera's popularity. The London public, who never really listened to the music anyway, were attracted away by the new type of ballad opera in which English words were set to 'well-known popular tunes and the action was carried forward by spoken dialogue between the songs, and not by incomprehensible recitative, as in Handel's offerings. The best-loved example of this type of work was Gay's *Beggar's Opera* (1728). Eventually, at the end of the 1728 season, the Academy was forced to close down.

Handel, however, showed remarkable resilience. Always a robust character, in personality as much as in physique, he travelled abroad again in 1729 to get new singers for a new venture, once more staged at the King's Theatre. In 1729 too he visited his ailing mother in Halle. She died the following year.

During the 1730s, Handel introduced some new operas, including *Orlando* (1733) and *Arianna* (1734), and there were a number of revivals and pastiches drawn from some of his earlier works. But competition from rivals forced him out of the King's Theatre into Covent Garden in 1734, and the popularity of the opera itself continued to decline. In 1737 he was financially almost ruined, and a stroke and subsequent paralysis laid him low for a time.

Handel was reluctant to give up the struggle for opera. *Serse* was staged in 1738 and his last work for this medium, *Deidamia*, was produced as late as 1741. Yet as early as 1732 he had been encouraged to turn to a new type of presentation, as dramatic musically as opera but more forceful and profound. This was the English oratorio, the musical collection that is Handel's lasting monument. In 1732 Handel revived his earliest efforts in this field, *Esther* and *Acis and Galatea*. Their popularity encouraged him to write new pieces of a similar design. 1733 saw *Deborah* and also *Athalia* performed at Oxford. In 1735 came a

setting of *Alexander's Feast*, Dryden's poem on the power of music. *Saul* and *Israel in Egypt* were first heard in 1739. In 1740 Handel set words selected from Milton's 'L'Allegro' and 'Il Penseroso' by a rich amateur, Charles Jennens. Jennens had already provided the libretto for *Saul* and it was Jennens also who collaborated with Handel on his most glorious and enduringly popular work, *Messiah*.

Messiah, which may be said to introduce his last phase of creative work (he wrote no more operas after 1741), is a milestone in musical history. It is a moving and uplifting work, with a quality that transcends its time. Handel wrote it in the short space of three weeks in August and September 1741 and it was first staged in Dublin on 13 April 1742. It was an instant success. It was not performed in London until the Covent Garden performance of 1748, but thereafter it enjoyed and continues to enjoy innumerable performances.

Other oratorios quickly followed, both on biblical and secular subjects: *Samson* (1743), *Semele* and *Joseph* (1744), *Hercules* and *Belshazzar* (1745), *Judas Maccabaeus* (1747), *Alexander Balus* and *Joshua* (1748), *Susanna* and *Solomon* (1749). *Theodora*, written in 1750, was a failure, but *Messiah*'s popularity was really rising now. Handel performed it at the Foundling Hospital with an organ presented to the institution by himself. His last oratorio, *Jephtha*, was written in 1753, and while he was writing it his sight failed. Though not totally blind, he now had to rely on his secretary, John Christopher Smith, with whose help he continued working, even to the extent of making an English version of his early Italian oratorio *Il Trionfo de Tempo*. This, *The Triumph of Time and Truth*, was first heard in 1757. By March 1759 his health was poor. At a performance of *Messiah* in London he collapsed, and after a short illness he died on 14 April 1759.

Handel represents the pinnacle of the late baroque tradition in music. He was a man of international standing and wide first-hand experience of various continental styles and tastes. We may compare the dignified and highly disciplined craftsmanship of Bach with the flamboyant easy mastery of Handel, both musical styles being equally polished. Yet for all his panache, Handel was still capable of the most poignant music, as his anthem for the funeral of Queen Caroline (1737) shows. Indeed, some of his best works are occasional pieces. 'Zadoc the Priest' was one of four anthems he wrote for George II's coronation (1727). The Dettingen *Te Deum*, celebrating the victory over the French, appeared in 1743. The *Music for the Royal Fireworks* (1749), celebrating the peace of Aix, was rehearsed before 12,000 people in Vauxhall Gardens and was more successful than the firework display itself, which was a fiasco.

Handel's operas are only now being revived, although isolated arias have been popular for generations. He also wrote numerous chamber works including organ concertos, concerti grossi, and harpsichord pieces. But his fame rests on his oratorios. Here, as the heir of Henry Purcell, he brought choral singing in England to a point not reached since.

G. E. H. Abraham (ed.), *Handel, A Symposium* (1954).

F. Chrysander, *Georg Friedrich Händel* (Leipzig, 1858–67).

O. E. Deutsch, *Handel: A Documentary Biography* (1955).

P. H. Lang, *George Frederick Handel* (1966).

Stanley Sadie, *Handel* (1962).

John Tobin, *Handel's Messiah* (1969).

Performing editions of Handel's works are published chiefly by Novello (Sevenoaks, Kent) and Peters (formerly Leipzig, now Frankfurt).

Portraits: oil, three-quarter length, after T. Hudson, 1756: N.P.G.; oil, quarter-length, by unknown artist, *c*.1730: N.P.G.; oil, full-length, by T. Hudson, 1756: N.P.G.; oil, by W. Chapman: Graves Art Gallery, Sheffield; statue, by L. F. Roubillac: Fitzwilliam Museum, Cambridge.

Hardinge, Sir Henry (1785–1856), Viscount Hardinge; military commander; became Governor-General of India, see *Lives of the Victorian Age*.

Hargreaves, James (d. 1778), inventor of the spinning jenny, the first practical application of multiple spinning by machine.

James Hargreaves was born, probably in Blackburn, at an unrecorded date. Little is known of his early life. He seems to have worked in his youth as a carpenter and handloom weaver at Standhill. About 1760 he was employed by Robert Peel (the grandfather of the statesman) to construct an improved carding machine. The invention of the spinning jenny occurred, it is thought, about four years later.

Hargreaves is supposed to have conceived the idea for the jenny from observing a spinning wheel which had been accidentally overturned. As it lay on the ground, both the wheel and the spindle, now in an upright instead of a horizontal position, continued to revolve, and it struck Hargreaves that if several spindles were likewise turned sideways, several threads might be spun at once. Accordingly, he set up a machine with eight 'rovings' (for the loose fibre), and eight spindles (for the thread). With this spinning jenny a single operator could spin a number of threads of wool, cotton, or flax.

There was at this time a considerable need for an invention of the nature of Hargreaves's spinning jenny. John Kay's flying shuttle had accelerated the production of weavers, thereby causing a demand for thread which manual spinners found it difficult to fulfil. The spinning jenny multiplied production eightfold. It did not entirely supersede the spinning wheel, however, for in the manufacture of cotton the rovings, which the jenny converted into yarn, had themselves still to be spun in the old fashion. On the other hand, in the woollen industry the spinning jenny continued in use for production of both the warp and the weft long after it had been superseded in cotton manufacture by Compton's mule, which was itself derived from Hargreaves's original idea.

At first, the jenny was worked solely by Hargreaves and his children to make weft for their own loom, but in order to support his large family he sold some of the machines and built others. In 1768 a group of hand spinners, fearing for their livelihood, broke into Hargreaves's house in Blackburn, gutted the building, and destroyed the jenny and loom. Hargreaves and his family were uninjured.

After this disaster Hargreaves moved to Nottingham and formed a partnership with Thomas James, who built a small cotton mill at Hockley in which the jenny was utilized. In 1770 Hargreaves (probably assisted by James) took out a patent for the jenny, but it proved impossible to enforce this, because of the early sales of his machines in Blackburn. Nonetheless, Hargreaves was moderately successful, although he missed the fortune he might have made, for by the time of his death there were at least 20,000 jennies in use. As for their inventor, he continued to work at his mill until the last. He died on 22 April 1778.

T. S. Ashton, *The Industrial Revolution, 1760 to 1830* (1948).

T. S. Ashton, *An Economic History of England: the Eighteenth Century* (1955).

Hastings, Warren (1732–1818), British colonial Governor in India.

Warren Hastings was born on 6 December 1732, the son of an Oxfordshire clergyman, Pynaston Hastings. Orphaned early, he was brought up by relatives. He entered Westminster School and by the influence of a distant kinsman, who had become his guardian, he secured an appointment in the East India Company, going out to Calcutta in 1750. In 1753 he was sent to an outlying Company post at Kasimbazar, where he devoted much study to the languages and culture of the inhabitants. In 1756, with other Company servants, he was seized on the orders of the local ruler, the Nawab of Bengal, Siraj-ud-daula, and taken to the native capital, Murshidabad. Hastings, however, was given parole, and he was able to be of service to the survivors of the notorious 'Black Hole' incident. The atrocity, in which 146 Europeans were packed into a tiny prison for one night, only twenty-two of them managing to survive, horrified everyone who subsequently heard of it. In December 1756 the refugees from this incident were reached by a relief expedition under Clive (q.v.), and Hastings joined the force as a volunteer for the ensuing campaign.

In August 1758 he was appointed the Company's representative at the court of the puppet Nawab installed by Clive, Mir Jafar. Hastings worked under Clive's direction, and probably owed the appointment to his suggestion. He regarded Clive's support as essential to the stability of Mir Jafar's government, and attempted unsuccessfully to persuade Clive to postpone his return to England in 1760. He had not himself sufficient seniority to prevent the subsequent disintegration of both the native province and the Company's local affairs.

What influence he could assert was used to back Mir Jafar's son-in-law as better fitted to exercise rule, and Mir Kasim was accordingly installed as Nawab in

October 1760 by Clive's successor, Vansittart, who appointed Hastings to his Council in Calcutta the following year. Mir Kasim, however, was not inclined to accept Company direction and Hastings was frequently employed as an intermediary in the growing state of friction between the two parties, which, despite Hastings's efforts, erupted into ferocious warfare in mid-1763. Monro's victory over the combined Indian army at Buxar (23 October 1764) decisively established the British grip on Bengal, the immediate token of which was the restoration of Mir Jafar. Vansittart and Hastings, who had endeavoured to modify the Council's consistently overbearing attitude towards the Nawab, now received the odium for their nominee's acts of terror. They both resigned and returned to England in December, where they were equally unsuccessful in defending their joint reputation.

Eventually Clive was moved to exert his personal influence on behalf of Hastings, and in 1768 the Company appointed him to the Madras Council. He sailed for India in 1769.

In 1772 Hastings was appointed Governor of Bengal on the basis of his previous experience, with a brief to reorganize the administration and silence the criticism that was becoming politically embarrassing to the directors at home. Working pragmatically, he removed the seat of government to Calcutta, directly under Council supervision, and brought the total conduct of administration into the hands of the Company. The result of this was to encourage the directors to strengthen the regulations against the private trading of the Company's servants, which adversely affected native trade, the government's revenue that was based on it, and also Company profits. However, Hastings could work effectively only with the

goodwill of those same Company servants.

The British government intervened, however, its collective conscience being disturbed by the stream of information, true and false, that had emanated from India over the years. Among other provisions of the Regulating Act of 1773, by which parliament attempted to reform the Company's scandalous affairs, the authority over Bengal was to be vested in a Governor General and a Council of four, with limited control over Bombay and Madras. The Act nominated Hastings for the principal office. His government-nominated councillors, however, were not sound appointments, and one, Philip Francis (q.v.), was well primed with second-hand prejudices, particularly against Hastings himself. He made it his duty to harass Hastings and undo his work where he could, contriving to carry a majority of the Council with him. In 1780 the two fought a duel and Francis was wounded, leaving for England soon afterwards to continue his vendetta there. Ironically, both men shared the same general belief that the government of Bengal should be Indian rather than British in character, and that there should be no extensions of British sovereignty beyond it.

Nevertheless it proved impossible to preserve the East India Company from entanglement in the native struggles for power in the subcontinent. Of particular concern were the aggressive Maratha chieftains of Central India, and Company forces were periodically used to defend the territory of the Vizier of Oudh against them. In the interest of further strengthening Oudh, Hastings agreed in 1773 to provide Company support to the Vizier's occupation of Rohilkhand on a cash basis, from which transaction arose the successful Rohilla War of 1774.

It was the Bombay Council, however, which embroiled Hastings directly with the Marathas when in 1775 it promised aid to a principal contender in a Maratha civil war, following this up with a series of miscalculations that united the Marathas against the Company in open war by 1778. Hastings was compelled to send a force across Central India to rescue the Bombay authorities from their own folly, and a peace was negotiated in 1782 without significant loss to either side.

By that time, a third war was in progress. In July 1780 the combined efforts of the Nizam of Hyderabad, the Maratha Rajah of Berar, and Haidar Ali, the ruler of Mysore, were pitted against the Company in Madras. The Madras government relied upon Hastings to deliver the presidency from Haidar, whose forces had invaded the Carnatic, and who was to be supported a year later by the French. Hastings sent Sir Eyre Coote (q.v.) to take over military operations in the Carnatic, followed by a substantial portion of the European troops in Bengal, while Colonel Pearse, with a strong column of native troops,

was dispatched overland to link up with them. For his part, Hastings used his personal influence to detach the Rajah from the alliance. The war outlasted both Coote and Haidar, and it was not until March 1784 that Hastings was able to negotiate peace with the latter's successor, Tipu Sultan, with a mutual restoration of conquests.

At this point, the British government tried again to improve India's administration by passing Pitt's East India Act. Hastings took it as a personal criticism and chose to retire, leaving India in February 1785. More than any other governor, he had entered sympathetically into the culture of the Indians themselves, and had encouraged his colleagues to do the same. He had patronized English scholars anxious to undertake studies in Indian learning and arts, and had been instrumental in founding the College of Arabic Studies at Calcutta (1781) and the Asian Society of Bengal (1784). In consequence, his reputation among the Indians was considerable.

His initial reception in England was gratifyingly warm, but his personal opponents in the Company joined forces with the party hacks of the parliamentary opposition in an endeavour to topple Hastings, the Company, and Pitt's administration in the same ruin. The attack was led by Burke, a friend of Francis. He opened his parliamentary campaign to bring about the impeachment of Hastings in February 1786, on specific charges of maladministration and abuse of office.

His trial before the House of Lords opened in February 1788 in Westminster Hall, which was packed with a distinguished audience. The impeachment was managed by Burke, Fox, and Sheridan, and proceeded at a leisurely pace until Hastings's complete acquittal in April 1795. His defence had cost him over

£100,000, more than he had brought back from India. He failed to recover his costs from the government or the Company, but the directors relented sufficiently to grant him an annuity of £4,000 and an interest-free loan, and he was made a Privy Councillor and a D.C.L. of Oxford University. He passed the rest of his life undisturbed as a country gentleman, and died at his estate of Daylesford, in Oxfordshire, on 22 August 1818.

K. Fielding, *Warren Hastings* (1954).

Abdul Majed Khan, *The Transition in Bengal, 1756–1775* (1969).

P. J. Marshall, *The Impeachment of Warren Hastings* (1965).

P. Moon, *Warren Hastings and British India* (1947).

Lucy Sutherland, *The East India Company in Eighteenth Century Politics* (1952.)

Patrick Turnbull, *Warren Hastings* (1975).

Portraits: oil, half-length, by T. Kettle: N.P.G.; oil, half-length, by T. Lawrence, 1811: N.P.G.; oil, full-length, by J. Reynolds, 1766–8: N.P.G.

Hawke, Sir Edward (1705–81), Baron Hawke; admiral, whose victory over the French at Quiberon Bay was one of the most decisive actions of the Seven Years War.

Edward Hawke was born in 1705, the son of a lawyer. He entered the Royal Navy in 1720 as a volunteer and served a hard apprenticeship, receiving his lieutenant's commission in 1729. He received his first command, aboard the 10-gun sloop *Wolf*, in 1733, and served for a time in the West Indies in command of the 50-gun battleship *Portland*.

Towards the end of 1743 Hawke was sent to serve in the Mediterranean aboard the 70-gun *Berwick* and he saw his first real action at the Battle of Toulon in 1744. In this battle *Berwick* alone secured a prize. Having been elevated to the status of squadron commander, Hawke returned home in 1745.

In July 1747 Hawke was promoted rear admiral of the White and given charge of Plymouth. The following month he took temporary command of the vital Western Squadron and, flying his flag aboard the *Devonshire*, encountered on 2 October 1747 a French convoy escorted by nine ships commanded by Admiral de l'Etenduère. The subsequent engagement on 14 October, known as the second Battle of Cape Finisterre, is remarkable for the freedom with which Hawke, with fourteen ships under his command, interpreted the rigid Fighting Instructions that stifled the tactical sense of British admirals for most of the eighteenth century. Four French ships struck, and casualties in the remainder were considerable. Hawke's reward was the Order of the Bath and promotion to vice admiral of the Blue in 1748.

Hawke was immediately given the important Portsmouth command, and he also became one of Portsmouth's M.P.S, retaining the seat until 1776. At the end of 1752 he again went on half-pay, but as a resumption of war with France became increasingly likely, he was advanced to vice admiral of the White and, although in rather poor health, returned to Portsmouth in February 1755. In July he was ordered to sea.

The early stages of the Seven Years War were uneventful for Hawke. In June 1756 he superseded John Byng (q.v.) as commander in chief in the Mediterranean, for his failure to relieve Minorca. In trying to save the British garrison there, however, Hawke fared no better than Byng. His arrival was far too late.

Promoted to admiral of the Blue in February 1757, Hawke was in August put in charge of the naval element of the projected combined army and navy expedition against the port and arsenal at Rochefort. The subsequent disastrous failure of the expedition was due to the irresolution of the senior army officers.

No blame was attached to Hawke, who was promptly sent back to sea with a squadron in the Bay of Biscay.

In May 1759 he was given the Western Squadron again, entrusted with the blockade of Brest, where an expedition for the invasion of Great Britain was in preparation. The blockade was sustained until early November, when a prolonged gale forced a return to Torbay. The French admiral, Conflans, took the opportunity to bring out his fleet, but Hawke was already heading back for his station and on 20 November 1759 came up with the enemy making for the military transport rendezvous at Morbihan. Hawke, aboard the 100-gun *Royal George*, had two ships more than the French. The French ran for the coast, but were brought to battle inshore in a heavy gale and lost four ships. Action was broken off as the French took refuge among the rocks and reefs of Quiberon Bay, but Hawke followed them in and captured or destroyed all but eight ships for the loss of two of his own, which were driven ashore and wrecked.

For what we may assume to be political reasons, Hawke was not awarded the peerage which his victory had clearly earned. He professed himself satisfied with the pension of £2,000 awarded to him. For the remainder of the war he maintained a steady watch over a stretch of sea extending from Ireland to the Channel and the Bay of Biscay. He retired in the autumn of 1762, with the rank of admiral of the White.

The war ended in 1763, and Hawke's retirement was sweetened with the grant of the sinecure appointment of Rear Admiral of Great Britain, which he held for two years until it was exchanged for the senior and more lucrative vice-admiral's office. In December 1766 he somewhat unexpectedly became First Lord of the Admiralty in the Chatham government, but it was not a post in which he distinguished himself. As always, Hawke rendered honest and efficient service, but his health was now bad, and it was for this reason that he eventually resigned in January 1771. In 1776 he was finally given a barony, and he held the post of Admiral of the Fleet, awarded to him in 1768, until his death at Sunbury on 17 October 1781.

G. Marcus, *Quiberon Bay* (1960).

Portrait: oil, full-length, by Francis Cotes, 1768–70: National Maritime Museum, Greenwich.

Hawksmoor, Nicholas (1661–1736), architect, see *Lives of the Stuart Age*.

Haydon, Benjamin Robert (1786–1846), painter of historical and religious subjects.

Haydon was born on 26 January 1786 at Plymouth. His father was a printer and publisher, and the books in his shop provided the young boy with abundant material for the early development of his interest in historical subjects. At Plympton Grammar School, which he entered in 1798, he combined an enthusiasm for drawing and etching with more academic accomplishments in Latin, Greek, and French. On leaving school, Haydon worked for six months for an accountant in Exeter and then served as an apprentice to his father, but already he was obsessed by an awareness of his individual talents as a painter: in May 1804, in deliberate rebellion against his father, Haydon set out for London.

He took lodgings in Broad Street, Carnaby Market, and, after satisfying himself by a visit to the Royal Academy that he had no potential rival as a historical painter he immediately bought some plaster casts and set up his easel. For two years Haydon attended lectures at the Royal Academy and worked on a list of thirty-eight historical subjects; then, in October 1806, he began work on *Joseph and Mary resting on the Road to Egypt*. While painting this picture Haydon was commissioned by Lord Mulgrave to paint *Dentatus*, and also patronized by Sir George and Lady Beaumont. A brief visit to Plymouth, where his father was ill and his mother lay dying, served only to reinforce Haydon's commitment to his career as a painter in London, and his first sight of the Elgin Marbles on their arrival at Lord Elgin's Park Lane house helped him to realize that heroic ideal towards which all his painting would henceforth aspire.

In March 1809 *Dentatus* was completed, and the following year it was awarded a prize of 100 guineas by the British Gallery. Under the patronage of Lord Mulgrave, Haydon now acquired fame and temporary prosperity, but in a dispute with the Royal Academy over the hanging of *Dentatus* he displayed all the arrogance and intemperance that continually was to disrupt his career. From 1809 to 1812, during the painting of *Macbeth*, Haydon was living largely on credit, and the true nature of his personality is recorded with painful intimacy in the daily journal that he wrote during these years. In 1810 Haydon submitted his *Romeo and Juliet* to the Royal Academy but then withdrew it on learning where it was to be hung; on the completion of *Macbeth* he argued violently with Sir George Beaumont, who had originally commissioned this work; in early 1812 he wrote three letters to the *Examiner* in which he attacked both the Royal Academy and the British Gallery.

For the following two years Haydon worked feverishly: heavily in debt and wholly dependent upon the generosity of his friends, he often worked for fifteen hours without a break and lived on a diet of potatoes alone. His health – both physical and mental – inevitably deteriorated. The completion of *The Judgment of Solomon* in 1814 brought temporary financial relief but no further commissions; after selling this picture for 600 guineas, Haydon spent the money on a brief visit to Paris and then immediately began work on another of his own projects, *Christ's Entry into Jerusalem*. This picture was eventually finished in 1820, but the profits made by its exhibition in London, Edinburgh, and Glasgow were insufficient to rescue Haydon from the debts he had now incurred. In October 1821 he married Mary Hymans, a respectable widow; in the same year he was twice arrested for debt; two years later he was briefly imprisoned, and the recently completed *Raising of Lazarus* was seized by his creditors and sold to an upholsterer for £30.

Haydon's lack of financial success may be attributed to his own wilful refusal to paint marketable pictures and the extravagant manner in which he antagonized his potential benefactors, but for all this misplaced energy, some of his ideas did have positive effects. In 1812 Haydon's own impassioned voice was instrumental in persuading the British government to buy the Elgin Marbles for the nation, and he also suggested to parliament that artists should be commissioned to decorate public buildings and that schools of design should be established throughout the country.

On his release from prison Haydon immediately began work on his next painting, *The Crucifixion*. Attempts were made to persuade him to paint some smaller canvases and portraits, which he might sell more easily, but he knew instinctively that he had little talent for this type of painting. In 1826 he attempted a reconciliation with the Royal Academy, and for three years his paintings were hung in their exhibitions, but after another argument in 1828 the mutual mistrust was again resumed. During the years 1823–37 Haydon painted several more large canvases, quarrelled with his patrons, and watched five of his children die; he was sustained only by his own will-power and his wife's loyalty. In the late 1830s, after his radical opinions as expressed in a series of letters to *The Times* had attracted wide attention, Haydon began to give lectures on painting and design; he travelled to Liverpool and Manchester and was particularly pleased by his reception at Oxford University in 1840. Briefly, it seemed that Haydon had at last found his audience, but when he asked for commissions to provide paintings for the new House of Commons he was rejected by the authorities just as before. In 1845 Haydon commenced work on his own project for six pictures illustrating political themes. He completed two; on 22 June 1846, in a fit of what the Coroner's jury defined as insanity, he committed suicide.

E. George, *The Life and Death of Benjamin Robert Haydon* (1967).

T. Taylor (ed.), *Life of Benjamin Robert Haydon, from his autobiography and journals* (1853).

Portraits: oil, half-length, by Georgina Zornlin, 1828: N.P.G.; pencil, full-length, by D. Wilkie, 1815: N.P.G.; pen and ink, quarter-length, by J. Keats, 1816: N.P.G.

Hazlitt, William (1778–1830), essayist and critic.

William Hazlitt was born on 10 April 1778 at Maidstone, Kent, the fourth child of a Unitarian minister. The family moved to Cork in 1780 and thence to America in 1783, where the writer's father founded the first Unitarian church in Boston. They returned to England in 1786, settling at Wem in Shropshire.

Hazlitt was educated privately until 1793, when he went to the Unitarian college at Hackney. After two years, he returned home, preferring to continue his own education with the help of his father's considerable library. In 1798 Coleridge visited Wem and deeply impressed Hazlitt, who later went with him to visit Wordsworth at Alfoxden. Hazlitt continued to live at his father's house and read avidly all the great English and French philosophers – his favourites were Burke, 'Junius', and Rousseau – and also several novelists. He was particularly excited by Fielding's *Tom Jones*, and he also loved Sterne.

In 1802 he wintered in Paris, copying the Louvre paintings with the intention of becoming a painter, and on his return he toured England, painting portraits of his friends. Though several of these – notably the picture of Charles Lamb – were certainly good, he gradually decided to abandon painting and, becoming intimate with Godwin (q.v.) and his circle, began writing and publishing philosophical essays, abridgements of parliamentary speeches, and a grammar based on Horne Tooke's work.

In 1807 Hazlitt became engaged to Sarah Stoddart, sister of an editor of *The Times*. They were married in 1808, settling in Winterslow, Wiltshire, where his son was born in 1811: on this occasion Charles Lamb wrote, 'Make him like his father, with something a better temper and a smoother head of hair, and then all the men and women must love him.' Lack of money soon forced him and his family to move to London to be nearer the centre of the literary world. Arriving in Westminster in 1812, he gave a course of lectures in philosophy at the Russell Institution and then became parliamentary reporter for the *Morning Chronicle*. He became theatre critic on the *Chronicle* and also wrote for the *Champion*, *The Times*, the *Edinburgh Review*, and the *Examiner*. This last paper belonged to John and Leigh Hunt, who became close friends of Hazlitt, collaborating with him in a successful series of papers called *The Round Table*.

In 1817 he published his *Characters of Shakespeare's Plays*, dedicated to Lamb, which was a moderate success, and in 1818 *A View of the English Stage*, a collection of theatre criticism, and *Lectures on the English Poets*, a series of lectures given at the Surrey Institution. He was now being invited to contribute regularly to various magazines, including *Yellow Dwarf*, *The London Magazine*, and *The Liberal*, started by Byron. However, his short temper and obstinately individual politics – he viewed Whigs, Tories, and Benthamite radicals with equal scorn – left him isolated and friendless. Moreover, his wife was vain and incompetent and their only bond was love of their son William. In 1819 they separated, and in 1820 Hazlitt moved to Chancery Lane, where he fell in love with his landlord's daughter, Sarah Walker. Intending to marry her, he (and Mrs. Hazlitt) went to live in Scotland for the forty days necessary for a divorce, but on his return to London he decided that Miss Walker had always deceived him. This almost mad love haunted him even on his deathbed, and was the subject of a strange book called *Liber Amoris*, a work which he considered rivalled Rousseau's *Confessions*, but which De Quincey described as an 'explosion of frenzy'.

In 1824 Hazlitt did decide to marry again. He chose Mrs. Arabella Bridgwater, a barrister's widow with a comfortable income, and after their marriage they immediately set off on a Grand Tour through Paris, Turin, Florence, Rome, Venice, and Milan, Hazlitt writing his impressions for publication in the *Morning Chronicle*. They returned via Holland in October 1825, and almost immediately the second Mrs. Hazlitt announced that she had left him. 'That superior woman, who will make him a decent being in regard to

washing his face and hands,' as Haydon described her, gave as her reason 'the ill-conduct of the boy': her stepson certainly resented her and always championed his mother, but the blow of being abandoned hit Hazlitt hard, and he lived the rest of his life alone in lodgings. He published two excellent collections of essays, *The Spirit of the Age* (1825) and *The Plain Speaker* (1826), and some remarkable anecdotal conversations with the eccentric painter Northcote, which appeared as 'Boswell Redivivus' in Colburn's *New Monthly Magazine*. After this he devoted himself to a *Life of Napoleon*, which was doomed because of his inadequate research and the strong bias of the book, alien to most Englishmen of the time. Disappointed by its failure and afflicted by stomach cancer, he died in the presence of his son William and Charles Lamb in Soho on 18 September 1830. His last words were, 'Well, I've had a happy life.'

Hazlitt's 'happy life' can best be seen in the finest of his essays, where he extols the joys of long country walks, vigorous games of fives, and lively conversation. His human relationships seem seldom to have been happy. Selfish, egotistical, and unbearably shy, he had few friends and suspected everyone. Yet, at ease, he could talk frankly and cheerfully, and had great aesthetic and intellectual capacities. Though a hard-line Dissenter, who boasted never to have changed an opinion after the age of sixteen, he was sensitive and, albeit with effort, able to conquer personal bias in favour of artistic objectivity.

H. Baker, *William Hazlitt* (Cambridge, Mass., 1962).

P. P. Howe (ed.), *The Complete Works of William Hazlitt* (2 vols.; 1930–4).

P. P. Howe, *Life of Hazlitt* (1922 and 1928).

G. L. Keynes (ed.), *Selected Essays* (1930).

C. M. Maclean, *Hazlitt* (1943).

E. W. Schneider, *The Aesthetics of Hazlitt* (Philadelphia, 1933).

Portraits: chalk, quarter-length, by W. Bewick: N.P.G.; oil, by John Hazlitt: Maidstone Museum and Art Gallery, Kent.

Hepplewhite, George (d. 1786), cabinet-maker and furniture designer.

The place and date of Hepplewhite's birth are unknown and few facts about his life are recorded. It is generally accepted that he was appointed to the well-known Lancaster firm of cabinet-makers run by Robert Gillow, though the sophistication of Hepplewhite's work has led some experts, like C. Cescinsky in his *English Furniture of the Eighteenth Century* (1913), to conclude that Hepplewhite was trained in London.

About 1760 Hepplewhite was established in business as a cabinet-maker in Redcross Street, Cripplegate, London. The name of Hepplewhite is not in the contemporary trade directories and he does not seem to have enjoyed much of a reputation in his lifetime. It is probable that he worked as a maker of practical furniture for the architects of the period rather than aiming at establishing a prominent business of his own. After his death in 1786 the administration of his estate (which was recorded as being less than £600) was granted to his widow, Alice. Alice subsequently continued the business for about ten years under the name of A. Hepplewhite & Co. The famous *Cabinet-maker's and Upholsterer's Guide* was published by the firm in three editions (1788, 1793, and 1794). The final revised edition of 1794 consisted of 300 designs on 128 plates and was meant, according to the preface, 'to unite elegance and utility, and to blend the useful with the agreeable'. The drawings were intended to be 'useful to the mechanic and serviceable to the gentleman'. The publication was a success, being the most comprehensive and useful catalogue to appear since the Chippendale

Director of 1754. It undoubtedly aided the dissemination of the Hepplewhite style, and accounts for the great variety of furniture in that style.

Attribution of eighteenth-century English furniture to particular makers is difficult, and is generally made on the evidence of bills or trade labels. In the case of Hepplewhite no such evidence has come to light. Therefore his name is more indicative of a style and character of furniture than of specific work. The style is refined and light; it exploits fine craftsmanship without flamboyance. The designs in the *Cabinet-maker's and Upholsterer's Guide* probably represent a selection of those contemporary styles that had satisfied Hepplewhite's standards. Only a few of the plates are signed, and some were produced by Shearer. There is also clear evidence of the influence of Robert Adam (q.v.) and of the French Louis XVI style in the drawings.

Although Hepplewhite produced the whole range of furniture needed to equip households, his name is particularly associated with certain items, such as chairs. These were considerably lightened by a change of the massive proportions formerly customary and by designs that did not use stretcher rails to brace the legs. This innovation was a major contribution, allowing further exploitation of leg design. The backs of Hepplewhite chairs are of great variety but the shield shape is always associated with him, as is the use of the Prince of Wales feathers (either carved or painted). Small window seats and upholstered confidantes and duchesse settees (developments of the chaise longue and sofa) are in the French taste which Hepplewhite so admired. The same French influence affects much of the dainty drawing room and boudoir furniture produced by using satinwood veneers with inlays and bandings of exotic woods. These items are much esteemed today for their smallness and fine workmanship. Less esteemed are examples of painted furniture in the same idiom because of the impermanence of the decoration.

It is in the use of classical ornament that the Adam influence declares itself. The classical ornaments, derived from the Adelphi, were used both in carving and painting by Hepplewhite, and it is in restraint that his manner is seen. Mouldings on bookcase pediments, which in the Adam originals appear heavy (being architectural in form but without modification), are lightened and altered by Hepplewhite, but not at the cost of loss of purity of design.

The Hepplewhite style and the designs in the *Guide* are thus a comprehensive statement of the English furniture fashion in the late eighteenth century. The manner, derived from Hepplewhite's digest of the less extreme forms of the rapidly changing fashions of the eighteenth century, is characterized by a new grace and refinement that continued its influence into the twentieth century.

R. Edwards, *Hepplewhite Furniture Designs* (1947).
R. Edwards and M. Jourdain, *Georgian Cabinet Makers, c. 1700–1800* (1955).
R. Edwards and P. Macquoid, *The Dictionary of English Furniture* (1954).

Herschel, Sir (Frederick) William

(1738–1822), original name Friedrich Wilhelm Herschel; German-born astronomer, who discovered Uranus.

William Herschel was born on 15 November 1738 in Hanover, the fourth of ten children born to Isaac Herschel, a military bandsman, and Anna Ilse Moritzen. Brought up as a musician, at the age of fourteen he followed his father in joining the band of the Hanoverian Guard as an oboist. In 1755 he paid a brief visit to England with his regiment, returning shortly afterwards to a homeland that soon became embroiled in the Seven Years War. Hanover was early invaded by the French, and in 1757 the young Herschel again came to England, this time as a refugee.

For several years Herschel made his living as a musician, first in northern England and later in Bath, where in 1766 he was appointed organist at the Octagon Church, residing there for sixteen years, teaching and composing music as well as carrying out his church duties.

While engaged in this substantially lucrative though rather unremarkable employment, Herschel, whose talent as a composer seems to have been indifferent, took up the spare-time study of mathematics and science, and especially astronomy, which became his first love. With his brother Alexander, who had been in Bath since 1760, and his sister Caroline Lucretia, who joined him there in 1772, he began to make observations of the night sky in earnest. For this he hired a modest reflecting telescope but soon exhausted its possibilities. The high cost of buying the rather inefficient astronomical instruments then available forced him to learn to make his own. He taught himself the techniques of metal-casting, grinding, and polishing, and while he remained for a time a musician by profession, he soon took up the role of astronomer by choice.

Herschel's aims as an astronomer were twofold: 'to carry improvements in telescopes to their utmost extent', and 'to leave no part of the heavens unexplored'. His career in astronomy bears out these intentions to the full: the forty-seven years from 1774, when he made his first observations of the Orion nebula with the earliest of his own successfully made Newtonian reflectors, to 1821, when he sent his last communication to the Royal Astronomical Society, tell the tale of a dedicated scientist who rose to eminence

through unceasing hard work and reasoned judgment as much as through fortuitous discoveries.

Of these discoveries, the first, and at the time the most momentous, came in March 1781, when Herschel, using his vastly improved optical equipment, first sighted the planet Uranus. Already becoming known to other astronomers, he had only recently sent papers to the Royal Society, one on observations that he had made on the periodical variable star, Mira Ceti, another on the mountains of the moon, and yet another on the rotation of the planets. But his detection of a new planet drew considerable attention: he was awarded the Copley Medal and was elected to the Royal Society in December 1781; and in the following year he came to London, both to exhibit his instruments (which turned out to be superior to those at Greenwich) and also to have an audience with George III, who appointed him Court Astronomer on a salary of £200 a year.

In the wake of his fame, Herschel gave up his professional musical career and left

Bath in 1782, moving first to Datchet, then to Clay Hall near Windsor, and finally (in 1786) to Slough, where he stayed for the rest of his life. His industry was prodigious, but throughout his long active career he relied on the assistance of Caroline, herself a more than competent astronomer. He was a man of geniality and charm, qualities that attracted an accolade from Fanny Burney, who describes him as 'a man without a wish that has its object in the terrestrial globe'.

In 1786 Herschel was elected a Fellow of the Royal Society of Göttingen, and in 1802 he became a foreign member of the French Institute, visited the French astronomer Laplace in Paris, and had an interview with Napoleon. His instruments too became known outside Britain, and as well as making them on a commercial basis, he carried out several commissions from foreign establishments.

His monumental instrument was, however, constructed for his own purposes at Slough. Completed with royal aid in 1789 after some failures, it consisted of a giant 50-inch mirror and a tube nearly 40 feet long that was wide enough to walk through. The giant reflector proved its worth immediately with the detection of the sixth and seventh moons of Saturn in August and September of that year.

With this new instrument, as with some of his others, Herschel turned his attention to nebulae, and it is here that much of his most important work was done. Throughout his whole career he catalogued 2,500 of these misty patches of light, and with his highly developed equipment he was early able to discern that they were not all alike. Some were 'nebulous stars', as he called them, containing material out of which stars might be formed; some, like the nebula in Taurus, later known as the Crab, were thought by Herschel to be stars surrounded by a 'shining fluid', a 'nebulosity ... not of a starry nature'; and undoubtedly the most interesting group of misty objects were those that through the telescope appeared to be resolved into uncountable separate stars, the so-called 'island universes'.

Continuing a line of thinking dating back to Newton, Herschel assumed that matter had been originally distributed equally throughout space, and later drawn together into one place or another by gravitational attraction to form stars. Gravitation was certainly a concept that was obvious in stellar space as well as within the solar system; Herschel proved as much by his examination of double stars, of which he catalogued over 800 during his lifetime. But as his observations progressed with bigger and better telescopes, he saw that all stars, even the dimmest, were seen to be concentrated unequally, lying mainly about the plane of the Milky Way and forming a lens-shaped system that thickened considerably at the centre. Herschel's intuitive discovery that the sun and its planets shared in the composite revolving motion of this system, which to him and his contemporaries was the entire universe, was the final clue that established the sun's status as but a single star among many hundreds of thousands all rotating in one single mass, now known to us as the Galaxy.

Of his other work mention may be made of his experiments in spectroscopy, his research into stellar luminosities, his investigations of Mars and its polar caps, his speculation about comets, and his exhaustive studies of the sun. Some of his theories were wildly erroneous, but this detracts little from his outstanding merit as the foremost astronomer of his time.

In 1788 Herschel married a wealthy widow, Mary Pitt, and for a brief period relations between her and Caroline were strained. In general, however, life at Slough was serene and, with Mary's money, free from want. Herschel continued working and maintained a stream of material to the Royal Society up to 1818. He was awarded honorary doctorates by Edinburgh and Glasgow universities, received a knighthood in 1816, and became the first President of the Royal Astronomical Society. A severe illness in 1807 had a marked effect on his health, however, and frequent rests were obligatory. In 1821 he issued his last communication, on binary stars, to the Royal Astronomical Society. He died at Slough, aged eighty-three, on 25 August 1822.

With Herschel, the father of sidereal investigation, astronomy breaks forth from its preoccupation with the solar system and Copernicus's heliocentric theory into the vast regions of interstellar space. His best epitaph is his own comment, allegedly made to the poet Thomas Campbell in 1813: 'I have looked further into space than ever a human being did before me.'

A. Armitage, *William Herschel* (1962).

E. S. Holden and C. S. Hastings, *Synopsis of the Scientific Writings of Sir William Herschel* (1881).

M. A. Hoskin, *William Herschel and the Construction of the Heavens* (1963).

C. A. Lubbock (ed.), *The Herschel Chronicle: The Life-story of William Herschel and His Sister Caroline Herschel* (1933).

J. B. Sidgwick, *William Herschel, Explorer of the Heavens* (1963).

Portraits: oil, half-length, by L. F. Abbott, 1785: N.P.G.; plaster cast of bust, by J. C. Lochee: N.P.G.; oil, half-length, by John Russell, 1794: Science Museum.

Herschel, Sir John Frederick William (1792–1871), astronomer, see *Lives of the Victorian Age*.

Hervey, John, Lord (1696–1743), Baron Hervey of Ickworth; politician and writer.

Hervey was born on 15 October 1696 at Ickworth in Suffolk, son of John Hervey, 1st Earl of Bristol, and educated at Westminster School and at Clare Hall, Cambridge, from which he graduated M.A. in 1715. A year after leaving Cambridge he made the Grand Tour of Europe. On his return to England he made a politically useful marriage in 1720 to Mary Lepell, a maid of honour to Princess (later Queen) Caroline.

In 1725 Hervey was elected M.P. for Bury St. Edmunds. His first commitment was to the anti-Walpole faction within the Whig party led by William Pulteney, but when George II declared his favour for Sir Robert Walpole Hervey quickly changed his allegiance.

As a pamphleteer and as an influential favourite of Queen Caroline, Hervey proved useful in advancing Walpole's policies, and his services were rewarded in 1730 by his appointment as a Privy Councillor and as Vice Chamberlain of the Royal Household. After one particular exchange of pamphlets Hervey fought a duel with his former leader, Pulteney, in 1731: both were slightly wounded and honour was apparently satisfied.

Hervey succeeded as Baron Hervey in 1733, and became one of the leading advocates of Walpole's policies in the House of Lords. Not a politician of any originality himself, he is chiefly remembered for his accurate and witty portrayal of the contemporary political scene in his *Memoirs of the Reign of George II* (not published until 1848). His friendship with both political and literary personalities afforded a significant range for Hervey's caustic social observation, and his direct literary style is the expression of a man who was clever, cynical, and often gifted with acute insight: it was perhaps inevitable, therefore, that he should have attracted as many enemies as friends.

Alexander Pope referred to him as 'Lord Fanny' in the *Dunciad* and attacked him again in the character of 'Sporus' in the 'Epistle to Dr. Arbuthnot'. At a later stage of his career Hervey quarrelled with the Prince of Wales over their rivalry for the affections of a certain maid of honour to the Queen, and the combination of his acid wit and affected manners did little to enhance his popularity.

In 1740, after a long and impatient wait for some reward from Walpole for the use of his influence upon Queen Caroline, Hervey was appointed Lord Privy Seal. Prosperity was brief, for two years later (1742) he was deprived of office as the Walpole administration fell. During the remaining months of his life Hervey retained his seat in the House of Lords as an active member of the opposition. He died at Ickworth on 5 August 1743.

Earl of Ilchester (ed.), *Hervey and his Friends 1726–38* (1950).

R. Sedgwick (ed.), *Memoirs of the Reign of George II* (3 vols.; 1931: 1952 rev. ed.).

Portrait: oil, full-length, studio of J. B. van Loo, c. 1740–1: N.P.G.

Hobhouse, Sir John Cam (1786–1869), politician, see *Lives of the Victorian Age*.

Hogarth, William (1697–1764), painter and engraver; the first English-born artist to achieve international status.

William Hogarth was born on 10 November 1697 in London, the only son of a schoolmaster who also undertook literary hack-work for various publishers and booksellers. As a young child he enjoyed making rough drawings of scenes from the streets in which he grew up. At the age of fifteen he was apprenticed to a silversmith, but had little appetite for the dull work of copying heraldic designs, and after the death of his father in 1718 he established himself in his own shop as an engraver on copper. From the routine business of engraving tickets, cards, and book illustrations he quickly progressed to the execution of satiric prints on contemporary fashions, such as the *Masquerades and Operas* of 1724, and this early success enabled him to commit himself wholly to an artistic career.

Hogarth's lack of formal training turned out to be no disadvantage, and it led to the early development of his very individual working methods. Rather than make several preliminary drafts before attempting the final composition, Hogarth trained his memory to retain 'in my mind's eye without drawing on the spot whatever I wanted to imitate'. The finished picture thus became an improvization upon life, and the full vigour and coarseness of London street life – of which Hogarth had wide experience – was translated into visual terms with unprecedented realism. Hogarth himself, who acquired a wide knowledge of European art from reproductive engravings, was fully conscious of his own technique, and despite his impatience with formal training he was eager to learn from any teacher who might relate to his personal talent: in 1720 he attended a private drawing school in St. Martin's Lane, and in 1724 he joined a free drawing school that had recently opened in the house of Sir James Thornhill.

Both the dramatic subject matter and the detailed realistic style of *The Beggar's Opera* (1728) demonstrate Hogarth's determination to obey his own talent rather than contemporary fashion. In the same year he brought a successful lawsuit against a patron who had commissioned and then rejected another of his paintings. His scorn for the affected tastes of the so-called connoisseurs was deeply felt, and the satire of his later art was offered as honest criticism rather than as light entertainment. In 1729 Hogarth eloped with the daughter of Sir James Thornhill.

By 1731 Hogarth had completed *A Harlot's Progress*, the first of his series of satirical pictures on contemporary morals, and in 1733 his ability to record the boisterous reality of London life was further developed in *Southwark Fair*. Ironically, the consequence for the artist of these revolutionary paintings was that his reputation was enlarged and his personal prosperity increased. The engravings of Hogarth's next satirical series, *A Rake's Progress*, were withheld from publication until he managed to secure the passing of a copyright act (still known as 'Hogarth's Act') to protect them from piracy. The artistic conventions that Hogarth was developing in these series of pictures were influenced more obviously by his literary and theatrical interests than by the work of other painters, and according to his own testimony this influence was not accidental:

> I therefore wished to compose pictures on canvas, similar to representations on the stage ... I have endeavoured to treat my subjects as a dramatic writer; my picture is my stage, and men and women my players. ...

Among Hogarth's closest friends were Garrick and Fielding (qq.v.), and he was influenced not only by the formal conventions of drama – the series of separate pictures corresponding to the acts of a play – but also by its underlying moral and aesthetic philosophy: the debauched progress of the rake, for instance, is painted to instruct as well as to entertain.

In 1733 Hogarth bought a large house in Leicester Square; in the following year he inherited Sir James Thornhill's art school, which he transformed into a study and debating centre for leading artists; and in 1735 he was elected a governor of St. Bartholomew's Hospital. This worldly prosperity allowed Hogarth the freedom to experiment with his talents in

the genre of historical painting, and he produced two large religious pieces (*The Pool at Bethesda* and *The Good Samaritan*) to decorate the main staircase at St. Bartholomew's Hospital. He was most widely known, however, for his satirical engravings, and it was perhaps inevitable that these new historical paintings were poorly received. But Hogarth, despite the essential independence of his character, was in this case disappointed by the unfavourable criticism: it was his ambition to be respected as a major artist rather than as a mere caricaturist or illustrator. The need to gain full recognition of his talent also motivated a series of portraits of middle-class patrons that Hogarth painted in the early 1740s; the first of these was his major full-length portrait of the philanthropist Thomas Coram, a work that infused new realism into a decaying tradition. In 1745 Hogarth persuaded various other artists to contribute paintings to the Foundling Hospital (where his own portrait of Coram was hung), and the success of the consequent exhibition contributed much towards the

eventual establishment of the Royal Academy in 1768.

In 1743 Hogarth completed his next satirical series, *Marriage à la Mode*, but he delayed its exhibition until after he had travelled to Paris to recruit skilled French craftsmen for the engraving of the plates. Further didactic prints, executed mostly from drawings rather than paintings, included *Industry and Idleness* (1747), and *Beer Street, Gin Lane*, and *Four Stages of Cruelty* (all 1751).

After moving to Chiswick in 1749 Hogarth retreated from social involvement in order to write his *Analysis of Beauty*, the first attempt ever by a practising English artist to compose his theories concerning the form and structure of painting into a formal aesthetic. One of the chief features of this work is Hogarth's theoretical explanation of his 'precise serpentine line', which he used as his expressive symbol for the infinite variety and intricacy of the natural world. (This line is depicted on the palette in his self-portrait of 1745, now in the Tate Gallery, London.) The *Analysis* was published in 1753, and though in England it stimulated only misunderstanding and hostility from the artistic establishment, it was received with much respect on the Continent.

Hogarth returned to painting in 1754 with a large series entitled *Election*, but though he continued to produce occasional portraits and prints until a few months before his death, the lack of public sympathy with the deeper themes of his art prevented Hogarth from developing his talent any further. In 1745, as a result of a quarrel with his official art dealers, Hogarth had himself conducted an auction of his best-known paintings: the prices bid had been absurdly low, and for the rest of his career Hogarth was conscious of the futility of his single-handed struggle to attain for indigenous

English art the same respect that was given willingly and blindly to anything painted either abroad or by the Old Masters. In 1757 he was appointed Serjeant Painter to George III, but this honour was a reflection more of his superficial popularity than of any real understanding of his art.

Suffering from ill health and frustration, Hogarth became involved in a political dispute in 1762 and was attacked by John Wilkes (q.v.) and his former friend Charles Churchill, against whom he retaliated with savage caricatures. He died suddenly at his house in Leicester Square on 26 October 1764, and was buried at Chiswick under an epitaph written by Garrick. It was left to later generations – and in particular the Romantics, who responded enthusiastically to the first major exhibition of Hogarth's paintings in 1814 – to recognize the fact that England had at last produced a painter of true greatness.

F. Antal, *Hogarth and His Place in European Art* (1962).
J. Burke (ed.), *The Analysis of Beauty with the Rejected Passages from the Manuscript Drafts and Autobiographical Notes* (1955).
J. Burke and C. Caldwell, *Hogarth: The Complete Engravings* (1968).
F. D. Kligender (ed.), *Hogarth and English Caricature* (1943).
R. E. Moore, *Hogarth's Literary Relationships* (1948).
A. P. Oppe, *The Drawings of William Hogarth* (1948).
R. Paulson, *Hogarth's Graphic Works* (2 vols.; 1965).
R. Paulson, *Hogarth: His Life, Art and Times* (2 vols.; 1971).
R. Paulson, *The Art of Hogarth* (1975).

Works in:
National Gallery, London.
National Portrait Gallery.
Tate Gallery.
Soane Museum.
Dulwich Collection.
National Maritime Museum.
National Gallery of Scotland, Edinburgh.
Also works in many provincial galleries, and in various galleries in America.

Portraits: oil, quarter-length, self-portrait, 1745: Tate Gallery; oil, full-length, self-portrait, *c.* 1757: N.P.G.

Hogg, James (1770–1835), Scottish poet and novelist.

James Hogg was born at Ettrick, Selkirkshire, and baptized there on 9 December 1770, the second son of Robert Hogg, member of a long-established family in the Border area. Because of continual work on his father's farm, he received very little formal education, his sole reading material (according to his own account) being the Bible. His work was mainly that of herding sheep, and by the age of sixteen he was known as a skilled shepherd – the trade from which developed his later nickname, 'The Ettrick Shepherd'. In 1790 Hogg was employed as a shepherd by a Mr. Laidlaw of Blackhouse on the River Yarrow, and his enthusiasm for literature was developed rapidly by his friendship with Laidlaw's sons (one of whom, William, later became a close friend of Sir Walter Scott). During his employment with Laidlaw Hogg made several journeys with his sheep to the Scottish Highlands, and it was the experience of hearing a crofter's recitation of 'Tam o' Shanter' (by Robert Burns, q.v.) that stimulated Hogg to write his own first verses.

In 1800 Hogg returned to Ettrick to manage the farm and care for his ageing parents. He published his first poems at Edinburgh in 1801; this volume, *Scottish Pastorals, Poems, Songs, Etc.*, led to a meeting in 1802 with Sir Walter Scott, for whom Hogg agreed to supply a number of local ballads for the *Border Minstrelsy*.

On the expiry of the lease on the family farm in 1803 Hogg made plans with a neighbouring farmer to establish a new farm on the Isle of Harris, but a dispute destroyed this project and Hogg, now virtually penniless, was forced to hire himself out again as a shepherd. While working at Mitchelstacks in Nithsdale Hogg met the Scottish writer Allan Cunningham, and was encouraged by this friendship to persevere with his own writing. In 1807, largely through the help of Sir Walter Scott, a second collection of Hogg's verses was published, *The Mountain Bard*; this volume brought Hogg a welcome £300, but he lost the money in a failed farming venture in Dumfriesshire, and in 1810, again bankrupt, he decided to move to Edinburgh to see whether he could earn his living by literature alone.

Together with several other struggling writers, Hogg published in 1810 a miscellany of verses entitled *The Forest Minstrel*. This volume was cannily dedicated to the Countess of Dalkeith, who rewarded Hogg with 100 guineas. In his determination to make money Hogg did not limit himself to poetry alone; he also wrote several plays and established a weekly critical journal entitled *The Spy*. The plays are weak and the journal did not last beyond its first year, but in *The Queen's Wake* (1813) Hogg displayed a more enduring talent: the several tales, supposed to have been recited by seventeen bards at the Holyrood court of Mary, Queen of Scots, are picturesque and imaginative, and the success of this volume led to meetings with Southey, Wordsworth, and John Murray (qq.v.), the last of whom agreed to act as the English publisher for all Hogg's work. Hogg attempted to repeat this success with two similar volumes in 1815 and 1816, but found to his distress that this device would not work twice. Again running out of money, Hogg now composed a careful letter to the Duchess of Buccleugh, whose husband generously provided him with a farm at Eltrive, on the River Yarrow, at a nominal rent.

Though he had abandoned Edinburgh, Hogg had certainly not abandoned literature, and in 1816 he wrote *The Poetic Mirror*, a volume of ingenious and effective parodies of Wordsworth, Cole-

ridge, Scott, Southey, and even himself. In 1817 Hogg helped to inaugurate the *Edinburgh Monthly Magazine* (later known as *Blackwood's Magazine* after the publisher William Blackwood), and the following year he dedicated a new illustrated edition of *The Queen's Wake*, published in London, to Queen Charlotte. Several volumes of tales in verse and prose confirmed Hogg's reputation as a prolific writer who could produce exactly what his public wanted, and in 1820 he married Margaret Phillips, the daughter of a local gentleman, and leased a neighbouring farm. His volume of 1822, *The Three Perils of Man : War, Women, and Witchcraft*, had its success guaranteed by its title, and a complementary volume on the perils of woman was the inevitable sequel in the following year.

The work by which Hogg is chiefly remembered, *The Private Memoirs and Confessions of a Justified Sinner*, was published in 1824. In this work, largely ignored by his contemporary public, Hogg treats the individual personality with a far greater insight than any of his other works suggest that he possessed: superficially a historical novel about a man who justifies his murder of his brother as being in accordance with the Calvinist doctrine of predestination, the narrative reflects moral tensions in the society of early-nineteenth-century Scotland with disturbing accuracy. The sophisticated technique of balancing the first-person account of the murderer against the narrative of a disinterested editor is the one success among Hogg's continual attempts at originality. Two years later he published an ambitious epic poem, *Queen Hynde*, but in this case Hogg's talents were insufficient to realize his intentions.

Throughout his career the pace at which Hogg wrote was never relaxed, and his work on the farm at Eltrive was constantly interrupted by publishers' deadlines and visits from literary acquaintances. To make arrangements for a cheap reissue of all his works he travelled in 1832 to London, where he was lavishly entertained for three months. On his return to Scotland he published a volume of *Lay Sermons*, and in 1834 there followed a hastily written biography of Scott, *The Domestic Manners and Private Life of Sir Walter Scott*. This last volume caused offence to Scott's son-in-law, J. G. Lockhart, whose own massive but partisan biography was published three years later.

Much of Hogg's success was due to good advice and influential connections, but his career remains remarkable nevertheless for the energy and facility with which he continued writing. Neither his farming nor his marriage was equally successful, but this was perhaps inevitable in the case of a man who was concerning himself only with the publication arrangements for his latest book. Hogg died on 21 November 1835, and was buried in the churchyard at Ettrick.

J. Carey (ed.), *The Private Memoirs and Confessions of a Justified Sinner* (1969).

J. W. Oliver (ed.), *Selected Poems of James Hogg* (1940).

L. Simpson, *Hogg: A Critical Study* (1962).

A. L. Strout, *The Life and Letters of Hogg*, vol. 1, *1770–1825* (Lubbock, Texas, 1946).

Portraits: water-colour, half-length, by S. P. Dennling: N.P.G.; oil, by W. Nicholson: Scottish N.P.G.

Hood, Thomas (1799–1845), poet, humorist, and journalist.

Thomas Hood was born on 23 May 1799 in London, the son of a Scottish bookseller who was also an unsuccessful novelist. He was educated at a suburban boarding school and later at a day school in Clerkenwell. He was brought up in a family of good literary tastes, eventually consisting of four daughters and two sons.

His elder brother, James, died early of tuberculosis, and this disease was later to claim the lives of his parents and two of his sisters.

On the death of his father in 1811, his mother moved to Islington and Hood himself came under the tutelage of a schoolmaster who recognized him to be a child of some promise. Soon afterwards Hood became apprenticed to an engraver in order not to burden his mother. After a short time in this post, however, he left to become a clerk in a counting-house in the City. His health began to fail, and in 1815 he was sent to live with relations of his father in Dundee.

During his three years in Scotland, Hood began to sketch and write, and many of his verse and prose works were published in local newspapers and periodicals. In 1818 he returned to London and began to work for his uncle, who was an engraver. After a two-year apprenticeship, Hood started to work on his own, and at the age of twenty-two he was appointed a sub-editor of the *London Magazine*. Through this he became acquainted with Lamb, Hazlitt, Coleridge, De Quincey and others, and he also began his career as a humorist. As his reputation grew so did the demand for his more witty works.

The most eventful of the friendships that Hood now formed was with John Hamilton Reynolds. In May 1824 he married Reynolds's sister, Jane, and in the following year the two men published a small anonymous volume entitled *Odes and Addresses to Great People*, of which the authorship was recognized quickly by Coleridge, among others.

In 1827 there appeared *Plea of the Midsummer Fairies*, a short book of serious verse of real quality. Both this work and the dramatic romance *Lamia* failed commercially. In 1829 Hood published a serious poem, 'The Dream of Eugene

Aram', in *The Gem*, a journal which he helped to edit. But the public wanted work by Hood the jester, and he supported himself mainly by hack work for various periodicals, including the *Comic Annual* (1830–9), the *New Monthly Magazine* (1841–3), and *Hood's Magazine* (1843).

Over the years, Hood developed from the popular humorist, through the genial satirist, into the sympathetic social commentator. In 1843 appeared one of his best-known poems, 'The Song of the Shirt' – a social protest against the unfair labour practices of the day. Its publication in the Christmas issue of *Punch* did much to enhance that journal's reputation. But it was with his comic poetry that Hood captured current interest most firmly. His ridiculous puns, as in his poem 'Faithless Nelly Gray', continue to be a joy for modern readers:

> Ben Battle was a soldier bold,
>   And used to war's alarms;
> But a cannon-ball took off his legs,
>   So he laid down his arms.

Among his other works are an unsuccessful novel, *Tylney Hall* (1834), *Whims and Oddities* (1826), and *Up the Rhine* (1840), the last being a series of sketches satirizing the English tourist.

Hood ran into financial difficulties soon after the collapse of his publisher, and his failing health made the final years of his life most difficult. For a time he lived abroad, but in 1840 he returned to England through the help of friends. During the last year of his life, the British government granted his wife an annual pension of £100 – a fact which greatly relieved the emotional if not the physical stress under which he had been living. Hood died on 3 May 1845.

W. Jerrold (ed.), *Poetical Works* (1906).
L. Marchand (ed.), *Letters of Hood from the Dilke Papers in the British Museum* (New Brunswick, 1945).
F. Morgan-Peter (ed.), *Letters* (1973).
J. C. Reid, *Thomas Hood* (1963).

Portrait: millboard, half-length, by unknown artist, c. 1835: N.P.G.

Hoppner, John (1758–1810), portrait painter.

Hoppner was born on 4 April 1758, the son of German parents. He became a chorister at the Chapel Royal at an early age and commenced his studies as a painter when he was still very young, thanks to a small allowance from George III. Hoppner's mother was one of the German ladies-in-waiting, and the King's interest in him was rumoured to be a truly paternal one. There seems little evidence to substantiate this rumour, but Hoppner encouraged it.

In 1775 he was admitted as a student at the Royal Academy and in 1778 was awarded the Silver Medal for drawing from life. In 1782 he carried off the Academy's highest award, the Gold Medal for Historical Painting, with his most original presentation of a scene from *King Lear*. Hoppner made his first exhibition at the Academy in 1780 and continued to exhibit there regularly until 1809.

In 1782 he married Phoebe, the youngest daughter of Mrs. Patience Wright, an American lady noted for her sculptured portraits modelled in wax, for her social qualities, and for her patriotic ardour. It was in his mother-in-law's house that Hoppner met Benjamin West, and Benjamin Franklin.

Hoppner was successful with his paintings right from the beginning of his career and was never lacking in wealthy and fashionable sitters. His first love was landscape, but, constrained by his small financial means and the fashion of the day, he was obliged to turn to portrait painting. He was at his best when drawing women and children, which he did with great simplicity and naturalness. He did, however, produce one or two outstanding male portraits, as is shown in his painting of Lord Nelson, but usually his style was too restrained to depict men successfully. In 1785 he exhibited the portraits of the three youngest royal princesses, Sophia, Amelia, and Mary; the last of these is often considered to represent the peak of his achievement. Hoppner was often accused of plagiarizing from his contemporaries, and in this painting he managed to combine elements from the work of Reynolds and Romney to give his own work a peculiar grace and charm.

In 1789 Hoppner was appointed Portrait Painter to the Prince of Wales. Shortly afterwards, in 1792, he was elected an associate of the Royal Academy, becoming a full academician in 1795. By this time Reynolds was dead and the popularity of Romney was declining. Thus the favour of society was divided between Hoppner and his well-matched rival, Sir Thomas Lawrence (q.v.). Their rivalry was keen and tinged with bitterness on the side of Hoppner, who exclaimed against the impropriety of Lawrence's portraits. Lawrence was, for his part, more generous in his comments on Hoppner's talents, and was genuinely sorry when his rival died.

Hoppner never exhibited anywhere but the Academy and the majority of his paintings were portraits. However, in his early years he occasionally depicted ideal subjects in his works, the most notable of which are *Primrose Girl* (1780 and 1785), *Jupiter and Io* (1785), *Belisarius* (1787), *A Bacchante* (1789), and *Cupid and Psyche*. He also did a number of chalk landscapes, which are now in the British Museum, and indeed his love of landscapes is reflected throughout his work in the backgrounds of his portraits, which are very delicately done. In 1803 he and Sir

Charles Wilkin published a series of *Portraits of Ladies* and in 1805 Hoppner published a volume of *Eastern Tales*, which was not a great success.

During his last years Hoppner had to contend with a chronic state of ill health, resulting from a naturally weak constitution. He died in his London home on 23 January 1810 and was buried in the cemetery of St. James's Chapel, Hampstead Road.

W. McKay and W. Roberts, *John Hoppner, R.A.* (1909–14).

Works in:
N.P.G.
National Gallery.
Tate Gallery.
V. & A.

Horne, John (1736–1812), see Tooke, John Horne.

Howard, John (1726–90), philanthropist and prison reformer.

John Howard was born on 2 September 1726, probably in Hackney. His father was a partner in an upholstery and carpet business. His mother died soon after her son's birth, and he grew up a sickly child. He spent his early days at Cardington, near Bedford, where his father had some property. Educated at school in Hertford, he was subsequently apprenticed to a wholesale grocer. In 1742, however, his father died, leaving a handsome fortune to him and his sister. Having bought himself out of his indentures, Howard made a tour of the Continent, but returned in very poor health. His landlady, Sarah Loidore, nursed him devotedly, and despite her twenty-seven years' seniority, the two were married in 1751, but she died only four years later.

In 1756 Howard sailed for Portugal, and his ship was captured by French privateers. He was imprisoned and suffered considerable hardship. Returning to England on parole, he negotiated an exchange of prisoners, giving details of his fellow-prisoners' sufferings to the Commissioners of Sick and Wounded Seamen.

In 1756 Howard was made a Fellow of the Royal Society and returned to Cardington. Two years later he married Henrietta Leeds, and set about improving the lot of the local villagers, erecting houses, providing elementary education for children irrespective of their religion, and encouraging self-help. In 1765 his second wife died, four days after the birth of their son, and Howard endured another period of ill health.

In 1773 he was appointed High Sheriff of Bedfordshire. He visited the county jail and, appalled at what he saw there, began the work on prison reform that was thereafter to be his central concern. He discovered that in many cases people who had been found not guilty or had not even had a case made against them were still kept in prison until they had paid certain fees to their jailers. Howard suggested that the jailers be paid salaries instead of this invidious form of virtual ransom, and was requested by the justices to supply a precedent. Subsequent investigations revealed the same situation, together with deplorable sanitary conditions, in penal institutions throughout England. On 4 March 1774 he gave evidence of his researches to a House of Commons committee, and was called to the bar to be thanked for his 'interesting observations' and commended for his 'zeal and humanity'. Two bills were passed: one for abolishing jailers' fees, the other for improving sanitary conditions in prisons and for making better provision for the prisoners' health. Howard had copies of these bills printed at his own expense and sent to every county jail, but in general their provisions were ignored.

Howard carried out prison visits in Scotland, Ireland, and France (where, however, he failed to gain entrance to the Bastille). He made another tour of inspection in northern Europe, and in November 1776 began a second round of English prisons which resulted in a book, *The State of Prisons in England and Wales with Preliminary Observations and an Account of Some Foreign Prisons*. His sister died in 1777, leaving Howard her fortune and a house in Ormond Street.

In 1778, the House of Commons appointed Howard to inquire into the 'hulk' system of imprisonment, to establish whether abandoned ships were more or less suitable than buildings for housing prisoners. His investigations led to the passing of an act authorizing two new-style penitentiaries intended to reform convicts through religious instruction and supervised daily labour; as part of the better conditions, prisoners were to have their own cells at night. The scheme failed, however, owing to the death of one of the three supervisors and the resignation of Howard.

In 1780 Howard published an appendix to his *State of Prisons*, followed by *Historical Remarks and Anecdotes on the Castle of Bastille*. He continued in his role as travelling investigator, taking particular note of the high level of jail fever and smallpox, and in 1782 the Irish House of Commons appointed him to inquire into the situation in Ireland, where he received an LL.D. from the University of Dublin.

In 1785 he commenced first-hand research into the conditions of lazarettos or quarantine houses, travelling to Venice on a vessel with a foul bill of health. In 1789 he published *An Account of the Principal Lazarettos in Europe with Various papers relative to the Plague*, and extended his inquiries into the state of hospitals. Later that year he began his last journey, a tour of Russian hospitals. He died of camp fever at Kherson in southern Russia on 20 January 1790. He was buried near by and a brick pyramid was erected over his grave. The achievements of Howard's life were slow to take effect, many requiring more than a century for action to be taken. Nevertheless his integrity and humanity brought great public acclaim, and his was the first statue to be admitted to St. Paul's Cathedral.

D. L. Howard, *John Howard, Prison Reformer* (1958). M. Southwood, *John Howard: Prison Reformer* (1959).

Portrait: oil, half-length, by M. Brown: N.P.G.

Howe, Richard (1726–99), Earl Howe; admiral; brother of William Howe (q.v.).

Richard Howe was born on 8 March 1726, the second son of Emanuel Scrope Howe, 2nd Viscount. He joined the navy in 1739. During the War of the Austrian Succession, his career was advanced by the influence of an eminent and valuable patron, Sir Charles Knowles, and he saw action as commander of the sloop *Baltimore*, operating mainly off the Scottish coast.

At the end of the war, Howe became Knowles's flag captain aboard the *Cornwall* and, after two peace-time commissions, obtained command of the 60-gun *Dunkirk* in 1755. In this ship he served with Admiral Boscawen, who in April 1755 sailed out from England to intercept a French fleet carrying reinforcements to Canada. Boscawen encountered the French off the St. Lawrence on 7 June, but lost them in a fog. On the following day chance put the *Dunkirk* nearest to some stragglers, and her gunfire overwhelmed the *Alcide*, giving Howe the dubious distinction of having performed the first act of aggression in the Seven Years War – on his admiral's orders.

In 1757, the year in which he also became M.P. for Dartmouth, Howe transferred with his crew to the 74-gun

Magnanime, in which he inaugurated the practice of giving leave to the crew watch by watch. Always popular with his men in view of the concern he always showed for them, Howe was felt by some of his contemporaries to be too lax.

Later in 1757 Howe led an expedition against Rochefort, and despite the fact that he captured the island of Aix against all probabilities, it turned out to be a fiasco. A second expedition, in 1758 against St. Malo, was equally unsuccessful.

Throughout the remaining stages of the war, *Magnanime* acquitted itself well, and in 1762 Howe, now a married man with an estate at St. Albans and a viscountcy inherited from his elder brother (killed in action in 1758), became flag captain to Prince Edward, Duke of York, George III's younger brother. At the end of the war in 1763 Howe became a Lord of the Admiralty, and two years later Treasurer of the Navy.

In 1775 he was promoted to vice-admiral and in the next year became commander in chief, North America, where his younger brother, William Howe (q.v.), already commanded the land-based forces. At first his duties were mainly in co-operation with the army, but the entry of France into the War of American Independence in 1778 made naval conflict inevitable.

Howe was not helped at all by the home government. In September 1778, having resigned his post, he sailed back to England and proceeded to attack Lord North's ministry in parliament. He refused any further commissions under the North administration. He was brought back in 1782, after North fell, and as admiral of the Blue aboard the *Victory* acted as commander in chief, Channel; Britain's naval supremacy had been partly recovered by Rodney's victory at the Battle of the Saints, and Howe was employed to keep an eye on the situation in Europe, especially Gibraltar, which had been under siege by Spain since 1779. On 11 September 1782 Howe sailed from Spithead with 183 sail, including thirty-four battleships, and reached the Straits by mid-October. Although he had fewer vessels than the Spaniards, Howe was able to manoeuvre his transports into Gibraltar behind the line of battle without interruption. In the same way, having relieved the besieged garrison, he was allowed to depart on 19 October with only some half-hearted distant cannonading. The absence of fighting should not detract from the fact that Howe showed impeccable ability both as a commander and as a seaman.

In January 1783 Howe was appointed First Lord of the Admiralty. He reduced the navy to peace-time establishment and carried out much dockyard reform. But he failed to carry the confidence of the younger Pitt and eventually felt compelled to resign in 1788. In this year he was created Baron and Earl Howe.

On the outbreak of the new war with France in 1793, Howe was given command of the Channel fleet again. In April 1794 the French mounted a large-scale naval operation to escort in a grain convoy from America. On 2 May Howe led out his thirty-two ships to escort an East India Company convoy down-Channel. Detaching six ships to proceed with the convoy, he took the remainder of his squadron to look for the French and their grain. On 28 May, 400 miles west of Ushant, he sighted a French fleet out on the same errand. The French attempted to draw the British fleet away from the grain convoy. A running battle developed, which reached its climax on 1 June, when Howe's fleet broke through the French line and precipitated a mêlée. In the fight, six Frenchmen were captured and one sunk by gunfire without corresponding British loss. The convoy, however, got through the area and reached France safely.

Nevertheless, Howe was congratulated by an overjoyed England. His exploits made this day the Glorious First of June, despite the fact that the French had saved their precious grain supply. George III presented Howe with a diamond-hilted sword and in 1796 he was at last promoted admiral of the fleet. In 1797 he was awarded the Order of the Garter and retired from the navy in declining health. His last offical act actually followed his retirement, when in May 1797 he mediated in a fleet mutiny. Howe died on 5 August 1799.

T. S. Anderson, *The Command of the Howe Brothers during the American Revolution* (1936).
Sir John Barrow, *Life of Earl Howe* (1838).
T. H. McGuffie, *The Siege of Gibraltar (1779–1783)* (1965).
O. Warner, *The Glorious First of June* (1961).

Portraits: oil, full-length, by H. Singleton: N.P.G.; oil, artist unknown: National Maritime Museum, Greenwich.

Howe, William (1729–1814), 5th Viscount Howe; British general in the War of American Independence.

William Howe was born on 10 August 1729, the younger brother of George Howe, 3rd Viscount, who was killed in America during the Seven Years War, and of Richard Howe (q.v.), 4th Viscount. In September 1746, after an education at Eton, William Howe was appointed cornet in an experimental corps of light horse raised by the Duke of Kingston after the Battle of Culloden, and re-formed as the Duke of Cumberland's Light Dragoons in the following year. It served in Flanders in the last year of the War of the Austrian Succession, by which time Howe was a lieutenant; it was disbanded in 1749.

In 1750 Howe became a captain in the 20th Regiment of Foot, which was then commanded by James Wolfe (q.v.) in the absence of its official commander, and which had been trained by him to a high degree of efficiency. That the two became personal friends indicates Howe's own military capabilities. He was appointed major in January 1756 in a newly raised regiment of foot, subsequently designated the 58th which, as lieutenant colonel, he took out to North America in 1758. It participated in the siege and capture of Louisbourg under General Amherst. With a team of hand-picked men, Howe participated in the capture of Quebec (1759) and, resuming command of the 58th, attended to the city's defence during the winter. He was in charge of a brigade in Murray's expedition to Montreal (1760) and another at the successful assault on Belle Isle (1761) and was adjutant general for Clanwilliam's force of 11,000 troops that took Havana in 1762. His distinguished service in the Seven Years War was duly rewarded by the colonelcy of the 46th Foot (1764) and the lieutenant-governorship of the Isle of Wight (1768). While campaigning, he had been elected to succeed his eldest brother as M.P. for Nottingham in 1758, retaining the seat until 1780. In 1772, he was made a major general.

The new infantry development, embodied in the 'light infantry' experiments in the North American campaigns, was given a fillip in 1774 when Howe was appointed to train companies detached for that purpose from several regiments. The aim was to produce troops capable of rapid and independent movement who could operate ahead of or on the flanks of the main body of a regiment or army in battle. As a result of Howe's efforts, such specialized 'light companies' became a normal part of British infantry regiments until the mid nineteenth century.

Although he disapproved of the government's policy towards the Ameri-

can colonists and had no confidence in General Gage (q.v.), Howe was sent to join him with reinforcements in May 1775 and exercised a subordinate command at the Battle of Bunker Hill (15 June). The British infantry, attacking uphill against a prepared position, paid dearly for their victory, and Howe lost all his staff, although he was unhurt himself. He continued to attract honours, receiving the colonelcy of the Royal Welch Fusiliers, promotion to lieutenant general, and the Order of the Bath, and succeeding Gage in local command (October 1775). Despite all this, he was clearly not reconciled to the war and, although he later denied it, this may have affected his conduct of operations, which failed to fulfil the promise of his earlier career. On the other hand, he was not supported by positive political direction from the home government, and rebels in a large country do not present an easy military problem, especially when the army's base lies across an ocean.

Howe spent the winter of 1775–6 in quarters at Boston and then, hemmed in by Washington's troops, withdrew to Halifax. Reinforcements began to reach him, together with his brother as naval commander with a joint commission to treat with the colonists if it was considered that limited concessions might provide a basis for a restoration of order. When this failed, Howe launched an offensive that captured Long Island and New York, where he established quarters for his second winter, while the morale of the Americans confronting him began to crack. Washington's leadership and a daring raid across the Delaware on 26 December 1776 completely reversed the situation, and Howe demanded an additional 20,000 men for the next year's campaign. He received 2,500 and did not take the field until June 1777.

The agreed strategic plan was for

Burgoyne to advance south from Canada and Howe to move north to meet him, so cutting off New England from the remaining colonies. Considering that it would be unwise to leave the local initiative in American hands while waiting for Burgoyne's approach, Howe left Clinton at New York with weak forces and took the rest by sea to Chesapeake Bay in August. He brought Washington's 8,000 men to battle at Brandywine (17 September) and defeated them with his own 18,000, going on to take Philadelphia on 27 September. Meanwhile Burgoyne, struggling down the Hudson valley, received no news of the force he assumed to be advancing to meet him and finding himself surrounded, surrendered at Saratoga to the American general, Gates, on 17 October 1777.

For a third winter Howe put his men into winter quarters, at Philadelphia, while near at hand Washington's own men reached the nadir of their spirits at Valley Forge, although they remained unattacked. Howe had already dispatched his resignation, and left America in May 1778. Political feeling about the war ran high at Westminster and the two brothers procured a Commons committee to inquire into the conduct of the war, in order to vindicate their own efforts. The investigation terminated in June 1779 without either their critics or themselves establishing a case.

In 1782 Howe was appointed lieutenant general of ordnance and later (1785) vacated his infantry colonelcy for that of the 23rd Light Dragoons. When Great Britain became involved in the war against Revolutionary France (1793) he was employed in various district commands in England before assuming the governorship of Berwick-on-Tweed in 1795, and transferring in 1805 to the same office in Plymouth, where he died on 12 July 1814. He had been promoted general in October 1793 and had succeeded to the viscountcy after his brother's death in 1799. The title lapsed on his death.

J. R. Alden, *The American Revolution, 1775–1783* (1954).

T. S. Anderson, *The Command of the Howe Brothers during the American Revolution* (1936).

P. Mackesy, *The War for America, 1775–1783* (1964).

Portrait: engraving, three-quarter length, by C. Corbutt, 1777: N.P.G.

Hume, David (1711–76), philosopher; a leading figure of the Enlightenment in Britain.

David Hume was born on 26 April 1711, the son of Joseph Hume, a descendant of Lord Hume of Douglas, who had fought in the French wars of Henry V and VI. The family home, a modest farmhouse called Ninewells, set in a small estate, lay on the banks of the Whitewater in Berwickshire. David was the third child. His father died when he was an infant, and it seems that it was his mother who was responsible for the intellectual athlete who emerged. He later described her in his autobiography *My Own Life* as 'a woman of singular merit, who although young and handsome, devoted herself entirely to the rearing and education of her children'. He considered himself to have the same constitution as her, and indeed died of the same affliction (haemorrhage of the bowels). Hume received little formal education, but nevertheless entered the Greek class at the University of Edinburgh at the age of twelve. He did not graduate, however, and it is not known how long he remained there.

Early on he steered his life onto a course of philosophical pursuits and an austere mode of living which he retained for most of his life. His greatest passion was the exercise of his mind in the disputes that had engaged scholars for centuries, and he 'found a certain boldness of temper growing on me, which was not inclined to submit to any authority in these subjects'. The excitement of intellectual discovery led to a nervous breakdown in 1729, from which it took him several years to recover.

At the age of seventeen Hume made a brief sortie into the legal profession, but found it distasteful and soon returned to his private studies. Six years later (in 1734) he embarked on a career in commerce in Bristol. He was unable to tolerate this for long, and in the middle of 1734 went to France. He spent the greater part of the three years in France conversing with the Jesuits at Descartes's old college of La Flèche. Here, at the age of twenty-six, he wrote his first work, the *Treatise of Human Nature*. It was an ambitious book and, although flawed, does represent the most thorough exposition of his thought. It is divided into three books, of which Book I ('Of the Understanding') is concerned with the process of knowing, Book II ('Of the Passions') with an elaboration of the emotional nature of man in which a subordinate role is assigned to reason, and Book III ('Of Morals') with Hume's conception of moral goodness in terms of mutable 'feelings'. It does not do justice to his more mature efforts. He returned to England in 1737 and set about publishing the *Treatise*. Books I and II were published in two volumes late in 1738 or early in 1739 and 'fell dead-born from the press' (his own words), as did Book III the following year. Hume was greatly disappointed with his lack of success. Nevertheless, he sent a copy of the book to the seventeen-year-old Adam Smith, then studying at the University of Glasgow, who became a lifelong friend.

After 1740 Hume turned his attention to political and historical works. In 1741 he published anonymously in Edinburgh the first volume of *Essays Moral and Political*, and followed it with a second volume in 1742. There followed a third essay, *That Politics may be reduced to a Science*, discussing the importance of forms of government, a fourth, *On the First Principles of Government*, and a fifth *On the Origin of Government*. Hume's political instincts were conservative, stemming from his social concept of a man and his analogy of the structure of government with that of the family. Absolute monarchy, in his eyes, was preferable to a republic because it proved a better bulwark against anarchy. The work gained some success and inspired Hume to apply for the chair of Ethics and Pneumatic Philosophy at Edinburgh in 1744. Objectors, however, alleged heresy and even atheism, pointing to the *Treatise* as evidence, and forced Hume to leave the city and search for more gainful employment.

He spent a year (1745–6) near St. Albans as tutor to the young and feeble Marquis of Annandale, and followed this by a few months in the employ of General James St. Clair on an abortive expedition to Brittany. After a brief spell back in England, he accompanied the general to the court of Turin, as his secretary and aide de camp. In 1748, while in Turin, he brought out his *Philosophical Essays of Inquiry Concerning Human Understanding*. This was essentially a re-write of Book I of the *Treatise*, abridged and reorganized for popular use with the addition of the essays 'On Miracles' and 'On Necessity'. Back in England in 1749 he worked until 1751 on the *Dialogues on Natural Religion* (published posthumously) and on the second volume of the *Inquiry*, published in 1751 and entitled *Inquiry Concerning the Principles of Morals*. Hume regarded this as the best of his works, but 'it came unnoticed and unobserved into the world'. His essays were by now increasing in popularity and his *Political Discourses*

(1752) were immediately successful. This work has been described as the 'cradle of political economy' and, remembering that the *Wealth of Nations* by his friend Adam Smith did not follow until 1776, it was an original and daring enterprise. The *Political Discourses* achieved for Hume a European reputation and influenced the French school of economists of the late eighteenth century.

Hume's mature philosophical works represent an attempt to define the principles of human knowledge. He holds that all knowledge is grounded in sense experience. Men do not create any ideas and their words have meaning only in so far as they conjure up something that derives from an impression. He held that all objects of awareness must either be a relation of ideas, which can be studied formally as logical connections between meanings, or matters of fact (for example, that fire burns), which are logically barren. Hence he concludes that any demonstrative science of fact is impossible. This leads on to Hume's distinctive doctrine of causality which so influenced Immanuel Kant. It states how an observer passes from an impression to an idea regularly associated with it through force of habit, although his scepticism denied that from impressions and ideas one can infer a persisting external world. Similarly in his ethical theory he stresses the importance of habits and feelings rather than rational obedience to general principles. His moral system is grounded on men's natural feelings of goodwill towards each other where happiness of self is combined with sympathy for one's fellows.

With a high reputation in the literary world and £1,000, which he had saved by being frugal, Hume was able to settle in Edinburgh and study in peace. In 1752 he was elected librarian of the Faculty of Advocates, a position which he retained

for the next five years. With the resources of a huge library he was now able to satisfy a desire of some years' standing to write a history book.

In 1754 Hume published the first volume of the *History of Great Britain*, and the next five volumes appeared at intervals until the last in 1762. As a historian he was no great stylist but a fairly impartial judge by contemporary standards. By now he had achieved fame and notoriety. In 1762 James Boswell (q.v.), the biographer of Samuel Johnson, called Hume 'the greatest writer in Britain', although to the majority of the public he was known merely as an atheist.

In 1763 Hume left England to become secretary to the British embassy in Paris under the Earl of Hertford. His reputation in France was higher than it was in England, and he proved an unlikely social success whose favours were courted by noble ladies at their receptions and in their boxes in the theatre. When he returned to London in 1766 he brought with him Jean-Jacques Rousseau, the French philosopher and author, and found him a refuge from persecution in a country house at Wootton in Staffordshire. Rousseau, however, suspected a plot and fled back to France with stories of Hume's treachery. Hume retaliated by publishing the relevant correspondence between them with a connecting narrative (*A Concise and Genuine Account of the Dispute Between Mr. Hume and Mr. Rousseau*, 1766).

In 1769 Hume returned to Edinburgh 'very opulent' and intent on taking the remainder of his life easily. In 1770 he arranged for the building of a new house in the new town of Edinburgh, where he lived, 'the centre of accomplished and refined society', and occupied himself by revising the text of his writings. He issued five further editions of his *History* between 1762 and 1773, as well as eight editions of his collected writings under the title *Essays and Treatises* (1753–72). The final edition of this collection, prepared by Hume, appeared posthumously in 1777. His autobiography, *The Life of David Hume, Written by Himself*, which appeared the same year, is actually dated 18 April 1776. After a long illness he died in Edinburgh on 25 August 1776.

M. Belgion, *Hume* (British Council pamphlet; 1965).

T. H. Green and T. H. Grose (eds.), *Philosophical Works of David Hume* (4 vols.; 1874–5).

J. Y. T. Greig (ed.), *Letters of David Hume* (1932).

R. Klibansky and E. C. Mossner (ed.), *New Letters of David Hume* (1954).

A. MacIntyre (ed.), *Hume's Ethical Writings* (New York, 1965).

E. C. Mossner, *The Life of Hume* (1972, rev. ed.).

N. Kemp Smith, *The Philosophy of David Hume* (1941, 1960).

F. Watkins (ed.), *Hume: Theory of Politics* (1951).

D. C. Yalden-Thomas (ed.), *Hume: Theory of Knowledge* (1951).

Portrait: oil, half-length, by A. Ramsay, 1766: Scottish National Gallery.

Hunt, (James Henry) Leigh

(1784–1859), poet, essayist, and journalist.

Hunt was born on 19 October 1784 at Southgate, Middlesex. He was descended from a family that had emigrated from Devon to the West Indies in the time of James I. His grandfather and great-grandfather were clergymen, as, for a brief period at least, was his father, who as a Royalist in America at the time of the American Revolution was forced to flee with his wife to England.

Leigh Hunt was educated at Christ's Hospital, London, known as the 'Blue-Coat School' because of the long blue gowns traditionally worn by the students. During his school days he began to write verses. These were collected by his father and published by subscription in 1801 under the title *Juvenilia*. The poetry was highly imitative, and in later years Hunt remarked, 'I was as proud perhaps of the book at that time as I am ashamed of it now. My book was a heap of imitations, all absolutely worthless.'

At an early age Hunt began to write theatre reviews for a Sunday newspaper, *The News*. The paper was published by his brother John, and enjoyed a mild success. His first regular job, however, was that of assistant to his brother Stephen, who was a lawyer. Becoming dissatisfied with the mundane nature of the work, he exchanged one bad position for another – that of a clerk in the War Office.

In 1808 he joined his brother John in a new publishing venture as editor of the *Examiner*. This journalistic work was more to his liking, although the politically radical ideas expressed in the journal proved to be expensive. In 1813, as the result of a damaging article he wrote on the Prince Regent (later to become George IV), he was fined £500 and sentenced to two years in jail. He took his imprisonment stoically and made the best of the situation by continuing to read, write, and cultivate a garden in the jail yard. Among those who were sympathetic and shared some of his views, his visitors included Lord Byron and Charles Lamb. Hunt tells us that he converted his two rooms in the jail into a cheerful study:

> I papered the walls with a trellis of roses; I had the ceiling coloured with clouds and sky; the barred windows were screened with Venetian blinds; and when my bookcases were set up, with their busts and flowers, and a pianoforte made its appearance, perhaps there was not a handsomer room on that side the water.

Hunt published his first major literary work, *The Story of Rimini*, in 1816. It was a 'verse story' of Paolo and Francesca, and although of some interest, showed no signs of poetical genius. In fact, very few of Hunt's poems demonstrate a lasting quality. His main contribution to the arts was as a critic of music and the visual arts, and it is in his essays that his best work lies. In these he followed eighteenth-century models, but sought to entertain rather than improve.

In spite of his lifelong impecuniousness, Hunt befriended many writers, especially the young poets Keats and Shelley. His home was always open to local artists and creative persons of all descriptions, including Benjamin Haydon, John Hamilton Reynolds, and William Hazlitt, to whose magazine *The Round Table* Hunt contributed during 1817.

In 1822 he was invited to Italy to edit a journal proposed by Byron and Shelley, *The Liberal*. Shortly after he arrived, Shelley died in a boating accident; the journal was to last for only four issues before Hunt was forced to return to England because of financial difficulties. He had been treated rather badly by Byron, and his feelings were reflected in what many of Hunt's friends thought was an ill-advised work, *Lord Byron and Some of His Contemporaries* (1828), subsequently reworked as his *Autobiography* (1850, rev. ed. 1860). His occasional adventures in journalism provided a modest income; from 1834 to 1836 he edited and contributed frequently to the *London Journal* and *Leigh Hunt's Journal* during 1850–1. Among his other works are *The Descent of Liberty: A Masque* (1815), dealing with the life of Napoleon; *Foliage, or Poems Original and Translated* (1818); his poem against war 'Captain Sword and Captain Pen' (1835); a novel, *Sir Ralph Esher* (1832); *Imagination and Fancy* (1844); *Wit and Humour* (1846); and *A Jar of Honey from Mount Hybla* (1848). Carried by time beyond the age of the early Romantics, Hunt lived to praise Tennyson, and be satirized by Charles Dickens as the character of Skimpole in *Bleak House*. He died at Putney on 28 August 1859.

E. Blunden, *Hunt: A Biography* (1930).

L. H. and C. W. Houtchers (eds.), *The English Romantic Poets and Essayists: A Review of Research and Criticism* (New York, 1958).

A. Landre, *Leigh Hunt* (1935–6).

J. E. Morpurgo (ed.), *The Autobiography* (1949).

Portraits: oil, half-length, by B. R. Haydon: N.P.G.; miniature, three-quarter length, by M. Gillies: N.P.G.; oil, three-quarter length, by S. Laurence, 1837: N.P.G.; pencil, three-quarter length, by T. C. Wageman, 1815: N.P.G.

Hunter, John (1728–93), Scottish anatomist, surgeon, and physiologist, considered to be the founder of scientific surgery.

John Hunter was born on 13 February 1728 at Long Calderwood, East Kilbride, Lanarkshire. He was the youngest of ten children, and had little formal education. In 1745 at the age of seventeen he went to Glasgow to assist one of his brothers-in-law in his cabinet-making business, but after three years at this unrewarding task was invited by his elder brother William, a lecturing anatomist, to join him in London as his assistant.

For nearly eleven years he worked hard learning the practical anatomy of the human body by assisting in the dissecting rooms. On certain occasions, when William was indisposed, John delivered anatomical lectures to his brother's pupils. In 1749 he began additional studies in surgery at Chelsea Hospital, and two years later he was admitted as a surgical student at St. Bartholomew's Hospital.

In 1756 John Hunter became house surgeon at St. George's Hospital. Shortly thereafter, William invited him into full partnership, which included sharing responsibilities for lectures on anatomy. Although not as eloquent as William, John soon gained the confidence of his students through the force of his enthusiasm and his knowledge of the subject. He worked so hard, however, that his health suffered and he was forced into temporary retirement (1759).

In 1760, Hunter obtained an army post as staff surgeon, and in the following spring he accompanied the expedition sent out to besiege Belle Isle. In 1763, with the coming of peace, he left the army and returned to London, where he established a surgical practice.

While in the army Hunter had collected over 200 live animals and innumerable preserved specimens for future study. These served to spark his increasing interest in comparative anatomy, physiology, and pathology. To house this miniature zoo Hunter bought a piece of land at Earl's Court. He eventually built a house there, which was used as a combined home, zoo, anatomical museum, and workshop for his experiments and dissections. The Royal Society elected him a Fellow in 1767.

Hunter had made great strides, of both theoretical and practical value, even at this relatively early stage in his career. As a result of his many experiments with living animals, he furthered the basic physiological understanding on which surgery must be based. His later investigations of venereal disease, inflammation, and gunshot wounds were received as significant contributions to the slender literature on these subjects. He offered valuable insight into the surgical repair of a ruptured Achilles tendon after suffering such a rupture himself (1767), supposedly while dancing.

His interests were growing to include every branch of natural science, and he pursued them at every moment left free by his lectures and rapidly growing surgical practice. Among his many pupils at this time was Edward Jenner (q.v.), who had come to study with him in 1770. They were to become lifelong friends and collaborate on many biological experiments and studies.

Hunter was appointed Surgeon Extraordinary to George III in 1776, and in 1786 he was named Deputy Surgeon General of the army. Four years later, in 1790, he was appointed Surgeon General and Inspector General of Hospitals. All these appointments were extremely lucrative.

Among his many anatomical discoveries were the distribution of the blood vessels of the uterus, which he traced from their source to the placenta, and the distribution of the branches of the nasal and olfactory nerves. Hunter also described the natural descent of the testicles into the scrotum in the male foetus. Among his most brilliant contributions to surgical technique was a means of repairing popliteal aneurysm – an abnormal bulging behind the knee due to weakening of the walls of the vein.

Most of Hunter's time was spent teaching, attending to his surgical practice, and experimenting. He managed to write several books, three of which were published before he died. They include a technical treatise on dentition, *The Natural History of the Human Teeth* (1771, 1778), a *Treatise on the Venereal Disease* (1786), and *Observations on Certain Parts of the Animal Oeconomy* (1786). Many consider his finest work to be *A Treatise on the Blood, Inflammation and Gunshot Wounds*, published posthumously in 1794. It stressed the need for greater understanding of physiology in practical surgical technique.

By 1788, Hunter was generally regarded as the leading surgeon in England. He had advanced surgery as far as it was possible to go before the introduction of anaesthetics in the next century. He was comfortably settled in both his professional and his private life, for in 1771 he had married Anne Home, an accomplished young lady who wrote verse. Over a period of several years Hunter had amassed a collection of some 10,000 anatomical specimens, which was sold to the government after his death. It was made the responsibility of the Royal College of Surgeons, and was destroyed by enemy action in World War II.

Hunter died of a heart attack in London on 16 October 1793. He was buried in the vaults of St. Martin-in-the-Fields, and in 1859 his remains were removed to Westminster Abbey.

Jessie Dobson, *John Hunter* (1969).
S. R. Gloyne, *John Hunter* (1950).
J. F. Palmer (ed.), *The Works of John Hunter* (5 vols.; 1835–7).

Portraits: oil, three-quarter length, by J. Jackson after Reynolds: N.P.G.; oil, three-quarter length, by Sir J. Reynolds, 1786: Courtauld Institute of Art; oil, by J. Zoffany: Buckingham Palace.

Huskisson, William (1770–1830), statesman; a leading advocate of the principles of free trade.

Huskisson was born on 11 March 1770 at Birch Moreton, Worcestershire. At the age of thirteen he went to Paris in the care of his maternal great-uncle, a physician named Gem, who was attached to the British Embassy there, and six years later witnessed the fall of the Bastille. He supported the moderate party of the French Revolution and became a member of the 'Club of 1789', which had been established to support the new form of constitutional monarchy in opposition to the anarchical schemes of the Jacobins. A dissertation that he delivered to the society in August 1790 regarding the issuing of assignats (paper currency) by the Revolutionary government revealed his financial knowledge but failed in its purpose. He withdrew from the society.

In January 1793 he was appointed by Henry Dundas to a new office, created under the Aliens Act, for making arrangements with the émigrés. His effectiveness in this post was greatly helped by his knowledge of French, and he soon also became acquainted with Canning. Moreover, his obvious talents

recommended him to William Pitt the Younger. In 1796 he entered parliament as the member for Morpeth but, perhaps out of shyness, did not speak in the House of Commons until February 1798. In 1800 he inherited from the deceased Dr. Gem an estate at Eastham, Sussex, which provided him with the necessary financial independence to pursue a public career.

In Pitt's administration of 1804 Huskisson was appointed Secretary of the Treasury and held office until January 1806. He occupied the same post under the Duke of Portland but resigned with Canning, now his close friend, in 1809. The following year saw the publication of his pamphlet on the *Depreciation of the Currency*, by which he acquired a reputation as an economist. His public career was retarded, however, by his continued adherence to Canning and by his espousal of free-trade principles which were unpopular among the Tory aristocracy.

In 1814 Huskisson entered Liverpool's ministry in the minor office of Chief Commissioner of Woods and Forests. His influence, however, was henceforward very great in the commercial and financial policy-making of the country. In 1819 he became a member of Peel's financial committee and his speech on the Chancellor of the Exchequer's income and expenditure resolutions probably saved the government from defeat. He became heavily involved in 1821 in a committee set up to investigate the causes of agricultural discontent, although his speeches on taxation in the same year gave rise to a permanent distrust of him among the agricultural party, who in 1822 came out in total opposition to him.

In 1823 Huskisson was appointed President of the Board of Trade and Treasurer of the navy. The post at the Board of Trade suited his particular abilities and gave him an outlet for his free-trade opinions. Notable in this respect were his efforts against the Corn Laws, the most recent of which had been passed in 1822. By this piece of protectionist legislation, the import of grain was completely banned unless and until British farmers could get 70s. a quarter on the home market. After this price was reached, grain imports were subject to a tariff, and duty-free imports were allowed only when grain prices reached 80s., under the terms of an earlier act passed in 1815. But the laws, designed to favour agricultural at the expense of industrial and mercantile interests, never operated. In the existing economic conditions the price never got anywhere near 70s.; in fact, prices and rents were forced down and poverty and universal discontent reigned. The Corn Laws represented an issue over which Huskisson was at variance with members of his own party, but this issue was only one of several.

After succeeding Canning as the member for Liverpool in the election of 1823, Huskisson became a leading supporter of mercantile interests in parliament. Much of his early work reflected his liberal ideas. He reformed the Navigation Acts (restrictions on foreign and colonial trade to protect home commerce), thereby admitting other nations to full equality and reciprocity of shipping duties. In 1825 he consolidated all the revenue laws into eleven acts. An act was passed that controlled the relations of capital and labour for the next forty years, and duties were reduced on a wide range of goods. When a minor economic slump occurred in 1825 Huskisson's free-trade policies were held responsible, and in order to appease the conservative members of his own party he was forced to advocate delay in the repeal of the Corn Laws. During 1826, however, he assisted Lord Liverpool in preparing a new corn bill – work that permanently damaged his health – which proved impossible to implement owing to the opposition of Wellington in the House of Lords.

Canning's death in 1827 grieved Huskisson enormously; it was out of respect for his former colleague that he accepted the posts of Secretary for the Colonies and Leader of the House of Commons, believing that there was no other way to secure the continuation of Canning's policy. Dissensions soon broke out in the party, resulting in Lord Goderich's resignation and the succession of Wellington. Huskisson and Wellington never really saw eye to eye, and although a compromise was reached over the Corn Laws – the Tariff being regulated according to price fluctuations – the tension was undiminished. A dispute over the reallocation of the disfranchised seats of East Retford and Penryn led to Huskisson's resignation. Huskisson, Peel, and others felt that the new seats should go to the large manufacturing towns, but the Commons voted in favour of giving them to the local hundreds. Wellington saw fit to regard Huskisson's threat of resignation as an actual withdrawal from office, and Huskisson departed in May 1828.

Although his health was now deteriorating fast Huskisson still made frequent appearances in parliament, and in 1828 supported the Roman Catholic Emancipation Bill. During the session of 1829 he made several speeches in favour of moderate parliamentary reform, and supported Lord John Russell's proposal to confer additional parliamentary representation on Leeds, Liverpool, and Manchester. On 15 September 1830 he went to Liverpool for the opening of the Manchester and Liverpool railway. While climbing into a carriage Huskisson, a man peculiarly prone to injury, fell back on to the rails in front of an oncoming engine, which ran over his leg. The shock proved too much for him, and he died the same day.

A. Brady, *William Huskisson and Liberal Reform* (1967, 2nd ed.).

C. R. Fay, *Huskisson and his Age* (1951).

Portrait: oil, half-length, by R. Rothwell, *c.* 1830: N.P.G.

J

Jackson, John (1769–1845), the prize fighter known as 'Gentleman Jackson'.

Jackson was born on 28 September 1769, the son of a London builder. Little is known of his life prior to the first of only three appearances he made in the prize ring. This took place on 9 June 1788 at Smitham Bottom near Croydon, and Jackson defeated Fewterel of Birmingham in an hour and seven minutes, watched by the Prince of Wales. The following year Jackson was defeated by George (Ingleston) the Brewer at Ingatestone, Essex, on 12 March. A heavy fall dislocated his ankle and broke a small bone in his leg. He offered to finish the fight tied to a chair, but his opponent declined. However, on 15 April 1795 he had a spectacular success in a contest with Mendoza at Hornchurch, Essex, when the prize money was 200 guineas on each side. Jackson was much younger than Mendoza (then thirty-two), and the latter was badly mauled in the contest, which lasted only ten and a half minutes. Mendoza had very long hair, which Jackson seized several times while punching vigorously with the other hand – an action which was quite within the rules of the time.

This win marks the golden age of English prize fighting. It established Jackson as Champion of England, which title he retained until 1803 when he retired, to be succeeded by Jem Belcher. In retirement Jackson set up a school, much patronized by the nobility, where he taught the art of self-defence. Thomas Moore tells us that he made 'more than a thousand a year by teaching sparring', and testifies to the respect paid to him everywhere. One of his most famous pupils, Lord Byron, manifested his great regard for the prize fighter publicly by being seen often in his company, and on being questioned about the choice of a companion so much his inferior in rank by his tutor at Cambridge, Byron replied that Jackson's manners were 'infinitely superior to those of the fellows of the college whom I meet at high table'.

In 1820 Jackson was employed with eighteen other prize fighters dressed as pages to guard the entrance to Westminster Abbey and Hall on the occasion of George IV's coronation. According to the inscription on a mezzotint engraving by C. Turner, Jackson later became landlord of the Sun and Punchbowl, Holborn, and of the Cock at Sutton. He died, aged seventy-seven, on 7 October 1845 in London, and was buried in Brompton cemetery, where a colossal monument was erected to his memory.

Jackson was 5 feet 11 inches in height and 14 stone in weight. He was a fine short-distance runner, and is said to have lifted $10\frac{1}{2}$ hundredweight and to have been able to write his name with an 84 pound weight attached to his little finger. His name is remembered by Byron in *Hints from Horace*:

> And men unpractised in exchanging knocks
> Must go to Jackson ere they dare to box.

Frank Butler, *A History of Boxing in Britain* (1972).

Portrait: pencil drawing, quarter-length, by Sir D. Wilkie, 1807: British Museum.

James Francis Edward Stuart (1688–1766), commonly called 'The Old Pretender'; recognized by the Jacobites as James III of England and James VIII of Scotland.

James was born in London on 10 June 1688, the son of James II and Mary of Modena. All previous children of the marriage having died in infancy, the Queen's bearing of a son came as something of a shock to the nation. Rumours abounded that the baby was not Mary's at all, but an impostor smuggled into her bed; but whether such rumours were true or not, with his birth it seemed unlikely that James II's policy of restoring Catholicism in England would die with him. Thus it was that, to safeguard Protestant supremacy, leading Whigs and Tories invited William of Orange to prosecute his claim to the English throne. In the ensuing Glorious Revolution James Francis Edward was sent with his mother to France, where his father joined them a few days later. Thrown on the mercy of Louis XIV, the family set up court at St. Germain.

The favourable reception in England of the House of Orange led to the Act of Settlement of 21 June 1701, by which the male line of the Stuarts was excluded from the English throne. Moreover, shortly before his death, William III gave his assent to an Act of Attainder against the young Prince, James. Even so, when the young man's father died, on 6 September 1701, he was proclaimed by Louis to be King James III of England and VIII of Scotland.

In 1705, after receiving reports that Scotland would definitely rise on behalf of the Jacobite cause, Louis XIV began to fit out an expedition, which the young James joined at Dunkirk. It was doomed to fail, however, and after several false starts, was driven off by stormy weather and also by the pursuit of an English fleet under George Byng (q.v.).

James returned in 1708 to France, where he fought with the French army, distinguishing himself at the Battles of Oudenarde (1708) and Malplaquet (1709). In 1713 he was exiled from France under the terms of the Treaty of Utrecht, but found cordial hospitality with the Duke of Lorraine.

The Hanoverian succession in 1714, the inauguration of a foreign dynasty, tended to strengthen the Jacobite claim, but the Jacobites were slow in acting. Preparations for a new expedition went ahead, while in Scotland the Earl of Mar (see Erskine, John) succeeded in gaining support for the first Jacobite rebellion of 1715. Though Mar and his army were defeated at Sheriffmuir, the news that reached France was of a Jacobite triumph, and James – called 'The Pretender' by the supporters of George I – left for Scotland, disguised as a servant. Landing at Peterhead on 22 December, he journeyed to Fetteresso, where he met Mar and others from the army at Perth. James formed them into a privy council, and plans were made for his coronation at Scone on 23 January 1716. The magistrates and clergy of Aberdeen received him enthusiastically and in his march southwards he met with no hostility. Yet despite this, it was becoming increasingly clear that James's position was untenable. The Highlanders considered him a most uninspiring leader, and when news reached Perth of the approach of the English forces they decided to retreat. Crossing the Tay on ice, the Jacobites soon put two days between themselves and the English and gained enough time for James and Mar to make good their escape to France; they arrived there safely in February.

At St. Germain, Mar now supplanted Bolingbroke (see St. John, Henry, in *Lives of the Stuart Age*) as James's Secretary of

State, the latter having been dismissed for alleged carelessness. Soon after this, the royal party moved to Rome. In 1719 Cardinal Giulio Alberoni offered Spanish help and James was encouraged to move to Madrid. Plans were made for the Duke of Ormonde (see Butler, James, 2nd Duke, in *Lives of the Stuart Age*) to lead a main expedition of 5,000 men, along with enough arms for another 30,000, while a subsidiary force of a single battalion under Earl Marischal was to raise the Highlands. However, the main expedition was driven back by a storm, while the smaller force had to surrender after a skirmish in the pass of Glenshiels.

James had remained in Madrid, where he was married by proxy, on 28 May 1719, to Princess Maria Clementina, granddaughter of the King of Poland, although the couple were not formally united until September. She bore him two sons, Charles Edward (q.v.), 'The Young Pretender', and Henry (1725–1807), the last of the Stuart line, who entered the Church and became known as the Cardinal Duke of York. The marriage between James and Maria Clementina was not altogether happy, and just after Henry's birth there was a temporary separation when Maria retired to a convent for two years. She died in 1735.

Expeditions to win back the English crown continued to be planned, but were rendered abortive by financial problems and dissension among the English Jacobites. To remedy this, plans were made to make Bishop Atterbury and the Earl of Oxford (see Harley, Robert, in *Lives of the Stuart Age*) heads of the Jacobite movement. But correspondence concerning these plans was intercepted by the English government. Mar, suspected of treachery, was dismissed by James, and John Hay, later Earl of Inverness, took his place in 1724. Yet despite this transfusion of new blood into his councils, James was

losing interest. He was daily afflicted by fits of incapacitating melancholia, so that gradually his former supporters came to pin their hopes of a Stuart revival on his son, Charles Edward. In the Forty-Five James gave only financial assistance, having lost all hope of his own restoration. He died, a worn-out man, on 1 January 1766, and was buried at St. Peter's, Rome, where in 1819 a monument was erected over his tomb by order of George III.

John Baynes, *The Jacobite Rising of 1715* (1970).
Brian Bevan, *King James III* (1967).
Sir C. Petrie, *The Jacobite Movement* (1959).
A. and H. Tayler, *The Old Chevalier* (1934).
A. and H. Tayler, *The Stuart Papers at Windsor* (1939).

Portraits: oil, half-length, studio of A. S. Belle, *c.*1712: N.P.G.; oil, full-length, by N. de Largillière, 1695: N.P.G.; pen and ink, quarter-length, by or after F. Ponzone, *c.*1741: N.P.G.

Jeffrey, Francis (1773–1850), Scottish judge and critic; one of the founders and the most famous editor of the *Edinburgh Review*.

Francis Jeffrey was born on 23 October 1773 in Edinburgh, the son of George Jeffrey, Deputy Clerk in the Court of Session. His father was a respected high Tory of severe, sensible, and gloomy disposition. Young Francis, a small but healthy child, leaned more towards his lively and humorous mother, Henrietta, a Lanark farmer's daughter; sadly she died when he was thirteen.

Educated first at Edinburgh High School, Francis Jeffrey then entered Glasgow University. In 1792 he went to The Queen's College, Oxford, but returned after a short stay, finding the company uncongenial and 'dissipated'. After this he studied for the bar at Edinburgh and qualified as a barrister in 1794. But the Whiggish attitudes he had now begun to cultivate militated against his having a profitable practice.

While studying for the bar, Jeffrey had

made the acquaintance of Scott and others in the Speculative Society. His declaration of himself as 'a philosophical Whig' in 1793 was a sore disappointment to his father as well as a hindrance to preferment, and in 1798 a journey made by him to London, despite the battery of introductions he carried with him, was a depressing failure.

In 1801 Jeffrey became engaged to Catherine Wilson, a second cousin, and despite a general lack of funds the couple married in the same year. In 1801 also, Jeffrey lost the reportership of the Court of Sessions, Judge Sir William Miller refusing support to anyone with Whig sympathies.

Baffled in his career, Jeffrey turned his energies elsewhere. Sydney Smith (q.v.), then resident in Edinburgh, suggested to Jeffrey and others the inauguration of a new magazine, and 1802 saw the preliminary preparation and launching of the *Edinburgh Review*. At first it was organized in committee with Smith as unofficial editor, but after a year Jeffrey was appointed to the editorship, a post he retained until 1829. The *Edinburgh Review* was published by Constable and it received instantaneous acclaim.

Its success lay largely in the fact that it was an independent voice, not influenced, as its predecessors had been, by its publishers. Moreover, as a matter of principle, it paid its contributors well. This ensured its continuing success, and well after the founder members had dispersed, notable writers found it worth while to work for the *Review*. Much of the credit for this success can be attributed to Jeffrey's editorship, under which the *Review* became a leading organ of public opinion and perhaps the most dreaded of critical censors.

It did not, particularly in its early issues, take a strong political line. Although most of its founders had Whig associations, its

contributors ranged over the political spectrum and included Scott and even Southey. A measure of the success of the *Edinburgh Review* was that it provoked from the opposite camp a rival, the Tory *Quarterly Review*.

Jeffrey, like most of the group concerned with the *Edinburgh Review*, thought of his involvement with it as a part-time activity. He regarded himself first as a man of the law. In 1803, however, fearing that invasion was imminent, he had joined a volunteer regiment, but being 'mortally afraid of the war', he was singularly unsuccessful as a soldier, and he returned to Edinburgh with a new zest for his old home and literary friends and society. In August 1805 his wife died and soon after this, in November, he was mourning the loss of their child, born in 1802.

About this time, Jeffrey's legal practice began to improve. In 1807 he appeared with success before the General Assembly, and he was also extending his practice in the courts. He was an effective if not a brilliant lawyer. In 1813 he visited America in pursuit of Miss Charlotte Wilkes (niece of John Wilkes), whom he married on 7 October 1813. While in America Jeffrey met President Monroe and Secretary of State Madison, and became an advocate of Anglo-American reconciliation.

In 1820 he was appointed Lord Rector of Glasgow University and ten years later he became Lord Advocate. From 1834 to 1850, as Lord Jeffrey, he was Judge of the Court of Session. As M.P. for Malton (1831–2) he was 'a timid politician', and his parliamentary career was of little note, although he did introduce the Scottish Reform Bill.

His claim to distinction lies in his function as editor and critic. His contemporaries thought highly of him. Carlyle and Cockburn considered him a brilliant critic, and Macaulay read and re-read his articles till he had them by heart.

A warm-hearted family man, Jeffrey made many lasting friendships. Out of sympathy with the Romantic movement and the mysticism of Scott, Wordsworth, Coleridge, and Shelley, he was neverthe-less respected as a fair opponent and an impartial and acute critic. Jeffrey died in Edinburgh on 26 January 1850 at the age of seventy-six.

Contributions to the Edinburgh Review (4 vols.; 1844: 3 vols.; 1846: 1 vol.; 1853).

Lord Cockburn, *Life of Lord Jeffrey* (1852).

T. Crawford, 'The *Edinburgh Review* and Romantic Poetry', *Auckland University College Bulletin*, 47 (1955).

J. A. Greig, *Francis Jeffrey of the Edinburgh Review* (1948).

Portraits: oil, three-quarter length, by A. Geddes, 1826: N.P.G.; pencil, quarter-length, by J. Linnell: N.P.G.; marble bust, by P. Park: N.P.G.; oil, by C. Smith, *c.* 1830: Scottish N.P.G.

Jenkinson, Robert Banks (1770–1828), 2nd Earl of Liverpool; Tory statesman; Prime Minister of England from 1812 to 1827.

Jenkinson was born on 7 January 1770, the eldest son of the 1st Earl of Liverpool. He received the conventional education of Charterhouse, Oxford, and the Grand Tour. His father had been one of George III's most trusted political advisers, and in 1790, Jenkinson became M.P. for Appleby. He served under William Pitt the Younger as a Commis-sioner of the India Board (1793–6) and Master of the Mint (1799–1801). He was a competent Foreign Secretary under Addington (1801–4), but in Pitt's last cabinet (1804–6) he moved to the Home Office. After declining to become Prime Minister he became Home Secretary in the Portland ministry (1807–12) under Spencer Perceval. In 1808 he succeeded his father as 2nd Earl of Liverpool.

Age, office, and a happy marriage transformed Liverpool from a reclusive theoretician into a modest, conciliatory politician. By 1809 he was the strongest unifying force among the Tories and the anchor man of any administration formed on Pittite-Tory principles, with the result that, after Perceval's assassination in June 1812, he was offered the premiership. He accepted the post on the understanding that his appointment was purely a stop-gap measure. In the event, he was to be Prime Minister for the next fifteen years.

The Liverpool administration was considered weak at the time of its formation, but it was given greater security by the victories of Wellington (see Wellesley, Arthur). Problems de-veloped with the Commons after the war over their demands for instant tax reductions; in addition, there was widespread discontent about the re-tention of the Corn Laws. The refusal of parliament in 1816 to renew income tax left the ministry with a revenue of twelve million pounds to meet an expenditure of thirty million. Liverpool engineered the return to the gold standard embodied in Peel's 1819 Act, which gave Britain the financial stability to undertake new commercial measures.

The disorder and violence that marked the economic depression of the post-war period was regarded by the government as part of a Jacobin conspiracy to overthrow the existing order of society. Liverpool felt that the first duty of a responsible government was the mainten-ance of public order; consequently, he sanctioned moderately repressive legis-lation at the outset to avoid the brutality of arbitrary government later. The government's main problem was that it had no regular police force or standing army to quell the disturbances, but was forced to rely upon inefficient local magistrates and a network of spies and informers whose loyalty went to the

highest bidder. The events in Manchester on 16 August 1819 highlight this governmental dilemma.

On that occasion, a crowd of 60,000 assembled at St. Peter's Field near Manchester to demonstrate their grievances about rising prices and listen to 'Orator' Hunt making demands for the reform of parliament. The local magistrates gave permission for the Manchester yeomanry to seize the speakers. The untrained militia took this as an opportunity to harass the crowd, and the magistrates, fearing mob violence, ordered the 15th Hussars and the Cheshire Yeomanry to make a charge. Some 500 people in the crowd were injured and eleven were killed. The news of the so-called 'Peterloo Massacre' stirred bitter hatred of the government in radical circles, but Westminster refused to repudiate the magistrates' action and indeed some intemperate members of the government rushed to congratulate the magistrates on their firm conduct.

In 1819 the Six Acts were passed, severely restricting civil liberties; they received almost immediate justification with the discovery of the Cato Street conspiracy in 1820. This was an ill-conceived plan devised by Arthur Thistlewood to assassinate the entire cabinet, seize various vantage points, and form a government. One of the plotters turned informer and the ringleaders were caught in Cato Street, Marylebone, on 23 February.

Liverpool's government was threatened again in 1820 when the proceedings against Queen Caroline (see Caroline of Brunswick) drew the Whigs and Radicals closer together, but the improvement in economic conditions after 1821 allowed the administration to enter on a more constructive and fortunate phase during the 1820s. A sound administrator and good judge of personality, Liverpool surrounded himself with talented ministers – Castlereagh, Canning, Peel, and Huskisson. His own interests were primarily in matters of trade and commerce; in matters of foreign policy he favoured Canning's isolationist approach. To Liverpool the period from 1821 to 1826 represented the fruition of his true conservative ideals. He believed in avoiding organic change by pursuing administrative reform and allowing the general prosperity ensuing from economic recovery to benefit both rich and poor alike. However, he resolutely opposed Catholic emancipation, and was never a supporter of parliamentary reform.

By 1826, when there was a renewal of economic distress, the strains of holding the cabinet together were beginning to tell on Liverpool, and he was reluctant to face the furore over the Corn Laws and the Catholic question. Early in the morning of 17 February 1827 he suffered a paralytic stroke, which forced him to resign from office. Without his moderation and sense of timing the Tories disintegrated, and within three and a half years the Whigs had returned to power. This, however, Liverpool was not to see. After lingering on for nearly two years, he died on 4 December 1828 at Fife House.

W. R. Brock, *Lord Liverpool and Liberal Toryism, 1820 to 1827* (1941).
C. Petric, *Lord Liverpool* (1956).
C. D. Yonge, *The Life and Administration of the 2nd Earl of Liverpool* (3 vols.; 1868).

Portrait: oil, full-length, by T. Lawrence, 1827: N.P.G.

Jenner, Edward

Jenner, Edward (1749–1823), physician who discovered the principle of vaccination (though not inoculation) against smallpox.

Jenner was born on 17 May 1749 at Berkeley, Gloucestershire, the third son of Stephen Jenner, the local vicar. His father died when he was five years old, and his early education was entrusted to his eldest brother, Stephen, who had followed his father into the Church. Edward Jenner showed a remarkable curiosity from an early age, and by his ninth birthday had a vast collection of the nests of the dormouse and a respectable collection of fossils. When he left school he decided to choose the profession of medicine. He moved to Sodbury, where he was apprenticed to Daniel Ludlow, an eminent surgeon. Jenner then went to London, where he studied under John Hunter (q.v.), one of the greatest surgeons of the day.

Hunter quickly recognized his abilities, and during two of his three years of study Jenner was a guest in the Hunter household. This was the beginning of a lifelong friendship. During his period of formal study with Hunter, we are told that Jenner became 'an expert practical anatomist, a careful observant experimenter, a sound pathologist, and a finished naturalist'. In 1771 Captain Cook (q.v.) returned from his first voyage of discovery, and Hunter recommended that Jenner be put in charge of preparing and arranging the specimens collected during the trip by Sir Joseph Banks (q.v.). Jenner was so successful in this task that he was offered the post of naturalist on the next expedition. He politely declined this offer, and in 1773 returned to Berkeley to organize his first medical practice. Here, he indulged in music-making with an amateur group and also in writing light poetry.

In 1788 he married Catherine Kingscote. During the same year he was elected a member of the Royal Society, partly because of his earlier submission to them of a rational and accurate scientific paper on the habits of the cuckoo. In 1792 Jenner obtained an M.D. from St. Andrews. From then on he was greatly concerned with a problem the solving of which would prove to be his greatest contribution to medical science.

For over seventeen years Jenner had studied the much-feared disease smallpox. At that time, about 2,000 persons a year died of this disease in England. He noticed,

253

as did many of the dairy farmers in Gloucestershire, that milkmaids often had cowpox sores on their hands from milking infected cows. It was also evident that few of these milkmaids ever contracted smallpox. It was not until 14 May 1796, however, that Jenner was able to test his theory. He inoculated a young boy, James Phipps, with material from cowpox vesicles taken from the hands of a milkmaid, Sarah Nelmes. About six weeks later, on 1 July, he inoculated the same boy with a smallpox mixture. The boy did not get smallpox.

It was nearly two years before Jenner was able to repeat his experiment. In 1798 he published the results of his studies and introduced the method of vaccine inoculation against smallpox. His paper was entitled *An Inquiry into the Causes and Effects of the Variolae Vaccinae, a Disease Discovered in Some of the Western Counties of England, Particularly Gloucestershire, and Known by the Name of The Cow Pox.*

The medical community was slow at first to accept the radical treatment. Before long, however, the new technique of vaccination was generally accepted, and thousands of people in England, Europe, and America were being routinely inoculated against smallpox. Parliament awarded Jenner a grant of £10,000 in 1802, in appreciation of his discovery; in 1806 it awarded him an additional £20,000. The success of his technique in India resulted in a subscription being raised, finally totalling £7,383.

Jenner received acclaim from royalty, governments, and the leading scientific societies around the world. In 1813 he was awarded an honorary M.D. by Oxford University. In spite of his world-wide fame, however, the Royal College of Physicians refused him membership unless he could pass an examination in the classics. He continued to inoculate the poor free of charge.

The remaining years of Jenner's life were spent mainly in the study of smallpox and in the dissemination of information relating to his discovery of vaccination. In 1822 he published a paper entitled *On the Influence of Artificial Eruptions in Certain Diseases.* A work in progress, *On the Migration of Birds*, was presented to the Royal Society shortly before his death. Jenner died of apoplexy at his home in Berkeley on 26 January 1823.

C. Creighton: *Jenner and Vaccination* (1889).
F. D. Drewitt: *The Life of Edward Jenner* (1931).
W. R. LeFanu, *A Bio-Bibliography of Edward Jenner, 1749–1823* (1951).

Portraits: oil, three-quarter length, by J. Northcote, 1803: N.P.G.; statue in a monument, by E. H. Baily: Gloucester Cathedral.

Jervis, John (1735–1823), Earl St. Vincent; naval commander and administrator.

John Jervis was born at Meaford, Staffordshire, on 9 January 1735, the second son of a barrister, and educated at the grammar school in Burton-on-Trent and then at a private school in Greenwich, where his father moved in 1747 to take up his new appointments as Solicitor to the Admiralty and Treasurer of Greenwich Hospital.

Although originally intended to follow his father in the legal profession, Jervis developed an interest in the sea, stimulated at Greenwich, and in 1749 he enlisted as an able seaman on a ship bound for Jamaica. In 1755 Jervis was promoted to the rank of lieutenant, and during the next few years he served in various ships in stations ranging from the Mediterranean to North America; in 1759 he was with Wolfe at Quebec.

In 1774 Jervis travelled overland to Russia, returning through the countries of Scandinavia, and on this and other Continental journeys he made extensive notes on the strength and organization of foreign navies. He married Martha, only daughter of Sir Thomas Parker, in 1775, and after distinguishing himself in an engagement during the French war, he was knighted in 1782.

In 1783 Jervis was elected M.P. for Launceston, and from 1784 to 1790, when he was elected for Wycombe, he represented the constituency of Yarmouth, but he seldom spoke in parliament except in debates concerning the navy. At the outbreak of war with Revolutionary France in 1793, Jervis, now a vice admiral, successfully led the naval forces in an expedition to the West Indies. On his return home to England he was made a full admiral.

As commander of the Mediterranean fleet in 1795 Jervis successfully blockaded the French fleet in Toulon, but after the French had gained control of Italy in 1796 and had allied with the Spanish fleet, Jervis was forced to retire. In February 1797 a Spanish fleet approached Jervis's fleet off Cape St. Vincent. In the ensuing battle Jervis failed to exploit the technical superiority of his own ships; it was due solely to Nelson's personal initiative that four Spanish ships were actually captured. Nevertheless, the British public, hungry for even the slightest of victories, acclaimed Jervis as a hero. With a title and a generous pension granted by parliament, Jervis, now Earl St. Vincent, had reached the peak of his career.

In 1798, the year of mutinies at Spithead and the Nore, St. Vincent used extreme punishments to prevent rebellion from spreading throughout the navy. He retired for short time to recover from the effects of mental strain and overwork, but returned to the command of the Channel fleet at the first signs of a fresh wave of seditious unrest.

Appointed First Lord of the Admiralty in 1801, St. Vincent took advantage of a brief period of peace to conduct a detailed inquiry into the corruption then being practised in almost every administrative department of the navy. The impeachment of Lord Melville and several much-needed administrative reforms were among the consequences of St. Vincent's investigation. His harsh and intolerant methods, however, provoked much hostility, including that of William Pitt the Younger, and when Pitt resumed the office of Prime Minister in 1804 St. Vincent resigned.

On Pitt's death in 1806 St. Vincent accepted the acting command of the fleet, but after another change of government in the following year he again resigned. On the coronation of George IV in 1820 he was promoted to the honorary title of admiral of the fleet. St. Vincent died on 14 March 1823, and was buried at Stone in Staffordshire.

C. Lloyd, *St. Vincent and Camperdown* (1963).
A. T. Mahan, *Types of Naval Officers* (1901).

Portraits: pencil, quarter-length, by Bouch, 1797: N.P.G.; oil, quarter-length, studio of L. F. Abbott: N.P.G.; oil, three-quarter length, by F. Cotes, 1769: N.P.G.; oil, quarter-length, studio of Beechey: N.P.G.

Johnson, Samuel (1709–84), LL.D.; poet, essayist, literary critic, and lexicographer; one of the most influential figures of the eighteenth century.

Samuel Johnson was born on 18 September 1709 in Lichfield, Staffordshire, the son of Michael Johnson, a bookseller and magistrate. According to Macaulay, his father was a man of considerable learning and a zealous churchman. Both father and son seem to have had an exclusive interest in the content rather than the sale of books.

At the age of three he was taken to Queen Anne's court to receive the sovereign's touch, which was supposed to cure scrofula. But the disease stayed,

permanently scarring his features, and Boswell (q.v.) tells us that he lost the sight of one eye at an early age. Between the ages of sixteen and eighteen he studied at home, where he used his father's books to read extensively, particularly in Latin authors and the writings of Petrarch.

Despite his debts, Samuel's father entered his son at Pembroke College, Oxford, where he stayed for three years in straitened circumstances. The poverty he learned to endure was to remain with him for most of his life. While still at college he translated the *Messiah* of Alexander Pope (q.v.) into Latin verse, which Pope read with approval. But he was forced to leave Oxford without a degree in the autumn of 1731 because of his debts to local tradesmen.

For the next five years Johnson remained in the Midlands. For a time he was usher of Market Bosworth School in Leicestershire, and then companion to a country gentleman. In 1733 he went to Birmingham, drudging for a printer. He produced a long-forgotten translation of a Latin book on Abyssinia by Lobo, and proposed a subscription edition of the poems of Politian that never materialized. In 1735 he married Elizabeth Porter, aged forty-eight, 'a widow who had children as old as himself', Macaulay tells us. They took a house in the near-by town of Edial, and Johnson advertised for pupils. Of the three he obtained, one was David Garrick (q.v.).

It was in the company of Garrick that Johnson set out in 1737 for London. Furnished with one or two letters of introduction and with three completed acts of a tragedy called *Irene*, Johnson was hopeful of literary fame. He could hardly have arrived at a time more inauspicious for the writer's calling. Few writers, even those of greatness, could hope to make a living from letters. About a year after his arrival he obtained employment from Cave, a bookseller and editor-proprietor of the *Gentleman's Magazine*. Under the guise of reports from 'the Senate of Lilliput', this journal was the chief source of news from parliament, since overt reporting was forbidden.

Shortly after starting work for the *Gentleman's Magazine*, Johnson anonymously published *London* (May 1738), a poem based on the Third Satire of Juvenal, for which he received only ten guineas but which attracted the favourable notice of Pope, who had done the same kind of thing with Horace.

The death of a friend among his London acquaintances, Richard Savage, inspired Johnson to write his biography. The piece was published anonymously, but the identity of the author was soon learned or guessed at. Although he produced nothing for the next three years, his reputation had been furthered, and in 1747 a group of leading booksellers asked him to prepare a new dictionary of the English language in two volumes. Johnson accepted the commission for 1,500 guineas, out of which he had to pay assistants. The *Dictionary* did not appear until 1755, by which time Johnson had exhausted the money he had received. In 1749 he produced *The Vanity of Human Wishes*, an imitation of the Tenth Satire of Juvenal. A few days after the appearance of this poem, the tragedy *Irene* was put on by David Garrick. But the balanced lucid style so successful in the stately *Vanity of Human Wishes* became a thing of monotony on the stage, and *Irene* was withdrawn after only nine performances.

About a year after this Johnson began to work on a series of essays. The first, *Rambler*, appeared in March 1750 and was immediately acclaimed. Here, the measured periods and balanced argument of Johnson's style could be employed to effect. In 1752 Johnson's wife died. The *Dictionary* which he had agreed to produce largely in order to give her security was far behind schedule, and for the next three years Johnson buried himself in the work. The book was finally issued in 1755, without a dedication. The prospectus which Johnson had prepared and submitted to Lord Chesterfield (see Stanhope, Philip Dormer) in 1747 had been ignored by him, and Johnson, always sensitive to slights though long used to them, used the occasion of Chesterfield's opportunistic puffing of the *Dictionary* in *The World* to compose his famous letter on patronage: 'Is not a Patron, my Lord, one who looks with unconcern on a man struggling for life in the water, and, when he has reached ground, encumbers him with help?'

The *Dictionary* finally established Johnson's reputation, if not his fortune. Though by any standards the etymologies are deficient, Johnson's *Dictionary* is unique in that it is never less than clear and authoritative, and at its best is a storehouse of the finest utterances of the great English writers and philosophers, with frequent examples of Johnson's own inimitable wit dotted throughout.

Johnson still found it necessary to take on hack work, such as abridging the *Dictionary*. He also contributed to the *Literary Magazine*, most notably a scathing review of Soames Jenyn's *Free Inquiry into the Nature and Origin of Evil*; and in spring 1758 he started work on a series of essays under the title of *The Idler*, which appeared in the *Universal Chronicle*. These essays contain some of Johnson's best prose. They were widely read and pirated and sold well in a collected volume. While Johnson was engaged on this work, his mother died, and to defray the funeral costs he wrote *Rasselas, Prince of Abyssinia* (1759) in seven days. The style, inimitably Johnson's, was the cause of much controversy in the *Monthly Review* and *Critical Review*, but what strikes us today is the thin disguise of Abyssinia for a dissertation on morals and manners in a very familiar European tradition.

Despite these successes, Johnson's life had now settled into a characteristic pattern of long periods of inactivity punctuated by frantic efforts to save himself from the consequences of debt. On the accession of George III, and the rise to power of Bute, Johnson, who had long ago shown his political colours by vociferous attacks on the Whig administration of Sir Robert Walpole, was offered a pension of £300 per annum. This regular income freed him from the pressing need to do hack work. He had received a large number of subscriptions for a new edition of Shakespeare, which showed no signs of appearing, but in a characteristic burst of activity Johnson completed the work and it appeared in October 1765. Its deficiencies in textual matters and in respect of Johnson's ignorance of other Elizabethan and Jacobean dramatists are great, but the comments on Shakespearean characters are in many respects unsurpassed for their lucidity. As a result of this work Johnson was awarded an honorary doctorate by Oxford, giving him the title 'Dr. Johnson' by which he is best known.

His awesome talents for verbal expression were sharpened by the company in which he now moved as an equal, including men such as Goldsmith, Gibbon, Reynolds, and Burke (qq.v.), with whom he founded in 1764 the 'Literary Club', now invariably known as 'Johnson's Club'. It is at this period of his life that we have the clearest picture of Johnson, and for this we are indebted to his meeting in 1763 with the young Scots lawyer, James Boswell (q.v.), whose *Life of Johnson* is perhaps the greatest biography of any Englishman.

Among the members of the Johnson Club was Henry Thrale, a rich and cultivated brewer with a clever and pretty young wife (see Thrale, Mrs. Hester). From 1765 onwards Johnson became a close friend of the Thrales, cherishing a particularly strong regard for Hester, who seems to have had the knack of rallying Johnson with her chatter. He was a constant visitor to the Thrales' house in Streatham and formed a close tie with them that lasted until 1783 when Henry Thrale died and his widow ran off with an Italian music master, an event which caused Johnson great pain.

In August 1773, accompanied by Boswell, Johnson set out for the Scottish Highlands on the first leg of a long-projected tour, initiated by his desire to see a society of an utterly different cast from that of London. In this project he was encouraged by Boswell, whose own Scottish origins may have had something to do with Johnson's prejudiced attitude towards that country. After two months wandering through mull, loch, and island, Boswell and Johnson returned to England, and Johnson's *A Journey to the Western Islands of Scotland* was published early in 1775. In spite of his abrasive attitude to the Scots, the book was received with pleasure even in Scotland, and it remains one of his most delightful works. The *Journal* also contains Johnson's celebrated exposure of the *Fingal* forgery of James Macpherson (q.v.). After threats to his life from Macpherson, Johnson took the precaution of walking the streets of London with a cudgel, but also characteristically challenged Macpherson in a famous letter to disprove his assertions.

Eager to seize on any indication of the diminution of his powers, many of Johnson's enemies and also some of his friends saw such signs in his publication of a poor anti-American pamphlet entitled *Taxation No Tyranny* in 1776. In 1777 he was approached by a consortium of leading booksellers to write short biographical prefaces for a new edition of the English poets. No one was better suited to the task. *The Lives of the Poets*, inflated from the planned few pages to ten small volumes, are among his greatest critical works.

The *Lives* proved to be Johnson's last major work. The death of an old friend, the quack doctor Robert Levet, was the inspiration of his last poem, a work which contains much of Johnson's own experience of life:

> Condemn'd to Hope's delusive mine,
>   As on we toil from day to day,
> By sudden blasts, or slow decline,
>   Our social comforts drop away.

The poem was apt and prophetic. In June 1782 Johnson had a stroke, recovered temporarily, but soon fell ill again. In great fear of death, he was attended without fees by the leading doctors of the court, and visited by Edmund Burke and Fanny Burney (qq.v.), among many others. He died on 13 December 1784, and was buried among his peers in Westminster Abbey.

W. J. Bate, *The Achievement of Samuel Johnson* (New York, 1955).

R. W. Chapman (ed.), *The Letters of Samuel Johnson* (1951, rev. ed.).

J. L. Clifford, *Young Sam Johnson* (New York, 1955).

J. L. Clifford and D. J. Greene, *Samuel Johnson: A Survey and Bibliography of Critical Studies* (New Haven, 1970).

D. J. Greene, *Samuel Johnson* (New Haven, 1970).

A. T. Hagen, J. H. Middendorf, *et al.* (eds.), *Complete Works* (New Haven, 1958–   ).

J. H. Hagstrum, *Samuel Johnson's Literary Criticism* (Chicago, 1967).

Christopher Hibbert, *The Personal History of Samuel Johnson* (1971).

G. B. Hill (ed.), Boswell's *Life of Johnson* (rev. L. F. Powell, 6 vols.; 1934–64).

G. B. Hill (ed.), *The Lives of the English Poets* (3 vols.; 1905, repr. 1967).

F. W. Hiller (ed.), *New Light on Dr. Johnson* (New Haven, 1959).

E. L. McAdam, Jr., and G. Milne (eds.), *Complete Poems* (New Haven, 1964).

John Wain, *Samuel Johnson* (1974).

Portraits: oil, quarter-length, by J. Barry: N.P.G.; oil, half-length, after Opie: N.P.G.; oil, head, after Reynolds: N.P.G.; oil, three-quarter length, by J. Reynolds, 1756: N.P.G.; oil, half-length, by J. Reynolds, *c.* 1778: N.P.G.; bust, by J. Nollekens: V. & A.,

Jones, Sir William (1746–94), judge, and scholar in Oriental studies.

William Jones was born in London on 28 September 1746, the son of Welsh parents. He was educated at Harrow, where he showed a great aptitude for languages. His main interest was in Latin and Greek, but he also took Hebrew and made his first beginnings in Arabic. At University College, Oxford, which he entered in 1764, he continued these studies, reading Persian and Arabic under the guidance of a Syrian Mirza, whom he had met in London and brought to Oxford at his own expense. During the vacations Jones taught himself French and Italian, later going on to Spanish, Portuguese, and German.

In 1766 he was awarded a fellowship at Oxford, two years before he received his B.A., and later he took a post as tutor to Lord Althorp (see Spencer, John Charles), but financial pressures made it necessary for him to take up a more lucrative employment. He chose law and studied at the Middle Temple, qualifying as a barrister in 1774. Two years later he was made a commissioner of bankrupts. In 1781 appeared his *Essay on the Law of Bailments*, a standard work on the subject, which prompted one American jurist to assert that, if Jones had written nothing else in his life, 'He would still have left a name unrivalled in the common law for philosophical accuracy, elegant learning, and finished analysis.'

In the meantime Jones had not laid aside his Orientalist pursuits. In 1770 appeared his translation from Persian into French of a manuscript biography of Nadir Shah, the ruthless warrior-king who ruled Persia from 1736 to 1747; in 1770 also, Jones published a *Traité sur la Poésie Orientale* and a French verse translation of some of the odes of the fourteenth-century Persian lyric poet, Hafiz; in 1771 he brought out a *Persian Grammar*; in 1772 he published *Poems, consisting chiefly of translation from the Asiatick languages*; and in 1774 there appeared his six-part Latin treatise on Asiatic poetry, *Poesos Asiaticae Commentariorum Libri Sex*.

In 1773 Jones was invited, along with Garrick, to be a member of Johnson's Literary Club. He was on intimate terms with such intellectuals as Burke and Gibbon, and his work as an Orientalist attracted considerable attention abroad. In 1780 he stood for election to parliament but withdrew his candidature in the face of what he took to be the undeniable superiority of his opponent.

In 1783 there came a change in Jones's fortunes when he was appointed to a judgeship in the Supreme Court in Calcutta. Newly married and with a knighthood from George III, he took up his duties in December 1783.

Jones's judicial work was arduous but he carried it out conscientiously. He was a fair-minded man who won the respect of Englishman and Indian alike. It is not, however, as a judge that we remember him today, but as a linguist and one of the earliest Indologists.

As soon as he arrived in Calcutta, Jones set about the formation of the Asiatick Society, later known as the Royal Asiatic Society of Bengal. At the first meeting he 'unfolded, in an elegant and appropriate address, the objects proposed for their [the Society's] researches'. Essentially, these were to improve knowledge and scholarship in Oriental studies, and the immediate task that he set himself was to learn Sanskrit.

Apart from the intrinsic value of a knowledge of Sanskrit, there were also very good practical reasons why Jones should learn it. One was connected with his day-to-day activities in court; to be fully conversant with all the intricacies of Hindu law he found the ancient language vital, if only for checking authorities cited by Indian attorneys. Another reason was that he had already projected a plan to compile a huge digest of Hindu and Muslim law. For this project, incomplete at his death, he employed a number of Indian scholars. He published his *Mohammedan Law of Inheritance* in 1792 and his *Institute of Hindu Law, or the Ordinances of Manu* in 1794.

In 1782 Jones had introduced to Western culture the seven pre-Islamic (sixth-century) Arabic poems of the *Mu'allagat* (*Moallakât* in his transliteration); now, from his situation in India, he proceeded to bring forth to Occidental eyes for the first time some of the finest literature in Sanskrit. His translations included the dramatic work *Śakuntalā* (*Sacontalá, or the Fatal Ring*, 1789) and the *Rtusamhāra*, attributed to the fourth-century Indian poet and dramatist Kālidāsa (published as *The Seasons* in 1792). He also translated some of the Vedic Hymns.

However, Jones's greatest achievement lies in his recognition of the affinity between Sanskrit and several of its European counterparts, which gave rise to the nineteenth-century wave of interest in Indo-European comparative philology.

Jones's acquaintance with Sanskrit and the intense literary activity that he felt obliged to engage in because of it were crammed into nine short years. On top of his judicial duties, the workload that he took upon himself broke his health. Calcutta's climate served to do the rest, and bouts of illness dogged him continually until his death on 27 April 1794, at the early age of forty-four.

A. J. Arberry, *Asiatic Jones* (1946).
A. J. Arberry, *Oriental Essays* (1960).
Garland H. Cannon, *Oriental Jones* (1964).
John Shore, Lord Teignmouth, *The Works of Sir William Jones, with the Life of the Author* (13 vols.; 1807).

Portrait: drawing, quarter-length, artist unknown: University College, Oxford.

Jordan, Dorothy, Dorothea, or Dora

(1761–?1816), actress noted especially for her lively comedy roles.

Dorothy Jordan was born on 22 November 1761 in London, the illegitimate daughter of Francis Bland, probably a soldier, and Grace Phillips, an actress. Educated chiefly by her mother, she had an unsettled childhood, travelling to Wales and Ireland and wherever her mother could get stage parts to support her fatherless family. After a period in a milliner's shop, she made her first recorded appearance on the Dublin stage, in Fielding's *The Virgin Unmasked*, although it is known that she had earlier appeared as Phoebe in *As You Like It* (1777). In 1781 she joined Richard Daly's theatre in Dublin's Smock Alley, where she played opposite John Philip Kemble (q.v.). Known as 'the general lover of the company', Daly was in the habit of seducing his actresses when they got into debt; when Dorothy discovered that she was pregnant by him, the family fled to England.

A three-year contract at 15s. a week with Tate Wilkinson's Northern Theatre Company gave the family financial security. Between playing 'sentimental and gay ladies, chambermaids, opera parts and breeches parts', she gave birth to Daly's daughter, Frances, disappearing from the stage for less than two months. Rumours abounded, but were smothered by the growing success of the neat-figured, not pretty, but animated actress, now calling herself Mrs. Jordan. Mrs. Siddons (q.v.), who saw her act in Leeds, pronounced that she should stay there, but others thought differently, and in 1785 she joined the Drury Lane Theatre under Sheridan's management.

Sated with Mrs. Siddons's grand tragic style, the London audiences were ready for a change, and the gaiety of Mrs. Jordan took London by storm. She opened on 18 October 1785 as Peggy in *The Country Girl* by Wycherley, which was seen by Lord North and the Prince of Wales. Her salary was doubled to £8 a week and she began to rival Mrs. Siddons in popularity.

Three illegitimate children were borne by Dorothy to Sir Richard Ford, a barrister and M.P. who promised to marry the actress when he was financially independent. During one of her confinements, the *Morning Post* remarked, 'The river [of Jordan, of course] in its present state of storm and agitation is no longer Ford-able.' With four children to support, Dorothy was in constant need of money and relations between herself and Kemble, now manager of Drury Lane, became strained. By 1790 it was clear that Ford would never marry her, although they shared a house in Richmond. The provinces were less tolerant of this arrangement than London, and it was after a particularly unpleasant tour that Mrs. Jordan turned to another protector, Prince William, Duke of Clarence, the future William IV.

Clarence was twenty-six, and the actress with whom he lived for the next twenty years was thirty. Loving letters passed between the two, and they began to 'prepare themselves for a thousand cruel storms' of public abuse. Within months, however, the fuss had died down and the couple settled in to a respectable but financially embarrassed existence.

With a growing family (she bore Clarence ten children), Dorothy welcomed the Duke's move in 1797 to the spacious Bushey House, where she lived for the next fourteen years. Her work on the stage was a financial necessity, but it was obviously also a continuing pleasure. She acted in the ill-starred *Vortigern* and in fashionable 'Gothick' plays, and in 1800 George III was shot at during her performance in *She Would and She Would Not*.

In 1809, after several retirements, she returned again to the stage to provide a dowry for her daughter, but now she admitted to being 'quite tired of the profession . . . a mere money-getting drudgery'. A period of decline began in 1811 with Clarence's sudden decision to separate from her, probably suggested by his legal and financial advisers as a way out of his money troubles. Despite the clause in her separation settlement that allowed her care of her four young daughters only on condition that she did not return to the stage, the pressing financial difficulties of her family forced her back for a final triumphant season at Covent Garden. Fearful of arrest after the bankruptcy of two sons-in-law, she fled to France in 1815. There is some evidence that Dorothy Jordan died on 4 July 1816 at St. Cloud, attended by Miss Sketchley, her children's governess, but there is also a legend that she returned incognito to England and lived on there for several years. Her children were raised to nobility under the name of FitzClarence; her eldest son, George Augustus Frederick, distinguished himself in the Napoleonic Wars, served in India, and was created 1st Earl of Munster.

A. A. Aspinall (ed.), *Mrs. Jordan and her Family* (1951).
B. Fothergill, *Mrs. Jordan, Portrait of an Actress* (1965).
Clare Jerrold, *The Story of Dorothy Jordan* (1914).
P. W. Sergeant, *Mrs. Jordan* (1913).

Portrait: oil, full-length, by John Hoppner, 1786: Buckingham Palace.

'Junius' (*fl.* 1768–72), pseudonymous author of a series of letters attacking the governments of the Duke of Grafton (see Fitzroy, Augustus Henry) and Lord North and also the political influence of King George III; identified, but far from conclusively, with Sir Philip Francis (q.v.).

The letters, most of them signed with the signature 'Junius' (recalling both the legendary Lucius Junius Brutus, who drove out Tarquin the Proud and established the Roman Republic in 510 B.C., and also his historical descendant, Marcus Junius Brutus, the slayer of the dictator Caesar), are essentially a product of the political situation obtaining at the time. They served to stimulate public opinion and in spite of their unrelieved invective, or perhaps because of it, they were possessed of some power and intensity.

The first letters, sent out privately in 1768 to the ailing Earl of Chatham (see

Pitt, William, the Elder) and George Grenville (q.v.), have as their main purpose unification of the opposition to Grafton. Opposition unity would be easier if Grenville, once a protégé of Chatham but now an opponent, could be reconciled with him. In October 1768 Chatham withdrew from parliament, and he did not return to the political arena again until 1770.

In November 'Junius' began his attacks in earnest and publicly, through the medium of the press. His publisher was Henry Sampson Woodfall, editor of the *Public Advertiser*; his collected edition of the letters, published in 1772, actually dates from 21 January 1769. At this time the Wilkes crisis was at its height, and Grafton's inept handling of it was excellent fuel for the fire of satirical attack. Indeed, 'Junius' leapt to Wilkes's defence. But the contempt of 'Junius' for Grafton and his ministers was on the level of personal hatred. Particular targets were John Russell, the Earl of Bute (see Stuart, John), and Lord Mansfield (see Murray, William).

Another Establishment figure who came under heavy fire from 'Junius' was John Manners. The attack provoked the spirited defence of Granby by another soldier, Lieutenant-General Sir William Draper.

The most sensational of the letters, however, was an attack on the King himself. George III's actions were capricious and based on personal prejudice. They had already worked with powerful effect against Grenville, and later his hostility was to be brought to bear on Fox (q.v.). On 19 December 1769 'Junius' published a famous letter to the King, the very encapsulation of the resentment and annoyance engendered by royal intervention in the running of the country. For this Woodfall was prosecuted on a charge of seditious libel, but the case could not stand.

'Junius' sustained his self-appointed task as public gadfly until January 1772. Stylistically, the letters are sententious and epigrammatic, utilizing antithesis to an extreme degree. Coleridge regarded them as 'a kind of satiric poems'. Satiric they are indeed, and shrewd and sarcastic and boldly abusive. But 'Junius' could afford to be (in Johnson's phrase) 'sarcastic in a mask'; sarcasm added bite to his purpose, which was to get people to do something about the political situation.

'Junius' remained unknown throughout his journalistic career. Notwithstanding exhaustive research, his identity continues to be a mystery. There are as many as fifty candidates, including Gibbon, Burke, John Wilkes, and even Chatham himself. Yet, despite the fact that the evidence is circumstantial, the best guess is still Sir Philip Francis. As a principal clerk in the War Office, Francis had in 1762–3 been a party to information concerning the peace negotiations with France. This matches well some of the more intimate references to Bedford in the letters of 'Junius'. Moreover, Francis was probably sending letters to the press, especially the *Public Advertiser*, as early as 1763, and was a known supporter of a scheme to bring down the Grafton administration. The idea that Francis might be 'Junius' was put forward as long ago as 1816 by John Taylor. Yet it does not entirely fit the facts; an element of mystery remains.

In 1772 'Junius' published his last letter (21 January). How much he had affected public awareness of the political situation is certainly questionable. 'Junius' himself was by no means confident of his effectiveness. On 19 January 1773 he wrote privately to Woodfall, more or less admitting defeat. With this communication the 'Junius' letters end: by October 1774 Francis, if it was indeed he who wrote them, was in India.

Francesco Cordasco, *A Junius Bibliography* (1949).
Alvar Ellegård, *A Statistical Method for Determining Authorship: the 'Junius' Letters* (1962).
Alvar Ellegård, *Who was 'Junius'?* (1962).
C. W. Everett (ed.), *The Letters of Junius* (1927).
B. Francis and E. Keary (eds.), *The Francis Letters* (2 vols.; 1901).
Abraham Hayward, *More about Junius* (1868).
John Taylor, *Junius Identified* (1816).
See also references under Francis, Sir Philip.

K

Kauffmann, (Anna Maria) Angelica (1741–1807), Swiss-born history and portrait painter, who was among the earliest members of the Royal Academy.

Angelica Kauffmann was born at Chur in the Swiss canton of Schwyz on 30 October 1741, the daughter of Johann Joseph Kauffmann, also a painter. From a very early age she revealed artistic talents, but she was also an accomplished musician, and in 1760 she was compelled to choose between the two careers. In the event, she chose painting, and having studied in Milan, Bologna, and Venice, she finally arrived in Rome. At this point she was concentrating on portraiture.

In 1766 Angelica arrived in England and was at once received into society as well as being extremely popular with royalty. She was a beautiful woman and a gay and charming personality. She befriended Sir Joshua Reynolds (q.v.) and a romantic relationship ensued; in 1767, however, she was tricked into an unfortunate marriage with a valet posing as a Swedish count, from whom she soon obtained a divorce.

Angelica was one of the founder members of the Academy in 1768 and contributed works until 1797. Her fifteen-year stay in England is marked chiefly, however, by the decorative work she produced in houses designed by the Adam brothers. Here she excelled in small-scale history pieces for walls and ceilings. She was also one of the artists employed in 1773 to decorate St. Paul's.

In 1781 Angelica married for the second time. Her husband, Antonio Zucchi, an Italian painter and an associate of the Royal Academy, took Angelica back to Italy within a few days of their marriage.

Angelica lead a stimulating social life in Rome and her friends included both Goethe and Herder. She died there on 5 November 1807 and her elaborate funeral was supervised by the Italian artist Antonio Canova.

Angelica Kauffmann's work has been much criticized for its faulty drawing and composition and the dull monotonous figures, but her paintings adapted well to engraving and undeniably had a certain grace and warmth of colour. She attempted with limited success to adapt mythological and allegorical scenes to classicist lines.

Adeline Hartcup, *Angelica* (1954).

Portrait: self-portrait, oil, half-length: N.P.G.

Kay, John (1704–64), engineer, the inventor of the flying shuttle, sometimes referred to as 'Kay of Bury'.

John Kay was born on 16 July 1704 at The Park, Walmersley, near Bury in Lancashire. It is believed that he was educated abroad. While still a young man he returned to England and was placed in charge of a 'woollen manufactory' in Colchester, owned by his father. By 1730 he had come back to Bury and was making reeds for looms, and in the same year he took out a patent for 'an engine for making, twisting, and carding mohair, and twining and dressing of thread'. At about the same time he effected a great improvement in the loom reeds, manufacturing the dents out of metal instead of cane, thus making them more durable and ensuring a fabric of a more even texture. These new-style reeds were rapidly put into general use.

In 1733 Kay took out a patent for the flying shuttle, possibly the most important improvement ever made in the loom. Up to that time the shuttle containing the weft (horizontal) thread had to be thrown from one weaver to another, through the alternate (vertical) threads of the warp. The weft was 'beat' or closed up after each throw of the shuttle by a 'layer' extending across the piece of material being woven. Kay added to the 'layer' a kind of grooved guide or 'raceboard' through which the shuttle was thrown rapidly from side to side, by means of a shuttle 'driver'. With the raceboard and shuttle driver attachment, one weaver could weave fabrics of any width more quickly than two men could previously have done, and with an improved quality. This 1733 patent also included a device for removing dust from wool. Five years later Kay patented an invention for working pumps.

In 1738 Kay moved to Leeds. His new shuttle was widely adopted by woollen manufacturers but, unwilling to pay Kay his royalties, a number of them formed the 'Shuttle Club' for the purpose of meeting legal costs in proceedings for infringements of the patent. Kay himself was nearly ruined by these lawsuits.

He returned to Bury and in 1745 took out a patent with Joseph Stell for a mechanical smallware loom. But this met with small success. In 1753 a mob broke into Kay's house in Bury and wrought serious havoc. Kay barely escaped with his life, and after this experience it is thought that he went to France, where he set up business with machines smuggled out of Lancashire. He died, as far as is known, in poverty and obscurity in 1764.

Kay was the instigator of most important improvements in the machinery for the weaving of cloth, and with more encouragement from the woollen and cotton manufacturers it is possible he might have achieved even more.

J. Lord, *Memoir of John Kay of Bury* (1903).

Portrait: lithograph, by Madeley: British Museum.

Kean, Edmund (1789–1833), actor.

Edward Kean was born on 17 March 1789 (some authorities give the date as 4 November 1787), the son of Anne Carey, who described herself as 'an itinerant actress and street hawker'. His father was one of two Irish brothers, Aaron and Edmund Kean.

Abandoned in a Soho doorway, he was adopted by a middle-class couple. At the age of two his mother arranged for him to appear at His Majesty's Theatre as a cupid in the ballet *Noverre*. This was followed by other similar appearances; at the same time he was receiving spasmodic education at Mr. King's school in Soho.

To obscure his humble origins, Kean was given to circulating rumours of his royal blood, Eton education, and countless daring escapades. While many of these contain no grain of truth, it is a fact that his life was full of adventures. The first happened in 1795, when he walked to Portsmouth and went as cabin-boy to Madeira, but he did not like the life and so, feigning illness, he was returned to England as a patient. He was taken in by his uncle Moses Kean, a ventriloquist, who gave him elocution lessons. His uncle's mistress was Charlotte Tidswell, a small-part actress at Drury Lane, and she did her best to give him a general education, as well as teaching him to act.

In 1801 Kean did his first real acting as Prince Arthur at Drury Lane. Soon after this he ran away, to reappear as a tumbler with Saunder's Circus, where he fell and broke both legs, an accident from which he never fully recovered. In 1802 he performed his first Hamlet at York, and for the next twelve years he travelled round the country acting wherever he could get work.

In 1808 he married Mary Chambers, an actress nine years older than himself, who bore him two sons, Howard and Charles. Life became rather hard for him with these new, unwonted responsibilities. He was earning very little and was ignored or slated by the press. In 1813 Howard, his adored elder son, died.

In 1814 Kean was offered a contract at Drury Lane. He insisted that his first performance should be as Shylock. After one walk-through rehearsal he had his first great triumph. His fellow actors cheered him from the wings and news of his performance spread fast, so that the box-office receipts for his next performance were doubled. He was given a weekly salary of £20, and later the theatre committee gave him a lump sum of £5,000. Presents were showered upon him but he was improvident and generous. His mother heard of his success and arrived for her share: Kean gave her an annuity of £50 until her death, and supported her other children as well, though he would never admit their relationship.

Kean played every great Shakespearean tragic hero, and was adored by most critics. But as time went on he became more and more uncontrollable and debauched, pleading illness when hangovers prevented his acting and even wearing a totally unnecessary sling to win over a grumbling audience. He was also vain and often said he would never play any secondary character at all.

In 1820 came his first American tour. He was a triumph in Boston and Philadelphia, but his wildness caused rather more mixed reactions in New York.

After his return to London he achieved more successes and travelled to Dundee, Paris, and Switzerland, playing to rapturous houses. In 1825, however, a scandal broke that shook even his most adoring fans. He was ordered to pay £800 damages after being sued for adultery with the wife of a city alderman. The unpopularity this caused led him to return to America, but the scandal led to rioting in New York where the audience threw things at him and a mob attacked the house where he was staying, so that he finally fled to Canada.

By 1827 he was forgiven for his behaviour and his Shylock at Drury Lane was once again drawing huge audiences and winning him new admirers. His health and memory, however, were failing. Nevertheless he went to Paris, where his Richard III was admired by Dumas, and in 1828 he went to Glasgow to play Brutus to his son's Titus in *Brutus, or the Fall of Tarquin.*

However, his health was rapidly deteriorating. In 1831 he went to live in a cottage at Richmond, doing occasional small parts at Richmond Theatre and drinking very heavily. 25 March 1833 was the day of his last performance, during which he collapsed and had to be taken home to Richmond, where he summoned his wife and was reconciled with her and where, on 15 May 1833, he died.

Kean was a small man with very expressive eyes, a fine voice and a powerful magnetic quality. He reintroduced the naturalistic style of acting, eschewing the posturing and declamatory passion of his precedessors, and preferring to give the illusion of being, not playing, his characters. His acting won him such acclaim that for eighteen years he earned an unprecedented average of £1,000 a year, but his profligacy, generosity, and drinking habits used it all up easily, and he died in debt. Coleridge put into words the general opinion of him when he wrote,

'To see Kean act is like reading Shakespeare by flashes of lightning.'

M. W. Disher, *Mad Genius, a Biography of Edmund Kean* (1950).

H. M. Hillibrand, *Edmund Kean* (New York, 1933).

G. W. Playfair, *Kean* (1950, 2nd ed.).

Portraits: pencil, quarter-length, by S. Cousins, 1814: N.P.G.; pencil, three-quarter length, attributed to T. Wageman: N.P.G.; oil, by D. Maclise: National Gallery of Ireland, Dublin.

Keats, John (1795–1821), Romantic poet.

John Keats was born on 31 October 1795 at the Swan and Hoop Livery Stables, Finsbury, London, the son of Frances Jennings and Thomas Keats, the manager of the stables. He received little formal education. At the age of about eight he, together with his brothers George and Tom, began attending a school in Enfield kept by the Rev. John Clarke, whose son, Charles Cowden Clarke, was to become Keats's teacher, friend, and devoted supporter. His only sister, Fanny, was born on 3 June 1803. The following April their father was killed in a riding accident, and two months after that their mother married a stable-keeper. The marriage proved unhappy, and she sent her children to live with their grandparents.

In March 1810 Keat's mother died of tuberculosis, watched over constantly during the final days of her illness by her eldest son. In July of the same year their grandmother placed the children under the care of Richard Abbey. At the suggestion of Abbey, Keats left the Enfield school in the summer of 1811 and was apprenticed to a surgeon and apothecary, Thomas Hammond, in Edmonton. There he stayed until 1815 when he left for London to continue his medical training, first at Guy's Hospital and later at St. Thomas's Hospital.

The medical life was not for Keats. He had become fascinated with the poetry of Spenser and the Elizabethans, introduced to him by Cowden Clarke. During his apprenticeship with Hammond, Keats had been a frequent visitor to his old school where he borrowed and read books of all descriptions, especially poetry and mythology. By 1814 he had written his first juvenile verses. These early efforts were hardly notable for their originality; he was as yet much too imitative, which he fully conceded in the title of one of his earliest poems, *Imitation of Spenser* (1814).

In December 1814 his grandmother died, and Keats was separated from his sister, Fanny, when she was sent to live with the family of Richard Abbey.

The journalist, political radical, and poet Leigh Hunt (q.v.) now played a significant role in the life of Keats. In 1813 Hunt had been sentenced to two years in prison as the result of articles he had written in the *Examiner*. On 2 February 1815 Keats wrote a sonnet entitled 'Written on the Day That Mr. Leigh Hunt Left Prison'. Keats did not meet Hunt until October 1816, but from that

moment they became close friends. During the next few months Keats fell under the influence of Hunt, and was captivated by his poetry and literary dogmas. Hunt was of the 'Cockney School' of poetry, and Keats was to suffer later at the hands of the critics as a result of this association.

During his schooldays Keats was known as a fighter, and his highly pugnacious spirit could be aroused by the slightest provocation, yet he was described by one of his contemporaries as having a face of 'almost feminine beauty'.

On 25 July 1816 Keats passed an examination at Apothecaries' Hall, London, which entitled him to practise as a surgeon or physician. However, the increasingly urgent sense of his vocation as a poet made it impossible for him to accept such a sensible and mundane profession. He laid down the scalpel and took up the pen, for good.

In October 1816 Keats composed one of his finest shorter poems, the sonnet 'On First Looking into Chapman's Homer'. Leigh Hunt was so impressed with the sonnet that in December of the same year he quoted it in the *Examiner*, in his article on 'Young Poets'.

Leigh Hunt introduced Keats to many of his friends, including Percy Bysshe Shelley, Benjamin Haydon, and William Hazlitt. From this period Keats spent much time at Hunt's cottage. He developed a close friendship with the painter Haydon, who in March 1817 introduced him to the Elgin marbles.

Keats published his first volume of poetry on 3 March 1817. In April 1817 Keats left for the Isle of Wight, where he began his plans to write a major poem to test his creative capacities as a poet. The result – *Endymion : A Poetic Romance* – was completed in November 1817 and published the following May. *Endymion* is a poem of over 4,000 lines. In it Keats attempted to deal with a classical subject at sufficient length to provide himself and his critics with room to judge his genius, believing that all great poets are ultimately judged by their longer poems. The reaction to this work was intense, if mixed.

Keats's circle of literary acquaintances continued to grow, and on 28 December 1817 he met Charles Lamb and William Wordsworth at a dinner party arranged by Haydon. In May 1818 his brother George married, and left the following month for America – leaving Keats to attend to his youngest brother, Tom, who had started the first symptoms of tuberculosis.

In June 1818 Keats set out on a walking tour of Scotland with his friend Armitage Brown. Keats over-exerted himself and was forced to end the tour abruptly on doctor's orders. When he returned to London he found Tom dangerously ill, and on 1 December he died. Keats was immediately invited to stay at Brown's house in Hampstead, and there he met Fanny Brawne. Keats fell in love with her almost immediately, but although Fanny professed her love, she was unable to reciprocate with the same intensity. Keats's bitter disappointment and sense of rejection did not prevent him from writing, and in the following year he channelled all his energies into producing some of his greatest poetry.

In January 1819 Keats wrote 'The Eve of St. Agnes', a poem in Spenserian stanzas based on the legend that on this evening each year young girls are permitted a glimpse of their future husbands. The imagery in this masterpiece is among his finest. The opening lines convey a stark scene of frozen beauty:

St. Agnes' Eve – Ah, bitter chill it
    was!
The owl, for all his feathers, was a-
    cold;

The hare limp'd trembling through
 the frozen grass,
And silent was the flock in woolly
 fold.

In the spring of the same year Keats composed 'La Belle Dame sans Merci' and the major odes, including 'Ode on a Grecian Urn', 'Ode to Psyche', 'Ode to a Nightingale', and 'Ode on Melancholy'. At Winchester he worked on *Otho the Great*, 'Lamia', and *Hyperion*. In July 1820, his last book of poetry was published: *Lamia, Isabella, The Eve of St. Agnes, and Other Poems*.

Towards the end of December 1819 Keats became engaged to Fanny Brawne. However, on 3 February 1820 he suffered a severe haemorrhage, and could no longer escape recognizing the fact that he was suffering from progressively worsening tuberculosis. He offered to break off his engagement with Fanny, but she refused. As his condition did not improve, his doctor ordered him to move to Italy, where the climate would be more healthful. Shelley invited him to stay but the offer was never actually accepted. Keats finally sailed for Italy with an artist friend, Joseph Severn. They arrived in Rome on 15 November 1820. On 10 December 1820 Keats had a severe relapse. He died on the morning of 23 February 1821, and was buried in the Protestant Cemetery in Rome.

W. J. Bate, *The Stylistic Development of Keats* (New York, 1945).

D. Bush, *Keats* (New York, 1966).

C. L. Finney, *The Evolution of Keats's Poetry* (2 vols.; Cambridge, Mass., 1936).

G. H. Ford, *Keats and the Victorians* (New Haven, 1944).

H. B. Forman (ed.), *Complete Works of John Keats* (5 vols.; 1900–1).

H. W. Garrod, *Keats* (1939, rev. ed.).

R. Gittings, *John Keats* (1968).

H. E. Rollins (ed.), *The Letters of Keats 1814–21* (Cambridge, Mass., 1958).

L. Trilling, *The Opposing Self* (New York, 1955).

A. Ward, *John Keats: The Making of a Poet* (New York, 1963).

Portraits: oil, full-length, by J. Severn, 1821: N.P.G.; oil, half-length, by W. Hilton after a miniature by J. Severn: N.P.G.; miniature, half-length, by J. Severn, 1819: Keats Museum, Hampstead; pencil, quarter-length, by C. A. Brown, 1819: N.P.G.; pen and ink, quarter-length, by B. R. Haydon, 1816: N.P.G.; drawing, quarter-length, by J. Severn, 1816: V. & A.

Kemble, Charles (1775–1854), actor and theatre manager; youngest brother of John Philip Kemble and Sarah Siddons (qq.v.).

Charles Kemble was born in Brecon, South Wales, on 25 November 1775. Like his brother John Philip, he studied at the English College at Douai; upon his return to England he entered the civil service. However, Charles gave up his position at the post office to play Orlando in *As You Like It* at Sheffield in 1792. After an apprenticeship on the northern circuit of theatres, he made his London début as Malcolm in his brother's memorable *Macbeth* of 1794 at Drury Lane.

Although in many ways a feeble copy of his elder brother, Charles Kemble had the same bearing and a similar appearance, the same solid classical education, and the same literary aspirations. Like John he had little success in farces and melodramas, but in many parts where his brother had failed he excelled, effectively playing such characters as Sir Charles Surface, Orlando, Benedick, and Romeo.

In 1803 Charles followed John Philip Kemble and Mrs. Siddons to Covent Garden. In 1820 he inherited his brother's debts and management difficulties. As manager, he recognized the genius of the actor William Macready. John Philip Kemble's great innovation had been to introduce classical dress, whatever the period of the play's action; this Charles changed – he was one of the first managers to attempt to introduce historical accuracy into theatrical costume.

Covent Garden's financial situation, however, was catastrophic, and the future continued to look bleak until 1829, when Charles's daughter Fanny first appeared on the stage. She was an instant success. In 1832 and 1834 Charles took Fanny to America along with his wife and they got a warm reception there.

Charles Kemble's last years were fraught with continuing financial worries, and his withdrawal from the stage was hastened by the onset and progress of deafness. He died on 12 November 1854.

P. Fitzgerald, *The Kembles* (2 vols.; 1871).

Kemble, John Philip (1757–1823), actor and theatre manager; brother of Charles Kemble and Sarah Siddons (qq.v.).

John Philip Kemble was born on 1 February 1757 at Prescott in Lancashire, the son of Roger Kemble, manager of a touring theatrical company, and Sarah Ward, a Birmingham actor manager's daughter. He was brought up in the Roman Catholic faith. His schooling was frequently interrupted by appearances on the stage, but in 1771, after attending Sedgley Park seminary at Wolverhampton, he was sent to the English College at Douai, where he became known for his oratory and phenomenal memory. After five years he abandoned his studies and returned to England to an outraged family and the precarious life of an unattached strolling player. His sister Sarah then intervened and obtained him a place in Joseph Younger's Liverpool troupe. The following year, 1778, he joined Tate Wilkinson's northern circuit.

His pretensions to literature brought Kemble little public acclaim but won him a place among the *literati*. A move to Richard Daly's Dublin company gained him more influential friends. Captain Jephson adapted Walpole's *Castle of Otranto* for Kemble, parading this newly

discovered 'Adonis of the buskin' before Dublin society. Drury Lane and Covent Garden then raced to hire the rising star, and 30 September 1783 saw him opening in *Hamlet* at Drury Lane. Success did not come immediately, but the public enjoyed seeing Kemble, whose popularity rose when he started acting with his sister in 1785. One critic remarked that Kemble 'had a muse of fire before him', and asked, 'Why did he not kindle at her inspiration?' But audiences welcomed Kemble's Lear to Mrs. Siddons's Cordelia, and his Othello to her Desdemona.

In 1786 Kemble was acting six nights a week, and London had gained a new tragic style. The slow studied delivery, the peculiar pronunciation, the haughty bearing and stiff movements were much criticized. Leigh Hunt said that Kemble was 'a teacher of elocution rather than an actor'; Charles Lamb declared that 'he took a stance and orated'; and the *Morning Chronicle* said his Richard III was full of 'coldness and degradation'; but all were agreed that he was supreme in those roles which displayed what Hazlitt called 'the beauty and grandeur of the theatre': Coriolanus, Wolsey, Cato in Addison's neo-classical play of that name, Percy in 'Monk' Lewis's *Castle Spectre*, and Rolla in Sheridan's reworking of Kotzebue's drama *Pizarro*. He was too formal for comedy but he continued to act parts such as Benedick and Sir Giles Overreach despite criticism.

London society nevertheless flocked to Drury Lane and Kemble was entertained by royalty, the aristocracy, the intellectuals, and artists of the day. Thomas Lawrence (q.v.) was a particular friend and painted the actor many times.

Drury Lane had been considerably mismanaged by Sheridan, and Kemble could not hope to restore its failing finances when he became manager in 1788. He was, however, methodical and stern: his journal records the plays and the receipts for every performance. He insisted on punctuality at rehearsals and supervised every detail of his productions. Many spectacular innovations were introduced under his management: his *Macbeth* was distinguished by weird costumes, singing witches, and the non-appearance of Banquo's ghost.

Wrangles with Sheridan and constant financial worries forced Kemble's resignation from Drury Lane, and in 1803 he became manager of Covent Garden. Now eclipsed by George Frederick Cooke in the leading tragic roles, his troubles were increased by a staggering financial loss in a fire that destroyed the theatre, followed by the 'Old Price' riots – demonstrations against the necessary increases in admission prices – which attended the opening of the newly built Covent Garden in 1809. Months of these demonstrations and frequent bouts of asthma and gout sent Kemble abroad for two years, a period of absence that saw the rise of Edmund Kean (q.v.) who, according to Hazlitt, 'destroyed the Kemble religion'. Kemble struck financial problems again and only a grant from the Duke of Northumberland kept him solvent. Brutus was his last new part, and on 23 June 1817 he made his final appearance, as Coriolanus.

His last years were spent living quietly in Switzerland with his wife Priscilla, until his death in Lausanne on 26 February 1823.

Herschel Baker, *John Philip Kemble: the Actor in His Theatre* (Harvard and London, 1942).
H. H. Child, *The Shakespearian Productions of John Philip Kemble* (1935).
P. Fitzgerald, *The Kembles* (2 vols.; 1871).

Portraits: oil, half-length, by G. Stuart: N.P.G.; pencil, full-length, by T. Lawrence: N.P.G.; engraving, quarter-length, by P. Thomson, *c.*1819: R. Mander and J. Mitchenson Theatre Collection.

Kendal, Duchess of (1667–1743), see Schulenburg, Countess Ehrengarde Melusina von der.

Kent, William (1686–1748), architect, interior decorator, and landscape gardener.

William Kent was born in 1686 at Bridlington, Yorkshire. At the age of fourteen he is believed to have been apprenticed to a coach-painter for five years. His talents were quickly recognized, and in 1709 he was sent to study painting in Italy where he remained for ten years. He returned to England with Richard Boyle, the 3rd Earl of Burlington, who was to become his most constant and influential patron.

Through Burlington's influence, Kent obtained many commissions for both decorative and portrait painting, but he was unsuccessful in these fields. However, adverse criticism did not mar his personal popularity, and indeed, with Burlington behind him, Kent was constantly in demand. From decorative painting he turned to architecture. In 1727 his edited version of the *Designs of Inigo Jones* was published, containing many of Kent's own decorative designs. His work at Kensington Palace for George I and at Chiswick House and Burlington House conformed largely to these early designs.

In 1730 Burlington sent Kent back to Italy for further study, and on his return Kent embarked on a scheme to redesign the public buildings of London according to the strictest principles of Palladianism. Examples of this are the royal mews in Trafalgar Square (1732) and the treasury buildings of Whitehall (1734). Many of Kent's plans were never to reach fruition, notably those for the Houses of Parliament and a palace in Hyde Park.

Probably Kent's most important work was Holkham Hall in Norfolk, begun in 1734 for Thomas Coke, Earl of Leicester.

Not only did he design the house – he was also responsible for the interior decoration and the furniture. In this respect, Holkham is the first example of a house planned both externally and internally in a unified design.

His imagination and fantasy were to find their natural expression and satisfaction in landscape gardening. Kent's work laid emphasis on informality and the Romantic, although his student, Lancelot ('Capability') Brown (q.v.), was later to develop Kent's idea of a natural landscape within the garden more successfully. His chief works can be seen at Rousham, Oxfordshire, and at Stowe House, in Buckinghamshire, where small classical temples are scattered amongst wooded glades and grassy vistas.

William Kent died on 12 April 1748, and was buried at Chiswick. Horace Walpole summed up his career as follows:

The Apollo of arts found a proper priest in the person of Mr. Kent. . . . He was a painter, an architect, and the father of modern gardening. In the first character, he was below mediocrity; in the second, he was a restorer of the science; in the last, an original and the inventor of an art that realizes painting, and improves nature. . . . He leaped the fence, and saw that all nature was a garden.

Margaret Jourdain, *The Work of William Kent* (1948).

Portrait: engraving, quarter-length, artist unknown: British Museum.

Knaresborough, Blind Jack of (1717–1810), see Metcalf, John.

Kneller, Sir Godfrey (1646–1723), painter and courtier, see *Lives of the Stuart Age.*

L

Lamb, Lady Caroline (1785–1828), socialite, novelist, and intimate admirer of Lord Byron (q.v.).

Lady Caroline Lamb was born on 13 November 1785, the only daughter of Frederick Ponsonby, 3rd Earl of Bessborough, by his wife Lady Henrietta Spencer. At the age of three she was sent in the care of a servant to Italy, where she remained for six years, and even after her return to England it was her maternal grandmother rather than her parents who worried about her education. She was an unpredictable child, full of contradictory emotions and sudden enthusiasms. By the time she entered London society she was already known to possess an independent, wilful, and excitable temper.

In June 1805 Lady Caroline married her cousin William Lamb (q.v.; later Lord Melbourne), but although Lamb proved a kind and enduring husband he soon recognized that his wife's volatile personality precluded any possibility of a long-term stable relationship. For her part, Lady Caroline was incapable of recognizing as love William's undemonstrative and tolerant affection. The most magnetic attraction for any woman's passion during Lady Caroline's heyday was undoubtedly Lord Byron, and despite her later bitterness, Lady Caroline's entry in her diary after their first meeting shows that she well knew what she was letting herself in for: Lord Byron, she wrote, was 'mad, bad, and dangerous to know'. Her affair with Byron was brief but passionate; it ended in 1813, after a party in July at which Lady Caroline first quarrelled with Byron and then tried to kill herself. This scene led to her social ostracism, and by the end of the summer she had left London for Ireland.

Caroline now undertook to revenge herself on an indifferent world by writing and publishing anonymously her first novel, *Glenarvon* (re-issued in 1865 as *The Fatal Passion*), which contained hostile caricatures of most of her acquaintances, including Byron. The book sold well; even Byron received it with characteristic sardonic humour: 'As for the likeness, the picture can't be good; I did not sit long enough.'

The book was a source of further distress to her husband, portrayed in the novel as Lord Avondale, a noble-hearted man who nevertheless corrupts his wife by his cynical moral views. Lamb's friends insisted that if he did not leave her, they would assume that he had connived at the book's publication and would have to drop him. Accordingly, separation papers were drawn up; the arrangements were thwarted, however, by a last-minute reconciliation. As William was going to bed one evening, he became aware of a scuffling at the door: it was Caroline, preparing to spend the night on his doormat as a final token of her remorse and devotion. The following morning the lawyers arriving for the final signature found her sitting on his lap, laughing merrily while he fed her bits of bread and butter.

During the next eight years Lady Caroline wrote three further novels, as well as some poetry that was circulated privately; none of these works was of any literary merit, but the writing served satisfactorily to pass away the time, which hung heavily on her hands.

A chance encounter with Byron's funeral procession on its route to Newstead Abbey in 1824 finally over-balanced her fragile mental stability, and in the following year she was at last parted from her husband by legal separation. He nevertheless continued to write affectionately to her, provided for her, and was present at her deathbed. Almost the only other companions of Lady Caroline's final years were her servants and her only surviving child, a mentally deficient boy who died in 1836 at the age of twenty-nine. Lady Caroline herself died at Melbourne House in London on 26 January 1828. In one of her last letters she wrote, 'Remember the only noble fellow I ever met with is William Lamb.'

Lord David Cecil, *The Young Melbourne* (1939).
E. Jenkins, *Lady Caroline Lamb* (1932).

Portraits: oil, half-length, by T. Phillips: Chatsworth, Devonshire Collection; drawing, quarter-length, by M. A. Knight: Newstead Abbey Collection.

Lamb, Charles (1775–1834), essayist, poet, and letter-writer, who was also the author, with his sister Mary (1764–1847), of *Tales from Shakespeare*.

Charles Lamb was born on 10 February 1775 in Crown Office Row in the Inner Temple, London, the son of a clerk and personal assistant to a lawyer. The Lamb family was poor, and of seven children only three survived beyond infancy, Charles Lamb being the youngest.

Lamb's earliest formal education was conducted at a small local day school, but at the age of seven he was sent to the famous school at Christ's Hospital. Lamb's contemporaries here included Leigh Hunt and Samuel Taylor Coleridge (qq.v.). Under the kindly discipline of James Boyer and Matthew Field (both clergymen), the pupils enjoyed an educ-ation that was stimulating and yet re-laxed. In 1791 Coleridge took up a place at Cambridge University, and Lamb would probably have accompanied him had it not been for a severe speech defect, a stutter that sapped his self-confidence whenever he was asked to speak in public.

On leaving Christ's Hospital in 1789 Lamb worked briefly in an accountant's office and then began his long career as an East India Company clerk. An unhappy love affair with a girl whom he had met while staying at his grandmother's house may partly account for a six-week period of confinement in an asylum during the winter of 1795. Several members of the Lamb family were subject to periods of mental disturbance, and the most drastic consequence of this trait occurred in 1796 when Mary, Lamb's sister, killed her mother with a carving knife. A verdict of temporary insanity was delivered at the inquest, and rather than see his sister confined in an asylum Charles Lamb undertook complete personal re-sponsibility for her welfare.

Included in *Poems on Various Subjects* (1796), the first volume of poetry published by Coleridge, were four sonnets by Lamb, and on a visit to Coleridge at Nether Stowey in 1797 Lamb met William and Dorothy Words-worth. In 1798 he collaborated with a friend on another volume of poetry, and also published a derivative prose work entitled *The Tale of Rosamund Gray and Old Blind Margaret*, but the urgent need for a sufficient income to support his sister and himself determined that most of Lamb's literary energies went into marketable journalism rather than private projects. In 1799, after the death of his father, Lamb set up house with Mary in the Temple district of London, and he became acquainted with many literary and theatrical per-sonalities.

In 1802 Lamb published *John Woodvil*, a poetic tragedy written in Elizabethan blank verse, but his only play to be performed, a farce entitled *Mr. H.*, was hissed off the stage at Drury Lane in 1806. A more successful venture was *Tales from Shakespeare*, the stories of the plays rewritten in prose for children in collaboration with Mary and published in 1807, and this was followed by a series of other books for children which included *The Adventures of Ulysses* (1808) and *Beauty and the Beast* (1811). Lamb's most ambitious work of literary criticism, *Specimens of the English Dramatic Poets who Lived about the Time of Shakespeare*, was published in 1808; to a certain extent this work justifies Lamb's claim to be one of the first critics to appreciate the merits of the Elizabethan and Jacobean dramatists, but the brief passages of criticism that accompany the dramatic extracts in fact demonstrate his limitation rather than his talents. Here, as in a later essay 'On the Tragedies of Shakespeare', Lamb shows that he is chiefly interested in the characters of the plays as vehicles for his own imagination.

The circumstances of Lamb's life, so much of which was devoted to the care of his sister and the daily routine of his job at India House, inevitably contributed to the development of his retiring and literary personality: he never married, he rarely travelled far from London. His wide correspondence, however, is evidence that he cared as much for his friends as for his books. In 1818 Lamb published two volumes of *Collected Works*, but the essays for which he is probably most famous, the *Essays of Elia*, were not started until two years later, when he was asked by his friend William Hazlitt to contribute to the newly-established *London Magazine*. For the pseudonym Elia, Lamb carefully constructed the persona of a mannered but knowledgeable literary gentleman: the miscellaneous subjects of his essays are treated in a wholly subjective manner and in an elaborate literary style, consciously dependent upon certain prose writers of the seventeenth century. Political, moral, and topical issues were all avoided, leaving personal fancy and autobiographical memories as the chief motivating forces for the lonely business of writing.

After two years of writing these essays at the rate of about one a month, Lamb arranged in 1823 for their publication in a single volume. He was disappointed by their poor sales, and also by Robert Southey's criticism that they lacked 'sound religious feeling'; but in this same year he met the person who perhaps more than any other helped to sustain his self-confidence. Emma Isola was a young orphan girl whom the Lambs met while on holiday in Cambridge. After being adopted as their child Emma became the responsive object of Lamb's affections as well as his educational theories.

In 1823 the Lambs moved house to the district of Islington, and two years later, after a severe illness, Lamb retired from his job at India House. Overjoyed to be free, and provided with a generous pension, Lamb moved to Enfield. He continued to write essays for the periodicals, including a series on 'Popular Fallacies' and another eventually published as *Last Essays of Elia* (1833), but after the brief happiness of the first few months, Lamb's retirement became a period of continual disillusion. Because of a deterioration in Mary's health he was compelled to sacrifice a measure of his independence and live with friends in a smaller house; a further deterioration in 1829 necessitated another move, again to live in the house of friends. In 1833 Emma Isola married and moved away from the Lambs; the following year Coleridge died, and Lamb's loneliness was intensified by deaths of other friends and by his own ill-health.

The muted tone of Lamb's later essays is an accurate reflection of his personal dejection. Early in December 1834 Lamb stumbled while out walking, and after a consequent illness he died on 27 December 1834. He was buried in Edmonton churchyard; Mary survived him by thirteen years, living harmlessly on in the care of friends.

E. Blunden, *Lamb and His Contemporaries* (1933).

M. Elwin (ed.), *Essays of Elia* (1952).

E. V. Lucas, *The Life of Lamb* (1921, rev. ed.).

E. V. Lucas (ed.), *Works of Charles Lamb* (7 vols.; 1903–5: 6 vols.; 1912).

F. B. Pinion (ed.), *A Lamb Selection* (1965).

E. M. W. Tillyard (ed.), *Lamb's Criticism: a Selection* (1923).

Portraits: pencil and chalk, half-length, by R. Hancock, 1798: N.P.G.; oil, half-length, by W. Hazlitt, 1804: N.P.G.; oil, half-length, by F. S. Cary, 1834: N.P.G.; oil, three-quarter length, after H. Meyer: N.P.G.

Lamb, William (1779–1848), 2nd Viscount Melbourne; Whig statesman who held the offices of Secretary for Ireland (1827–8), Home Secretary (1830–4), and Prime Minister (1834 and 1835–41).

William Lamb was born on 15 March 1779 in London. His mother, Elizabeth Milbanke, Lady Melbourne, was one of the great Whig hostesses of the period. Her husband, the 1st Viscount Melbourne, was idle and extravagant, and the general lack of family resemblance between him and William led to the general opinion that the boy was not the 1st Viscount's son. William's legitimacy, however, was never openly questioned.

After a childhood spent mainly in Hertfordshire, at Brocket Hall, the family seat, Lamb was educated at Eton and at Trinity College, Cambridge, graduating in 1799. Following a period of further study at Glasgow University, he returned to London and became prominent in the circles of the aristocratic Whigs. A debonaire young man, he led a rather rakish existence. In 1805 he married Lady Caroline Ponsonby (see Lamb, Lady Caroline).

Lamb's elder brother Peniston died in January 1805, making him heir to the title. Within the year he became a Whig M.P. (for Leominster, Herefordshire) and allied himself with the Whigs grouped around Charles James Fox (q.v.). He became known for his independent line, however, winning the respect of both sides of the house. He became a friend of George Canning (q.v.) and sometimes even voted with the Tories; in 1812 Liverpool offered him a post in the government, which he declined. Lamb was never to be a good party man, although throughout his career he remained more convinced of the importance of personal loyalties than of the rightness of any cause.

Embarrassed perhaps by Lady Caroline's very public infidelities, Lamb left politics in 1812 for four years, returning in 1816 to continue his own independent course. In 1816 he supported the government's move to suspend the Habeas Corpus Act; in 1819, on the other hand, he joined the radicals in calling for an investigation into the Peterloo massacre, and he was a consistent champion of Catholic emancipation.

In 1825 Lamb finally separated from Lady Caroline. Only now, after his forty-sixth birthday, did his political career start to gather momentum. In 1827 he joined the coalition ministry of his friend Canning, and was made Secretary for Ireland. In January 1828, however, a political crisis following the dismissal of Viscount Goderich (see Robinson, Frederick John) brought him back to London. Like other Whigs, he could not bring himself to serve in the Duke of Wellington's ministry and soon resigned, along with the Canningites.

In July 1828 Lamb succeeded as 2nd

Viscount Melbourne. After eighteen months out of office he was given a post in 1830 in the newly-formed Whig administration of Earl Grey. Back after nearly fifty years, the Whigs were keen to pursue a policy of moderate reform as a means of preventing full-scale revolution, a policy that Melbourne was prepared to support. Grey made him Home Secretary, an office that he filled with realism and harsh fairness. He insisted on the full application of the existing law, but avoided panic measures and took no special powers. His relations with the old King, William IV, were better than those of most of his colleagues. The main blot on his record at this time was his confirmation in March 1834 of the order of transportation for life on the Dorset trade unionists known as the Tolpuddle Martyrs. Not that he believed that trade unions were illegal; the Martyrs' offence had been the administering of a secret oath, and Melbourne seemed unable to understand what all the fuss was about.

The Whig government foundered over the Irish question in 1834 and, despite a continued Whig majority in the Commons, a vacuum was left in the leadership of the country. Acceptability to both of the Whig factions and also to the King was a prime requisite for a leader; of the members of the old cabinet Melbourne fitted the bill adequately, and he reluctantly accepted the office of Prime Minister in June. Melbourne's ministry was short-lived. The fall of the ministry in November was made worse by the fact that Lord Brougham (q.v.), the Lord Chancellor, leaked the news to the press before the other cabinet members had been informed.

The Tories under Peel (see *Lives of the Victorian Age*) took over the government, but were out again within five months. In April 1835 Melbourne unwillingly became Prime Minister

again, with a programme of moderate reforms that were continually baulked by the House of Lords. In these early years of a ministry that was to last with only a short interruption until 1841, Melbourne groped along. Out of touch with the new religious revival that was sweeping the country, he gave offence by his breezy attitude towards church affairs. The Irish question continued to trouble the government, but one of the mainstays of Melbourne's power was the support of O'Connell and his followers, who feared the return of the Tories.

Melbourne's private indiscretions proved an additional hindrance. Since his break with Caroline he had lost no opportunity for dalliance with the ladies, and in 1836 this led to a court case in which George Norton, husband of Caroline Norton, with whom Melbourne had spent a good deal of time, sued the Prime Minister for damages. Norton's case was thrown out of court, but Melbourne's reputation had not exactly been enhanced by the proceedings, despite his protestations of (probably genuine) innocence.

In 1836-7 William IV's growing hostility, interference, and stupidity hampered Melbourne greatly. He stayed on only in the fear that his resignation would lead to even greater chaos. To the Irish problem was added a rebellion in Canada and trouble over the post of Regius Professor of Divinity at Oxford.

On 20 June 1837, however, William IV died. Melbourne then found himself called on to instruct and support an attractive eighteen-year-old girl. Queen Victoria amazed everyone by her firm but modest self-confidence in her first public duties, but when she threw an inquiring glance at her Prime Minister he was quick to respond and steer her through the complexities of state affairs. He took on the role of her private secretary, tutor, and mentor, while she came increasingly to rely on him. Melbourne, at last feeling himself to be admired, valued, and happy, found a new zest for preserving his precarious government. It survived crisis after crisis. The worst came when, in 1839, radicals and Tories combined to reduce the government's majority to five in a vote on the emancipation of slaves in Jamaica. Melbourne felt forced to resign. But Victoria took a great dislike to Sir Robert Peel. She utterly rejected his suggestion that some of the Ladies of the Bedchamber, who were married to Whigs, should be replaced; Peel refused to form a government under a Queen surrounded by Whigs, and to Victoria's delight the deadlock was resolved by the return of Melbourne.

His government soldiered on for two more years. Despite continuing problems, it managed to introduce the first real step towards universal education, amended the Corn Laws to bring down the price of bread, and took further steps to placate the Irish. Under Melbourne's brother-in-law, Palmerston (see Temple, Henry John, in *Lives of the Victorian Age*), as Foreign Secretary, it also went to war in China, Afghanistan, and Persia, and narrowly avoided war with France over Syria. Nevertheless, the weakness of the government that had given Britain stability as well as much-needed reform was becoming increasingly clear.

Melbourne's own weakness was also becoming apparent. He was only just over sixty, but was clearly ageing prematurely. With the arrival of Prince Albert, Victoria's future husband, Melbourne's influence declined sharply. After the royal marriage in 1840, the fundamental differences between Albert and Melbourne became apparent, particularly on the role of the monarchy.

In May 1841 the government was defeated on the budget, and in the subsequent election the Whigs lost heavily. Melbourne had spent much of his last few months in office, in concert with Prince Albert, persuading the Queen to be more diplomatic with Peel and advising Peel, through intermediaries, on how to handle the Queen.

After a stroke on 23 October 1842, Melbourne went into semi-retirement. His last years were comparatively lonely, although he was cared for by his brother and sister-in-law. He emerged occasionally to counsel the Liberals, notably advising them to vote for the outright repeal of the Corn Laws. Melbourne died on 25 November 1848.

Lord David Cecil, *The Young Melbourne* (1939).
Lord David Cecil, *Lord M.* (1954).
L. C. Sanders (ed.), *Lord Melbourne's Papers* (1889).
P. Ziegler, *Melbourne* (1976).

Portraits: oil, three-quarter length, by J. Partridge, 1844: N.P.G.; oil on panel, three-quarter length, by E. Landseer, 1836: N.P.G.; pencil and wash, half-length, by S. F. Diez, 1841: N.P.G.; pencil, full-length, by G. Hayter, 1837: N.P.G.

Lambton, John (1792–1840), 1st Earl of Durham; radical Whig politician and Governor General of Canada.

John Lambton was born of aristocratic Whig parents in County Durham on 12 April 1792. After an education at Eton (1805–9) he entered the army, and became an M.P. in 1813. Three years later, after the loss of his first wife, he made a politically advantageous marriage with Louisa Elizabeth, eldest daughter of Lord Grey (q.v.). In parliament Lambton formed a useful link between the Whig aristocracy and the new middle-class democrat section of the party. Early making friends with Brougham (q.v.), Lambton in the main supported electoral reform. His haughtiness and uncompromising attitude, however, led to a quarrel with the more moderate Brougham in 1825 over Catholic emancipation. But despite their differences, Lambton and Brougham both served in Grey's Whig ministry of 1830.

In 1828 Lambton was created Baron Durham. His task in Grey's cabinet two years later entailed drafting in committee the detailed proposals for the Reform Bill. The work on the great Reform Bill was done speedily and thoroughly and it became law in 1832, despite the delaying tactics of the House of Lords.

Durham – 'Radical Jack' as he had early been nicknamed – was a popular champion of reform with a large public following, but his uncompromising, haughty conduct and almost doctrinaire radicalism became acutely embarrassing to his father-in-law, and a way was sought to remove him.

He was sent, therefore, on what turned out to be a futile diplomatic mission to Russia, returning in 1833. His popularity was wide throughout England, and as an agitator he was very much a thorn in the side of the Whig party, of which he was obviously eager to become the leader. That honour, however, went to William Lamb, Viscount Melbourne (q.v.), who took steps to keep Durham out of the cabinet.

Durham was again sent as Ambassador to Russia in 1835, returning in 1837. In January 1838 he was sent out in the capacity of Lord High Commissioner and Governor General to Canada.

Canada at that time comprised two provinces, Upper and Lower Canada. The majority of the population in Lower Canada was French Canadian, and the recent rebellion of these French Canadians against British rule had caused the suspension of the constitution. Durham was vested with dictatorial powers when he left England, and dealt with the matter in an altogether high-handed manner. He declared an amnesty for all except eight of the rebels, whom he summarily ordered to be transported to Bermuda and held without trial. A storm of protest broke in England, led by Brougham, his former friend, who was still smarting over his exclusion from Durham's reform committee (1830–2). An Act of Indemnity was passed by the Commons, and the eight transportees were returned to Canada. Incensed at having his authority so undermined, Durham resigned and returned to England. During the transatlantic crossing, however, his temper was somewhat mollified and he contented himself with the task of writing up his Report on the Affairs of British North America. As it turned out, this document, put before parliament on 31 January 1839, laid down the principles that determined British colonial policy for a century to come.

In 1839 Durham became chairman of the New Zealand Company, which had been started by Gibbon Wakefield. His health, however, which had always been poor, gave way completely and he died on 28 July 1840.

L. Cooper, *Radical Jack* (1959).
Sir C. P. Lucas (ed.), *Lord Durham's Report on the Affairs of British North America* (3 vols.; 1912).
S. Maccoby, *English Radicalism, 1832–1852* (1935).
S. J. Reid, *Life and Letters of the First Earl of Durham* (2 vols.; 1906).

Portrait: oil, half-length, by T. Phillips, *c.*1819: N.P.G.

Lamerie, Paul de (1688–1751), silversmith.

Paul de Lamerie was born in the Netherlands in 1688, the son of Huguenot parents who had fled from persecution in France and eventually came to England. By 1691 the family had settled in Westminster and in 1712, after completing his apprenticeship to Pierre Platel, a London goldsmith, the young Lamerie registered his own mark and established his first shop.

Most of his early work was in the conventional Queen Anne style, plain and unadorned; it is only in his few commissioned works (such as a large wine cistern for the 1st Earl Gower) that he displays the more ornamental style characteristic of French Huguenot craftsmen. By the 1730s, however, he had developed his own version of the rococo style. He was now receiving commissions from the London livery companies and from prominent merchants and politicians, although he did produce speculative work that was not commissioned but rather kept in his shop for later sale.

Characteristic of the rococo style is its use of heraldic engraving and embossed decoration, and there is evidence that William Hogarth (q.v.) was among the many skilled engravers employed by Lamerie. The native English silversmiths at first greatly resented the influence of the incoming Huguenot workers, but Lamerie's work appealed strongly to the nobility who had travelled on the continent and it became increasingly popular. He continued to produce work of a high standard and great originality up to his death in 1751, and though he left no immediate successor, the number of his imitators was a testament to his influence on the English tradition.

P. A. S. Phillips, *Paul de Lamerie: Citizen and Goldsmith of London, 1688–1751* (1935).

Landor, Walter Savage (1775–1864), poet and prose writer.

Landor was born on 30 January 1775 at Warwick, the eldest son of a retired physician who was living entirely on the income from his estates. From the very beginning of his long life he showed an ebullient and impulsive temperament and the distinctive classical style of his later literary work has sometimes been seen as a deliberate attempt by a turbulent personality to attain serenity through art.

In 1793, after a period of tutelage by a Derbyshire vicar, Landor entered Trinity College, Oxford; but the system could not hold him, and after a spectacular incident in which he fired a gun towards the room of a fellow undergraduate (the shutters, fortunately, were closed), Landor was rusticated. His father was extremely angry; Landor himself retreated to London, where in 1795 he published his first volume of poems.

From London Landor moved to South Wales, and in 1798 he published his next work, *Gebir*. This long poem was not commercially successful, but it did attract the praise of Coleridge and Southey. Though aristocratic by temperament, Landor did share with these other young writers a commitment to radical politics, and in 1808 he went to Spain to offer his help to the Spanish guerrillas in their fight against French rule. The campaign failed to achieve any significant results and Landor was back in Wales within the year. The experience did, however, provide him with material for a tragedy, *Count Julian*, which he wrote in 1810–11.

Landor's father had died in 1805, but his inheritance was much reduced by the claims of his six brothers and sisters. However, this did not prevent him from now buying the estates of Llanthony Abbey in Monmouthshire and embarking on an extravagant campaign of modernization. In 1811, at a ball in Bath, he displayed a similar impulsiveness: he saw an attractive young girl, asked her name, and within weeks had married her.

Julia Thuillier, the daughter of a local banker of Swiss descent, was only seventeen years old when she married Landor. By 1814 relations between Landor and his neighbours were so strained that Landor found it necessary to move abroad; in Jersey he quarrelled with Julia and travelled on to France alone; a reconciliation was achieved and in Como in 1818 the first of their four children was born; then, inevitably, Landor quarrelled with the local authorities, and yet another move became necessary, this time to Florence.

The years that Landor spent in Florence between 1821 and 1835 were probably the happiest of his life, and the five volumes of *Imaginary Conversations* (published 1824–9) which he wrote there certainly contain his best prose writing. In these loose, free-flowing dialogues, purporting to be conversations between famous men and women of all periods of history, Landor at last discovered the literary form to which his talents were best suited.

The idyllic existence was ended in 1835 by another violent quarrel with his wife, and Landor returned to England alone. For the next twenty-two years he lived mostly at Bath, writing some further dialogues on Greek mythical subjects and other works modelled on classical forms, but unable now to recreate the freshness and originality of his former work. Most of Landor's long works in verse have little appeal for modern readers, and he is remembered chiefly for the *Imaginary Conversations*.

Despite the length of his life Landor's own temperament allowed him little tranquillity in his old age. In 1857 he became involved in a trivial case of libel and was advised to leave England; with characteristic generosity he had by now transferred all the income from his estates to his wife and children, and it was in Florence, in a state of total dependency on the goodwill of others, that he lived the last seven years of his life. Among those who helped and visited Landor were Swinburne and Robert Browning, both of whom bore witness to the essential nobility of Landor's character despite his occasional arrogance and intemperance. Landor died in Florence on 17 September 1864, aged eighty-nine.

H. Ellis (ed.), *Imaginary Conversations and Poems* (1933).

M. Elwin, *Landor: A Replevin* (New York, 1958; rev. ed.).

G. Grigson (ed.), *Selected Poems* (1964).

C. W. and L. H. Houtchens (eds.), *The English Romantic Poets and Essayists: a Review of Research and Criticism* (New York, 1966; rev. ed.).

R. H. Super, *Landor: A Biography* (New York, 1954).

T. E. Welby and S. Wheeler (eds.), *The Complete Works: Poetry and Prose* (16 vols.; 1927–36).

S. Wheeler (ed.), *The Poems* (1937).

Portraits: oil on panel, half-length, by W. Fisher: N.P.G.; pastel, quarter-length, by R. Faulkner: N.P.G.

Lansdowne, 1st Marquis of (1737–1805), see Petty, William.

Law, John (1671–1729), Scottish financier and speculator, for a time controller general of French finance; originator of the 'Mississippi scheme'.

John Law was born in Edinburgh in April 1671, the son of a goldsmith and banker, William Law, and educated in mathematics, commerce, and political economy at Edinburgh University. At the age of twenty he moved to London, where he led the frivolous life of a gambler. After a duel in which he killed Edward 'Beau' Wilson, he was sentenced to death for murder on 20 April 1694. He was later pardoned and detained in prison, but managed to escape to Holland, where he came into contact with finance and banking operations. Law returned to Scotland at the end of 1700. Early in 1701 a pamphlet entitled *Proposals and Reasons for Constituting a Council of Trade in Scotland* was anonymously published. When it was republished in 1751, it bore Law's name. There are some doubts about the originality of the work, since certain of its ideas had been propounded earlier by the English banker William Paterson (see *Lives of the Stuart Age*).

In 1705 Law published *Money and Trade*

Considered, with a Proposal for Supplying the Nation with Money. In this treatise, he identified the prosperity of a nation with the amount of its circulating currency – wrongly, as we now know. He suggested a need for a bank issuing notes on the security of land, and explained in detail the advantages of paper money over coin. He submitted his plan to establish such a bank to the Scottish parliament, but it was rejected.

Between 1708 and 1715 Law roamed the Continent earning his living by gambling. He tried to implement his projects in Paris but was baulked in this endeavour until the death of Louis XIV in 1715. By then France had become financially exhausted by wars and was on the brink of bankruptcy. Law believed that credit and paper money would regenerate the French economy. He reappeared in Paris and submitted his proposal for a state bank to the regent, the Duke of Orleans. The council of finance opposed the proposal. The regent, however, allowed Law to found his private *Banque générale* (May 1716) and authorized it to issue paper money.

Because the value of the notes was fixed, the paper currency soon rose to a premium over the fluctuating French coinage. Law's bank rapidly became successful and its reputation increased when a decree ordered that the paper currency be accepted in payment of taxes.

Law now contrived an enterprise known as the 'Mississippi scheme'. In 1717 he acquired a monopoly of commercial privileges in Louisiana and organized the *Compagnie de la Louisiane ou d'Occident*, which he united with his bank. In order to appease the indignant parliament, the regent converted the private *Banque générale* into the *Banque royale* (1718), and its issues of notes were guaranteed by the state.

In the meantime, Law continued to enlarge his Western company. By 1719 almost all French colonial trade was controlled by Law's *Compagnie des Indes*. The gigantic programme of the company attracted speculators. By spring 1720 the stock had risen 2,000 per cent over its original value. During this boom, Law was courted by the highest dignitaries of both church and state.

In 1720 Law, a Protestant, converted to Roman Catholicism so that he could become controller-general of finance. His success, however, soon began to decline. The successful speculators started to hoard specie (coin) in exchange for their paper money. Consequently, the country became flooded with notes and prices rose astronomically. In May 1720 a decree was issued reducing the value of the bank notes by fifty per cent. Within a week Law was removed from office. The devaluation was revoked, but the 'system' had irrevocably collapsed, leaving thousands of angry investors. Law was forced to leave France.

During his short stay on the Continent he had declined the offer of Tsar Peter to administer the finances of Russia. He returned to London in October 1721. The death of the regent terminated his hopes of being recalled to France. Harassed by the demands of his French creditors, Law was afraid to leave England until 1725, when he went to Italy. He died in Venice in poverty on 21 March 1729.

In spite of the eventual bursting of the 'Mississippi Bubble', Law made significant contributions to monetary reform, and is considered by many to have been a financial genius.

E. J. Hamilton, 'Prices and Wages at Paris Under John Law's System', *Quarterly Journal of Economics*, 1937.

P. Harsin, *John Law, Oeuvres Complètes* (3 vols.; 1934).

H. M. Hyde, *John Law* (1948).

Portrait: oil, half-length, by A. S. Belle (attrib.), 1715–20: N.P.G.

Lawrence, Sir Thomas (1769–1830), portrait painter.

Lawrence was born at Bristol on 13 April 1769, the son of an innkeeper. The pencil portraits he drew of the customers at his father's inn at Devizes gained him an early reputation. From 1782 to 1786 Lawrence developed his own talents without any formal training while living with his family in Bath, and the award of a prize from the Society of Arts in 1784 confirmed his confidence in his own abilities and gave him much encouragement.

In 1786 he travelled to London, where his name was already known to Sir Joshua Reynolds and other well-known painters, and enrolled as a student at the schools of the Royal Academy. Lawrence's enjoyment of fashionable society life contributed much to the rapid enlargement of his fame, and in 1789 he was summoned to Windsor to paint the portrait of Queen Charlotte. He became an associate of the Royal Academy in 1791, proceeding to the rank of full

Academician three years later. On the death of Reynolds in 1792 he succeeded the latter as official Painter to the King. By the end of the century he had become the leading portrait painter of the age.

Lawrence's respect for Reynolds ensured that his own style of painting remained essentially within the established eighteenth-century tradition, but his dramatic treatment of his subjects reflected contemporary tendencies in all the arts towards the ideals of Romanticism. Lawrence's rapid, fluid brushstrokes emphasized the more romantic aspects of his art, and though the quality of his work as a whole is uneven, his influence over younger artists determined the dominant style of English portraiture until much later in the century. He was knighted in 1815 and after the end of the Napoleonic wars his reputation was extended throughout Europe by his many commissions to paint the political and military leaders of the victorious nations. *Pope Pius VII*, one of the portraits from this European series, is often considered to be his masterpiece.

283

On his return to England in 1820 Lawrence was elected President of the Royal Academy, a position which he held until his death. He played a significant part in the acquisition of the Elgin marbles and in the founding of the National Gallery, and his collection of old-master drawings was one of the finest ever made by an individual collector.

Lawrence's occasional attempts at painting in the classical manner and at extending the range of his art by painting historical subjects are generally considered to be failures, and his place in the history of English painting rests securely on the quality of his portraits alone. Lawrence never married, but the vitality of his paintings bears witness to his full enjoyment of the social life into which his profession gained him entrance. He died in London on 7 January 1830.

K. Garlick, *Sir Thomas Lawrence* (1954).
D. Goldring, *Regency Portrait Painter* (1951).

Works in:
Windsor Castle.
Wallace Collection, London.
National Gallery, London.
National Portrait Gallery, London.
Tate Gallery, London.
British Museum.
Royal Academy, London.

Portraits: oil, self-portrait: Royal Academy; oil, half-length, by R. Evans after a self-portrait, *c.* 1825: N.P.G.; marble bust, by E. H. Baily, 1830: N.P.G.

Le Despencer, 15th Baron (1708–81), see Dashwood, Francis.

Leicester of Holkham, Earl of (1752–1842), see Coke, Thomas William.

Lewis, Matthew (1775–1818), known as 'Monk' Lewis; novelist and dramatist.

Lewis was born in London on 9 July 1775, the eldest son of Matthew Lewis, Deputy Secretary at the War Office and the wealthy owner of Jamaican plantations. He was a precociously gifted child, very musical, and devoted to his mother. He attended Westminster School, where he distinguished himself as an actor. While he was still a schoolboy Lewis's parents separated, and he took great pains to ensure that they still communicated. In 1791 he wrote his first play, the genial comedy *The East Indian*, and the following year he paid an extended visit to Weimar, where he met Goethe and became deeply interested in German Romantic literature.

In 1794 Lewis, an excellent linguist, was appointed attaché at the British Embassy in The Hague; while there he read Mrs. Radcliffe's novels and was inspired to write his most famous work, *The Monk*. Published in 1795, the novel enjoyed considerable notoriety, since its alleged indecency provoked the Attorney General to try to have it suppressed; an expurgated second edition was swiftly issued. *The Monk* is a naïvely contrived succession of melodramatic horrors but it is nevertheless an important document for the history of taste.

Lewis was now a celebrity. In 1796 he succeeded Beckford as M.P. for Findon, and he used a £1,000-a-year allowance from his father to buy an impeccably 'Gothic' cottage at Barnes and rent elegant chambers in Albany. He saw much of the royal family, particularly the Duke of York and the Princess of Wales. Lewis was a small dapper man who talked a great deal but seems to have been universally liked. His literary output was considerable, and included twelve tragedies with titles like *Alphonso, King of Castile*, dramatic spectaculars for which he also, in many cases, wrote the music, several good translations from German, and a quantity of facile but pleasant verse. He even wrote a monodrama, *The Captive*, which is reported to have sent a Drury Lane audience 'into fits'. Lewis's greatest commercial success was the sixty-day run of *The Castle Spectre*, produced by Sheridan at Drury Lane in 1798.

At this time Lewis developed a hopeless passion for Lady Charlotte Bury, the Duke of Argyll's married daughter, and in 1798 met the still obscure Walter Scott at her Inverary house. Scott, flattered by the attentions of an established writer, helped Lewis compile *Tales of Wonder*, and in return Lewis got some of Scott's translations of Goethe published. In 1805 Lewis, still loyal to his mother, took exception to his father's latest mistress, but the quarrel must have been patched up by the time Lewis senior died in 1812, for he left his entire estate to his eldest son. Lewis promptly installed his mother in a beautiful cottage at Leatherhead.

Now the owner of large Jamaican estates, Lewis took a philanthropic interest in the conditions of his Negro slaves, and during a visit to Jamaica in 1816 stipulated firmly that they be treated humanely. One of his most attractive books is his *Journal of a West Indian Proprietor* (1834). In spring 1817 Lewis visited Byron and Shelley at their Geneva villa, and went on to Venice with Byron. Later that year, still concerned about his slaves, Lewis paid another visit to Jamaica, but during the return voyage died of yellow fever, and was buried at sea on 14 May 1818.

L. F. Peck, *A Life of Lewis* (Cambridge, Mass., 1961).

Portrait: oil, by H. W. Pickersgill: N.P.G.

Liverpool, 2nd Earl of (1770–1828), see Jenkinson, Robert Banks.

Lovat, 12th Baron (?1667–1747), see Fraser, Simon.

M

McAdam, John Loudon (1756–1836), Scottish engineer, the 'macadamizer' of roads.

McAdam was born at Ayr in 1756, the son of James McAdam, the founder of the first bank in Ayr, and Suzannah Cochrane of Waterside. While a baby he narrowly escaped death in a fire in the family house, after which the McAdams removed to Blairquhan on the Girvan, near Staton. John was sent to the parish school of Maybole, where his activities in constructing a model section of the Maybole–Ayr road presaged his future career. In 1770, on the death of his father, John went to stay in New York with a merchant uncle, where he remained until the end of the American war.

He had begun well in business, and at the end of the war was able to return to Scotland and to purchase the estate of Sauhrie, situated between Maybole and Ayr, where he stayed for the next thirteen years. He became a magistrate and Deputy Lieutenant for the county and Road Trustee, and in 1798 he was appointed agent for revictualling the navy in the western ports, and moved to Falmouth.

As Road Trustee, McAdam had acquired considerable first-hand knowledge of the condition of highways, and he recognized the urgent need for rebuilding roads that were 'dangerous to travel on, and very costly to repair'. McAdam conducted a number of experiments for road improvement, which he continued when he moved to Falmouth. He concluded that roads should be constructed of pieces of broken stone of equal size, none exceeding a weight of six ounces, and that the tracks should be raised and have a system of drainage. The thin layers of broken stone would gradually consolidate with the passage of traffic, becoming solid and durable. He recommended granite and greenstone as material for the new roads. This method of construction proved admirable for roads bearing horse-drawn traffic, and it was adopted throughout the nineteenth century, until the advent of faster, heavier motor traffic necessitated a modification whereby the stones were covered with tar to hold them in place.

In 1815 McAdam became Surveyor General of Bristol Roads, and a number of new highways were built according to his specifications. He also published *A Practical Essay on the Scientific Repair and Preservation of Roads* and *The Present State of Roadmaking* to disseminate his ideas more widely, the latter going into its fifth edition by 1820. By 1823 the 'macadamization' of highways was gaining general approval, and a House of Commons committee took evidence from McAdam; endorsing his views, parliament awarded him financial recompense for the work he had undertaken on tours of inspection. He was appointed General Surveyor of Roads in 1827 and granted a gratuity, which he accepted, though he refused a knighthood. McAdam died on 26 November 1836 while on a visit to Moffat in Dumfriesshire.

McAdam was of generous character, if outspoken, and an able writer with a genuine interest in science. He was married twice, and had four sons and three daughters by his first wife. His eldest son predeceased him, but the second became Surveyor General of Roads, and the third accepted a knighthood, and was Chief Trustee and Surveyor of Turnpike Roads.

R. Devereux, *Life of John McAdam* (1936).

Portrait: oil, full-length, by unknown artist: N.P.G.

Macdonald, Flora (1722–90), Jacobite heroine who aided Prince Charles Edward Stuart (q.v.) to escape after the defeat of Culloden.

Flora Macdonald was born in 1722, the daughter of Ranald Macdonald, farmer or tacksman of Milton, South Uist, a small island in the Outer Hebrides. Her father died when she was an infant and from the age of six she had to manage without her mother, who was taken to Skye by Hugh Macdonald of Armadale, who later married her. Flora, however, remained at Milton with her brother Angus until she was twelve, when it was decided that she should benefit from the services of the Clanranalds' family governess at Benbecula in North Uist. She accepted the change readily and developed a taste for music; she is said to have taken a particular interest in the spinet and in singing Gaelic songs. In 1739 she was invited to Monkstadt in Skye by Margaret, wife of Sir Alexander Macdonald of the Isles, and there it was arranged that she should complete her education in Edinburgh. She remained in Edinburgh until 1745, and then returned to Skye.

It was in Benbecula, on a visit to the Clanranald family, in 1745, that she met Prince Charles Edward Stuart in flight from his defeat at Culloden and agreed to help him escape. Flora later told the Duke of Argyll that her motive was simply to succour a person in distress, and she told Frederick, Prince of Wales, that she would similarly have befriended him.

Mobility during the period following the rising was severely restricted, as the English hoped to cut Charles Edward off in his flight. Boat journeys from North Uist were forbidden, but on the pretext of needing to visit her mother, Flora managed to obtain a pass to leave the island from her stepfather, Hugh Macdonald, who was in charge of the militia. This pass enabled Flora and her maidservant, Betty Burke, together with a crew of six men, to take to the water without impediment. Hugh Macdonald himself was probably under no delusion as to the identity of Betty Burke. On 27 June 1746 the party set off and, after running into gunfire from the McLeod militia at Waternish, they held out again to sea and disembarked eventually at Kilbride, near Monkstadt. Leaving the Prince to shelter in a cave, Flora went on to seek out her kinsmen. She made contact with Lady Macdonald. She also encountered John McLeod, a captain in the Hanoverian militia, and was thoroughly questioned by him in view of her recent journey at a time when all travel was prohibited. She managed, however, to keep her self-possession and to divert suspicion.

Flora confided in Lady Macdonald, who was a secret Jacobite, and together they planned the next stages of the Prince's journey. He was sent with Flora and a servant to Kingsburgh, from where he went to Portree, to take a boat on to Raasay. This was duly accomplished and in gratitude, when he departed, the Prince gave Flora a portrait of himself in a golden locket.

The secret of the escape was soon common knowledge, probably let out by the boatmen on their return to Benbecula. Flora was summoned by McLeod and, against all advice to flee to the hills, went to her mother on Skye. She was sent to imprisonment in the Tower of London.

She was set at liberty in 1749 by the Act of Indemnity and before returning to Scotland enjoyed the company of the most distinguished members of London society. Her return home was greeted by a huge banquet attended by all the principal families of Skye. On 6 November 1750 she married Allan Macdonald of Kingsburgh, accompanying him in 1774 to North Carolina. At the outbreak of the American war, her husband was appointed brigadier general and Flora accompanied him on campaigns, but on his being taken prisoner in Halifax, Virginia, in 1779, she returned to Scotland. After a hazardous voyage, she arrived at Milton, where she awaited the return of her husband, eventually settling with him at Kingsburgh. It was there that she died, on 5 March 1790, having borne him eight children.

A vast romantic legend surrounds Flora Macdonald, extending even to a false autobiography of her, which first appeared in 1870. Yet her character comes through all this as that of a resourceful and sensible person, if not as remarkable as the stories would have us believe.

A. Macdonald of Bellfinlay, *The Truth about Flora Macdonald* (1939).
A. MacGregor, *The Life of Flora Macdonald* (1882).

Macdonell, Alastair Ruadh (?1725–61), 13th Chief of Glengarry; Jacobite sympathizer who betrayed the cause to the Hanoverian government.

Macdonell was probably born in 1725, the eldest son of John Macdonell, 12th Chief of Glengarry, and a member of a branch of the Clan Macdonald. In 1738 Macdonell was sent to France, where five years later he joined Lord Drummond's regiment of Royal Scots Guards. Early in 1745 he was sent to Scotland to give information in connection with certain Jacobite disputes. The Highland chiefs dispatched him to France in May 1745 to warn Charles of the unprepared state of the Highlands, while assuring him of their allegiance to his cause. However, since Charles had set sail before Macdonell arrived in France, he decided to return immediately with a detachment of Drummond's guards; but he was captured by H.M.S. *Sheerness* on 25 November 1745 and sent to the Tower.

Macdonell was released in July 1747, and in December 1749 helped himself to the Jacobite treasure concealed in Loch Arkaig. It was then, or shortly afterwards, that he decided to betray the Jacobite cause. He introduced himself to Henry Pelham and was hired to spy on Prince Charles and his adherents, corresponding with the government under the pseudonym of 'Pickle'. It has been suggested that he bore a grudge against the Prince, for at the Battle of Culloden (1746) the Macdonell clan had been prevented from taking the post of honour on the right. Later in the battle the clan refused to join the general advance and virtually deserted the Prince's cause. Though the clan sheltered the Prince during his later wanderings, Macdonell may early have persuaded himself that he was saving his clan and the Highlands generally from much needless further suffering by frustrating Charles Edward's foolish schemes.

Macdonell was in Rome during 1750 and in France during 1751–3. While making impassioned and plausible appeals to the King and Princes, he was betraying the Jacobite cause to the British government. However, Pelham's death in 1754 blighted his main hopes of personal reward, and in addition the leading Jacobites knew perfectly well what his true character was.

In September 1754 Macdonell succeeded to the impoverished fortunes of his father on the latter's death, also becoming chief of the clan. He died without issue on

23 December 1761, and was succeeded as chief by his nephew Duncan, the son of his brother Aeneas, who had been slain at Falkirk.

Andrew Lang, *Pickle the Spy* (1897).
Henrietta Tayler, *Jacobite Epilogue* (1941).

Macpherson, James (1736–96), Scottish poet, author of the 'Ossian' fragments.

James Macpherson was born at Ruthven, Inverness-shire, on 27 October 1736, the son of an impoverished farmer. After an elementary education at home and at a local school he briefly studied divinity at the universities of Aberdeen and Edinburgh, but he left these without taking a degree and returned to his native parish to become a school-teacher.

Macpherson was already ambitious to make himself known as a poet, and in 1758 he published a long but unsuccessful heroic poem called *The Highlander*. While working as a tutor he met Dr. John Hume and Dr. Carlyle, two amateur scholars interested in ancient Scottish poetry, who were greatly impressed by the young man's reciting several Gaelic verses and showing them sixteen translated fragments that he claimed were sections of a much longer work. In 1760, with the assistance of these scholars, Macpherson published *Fragments of Ancient Poetry Collected in the Highlands of Scotland and Translated from the Gallic or Erse Language*.

Soon after publication Macpherson, financed by his new patrons, made a series of journeys to the Highlands and Western Isles to gather more material from the oral cultures of the isolated Scottish communities, and after rapidly translating his findings he published, in quick succession, *Fingal, an Ancient Epic Poem* (1762), *Temora* (1763), and *The Works of Ossian* (2 vols.; 1765). All these books, Macpherson claimed, were translations of the Gaelic works of Ossian, a legendary warrior and bard of the third century A.D.

Accusations of forgery were met by Macpherson with almost careless disdain: the original manuscripts from which he had worked did exist, he declared, but lack of both time and money prevented their publication. There was much animosity between Macpherson and Samuel Johnson, who openly accused him of dishonesty in *A Journey to the Western Isles of Scotland* (1775).

In 1764 Macpherson was appointed secretary to the Governor of West Florida, but after quarrelling with his employer he returned to England in 1766. As well as books of history and a translation of the *Iliad* (1773) Macpherson wrote many political pamphlets, and in particular was employed by Lord North's ministry after 1776 to defend its American policies. In 1780 Macpherson succeeded a relative as the London agent of a wealthy Indian nabob, a position which he found extremely profitable, and in connection with this work he entered parliament as M.P. for Camelford, Cornwall. Although he retained this seat until his death, there is no record of his ever having spoken in a debate; instead, he used much of his new wealth to build himself a mansion in his native Inverness-shire, where he died on 17 February 1769. He was survived by his four illegitimate children, and his will contained provisions for his burial in Westminster Abbey. In 1805 an official report by the Highland Society of Scotland on the authenticity of Macpherson's publications stated that the legends treated by Macpherson were still current, but that in his transcriptions he had edited, rewritten, and inserted much new material.

O. L. Jiriczek (ed.), *The Works of Ossian* (3 vols.; Heidelberg, 1940).
T. B. Saunders, *The Life and Letters of Macpherson* (1894).
E. D. Snyder, *The Celtic Revival in English Literature* (Cambridge, Mass., 1923).

D. S. Thomson, *The Gaelic Sources of Macpherson's Ossian* (1952).

Portrait: oil, half-length, after J. Reynolds: N.P.G.

Malthus, Thomas Robert (1766–1834), political economist.

Malthus was born on 14 February 1766 near Dorking, Surrey, the second son of Daniel Malthus, a scholarly man who ofted visited Oxford and had produced some useful work. Daniel Malthus was a friend and disciple of Jean-Jacques Rousseau. The boy Thomas was brought up on the lines recommended in Rousseau's educational treatise *Émile*, being taught first by his father and then by a succession of hand-picked tutors. These included Gilbert Wakefield, later a classics master at the Dissenters' academy at Warrington, which Malthus also attended for a short time.

In 1784 Thomas Malthus entered Jesus College, Cambridge, where he came under the influence of another tutor who, like Wakefield, was a Unitarian. Both these men encouraged Malthus to develop the independence of mind and uncompromising honesty that were later apparent in his work. Malthus read history, poetry, and modern languages, incidentally winning prizes in classics and mathematics. He graduated in 1791 and was made a fellow of Jesus College in 1793.

Malthus took holy orders in 1798 and held a curacy in Surrey for several years. In 1804 he married a Miss Harriet Eckersall of Bath, and in 1805 he took up a post teaching history and political economy at Haileybury, where he lived quietly for the rest of his life.

While still at Cambridge, Malthus had found himself moving away from his father's simple faith in Rousseau's concept of the 'perfectibility' of man through a basic faith in the essential goodness of human nature. He found difficulty in equating this idealistic concept with life as he saw it around him. At this time he still supported the more liberal poor-law schemes under consideration by Pitt's government, but he was already beginning to wonder if it really was in the best interests of the poor to continue the Speenhamland system of fairly generous outdoor relief. He believed in the work ethic, deploring intellectual idleness in the wealthy as much as physical laziness in the poor. He saw the ideal working man as a sturdy yeoman, hard-working and self-supporting. He was unaware as yet of the full implications of the new industrial society for a proletariat no longer protected by a patriarchal system, and felt that to allow able-bodied men outdoor relief was bad for them. The fact that the money allowed barely kept a poor family alive does not seem to have been noticed by the otherwise clear-sighted Malthus. His sheltered existence in Haileybury was, after all, remote from the realities of northern industrial life.

In 1798 Malthus published his *Essay on Population* anonymously. In it he lays down his pessimistic dictum that 'population increases in a geometrical, and subsistence only in an arithmetical, ratio'. If allowed to expand unhindered, population would eventually be checked by famine, pestilence, and war. Only 'vice', 'misery', and 'self-restraint' (the deliberate limiting of a poor man's family) prevented this from happening.

Some weaknesses exist in Malthus's presentation of the issues involved and his handling of statistical data is weak. Anxious to be empirical, he failed to take account of what later socialist philosophers saw as the attempt by capitalists to keep the poor poor. Nor were any of the 'classical' economists yet aware of the problem of unemployment that was becoming an integral part of the new capitalist society.

Between the first appearance of the *Essay on Population* and the second, expanded edition (1803) Malthus profited from an extensive tour, ranging from Scandinavia to Russia, combing the libraries and talking with fellow European economists. Malthus felt deeply about the implications of the problem as he saw it, and in this light the bitter attacks of idealists like Cobbett on him merely for having voiced what seemed at the time an unpleasant truth seem rather unfair.

The 1803 edition of the *Essay on Population* showed some modifications of opinion. Though still forced to recognize the necessity of a 'providential check', Malthus no longer saw this as an insuperable obstacle to social improvement. Reformers might even be positively helped by being aware of the natural tendencies that they had to combat. From this time onwards Malthus was fully in favour of factory acts, national schools, and everything else that might be done for the poor within the existing system. Radicals continued to attack 'Parson Malthus' (as Cobbett called him), but on the whole they failed to provide an effective answer to his arguments.

A man of diverse interests, Malthus was elected a Fellow of the Royal Society in 1819. In 1821 he became a member of the Political Economy group, where he had many bitter disputes with John Stuart Mill (see *Lives of the Victorian Age*). He was made a member of the Institut de France and became one of the five distinguished foreign associates of the French Academy of Sciences. He was also a member of a similar society in Berlin. In 1834 he became a founder member of the new Statistical Society of London.

In 1820 Malthus published the *Principles of Political Economy*, a summary of his views on economics. He spent his last years revising this and the *Essay on Population*, which entered its sixth edition in 1825. He died at Bath on 23 December 1834.

A. Flew (ed.), *An Essay on the Principle of Population* (1971).
D. V. Glass (ed.), *Introduction to Malthus* (1953).
P. M. Houses and O. D. Duncan (eds.), *The Study of Population: An Inventory and Appraisal* (Chicago, 1959).
Jane Soames Nickersen, *Homage to Malthus* (1975).
K. Smith, *The Malthusian Controversy* (1951).

Portrait: engraving, after J. Linnell, 1833: British Museum.

Mansfield, 1st Earl of (1705–93), see Murray, William.

Mar, 6th or 11th Earl of (1675–1732), see Erskine, John.

Marlborough, 1st Duke of (1650–1722), courtier, politician, diplomat, and general, see Churchill, John, in *Lives of the Stuart Age*.

Martin, John (1789–1854), known as 'Mad Martin', historical and landscape painter of large-scale canvases.

John Martin was born on 19 July 1789 at Haydon Bridge in Northumberland, the son of a fencing master. He was first apprenticed to a coach-painter and later to a china painter. At the age of seventeen he left for London, where for a period he attempted to make his living as an enamel-painter while studying architecture and perspective. *Sadak in Search of the Waters of Oblivion* was his first exhibit at the Royal Academy, in 1812. However, his first claim to fame came in 1816 when he exhibited *Joshua commanding the Sun to stand still* and received a prize from the British Institution. He had developed a style based on an enormous canvas crowded with figures set in a fantastic, threatening, apocalyptic landscape. This first success he followed with a series of canvases, including the celebrated *Fall of Babylon* (1819), *Macbeth* (1820), and

Belshazzar's Feast (1821), probably his finest work. He was able to sustain his reputation for several years with paintings such as *The Destruction of Herculaneum* (1822) and *The Seventh Plague* (1823).

The Deluge, painted in 1826, was exhibited eight years later in the Salon, where it made a strong impression on the French Romantic movement. Gustave Planché described Martin as essentially the 'poet's painter', since his work exercised such a powerful appeal on imaginative writers.

Engravings of many of Martin's works received wide circulation and Martin had very soon created quite a name for himself abroad. It was through the engravings that Louis-Philippe of France first became aware of Martin's talents and so awarded him a special medal.

Further acknowledgement came when, as a result of exhibiting *The Fall of Nineveh* in Brussels in 1833, he was elected a member of the Belgian Academy and presented with the Order of Leopold by the King of Belgium.

His spectacularly sublime works, notably *The Fall of Babylon*, were responsible for his greatest success, and the *Magazine of Fine Arts* spoke in 1833 of Martin's works as revealing a 'greatness and a grandeur'. Before his death, however, public taste had changed and Martin's faulty drawing and use of colour were the object of heavy criticism. On a small scale, his illustrations for Milton's *Paradise Lost*, although representative of his grandiloquent style, are less rough in draughtsmanship.

Martin died on 17 February 1854 on the Isle of Man, where he had been convalescing following a stroke. At the time of his death he was working on a series of three large paintings; these were subsequently exhibited and received moderate acclaim.

His interests had not been solely confined to art. He had long been concerned with projects for the improvement of London's sewerage system and many of his London water landscapes were drawn while wandering around docks and sewers. His nickname 'Mad Martin' derives from the fact that all three of his brothers were certified lunatics.

T. Balston, *John Martin, 1789–1854, His Life and Works* (1947).

Works in:
South Kensington Museum.
Tate Gallery, London.

Portrait: oil on panel, half-length, by H. Warren, c.1839: N.P.G.

Melbourne, 2nd Viscount (1779–1848), see Lamb, William.

Melcombe of Melcombe Regis, 1st Baron (1691–1762), see Dodington, George Bubb.

Mendoza, Daniel (1764–1836), pugilist, noted for his speed and scientific style of fighting.

Mendoza was born in July 1764 of Jewish parentage in the parish of Aldgate, London. He was apprenticed at thirteen to a glazier, and then had various jobs, during which he became involved in several fights, encouraged and seconded by Richard Humphries, from whom initially he learned his scientific approach to boxing. By the age of nineteen he was challenging professionals. His first bout took place in 1784 at Mile End, where he beat Harry the Coalheaver, but his fame really spread after his win over Samuel Martin, 'the Bath butcher', at Barnet racecourse on 17 April 1784, when £40,000 was wagered on the result.

Virtually a middleweight at 11st. 6lb., standing 5ft. 7in. tall, Mendoza yet beat his heaviest antagonists. His style, which caused much discussion, was neat and quick rather than forceful, and he usually got in more blows than his opponents. In 1789 he published a small volume, *The Art of Boxing*, enshrining his style – a new and successful union of the theory of sparring and the practice of boxing.

Mendoza opened a boxing academy at Capel Court in the City of London, where royal patronage ensured a stream of noble pupils. After initial mutual admiration between him and Humphries they became bitter enemies and fought three times, the first fight taking place on 9 January 1788. After twenty-nine minutes Mendoza fell, sprained a foot, and fainted; a second contest was therefore arranged for 6 May 1789 when, after a long fight, Mendoza won. His superiority was emphasized when he beat Humphries again on 29 September 1790.

During 1791 Mendoza made a sparring tour of Ireland, before taking the championship from William Warr of Bristol. Warr was not satisfied, however, and a second contest was arranged in which Mendoza took only fifteen minutes to repeat his success. However, he lost the championship in 1795 when, for 200 guineas a side, he met John Jackson (q.v.) at Hornchurch, Essex.

Mendoza's health was now failing and he had accepted this last challenge because of pressing debts. He later became the landlord of a public house in Whitechapel, acting occasionally as an officer of the Sheriff of Middlesex. In prison for debt during 1805, he subsequently defeated the young Henry Lee on 21 March 1806, after fifty-three rounds. In 1816 he published his memoirs. He made sparring tours for many years, visiting the chief towns in Britain, before his last appearance in 1820, when Mendoza, then fifty-six, was defeated by the young Tom Owen.

After a public benefit in August 1820, Mendoza was seen occasionally in the fives court. He died on 3 September 1836 in a small house in London, leaving a wife and eleven children. The first of many Jewish champion boxers, Mendoza had stimulated a revival of boxing in England.

Frank Butler, *A Short History of Boxing in Britain* (1972).
John R. Gilbert, *Famous Jewish Lives* (1970).

Metcalf, John (1717–1810), road-maker, known as 'Blind Jack of Knaresborough'.

John Metcalf was born on 15 August 1717 at Knaresborough, Yorkshire, the son of impoverished parents. At the age of six he contracted smallpox, as a result of which he became almost totally blind. His family taught him to play the fiddle, since the calling of a musician was in those days one of the few careers open to a blind man.

Jack, however, had other ideas. Even as a boy, he decided that he would live as normal a life as possible in spite of his disability, and astonished his friends by leading bird's-nesting and apple-scrumping expeditions, and also by his prowess as a swimmer and as a horseman. He thought of becoming a professional jockey, but abandoned this scheme because of his size – he was six foot two.

In 1739 he eloped with and married Dorothy Benson, on the eve of her marriage to someone else. Their association appears to have been a happy one, and it was certainly fertile: by the end of his life he had ninety great-grandchildren. His next exploit was to walk to London and back, racing on the return journey against the coach of a certain Colonel Liddel, which he beat into second place. He spent much of his time tramping along the roads of northern England, aided only by a long staff, and he appears to have memorized every step and to have been able to recall details of the roads and their exact condition decades after he traversed them.

Northern England fell under the threat of a Jacobite invasion from Scotland in 1745, and so Blind Jack decided that he would become a recruiting sergeant for George II. Accordingly, in a few days he enlisted 140 men from Knaresborough and the surrounding district and presented himself at their head to General Wade at Newcastle. In spite of his blindness, he seems to have been accepted into the army; he fought at Falkirk and at Culloden.

For the next twenty years he followed various occupations – horse-dealer, transport contractor to the army, cotton-goods wholesaler, corn and timber merchant – as well as engaging in smuggling from time to time. His other senses were highly developed and compensated for his lack of sight.

In 1765 parliament authorized the construction of a new turnpike road between Harrogate and Borough-bridge. Metcalf tendered for the con-struction of a three-mile stretch of the new road. He was well known to the master surveyor, got the contract, and completed it with great speed and efficiency. In 1766 he got a contract for the construction of a new bridge at Boroughbridge, which he completed with similar efficiency. He devoted most of his time for the next thirty years to road-building. He would do most of the surveying himself, aided only by a long staff, and direct gangs of workmen with precise instructions, often achieving feats of engineering considered impossible by less imaginative, sighted men. He built roads all over the north, altogether engineering over 180 miles of new routes. Metcalf continued building roads until 1792 when, his wife having died in 1778, he retired at the age of seventy-five to spend his remaining years farming near Wetherby. Blind Jack died on 26 April 1810, aged ninety-two.

E. A. Pratt, *A History of Inland Transportation and Communication in England* (1912).

Mill, James (1773–1836), philosopher, historian, and economist.

James Mill was born in Forfarshire, Scotland, on 6 April 1773, the eldest son of a shoemaker in the village of Northwater Bridge. His mother was determined that her son should be educated as a gentleman and not follow in his father's trade. Near to the village of Northwater Bridge was Fettercairn House, the summer residence of Sir John and Lady Stuart, and it was due to the patronage of Lady Stuart that Mill was able to go from Montrose Academy to the University of Edinburgh in 1790 to study divinity. While at the university Mill read Plato and Rousseau, and though he was licensed to preach in 1798 it was already apparent that his own ideas were developing in other directions; his first sermons were not successful and, rather than pursue a career in the church, he took a series of tutoring jobs.

In 1802 Sir John Stuart travelled south to London to take his seat in the House of Commons and Mill travelled with him. For three years he earned what money he could by contributing to periodicals, and in 1805 he became editor of the *St. James's Chronicle*; in the same year he married Harriet Burrow, and moved into a house bought by his mother-in-law. His financial position was not easy, however, as by now his mother and his brother William had died and his father was paralyzed and heavily in debt; in addition Mill himself became the father of nine children, for which rashness he later apologized to his son, John Stuart Mill (see *Lives of the Victorian Age*).

Then, in 1808, came a meeting with Jeremy Bentham (q.v.) that was to influence the entire subsequent develop-ment of Mill's life. Bentham provided him with a house near to his own at a low rent, and Mill became his close companion and the chief exponent of his Utilitarian ideas in England. Mill worked extremely hard, and in influencing his master's ideas towards philosophic radicalism he demonstrated the continuing originality of his own intellect. Mill's attempt in 1820 to establish a chrestomathic school was not successful, but his undefeated enthusiasm promoted the eventual foundation of London University five years later. Between 1816 and 1823 Mill wrote several articles on Utilitarianism for the *Encyclopaedia Britannica*. For the *Westminster Review*, established in 1823 with money provided by Bentham himself, he wrote a series of powerful essays attacking the Church and the incapacity of the governing classes.

In 1818 Mill published his *History of India*, and its success brought the financial prosperity that he had needed for so long. On the strength of this work, Mill was appointed an official of the East India Company, and by 1830 he had risen to become head of his department. Mill became increasingly friendly with David Ricardo, and it was on Ricardo's economic theories that he based his *Elements of Political Economy* (1821). Mill was also working at this time on his *magnum opus*, the *Analysis of the Phenomena of the Human Mind*, in which he atttempts to provide for Utilitarianism a psychological framework based on the doctrine of associations of David Hartley.

In August 1835 Mill was severely weakened by a haemorrhage of the lungs. But an article on Church reform written in this year for the *London Review* demonstrates his continuing intellectual vigour. Further weakened by an attack of bronchitis, he died peacefully on 23 June 1836. From the humblest of beginnings Mill had achieved success by force of character and rigid commitment to rationalist ideals. His opinions on education and government were often criticized for being doctrinaire and without historical backing, but his dogmatism and intellectual arrogance led him to disregard criticism.

A. Bain, *James Mill* (1882).

S. Catlin, *The Later Utilitarians: James Mill and J. S. Mill* (New York, 1939).

F. A. Cavanagh (ed.), *James and John Stuart Mill on Education* (1931).

J. Hamburger, *James Mill and the Art of Revolution* (New Haven, 1963).

B. Mazlish, *James and John Stuart Mill* (1975).

D. Winch (ed.), *Selected Economic Writings of James Mill* (1966).

Portrait: drawing, half-length, artist unknown: British Museum.

Montagu, John (1718–92), 4th Earl of Sandwich; statesman, First Lord of the Admiralty during the American Revolution.

John Montagu was born on 3 November 1718, the eldest son of Edward Richard Montagu, Viscount Hinchinbroke, and grandson of Edward, 3rd Earl of Sandwich, whose title he inherited at the age of eleven. He was educated at Eton and then at Trinity College, Cambridge, but did not take a degree. In July 1738 he undertook an extensive tour of the Mediterranean countries, a record of which was eventually published in 1799 with the title, *A Voyage . . . Round the Mediterranean in the Years 1738 and 1739*.

Sandwich took his seat in the House of Lords in 1739, and immediately attached himself to the Whig group led by John Russell, 4th Duke of Bedford. In December 1744 he was appointed a Lord Commissioner of the Admiralty and began to develop a real interest in naval affairs. Much of his work was done abroad and in 1746 he was sent as plenipotentiary to the Congress at Breda, where he took an important part in the negotiations that culminated in the 1748 Treaty of Aix-la-Chapelle. In February 1748 he was appointed First Lord of the Admiralty and, aided by Anson, conducted a number of investigations into abuses at naval

establishments and dockyards. Together they put through in 1749 an act regulating the discipline of the navy. Sandwich's position was relatively secure until, in 1751, the Duke of Newcastle succeeded in resolving a feud with Bedford by having Sandwich, Bedford's protégé, removed from office, thereby securing Bedford's own resignation. Sandwich then spent a number of years out of office or in minor posts until in February 1763 he was appointed First Lord of the Admiralty once more, and Secretary of State for the Northern Department. It was in the latter capacity in November 1763 that he took a leading part in the prosecution of John Wilkes (q.v.).

Some years previously Sandwich had been a friend and associate of Wilkes in the infamous Brotherhood of Medmenham (see Dashwood, Francis). Apparently in retaliation for a trick played on him by Wilkes at one of the Brotherhood's meetings, he appeared against the journalist, producing as evidence in the trial a pornographic poem that had been privately printed by Wilkes for circu-

lation amongst his friends. Moreover, Sandwich insisted on reading the verse out loud to the Lords. This may have damaged Wilkes's case, but certainly the hypocrisy of it all rebounded on Sandwich, who suffered a large measure of public opprobrium and was pilloried as 'Jemmy Twitcher' (the name being derived from a treacherous character in John Gay's *Beggar's Opera*).

In January 1768 he was appointed Postmaster General in the Duke of Grafton's ministry, and then served (1770–1) as Secretary of State for the Northern Department again. When Lord North came to power in 1771 Sandwich was for a third time appointed First Lord of the Admiralty. However, the naval department had for some time been the victim of inefficient leadership; Sandwich was left with the impossible task of trying to run an effective navy with inadequate resources and equipment. The funds that were required were continually withheld because North's administration had undertaken a programme of rigorous economy in government expenditure; thus the outbreak of the War of American Independence and the threat, in 1779, of a combined Franco-Spanish invasion served only to throw the depleted state of the British navy into sharp perspective. The sense of national shame induced by the defeats in America led the public and the government opposition to denounce North's ministry in the bitterest terms. Sandwich, whose personal unpopularity made him the ideal scapegoat, was a special target for attack. Bitterness intensified towards him after the part he played in the court martial of Admiral Keppel, a popular figure who, it seemed likely, was being made to suffer more because of his association with the opposing Rockingham Whig group than for any true misdemeanour. This case led to a serious rift between the Admiralty and the fleet and many young officers were unwilling to accept a command as long as Sandwich remained in authority.

Amid these tribulations, Sandwich's career drew to a close. After North's fall in March 1782 he more or less retired from public life. A man of many unpleasant personal characteristics, including debauchery and hypocrisy, Sandwich was always portrayed by his contemporaries in a way that tended to obscure his administrative abilities, which were not inconsiderable, given the constraints within which he had to work. Sandwich died in London on 30 April 1792.

G. R. Barnes and J. H. Owen (eds.), *The Private Papers of John, Earl of Sandwich, 1771–1782* (4 vols.; 1932–8).

G. Martelli, *Jemmy Twitcher* (1962).

Portraits: oil, half-length, after Zoffany, *c.*1774: N.P.G.; oil, three-quarter length, by J. Highmore, 1740: N.P.G.

Montagu, Lady Mary Wortley

(1689–1762), essayist and letter-writer, also distinguished as a poet, feminist, medical pioneer, traveller, and eccentric.

Lady Mary was born in London in 1689, the daughter of Evelyn Pierrepont, 5th Earl and later 1st Duke of Kingston, and Lady Mary Fielding, cousin of Henry Fielding (q.v.), the novelist. Her exact date of birth is not known, but she was baptized on 26 May 1689 at Covent Garden. Her mother died in 1694 and the girl grew up mainly in the company of her father and brother. When she was eight, her father toasted her at the Kit-Cat Club, to which she was later to be elected. She spoke French and learned Latin, and by 1710 was competent enough in the language to send a translation of Epictetus' *Encheiridion* to Bishop Burnet (see *Lives of the Stuart Age*).

Though she contributed a letter to the *Spectator* in 1714, the first of her real literary works to be published were the *Town Eclogues* (1716) which she wrote in collaboration with Gay and Pope (qq.v.). These were pirated by the notorious bookseller, Curll, and in revenge Pope is said to have administered an emetic to the offending Curll.

While in her early twenties, Lady Mary captivated the Whig M.P. Edward Wortley Montagu who paid court to her. She, however, responded with a series of well-constructed arguments putting the case against marriage. He persisted and approached her father for her hand. It was only after this consent had been withheld that Lady Mary made her own decision, and was married in 1712 by special licence.

She was at this time much in favour with the Princess of Wales, later Queen Caroline, and was often at court. There, as always, her lively tongue made her both friends and enemies. Pope had a special admiration and affection for her, which he was to celebrate in the 'Epistle to Mr. Jervas' (1717). 'Eloisa to Abelard' was also inspired by Lady Mary, but the friendship between her and Pope was later to falter, and after 1727 he made only unflattering references to her.

A son was born to the Montagus in 1713, followed five years later by a daughter (later Lady Bute). In 1715 Lady Mary narrowly escaped death from an attack of smallpox. Edward Montagu was appointed Ambassador to Constantinople in 1716, and the family's sojourn in Turkey provided the material for *Letters from the East*. The preface to these epistles was written by her friend Mary Astell, an early defender of women's rights and author of *A Serious Proposal to Ladies*.

In her readiness to respond to the life and customs of the East, Lady Mary was ahead of many of her contemporaries. She learned Turkish and took considerable interest in the practice of inoculation against smallpox, to the extent of having her own small son and later her daughter inoculated. She tried to introduce the practice in England on her return in 1718, receiving acclaim from Steele for her efforts, but failed to convince the medical profession.

Back home in England, Lady Mary resumed her place in society while her husband, M.P. for Huntingdon and later for Peterborough, seems from this time to have been principally 'devoted to making money'. The friendship with Pope, continued by letter during the time abroad, prospered, and in 1718 the Montagus took a cottage near Pope's in Twickenham. Sir Godfrey Kneller (see *Lives of the Stuart Age*) painted Lady Mary for Pope in 1719 and there is an affectionate letter from Pope to her dated 1721. However, the friendship seems to have ended the following year. There is no complete explanation of the rift, but Lady Louisa Stuart, her granddaughter, believed that Pope had made some kind of a declaration of love and had been rebuffed by Lady Mary.

Whatever the cause of the quarrel, the effects were long-lasting. In the Pope–Swift *Miscellanies* (1727) Lady Mary was lampooned in the 'Capon's Tale'. Worse was to come with the 'First Satire of the Second Book of Horace' (1732–5). Lady Mary asked one of her friends to remonstrate with Pope after this piece, but the poet disclaimed any slur. At this Lady Mary, together with Lord Hervey (q.v.), who had also been a victim of the 'Satire', responded in kind with the scurrilous 'Verses addressed to an Imitator of Horace'.

The abuse was resumed in Pope's 'Epistle to Miss Blount' (1734–5), and there are insulting references to Lady Mary in the 'Epistle to Dr. Arbuthnot' (1734–5), 'The Satires of Dr. John Donne, versified' (1735), and 'Epilogue to the Satires' (1738). Although he suspected

Lady Mary, probably mistakenly, of the authorship of *A Pop on Pope*, a retaliatory piece to the *Dunciad*, Pope is clearly the aggressor, showing throughout considerable vindictiveness.

The squabbles with Pope were, however, only a small part of Lady Mary's life. She read Fielding's *Modern Husband* for him, and he dedicated his first comedy to her. Her favour was courted by Edward Young (q.v.), who consulted her about his tragedy *The Brothers*. Nor did she neglect her own writing. In 1735 she wrote the 'Answer', a sensible and realistic reply to James Hammond's 'Elegy to a Young Lady in the Manner of Ovid', and a year later penned a spirited attack on Swift entitled 'The Dean's Provocation for writing the Lady's Dressing Room'. In 1735 she also wrote a play, *Simplicity*. 1737 saw her occupied with *The Nonsense of Common Sense*, nine essays written in answer to the paper *Common Sense*, which was at the time attacking Sir Robert Walpole's government.

In 1739 Lady Mary suddenly left England alone. There is no account of a rift with Edward Montagu, but she seems to have become infatuated with Francesco Algarotti and to have intended to live with him in Italy. When this plan miscarried, she moved restlessly over Italy and France, and settling in 1742 at Avignon. She moved in 1746 to Brescia, where she lived for a time with the young Count Ugolino Palazzi, but in 1758 she was in Venice once more. During these years she wrote to her daughter, Lady Bute, about a variety of subjects, from English literature to her impressions of Italian society. She wrote that she hoped her granddaughters would acquire some learning, but not marry. She numbered among her friends Voltaire, Montesquieu, and Sir James Denham Stuart.

Edward Montagu died in 1761, having lived the last years of his life in miserly economy, his only indulgence being Hungarian wine. Young Edward Montagu had alienated both his parents, and the Montagu fortune, amounting to £1,350,000, was left to their daughter Lady Bute.

Lady Mary's health was beginning to fail, and she survived her husband by less than a year. She died of cancer in London on 21 August 1762, and was buried in Grosvenor Chapel, South Audley Street.

Lady Mary Wortley Montagu's *Letters from the East* burst upon the literary world most dramatically. Successive editions of these and her other epistles, together with her verse, won general posthumous acclaim. Her entire correspondence numbers about 1,000 letters. They are as many-sided as the personality of their author; through them we can trace the development of a vivacious young woman into a mature blue-stocking, occasionally cynical, occasionally passionately romantic, but always eloquent, versatile, and witty.

R. Halsband (ed.), *The Nonsense of Common Sense* (1947).

R. Halsband (ed.), *The Complete Letters of Lady Mary Wortley Montagu* (3 vols.; 1965–7).

R. Halsband, *The Life of Lady Mary Wortley Montagu* (1956).

Lord Wharncliffe and W. M. Thomas (ed.), *Letters and Works* (1861).

Portrait: oil, full-length, attributed to J. B. Vanmour, *c.* 1717–18: N.P.G.

Moore, Sir John (1761–1809), lieutenant general; commander of the retreat to Corunna during the Peninsula campaign.

Moore was born in Glasgow on 13 November 1761, the son of John Moore, a doctor and minor author. In 1772 he accompanied his father on a tour through Europe in the service of the 8th Duke of Hamilton. His ambition to become a soldier was early discernible, and in 1776 he was commissioned into the 51st Regiment of Foot, becoming a captain-lieutenant in a regiment raised by Hamilton two years later. From 1778 to 1783 Moore served with this latter regiment in America.

Between 1784 and 1790, Moore held a seat in parliament as M.P. for a constituency composed of the Scottish boroughs of Lanark, Selkirk, Peebles, and Linlithgow; he took an independent line, although in most issues he supported the younger Pitt. As well as being friendly with Pitt, however, he was on good terms with Burke and the Duke of York.

In 1788 he rejoined the 51st Foot, and at the outbreak of war with France (1793) he went as a lieutenant colonel to the Mediterranean. After distinguishing himself at the siege of Calvi in Corsica in 1794 he was appointed adjutant general to Sir Charles Stuart, but owing to petty jealousy and the dislike of the newly appointed Viceroy, Sir Gilbert Elliot, he was recalled to England in 1795. Pitt soon gave him another posting, this time to the West Indies, where he once again demonstrated his remarkable abilities as a military leader.

In 1797 Abercromby, his superior in the West Indies, having been transferred to Ireland, requested Moore's services there. Moore was appointed major general and saw action during the rebellion at Vinegar Hill (1798).

In 1799 he was severely wounded during Abercromby's unsuccessful Helder expedition against the French and the Dutch, but he recovered in time to accompany Abercromby to Egypt in 1801. Here, at the Battle of Alexandria, Abercromby was killed and Moore was again wounded, but after the fall of Cairo Moore escorted the defeated French army to the coast; he later received the official gratitude of the British parliament.

Soon after his return to England in late 1801, Moore, now a full colonel, began to implement his ideas concerning discipline, drill, and manoeuvrability in a training programme for his new regiment, the 52nd, at Shorncliffe. Many of his ideas were later adapted for the training of the first police forces. Moore was knighted in 1804 and made lieutenant general in 1805. In 1806 he was appointed deputy commander in the Mediterranean, and almost immediately assumed the full command; in 1807, while on a mission to aid Gustavus IV of Sweden, he displayed great ingenuity in avoiding British commitment to Gustavus's wholly impractical plans.

On his return to England, Moore was directed to take his division to Portugal to aid resistance against the French invasion of the Peninsula. Here he served under Sir Hew Dalrymple and Sir Harry Bussard, chafing under their complete incompetence. However, after the Convention of Cintra (September 1808), the two senior officers were recalled and Moore assumed complete command, with the object of expelling French forces from Spain.

Following instructions to aid the Spanish government against the French, he advanced into Spain as far as Salamanca, where he was enthusiastically welcomed, but because of lack of money and discouraging reports about the morale of his Spanish allies, he planned to return to Portugal. After desperate pleas for aid from the Spanish government in Madrid, however, he decided to advance northward against the French army under Soult, positioned on the Carrion River; here, learning from an intercepted message that Madrid had already fallen and that Napoleon's army had cut off his line of retreat into Portugal, he realized that to save his troops he must retire as quickly as possible to Corunna.

After a forced march of 250 miles over rugged country and in winter conditions, Moore's army reached Corunna on 13 January 1809 and embarkation began. Three days later the pursuing French army arrived. In a fierce action on 16 January the French were repulsed, but Moore himself was not to share in the victory. Wounded in the early stages of the fighting, he died in the evening of the same day. His burial at dawn in the citadel at Corunna is the subject of a well-known poem by Charles Wolfe.

Moore was an extremely popular commander with his own troops, and tributes from Wellington and the French general Soult testified to his military ability. The Peninsula expedition had been, as parliament later acknowledged, a wholly impractical venture, and in these circumstances Moore's delaying of the French conquest of Spain for a whole year was a considerable achievement.

J. F. C. Fuller, *Sir John Moore's System of Training* (1925).

J. F. Maurice (ed.), *The Diary of Sir John Moore* (1904).

Carola Oman, *Sir John Moore* (1953).

Portraits: oil, half-length, by Sir T. Lawrence, *c.* 1800: N.P.G.; oil, by Sir J. Northcote: Scottish N.P.G.

Morland, George (1763–1804), popular landscape and genre painter.

George Morland was born on 26 June 1763 in London, where his father, Henry Morland, was himself a painter and also a restorer of pictures. His talent as an artist emerged early. At the age of ten he exhibited drawings at the Royal Academy and in 1777 he became his father's apprentice. Influenced by Gainsborough, Reynolds, and Stubbs, as well as by older painters, he produced his first engraving in 1780 and exhibited his first oil painting, *Hovel with Asses*, in 1781. In 1784 he was released from his apprenticeship and studied for a time at the Royal Academy schools. Now beyond parental control, Morland took openly to a life of dissipation and bohemianism. He had already produced some clandestine *galanteries* (paintings on amorous subjects) for a Drury Lane publisher. In 1786 he was to produce the series *Laetitia, A Harlot's Progress*, engraved by J. R. Smith. In the two years before that date, however, he held a one-man show in private rooms; went off to France; and took part as an amateur jockey in horse races at Margate. In July 1786 he married Anne, the sister of William Ward, an engraver with whom Morland now began a long association.

Morland's arrival upon the artistic scene coincided with or even helped to stimulate popular demand for the picturesque. From 1787 he devoted himself to the sentimental and the rustic, and was able to reach a wide public, partly through Ward's engravings of his work, but mainly because he was one of the first painters to eschew private patrons who could dictate his subject matter to him. Instead he sold through an agent, which meant that his work was more readily available, although it did not altogether free him from exploitation.

Morland's genre painting was styled closely on the seventeenth-century Dutch and Flemish painters, notably Brouwer. His pictures deal with the domestic and leisure-time aspects of country living, and among the best of them are *Industry* and *Idleness*, while the *Inside of a Stable* (1791) is a typical example of his rustic painting, revealing his great sensitivity to colouring and conception.

By 1794 Morland's powers were beginning to decline and he ran up huge debts. In 1799 he was arrested and imprisoned until 1802. He produced a large quantity of hurriedly executed and mechanical work for his creditors during his confinement, but was very ill on his release, and still in debt. He was arrested again in October 1804, and died of brain fever in prison some days later, on 29 October.

G. C. Williamson, *George Morland, His Life and Works* (1904).

See also David Thomas, *George Morland* (Arts Council exhibition catalogue; 1954).

Portraits: self-portrait, oil, quarter-length: N.P.G.; self-portrait, chalk, quarter-length: N.P.G.; pencil and chalk, half-length, by Sophia Jones, 1805: N.P.G.

Mornington, 2nd Earl of (1760–1842), see Wellesley, Richard Colley.

Murray, Lord George (1694–1760), Jacobite; lieutenant general of the Young Pretender's forces in 1745.

Lord George Murray was born on 4 October 1694 at Huntingtower, near Perth, the fifth son of John Murray, 2nd Marquis and 1st Duke of Atholl. He was educated at Perth, and spent six months at Glasgow University before going to Flanders as an ensign of the First Regiment, the Royals, in 1711. He returned to England with them in 1713 and joined his father at Dunkeld in July 1715. In the rising of that year he served with the Jacobites under his brother William, the Marquis of Tullibardine, and commanded a battalion at Sheriffmuir, subsequently escaping to the Continent on the collapse of the rebellion.

In 1719 Murray accompanied the expedition under Marischal and Tullibardine to the north-western Highlands and was wounded at the Battle of Glenshiels, but escaped, finally reaching France in 1720. He returned secretly to Scotland in 1724 while his father was negotiating a pardon for him which was granted in 1725. In 1728 Murray married and took no part in political intrigue for the next seventeen years.

In 1745 Murray was nominated Deputy Sheriff to his brother and was induced by him to join the rebellion. Murray's initial hesitation has been much debated. Some argue that after his pardon he had wanted no more to do with politics. Yet other Jacobites had always reckoned on his support, and Murray himself asserted that he would always support a cause that he thought 'just and right, as well as for the interest, good, and liberty of my country'.

Prince Charles Edward Stuart made him lieutenant general as soon as Murray entered Perth with a number of Atholl men on 26 August 1745. The Jacobites then marched south, obtaining possession of Edinburgh without opposition. Murray decided that a surprise dawn attack would defeat Cope's government troops at Prestonpans, and his judgment was vindicated by the ensuing Jacobite victory on 21 September. After this success the Jacobite army delayed for six weeks near Edinburgh, but on 30 October Charles appointed Murray and the Duke of Perth lieutenant generals for a march into England, which began the next day. Soon Carlisle was besieged, but Murray, annoyed at the prominence assigned to the Duke during the siege, resigned his command; he accepted it again later on the Duke's resignation.

After Carlisle's surrender (18 November 1745) Charles proposed the march on London. Whatever reservations Murray may have had about attacking with such a small army in the face of strong opposition were voiced plainly when they reached Derby on 4 December. On Murray's advice, they determined to retreat north until reinforced by Scottish recruits. Having led the advance, Murray now commanded the rear, and the retreat was silent, swift, and orderly.

On 18 December Cumberland (see William Augustus) came within sight of Murray's rearguard forces, the latter having been detained at Clifton. Murray, wishing to check the pursuit by the English forces by means of an early-morning surprise attack on Cumberland, was furious when Prince Charles refused his request for 1,000 men as reinforcements; instead the Prince ordered him to rejoin the main body at Penrith without any engagement. Murray disregarded the order, made the attack most successfully, and joined the Highlanders when they entered Scotland on 20 December. On 6 January 1746 he presented the Prince with a request for discretionary power to be vested in his commanders in time of emergency; the Prince declined, complaining at the attempt to limit his prerogative.

Reinforcements from the Highlands and France enabled an army of 9,000 to march from Stirling to meet the government troops under Lieutenant-General Henry Hawley at Falkirk on 17 January. Hawley's men were defeated, yet the Jacobites hesitated to pursue them. The nearness of Cumberland compelled Charles to retreat to Inverness, a move that Murray deemed most imprudent, since it was likely to discourage Jacobite support elsewhere. He offered to make a stand with 2,000 men at Atholl, but was again overruled.

During March 1746 Murray, with a picked force of 700 men, was almost successful in freeing the Atholl country from occupation by government troops, but on 31 March he was recalled to the Prince at Inverness because of the approach of Cumberland. Charles intended to await the attack at Culloden, but Murray, in total opposition, suggested a retreat to the hills to await reinforcements, since the terrain did not favour the Highland mode of attack. Failing this, he urged a night attack, but in the attempt on the eve of 15 April the rebels were unable to reach the enemy before daybreak. The Prince's original plan was then revived, but to no purpose. On 16 April the Highlanders fled before the enemy's artillery.

On 17 April Murray sent the Prince a letter of resignation from Badenoch, where he and a number of Highland chiefs were in retirement with a force of 3,000. However, on learning that Charles considered his cause lost and was determined to retire to France, Murray at first vainly entreated him to remain, and then disbanded his forces and joined the Prince on the Continent. Charles received him in Rome on 27 March 1747, but continued to harbour resentment over the tone of Murray's resignation. Thus Murray was not invited to join the other Jacobite exiles in Paris later that year. Instead, he spent the remainder of his life wandering through Germany, Silesia, Poland, and Prussia, before settling first at Emmerich and then at Medemblik in Holland. It was at Medemblik that he died thirteen years later on 2 October 1760.

Murray was probably the most able of the Jacobites. He had undoubted military ability, but was haughty and proud and had a temper that brooked no opposition and led to discord among his fellow officers.

Winifred Duke, *Lord George Murray and the Forty-Five* (1927).
John Prebble, *Culloden* (1970).
Kathleen Thomasson, *The Jacobite General* (1958).
Henrietta Tayler, *Jacobite Epilogue* (1941).

Murray, John (1778–1843), publisher.

John Murray was born on 27 November 1778 in London, the third and only surviving son of John MacMurray, the founder of the family publishing business. His father had bought the bookselling and publishing business of William Sandby at 32 Fleet Street on his retirement from service in the marines in 1768. Business was slow at first, and it was only after John Murray had taken personal control in 1803 that it became a successful and influential concern.

His father died in 1793, and until Murray came of age the firm was managed by its former senior assistant, Samuel Highley. But in 1803 Murray dissolved the partnership with Highley and proceeded to develop the business according to his own ambitions.

Murray's first action on assuming control was to buy the copyright of George Colman's play, *John Bull*. His first important publication, *The Revolutionary Plutarch*, came out in December 1803. After corresponding with Archibald Constable, an Edinburgh publisher, Murray became London agent for Constable's publications and also for *The Edinburgh Review*. His several journeys to Scotland during the completion of these arrangements were also put to the purpose of courting Anne Elliott, and in March 1807 Murray and Anne Elliott were married in Edinburgh.

In 1812 Murray moved his business premises from Fleet Street to 50 Albemarle Street. The previous year he had met Byron (q.v.), for whom he agreed to publish the first two cantos of *Childe Harold*, and he also bought the copyright of these works from R. C. Dallas. This was the beginning of a long and mutually beneficial relationship between Byron and Murray: their business partnership ended in 1822, but their personal friendship continued until Byron's death and their correspondence is one of the major literary documents of the age.

In 1813 Murray discontinued his business arrangements with Archibald Constable. This was partly due to his dissatisfaction with Constable's inefficiency, but more important, it allowed him to introduce a rival magazine to the *Edinburgh Review*, devoted to Tory rather than Whig principles. Having secured the enthusiastic support of Robert Southey and Sir Walter Scott (qq.v.), Murray had launched the first number of the *Quarterly Review* in February 1809, but until the break with Constable the magazine consistently lost money and appeared only at irregular intervals. Despite the personality of its first editor, William Gifford, whose chief characteristic was his contempt for all radicals and creative authors, the *Quarterly Review* eventually established itself as an influential literary organ for young writers, and this policy was developed further after 1824 when Gifford was succeeded as editor by John Gibson Lockhart.

Albemarle Street became one of the major literary centres of London; among the famous authors whose works he published were Jane Austen, George Crabbe, and Washington Irving. He tried to secure publication rights for Sir Walter Scott's Waverley novels, but Scott's previous commitment to his Edinburgh publishers could not be broken. The one major professional mistake that Murray made was his publication of *The Representative*, a daily newspaper that failed after only six months because of heavy losses and a financial dispute with its original sponsor, Benjamin Disraeli. In 1824 Murray was involved in the unfortunate destruction of Byron's *Memoirs*, but this was an incident in which he characteristically allowed personal loyalty to come before professional interest: the publication of these memoirs had been forbidden by Byron himself after protests from his wife, and after Byron's death in 1824 Murray agreed that they should be destroyed.

During the 1830s Murray published an increasing number of biographies (such as Croker's *Boswell*) and works of history (such as Napier's *Peninsular War*); his interest in travel books was to be continued by his son, whose own series of *Handbooks* was used as a model for the classic guidebooks of Baedeker. Murray's continuing enterprise was demonstrated by his establishment of *The Family Library*, a series of popular treatises by such writers as Scott, Southey, and Palgrave. A four-volume collected edition of Byron's poems was published in 1828, and an eight-volume edition in 1832–5, the latter including a biography of Byron by Thomas Moore.

In the autumn of 1842 Murray's health broke down, and he died on 27 June 1843. Not least among the many who had cause to be grateful to Murray were the writers whose works he published and to whom his generosity was abundant. By a combination of sound business sense, skilful opportunism, and confidence in his own literary tastes, Murray transformed a risky family venture into a publishing firm of national importance.

G. Paston, *At John Murray's* (1932).
S. Smiles, *A Publisher and his Friends* . . . (2 vols.; 1891).

Murray, William (1705–93), 1st Earl of Mansfield; Lord Chief Justice (1756–88), noted for his contribution to commercial law.

William Murray was born at the Abbey of Scone on 2 March 1705, the fourth son of David Murray, 5th Viscount Stormont. He was educated successively at Perth grammar school, at Westminster school, and at Christ Church, Oxford. It was at Oxford that he developed an interest in the classical orations of Cicero, which impressed upon him the value of reasoned argument and clear enunciation. He eventually acquired an M.A. in 1730, and was called to the bar at Lincoln's Inn, becoming a bencher in 1743.

Murray enjoyed only a moderate practice in England until, in 1737, an eloquent speech made by him to the House of Commons took him to the top of the legal profession, and on 27 November 1742 he was made a King's Counsel and Solicitor General to Lord Wilmington's government. In the House of Commons he established himself as the ablest defender of the government when in February 1744 he delivered a speech supporting the Habeas Corpus Suspension Bill in view of the threatened Jacobite insurrection. By 1747 he was the acknowledged leader of the House and earned further praise by defending the Treaty of Aix-la-Chapelle (1748) and the Regency Bill (1751). Inevitably, such a swift rise to power produced some detractors, notably William Pitt the Elder, who imputed charges of Jacobitism against Murray. These had little effect, however, since his loyalty to the Crown was obvious, despite his Jacobite family origins.

In April 1754 Murray became Attorney General to the Duke of Newcastle's administration, and his reputation as a skilful debater was severely tried as Pitt launched incessant attacks against the government. Murray had no stomach for politics and was pleased to be accepted in 1756 for the vacant post of Lord Chief Justice; at the same time he was created Baron Mansfield. Henceforward he refrained from obvious support of any administration, except that in 1761–3 of John Stuart (q.v.), Earl of Bute, although he continued as a member of the cabinet for the next fifteen years.

As Lord Chief Justice Mansfield developed an imposing personality, and in his first twelve years hardly any lawyer demurred from his judgment. Much of the real achievement of Mansfield, however, took the form of establishing new rules and regulations and codifying new forms of behaviour for a country that was being transformed from a predominantly agrarian society to an industrial one depending for its survival upon trade and commerce. The law had to reflect this change and Mansfield's wisdom in absorbing the international law of commerce into the general law of England and his establishment of procedures to deal with such features of the new industrialism as bills of exchange, bank cheques, and marine insurance went a long way in helping the country through this period.

Much better known are Mansfield's judgments in certain test cases. In 1768 he reversed the sentence of outlawry imposed on John Wilkes (q.v.) on a technicality, despite royal pressure. Although in 1770 in the debate on Wilkes's exclusion from the House of Commons he succeeded in defeating Lord Chatham's attempt to involve the House of Lords in the struggle, it looked at the time like a sign of weakness. His popularity was not increased by his attitude towards the laws of libel demonstrated in three cases between 1770 and 1784 that concerned the 'Junius' letters. Each time he concluded that the role of the jury was limited to deciding on the fact of a sale or publication of a work, the question of libel itself being a matter of law for the judge to decide. His judgment in the Somersett case of 1772 was a single momentous decision: that a slave who had escaped to England could not be forcibly removed on the grounds of his being a slave.

On 31 October 1776 he was raised to an earldom. By now the situation in the American colonies had become serious; Mansfield was a staunch advocate of coercion. In November 1779 he proposed a coalition of all parties to deal with the problem, but his advice was ignored. After this rebuff he took little further part in politics. He was known, however, to support the Roman Catholic Relief Bill of 1778, and on the outbreak of the Gordon riots of 1780 he suffered the vengeance of the mob, who sacked and burned his house in Bloomsbury Square. Subsequently Mansfield conducted the treason trial of Lord George Gordon (q.v.) with such impartiality that an acquittal resulted.

Mansfield served as Speaker in the House of Lords until ill health forced him to resign his office. He retired to his house, Caen Wood (Kenwood, recently improved for Mansfield by Robert Adam), in Highgate, London, where he died on 20 March 1793 at the age of eighty-eight.

Cecil Fifoot, *Lord Mansfield* (1936).

Portraits: oil, full-length, by J. S. Copley, 1783: N.P.G.; oil, half-length, by J. B. Van Loo: N.P.G.

N

Napier, Sir Charles James (1782–1853), general and colonial administrator, see *Lives of the Victorian Age*.

Nash, John (1752–1835), architect and town planner.

John Nash was probably the son of a prosperous Lambeth millwright, and may have served his architectural apprenticeship with Sir Robert Taylor. In about 1780 a legacy enabled him to set up his own practice, and he soon introduced the stucco house to London's streets (some still survive in Great Russell Street). By 1783, however, Nash was bankrupt, and retired to an estate in Carmarthenshire until 1793, when his friend Samuel Cockerell persuaded him to take up architecture again.

Nash resumed modestly, with such local commissions as Cardigan jail (1793) and a new west front for St. David's Cathedral, but his fortunes improved rapidly after 1795, when he went into partnership with the landscape gardener Humphrey Repton. The two men became the country's most celebrated practitioners of the fashionable picturesque style. Many wealthy landowners employed Repton to 'improve' their grounds with canals, Chinese bridges, and artful vistas, and Nash to rebuild their mansions in a style both asymmetric and eclectic – for example, East Cowes Castle, on the Isle of Wight (1798) is a vast pseudo-Gothic pile, whilst Cronkhill, in Shropshire (1802) is based on Italian provincial architecture. However, Nash's greatest tribute to the picturesque is Blaise Hamlet (1811), a group of whimsical *cottages ornés* heavy with thatched roofs, dormer windows, barge-boarded gables, and leaded lights.

Although he broke with Repton in 1802, Nash remained the darling of the nobility, and continued to design their huge mansions in Ireland, such as Rockingham (1810). At this time he met his finest patron – George, Prince Regent, the future George IV. Nash prudently cemented this new alliance by entering into a marriage of convenience, and his earliest rewards included a house in Mayfair and a sinecure at the Office of Woods and Forests (1806).

The Prince Regent owned the Royal Pavilion at Brighton, a house with an extraordinary history: originally nothing more than a substantial farmhouse, it had been turned into a Palladian villa by Henry Holland in 1787, and in 1808 it was equipped with huge Moorish-style stables by William Porden. In 1815 Nash was employed to turn the Pavilion into a fairytale Indian palace. Although preserving its Palladian symmetry, he added onion domes, minarets, and delicate pierced stone balustrades to the exterior, festooned the interior with rich Chinese and Gothic detail, and produced a masterpiece of the picturesque.

Even greater things were afoot. In 1811 Nash had won the contract to turn Marylebone Park into a public park and residential area. The winning design demonstrated Nash's genius for large-scale town planning. Within a huge horseshoe of formal terraces, the new Regent's Park was to contain a lake, a pleasure garden, an ornamental canal, and

In 1827 the King asked Nash to turn Buckingham House into a grand royal residence. But Nash was now seventy-five and his powers were failing – he hurriedly designed a palace as big as Blenheim but hopelessly muddled in concept. Buckingham Palace was completed at huge expense in 1828, but provoked such mockery that most of it was immediately pulled down (with the entrance gateway known as the Marble Arch eventually being re-erected at Cumberland Gate, Hyde Park, in 1851), and Nash was hauled before a select committee. The death of George IV in 1830 left him at the mercy of his enemies, and he was summarily dismissed. The aged architect retired to his castle at Cowes, where he died on 13 May 1835.

Nash has been accused of 'hasty, universal, slick eclecticism', and it is certainly arguable that, taken singly, not one of his buildings shows the stuff of genius. But in his breadth of vision and his grasp of the fundamentals of town planning he has few equals amongst English architects.

T. Davis, *The Architecture of John Nash* (1960).
J. Summerson, *John Nash, Architect to George IV* (1935).

Portraits: oil, by Sir T. Lawrence: Jesus College, Cambridge; wax medallion, quarter-length, by J. A. Couriguer, *c*. 1820: N.P.G.

fifty exquisite villas half-hidden by trees. Although the details were derivative, the overall concept was entirely novel. On his own initiative, the Prince Regent also asked Nash to design a 'royal mile', to be called Regent Street, connecting his residence, Carlton House, with the new park – an additional expense, which the Treasury strongly resented.

In terms of specifically architectural merit, the terraces at Regent's Park show a gradual decline from the pleasing simplicity of Park Crescent (1812) to the ornate flabbiness of Cumberland Terrace (1827) – Nash's unerring sense of the monumental was too often vitiated by weak detailing. True, his task was made harder by official parsimony: even after the accession of George IV, the Treasury contrived to cancel all the northern terraces, the pleasure gardens, and most of the villas. Similarly, owing to difficulties in buying the sites required, Regent Street assumed a rather crooked path; nevertheless, Nash extemporized bravely, managing to fit in two grand circuses and the church of All Souls, Langham Place.

Nelson, Horatio (1758–1805), 1st Viscount Nelson; admiral in the Napoleonic War; one of the greatest and most colourful naval commanders in British history.

Horatio Nelson was born on 29 September 1758 at Burnham Thorpe, Norfolk, the fifth son of the Rev. Edmund Nelson, the local rector. After a local education he became a midshipman in 1770, and early benefited from the guiding influence of his maternal uncle, Captain Maurice Suckling (Comptroller of the Navy, 1775–8). He served in two battleships commanded by Suckling himself and also a merchantman; in 1773 he was among the crew on a voyage of northern exploration; and he saw further service in the East Indies (1773–6), on a battleship escorting Gibraltar convoys (1776) and, after promotion to lieutenant in 1777, in the Caribbean.

After Suckling's death in 1778, Nelson won the patronage of Sir Peter Parker, who provided him with the decisive promotion (June 1779) to post-captain in command of the frigate *Hinchinbroke*. Thereafter he could expect steady promotion by seniority, although sea-going appointments depended upon a professional reputation.

In 1781 Nelson took command of the frigate *Albemarle* on convoys, until a direct approach to Lord Hood obtained her posting to the admiral's successful battle squadron in the West Indies. The war with France, however, ended in 1783 without giving Nelson an opportunity to distinguish himself in a serious engagement.

In the reduced peacetime navy Nelson commanded the frigate *Boreas* in the Leeward Islands (1784–7). His conduct there was marred, however, by an open dispute with the commander in chief, Sir Richard Hughes, over the interpretation of imperial trading regulations. At the behest of local commercial interests, Hughes indulged the Americans' assumption that political independence did not debar them from economic privileges in British waters. Disobeying his superior's instructions, Nelson consistently turned back such intruders, thereby jeopardizing his career. Meanwhile he had married Frances Nisbet, a widow with a small son, Josiah, with whom he settled at Burnham on half pay after their return to England.

In 1793, at the outbreak of a new war with France, he received command of the battleship *Agamemnon*, subsequently joining Hood's Mediterranean fleet operating in support of the Austrian army in northern Italy. In August Nelson was sent with dispatches to the British Ambassador in Naples, Sir William Hamilton, and exceeded his orders by remaining to assist Hamilton in cajoling troops for the allied cause out of the King of Naples. Since their combined diplomacy succeeded, Hood could not but endorse his initiative. This visit also saw the first meeting between Nelson and Hamilton's wife, Emma (q.v.).

On 22 October, sailing off Sardinia, *Agamemnon* encountered a French squadron. Before retiring Nelson severely damaged the frigate *Melpomène* and Hood acknowledged his first notable engagement by giving him charge of a frigate force, with which he made coastal raids on Corsica in order to divert attention from the main landing there. During 1794 he captured the town of Bastia with a force of marines and took part in the assault on Calvi, during which the sight of his right eye was permanently impaired by a wound received ashore.

In 1795 Nelson, under the command of the cautious Hotham, Hood's temporary successor in Corsica, took part in an action against the French fleet out of Toulon. On 12 March 1795 the *Agamemnon* overhauled *Ça Ira*, which Nelson reduced to a wreck before being recalled by Hotham to prevent him from being isolated. The *Ça Ira* and the *Censeur*, by which it was being towed, were captured next day and the French descent on Corsica was frustrated. The seventeen-strong remainder of the French fleet was encountered again by the *Agamemnon* on 6 July. Eager as ever, Nelson ran for Corsica, the British base, and Hotham brought out the fleet, coming up with the French within sight of Toulon. The *Agamemnon* was one of the few ships to get into action (13 July) before the French reached safety with the loss of one ship. Nelson's last action in the *Agamemnon* (30 May 1796) was the capture of Bonaparte's siege train, being taken by sea to Italy. By then he had become a commodore and Sir John Jervis (q.v.) commanded the fleet.

In September 1796 the strategic situation forced the withdrawal of the fleet to Lisbon. Nelson now transferred to the *Captain*, but it was in the frigate *Minerve* that he assisted the evacuation of British garrisons endangered by Britain's new enemy, Spain. Off Cartagena in December, in company with the frigate *Blanche*, Nelson brushed with two Spanish frigates and forced one, the *Sabina*, to strike her colours. Finding Cartagena deserted and learning at Gibraltar on 9 February 1797 that the Spanish fleet had passed through the straits, Nelson made for Cape St. Vincent. During the journey he was chased by two Spanish battleships, ran into the middle of the entire Spanish fleet in a fog, and escaped undetected to reach Jervis with the news of the movements of the Spaniards.

The Battle of Cape St. Vincent (14 February 1797) began as a set piece. Jervis intercepted the Spaniards, sailing his fifteen ships in line ahead to exploit a gap developing in the loose enemy formation of twenty-seven ships. The Spanish rear division endeavoured to work around the back of the British line to close the gap, to prevent which Jervis ordered his line onto a reverse course. The *Captain* was thirteenth in line, and Nelson perceived that the leading British ships would not come up in time, whereupon he took his ship out of the line to attack and delay the enemy. This was a breach of naval discipline and established tactical method, but Jervis saw his purpose and ordered the last ship in line to his aid. The unexpected move succeeded. In the mêlée four

Spaniards were taken, two by Nelson himself. His reward was the Order of the Bath (his promotion to rear-admiral had been reached by seniority on 2 February). Jervis became Earl St. Vincent.

Three months later, Nelson, frustrated by the routine duties of blockades, pressed for an expedition against the Canaries. Eventually a purely naval attack on Santa Cruz was sanctioned, and entrusted to Nelson with four battleships, three frigates, and a cutter. Surprise was lost when winds and currents hampered the landings and the operation was a costly failure; the more so since Nelson's right arm, shattered by grape shot, had to be amputated.

Having recuperated in England, he returned to Lisbon aboard *Vanguard* (April 1798) and was promptly sent into the Mediterranean to investigate rumours of military preparations in Toulon. The Admiralty believed that the projected expedition was intended for Ireland or Portugal; St. Vincent therefore dispatched ten additional battleships to join Nelson. Repairing his storm-damaged flagship in a Sardinian bay, Nelson missed the sailing of the Toulon armada on 11 May. Having to guess about the French progress as far as Malta (19 June), Nelson estimated his quarry was bound for Egypt. Alexandria was empty on his arrival there (29 June), so he returned to Sicily, failing to intercept on its indirect course the slower French fleet which put Bonaparte's army ashore near Alexandria on 1 July. New information caused Nelson's return. On 1 August he discovered Admiral Bruey's thirteen battleships in Aboukir Bay and attacked them at their moorings. The *Genereux* alone escaped. As a result, Bonaparte's army was marooned in Egypt, and the Austrians, Russians, and Turks were emboldened to enter the war. Nelson became Baron Nelson of the Nile – and the object of Lady Hamilton's ambition, when he again came to Naples.

For his part he contrived to remain there, officially discharging his orders to operate in Italian waters. King Ferdinand of Naples was persuaded to declare war, whereupon his state was immediately invaded by the French. The Neapolitan court, the Hamiltons included, withdrew in Nelson's ship to Palermo (December 1798). Nelson insisted that the restoration and security of the discredited monarchy was his fleet's prime function, leaving others to conduct the naval war without him. In June 1799 his ships were thus engaged while the French fleet from Brest was at large in the Mediterranean and uniting at Cartagena with the Spaniards out of Cadiz. In July he ignored three orders from Lord Keith, St. Vincent's successor, to deploy his ships in accordance with his commander's strategy to meet the situation. Nelson was censured by the Admiralty, but Ferdinand created him Duke of Bronte and gave him estates in Sicily.

After pursuing the French to Brest, Keith returned in January 1800, ending Nelson's brief reign as acting commander in the Mediterranean during his absence. He then gave Nelson an opportunity to recover his sense of purpose, even indulging his reputed thirst for action by detaching his flagship *Foudroyant*, with two consorts, to search for a French convoy bearing reinforcements to beleaguered Malta. On 18 February the *Foudroyant* and the *Northumberland* fought and captured the convoy's flagship. Nelson mendaciously claimed that the success followed his rejection of Keith's orders regarding the search. When Keith forbade the use of Palermo as a base – the Hamilton residence was there – Nelson shifted his flag to a transport in the harbour and sent the *Foudroyant* away. On 13 July Nelson struck his flag and accompanied

Sir William and Lady Hamilton back to England overland. The Admiralty willingly accepted his voluntary return to save the embarrassment of recalling him. A triumphal procession through Central Europe culminated in a hero's welcome in England, where his wife discovered herself completely supplanted by Lady Hamilton, who bore Nelson's daughter, Horatia, on 29 January 1801.

Having ostensibly returned for his own health's sake, Nelson sought re-employment and joined St. Vincent's Channel fleet. Meanwhile a fleet was assembling for use as a threat against the hostile 'Armed Neutrality' of Baltic states. Sir Hyde Parker, a prudent admiral, was appointed to the command with Nelson as his second, a combined leadership designed to enable the fleet to achieve its purpose by diplomacy or action. Nelson transferred to the *St. George* (February) and the fleet sailed in March. Parker wished to proceed cautiously, but yielded to Nelson's arguments for forcing the approaches to Copenhagen in order to confront the Danish fleet before those of Sweden and Russia could arrive. Nelson, in the *Elephant*, took in ten battleships to anchor opposite the line of moored ships and supporting batteries (2 April) but the Danes were not overawed by his guns or his reputation. A three-hour duel ensued, the apprehensive Parker hoisting the recall signal to give Nelson the freedom to withdraw if necessary and knowing that he would disregard it if possible. Nelson did disregard it and the Danes were hammered into surrender, after which he urged the reluctant Parker to strike at the other fleets. In fact the opportune death of the Tsar ended the alliance without further action. The unfortunate Parker was recalled and Nelson received a viscountcy and the command, but the brutal triumph over a small neutral was not generally rewarded or acclaimed.

Nelson soon gave up his profitless duty and St. Vincent, now First Lord of the Admiralty, put him in charge of a motley collection of ships guarding the southeastern coasts against invasion. Only minor operations followed, all part of the posturing that led up to the signing of the Peace of Amiens on 25 March 1802. Nelson struck his flag in April to set up house with the Hamiltons on half pay. Early in 1804 Emma gave birth to his second daughter, who died soon after.

By 1804 Nelson, in the *Victory*, was Commander in Chief, Mediterranean, having been appointed on the resumption of war in 1803. His task was to blockade the Toulon fleet, and he maintained his battleships permanently at sea by means of store-ships. To entice the French out to battle he kept a distant station, with his frigates watching inshore.

Napoleon's plan for the invasion of England depended upon a naval diversion in the West Indies to draw off British squadrons from the Channel area. Villeneuve's Toulon fleet came out on 30 March 1805, eluded Nelson's frigates, linked up with the Spanish fleet from Cadiz while Nelson was still deployed to guard the Mediterranean, and reached the Caribbean on 14 May. The British naval commanders did not react as anticipated but kept station, and the French could not co-ordinate their own movements at sea in consequence. When Villeneuve's ships re-entered Cadiz (20 August) the projected invasion had collapsed. Nelson, who had failed to hold Villeneuve at the outset, had trailed in his wake to the West Indies and arrived there on 4 June. Having forced him to leave the area earlier than planned, Nelson also failed to come up with Villeneuve on the return passage, sailing first for Cadiz and then heading back into the Atlantic. Thus he missed his quarry, who took a more northerly course and entered Ferrol. Dispirited, Nelson returned to England on shore leave.

Nelson rejoined his fleet off Cadiz on 28 September. On 19 October, in response to orders to return to the Mediterranean, Villeneuve led out the combined fleet, and Nelson held off as far as Cape Trafalgar to make sure he cleared. On 21 October 1805 Nelson attacked from windward, disposing his ships in two columns to cut the enemy line and reduce the adverse numbers of thirty-three to twenty-seven sail-of-line, a tactic for which successful precedents existed. Villeneuve, caught without sea room inshore of the British and commanding a mixed fleet further confused by a late reversal of course, lost eighteen ships after three-and-a-half hours of gunnery. Nelson lost none, but was wounded on the quarter deck of the *Victory* soon after firing commenced. He died just as it petered out. The grief shown by the lower ranks and officers who worked under him was real and ample evidence of his ability to inspire subordinates. His body was given a state funeral in St. Paul's Cathedral.

G. Bennett, *Nelson the Commander* (1972).

Ludovic Kennedy, *Nelson and his Captains* (1975).

A. T. Mahan, *The Life of Nelson* (2 vols.; 1897).

G. P. B. Naish, *Nelson's Letters to His Wife and Other Documents* (1958).

Carola Oman, *Nelson* (1947).

T. Pocock, *Nelson and His World* (1968).

T. Pocock, *A Portrait of Lord Nelson* (reprinted 1971).

T. Pocock, *Trafalgar* (1959).

O. Warner, *The Battle of the Nile* (1960).

Portraits: oil, quarter-length, by H. Fuger, 1800: N.P.G.; oil, half-length, by W. Beechey, 1800–1: N.P.G.; oil, full-length, by L. Acquarone after L. Guzzardi: N.P.G.; oil, half-length, by L. F. Abbott *c.* 1797: N.P.G.; monument, by J. Flaxman: St. Paul's Cathedral, London.

Newcastle, Duke of (1693–1768), see Pelham-Holles, Thomas.

Newcomen, Thomas (1663–1729), inventor of the first practical steam engine, see *Lives of the Stuart Age*.

Nollekens, Joseph (1737–1823), sculptor.

Joseph Nollekens was born in London on 11 August 1737, the second son of Joseph Franciscus Nollekens, an Antwerp painter. His father died in 1747 and his mother then married a man named Williams and went with her husband to Flanders. Nollekens's education was consequently neglected. Early in life he set to work to train himself as an artist; back in England, he studied for a short time at Shipley's school and then, at the age of thirteen, went as an apprentice to the studio of the sculptor Peter Scheemakers, who also came from Flanders. Nollekens was regarded by the inhabitants of Vine Street (the area around Scheemakers's London studio) as a 'civil inoffensive lad, not particularly bright'. He was, however, bright enough to win three premiums at the Society of Arts before he left Scheemakers.

By 1760 Nollekens had amassed enough money from various sources to visit Italy and go to Rome, where he stayed for ten years. In 1762 he won a prize of fifty guineas at the Society of Arts for a marble bas-relief, *Timocles conducted before Alexander*. While he was in Rome, Nollekens worked for Thomas Jenkins, repairing and making replicas of antiques for the English market. He made many friends among English collectors and later gained commissions from them.

It was during his stay in Rome that Nollekens met David Garrick, who commissioned a bust, Nollekens's maiden attempt at portraiture. The result was so good that Garrick's friend Laurence Sterne agreed to sit for a bust, which was again most successful.

Nollekens returned to England in 1770 with enough capital to be able to acquire a house at 9 Mortimer Street, London, and to set up a studio there. His reputation had already reached England, and his busts were almost as much sought after as Reynolds's portraits. In 1771 he was made an associate member of the Royal Academy and the following year became a full academician. From 1772 until 1816 he was a regular contributor to the Academy. In 1772 he married Mary Welch, a beauty by all reports, but according to J. T. Smith, she was a woman with an even more mercenary character than Nollekens himself. Money was an obsession with him, and he was prepared to adopt almost any style of sculpture to curry the favour of the public. Despite his almost legendary parsimony, however, he reckoned Reynolds and Johnson among his acquaintances and was capable of sudden freaks of generosity, especially in his latter years.

Nollekens was an exceedingly industrious artist who rose at dawn each morning to start work; few commissions that came his way were rejected. He did a considerable number of statues including some idealized ones, the most popular of which were his nude female figures of Venus: *Venus Chiding Cupid, Venus anointing her Hair,* and *Venus with the Sandal.* In his statues he was content to follow rather than create fashion, as is demonstrated in the statue of Charles Stuart in Westminster Abbey, which was finished in 1787. Here he stuck fairly closely to the neo-classical style. Occasionally, however, he produced a more original work, such as *Sir Thomas and Lady Salisbury* (1777).

Nollekens also accepted several commissions for monuments; one of his most successful smaller works of this genre was the monument to Oliver Goldsmith (q.v.), who died in 1774. The combination of simplicity and cleanness of cut endows this work with an impressive dignity. By way of comparison, Nollekens's largest and perhaps best-known monument, to three naval captains who fell under Rodney, for which he was paid 3,000 guineas in 1782, does him little credit.

Nollekens's reputation as a portrait sculptor rests on his busts. He was not an intellectual artist and this very fact accounts, to a large extent, for his success; he was able to present each sitter as he found him and create each bust separately, with no rigid formula of design. The general feeling of his busts became increasingly more natural and less ornate as he grew older. They were greatly in demand, and he counted among his sitters such celebrities as George III, the Prince and Princess of Wales, and Lord Castlereagh. He varied his style to suit the character of his sitter, from classical to quasi-rococo and baroque.

Nollekens worked with tremendous industry until February 1819, when he had a sudden paralytic attack, but recovered sufficiently to continue working in his studio for about two years. He died in London on 23 April 1823, leaving

£6,000 to his servants and assistants and over £200,000 between four of his friends.

Nollekens did not exert a dramatic influence on the work of his successors but he was indubitably the leading portrait sculptor of his day; he is without rival in the period between Roubillac and Chantrey (qq.v.). The quantity and variety of his busts are as impressive as their quality.

Nollekens was allegedly of grotesque appearance, of small stature, with an extremely large head, a short neck, and narrow shoulders. His biographer, J. T. Smith, Keeper of the Prints at the British Museum, goes so far as to portray him as habitually dirty. This malicious biography of Nollekens, *Nollekens and His Times,* by his pupil was prejudiced by Smith's angry disappointment over his legacy under Nollekens's will. He had expected thousands after long years of good service; he received only £100. Despite this bias, however, the book is still a valuable portrait of Nollekens and an even more valuable observer's guide to the London of the period.

J. T. Smith, *Nollekens and His Times,* with introduction by G. W. Stonier (1949).

Portraits: oil, half-length, by L. F. Abbott: N.P.G.; oil, quarter-length, by J. Lonsdale: N.P.G.

North, Frederick (1732–92), 2nd Earl of Guilford; statesman who, as chief minister by request of George III, was in power when the American colonies were lost.

Frederick North was born on 13 April 1732 in London, the only son of Francis, 1st Earl of Guilford, by his first wife, Lady Lucy Montagu, daughter of George, 2nd Earl of Halifax. His godfather was the Prince of Wales, so he was frequently at Leicester House as a child. He went up to Trinity College, Oxford, from Eton, matriculating in 1749. The following year he received an M.A. before travelling for three years on the Continent, returning to represent the family borough of Banbury in the Commons after the general election of April 1754. Though he inclined to Toryism, North acted at first as a follower of his kinsman, the Duke of Newcastle, who recommended his appointment as a junior lord of the Treasury in 1759.

Taking a leading part in the proceedings against Wilkes (q.v.), North retired from office with his colleagues on the formation of the Rockingham ministry in July 1765. In May of the following year, after much hesitation, he declined Rockingham's offer of the vice-treasurership of Ireland. Chatham appointed him joint Paymaster of the Forces with Cooke in 1766, and he became a member of the Privy Council the same year. North now championed George III's principles of government. Although he had refused the post in March 1767, he overcame his fear of the opposition, led by George Grenville (q.v.), and accepted the office of Chancellor of the Exchequer in October, after resigning the office of Paymaster of the Forces.

With the King's encouragement and a steady majority in the Commons, North, as Leader of the House, succeeded in having Wilkes declared incapable of sitting in parliament and in replacing him with the ministerial candidate, Colonel Luttrell. In his review of his political career on 2 March 1769 North revealed a great contempt for popularity, stating that for the last seven years he had voted for none of the popular measures.

Townshend's American tea duty was retained by a majority of one in the cabinet on 1 May 1769, a decision (confirmed in the Commons in 1770) that rendered war inevitable. In January 1770 Grafton resigned as First Lord of the Treasury, and North assumed the office on the King's

entreaties. Grenville's death in November weakened the opposition, which was now led by Chatham and Rockingham.

Between 1772 and 1774 North successfully opposed proposals for the relief of the clergy and others from subscription to the Thirty-nine Articles. In 1772 and 1773 he allowed bills for the relief of Dissenters to pass through the Commons to rejection in the Lords, and he supported the Royal Marriage Act (1772) with considerable reluctance. In the same year he appointed two committees, the reports of which resulted in an act imposing a tax on tea exported by the East India Company to North America.

Ships carrying tea under the terms of the act were raided in Boston Harbour on 16 December 1773 and their cargoes tipped overboard, in the well-known 'Boston Tea Party' incident. Retaliatory measures – the Boston Port Bill and the Massachusetts Government Bill – were passed by large majorities in March 1774. On 20 February 1775 North carried a resolution that so long as the colonies taxed themselves, with the consent of the

King and parliament, no other tax should be laid upon them. This concession, however, came too late and a skirmish at Lexington on 19 April 1775 signalled the opening of war.

The first two years of the War of American Independence ended in British failure. North, despairing of success, repeatedly asked permission to resign, a permission which King George refused.

During the 1779–80 session North succeeded in granting free trade to Ireland, and on 6 April 1780 opposed a parliamentary resolution against the influence of the crown. North's house in Downing Street, threatened by the mob during the Gordon riots, was saved only by the timely arrival of the troops. For some time North had been uneasy about the policies that circumstances and the King required him to carry out, and on at least one occasion he wrote to the King confessing that he was inclined to share the opinions of some of his opponents.

He is said to have received the news of Cornwallis's surrender at Yorktown (19 October 1781) 'as he would have taken a ball in his breast, opening his arms and exclaiming wildly, "O God! it is all over!"' On 27 February 1782 a motion against the further prosecution of the American war was carried, and on 15 March a vote of no confidence in the government was narrowly rejected. North, however, was now determined to resign in spite of the King, and made his announcement in the Commons five days later.

North afterwards described his ministry as a 'government by departments'; he felt himself to be rather the agent than the responsible adviser or minister of the King. North would not allow himself to be called the Prime Minister, maintaining, 'There is no such thing in the British Constitution.' Earlier budgets had gained him a considerable reputation, but his later financial policy was unpopular, especially because of the extravagant terms of a loan for the government in 1781.

North still had a following of nearly 200 in the House. When Fox and Shelburne quarrelled, a coalition between one of them and North was necessary to carry on the government. Eventually a coalition with Fox was effected, and the combined followers of North and Fox obstructed and defeated Shelburne's ministry twice during February 1783. Shelburne resigned and the King charged North 'with treachery and ingratitude of the blackest nature'; vainly he tried to detach him from Fox and induce him to take the Treasury again. But George could not have one without the other, and in April 1783 was compelled to appoint North and Fox joint Secretaries of State under the Duke of Portland (see Bentinck, William Henry Cavendish). This coalition was successful as a personal arrangement, but unpopular in the country. Its only important attempt at a public measure was the East India Bill, which was defeated in the Lords on 17 December 1783. The King dismissed the ministry the next day.

Subsequently, North acted with the opposition against Pitt. He supported union with Ireland (May 1785), approved the impeachment of Warren Hastings (March 1787), and opposed the repeal of the Test and Corporation Acts (1787 and 1789). But declining health soon supervened to curtail his continued presence in parliament. He became blind, and his personal following in the House diminished. He succeeded his father as 2nd Earl of Guilford on 4 August 1790, and took his seat in the Lords on 25 November; he spoke there only four times.

His last years were spent chiefly in retirement with his wife and family, to whom he was deeply attached. Horace Walpole, visiting him in 1787, testified that 'His spirits, good humour, wit, sense, drollery, are as perfect as ever.' He died of dropsy on 5 August 1792, at his house in Grosvenor Square, London, and was buried on 14 August in the family vault at All Saints Church, Wroxton, Oxfordshire. He had married Anne, daughter and heiress of George Speke of White Lackington, Somerset, in 1756; by her he had four sons and three daughters.

North had received numerous personal distinctions, including a knighthood and honorary degrees at Oxford and Cambridge. He had a quick wit, some financial ability, unfailing tact, and unquestionable debating powers, but these qualities were offset by a certain timidity or indolence that prevented him for the better part of his career from following his own judgment rather than the King's and too often rendered him indecisive in a crisis.

H. Butterfield, *George III, Lord North and the People, 1779–1800* (1949).

J. Cannon, *The Fox–North Coalition* (1969).

I. R. Christie, *The End of Lord North's Ministry, 1780–1782* (1958).

W. B. Pemberton, *Lord North* (1938).

P. D. G. Thomas, *Lord North* (1976).

A. Valentine, *Lord North* (2 vols.; Oklahoma, 1967).

J. Steven Watson, *The Reign of George III* (1960).

Portraits: pastel, half-length, by N. Dance, *c.* 1775: N.P.G.; oil, three-quarter length, by N. Dance: N.P.G.

Nottingham, 2nd Earl of (1647–1730), Tory politician, see Finch, Daniel, in *Lives of the Stuart Age.*

O'Connell, Daniel (1775–1847), Irish nationalist leader.

O'Connell was born on 6 August 1775 at Carhen House, Cahirciveen, County Kerry, the eldest son of Morgan O'Connell, gentleman. He was descended from an Irish Catholic family of ancient though minor nobility. He was adopted at an early age by the childless head of his father's family, whose estate he later inherited. Educated first at a school run by a priest at Cobh, he went on to the English College at St. Omer in 1791, as at that time Trinity College admitted no Catholics. In 1794 he entered Lincoln's Inn to study law. In London he set about the attainment of knowledge and the cultivation of polite society.

In 1798 he was called to the Irish bar. In Dublin he lived the life of a gentleman in the clubs. Having seen at first hand, in his student days, the worst excesses of the French revolution, O'Connell had a lifelong aversion to mob violence, and for this reason he spoke out so strongly against the United Irishmen that he found it prudent to leave Dublin during the 1798 rebellion. He later went on the Munster circuit. His wit, charm, and considerable legal knowledge made him extremely successful as a lawyer, and he continued on circuit for twenty-three years.

In 1802 O'Connell married a woman without fortune – his cousin Mary, the daughter of a country doctor, to whom he remained devoted all his life. She bore him seven children.

About this time O'Connell began to speak out against the unpopular Act of Union of 1800. In 1805 his name was among those on the first Catholic petition for emancipation presented to the English parliament.

Since 1793 Catholics had been allowed to vote, but this was of little value while they were still denied the right to sit in parliament. O'Connell also wanted the Catholic Church to be free to appoint its own bishops and no longer subject to the English right to veto such appointments. O'Connell's scheme was firmly supported by both priests and people, against the hierarchy of the Church. When the Pope finally spoke in favour of the veto, O'Connell turned his energies instead to the work of ridding Ireland of the Penal Code. This group of laws still debarred Catholics not only from public office, but also from education in their own university; they even curtailed the right of an eldest son to inherit his father's land undivided.

In 1813 a man called Magee, proprietor-editor of the *Dublin Evening Post* and a firm supporter of O'Connell, was sued for libel against the Viceroy, the Duke of Richmond. In speaking for his friend in court, O'Connell openly castigated both the jury, which consisted entirely of Orangemen, and the entire system of government in Ireland, and although such rash boldness gained him much local popularity, it also resulted in a heavy fine and a sentence of imprisonment for Magee.

In 1823 O'Connell formed the Catholic Association, an organization that provided practical relief for the poor and which attracted the support of both the priests and educated Catholic laymen.

The size and effectiveness of this movement both precluded its suppression and gained liberal support in England, although the English House of Lords continued to reject any bills for Catholic relief that were presented to them. In 1826 O'Connell reorganized his movement into the New Catholic Association and also formed a patriotic society known as the 'Liberators'.

In 1828 O'Connell successfully contested a by-election against Lord Fitzgerald in County Clare, and although as a Catholic he was still unable to take his seat in the English parliament, his success convinced the Prime Minister, the Duke of Wellington, of the need to make concessions. In 1829 the Catholic Emancipation Act duly appeared, and O'Connell was able to take his seat in the Commons. Finding himself in the position of holding the balance of power between the Whigs and the Tories, O'Connell made a bargain with the Whigs (known as the Lichfield House compact) by which he promised peace in Ireland in exchange for the passing of some useful reforms in Irish local government. These reforms were probably of more practical value than the immediate repeal of the 1800 Act of Union would have been, though O'Connell continued to pay lip-service to the need for repeal in order to placate his nationalist supporters.

O'Connell and his followers in the Commons (known as 'O'Connell's tail') succeeded in keeping the weak Whig administration of Lord Melbourne in office until 1841, but when it became apparent that the Whigs could do little more than the Tories to help Ireland, O'Connell decided to make the repeal of the Act of Union his chief aim and founded an association for this purpose. The sufferings of the Irish Catholic peasants ensured immediate and over-

whelming support for the new Repeal Association. Mass meetings were held throughout Ireland during the summer of 1843, and a gathering of over a million supporters was planned for 8 October at Clontarf. Tension mounted, and when British troops arrived in Dublin, supported by warships in the bay, O'Connell cancelled the meeting. He and his chief colleagues were arrested for seditious conspiracy, but were released from imprisonment in the following year after a successful appeal to the House of Lords.

O'Connell's health was now failing, and the rise of the radical Young Irelanders, of whom he declared his strong disapproval, signalled the end of his own effective political role. The potato famine of 1845, during which O'Connell tried to gain government relief, weakened the morale of the Repeal Association to the extent of making its aims clearly unattainable within O'Connell's own lifetime. He died at Genoa on 15 May 1847 while travelling to Rome in search of sunshine.

R. Dudley Edwards, *Daniel O'Connell and His Work* (1975).

D. R. Gwynn, *Daniel O'Connell* (1947, rev. ed.).

A. Macintyre, *The Liberator: Daniel O'Connell and the Irish Party, 1830–1847* (1965).

Portraits: miniature, by B. Mulrenin, 1836: N.P.G.; board, quarter-length, by G. Hayter, 1834: N.P.G.

Old Pretender, The (1688–1766), see James Francis Edward Stuart.

Orford, 1st Earl of (1676–1745), see Walpole, Sir Robert.

Orford, 4th Earl of (1717–97), see Walpole, Horace.

Ormonde, 2nd Duke of (1665–1745), Anglo-Irish aristocrat, politician, and general, see Butler, James, 2nd Duke, in *Lives of the Stuart Age*.

Owen, Robert (1771–1858), Welsh industrialist and social reformer.

Robert Owen was born on 14 May 1771 at Newtown, Montgomeryshire, the son of a small businessman. He attended local schools until the age of ten, when he left to take up an apprenticeship with a clothier. Despite his lack of formal education he was an avid reader, and his inquiring mind led him to serious doubts about the value of religion. He then took a job as an assistant in a haberdasher's shop in London, but finding the conditions unsatisfactory, he moved to Manchester. At this time the cotton trade was booming, and soon Owen was running his own workshop. On being given, at the age of nineteen, the post of superintendent of a large mill, he proceeded to display a precocious confidence in business affairs and a special skill in the delicate business of man-management. His workers were readily distinguished by their sobriety and good order, and Owen was in the forefront of technical innovations.

In 1794–5 he became manager and one of the partners of the Chorlton Twist Company in Manchester. His duties led him frequently to Glasgow where he fell in love with Anne Caroline Dale, the daughter of the proprietor of the New Lanark mills, David Dale. His attraction to Miss Dale led Owen to offer to buy the mills for £60,000, to be paid in twenty annual instalments. On 30 September 1799 Owen and Anne Dale were married, and Owen left the Chorlton mills to his partners, in order to undertake the management of the mills at New Lanark.

The population of New Lanark, swelled by the young children of the poorhouses of Edinburgh and Glasgow, lived in squalid conditions which Owen's strong social conscience prompted him to attempt to improve. He began by banning the employment of young children and introducing schooling, and then went on to the improvement of the houses themselves. A store was opened at which goods could be purchased for little more than the cost price, while the sale of alcohol was strictly regulated. Although the mills thrived commercially, many of Owen's schemes entailed considerable expense, which was not to the liking of his profit-hungry partners. Consequently, in 1813 Owen organized a new firm whose members were content with a five per cent return on their capital and sympathetic to the cause of social reform.

In *A New View of Society, or Essays on the Principle of the Formation of the Human Character*, published in 1813, Owen repudiated man's individual responsibility for his actions and suggested that environment conditions character: hence his insistence on education. Another aspect of this theory was his belief that good working conditions are essential to productivity. He also started a scheme of old-age and sickness insurance.

The word spread about his achievements at New Lanark and very soon his work acquired European significance. The village became a place of pilgrimage for social reformers, statesmen, and royal personages. The future Tsar Nicholas I personally invited Owen to supervise similar schemes in Russia, and the Tory government of Lord Liverpool declared an interest, reassured by Owen's devotion to autocratic paternalism.

By about 1817, however, Owen's work as a practical reformer had given rise to more advanced, communistic ideas. Villages of 'unity and co-operation' were to be established for workers and unemployed alike, where housing and dining were to be communal and the care and education of the children the responsibility of the community. The fruits of labour would be shared among the inhabitants of these self-contained communities. These plans were well received in influential circles and the Duke of Kent, father of Queen Victoria, promised his support. Owen also joined in the agitation for factory reform, but the bill that did get passed in 1819 was no more than a compromise measure. Although a good number of his potential supporters were alienated at a meeting in London in August 1817, when he declared himself opposed to religion, the warmth and sincerity of Owen's personality carried him through this crisis.

During the period 1817–18 Owen travelled in Europe, spreading his gospel of co-operation. On returning to England in 1819 he found that the tide had turned against him and he was condemned in the newspapers as a heretic. He therefore turned his attention back specifically to the building of his model communities. A first attempt at Orbiton, near Glasgow, failed and in 1824 he sailed for America, where he bought the

holdings of a religious sect called the Harmony Society and christened the village New Harmony. For a time life in the community was well ordered but differences arose over the form of government and the role of religion. By 1828 he had broken off all contact with the place, having lost £400,000.

Owen returned to England and withdrew from the New Lanark mills. He was no longer a flourishing capitalist but the head of a working-class movement that embraced socialism and secularism. He devoted his considerable energies to public speaking and the launching of periodicals like *The Economist* and *The Crisis*, which provided a forum for socialist discussion. In September 1832 he started the Equitable Labour Exchanges, where exchange was effected by means of labour notes. The Grand National Consolidated Trades Union, founded in 1834, was an ambitious but premature attempt to create a national, all-embracing union. He was a natural champion of the Tolpuddle Martyrs in 1834, and prominent in the early stages of the Co-operative movement as well as in the socialist congresses from 1835 to 1846. Despite enthusiasm among the working classes, determined opposition from the employers and severe repression by the government and the law courts prevented the growth of socialism at this time.

In later life Owen began to lose touch with reality. He was far more interested in his ideal, the 'New Moral World', than in the day-to-day bargaining of politics. The converts that he made were very few. He tended to regard those who differed from him as children who had suffered the misfortune of not sharing in his experience. He was unable to discuss his ideas with the intellectuals of his day because he was unreceptive of ideas other than his own. He was a capitalist who stood up for good factory conditions and humane treatment of workers, envisaging a system based on co-operation and human fellowship.

In the end all Owen's schemes came to grief and in his later years he turned to spiritualism and millennarian notions.

Further Owenite communities were started at Queenswood in Hampshire (1839–45), where Owen himself took part for three years, and at Ralahine, County Cork (1831–3). He visited America again in 1844–7 and on his return published *Revolution in Mind and Practice* (1849) and *Letters to the Human Race* (1850). Converted to spiritualism by a medium in America in 1854, he began in the same year to write a work entitled the *New Existence of Man upon Earth*. His *Autobiography* appeared in 1857–8 and he died at Newtown on 17 November 1858.

G. D. H. Cole, *The Life of Robert Owen* (1965, 3rd ed.).

M. Cole, *Robert Owen of New Lanark* (1953).

J. F. C. Harrison, *Robert Owen and the Owenites in Britain and America. The Quest for the New World* (1969).

R. Owen, *Life of Robert Owen Written by Himself* (2 vols.; 1857–8).

Portraits: chalk, quarter-length, signed 'SB', 1851: N.P.G.; oil, half-length, by W. H. Brooke, 1834: N.P.G.; water-colour, quarter-length, by A. Hervieu, 1829: N.P.G.; water-colour, half-length, by E. Morley, 1834: N.P.G.

P

Paine, Thomas (1737–1809), radical political journalist and author of *The Rights of Man.*

Thomas Paine was born on 29 January 1737 at Thetford, Norfolk, the son of Joseph Paine, a farmer and corset-maker, and educated at the local grammar school. At the age of thirteen he left school to work for his father as a corset-maker; three years later – according to his own account – he ran away to sea, but by 1758 he was back in Dover, again working as a corset-maker. The following year Paine established his own business at Sandwich and married a local girl named Mary Lambert, but in 1750 she died and his business failed.

His next attempt at a career was as an officer in the excise service: he retained this post for over ten years, and when in 1771 he married Elizabeth Ollive, the daughter of a Sussex publican, it seemed that his future was determined. Again, however, neither marriage nor work gave him permanent security. In 1774, having written a pamphlet in support of his fellow workers' claim for higher pay, Paine was dismissed from the excise service; in the same year he separated from his wife, and travelled alone to London.

In London he met Benjamin Franklin, then working as an agent for several American companies. Franklin advised Paine to travel to America. In November 1774 he arrived in Philadelphia, and gained employment as a co-editor of the *Pennsylvania Magazine.* Among Paine's early articles for this magazine were strongly-worded arguments for the abolition of slavery and the emancipation of women, and the general surge of revolutionary feeling in America undoubtedly did much to confirm his personal convictions. In April 1775 the first military engagement of the revolutionary war took place at Lexington, and Paine published in January 1776 his first major political tract, *Common Sense.* Within a few months more than half a million copies of this tract had been sold and Paine himself had moved from obscurity to national fame. His rejection of his native country appears to have been swift and complete.

Paine served as a volunteer aide-de-camp to General Greene in the subsequent war, and published a series of sixteen pamphlets under the title of *The Crisis.* The first of these pamphlets was publicly read out to the troops of George Washington, and Paine was subsequently employed in liaison between Congress and Washington's army. In 1777 he was appointed secretary to the Committee of Foreign Affairs; two years later, however, while attempting to convict a member of Congress named Silas Deane of profiteering, he was betrayed by his own impetuosity into quoting from secret documents and had then to resign his post. Famous but still poor, Paine's next employment was as clerk to the General Assembly of Pennsylvania. In 1780 he began a subscription for the relief of the underpaid American soldiers with $500 from his own salary; the following year he was employed on a mission to France to request a loan from the sympathetic French government, and the equipment and money with which he returned

contributed much to Washington's victory at Yorktown in 1783.

In 1784, after repeated petitions to Congress, Paine was given the confiscated estate of a loyalist at New Rochelle by the State of New York, and a grant of money from Pennsylvania in 1785 enabled him to retire briefly from political involvement and devote himself to scientific interests. Chief among his inventions was an iron bridge without piers, and it was to promote this bridge that in April 1787 he travelled to Paris and then to London. In the emotional climate engendered by the French Revolution Paine revived his political interests: in December 1789 he published anonymously a warning against William Pitt's threatened involvement of Britain in a war against France, and in March 1791, in response to Edmund Burke's *Reflections on the Revolution in France*, he published the first part of his most famous work, *The Rights of Man*.

Progressing from a defence of the French Revolution, Paine develops in *The Rights of Man* a theory of the

principles of government. Man, according to Paine, though by nature a benevolent and social being, is incapable of satisfying his natural wants except through the organized government of society; this government, however, should never be allowed to become an end in itself. Using the new republican governments of France and America as his examples, Paine strongly emphasized the need for a written constitution as a guarantee of the civil rights of individuals. Later critics have pointed to the naïvety of Paine's assumption that with the overthrow of established government man's noble instincts and not chaos would prevail, but many of the reforms advocated in the second part of *The Rights of Man*, published in February 1792, have proved prophetic: family allowances, relief for the aged poor, public education facilities, and a graduated income tax.

Eight editions of *The Rights of Man* were published in England within one year and copies were immediately distributed in America and France, but in May 1792 the authorities issued a summons for Paine's arrest. The trial was postponed until December, but in September he sailed for France from Dover, evading by only twenty minutes the arrival of a warrant for his arrest. Later that year Paine was tried in his absence and found guilty of seditious libel, and his book was officially suppressed.

Paine arrived in France to find that he had already been elected a member of the National Convention, but his prominence was almost immediately placed in jeopardy by his early quarrels with Marat and other revolutionary leaders concerning the terrorist policies being used against the royalists; although he applauded the deposition of Louis XVI, he objected strongly to his execution. In December 1793 Paine was arrested and imprisoned, but escaped execution. He was released in November 1794 after the fall of Danton and Robespierre.

During his imprisonment, Paine had managed to write and publish the first part of *The Age of Reason* (1794), and after his release he completed the second part (1796). The publication of this work made its author vulnerable to charges of atheism as well as sedition.

Paine spent his last months in France in increasing loneliness, but eventually managed to accumulate enough money for the return voyage to America, and in October 1802 he arrived back in Baltimore. But the odium with which he was regarded in England was now manifesting itself in America because of his opposition to Washington and the federalists. His appeals for financial aid were repeatedly ignored; he was forced to let and eventually to sell his farm at New Rochelle, and in New York succumbed to illness and drunkenness.

Despite suffering the ingratitude of the people whose independence he had helped to promote, Paine remained stubbornly committed to his first principles, and continued his attacks on church and state. The later influence of his writings is as much due to their style as to their actual content: there is little wholly original in Paine's political philosophy, and his main achievement lay in his ability to translate the abstract ideas of his period into a language that made practical sense to his fellow men.

In 1806, his health deteriorating steadily, Paine suffered a bout of apoplexy. During his last years he was cared for by Madame Bonneville, a journalist's wife he had met in Paris; she had followed him to America, and in his last will he left what little property he still possessed to her and her children. Thomas Paine lived just long enough to witness the final fruits of the French Revolution, exemplified in the tyranny of Napoleon Bonaparte; ironically, during these final years it was the despised England that acted for the cause of liberty.

Paine died in New York on 8 June 1809, and was buried on the estate at New Rochelle. In 1819 his bones were exhumed by William Cobbett (q.v.), whose intention was to give Paine an honourable burial and to promote his reputation in his native land, but after their arrival in England the bones were lost and Cobbett's plan was not fulfilled.

A. O. Aldridge, *Man of Reason: Life of Thomas Paine* (Philadelphia, Pa., 1959).
H. H. Clark (ed.), *Thomas Paine: Representative Selections* (New York, 1965).
E. Foner, *Tom Paine and Revolutionary America* (1976).
P. S. Foner (ed.), *The Complete Writings of Thomas Paine* (2 vols.; New York, 1945).
R. McKown, *Thomas Paine* (1962).

Portrait: oil, half-length, by A. Millière, after an engraving after Romney, 1793: N.P.G.

Paley, William (1743–1805), clergyman and philosophical author.

William Paley was born at Peterborough in July 1743. His father was headmaster of Giggleswick School, and Paley began his education there, subsequently going on to Christ's College, Cambridge, from which he graduated as a senior wrangler in 1763. He was appointed a fellow of Christ's College in 1766 and a tutor in 1768. The lectures that Paley delivered at Cambridge between 1768 and 1775 dealt mainly with moral and political philosophy. His sources included the works of Locke, Butler, and others. He also involved himself with religious reform, supporting in an anonymous pamphlet the retrenchment and simplification of the Thirty-Nine Articles.

In 1775 Paley was appointed rector of Musgrave, moving to Dalston the following year. In 1777 he moved again, to Appleby, where he stayed until 1782, the year in which he was appointed Archdeacon of Carlisle.

It was at Carlisle that Paley began his career as an author. In 1785 he published a collection of his lectures, *The Principles of Morals and Political Philosophy*. His ethical system, as expounded in these lectures, has a firm religious basis: 'God Almighty wills and wishes the happiness of His creatures,' and adequate incentive to virtue is provided by a system of future rewards and punishments. A belief in Christianity is fundamental to an understanding of any of Paley's writings.

Besides the *Principles*, which ran to fifteen editions during its author's lifetime, Paley wrote three other substantial works. His *Horae Paulinae* appeared in 1790; *A View of the Evidences of Christianity*, a work examining the revelation of the truth of Christian belief through natural phenomena, was published in 1795; and *Natural Theology*, his last and perhaps his most notable work, appeared in 1802.

Natural Theology, or Evidences for the Existence and Attributes of the Deity Collected from the Appearance of Nature is one of the classic statements in teleology, which seeks to trace the ultimate reason or purpose that accounts for the origin and continuing existence of things in nature. During the sixteenth and seventeenth centuries, the advance of science brought about the mechanistic conception that all things in nature, including biological organisms, had forms directly related to their functions and functioned according to the plan of an external mind, an intelligent Being who was the Creator of all things. Thus everything, including human conduct, could be explained in terms of the Creator's ultimate purpose. Paley's book, based on John Ray's *The Wisdom of God Manifested in the Works of Creation* (1691), is the crystallization of the whole system of teleology. Like all his books, it presents its arguments with sound and lucid reasoning, and it even influenced Charles Darwin, who was ultimately to demolish its doctrine.

All Paley's works are models of logical presentation, and their influence was very strong: *Evidences of Christianity* was for over a hundred years compulsory reading for a student wishing to enter Cambridge. But Paley was not an original philosopher; his historical significance is as an expositor.

Paley was politically a liberal – he wrote a pamphlet supporting the abolition of slavery in 1789 – and he was also a religious liberal. His latitudinarian views might have prevented him from rising high in the church hierarchy, but he had some influential friends, and it was through their interest that he became in his latter years a canon of St. Paul's, London (1794), and sub-dean of Lincoln and rector of Bishop-Wearmouth (1795). Paley died at Bishop-Wearmouth on 25 May 1805. His collected works were published in seven volumes in 1825.

G. W. Meadley (ed.), *Memoirs of William Paley* (1809).

Portrait: oil, three-quarter length, by G. Romney, 1789: N.P.G.

Palmerston, 3rd Viscount (1784–1865), Whig statesman; one of Britain's most outstanding foreign ministers, see Temple, Henry John, in *Lives of the Victorian Age*.

Peacock, Thomas Love (1785–1866), satirical novelist and minor poet.

Peacock was born at Weymouth in Dorset on 18 October 1785, the son of a London glass merchant. When he was three years old his father died, and his mother took him with her to Chertsey, to live with her father, a retired naval officer. He was educated at a local school and, at the age of sixteen, went to London to find a job.

His first employment was not long, however. His interest in reading took hold of him and turned him into an excellent classical scholar, who also had a wide knowledge of contemporary literature in French and Italian as well as in English. In 1804, when he was eighteen, he published at his own expense a small volume of poetry, *The Monks of St. Mark*. Two years later followed *Palmyra*, the verse of which, like most of Peacock's poetry, could well have been written sixty or seventy years earlier, having nothing in common with the work of the Romantics.

In 1807 Peacock had an abortive affair with an unidentified young woman. Three years later he moved to North Wales, where he met his future wife, Jane Gryffydh. Peacock appears to have conceived a particular affection for North Wales; it is the setting of several of his novels, as well as a verse fragment, *Sir Calidore*; and he even went so far as to learn Welsh.

In 1812, the year in which Peacock produced some sad verses entitled 'The Philosophy of Melancholy', his publisher introduced him to Shelley (q.v.), and the two men, in spite of their dissimilar temperaments, became close friends. In 1816 Shelley settled in Marlow, where Peacock was living. Their friendship and daily contact continued over the next two years. Peacock's means were modest and thus it seemed only natural that Shelley, a wealthy man, should support his friend.

By 1818, the year of Shelley's final departure for Italy, Peacock's literary activities had taken a different and more successful turn. In 1814 he had published a satirical ballad, 'Sir Proteus'. There followed three satirical novels, *Headlong Hall* (1816), *Melincourt* (1817), and *Nightmare Abbey* (1818). In 'Rhodo-daphne' (1818), the most ambitious of his poems and the only one to show any significant influence of Shelley, the verse is competent but, again cast in an old-fashioned mode, lacks vigour and relevance. Henceforward, except for a few occasional – and satirical – verses, Peacock abandoned poetry.

Headlong Hall established a peculiar and individual pattern and style that was followed by all of Peacock's novels; it owed little to any precursor and has never been successfully imitated. The novels are uniformly short, consisting chiefly of dialogue, especially over the dinner table and in the drawing room, and their plots, which deal with the more absurd aspects of love and romance, serve as vehicles for the author's true purpose, which is to parody current opinions and satirize contemporary figures. Favourite targets are Coleridge, Shelley, Byron, Southey, Sir Walter Scott, Malthus and the Malthusians, Wordsworth, and Canning. Peacock's favourite types include epicurean parsons, eccentric antiquarians, and languid noblemen. The pungency of his wit makes him entertaining and readable even when the subject of his satire is unknown to the reader.

Shelley's departure for Italy had left Peacock deprived of financial support. Aged thirty-three, he applied to and entered the service of the East India Company, and gave some thought to the question of marriage. Two unhappy emotional attachments, and an intimate acquaintance with the affairs of Shelley, his wife Harriet, and Mary Godwin (a triangle satirized in *Nightmare Abbey*) had given him no illusions about the adequacy of love as a basis for happy marriage; accordingly he wrote off a remarkably businesslike proposal to Jane Gryffydh, whom he had neither seen nor written to for ten years. She accepted him; they were married in 1819 and set up house in London, later moving out to Lower Halliford, on the Thames near Chertsey. The marriage was a happy one, even after Jane Peacock became an invalid in the 1830s. Peacock took his duties at the East India Company very seriously and eventually rose, in 1836, to be chief examiner, in which post he remained for twenty years.

His job left him little time for literary work. In 1822 he published *Maid Marian*, a fantasy on the theme of Robin Hood that had been written three years earlier. His next work, *The Misfortunes of Elphin* (1827), is a comic medieval romance, set in Wales. In 1831, with *Crotchet Castle*, Peacock returned to the satire of contemporary thought and personalities, conversation again being dominant.

After *Crotchet Castle*, Peacock was more or less fully occupied at East India House. He wrote a few book reviews, some essays, a poem or two, and a memoir of Shelley, but nothing else. However, after he retired in 1856, he returned to the satirical conversation-piece novel. *Gryll Grange*, his last work, appeared in 1860, satirizing the Victorian passion for progress as personified by the educationists and scientists who so irritated him. Peacock's remaining five years were passed in peaceful seclusion and he died, aged eighty, on 23 January 1866.

H. F. B. Brett-Smith and C. E. Jones (eds.), *The Works of Thomas Love Peacock* (10 vols.; 1924–34).

A. M. Freeman, *T. L. Peacock: A Critical Study* (1911).

D. Garnett (ed.), *The Novels of Thomas Love Peacock* (2 vols.; 1963).

J. J. Mayoux, *Un Epicurien Anglais: Thomas Love Peacock* (Paris, 1933).

C. van Doren, *The Life of T. L. Peacock* (1911).

Portraits: miniature, quarter-length, by R. Jean, c.1805: N.P.G.; millboard, head, by H. Wallis, 1858: N.P.G.

Peel, Sir Robert (1788–1850), statesman, see *Lives of the Victorian Age*.

Pelham, Henry (1696–1754), statesman; First Lord of the Treasury from 1743 to 1754.

Henry Pelham was born in 1696, the second son of Thomas, first Lord Pelham, and Lady Grace Holles, daughter of the 3rd Earl of Clare. He was educated at Westminster school and Hart Hall (later Hertford College), Oxford, but he did not take a degree. After serving briefly as a volunteer in the army, he entered parliament in 1717 as an M.P. for Seaford. His elder brother, Thomas Pelham-Holles (q.v.), the Duke of Newcastle, had inherited most of the family wealth and power and it was he who, in 1722, secured for Pelham the county seat of Sussex. On his marriage in 1726 to Lady Catherine Manners he was granted half the family estate, and henceforth was assured of an independent and substantial income.

In parliament Pelham gave consistent support to Robert Walpole (q.v.) and Townshend (see Townshend, Charles, 2nd Viscount), with both of whom he was connected by marriage. His devotion earned him consecutively one of the lordships of the Treasury (1721), the post of Secretary for War (1724), and that of Paymaster to the Forces (1730). After Walpole had lost office in 1742 Pelham still defended him stoutly and began to emerge as his most likely successor, taking office in 1743. However, his authority was by no means clear among Walpole's former supporters, and influence at court lay in the hands of John Carteret (q.v.), Earl Granville. For the next three years Pelham and his brother, the Duke of Newcastle, strove to achieve an ascendancy in the House of Commons by means of a complex system of patronage. Granville had little grasp of parliamentary tactics and this, combined with his advocacy of further aggression in the War of the Austrian Succession, led to his virtual isolation in politics. In 1746 a mass resignation by the cabinet forced a final decision. Lord Bath (see Pulteney, William) and Granville failed to form an administration, thus leaving George II with no alternative to accepting the Pelhams and their own choice of ministers, which included William Pitt the Elder (q.v.), scarcely a royal favourite.

After 1747, however, no great issues emerged and Pelham, a tolerant and peace-loving individual, was left free to concentrate on the dual policy of economizing on government expenditure at home and ensuring peace abroad. In 1748 he made some drastic staff cuts in the army and navy and in 1749 reduced the interest on the national debt to three per cent. By the provisions of the treaty of Aix-la-Chapelle (1748), Britain accepted the French proposals for peace. The death of Frederick, Prince of Wales, in 1751 wiped out the last vestige of potential opposition, and in 1752 Pelham introduced further measures for consolidating and simplifying the national debt.

The problems that occurred in the administration were largely due to the jealousy of Newcastle, who was prone to dabble dangerously in domestic affairs even though it had been agreed that his main sphere of influence lay in the field of foreign policy. In 1750 quarrels between Newcastle and Pelham over the Duke of Bedford's resignation nearly broke up the ministry, and there was a serious dispute over Newcastle's decision to reinstate the policy of subsidizing foreign princes. However, there did exist a genuine attachment between the two brothers and Newcastle was grieved at Pelham's sudden death in Piccadilly, London, on 6 March 1754.

So unassuming was the style of Pelham's administration, aided by his skilful management of House procedures, that his real value was not realized till he had gone. King George II summed it up when he exclaimed on hearing of Pelham's death: 'Now I shall have no more peace!'

S. H. Nulle, *Thomas Pelham-Holles, Duke of Newcastle: His Early Political Career, 1693–1724* (Philadelphia, Pa., 1931).
J. B. Owen, *The Rise of the Pelhams* (1957).
J. W. Wilkes, *A Whig in Power* (Chicago, Ill., 1964).

Portraits: oil, half-length, by W. Hoare, *c*.1752: N.P.G.; oil, half-length, by J. Shackleton, *c*.1752: N.P.G.

Pelham-Holles, Thomas (1693–1768), Duke of Newcastle; statesman; First Lord of the Treasury in 1754–6 and 1757–62.

Thomas Pelham-Holles was born in 1693, the elder son of Thomas, 1st Lord Pelham, and Lady Grace Holles, younger sister of John Holles, Duke of Newcastle. Educated at Westminster School and Cambridge, he added the name Holles to his own on inheriting the estates of his mother's family in 1711. In the following year he succeeded his father as Lord Pelham and by 1714, when he came of age, he was one of the wealthiest and most influential landowners in England. Having used his influence for the good of George I and the return to power of the Whigs, he was rewarded for his loyalty in 1715, with the marquisate of Clare and the dukedom of Newcastle-upon-Tyne. He was made Lord Chamberlain in 1717, and in 1718 made an excellent Whig marriage with Lady Henrietta Godolphin, granddaughter of the Duke of Marlborough. In 1724 Robert Walpole made him Secretary of State for the Southern Department in place of Lord Carteret, and he was to hold this important office for the next thirty years. Newcastle remained in power for so long because of his shrewd grasp of the realities of eighteenth-century politics. He succeeded where abler men failed.

Contemporary commentators like Horace Walpole were unanimous in their contempt for Newcastle's constant fuss-ing, incessant intrigues, and general mediocrity, and did not give him due credit for his untiring devotion to the mundane business of managing elections and his astute handling of crown patronage. What distinguished New-castle from his colleagues was the time and money he was prepared to spend on the tedious and often dirty business of borough-mongering and the distribution of posts, sinecures, and pensions. It was an unheroic task, yet it made him an indispensable manager to the adminis-trations of Sir Robert Walpole and of his younger brother Henry Pelham (q.v.). In the 1740s and 1750s Newcastle was the chief link in the patronage system and the main channel through which preferments flowed.

In his official capacity as Secretary of State, Newcastle was conscientious and industrious but far too concerned with the minutiae of daily life ever to formulate a coherent policy. He was jealous of men of superior ability like Pitt, and was anxious to prove his leadership qualities. His chance came in March 1754, with the death of his brother, Henry Pelham.

In the ensuing scramble for power Newcastle outmanoeuvred all his rivals to secure the post of First Lord of the Treasury. George II had little respect for him but was familiar with his methods. There could, however, be little hope of an effective ministry unless Newcastle could appoint a first-rate minister to control the Commons while he was attending to business in the Lords. The two most gifted parliamentarians were Henry Fox and William Pitt. Fox was unable to come to terms with Newcastle, and Pitt was unacceptable to George II, so a compro-mise was found in Sir Thomas Robinson, a political nonentity who effectively forfeited any power that Newcastle ever had in the Commons. By 1754 Britain was

drifting into war with France; in order to stave off criticism Newcastle appointed Fox as Secretary of State and Leader of the Commons, but made the tactical error of excluding Pitt, who proceeded to denounce the government in several memorable speeches. War was finally declared in May 1756, but the half-hearted approach of the Newcastle administration incensed the public, who rallied round Pitt. Fox deserted the ministry and although Newcastle still commanded a majority in the Commons, he too resigned in October 1756.

The Devonshire administration proved equally incapable of coping with the crisis, however, and in June 1757 George II reluctantly acceded to a joint Pitt–Newcastle administration. Although Newcastle was once more the premier, it was Pitt who was responsible for all the major decisions. Newcastle used his influence in the City of London to finance Pitt's world-wide campaigns, but grew increasingly concerned at the spiralling cost of the war. Pitt, anxious to expand the war by attacking Spain, could not accept any restrictions and resigned in October 1761. By now George III had begun to exert his influence in govern-ment, and installed his favourite, the Earl of Bute (see Stuart, John), as head of the ministry. Newcastle continued in office but his influence had been severely reduced. He resigned in May 1762 but still entertained hopes of returning to power in alliance with Pitt or with the support of the younger Whigs, who resented the ascendancy of Bute. Circumstances, however, had changed with the advent of a new monarch, and Newcastle was unable to rally the support of his former allies. The last five years of his life were spent mainly in opposition, although for a few months in 1765 he became Lord Privy Seal. To his credit he left office considerably less wealthy than when he first entered it, and although he lacked statesmanship, he performed a necessary role in Whig politics. He died in London on 17 November 1768.

Reed Browning, *The Duke of Newcastle* (New Haven, Conn., 1975).

Sir L. Namier, *The Structure of Politics at the Accession of George III* (1957, 2nd ed.).

S. H. Nulle, *Thomas Pelham-Holles, Duke of Newcastle: His Early Political Career, 1693–1724* (Philadelphia, Pa., 1931).

J. B. Owen, *The Rise of the Pelhams* (1957).

J. W. Wilkes, *A Whig in Power* (Chicago, Ill., 1964).

B. Williams, *Carteret and Newcastle, a Contrast in Contemporaries* (1943).

Portraits: chalk, half-length, by W. Hoare: N.P.G.; oil, three-quarter length, by G. Kneller, *c.* 1721 (painting includes Sir Henry Clinton, 7th Earl of Lincoln): N.P.G.

Pepusch, John Christopher (1667–1752), original name Johann Christoph Pepusch, German-born musician, antiquarian, theorist, and teacher.

Pepusch was born in Berlin in 1667, the son of a Protestant pastor. After studying musical theory and the organ he had by the early age of fourteen earned himself a position at the Prussian court, teaching Prince Frederick William. During the six years he spent at court he continued his own studies. In 1687 he went briefly to Holland, and a year later made his way to England.

His first post was as viola player at Drury Lane, where in 1700 he took over the orchestral director's place at the harpsichord. From 1707 he revised and produced operas, adding to them some of his own music. He composed sonatas, songs, and chamber music, and one of his large-scale efforts, consisting of cantatas in the Italian manner, was performed but achieved very little success.

In 1712 Pepusch was appointed musical director to the Duke of Chandos, a post that he held for some seven years, until he was succeeded by his more famous countryman, Handel. After 1711 Handel came to dominate the musical stage, and Pepusch's more artificial and elaborate style did not please public taste. Pepusch recognized Handel's superiority somewhat grudgingly, deeming him 'a good practical musician'. Yet he did not give up his own composing for some time. His *Venus and Adonis* and *Apollo and Daphne* were produced in 1715, followed in the next year by *The Death of Dido*. His *Union of the Sister Arts* (1723), an entertainment for St. Cecilia's Day, achieved some success, but it was his collaboration with John Gay on *The Beggar's Opera* (1728), the first of the so-called 'ballad operas', that really caught public fancy. For this work, Pepusch skilfully arranged Gay's words around popular tunes of the day, adding a little of his own music for good measure. The result was a great success and was followed by others of the same type: *Polly* (1729) and *The Wedding* (1734). Beside his theatre music stand some quite pleasant sonatas and concertos. The church anthem 'Rejoice in the Lord, O Ye Righteous' is also his work.

Pepusch's fame, however, derives from his skill as a teacher and musicologist rather than as a composer. He became an acknowledged authority on theory, receiving a doctorate in music from Oxford University in 1714. His great love was for old music, especially the music of ancient Greece and Rome and of the Renaissance. Preserving ancient traditions for posterity, he amassed over the years a huge library of scores and music books, part of which is now in the British Museum.

Hand in hand with this love of old music went an aptitude for teaching. In 1710 Pepusch had established the Academy for the Practice of Ancient Music, and was its director for many years. One of his pupils during this period was William Boyce (q.v.) and it can hardly be doubted that Pepusch's influence on Boyce induced the latter to set about the task of compiling his *Cathedral Music*.

The Academy flourished until 1734, when the withdrawal of the choirboys caused it to languish for lack of sopranos. (No women were allowed, even in the audience.) To remedy this deficiency, musical instruction was offered at considerably reduced fees for children. Such was Pepusch's fame as a musical instructor that parents eagerly responded to his generous offer.

In June 1745 he became a Fellow of the Royal Society and presented a number of papers there, notably one on the modes of ancient Greek music. In 1737 Pepusch accepted the post of resident organist at the Charterhouse, and in his later years he became something of a recluse, seeing only old friends and pupils. He died on 20 July 1752, aged eighty-five, and was buried in the chapel at the Charterhouse.

A. B. Berger, 'The Beggar's Opera, the Burlesque and Italian Opera', *Music and Letters*, 17 (1936).
C. W. Hughes, 'J. C. Pepusch', *The Musical Quarterly*, 31 (1945).

Portrait: oil, three-quarter length, by T. Hudson (?): N.P.G.

Perceval, Spencer (1762–1812), statesman; the only British Prime Minister to have been assassinated.

Spencer Perceval was born in London on 1 November 1762, the second son of the 2nd Earl of Egmont. Educated at Harrow and at Trinity College, Cambridge, he was called to the bar at Lincoln's Inn in 1786. His marriage in 1790 to Jane Spencer-Wilson resulted in six sons and six daughters, and the need to support this ever-growing family made him extremely industrious. Two cases in particular – the prosecutions of Tom Paine (q.v.) in 1792 and of Horne Tooke (q.v.) in 1794 – drew attention to Perceval's formidable powers of oratory.

In 1796 he entered parliament as member for Northampton and quickly identified himself with the policies of William Pitt the Younger. On the formation of the Addington administration in 1801 he was appointed Solicitor General, and from 1802 till Pitt's death in 1806 he was Attorney General.

By this time Perceval had built up a solid reputation as both lawyer and politician. He was a devout Anglican and remained aloof from all the bribery and corruption associated with public figures of the day. His rise to prominence had been achieved by a combination of steady, plodding industry and a wholesale adherence to the constitution and the fundamental correctness, as he saw it, of the struggle against Napoleon. In common with the established ruling *élite* and with George III in particular, he opposed any moves towards Catholic emancipation, and it was his speech on this topic in 1807 that dealt the death blow to Grenville's Ministry of All the Talents. With the formation of the Portland administration Perceval was appointed Chancellor of the Exchequer and Chancellor of the Duchy of Lancaster. In this capacity he proved himself a master of parliamentary technique, and on the fall of the Portland government in 1809 he was made Prime Minister.

In order to unite the country to cope with the war crisis, Perceval wished to form a broad-based administration composed of Whigs and Tories; but with Canning and Castlereagh temporarily ruled out and Earl Grey (q.v.) remaining aloof, he was left with a ministry conspicuously lacking in talent. Very few commentators rated high its chances of survival, but the commentators were proved wrong. Perceval and his cabinet came to power at a time when very little progress was being made in the war, and many influential voices were being raised in favour of an early peace. Instead of giving in to pressure, Perceval stuck to his guns and urged a steady and unremitting exertion in support of the Peninsular campaign; slowly but surely the tide began to turn in England's favour. It was a victory for dogged persistence, a quality personified by Perceval, and he surprised everyone by not only clinging to power but actually consolidating it. Other problems were met in a similarly straightforward fashion. The Luddite riots, which appeared as a threat to the social order, were ruthlessly suppressed. The succession crisis of 1811 brought on by George III's recurrent bouts of madness did not result in a purge of the Perceval administration. No greater contrast could have been found than that between the flamboyant and dissolute Prince Regent and the puritanical Perceval, and it was this contrast that engendered mutual dislike. The Prince, however, was unable to persuade the Whigs to form a coalition administration and so Perceval continued in power, with the welcome addition of Castlereagh and Sidmouth to the ranks.

By early 1812 Perceval was showing himself to be an excellent leader in the Commons. It was generally acknowledged that here was the undramatic exponent of the policy upon which the English ruling classes were agreed. During March and April he grew in strength. But on 11 May 1812 while making his way through the lobby of the Commons, Perceval was shot through the heart. The assassin, John Bellingham, was exacting personal revenge for the failure of the government to provide him with financial redress after he was arrested and imprisoned while trading in Russia.

D. Gray, *Spencer Perceval: the Evangelical Prime Minister, 1762–1812* (1963).

Portraits: oil, half-length, by G. F. Joseph: N.P.G.; oil, three-quarter length, by G. F. Joseph, 1812: N.P.G.; marble bust, by unknown artist: N.P.G.

Petty, William (1737–1805), 1st Marquis of Lansdowne and 2nd Earl of Shelburne; statesman who was chief minister from July 1782 to February 1783.

William Petty was born in Dublin on 13 May 1737, the son of John Fitzmaurice, who took the additional name of Petty on succeeding to the Irish estates of his uncle. In 1760 Petty was created Baron Wycombe in the peerage of Great Britain, and a year later Earl of Shelburne in the peerage of Ireland. He was educated privately in southern Ireland before entering Christ Church, Oxford, in 1755. He left Oxford without a degree and joined the army, in which he gave distinguished service during the Seven Years War, reaching the rank of colonel and aide-de-camp to the King.

While abroad he was elected to parliament for the family borough of Chipping Wycombe. His father's death in 1761 made him ineligible to sit in the House of Commons, so he took his place in the House of Lords. Shelburne declined office under Lord Bute, but maintained a close relationship with George III, who used him as a go-between with Fox and Bute. He thereby gained a reputation for intrigue that he was never to lose.

In 1763 he was appointed President of the Board of Trade in the Grenville ministry, but he resigned a few months later after incurring the displeasure of the King by supporting Chatham's objection to the expulsion from the Commons of John Wilkes (q.v.). He had developed a close attachment to Chatham, with whom he shared a distaste for political parties, and on the latter's assumption of power in 1766 he was appointed Secretary of State for the Southern Department. In this capacity he attempted to pursue a policy of conciliation with the American colonies; by 1768, however, all the members of the cabinet except Shelburne and Chatham (who rarely attended meetings because of ill health) supported coercive measures against the American colonists, and in October of that year Shelburne resigned.

At Bowood, his country estate, Shelburne gathered around him a number of rational dissenters and radicals, including Priestley and Jeremy Bentham. By now he was an advocate of many 'advanced' opinions, and during the 1770s made speeches in the House in favour of parliamentary reform and tolerance towards nonconformity. He remained aloof from his colleagues in the House, and preferred to obtain private advice. This secrecy and intellectual radicalism made Shelburne a much disliked character whose association with the Rockingham Whigs was always distinctly uneasy. His opposition to complete American independence in favour of a federal alliance based on free trade and his support for an increase in the royal prerogative were both views that were diametrically opposed to those of his Whig colleagues.

In 1782 Shelburne took office under Lord Rockingham as Home Secretary. He tried to introduce a programme of public finance involving a simplification of taxation and a revision of customs duty along the lines laid down by Adam Smith, but his plans were not accepted.

On the death of Rockingham in July 1782, Shelburne was appointed first minister by the King. He formed a cabinet that consisted mostly of Chathamite Whigs, but Fox and his supporters resigned and went into opposition. With Lord North and his followers in opposition too, the Shelburne administration was exceptionally insecure. As long as the opposition remained divided, however, there was a chance of success. Unfortunately, Shelburne lost his opportunity through a lack of tact in conducting the peace negotiations with America. Shelburne was unable to explain his highly sophisticated ideas to parliament, nor could he explain them to his colleagues in the cabinet. He was criticized for his autocratic manner and his deviousness, and when the supporters of Fox and Lord North joined forces against him in a most unlikely alliance, Shelburne was doomed. He resigned in February 1783, and never again held office. For the remainder of his career he gave general support to William Pitt the Younger, and then, after the French Revolution (which he supported) to Fox. He was always more of a philosopher than a practical politician and lacked the qualities of leadership that might have enabled him to impress his personality upon others. He died in London on 7 May 1805.

J. Cannon, *The Fox–North Coalition* (1969).

Lord E. Fitzmaurice, *Life of William, Earl of Shelburne* (3 vols.; 1875–6).

D. Jarret, *The Begetters of Revolution, 1759–89* (1973).

J. Norris, *Shelburne and Reform* (1963).

Portrait: oil, half-length, after Reynolds: N.P.G.

Picton, Sir Thomas (1758–1815), general, who served with Wellington and fell at the Battle of Waterloo.

Picton was born in 1758, the younger son of Thomas Picton of Pembrokeshire. His early years are obscure, but it seems that he began his military career under the patronage of his uncle, William Picton, who was commanding the 12th Foot at Gibraltar when his nephew was gazetted ensign in 1771. Picton did not join the 12th until 1774, after finishing his studies at a private military academy in London, and he remained with the regiment until 1778, by which time he was a lieutenant. He then returned to England to take up a captaincy in the newly raised 75th Foot, but did not see action. The 75th stayed at home and was disbanded at the peace, Picton among others being placed on half pay.

The outbreak of the war against the Revolutionary French in 1793 found him an unemployed captain, living in retirement on his family estate. At the end of 1794 he sailed to the West Indies to seek the patronage of the commander in chief of the Leeward Islands, Sir John Vaughan. Vaughan found him a vacancy in the 17th Regiment and made him a supernumerary aide. Picton was a conscientious soldier and was quickly rewarded with the rank of major in the 68th Regiment and a brevet lieutenant-colonelcy.

Vaughan died in 1795, but Picton found a new patron in his successor, Sir Ralph Abercromby. He took part in the capture of St. Lucia, and was given the vacant command of the 56th Regiment. When Abercromby returned to England in 1797, he ensured Picton's future by making him military governor and commander of the recently captured island of Trinidad. His task was to maintain order where the decayed Spanish administration had failed; in this he succeeded completely and won the admiration of the inhabitants.

Although Picton's authority had been endorsed and he had been promoted to brigadier general in the previous October, the governorship was put into the hands of a commission in July 1802. It was a matter of political principle, not a reflection on himself, and Picton continued as the military member of the three-man commission. He took it badly, however, and clashed with the officious civil commissioner, William Fullerton. Picton participated in the assault on St. Lucia in June 1803, but shortly afterwards Fullerton returned to England, and Picton was forced also to return to England on hearing that Fullerton was bringing legal proceedings against him on the grounds that he had sanctioned the use of torture in a criminal examination. The case continued in a dilatory manner until 1810 and,

although Picton was technically exonerated, his judgment was brought into question. As a result, he was permanently embittered.

In April 1808 Picton was promoted to major general and in July 1809 took part in the ill-fated Walcheren expedition. In 1810 he joined Wellington's army in Portugal, where he was put in command of the reformed Third Division, which acquired a reputation for firm discipline and vigour in assault. In 1811 the Third fought at Fuentes de Onoro and in 1812 it was engaged in the successful assaults on Cuidad Rodrigo and Badajoz. During the latter, Picton was shot in the groin and was compelled to return to England to recover.

In February 1813 he was created a Knight of the Bath, and he was promoted to lieutenant general in June, by which time he was back with his division. He had now become something of a legend in the army and the subject of many apocryphal stories, although his men viewed him with respect rather than love. The Division fought hard at Vittoria, and at Sorauron, where Picton earned Wellington's displeasure by an unauthorized withdrawal in the face of superior numbers.

He returned briefly to England in 1813 to take his seat in the Commons as member for Carmarthen, rejoining to take part in the final battles on French soil at Orthez and Toulouse (both 1814). At Toulouse he incurred heavy and unnecessary losses, a fact made worse because a general armistice had already been signed elsewhere in France.

Despite some public agitation on his behalf, Picton did not receive the peerage that was awarded to some of Wellington's other officers. Nevertheless, he was appointed to the allied army in the Low Countries after Napoleon's escape from Elba in 1815, and was placed in command of the Fifth Division. At Quatre Bras (16 June), two of his ribs were broken by a musket ball, but he concealed the wound, and was thus present with his Division at Waterloo on 18 June 1815, at the precise point where the initial attack of the French infantry was directed. Putting himself at the head of two of his battalions for a counter-attack, Picton was again hit by a musket ball at the very moment of the charge and was killed. His body was recovered after the battle and was buried at St. George's, Hanover Square, London.

H. B. Robinson, *Memoirs of Lieutenant General Sir Thomas Picton* (2 vols.; 1836).

Portrait: oil, half-length, by M. A. Shee: N.P.G.

Piozzi, Mrs. Hester Lynch (1741–1821), see Thrale, Mrs. Hester.

Pitt, William (1708–78), 'the Elder', also known as 'The Great Commoner', 1st Earl of Chatham; statesman; Foreign Minister during the Seven Years War.

William Pitt was born at Golden Square, Westminster, London, on 15 November 1708, the fourth son of Lady Harriet Villiers, daughter of Viscount Grandison, a member of the Anglo-Irish nobility, and Robert Pitt, M.P., the son of Thomas ('Diamond') Pitt, a wealthy East India merchant and former Governor of Madras. Pitt was educated at Eton and Trinity College, Oxford. He left Oxford without a degree after a year because of gout, a complaint which was to be a lifelong inconvenience to him. He then spent several months at the University of Utrecht in the Netherlands, probably studying law.

The marriage in 1728 of his brother to Christian Lyttleton, sister of his school-friend George Lyttleton, brought the Pitts into one of the most influential families in the land-owning oligarchy that under the Hanoverians virtually controlled the British government. Through Viscount Cobham Pitt was in 1731 appointed a cornet in the King's Own Regiment of Horse. With an income of £150 a year from this commission, he now made his entrance into public life and court politics.

In 1735 Pitt was elected to parliament as M.P. for Old Sarum, one of his brother's pocket boroughs. He belonged to the small group known as the 'Boy Patriots', the clique of family friends and place-seekers established by Cobham to oppose Sir Robert Walpole's administration. The 'Patriots' joined other discontented Whigs grouped around Frederick Louis (q.v.), Prince of Wales, who was an opponent of his father, George II, and therefore of the Walpole government.

In 1737 the Prince of Wales appointed Pitt one of his court officials with a salary of £400 a year. Though still dependent on patronage, Pitt already showed an independent spirit and a willingness to exploit public opinion outside parliament. This appeal to the 'voice of England' was enhanced by his ability as an orator, and was a wholly new factor in English political life; to some extent it indicated the degree to which parliament, full of sinecurists, was becoming unrepresentative.

When Walpole fell in 1742 Pitt failed to obtain office in the new ministry and remained in violent opposition. In the War of the Austrian Succession (1740–8) Pitt's chief attacks were directed at Carteret's policy of forming a coalition of German states against France to protect Hanover. Inevitably, he came into direct conflict with King George II, who was also Elector of Hanover, and as a result he was kept out of any ruling ministry until 1746. In that year Henry Pelham (q.v.), seeing Pitt's value as an ally and fearing him as an opponent, finally admitted him to the government, first as Vice-Treasurer for Ireland, and then, a few months later, as Paymaster General of the Forces.

During the nine years that he held this office Pitt refused to take advantage of the personal profit to be made through bribery and corruption and so acquired a remarkable reputation for honesty. In 1754 he further consolidated his connection with the Temples by marrying Hester Grenville, daughter of the Countess of Temple, a union that proved singularly happy.

In the same year Henry Pelham died and was succeeded as First Lord of the Treasury by his brother, Thomas Pelham-Holles, Duke of Newcastle (q.v.). Pitt, disappointed of the leadership of the House of Commons, which Newcastle awarded to a nonentity named Robinson, began to express dissatisfaction with Newcastle's policy. He was unsparing in his attacks even after he had been dismissed from the post of Paymaster of the Forces in 1755. The outbreak of war with France in America in April 1755, however, was to turn the political tide in his favour.

The early phase of the war was marked by reverses for Britain, and in November 1756 Newcastle's government resigned and Pitt was asked to form a ministry. Pitt, however, had no real understanding of party politics and proved unable to hold a majority together. He failed to make the war against France more successful and in April 1757 had to resign.

In June Pitt returned to office, this time with Newcastle as his ally. Pitt was to control the war and foreign affairs, while Newcastle was to secure parliamentary support. Pitt, now free to concentrate on war policy, determined that the conflict should be a national war, in which Britain would use her superior command of the sea. He seized upon America and India as the main objects of British strategy: his main expeditions went to America, while he gave support to the East India Company and its 'heaven-born general'

Robert Clive in their struggle against the French in the subcontinent. He subsidized and reinforced the armies of Frederick the Great of Prussia to engage the French on the Continent, while the British navy harassed the French along their own coasts, in the West Indies, and in Africa. This resolute and concerted policy was too much for Bourbon France and her allies and, by the terms of the Treaty of Paris in 1763, Great Britain remained supreme in North America and India, and won territory in Africa and the West Indies.

But even before peace was made, Pitt was out of office. When King George III succeeded to the throne in 1760, he showed a determination to have ministers who pleased him and who desired to end the war, and Pitt felt obliged to resign. He left office in October 1761, the only minister who was not tired of war. His haughty and aloof manner and his high-handed treatment of affairs had earned him respect and admiration but little friendship. It was some measure of his unique reputation for high-minded disinterest that his acceptance, on his resignation, of a peerage and an annuity for his wife Hester should provoke bitter disillusionment. His effigy was burned in the city, and Hester was reviled as 'Lady Cheat 'em'.

In July 1766 the King asked him to form a ministry drawn from all sections of the Houses of Parliament. By this time, however, Pitt, a manic depressive, had lost his sense of judgment and found it difficult to form a coherent ministry. Pitt himself chose the secondary post of Lord Privy Seal, for which he was created Earl of Chatham. The 'Great Commoner' retired to the Lords and fell ill for two years, leaving a rudderless government, under the luckless Duke of Grafton (see Fitzroy, Augustus Henry) and Charles Townshend (q.v.), to abandon his policies. Engulfed in a black fit of insanity, Chatham withdrew completely and in 1768 resigned his office.

Chatham's last years were clouded by illness, yet he was to reappear in the House of Lords – with ever greater difficulty – as an elder statesman. Both before and after the outbreak of the War of American Independence, he spoke with great eloquence against the policy that the government was pursuing towards the American colonies, but he did not have English public opinion behind him, and he misunderstood the attitude of the Americans when he believed that if only they were treated with civility they would be, as he said, 'willing, giving, people'. His last speech, against any diminution of an empire based on freedom, closed a political career that had become devoted to a reconciliation of imperial power with constitutional liberty. On 11 May 1778, Chatham died in the arms of his son William.

Stanley Ayling, *The Elder Pitt, Earl of Chatham* (1976).
J. Brooke, *The Chatham Administration* (1954).
J. H. Plumb, *Chatham* (1953).
Sir C. G. Robertson, *Chatham and the British Empire* (1946).
O. A. Sherrard, *Lord Chatham: A War Minister in the Making* (3 vols.; 1952–8).
B. Tunstall, *William Pitt, Earl of Chatham* (1938).

Portraits: oil, half-length, after R. Brompton, 1772: N.P.G.; oil, three-quarter length, by W. Hoare, c.1754: N.P.G.; black chalk, after Gainsborough: Walker Art Gallery, Liverpool.

Pitt, William (1759–1806), 'the Younger'; statesman; Prime Minister of Great Britain, 1783–1801 and 1804–6.

Pitt was born at Hayes, Kent, on 28 May 1759. His career was in every way exceptional. He was Chancellor of the Exchequer at the age of twenty-three and Prime Minister before he was twenty-five, an appointment which provoked the popular jingle:

> A sight to make surrounding nations stare,
> A nation trusted to a schoolboy's care.

However, Pitt had been no ordinary schoolboy. He was the second son of William Pitt the Elder (q.v.) and Hester Grenville; from an early age Pitt himself saw his future as being in the political arena. In 1766, when his father became Earl of Chatham, he is said to have remarked, 'I am glad I am not the eldest son . . . I want to speak in the House of Commons like papa.'

In 1773, aged fourteen, he went to Pembroke Hall, Cambridge. There he led an austere life, taking no interest in games or sport. He had few friends or even acquaintances. Soon after he left Cambridge his father died, and Pitt – with only £300 a year of his own – embarked on a legal career. He was called to the bar in 1780, but in the same year stood as a candidate for one of the parliamentary seats of the University of Cambridge in the general election. He failed to be elected, but was then offered a seat by Sir James Lowther, a northern magnate who controlled nine boroughs. In 1781 he took his seat as member of parliament for Appleby.

His maiden speech in the House of Commons was eagerly awaited, and he more than fulfilled the expectations of his audience when he spoke in support of Burke's plan of economic reform in public administration; Burke declared that young Pitt was 'Not a chip off the old block . . . but the old block itself.' Pitt advocated the objectives of peace, retrenchment, and reform that were to remain the fundamental aims of his political career. The House of Commons was in a fluid state following the loss of the American colonies. Rockingham (see Watson-Wentworth, Charles) replaced Lord North (q.v.) in 1782 as First Minister, and offered Pitt the post of Vice-Treasurer of Ireland, a sinecure carrying a salary of £5,000 a year. Pitt refused, holding out for a seat in the cabinet. Three months later when Rockingham died he was offered the post of Chancellor of the Exchequer in Shelburne's ministry.

His tenure of this position was short, for the infamous Fox–North coalition brought Shelburne's ministry down, and the King, reluctant to call on the odious Fox (q.v.) to form a government, offered Pitt the position of First Lord of the Treasury. Pitt declined the offer twice, shrewdly judging that the time was not yet right. Thus the Duke of Portland (see Bentinck, William Henry Cavendish) now became the nominal head of a Fox–North administration.

During the summer recess of 1783 Pitt went abroad – to France – for the only time in his life. In the autumn he returned to attack the coalition government, which fell, after the failure of Fox's India Bill, in November 1783. George III once more approached Pitt with the offer of the

premiership, and Pitt accepted the seals of office on 19 December 1783, becoming at twenty-four England's youngest-ever Prime Minister. He was to remain in office for the next seventeen years. Despite suffering sixteen defeats in the House of Commons, Pitt clung to office, convinced that public opinion was moving in his favour. He had the great advantage of being untainted by past connections and errors. His integrity became apparent when, despite heavy debts, he refused to appropriate the clerkship of the Pells (a valuable sinecure) for himself. Waverers and place-seekers in the House began to shift to his side.

After three months as leader of a minority government, Pitt asked the King to dissolve parliament. He had judged the time perfectly, and was returned to power with an overwhelming majority. 160 coalition members ('Fox's martyrs') lost their seats.

Despite his youth, Pitt remained composed and confident and seemed to wield power as a natural right. His behaviour in the Commons is described by a contemporary, Sir N. W. Wraxall, as

> grave and firm, showing no favour to anyone, and marking no one with a nod or a glance. Pitt seemed made to guide and to command, even more than to persuade or to convince, the assembly that he addressed.

Pitt's career is often seen as falling into two distinct halves, the younger Pitt being viewed as a reformer and the middle-aged Pitt being labelled as a reactionary. This rigid dichotomy oversimplifies matters considerably. Pitt's foremost concerns were always efficient administration and sound finance. The measures he introduced were essentially *ad hoc* reforms of things that he felt were inefficient or wasteful, rather than the reflections of a doctrinaire ideology. Hence Pitt's introduction of a 'sinking fund' to reduce the national debt (1786). He also consolidated customs duties, and in 1784 reduced the tax on tea by 87 per cent. To offset the loss of revenue, windows in buildings were taxed at a graduated rate. Pitt also instituted the raising of state loans by competitive tender and the abolition of many sinecures.

In other spheres, Pitt was perhaps less successful in achieving what he set out to do. He established a new constitution for the East India Company (1784), settling the problem that had caused the Fox–North coalition's downfall. However, in 1785 a modest measure of parliamentary reform introduced by Pitt was rejected by the Commons. Pitt was the first statesman to attempt the practical application of the economic doctrines of Adam Smith (q.v.), and he tried to increase trade with Ireland, America, and France, although he was successful in obtaining a commercial treaty only with France (in 1786). He also failed to carry the House of Commons in support of Wilberforce's proposed abolition of the slave trade in 1792. The more permanent Pitt's administration was seen to be, the stronger it became, as men of ability and ambition in the House of Commons adhered to it. Yet there was no recognizable 'party' in the modern sense behind Pitt, and his supporters retained the right to reject his legislation without rejecting his administration.

After 1792 Pitt was compelled to turn his attention from domestic reform to foreign affairs. He had ignored the French Revolution as long as he could, believing that it was a domestic event which need not concern him. That he had misjudged the situation was soon obvious, as France went to war with Austria and Prussia, and Britain's ally, Holland, was threatened by the opening of the Scheldt. France declared war on Britain in February 1793. Pitt believed that the war would be short and that France's finances would soon be exhausted. But the war dragged on until 1815, first with Revolutionary and then with Napoleonic France. Pitt saw Britain's role as that of paymaster, and he helped to organize and finance three coalitions of European powers against France between 1793 and 1806.

After 1793 Pitt saw the restoration of peace and stability as his prime objective. He now opposed the idea of parliamentary reform in the belief that it was not 'a time to embark on a constitutional change'. War was contrary to everything Pitt believed in and had a disastrous effect on such measures as the 'sinking fund'. Pitt saw the successful conclusion of the war as the prime objective, and as societies promoting revolutionary ideals flourished in Britain and seemed to threaten internal stability, he introduced repressive measures, such as the suspension of Habeas Corpus (1794), and the Seditious Meetings Act and the Treasonable Practices Act (both 1795). Pitt entered the war with France not fired with any fervid antirevolutionary feeling but to protect British spheres of interest. Similarly, his defence of the constitution and repressive measures at home were, he felt, in the public interest until the war was ended.

By 1800 a legislative union had been effected with Ireland and Pitt felt that this would enable Catholics to be safely admitted to the franchise. George III, however, refused to consider the idea and Pitt resigned in February 1801. Addington (q.v.) replaced him as Prime Minister, but the idea that he could seriously rival Pitt as a leader was ridiculed in the popular rhyme:

> Pitt is to Addington
> As London is to Paddington.

While out of office, Pitt spent much of his time at Walmer Castle, and from 1803 his household was presided over by his niece, Lady Hester Stanhope (q.v.), who seems to have been the only woman with whom he was ever at ease. At this time Pitt was heavily in debt, but he refused free gifts from merchants of the City of London and from the King's privy purse. He did, however, accept a loan from friends.

Pitt supported Addington's administration loyally, but as war broke out with France again in 1803 his young adherents urged him to return to office. As Addington's inability to conduct the war became increasingly apparent, Pitt went into open opposition (1804) and was soon returned to power. He wanted to form a coalition government including Fox, but the King refused and Pitt took office with less support than previously. He embarked on vigorous measures against France and organized a third coalition against her. However, he was not in good health and charges of corruption against his old friend Henry Dundas (now Viscount Melville) hurt him greatly. Despite Nelson's victory at Trafalgar

(1805), the war went badly and Napoleon's crushing victory over Britain's allies at Austerlitz finally shattered Pitt's health completely. He died on 23 January 1806, at the age of forty-six. The House of Commons voted £40,000 to pay Pitt's debts, and he was buried in Westminster Abbey in a grave adjoining his father's.

A. Aspinall (ed.), *The Later Correspondence of George III, December 1783–December 1810* (5 vols.; 1962–70).

D. G. Barnes, *George III and William Pitt, 1783–1806* (1939).

G. C. Bolton, *The Passing of the Act of Union* (1966).

J. Brooke, *King George III* (1972).

J. Ehrman, *The Younger Pitt: the Years of Acclaim* (1969).

R. J. White, *The Age of George III* (1968).

Portraits: oil, three-quarter length, by J. Hoppner, 1805: N.P.G.; watercolour, quarter-length, by J. Gillray: N.P.G.; marble bust, by J. Nollekens, 1808: N.P.G.; oil, three-quarter length, by T. Lawrence, 1808: Windsor Castle.

Pope, Alexander (1688–1744), Augustan poet and verse satirist.

Alexander Pope was born on 21 May 1688 in Lombard Street, London, the son of a wholesale linen merchant. His family was Catholic, a factor which was important throughout his life: at that time his co-religionists were debarred from the best careers and also subjected to such financial disadvantages as double taxation. For this reason, Catholics tended to stick together, and friends such as John Caryll and Martha Blount, who shared the same faith as Pope, were to play an important part in his life. Also because of his religion his education was mainly restricted to tutoring at home, though he did attend Catholic schools at Twyford and in London. In the year that he was born his father retired and took his family to Binfield, in Windsor Forest.

All accounts agree that he was a precocious child. He told his friend

'Eloisa to Abelard', a form of Ovidian heroic epistle dealing with thwarted sexual love, is more dramatic than his previous work and was much admired by Dr. Johnson.

But another aspect of the poet had been gradually emerging, one evident since the publication of the 'Pastorals', and again in an established tradition – that of the verse essay of Horace. *An Essay on Criticism*, published in 1711, shows the emergence of a poet who wanted to occupy the centre of the stage of critical discrimination – in art, morals, and society. The memorable epigrams in this poem – 'To err is human, to forgive divine', and 'For fools rush in where angels fear to tread' are among them – have their sources in the classical authors, but the polish and wit is all Pope's own; as he said in another context, 'true wit' (poetical genius) is the talent to give form to 'what oft was thought, but ne'er so well expressed'.

The *Essay on Criticism* not only broadened and deepened Pope's claim to be the new voice of the age; it also introduced him to a more specialized and influential area of criticism, and to the friendship of such men as Steele and Addison (qq.v.). His interest in the idea of the poet as the spokesman for his time grew, and the two strands found in his early works – the powerful description of the early pastorals and Georgics, and the more sober, 'thinking' didacticism of the *Essay on Criticism* – were united in his first truly great work, 'The Rape of the Lock', which was drafted in two cantos in 1712 and then in five in 1714, and published in the 1717 collection. To the two imitative elements of his early work that had eventually flowed together, Pope added the striking originality of his conception of a mock epic.

The subject of 'The Rape of the Lock' – the unauthorized seizure of a lock of a

Joseph Spence that when he was only twelve he had written 'a kind of play' based on the *Iliad*. Soon after this he began work on a poem which was essentially a series of imitations of the great epic poets, including Milton, Spenser, Homer, Virgil, and Ovid.

Despite the doubt cast by later scholars upon some of Pope's more extravagant claims, it is clear that he had ambitions to be a poet from his boyhood and that his earliest talent was for imitation. His first appreciable works, the 'Pastorals', are in the established tradition of such verse. They were first published in Jacob Tonson's *Poetical Miscellanies* (1709). These early efforts show a side of Pope that is not usually remembered, a descriptive power present also in 'Windsor Forest' (1713) and 'The Temple of Fame' (1715) that fits more understandably with his later development when it is remembered that Pope was interested in painting and even took some lessons in it. Pope's other early poems also showed both this descriptive power and the imitative vein, though the tone of his girl's hair – was suggested to Pope by John Caryll after a similar incident, which had led to two families falling out. It was partly to reconcile them that Pope wrote the poem, but its warm humanity and ingenuity of concept have made a trivial subject eternal. Pope's method was to give the events and characters mock-heroic status, puffing the trivial with the swollen air of epic language, and deliberately causing rhetoric to descend to bathos:

> Here thou, great Anna! whom
>   three realms obey:
> Dost sometimes counsel take – and
>   sometimes tea.

Pope himself described his technique as 'using a vast force to lift a feather'. The term 'mock-epic' signifies the mockery, not of epic, but of the lack of a sense of proportion in human affairs.

By the time of the publication of the five-canto version of 'The Rape of the Lock' in 1714, Pope had already started on the work that was to secure him financially. His verse translation of Homer was announced in 1713, and the first four books of the *Iliad* appeared in 1715, followed by the remaining two in 1720. His *Odyssey* appeared in 1725–6. Pope's Homer was essentially of the eighteenth century, and some would say more Virgilian than Homeric, but it was a great success and made his fortune – he is estimated to have made about £10,000. Pope thus became the first and only professional poet of the eighteenth century able to support himself (and his parents) from his labours.

The success of Pope's Homer was helped considerably by the new friends he had found among the Tory clique that included Swift, Gay, Arbuthnot (qq.v.), and Bolingbroke (see St. John, Henry, in *Lives of the Stuart Age*). Pope was associated with most of these in the creation of the 'Scriblerus Club', formed to write collaborative satires on poetry. In the well-known 'Epistle to Dr. Arbuthnot' (1735), Pope immortalized Addison, with whom he had fallen out for political reasons, as the insincere 'Atticus', who would not condemn outright, but

> Damn with faint praise, assent with
>   civil leer,
> And without sneering, teach the rest
>   to sneer.

It was literary warfare of this kind that lay behind Pope's mock-epic *The Dunciad* (1728), which is essentially a satire on bad writing in the tradition of Dryden's *Mac Flecknoe*. Full of passages of individual brilliance, the poem lacks a unifying viewpoint, and at three books it is too long. *The New Dunciad* is considerably more effective and was considered by Pope himself to be his masterpiece.

Pope had moved with his parents from Binfield to Chiswick in 1716. His father had died in 1717, and in the following year he had rented a villa at Twickenham, then a small country town. He stayed there for the rest of his life, frequently entertaining such luminaries as Swift and Bolingbroke. He was particularly interested in gardening, and advised on and supervised the layout of the grounds of many of his aristocratic friends. Many of Pope's aesthetic principles on this practical scale are contained in the 'Epistle to Richard Boyle, Earl of Burlington', which was later rearranged with three others as 'Moral Essays, I–IV'. In these Pope showed his predilection for and skill in the Horatian epistolary form, while still employing the mock-epic verse form of the heroic couplet. During 1733–8 Pope published ten more of these Horatian imitations, collected with two verse dialogues as 'Epilogue to the Satires' in 1738.

But Pope had probably always been

bent on writing the eighteenth century's answer to Milton. The *Essay on Man* was his attempt at this, inspired in part by the philosophy of his friend Bolingbroke, but essentially a work of didactic poetry that superficially organizes the indication of the 'ways of God to man', though it lacks Milton's profound insight and grand design. The *Essay on Man* gained Pope a European reputation, though it is generally agreed not to be among his greatest works.

Pope's last years were occupied in rather elaborate – and seemingly pointless – manoeuvrings designed to ensure that his own favoured version of his correspondence was published while he was still alive. One of his stratagems was the editing of a selection of his own letters, which he then allowed to fall into the hands of the notorious pirate publisher Edmund Curll, who could be expected to – and did – bring them out as fast as they could be got into hot metal. This being done, Pope immediately protested and declared that he must bring out an authentic version, which he did in 1737. Similarly unorthodox devices were used to secure the publication of his letters to Swift, and Pope was apparently not above readdressing some of his letters to persons different from the original recipients for the sake of variety.

All this would seem to continue the habit of self-justification that some critics have noted in the nobler terms of the *Essay on Criticism* and the *Essay on Man*. It also accords well with the assessment of Pope's character that has been passed on via the Whig version of history, principally in *The Dictionary of National Biography*. This and similar versions, deriving principally from the rhetoric of Macaulay's sympathetic essay on Addison, relates Pope's satirical virtuosity to a personality characterized as a waspish, vindictive, and unforgiving. Modern biographers, nota-

bly Edith Sitwell and George Sherburn, have, however, painted a rather more sympathetic portrait of the artist. As Professor Ian Jack has pointed out, as well as the restrictions imposed upon him by his religion, Pope also had to endure physical disadvantage to an intolerable degree. Though, as portraits show, he had a fine, sensitive face, he was only four feet six inches tall, and suffered from spine curvature as the result of infantile tuberculosis. In the light of this, his bouts of melancholy and his frequent suspicions of enemies are perhaps not so surprising.

Alexander Pope died at Twickenham on 30 May 1744, and is buried in Twickenham Church.

N. Ault (ed.), *The Prose Works of Alexander Pope*, vol. 1, *The Earlier Works, 1711–20* (1936).

J. Butt (ed.), *The Poems of Alexander Pope* (6 vols.; 1939–61).

Bonamy Dobrée, *Alexander Pope* (1951).

M. Mack (ed.), *An Essay on Man* (1962).

M. Mack (ed.), *Essential Articles for the Study of Alexander Pope* (Hamden, Conn., 1968; rev. ed.).

M. Mack et al. (ed.), *The Translations of Homer* (4 vols.; 1967).

R. M. Schmitz (ed.), *An Essay on Criticism* (St. Louis, 1962).

G. Sherburn, *The Early Career of Alexander Pope, 1688–1727* (1934).

G. Sherburn (ed.), *The Correspondence of Alexander Pope* (5 vols.; 1956).

Joseph Spence, *Anecdotes of Pope and Others*, ed. J. M. Osborn (2 vols.; 1967).

A. L. Williams, *Pope's Dunciad: a Study of Its Meaning* (Baton Rouge, 1955).

Portraits: oil, full-length, by C. Jervas, 1715–27: N.P.G.; oil, half-length, studio of M. Dahl, 1727: N.P.G.; oil, head, attributed to J. Richardson, 1737: N.P.G.; chalk, half-length, by W. Hoare, c. 1739: N.P.G.; oil, studio of Kneller: York City Art Gallery; bust, by L. F. Roubillac: National Gallery of Scotland; engraving, half-length, by J. Smith after painting by G. Kneller, 1716: V. & A.

Portland, 3rd Duke of (1738–1809), see Bentinck, William Henry Cavendish.

Priestley, Joseph (1733–1804), theologian and scientist, Dissenter in religion and pioneer in the study of chemistry.

Joseph Priestley was born on 13 March 1733 at Birstall Fieldhead, near Leeds, Yorkshire, the eldest son of Jonas Priestley, a cloth-dresser, by his first wife, Mary. Poor health in childhood did not prevent him from studying with a local Dissenting minister in preparation for a religious career, and in 1752 he entered a new Dissenting Academy at Daventry, Northamptonshire. In September 1755 he became assistant minister to the independent Presbyterian congregation in Needham Market, Suffolk. Despite his sincerity and piety, his increasingly unorthodox opinions made him unpopular.

In 1758 Priestley moved to a more sympathetic congregation in Nantwich, Cheshire, where he opened a day school with thirty-six pupils. His teaching success led to his appointment as Tutor in Languages and Literature at Warrington Academy in 1761, where, since the universities and learned professions barred Dissenters, Priestley developed new courses for students intending to enter industry and commerce, writing the textbooks himself. He was ordained as a Dissenting minister at Warrington in 1762; married an industrialist's daughter, Mary Wilkinson, in the same year; and on 4 December 1764 became a Doctor of Laws at Edinburgh university.

Priestley now became interested in science, especially chemistry, and after 1765 he spent one month annually in London meeting leading scientists, including Benjamin Franklin. Priestley's electrical experiments led to his election to the Royal Society in 1766, and the following year, with Franklin's encouragement, he published *The History and Present State of Electricity* (reprinted 1966), in which he anticipated the inverse square law of electrical attraction, and noted the relationship between electricity

and chemical change. Writing this work led him to a large field of original experiments outside electricity, and to reflections on the similarity between the process of burning and respiration.

In September 1767 Priestley became minister of Mill Hill Chapel, in Leeds. From 1769 to 1788 at irregular intervals he published a magazine on biblical sciences, the *Theological Repository*. Priestley's political theories also developed rapidly at this time: his *Essay on the First Principles of Government, and on the Nature of Political, Civil, and Religious Liberty* (1769) represents eighteenth-century liberal thought.

Priestley's work on gases began about this time; he discovered, in addition to the three gases already known (air, carbon dioxide, and hydrogen), ten new 'airs', four of them between 1767 and 1773: nitric oxide, nitrogen dioxide, nitrous oxide, and hydrogen chloride.

In his experiments Priestley showed that the volume of air decreases by one fifth during respiration, putrefaction, and combustion. In 1772 he made possible quantitative tests of chemical changes that involve gases when he used nitrous oxide instead of mice as a means of measuring the 'goodness of air'. Lavoisier, interested by Priestley's summary of his work in *Philosophical Transactions* ('On Different Kinds of Air', 1772), proceeded to interpret the latter's observations theoretically. 1772 also saw the publication of a work on optics, *The History and Present State of Discoveries Relating to Vision, Light, and Colours*.

In December 1772 the 2nd Earl of Shelburne appointed Priestley as librarian, literary companion, and tutor to his sons. Accordingly Priestley moved to the Shelburne estate at Calne, Wiltshire, in July 1773. On 1 August 1774, by heating red mercuric oxide he obtained a colourless gas in which a candle would burn 'with a remarkably vigorous flame'; he called it 'dephlogisticated air' (phlogiston being thought to be a material transferred during burning and respiration). Not yet sure that he had discovered 'a new species of air', Priestley accompanied Shelburne to the Continent in October. Lavoisier, who met Priestley in Paris, immediately realized the significance of the latter's experiments, and went on to name the gas (oxygen), deduce its elementary nature, recognize it as the active 'principle' of the atmosphere, and interpret its role in combustion and respiration – though Priestley clung to the phlogiston theory into old age. Priestley's experiments also led to the discovery of ammonia, sulphur dioxide, nitrogen, and a gas later identified as carbon monoxide, and they also had fundamental significance for work on photosynthesis.

In 1779 Priestley became minister of the New Meeting congregation in Birmingham, where he met Josiah Wedgwood and James Watt at Lunar Society meetings, and where he wrote the *History of the Corruptions of Christianity* (1782), in which he rejected most of the faith's fundamental doctrines. By the outbreak of the French Revolution he had acquired a reputation as the antagonist of all establishments, both political and religious, and on 14 July 1791 his house, library, and laboratory were destroyed by mob violence.

Priestley was driven from Birmingham and eventually, in April 1794, he was forced to leave the country, joining his three sons in the United States. Refusing any public office, Priestley continued his literary and religious activities, corresponding with two leaders of the American Revolution, John Adams and Thomas Jefferson. He died at Northumberland, Pennsylvania, on 6 February 1804.

J. G. Crowther, *Scientists of the Industrial Revolution* (1962).

F. W. Gibbs, *Joseph Priestley: Adventurer in Science and Champion of Truth* (1965).

Anne Holt, *A Life of Joseph Priestley* (1931).

J. R. Partington, *A History of Chemistry*, vol. 3 (1962), pp. 237–301.

Caroline Robbins, 'Honest Heretic: Joseph Priestley in America', *Proceedings of the American Philosophical Society*, 1962.

Portraits: chalk, quarter-length, by Ellen Sharples, c.1780: N.P.G.; medallion, attrib. Hackwood: Wedgwood Museum, Barlaston, Staffs.

Prince, Thomas (1687–1758), American theologian, historian, and bibliophile.

Thomas Prince was born on 15 May 1687 at Sandwich, Massachusetts. On graduating in 1709 from Harvard he spent two years travelling abroad in the West Indies and Europe before deciding to settle in England, where he held a ministry for a short time at Coombs in Suffolk. He became homesick for his native New England, however, and in 1717 landed in Boston. There he was offered a post as a minister, and with a devoted wife and family behind him he became fully involved in the social and political life of New England.

As a theologian he was not a deep thinker. As a historian, on the other hand, he was far more adventurous, and his *Chronological history of New England in the form of Annals*, published in 1736, shows a fine facility and flexibility of prose style. He became a faithful supporter of the Evangelical, George Whitefield (q.v.), and when the Boston ministry split into two factions over Whitefield's preaching Prince became his leading champion.

Prince is mostly remembered, however, for his vast collection of books. The only comparable libraries in New England at this time were those of the Mather family, whose papers he collected, and Governor Hutchinson. Most of the books and tracts were concerned with the religious and civil history of New England. Many have been preserved, and are now in the Boston public library.

In 1758 Prince published a translation of the psalms. He died soon after, on 22 October 1758.

S. G. Drake, *Some Memoirs of the Life and Writings of the Rev. Thomas Prince Together With a Pedigree of His Family* (1851).

Pulteney, William (1684–1764), 1st Earl of Bath; Whig politician, who became an active opponent of Sir Robert Walpole.

William Pulteney was born on 22 March 1684, the son of William Pulteney, a member of an established Leicestershire family. Pulteney's father died before he came of age, and thus he inherited considerable property while still young. With Sir Henry Guy as his guardian, Pulteney received his education at Westminster School and at Christ Church, Oxford, where he distinguished himself in classics. He later undertook the Grand Tour, and after the death of Guy in 1710, added to his already great wealth a legacy of £40,000 and an annuity of £500.

In 1705, as a result of the interest of Guy, Pulteney had entered parliament as M.P. for Hedon, in Holderness, Yorkshire. Early showing himself as one of Walpole's many Whig supporters, Pulteney was appointed Secretary at War in 1714 (the year also of his marriage to Anna Maria Gumley) and in 1716 he joined the Privy Council. In the critical year 1717 Pulteney backed the policies and leadership of Walpole and Townshend and resigned with them in April when they were driven from office by the machinations of Stanhope and Sunderland.

Walpole's return to power in 1721 was naturally welcomed by Pulteney, but the latter was bitterly angry when he failed to receive the expected award of office. Declining an elevation to the peerage, he was given the rich but otherwise nugatory post of Cofferer of the Household in 1723; his antagonism towards Walpole grew apace and, after a confrontation over Walpole's proposals regarding the discharge of the debts of the civil list, he was dismissed (April 1725).

The partisan violence now unleashed found expression in a new journal, *The Craftsman*, under the general management of Pulteney and Bolingbroke (see St. John, Henry, in *Lives of the Stuart Age*). Dedicated to the destruction of Walpole's power, this periodical for ten years held the stage as the leading political journal of the time. Pulteney displayed great journalistic versatility in his attacks on all aspects of Walpole's domestic and foreign policies. In parliament he joined the Jacobite Sir William Wyndham in forming a new political group made up of dissident Whigs, called the 'Patriots'. All efforts were directed at removing Walpole, and after the change of monarch in 1727, Pulteney and his associates attempted to solicit royal aid, but without success. In addition to his work published in *The Craftsman*, Pulteney kept up a stream of attacks in individual pamphlets on such matters as the national debt, which had risen by £9 million during the period 1716–26.

After breaking with Townshend in 1730, Walpole attempted to make peace with Pulteney by offering him a peerage and the post of Secretary of State, but both offers were stiffly rejected. The vituperative pamphlets and articles continued. One of these, 'A Proper Reply to a Late Scurrilous Libel' (published in *The Craftsman* of 1731), led to a duel with one of Walpole's supporters, Lord Hervey. Following another article, published in the same year (1731) and entitled 'An Answer to One Part of an Infamous Libel . . .', Pulteney encountered the full wrath of Walpole and his name was crossed off the list of Privy Councillors.

In parliament in 1733 Pulteney attacked Walpole's appropriations from the sinking fund without success, but his denunciation of the excise scheme played a large part in its defeat. In the general election of the following year (1734) Pulteney was returned for Middlesex and continued his attacks in the Commons.

Bolingbroke's retirement to France in 1735 weakened the opposition and for a time Pulteney contemplated his own withdrawal from politics. But as Frederick Louis (q.v.), the Prince of Wales, began to take over as the focus of the anti-government groupings, Pulteney returned to the fight.

By January 1742 Walpole's government had all but collapsed. After unsuccessful overtures from the King inviting him to form a government, Pulteney accepted a place in the cabinet in February and was returned to the Privy Council. Accepted back into the establishment after years as a vigorous member of the opposition, Pulteney now saw his political prestige fall away dramatically. He suffered a personal tragedy in March when his only daughter died. A few months later he made his last speech in the House of Commons and in July 1742 accepted the title of Earl of Bath and retired to the Lords.

For some time afterwards he made vain attempts to get back into active politics; on Wilmington's death in 1743, he applied for the vacant post of First Lord of the Treasury, and early in 1746 he co-operated unsuccessfully with Granville (see Carteret, John) to form an administration. After these fruitless endeavours he retired from political life to spend his last years in social and literary activities. He died of a fever brought on by a chill on 7 July 1764. Erudite and pleasure-loving, Pulteney nevertheless had a factious spirit, and was guilty of deliberately narrowing the politics of the Whig supremacy to the pettiness of a duel.

J. H. Plumb, *Sir Robert Walpole*, vol. 2 (1961).

Portraits: oil, three-quarter length, after J. Reynolds, 1755–7: N.P.G.; oil, three-quarter length, by J. Reynolds, 1761: N.P.G.

R

Radcliffe, Mrs. Ann (1764–1823), novelist.

Ann Ward was born on 9 July 1764 in London, the only daughter of William Ward, a wealthy businessman. Her childhood was both comfortable and cultured, and she was taken under the wing of her uncle Mr. Bentley, Josiah Wedgwood's partner. Early on she developed a taste for the visually imaginative – the paintings of Claude and Richard Wilson, the topographical poetry of Gray and Thomson. In 1787 Ann Ward married William Radcliffe at Bath; her husband, then a law student, later became a journalist, and eventually editor of the influential *English Chronicle*.

Mrs. Radcliffe's first published work was the short 'Gothick' novel, *The Castles of Athlin and Dunbayne* (1789); in writing it she naïvely assumed that the historically remote setting justified gratuitous violence and an illogical plot. Her next novel, *A Sicilian Romance* (1790), showed greater maturity, and was much praised by Walter Scott, always Mrs. Radcliffe's most perceptive critic. Her first best-seller was *The Romance of the Forest* (1791), which typified her artistic strengths and weaknesses: her genuine gift for poetic language and evocative descriptions was vitiated by wooden characterization and an excessively ingenious plot.

Nevertheless, Mrs. Radcliffe was now popular enough to command an unprecedented £500 advance for her next work, *The Mysteries of Udolpho* (1794). This long and ambitious romance introduces a new kind of 'Gothick' writing: Mrs. Radcliffe's sensual and 'atmospheric' prose plays subtly on the reader's emotions (rather than bludgeoning him with horrors), and induces a state of perpetual and almost painful apprehension.

After the success of *Udolpho*, Mrs. Radcliffe temporarily gave up writing fiction, to accompany her husband on a long carriage excursion through Europe. In 1795 they jointly published *A Journey through Holland and the Western Frontier of Germany*; Mr. Radcliffe contributed the political comments, while his wife painted exquisite verbal pictures of Alpine scenery.

Such experiences affected Mrs. Radcliffe's last major work, *The Italian* (1797), for which she received an £800 advance. It is ostensibly a *frisson*-filled tale of the Inquisition and the evil machinations of Schedoni the monk – stock villains of the 'School of Terror'. But it contains many serious reflections – 'to be a guard over prisoners is nearly as miserable as being a prisoner oneself' – and the harsh tyranny it describes was perhaps suggested by the recent Terror in Paris. Furthermore, Schedoni was the first relatively credible character, with logical motives, that Mrs. Radcliffe had created, and accordingly she felt obliged to elucidate carefully the supernatural events surrounding him.

But this was as far as Mrs. Radcliffe was able to go – she was a brilliant romancer, skilled at evoking delightful shivers, rather than a genuine novelist, dedicated to analysing human nature – and from then on she only wrote occasional pieces. The best of them is *Gaston de Blondeville*

(1802), a somewhat academically 'medieval' ghost story, written to appeal to her husband's antiquarian tastes.

After 1810 she suffered from worsening asthma, and on 7 February 1823 she died after a particularly severe attack, and was buried at the Bayswater chapel of ease.

A. Grant, *Ann Radcliffe* (1951).

C. F. McIntyre, *Ann Radcliffe in Relation to her Time* (1920).

Raeburn, Sir Henry (1756–1823), Scottish portrait painter.

Raeburn was born on 4 March 1756 at Stockbridge, near Edinburgh. Orphaned while young, he entered employment with a goldsmith on leaving school and probably began to paint miniatures during his apprenticeship. Little is known of his early career, but some technical faults of draughtsmanship in his earliest known portrait, painted in 1776, indicate that he was probably completely self-taught. In 1780 he married a wealthy widow, Ann Edgar, and so was able to devote himself to developing his career as a professional portrait artist. Edinburgh, the 'Athens of the North' in which so many distinguished writers, lawyers, and scholars lived, provided him with abundant material and his talents developed rapidly. His painting of *The Rev. Robert Walker skating*, probably his most famous portrait, was painted in 1784.

In 1785 Raeburn travelled to Italy, but the style of his painting after his return to Edinburgh two years later was influenced more by the example of Sir Joshua Reynolds, whom he had met in London, than by what he had seen in Europe. During the last decade of the century Raeburn's art developed into its full maturity and he became the leading portrait painter in Scotland. With increased confidence his style became more simple and direct, less concerned with elaborate details of composition and more with the direct expression of essential features. Often he worked directly onto canvas without preliminary sketches or drawings.

After the death of John Hoppner in 1810 Raeburn travelled to London, probably with the intention of taking over Hoppner's practice, but the friendships that he had formed in Edinburgh, as well as the continuing opportunities in that city, persuaded him to return north. In 1812 he was elected President of the Edinburgh Society of Artists, and three years later he became a Royal Academician. On the occasion of George IV's visit to Edinburgh in 1822 Raeburn received a knighthood and was appointed King's Limner for Scotland.

Several of Raeburn's later portraits are weaker than those of his maturity, but his popularity and status in Edinburgh remained undiminished until his death on 8 July 1823. Many of his portraits are still in the possession of those families for whom they were originally painted, and because of this and also his relative isolation in Edinburgh, Raeburn's talents have perhaps not been so widely recognized as they deserve to be.

W. Armstrong and J. L. Caw, *Sir Henry Raeburn* (1909).

J. Greig, *Sir Henry Raeburn* (1911).

Works in:
National Gallery of Scotland, Edinburgh.
Scottish National Portrait Gallery, Edinburgh.
National Gallery, London.
Tate Gallery, London.
National Portrait Gallery, London.

Portrait: oil, self-portrait, half-length: National Gallery of Scotland, Edinburgh.

Raffles, Sir Thomas Stamford (1781–1826), colonial administrator and founder of Singapore.

Raffles was born on 5 July 1781, the son of a captain in the West India trade, aboard the merchant ship *Ann* off the coast of

Jamaica. He received his early education at an academy in Hammersmith. At the age of fourteen he left to become a clerk at East India House. His abilities and his patient and unremitting discharge of his duties secured him rapid promotion.

In 1805 the court of directors resolved to found a new settlement at Penang. Raffles had recommended himself so strongly by his diligent work that Sir Hugh Inglis appointed him assistant secretary to the new establishment. During the voyage out he applied himself to the study of the Malay language. This gave him an immediate advantage over other officials, and in 1806 he was appointed secretary and also registrar to the new court of judicature at an annual salary of £1,500.

In the next two years the fatigue and responsibility of organizing a new government and compiling all the official documents connected with it had a telling effect on Raffles's health. In 1808 he proceeded to Malacca to recover, and there he was able to spend some time learning the local customs and studying trading patterns. In 1811 Raffles joined the expedition against Java, and following the British victory there he was appointed Lieutenant Governor of the island. He had been instrumental in suggesting the conquest of this important trading area 'to save it from the French'. Raffles soon initiated important economic and administrative reforms, and increased the trade revenue eightfold.

In 1816 ill health brought Raffles home to England. The following year he published his most important work, *A History of Java*, and was knighted by the Prince Regent.

In October 1817 Raffles embarked for Sumatra after the court of directors had conferred upon him the post of Lieutenant Governor of Bencoolen. He arrived in March 1818 and found the social conditions atrocious. He immediately set to work to abolish slavery, to reform and gradually liberate the many convicts who had been sent there as part of a penal colony, to educate the natives, and to gain the confidence of the local chiefs.

Raffles was anxious to counteract the expansionist policies of the Dutch, who were attempting to exclude British trading from the area. He recommended that a new settlement be made to afford protection to British shipping. His proposals were met with great interest, and in February 1819 Raffles hoisted the British flag over the colony of Singapore – ideally situated for trading purposes at the mouth of the straits of Malacca. Under his care and guidance, Singapore quickly developed into an important British outpost and a key port for shipping. He remained there until 1824, when once again ill health demanded that he return to England. He embarked on the *Fame*, confident in the knowledge that his efforts had secured Malaya for the British. During the voyage home the ship caught fire, and although all the passengers were saved, his priceless collection of papers, maps, drawings, zoological and botanical specimens, and miscellaneous books on the local languages was lost.

He finally reached England in August 1824, disheartened but justifiably proud of his administrative achievements. His long interest in natural history, however, resulted in a successful campaign to establish a zoological garden in London, and when the English Zoological Society was founded, he was elected its first president. He died suddenly of apoplexy in July 1826 at Highwood Hill, Middlesex.

J. Bastin, *The Native Policies of Sir Stamford Raffles in Java and Sumatra* (1957).

J. Bastin, *Sir Thomas Stamford Raffles* (1969).

R. Coupland, *Raffles of Singapore* (1946).

H. R. C. Wright, *East-Indian Economic Problems of the Age of Cornwallis and Raffles* (1961).

C. E. Wurtzburg, *Raffles of the Eastern Isles* (1954).

Portrait: oil, full-length, by G. F. Joseph, 1817: N.P.G.

Ramsay, Allan (1713–84), Scottish portrait painter.

Ramsay was born in Edinburgh on 13 October 1713, the son of Allan Ramsay, the poet. After elementary training he went to London, where he studied briefly under the Swede, Hans Hysing. In 1736 he left for Italy, where he underwent two full years of training, first under Francesco Imperiali at Rome and then under Francesco Solimena at Naples. In Italy his style became fully formed, and on his return to London, where he based himself permanently, he immediately became popular. His best work achieved a certain cosmopolitan air new to British portraiture, while his Italian grand style, exemplified by such work as the portrait of Dr. Mead (1747), preceded the great portraits of Sir Joshua Reynolds (q.v.) by several years.

Reynolds's emergence in 1754, however, prompted Ramsay to visit Italy again for a further two years. In 1759 Walpole wrote:

> Mr. Reynolds and Mr. Ramsay can hardly be rivals. The former is bold and has a kind of tempestuous colouring, yet with dignity and grace; the latter is all delicacy. Mr. Reynolds seldom succeeds in women, Mr. Ramsay was formed to paint them.

Indeed, Ramsay's portrait of his wife is one of his best works, combining simplicity and grace with considerable delicacy of treatment and approach.

From 1757 to 1766 Ramsay painted solely for royal and government commissions, and in 1767 he was appointed Painter in Ordinary to George III, but refused a knighthood. Ramsay's intellectual interests and love of travel led him finally to abandon his artistic career. Among his friends were Hume, Voltaire, and Rousseau, and of his conversation Dr. Johnson said to Boswell: 'I love Ramsay. You will not find a man in whose conversation there is more instruction, more information, and more elegance.'

After 1754 Ramsay made two more trips to Italy, but on the way back from his fourth visit he died at Dover on 10 August 1784. Considered by many contemporaries to be the Scottish counterpart of Reynolds, he was the most successful of the Scottish predecessors of Sir Henry Raeburn (q.v.).

Alastair Smart, *The Life and Art of Allan Ramsay* (1952).

Works in:

National Gallery of Scotland, Edinburgh.
Scottish National Portrait Gallery, Edinburgh.
Tate Gallery, London.
National Portrait Gallery, London.

Portraits: self-portrait, chalk, quarter-length: Scottish N.P.G.; self-portrait, oil, quarter-length: N.P.G.

Reynolds, Sir Joshua (1723–92), portrait painter; the most distinguished figure in the history of British portraiture.

Joshua Reynolds was born at Plympton, near Plymouth, on 16 July 1723, the son of the Rev. Samuel Reynolds, a clergyman and headmaster of the local grammar school. His education was comprehensive and he was well read in the classics, but his early aspirations were those of a painter and at the age of seventeen he began his apprenticeship to Thomas Hudson in London. After a dispute, Reynolds set up his own practice, partly in London and partly in Devon. The first works to attract any attention were *Captain the Hon. John Hamilton* and the large group portrait of the Eliot family, directly modelled on the famous Van Dyck portrait in Wilton House.

In 1749 Reynolds had the opportunity

of sailing to Italy with a friend, Commodore Keppel. He spent the next three years in Rome, 'with measureless content', making extensive studies of the great Italian masters. His brief stay in Venice on the way home was to be of greater influence on his style of portraiture, and it was during his intensive vigils copying Raphael in the cold of the Vatican that he contracted the deafness from which he was to suffer for the rest of his life.

In 1752 he returned to London; his success was both immediate and constant and set his rivals, chiefly followers of Kneller (see *Lives of the Stuart Age*), at a safe distance. His first great work was *Commodore Keppel*, a lively and vigorous portrait now in the National Maritime Museum. A great number of the aristocracy sat for him, as well as members of the royal family, and his practice was such that he was soon obliged to employ assistants, for in his own words, 'No man ever made a fortune with his own hands.' His considerable practice rapidly made him an extremely wealthy man, while his professional success was matched by his social status.

Although he did not readily associate with fellow artists, he contracted a great intimacy with the outstanding literary figures of the time – Johnson, Garrick, Goldsmith, and Burke, among others. In 1764, when a sudden illness threatened Reynolds's life, Johnson wrote: 'If I should lose you, I should lose almost the only man whom I call a friend.' Reynolds was, in fact, chiefly responsible for the founding of the Literary Club, whose primary objective seems almost to have been to give Dr. Johnson ample opportunity to show off his witty conversation.

In 1768 the Royal Academy was founded, having as one of its purposes the public exhibition of the works of British artists, and Reynolds became its first

president. In the following year he received a knighthood, and he delivered the first of his many famous and authoritative 'discourses' in the Academy. Over the next twenty years Reynolds was to give a further fourteen 'discourses'.

It was also at this time that Reynolds's name was romantically linked with that of Angelica Kauffmann (q.v.), for whom Reynolds was both painter and sitter. From this time onwards, most of Reynolds's chief works appeared regularly at the Academy, and paintings such as the historical piece *Ugolino* and *The Strawberry Girl* were extremely popular.

The arrival of Gainsborough (q.v.) on the scene in 1775 meant serious competition for Reynolds, and it may have been this that caused his style to revert to its former informality, a tendency that was reinforced after his brief visit to Holland and Flanders in 1781. Greater warmth and sensitivity and less classicism and rigidity emerged, and lasted right up to the time when the failure of his eyesight compelled him to stop working (1789). He now devoted his time almost entirely to the portraiture for which he is especially renowned. Notable examples of the work of this later period are *Master Crewe as Henry VIII* and *Lady Caroline Scott as Winter*.

Despite a paralytic stroke in 1782, Reynolds persevered with his work and exhibitions, and managed to produce some of his most celebrated paintings, notably *Mrs. Siddons as the Tragic Muse* (1783). The death in the following year of his dearest friend for thirty years, Samuel Johnson, was a heavy blow.

He delivered his final 'discourse' to the Academy in 1790, an occasion marked by the collapse of the ceiling, which he failed to notice. Deaf and almost blind, he died in London on 23 February 1792, leaving behind nearly 3,000 portraits. He was buried in the crypt of St. Paul's, with impressive ceremonial respect.

Reynolds was without doubt the greatest portrait painter that England has produced and ranks with the greatest in the world. He is remembered for his creative versatility and his ability to alter his style and poses at will, something Gainsborough evidently had in mind when he said, 'Damn him, how various he is!' Unfortunately, however, the technique that he used and his choice of pigments for its execution have caused many of his works to fade uncontrollably, some even beginning this process in his own lifetime.

A. Graves and W. V. Cronin, *A History of the Works of Sir Joshua Reynolds* (4 vols.; 1899–1901).
F. W. Hiller, *The Literary Career of Sir Joshua Reynolds* (1936).
D. Hudson, *Sir Joshua Reynolds* (1958).
E. K. Waterhouse, *Reynolds* (1941).

Works in:
The National Gallery, London.
National Portrait Gallery, London.
Wallace Collection, London.

Portraits: self-portrait, oil, quarter-length: Dulwich Portrait Gallery; self-portrait, oil, half-length, 1753–4: N.P.G.; oil on copper, quarter-length, after a self-portrait: N.P.G.; oil, by Angelica Kauffmann: National Trust, Saltram House, Devon.

Ricardo, David (1772–1823), financier and one of the earliest and most influential writers on the new science of economics.

David Ricardo was born on 19 April 1772 in London, the third of seventeen children born to Abraham Ricardo, a London stockbroker. His father was a Jew from Amsterdam who settled in England and became a highly respected member of the London Stock Exchange. Of his nine surviving sons, six became stockbrokers like himself.

The boy was educated at first in England, and towards the time of his *bar mitzvah* (around the age of thirteen) he was sent for two years to a good school in Amsterdam, run by the Portuguese Synagogue. As a Jew he could not attend an English public school and did not, therefore, have the usual classical education. However, the subjects in which he did become proficient, namely mathematics, science, and geology, kept him well abreast of the best contemporary thought, and were ultimately of far more value to him in his career than the classics would have been. It was as a businessman that he was to earn his living, and it is a tolerable indication of his ability that he had amassed a considerable fortune before he was thirty.

In 1793 his deep love for a Quaker caused him to split with his parents. The girl, Priscilla Wilkinson, was a surgeon's daughter. After the marriage the estrangement with his parents lasted eight years. It seems certain that Ricardo himself was an atheist, but he found it socially more convenient to pass as a lapsed Jew.

The name of David Ricardo first appeared as a stock-exchange jobber in the year of his marriage. He had £800 at this time, yet within a few years he was a wealthier man than his father. He had a natural flair for the market as well as a sharp intelligence. He was unmoved by panic in the market and weathered crises by keeping calm. He never indulged in speculation, preferring to achieve steady returns on large capital sums by selling judiciously on the turn of the market.

Having amassed enough capital, Ricardo moved up to the position equivalent to a modern underwriter. He became a member of a syndicate that contracted for loans. These were mainly war loans, offered by financiers to the Exchequer in exchange for low-priced stocks. The contractors drew up a list of subscribers willing to share the load, and as profits on government stocks had no fixed limits, there was no shortage of subscribers. There was obviously considerable scope for bribery in such a situation, but Ricardo remained scrupulously honest in all his dealings.

After Waterloo (1815), Ricardo made the largest single profit of his life. He had contracted successfully for the government loan before the battle, when share prices were exceptionally low, reflecting the national mood of pessimism. After the victory share prices rocketed, and dealers made fortunes. Ricardo was chief among them, and as a result appears to have decided that he could afford to retire and devote himself to his other interests, economics and politics. After buying several country estates, both as places of residence and as investments against his retirement, Ricardo therefore withdrew from the stock exchange in 1819.

In that year he bought the Irish pocket borough of Portarlington and entered parliament. An outspoken radical, Ricardo supported the entire gamut of liberal measures, including religious tolerance and parliamentary reform. He strongly opposed the repressive Six Acts, following the Peterloo incident, and denounced measures curbing the freedom of the press. In this he generously supported the persecuted freethinker, Richard Carlile.

It is, however, to his writings as an economist that Ricardo owes his historical fame. He first became interested in economics when he came upon Adam Smith's *Wealth of Nations* while on a visit to Bath. Ten years later Ricardo felt he knew enough about economics to write a newspaper article on the alarm caused at the time by a serious depreciation in the currency. This was later published as a pamphlet, *The High Price of Bullion* (1809), advocating a currency standard based on gold bullion to combat the continual depreciation of paper money and the lack of small change resulting from the uncontrolled export and non-monetary use of sterling silver. The gold standard was set up eventually, as Ricardo had recommended, in 1816.

In 1815 he produced another pamphlet, an *Essay on the Influence of a Low Price of Corn upon the Profits of Stock*. This was one of the first attempts to make a systematic analysis of the relationship between rents, wages, profits, and markets in agriculture. By a process of logical deduction, Ricardo evolved what he called his 'theory of diminishing returns'; namely, that after a time, given constant conditions of labour and methods used in farming, the need to buy up inferior land, in order to feed a rapidly growing population, and farm it at the normal expense, must lead to a decrease in profits and ultimately in wages and employment. Though differing in details, this was an idea shared by Malthus (q.v.) and other economists.

Ricardo's *Principles of Political Economy and Taxation* (1817) was the first important textbook on the new science of economics. It was a technical study of a very complex subject, the interrelation of rents, wages, profits, and taxes in an industrial society. This book, unlike the *Wealth of Nations*, is difficult for a modern lay reader, although it remains a brilliant, comprehensive, and profound piece of economic thinking. Although his work was never as widely received as Adam Smith's, being too technical for the layman, Ricardo probed more deeply than Smith; where Smith was content to carry on from a working hypothesis, Ricardo needed by nature to be more precise and based theories and convictions on experience.

In private life Ricardo was both a popular clubman and a devoted husband and father. At Gatscomb Park, an estate in Gloucestershire he had bought in 1814, he enjoyed retirement and good country living, and entertained most hospitably. Malthus was a devoted friend and they kept up a voluminous and affectionate correspondence. Ricardo died from an ear infection on 11 September 1823, aged fifty.

M. Blaug, *Ricardian Economics: A Historical Study* (New Haven, 1958).

M. Blaug, *Economic Theory in Retrospect* (New Haven, 1968, rev. ed.).

J. H. Hollander, *Ricardo: A Centenary Estimate* (Baltimore, 1910; reprinted 1960).

O. St. Clair, *A Key to Ricardo* (1957).

P. Sraffa and M. H. Dobb (eds.), *Works and Correspondences* (11 vols.; 1951–7).

Richardson, Samuel (1689–1761), novelist.

Samuel Richardson was born at Mackworth in Derbyshire, where he was baptized on 19 August 1689. His father, the impoverished descendant of a middle-class family from Surrey, was a carpenter and joiner. His mother, too, was said to be 'not ungenteel'. Samuel was one of nine children and, although he later claimed to have been intended for the church, lack of money ensured that he must be apprenticed to a trade.

In 1706 Richardson was sent to London to be apprenticed to John Wilde, a printer and stationer. He completed his apprenticeship, served several years as a compositor and proofreader, and in 1719 set up his own business – at first in Fleet Street, afterwards in Salisbury Court. His business was highly successful; among other jobs, he obtained a contract worth over £3,000 for the printing of the Journals of the House of Commons. In 1724 he married one Martha Wilde, probably a niece or cousin of his former master. She died in 1731 and Richardson remarried not long after her death; his second wife was the sister of a Bath bookseller. As the printing business prospered, he was able to buy a country house at Hammersmith, which was then still a rural or suburban area.

It was not until 1739, when Richardson was fifty, that he embarked upon his literary career. In that year two booksellers and fellow stationers, Charles Rivington and John Osborn, suggested to Richardson that he should write a manual of practical advice for the conduct of life, in the form of a small volume of 'familiar letters'; Richardson decided to link his letters on a moral theme by means of the story of an incident in the life of a servant girl, and the result was *Pamela, or, Virtue Rewarded*. The book consists of a series of letters written by the heroine, Pamela Andrews, a young servant girl, recounting at great length her resistance – always properly respectful and genteel – to the sexual advances made by her employer, Mr. B., until at last Mr. B. comes to terms and marries her. The book was published towards the end of 1740 and provoked a widespread though varied reaction. It was recommended in sermons, but several slashing parodies appeared; one of Richardson's achievements with *Pamela* was to provoke Henry Fielding (q.v.) into the writing of novels – Fielding's *Joseph Andrews* started as a parody of *Pamela*, and he was almost certainly the author of *An Apology for the Life of Mrs. Shamela Andrews*.

To counter the appearance of an unauthorized sequel to *Pamela*, Richardson wrote a continuation himself in two volumes (1742). But even though *Pamela* took on a life of its own, Richardson did, in 1741, fulfil his original commission; the book appeared anonymously under the title *Letters written to and for Particular Friends, on the most Important Occasions. Directing not only the Requisite Style and Forms to be Observed in Writing Familiar Letters; But How to Think and Act Justly and Prudently in the Common Concerns of Human Life*. The letters include models for recommending servants, for dunning debtors and for excusing non-payment of debts, for acting properly in business, for courtship, and for applications for a daughter's hand in marriage.

In 1744 Richardson began his second novel, *Clarissa Harlowe*, which eventually appeared in 1747–8, in seven weighty volumes. Like Pamela, Clarissa is wooed by a gifted but unscrupulous man, Robert Lovelace, to whom she is secretly attracted. Unlike Pamela, she eventually succumbs to his advances; she then dies of shame. Lovelace gets his just deserts, being killed in a duel by Clarissa's cousin. Richardson devoted most of the last volume to a postscript analysing just how each character received moral justice.

Clarissa Harlowe established Richardson's European reputation. Several translations were made, and it provoked a flood of admiring letters, mostly from female readers. A circle, including the playwright Colley Cibber (q.v.), formed around Richardson, mainly of friends and confidants with

whom he discussed his work. Richardson reacted very badly to hostile criticism – he never forgave Fielding for satirizing *Pamela* – but within his own circle he was quite willing to examine the shortcomings of his compositions. One serious fault of his male protagonists – both Lovelace and Mr. B. – so far had been the difficulty of reconciling the demands of the plot upon their characters with the demands of Richardson's purpose.

In his last work Richardson set about delineating a male hero to match the moral virtue of Pamela and Clarissa. *Sir Charles Grandison* (1753) contrasts its hero, Sir Charles, who puts his moral obligation before self-interest, with the arrogant seducer Sir Hargrave Pollexfen. In many ways this is Richardson's most assured novel; however, its reputation never rivalled that of *Clarissa Harlowe*. In spite of the author's strenuous attempts to show his hero as courageous and impeccably manly, Grandison has been unkindly described as 'one of Richardson's finest female creations'.

This remark serves to emphasize

Richardson's achievement as a novelist – the detailed understanding of female emotion and personality. He simply did not understand men and he confused virility, courage, and love of action with lust, selfishness, and bullying. He sought to replace such qualities with the virtues of dignity, self-composure, and considerateness. Other criticisms are made of his extraordinary long-windedness, of his pompousness, of his thin-skinned vulnerability to criticism, and of his failure to see anything unpleasant in the subterfuges of his heroes and heroines. All these factors contribute to the lack of popular interest in Richardson's work today. Yet of those who have read him, even those critics to whom his pettiness and bourgeois moralizing are most repugnant have been forced to acknowledge the sustained power of his insight. His talents, when used to the best effect, combine to make him the true precursor of Jane Austen, Thackeray, and George Eliot.

After *Sir Charles Grandison* Richardson wrote no more, except for a querulous pamphlet complaining of his wrongs at the hands of the literary pirates. In 1754 he was elected Master of the Stationers' Company. His printing business continued to prosper, but as he grew older he became more and more eccentric, being given to attacks of nerves and of hypochondria. By design or good fortune, the foreman of his works was deaf; Richardson took to communicating with all his employees by leaving written notes for them. On 4 July 1761 he died of apoplexy; he was buried in St. Bride's Church.

J. Carroll (ed.), *Samuel Richardson: A Collection of Critical Essays* (1969).
J. Carroll (ed.), *Selected Letters* (1964).
T. C. Duncan Eaves and B. D. Kimpel, *Samuel Richardson: a Biography* (1971).
M. Kinkead-Weekes (ed.), *Pamela: or Virtue Rewarded* (1962).

W. M. Sale, *Samuel Richardson: Master Printer* (Ithaca, 1950).
G. Sherburn (ed.), *Clarissa: or the History of a Young Lady* (Boston, 1962).
I. P. Watt, *The Rise of the Novel* (1957).

Portraits: oil, quarter-length, by J. Highmore, 1747: N.P.G.; oil, full-length, by J. Highmore, 1750: N.P.G.

Ripon, 1st Earl of (1782–1859), see Robinson, Frederick John.

Rob Roy (1671–1734), Highland chieftain, see Macgregor, Robert, in *Lives of the Stuart Age*.

Robinson, Frederick John (1782–1859), 1st Earl of Ripon, better known as Viscount Goderich; statesman, who was Prime Minister from August 1827 to January 1828.

Robinson was born on 31 October 1782, the second son of Thomas Robinson, 2nd Baron Grantham. After an education at Harrow and St. John's College, Cambridge, from where he proceeded M.A. in 1802, Robinson entered Lincoln's Inn but never qualified as a barrister. In 1804 he became private secretary to one of his relatives, Philip Yorke, 3rd Earl of Hardwicke, the then Lord Lieutenant of Ireland. In November 1806 he became M.P. for the borough of Carlow, sitting as a moderate Tory. In the next year he was elected for Ripon, whose member he remained for nearly twenty years.

In 1803 Robinson was appointed Under-Secretary for War and the Colonies in the Duke of Portland's administration, but retired a few months later in sympathy with his friend, Viscount Castlereagh (see Stewart, Robert). Under Perceval he served as a Lord of the Admiralty and on the formation of Lord Liverpool's ministry in 1812 he was appointed a Lord of the Treasury. From 1813 to 1817 he was Joint Paymaster General, and in this capacity he was present with Castlereagh at the negotiations for the Peace of Paris. In 1815 Robinson introduced one of the famous and unpopular series of corn laws – the one that established the lowest internal selling price at 80s. a quarter. During the London riots that followed this measure, Robinson's house was attacked and severely damaged by the mob.

In 1818 he was appointed President of the Board of Trade and admitted to the cabinet. He gave cautious support to Catholic emancipation and was well-disposed towards lifting trade restrictions, but staunchly opposed parliamentary reform. The High Tories chose to regard him as a Liberal and it was with the advent of liberal Toryism and the improving economic conditions of the mid-1820s that Robinson established a fruitful partnership with William Huskisson. When Liverpool reconstructed his ministry in 1823 he appointed Robinson Chancellor of the Exchequer and Huskisson President of the Board of Trade. Huskisson provided most of the ideas but Robinson showed courage in giving them his full backing and in a series of budgets from 1823 to 1826 the duties on a number of items were reduced. He spoke to the House in such glowing terms of the prosperity of the country that William Cobbett felt compelled to dub him 'Prosperity' Robinson in 1825.

Canning succeeded Liverpool as Prime Minister in April 1827, and Robinson was granted the title of Viscount Goderich and the leadership of the House of Lords. He proved an ineffectual leader, however, and was unable to prevent the Duke of Wellington's amendment to the corn law being carried against the government. Nevertheless on the death of Canning in August 1827 George IV chose Goderich as his successor and requested him to form a ministry. He attempted to form a broad-based administration, but soon ran into

trouble; Goderich, in despair, pleaded with the King to admit Lord Holland and Lord Wellesley into the cabinet in order to strengthen the administration. George, however, was resolutely opposed to any extension of Whig influence in the government, and in January 1828, realizing that Goderich lacked the necessary qualities of leadership, he dismissed him. Goderich was not granted a post in Wellington's ministry.

In 1830 Goderich, whose conception of party ties was fairly loose, accepted the post of Secretary for War and the Colonies in Earl Grey's Whig ministry. He gave his full support to the Reform Act of 1832 but despite this change of heart he was unpopular with Grey, who forced him to resign from the colonial office in 1833 and accept the post of Lord Privy Seal. On 3 April 1833 he was created 1st Earl of Ripon. In the next year the proposed appointment of an Irish church commission seemed to him an attack on the established Church and, along with Stanley and Viscount Richmond, he handed in his resignation in May 1834. He joined forces with Peel and delivered a number of speeches condemning the financial incompetence of the Melbourne administration. In Peel's second ministry (1841–6) he was first appointed President of the Board of Trade, but moved from there in 1843 to the India Board. Like Peel, he had become a convinced abolitionist and assured the House that he had always opposed protection on principle. He spoke for the last time in the House of Lords in May 1847, and died at his house in Putney on 28 January 1859.

W. Devereaux Jones, *Prosperity Robinson: The Life of Viscount Goderich, 1782–1859* (1967).

G. I. T. Machin, *The Catholic Question in English Politics, 1820–30* (1964).

Rockingham, 2nd Marquis of (1730–82), see Watson-Wentworth, Charles.

Rodney, George Brydges (1718–92), 1st Baron Rodney; naval commander.

Rodney was born in February 1718. Despite good military connections, he entered the navy in 1732 as a 'king's letter boy' (the popular description of an official aspirant for commissioned service). He passed smoothly through the junior ranks, serving in various ships, and on 9 November 1742 he was appointed captain by Admiral Matthews in the Mediterranean in order to take home the 60-gun *Plymouth*, his commission being confirmed on arrival.

Other commands followed as the war, originally against Spain alone, widened in scope with the entry of France (1744). After being in control of two frigates in the North Sea, Rodney was given command of the new 60-gun *Eagle* in December 1745. He was employed on a successful cruise directed against French commerce early in 1747.

Peace came in 1748, and from then until 1752 Rodney was Governor of Newfoundland and in command of the 40-gun *Rainbow*. His promotion to rear-admiral came on 19 May 1759, and he flew his flag in the 60-gun *Achilles* for close operations against Le Havre well into 1760. In 1761 he was designated commander in chief in the Leeward Islands, in which capacity he advanced to vice-admiral's rank (21 October 1762), and gained a baronetcy (21 January 1764).

Rodney had returned to England in August 1763, peace having already been concluded. Since 1751, he had possessed a seat in the House of Commons in the Duke of Newcastle's interest, holding successively the pocket boroughs of Saltash, Okehampton, and Penryn. But unfortunately he was obliged to fight the general election of 1768 with his own resources, and won Northampton but ruined himself financially in the process. Extravagant living added to his woes, and

a command in Jamaica from 1771 to 1774 failed to improve his fortune, although in August 1771 he had been given the sinecure office of Rear Admiral of Great Britain. In 1775 he was forced to retire to France and remained there, stranded by his debts, until May 1778.

After the entry of France and Spain into the War of American Independence, Rodney became a full admiral (29 January 1778), but lacked a command until the end of 1779, when he was again given the Leeward Islands. On his way out to the West Indies he received the additional task of relieving Gibraltar. Off Cape St. Vincent, his squadrons fell in with a Spanish squadron, and from the resulting engagement (16 January 1780) only two Spaniards escaped. The relief accomplished, Rodney sailed on to the Leeward Islands with four ships only.

Rodney sighted the French off Dominica on 16 April, and an inconclusive battle took place the following day. Guichen sailed for France in the summer of 1780, and Rodney reposed in the satisfaction that he had at least restored a strong British naval presence in the area, even if his squadron's performance had been uninspiring.

The Dutch joined the conflict in 1780, and in January 1781 Rodney successfully attacked St. Eustatius. The island yielded a considerable amount of saleable booty, welcome enough to Rodney, whose extravagances continued to cause him difficulties. His justification for its seizure was that much of it belonged to British subjects. Unfortunately, what was sent home was captured by the French *en route*, while what remained was lost when the island itself was retaken later.

In August, poor health – chiefly the gout – forced Rodney to return to England for a rest, and on 6 November 1781 he was again appointed to a sinecure – Vice Admiral of Great Britain. He was back on station in February 1782 aboard the 98-gun *Formidable*. Meanwhile, the French Admiral de Grasse had, with thirty-five battleships, re-asserted French command of the waters on the far side of the Atlantic. He had swung the strategic balance of the war decisively in favour of France and her allies by the action on Chesapeake Bay (5 September 1781), had recaptured several of the West Indian Islands, and was threatening a junction with a strong Spanish squadron. Rodney came up with him on 9 April off the Saints Passage between Dominica and Guadeloupe. A running fight developed, which was closed on 12 April. Rodney had thirty-six ships-of-line, and employed a novel tactic later used by Nelson, that of breaking the enemy line in two places and precipitating a general action, rather than fighting in line. Five French ships were forced to strike, including that of Grasse himself. The battle could not now reverse the effects of Chesapeake Bay, but it ensured a better British posture at the peace conference.

To the embarrassment of the government, the supersession of Rodney by Admiral Pigot had already been decreed as a consequence of the St. Eustatius affair, and the latter was on his way out before news of the victory was received. There was a rush to make amends: votes of thanks were passed in parliament (22 May), a barony was conferred (19 June), the Commons voted him a pension of £2,000 a year (27 June), and the committee of inquiry into St. Eustatius was discharged, although private lawsuits arising from it continued to harass Rodney. He returned to England in September, and retired from public life. Rodney died on 23 May 1792, leaving five children by his two successive marriages.

D. Hannay, *Rodney* (1903).
David Spinney, *Rodney* (1969).

Portrait: oil, half-length, after Reynolds: N.P.G.

Romney, George (1734–1802), portrait painter, who for a time seemed likely to rival Reynolds and Gainsborough.

George Romney was born on 15 December 1734 at Dalton-in-Furness, Lancashire, the son of a local cabinet-maker. While working with his father he developed an aptitude for drawing and painting, and at the age of about twenty he went to Kendal in Westmorland to study with a provincial painter named Christopher Steele. He stayed with Steele for two years until 1756, when on impulse he suddenly married a local girl who had nursed him through an illness. Romney then set up on his own as a portrait painter, travelling all over northern England and producing likenesses at a few guineas a time. He also executed twenty figure paintings, which were exhibited in Kendal and subsequently sold by lottery.

In 1762 he abandoned his wife and family and went to London. He was immediately successful as a painter, winning an award from the Society of Arts with his *Death of Wolfe*. In awarding the first prize, however, the Royal Academy authorities deferred to the opinion of Sir Joshua Reynolds, who favoured J. H. Mortimer's *Edward the Confessor*, and Romney had to be satisfied with a £50 donation. The incident rankled: Romney reacted icily to Reynolds and thereafter refused to have anything to do with the Academy.

In the following year (1764) Romney visited Paris, where he met Joseph Vernet and was strongly influenced by the classical or antique flavour of the paintings of Nicholas Le Sueur. This influence pervades much of his work from 1763 to 1772; most notably, it is seen in *Sir George and Lady Warren and their Daughter* (1769) and *Mrs. Yates as The Tragic Muse* (1771).

On a visit to Italy (1773–5), Romney saw the work of Raphael and Titian and the experience inspired his best work.

Returning to London and to a reputation as a portrait painter that already rivalled that of Reynolds, Romney embarked upon a decade full of unquestionably fine work. His style, now much more graceful, is well seen in a number of works of this period, notably *Mrs. Carwardine and her Son* (1775), *The Gower Children* (1776), and *Earl Grey* (1784).

In his last years Romney went into a serious decline, both as an artist and as a man. Two personal relationships are associated with this decay: his friendship with William Hayley and that with Emily Hart, the future Emma, Lady Hamilton (q.v.). Hayley pandered to Romney's weaknesses of character and encouraged him to waste his talent on pretentious ideal and poetical subjects. Emily Hart exercised a morbid and bewitching influence over him that dominated his work. The two met in about 1781 and a torrid affair ensued. Emily modelled for Romney in over fifty paintings, posing as Circe, Calypso, Cassandra, even as Joan of Arc or Mary Magdalene.

Romney's love of ideal subjects bore little fruit, except for a few preliminary drawings for over-ambitious historical compositions and some unattractive specimens for John Boydell's Shakespeare Gallery, begun in 1787.

In 1797 Romney moved to a large studio in Hampstead but did not remain there long. In 1799 he went back to Kendal, to the wife whom he had deserted years before and who had remained faithful to him. He died at Kendal on 15 November 1802.

Anne Crookshank, 'The Drawings of George Romney', *Burlington Magazine* (February 1957).
T. H. Ward and W. Roberts, *Romney: A Biographical and Critical Essay* (2 vols.; 1904).

Works in:
Tate Gallery, London.
National Portrait Gallery, London.
Wallace Collection, London.
Kenwood House, London.
Fitzwilliam Museum, Cambridge.
Metropolitan Museum, New York.
Washington National Gallery.

Portraits: self-portrait, oil, half-length, 1782: N.P.G.; miniature, quarter-length, by Miss M. Barrett: N.P.G.; self-portrait, pencil, quarter-length: N.P.G.

Roubillac or Roubiliac, Louis François (?1705–62), sculptor, who worked in England and became one of the most eminent statuaries of the eighteenth century.

Roubillac was born of French parents at Lyons, probably in 1705. After receiving a fair general education he was sent as a pupil to the German sculptor Balthazar Permoser. He stayed for several years before returning to Lyons and working in the studio of Nicolas Couston. He first came to London probably in 1732, soon after winning a prize for a relief of an Old Testament subject at the Academie Royale de Peinture et de Sculpture in Paris (1730). The first record of Roubillac in England is his marriage in London to Catherine Helot in 1735.

Employed first by Thomas Carter, for whom he did mainly ornamental work, Roubillac was one day lucky enough to find a notebook containing a considerable sum of money belonging to Sir Edward Walpole. Returning the notebook and money to their owner, the young Frenchman struck up a friendship with Walpole, who subsequently became his patron.

Through Walpole Roubillac made the acquaintance of Cheeve and Jonathan Tyers, who in 1737 gave Roubillac his first independent commission, a statue of Handel for Vauxhall Gardens. This work foreshadows later executions very well: already there are traces of a rococo style that Roubillac was to use and develop.

By 1740 Roubillac, now prospering, had bought a house in St. Martin's Lane and set up a studio which was later to be occupied by the St. Martin's Lane Academy, where Roubillac taught sculpture. Besides statues Roubillac also executed several busts during this period, notably of Hogarth and Handel. They all have a certain element of intimacy and ruthless realism.

Roubillac was, however, chiefly employed in monumental works. One of the earliest and most famous of these was to the Duke of Argyll (Westminster Abbey). It is renowned for a highly praised figure of Eloquence. In this monument he introduced new patterns in order to break away from the traditional controlled balance of the seventeenth century and to add drama to his work. Later sculptors borrowed elements from it.

During the 1740s Roubillac began to obtain the occasional commission for work outside London; one of the most important of these was a tomb erected in Worcester Cathedral to Bishop Hough in 1746. Roubillac also did several monuments in the provinces, the most notable being those of the Duke and Duchess of Montagu at Warkton, Northamptonshire, and the statues of George I and Charles, Duke of Somerset, in the Senate House at Cambridge. All these works have a very elaborate and careful finish and are characterized by a highly decorative and ornamental style.

In 1752 Roubillac went to Italy for four months, only three days of which he spent in Rome. He was not very impressed by the ancient sculpture there but his enthusiasm for Bernini's work was almost unlimited.

Returning to England, he executed a full-length monument of Shakespeare, now in the British Museum. In 1757 the tomb of General Hargrave was completed and erected; in this Roubillac skilfully and pictorially combined the Christian theme of Resurrection with the pagan allegory of Time and Eternity, to make a quite remarkable effect.

It was in his tombs, where he was able to show a group in action, that Roubillac handled allegory most successfully. One of the best examples of this is the famous tomb of Lady Elizabeth Nightingale in Westminster Abbey, where a fleshless and shrouded Death menaces with his dart the figure of a young woman who is sinking into her husband's arms.

Roubillac's greatest strength, however, lay in the realism of his portraiture and his ability to create character by design: character rather than beauty was his aim. This is most evident in his later busts. Even in his own self-portrait Roubillac depicts himself with compelling and relentless realism. The majority of his portraits were executed in an informal style, where the introduction of innovations was relatively easy to achieve, but even in more formal compositions the mark of originality is still plainly seen.

Louis François Roubillac died on 11 January 1762 as a result of unskilful bleeding, and was buried in the churchyard of St. Martin-in-the-Fields, London. Although he had had a considerable number of commissions and was an industrious worker, he died impoverished.

K. A. Esdaile, *The Life and Works of Louis François Roubiliac* (1929).

Works in:
Westminster Abbey, London.
National Maritime Museum, Greenwich.
National Portrait Gallery, London.
Royal Academy, London.
Victoria and Albert Museum, London.
Royal Collection.
Trinity College, Cambridge.
Leeds Art Gallery.
Birmingham Art Gallery.
Worcester Cathedral.

Portraits: oil, half-length, by A. Carpentiers, 1762: N.P.G.; marble bust, attributed to himself: N.P.G.; oil, by Andrea Soldi: Dulwich College, London.

Rowlandson, Thomas (1756–1827), painter, caricaturist, and illustrator.

Thomas Rowlandson was born in July 1756 in the City of London, the son of a wealthy merchant and speculator. He was sent to Dr. Barrow's famous school in Soho Square, and later progressed to the Royal Academy; by nature high-spirited and mischievous, he was an excellent draughtsman with a rich pictorial imagination.

In about 1772 Rowlandson went to stay with an aunt in Paris and studied drawing at the Academie Royale. His style much improved by Gallic elegance, Rowlandson returned to the Royal Academy in 1774, to be acclaimed as its finest draughtsman; he sent his first contribution, a 'history painting' of Samson and Delilah, to the Academy exhibition in 1775.

At about this time Rowlandson's reckless father lost all his money gambling on the Stock Exchange, but fortunately the young painter's future was assured by a £7,000 bequest from his recently deceased Parisian aunt. By 1777 Rowlandson had opened a studio in Wardour Street and was doing a healthy trade in landscapes and portraits.

However, he was still restless, and made frequent expeditions to the inns and post roads of Holland and Germany, filling his sketchbooks with exquisitely drawn episodes from ordinary life. A vigorous and handsome man, Rowlandson was also fond of gambling and good living, and by 1782 he had squandered his aunt's legacy. Faced with the need to earn his money, he imitated his caricaturist friend Gillray (q.v.) and became a caricaturist himself.

Rowlandson's first mature satirical drawing was his *Vauxhall Gardens* (1784), which became notorious after being exhibited at the Royal Academy. This was followed by his *French Family* (1786),

English Review (1787), and dozens of other trenchant scenes, in which he turned an unsparing eye on various levels of society and subjected them to the boredom, indignity, and delights of everyday life. With equal insight he shows fashionable folk trying to cope with high winds in Hyde Park, or jolly hussars sitting at a stable door with local girls on their knees. Much of his work is good-naturedly obscene; in this he accurately reflects the attitudes of his time.

In 1800 Rowlandson married a Miss Stuart from Camberwell. He reached the height of his fame with the appearance, from 1812 on, of the three successive tours of Dr. Syntax, respectively in search of 'the Picturesque', 'Consolation', and 'a Wife'. These were produced in collaboration with William Combe (q.v.), who also provided the text for the *Dance of Death* (1815) and *Dance of Life* (1816).

When in more serious mood, Rowlandson revealed himself as a gifted book illustrator, contributing to editions of Goldsmith, Smollett, Sterne, and Fielding. Starting with a sixty-seven-plate series in 1782, describing a post-chaise journey to Spithead, he also drew many topographical subjects, perhaps his best being the *Microcosm of London* (1808).

In 1825 Rowlandson was struck down by illness and was forced to give up drawing. He lingered for two years, but died in his Adelphi chambers on 22 April 1827.

J. Grego, *Rowlandson the Caricaturist: a Selection from his works* (2 vols.; 1880).

A. P. Oppe, *Thomas Rowlandson: His Drawings and Water-Colours* (1923).

Portraits: pencil, quarter-length, by J. Jackson: N.P.G.; pencil, half-length, by G. H. Harlow, 1814: N.P.G.

Rumford, Count von (1753–1814), see Thompson, Sir Benjamin.

Russell, Lord John (1792–1878), 1st Earl Russell, see *Lives of the Victorian Age*.

Rysbrack, John Michael (1693–1770), original name Johannes Michiel Rysbraeck; portrait sculptor.

Rysbrack was born in Antwerp on 24 June 1693, the son of the landscape painter Pieter Rysbraeck. He was brought up in a cosmopolitan environment: his mother was French, and his father had worked for several years in both Paris and London. In 1706 the boy was apprenticed to Michiel van der Voort, a well-known Antwerp sculptor who had studied in Rome and absorbed baroque influences. After 1712 Rysbrack worked for some time in Antwerp, and in 1720 went to seek his fortune in London.

His talent was immediately noticed, and he worked for William Kent at Kensington Palace, and for James Gibbs at Westminster Abbey. Rapidly becoming dissatisfied with working for others, Rysbrack courageously set up on his own. Shortly afterwards the aged and celebrated Kneller (see *Lives of the Stuart Age*) commissioned him to carve the likeness for his tomb. This was an astonishing *coup* for a young foreigner against stiff local competition, and Rysbrack swiftly became England's most fashionable portrait sculptor, even in those sectarian times with Whigs and Tories alike.

This reputation was entirely justified, for Rysbrack not only had a penetrating gift for likeness, but also took immense pains over his work, making much use of preliminary models in terracotta. His personal style was an expressive fusion of baroque and classical, as typified by his bust of Daniel Finch (1723). However, if the subject demanded it, Rysbrack could be almost wholly classical, as in his portrait of Alexander Pope (1730), or wholly baroque, as in that of James Gibbs (1726).

Rysbrack was both industrious and versatile: besides carving sixty portrait busts before 1732, he did much sculpture for formal gardens, the best being his likenesses of Inigo Jones and Palladio at Chiswick House (1730). These were based on paintings and engravings, and demonstrate Rysbrack's skill at the three-dimensional rendering of two-dimensional sources. He also received many commissions for tomb sculpture, and indeed his masterpiece is probably the Isaac Newton monument in Westminster Abbey (1731), designed in collaboration with Kent. However, the Marlborough monument at Blenheim (1732) is less successful. Rysbrack also carved an impressive equestrian sculpture of William III at Bristol, based on Roman models but dramatically enlivened by a fluttering cloak.

By 1740 Rysbrack's pre-eminence was being strongly challenged by the theatrical style of Roubillac (q.v.). In response, Rysbrack attempted to diversify, carving almost rococo busts of Rubens and Van Dyck, as well as an elegant sculpture of the Duke of Somerset at Cambridge (1756). Although Rysbrack borrowed from Roubillac the use of asymmetrical compositions, as in the Beaufort tomb at Badminton (1754), his best work was still in his old style – for example the monumental calm of the John Locke bust (1755).

In 1765 Rysbrack disposed of his models and drawings in three great sales, and retired from business. He died at his house in Vere Street, London, on 8 January 1770, and was buried in Marylebone churchyard. Rysbrack was a talented and conscientious craftsman, and his achievement was to bring English sculpture from provincial isolation into the mainstream of European tradition.

M. I. Webb, *Michael Rysbrack, Sculptor* (1954).

Portrait: oil, three-quarter length, by J. Vanderbank, *c.* 1782: N.P.G.

S

Sackville, Lord George, later Lord George Sackville Germain (1716–85), 1st Viscount Sackville; general and politician.

Sackville was born on 26 January 1716, the son of Lionel Cranfield Sackville, 1st Duke of Dorset. He was educated at Westminster School and at Trinity College, Dublin.

George Sackville (who used that name up until 1770, when he added the name Germain in order to benefit from a will) was during almost the whole of his career the beneficiary of privilege: from the outset his father's friendship with George II guaranteed his advancement. In 1737, when Lionel Sackville was Lord Lieutenant of Ireland, young George became Clerk of the Council in Dublin and was given a captaincy in the 7th Regiment of Horse. Three years later he became a lieutenant colonel in Bragg's Regiment of Foot (renamed the 28th in 1742). He was wounded at the Battle of Fontenoy in 1745. Meanwhile, in 1741 he had, through his father's influence, become M.P. for Dover.

The 28th Regiment returned to England with the Duke of Cumberland (see William Augustus) in 1745 to meet the second Jacobite rising. Sackville was given the colonelcy of the 20th Regiment. He was not, however, present with that regiment when it fought at Culloden (16 April 1746), being unable to join it in time. When the 20th went on garrison duty, Sackville returned to Flanders (1747), leaving the regiment's administration to a competent young major, James Wolfe (q.v.). In 1749 Sackville joined the 12th

Dragoons on standby in Ireland. He sat for a time in the Irish parliament for the pocket borough of Portarlington.

At the outbreak of the Seven Years War Sackville was made a major general in command of an infantry brigade, and in 1757 he was transferred to the colonelcy of the 2nd Dragoon Guards. In 1758 Sackville was sent with some of his regiment to aid Prince Frederick of Brunswick. Marlborough commanded the British contingent, but on his sudden death in September 1758 Sackville took over the command. He was also made a Privy Councillor.

Up to that point in his career, Sackville seems to have enjoyed good relations with his military colleagues, but in Germany friction grew between him and the army commander on the one hand, and his immediate subordinate in the British contingent, the Marquis of Granby, on the other. It was brought to a head on the battlefield of Minden (1 August 1759). A confusion over orders led to the British infantry battalions carrying out their attack unsupported by the cavalry of Sackville, and then, when the French were in disorder, the cavalry failed to charge to complete the rout. Three direct requests for the charge came from the Prince, and a fourth messenger called Sackville to the Prince's side. The furious Granby added his appeals, and even put his own regiment, the Blues, into motion. By the time Sackville was persuaded to move, the moment had passed and the French had retired in good order.

Sackville had affronted an allied Prince

– a German Prince, just as King George II was. Granby used his own political influence, and Sackville was relieved of his command. He was dismissed from the service on 10 September and his name was struck from the role of the Privy Council. A court martial was eventually convened the following spring to listen to his defence and duly found him guilty and unfit to serve 'in any military capacity whatsoever'. George II instructed that the sentence be read out in front of every regiment in the army.

The accession of George III in 1760 allowed Sackville to repair his shattered fortune. The new King felt he had been ill-used and received him at court in 1763, restoring his name to the Privy Council list. Elected to parliament for East Grinstead and Hythe in 1761, he sat as M.P. for the latter, reverting to the former after the election of 1768 and holding the seat until 1782. In 1765 and 1766 he held the post of Joint Vice Treasurer for Ireland.

Sackville – or Germain, as he called himself after 1770 in order to benefit from the vast fortune of Lady Elizabeth Germain (died 1769) – made his mark as a parliamentarian. He attacked Townshend (see Townshend, George, 4th Viscount) over colonial taxation and was eventually (1775) brought into the North administration as Secretary of State for the American Colonies and President of the Board of Trade. Germain's early optimism about a quick settlement in America had turned by 1777 into a more realistic understanding of the situation. He conceived a workmanlike plan to isolate New England by having Burgoyne's Canadian-based forces link up with a northward-bound army from New York under Howe. The whole plan went awry, however, because Germain forgot that he had already authorized Howe's attack on Philadelphia. Burgoyne, stranded at Saratoga, surrendered to the French.

Sackville resigned in February 1782, only weeks before North's government collapsed. Despite opposition, he was given a viscountcy on his own request and went into retirement on his estate at Withyham, Sussex, where he died on 26 August 1785.

A. Valentine, *Lord George Germaine* (1962).

G. S. Brown, *The American Secretary: the Colonial Policy of Lord George Germaine, 1775–1778* (Ann Arbor, Michigan, 1963).

F. E. Whitton, *Service Trials and Tragedies* (1930).

St. John, Henry (1678–1751), 1st Viscount Bolingbroke; politician, see *Lives of the Stuart Age*.

St. Vincent, Earl (1735–1823), see Jervis, John.

Salomon, Johann Peter (1745–1815), musician and concert manager of German birth.

Salomon was born in Bonn, where he was baptized on 2 February 1745. His father, a musician of minor repute, had him educated for a career in the law; the boy also studied classics and gained a command of four modern languages, accomplishments which were later to stand him in good stead. However, he distinguished himself particularly in music, and decided to become a professional musician. About 1759 he was appointed court musician at Bonn Palace, a position which he left in August 1765 with the highest testimonials. As *Konzertmeister* under Prince Henry of Prussia, Salomon composed several operettas, and did much to make Haydn's 'music of the future' better known and appreciated in northern Germany. After some years the orchestra disbanded and Salomon travelled to Paris and London, revisiting Bonn frequently and making friends with the child Beethoven.

Salomon's first English appearance was

367

at Covent Garden on 23 March 1781, when he led the orchestra and played a violin solo of his own composition. He became well known among the principal London musicians, both as composer and performer, playing, as Burney records, with 'taste, refinement, and enthusiasm'. Having quarrelled with the directors of Professional Concerts soon after the foundation of that organization, Salomon took an independent course and began producing his own concerts.

While travelling abroad to engage opera singers for the impresario Gallini, Salomon heard of the death of Prince Esterhazy, Haydn's patron. He at once arranged for Haydn to come to England in the following year, and for Mozart to follow him the year after. The famous Salomon concerts began in 1791 in the Hanover Square Rooms, and were so successful that, when Mozart died that same year, Haydn agreed to stay for another year's concerts. He returned to England, again through Salomon's agency, in 1794. For these two visits Haydn composed twelve symphonies known as the 'Grand' or 'Salomon' symphonies. A few years later, it was again Salomon who suggested to Haydn that he should attempt an oratorio, and procured for him the libretto of the *Creation*. The oratorio was published in 1800, but first produced at Covent Garden by John Ashley, Salomon putting on the second performance at the King's Theatre on 21 April. The following year Salomon, in partnership with Doctor Arnold, took Covent Garden for the Lenten Oratorios.

In 1813 Salomon took an active part in establishing the Philharmonic Society and led the orchestra in its first concert. He also had plans for an Academy of Music. But a fall from his horse in 1815 brought on a severe attack of dropsy, from which he died at his house at 70 Newman Street on 25 November. He was buried in the south cloister of Westminster Abbey.

Salomon is best known as an organizer of concerts; the only composition of his that is still recalled is *Windsor Castle*, composed for the Prince of Wales's wedding in 1795. He was generous to excess, and it is said that only the vigilance of an old and faithful servant saved him from ruin through liberality. Haydn's last quartets were written to include a high violin part to suit Salomon's style of playing. He was much lamented at his death, and Beethoven remembered him affectionately as 'a noble man'.

'Memoir of Johann Peter Salomon', *Harmonicon*, February 1830.

Sandwich, 4th Earl of (1718–92), see Montagu, John.

Schulenburg, Countess Ehrengarde Melusina von der (1667–1743), Duchess of Kendal; mistress of George I.

Melusina von der Schulenburg was born on 25 December 1667 on the family estate at Emden. Her father was Count Gustavus Adolphus von der Schulenburg. Melusina's elder brother, Matthias Johann, achieved renown as a military commander.

Melusina found her way into the service of the Electress Sophia at Hanover where she attracted the attention of Sophia's son, George Louis (later George I of England). His wife Sophia Dorothea, suspected of adultery, was held prisoner for many years, and divorced in 1694; she died more than twenty years later, still a captive. George Louis, meanwhile, bestowed his favours on Melusina (among others), became Electoral Prince of Hanover in 1698, and acceded to the English throne in 1714.

The London populace disliked the two mistresses brought by King George I to England: 'Madame de Schulenburg', spare and thin – 'the maypole' – and

Baroness von Kielmannsegge, later Countess of Darlington – 'the elephant' – who for a period eclipsed, though she did not unseat, her rival. Shortly after their arrival in England Melusina gained ascendancy over the younger and prettier Baroness, and from then on her position of power and influence remained constant, though the King did not.

The Countess von der Schulenburg was naturalized in 1716 and titles were heaped upon her by King George. In 1719 she became Baroness of Glastonbury, Countess of Feversham, and Duchess of Kendal, the last principally a royal title. Charles VI, whose wife, a Wolfenbüttel-Brunswick princess, had been corresponding with the Duchess over the Anglo-Austrian alliance, decided to make her a Princess of the Empire in 1723. She was awarded an annual pension from the English exchequer of £7,500, but this sum represented only part of her income.

According to Sir Robert Walpole, the Duchess of Kendal 'would have sold the King's honour for a shilling advance, to the best bidder'. She is said to have been paid £5,000 by Bolingbroke's father for his viscountcy and also to have accepted the prodigious bribe of £11,000 from Bolingbroke's second wife, in expectation of influence exerted on her husband's behalf (see St. John, Henry, in Lives of the Stuart Age). The Duchess reaped a huge share in the South Sea Company profits, she made an extremely lucrative deal over a tenure in the customs house, and she also had an interest, to the tune of £10,000, in the affair of 'Wood's Ha'pence', which forced on the Irish at an extortionate rate a completely super-fluous copper coinage. Although she supported him and was said to be his 'fast friend', Walpole derided the Duchess, declaring her intellects mean and con-temptible. However the King, by no means a fool, obviously valued her judgment, and continued his custom of transacting state affairs in her apartments. She fostered the negotiations for a reconciliation between him and the Prince of Wales in 1720. She also had a hand in the 'partial' restoration of Bolingbroke, thereby honouring her promise to his wife, at least in part. In fact, Bolingbroke was allowed to return to England, but the King passed the matter over to the hostile Walpole, and Boling-broke's attainder was not reversed.

To the last the Duchess remained a vigilant companion to the King. In 1727 she accompanied him on the trip to the German dominions which turned out to be his last. On the journey she rested at Delden, while the King, concealing his illness, went on to Osnabrück. When the Duchess heard he was ailing she hastened after him, but tidings of his death reached her just after she crossed the Rhine.

The Duchess of Kendal at first retired to Berlin and later removed to Kendal House, Isleworth-on-Thames, where she stayed until her death on 10 May 1743. The King, it seems, had promised the Duchess that 'if he could, he would appear to her after death'. According to Horace Walpole's Reminiscence, 'soon after that event, a large bird flew into her window' and the Duchess, believing it to be the King's soul, cherished it 'and took utmost care of it'.

The Duchess of Kendal left two daughters, Petronella Melusina, who was made Countess of Walsingham in 1722 and married Philip Stanhope, 4th Earl of Chesterfield, and Margaret Gertrude, who married the Conte von Lippe. It was rumoured at the King's death that he left his mistress £40,000, but as the contents of his will were never known, this is unverified, as is the story that he and the Duchess had been secretly married.

J. M. Beattie, The English Court in the Reign of George I (1967).

Scott, Samuel (?1702–72), one of the earliest and most eminent English marine and topographical painters.

Samuel Scott is reputed to have been born in London about 1702. Little or nothing is known of his childhood. He is first heard of as an artist working in the capital in the late 1720s. He was a boon companion of Hogarth and in 1732 accompanied Hogarth and others on a trip by water to Gravesend. Ebenezer Forest wrote a journal of the five days spent at the coast, which was illustrated by Hogarth and Scott and later published.

Strongly influenced by the van de Velde brothers, Scott's early paintings were usually of naval battles. In 1732 he collaborated with George Lambert in a series of views of the East India Company's settlements.

An excellent draughtsman and expert user of colour, Scott executed a few water-colour paintings, but his major works were done in oil. He gained a great reputation for his sea pieces, the best examples of which are *The Engagement between 'The Lion' and 'The Elizabeth', 1745*, which Walpole described as Scott's best work, and *The Engagement between the Blast Sloop and two Spanish Privateers, 1745*. Both of these works manifest a mastery of tone and a dramatic sense of pattern which differentiate Scott's work from that of the van de Veldes and reveal him as an artist in his own right.

Canaletto, who came to England in about 1746, created a fashion for London views, especially reaches of the Thames diversified with characteristic figures. When he returned to Italy in 1751 Scott, having been profoundly influenced by him, became heir to this new market and abandoned marine paintings for the more lucrative views of London. In a manner similar to Canaletto, Scott added variety to his views with figures, which were often gay and amusing, but he made no attempt to endow them with the sparkle they had in the Italian's work. Like Canaletto too, Scott kept a repertory of drawings from which he produced painted versions and slightly altered repetitions, as in the case of his paintings of *Old London Bridge*, where he varied the size of the picture. Scott's talent is undeniable, and he manages to give his works a certain individuality and native quality; he does not reproduce Canaletto's Venetian brilliance in his works but portrays the watery aura of the English atmosphere. It is with good reason that he has since been dubbed 'The English Canaletto'.

In the 1760s Scott exhibited three times for the Society of Artists and in 1771 he made his only exhibition at the Royal Academy with a picture entitled *A View of the Tower of London*. He had spent most of his life in Twickenham, but he finally left London in 1765 and, after a short stay in Ludlow, Shropshire, where he painted some inland views, he moved to Bath, where he settled and eventually died of gout on 12 October 1772.

Works in:
The Tate Gallery, London.
The National Maritime Museum, Greenwich.
The British Museum, London.
The Guildhall, London.

Portrait: oil, quarter-length, by unknown artist: N.P.G.

Scott, Sir Walter (1771–1832), Scottish novelist, poet, and man of letters.

Walter Scott was born in Edinburgh on 15 August 1771, the fourth surviving son of a prominent solicitor. At the age of only eighteen months, he suffered an attack of poliomyelitis that left him permanently lame in his right leg, and for the good of his health he was sent to the country, in the care of his paternal grandparents, who had a farm near the Border town of Kelso. Full participation in various country pastimes rapidly developed in him a healthy and robust physique.

Scott's ancestors had lived in the Borders for generations, and during his convalescence he heard many traditional ballads and stories from his grandmother; nearly all his finest writing is consciously dependent on the oral tradition of the country people among whom he grew up.

Having received some education at Edinburgh high school and at Kelso, he began a five-year legal apprenticeship with his father. But although he applied himself conscientiously to his legal studies, his youthful exuberance found a more natural outlet in the Edinburgh taverns and literary societies. In the winter of 1786–7 he met Robert Burns during the latter's first and much-publicized visit to Edinburgh; in 1788 he heard a friend's lecture on German literature, and his own consequent interest in this subject led to his adaptation of two German ballads (published anonymously in 1796) and his translation of a tragedy by Goethe (published in 1799).

A further Continental theme to which Scott responded with animation was the outbreak of the French Revolution: his own sympathies were for the aristocracy, the representatives of chivalry and tradition, and in 1797 he helped to establish a volunteer cavalry corps to support the Royalist cause.

Despite these new literary and political interests Scott's chief personal pre-occupation during the early 1790s was his courtship of Williamina Belsches, the daughter of Sir John Belsches and Lady Jane Stuart of Fettercairn, near Montrose (see Mill, James). His disappointment when Williamina became engaged to a wealthy landowner in 1796 was acute. However, in December 1797 he married Charlotte Carpentier, the daughter of a French emigré, at Carlisle.

Having qualified as an advocate in 1792, Scott found his income was now sufficient to support a family, and he set up house with his wife in Edinburgh. In 1799 Scott was appointed Sheriff of Selkirkshire. Encouraged by meetings with the novelist Matthew Lewis (q.v.) he prepared a collection of Scottish ballads, eventually published in three volumes in 1802–3 as *The Minstrelsy of the Scottish Border*. The enthusiastic response to his emendations encouraged him to produce his own full-length narrative poem, *The Lay of the Last Minstrel* (1805).

The immediate commercial success of this colourful Romantic poem enabled Scott to commit himself wholly to a literary career. By his energetic participation in Edinburgh social life he gained the friendship of Southey, Wordsworth, Byron, and many other distinguished literary personalities. In 1804 Scott rented a large house at Ashestiel on the bank of the River Tweed near Selkirk, and the birth of his fourth child in the following year completed his family.

Despite his appointment to the well-paid position of Clerk to the Court of Session in 1806, Scott's literary activities rapidly increased. As well as contributing regularly to the *Edinburgh Review* he edited an eighteen-volume edition of the complete works of Dryden (1808) and another in nineteen volumes of the works of Swift (1814), but his income and his popular acclaim were chiefly the result of the long series of narrative poems that included *Marmion* (1808), *The Lady of the Lake* (1810), and *The Lord of the Isles* (1815). To a reading public that had only recently come to accept what the new Romantic movement in literature was offering, Scott's poems presented all the characteristic elements of this movement in their most palatable form: picturesque scenery, ideal heroines, dramatic action, and the occasional hint of melancholy and doom. Scott wrote at great speed – he was never ashamed of admitting that the money was more important than the art – and he frankly told his daughter that there were far better things for her to be reading than his own poems.

Scott's transformation from poet into novelist was the result of external pressures rather than of his own intention. With some of his first income from his literary work he had financed the establishment in Edinburgh of a printing press belonging to a former schoolfriend named James Ballantyne; in 1805 he had become an active partner in this firm, often making it a condition with his publishers that his works should be printed by Ballantyne; but his use of Ballantyne's press to publish antiquarian volumes with little public appeal meant that by 1813 the whole business was on the verge of bankruptcy. A further drain on his personal finances was his project for building a large country house on the estate of Abbotsford, near Melrose, where he had moved in 1812. Negotiations with the Edinburgh publisher Archibald

Constable and a grant from the Duke of Buccleuch managed to save the firm of Ballantyne, but Scott knew well that this was only a temporary reprieve – and it was in these circumstances of urgent financial need that, in the autumn of 1813, it happened to come across the uncompleted manuscript of a novel that he had begun several years previously and then forgotten.

The first of the Waverley novels was published anonymously in July 1814; the anonymity was probably occasioned by the social convention which deemed the practice of writing novels to be inappropriate for a gentleman, but by its effect in creating an atmosphere of mystery concerning the identity of the author, it served as an excellent publicity gimmick. Success was immediate, and for the rest of his career Scott was occupied in writing an apparently endless sequence of historical novels to satisfy the twin demands of his own financial need and the appetite of his reading public. Collected editions of Scott's works generally include at least thirty novels; among the best-known are *Old Mortality* (1816), *The Heart of Midlothian* (1818), *Ivanhoe* (1819), and *Redgauntlet* (1824). His choice of settings for his novels was determined by both love of tradition and intuitive historical awareness. A certain amount of Scott's writing was inevitably mere colourful pageant, but in dramatizing the personal conflicts of his heroes – whose loyalties are often divided between Scotland and England, family and self, past and future – Scott often demonstrated a profound understanding of historical processes.

Most of Scott's writing was done in the early hours of the morning in order that it should not disturb his social activities, and he allowed his social commitments to increase as his fame grew. In 1818 he helped to publicize the discovery of the long-lost regalia of the Scottish monarchy; in 1820 he received a baronetcy and was elected President of the Royal Society of Scotland, and two years later he organized the celebrations for George IV's visit to Edinburgh that launched the kilted Highlander as the national stereotype. Scott was not unjustified in claiming that his personal achievements had helped to stimulate a cultural renaissance for all of Scotland.

The glory was all too brief. The expenses of Abbotsford alone had amounted to over £75,000, and because of his complicated arrangements with various different publishers, Scott's income was never consistent. In January 1826 a financial collapse in London caused the publishing firms of Constable and Ballantyne to go bankrupt, and Scott himself became liable for debts that amounted to over £130,000. In May of the same year his beloved wife died, and Scott was thus faced at the height of his success with his greatest physical and moral challenge.

Undeterred by the apparent impossibility of raising the vast sums required, Scott dedicated the rest of his life to the fulfilment of what he willingly accepted as his personal responsibilities. This characteristic strength of character had always attracted loyal affection from his servants and acquaintances, and Scott's creditors proved generous in allowing him to retain his house at Abbotsford and an annual salary of £1,600 a year; the rest of his property, together with all profits from current and future work, was surrendered to a trust from which the debts might eventually be paid. A journal that Scott kept during these final years at Abbotsford records the stoic good humour with which he accepted his failing health and his necessary work. In June 1827 he published an eight-volume *Life of Napoleon*; on the day after its publication he began work on *Tales of a Grandfather*, a children's history of Scotland, and by Christmas enough money had been earned to pay the creditors a dividend of 6s. in the pound. Tom Purdie, Scott's bailiff and intimate friend for over twenty-five years, died in 1829, but Scott himself continued without rest: by December 1830 he was able to pay a further divided of 3s. in the pound, and his attendance at a rowdy political meeting at Jedburgh in 1831 to protest against the imminent Reform Bill demonstrated his continuing interest in all social and political issues.

Scott's physical health was inevitably weaker than his moral determination, and in October 1831, after he had suffered a series of paralytic strokes, a frigate of the British navy was placed at his disposal for a Mediterranean cruise. Scott visited Malta, Naples, and Rome, but he was now too ill for such superficial cures and on the return journey he suffered a further attack of apoplexy. Soon after his return to Scotland he sank into a state of semi-consciousness, in which he remained – intermittently aware of both the work yet to be done and his own incapability of performing it – until his death on 21 September 1832; that he died at Abbotsford and in the presence of his children was perhaps a certain consolation, for Scott's house and family were his deliberate symbols of tradition, growth, and all that he loved best about his native country.

At the time of Scott's death the debts still outstanding amounted to £54,000; over £20,000 was immediately realized from life insurance policies and the remainder was quickly raised from the sale of his copyrights. The irony that the most commercially successful of authors should have died while heavily in debt was a reflection of the paradoxical nature of Scott himself – talented and careless, rational and romantic, Tory and radical. Scott's character was as fascinating and as full of conflicts as any of his novels, and if his success was on an unprecedented scale, so also was the hard work with which he had earned it. He was the first British novelist to achieve mass public acclaim within his own lifetime.

The Waverley Novels (25 vols.; Centenary edition, 1870–1).

A. O. J. Cockshut, *The Achievement of Sir Walter Scott* (1969).

T. Crawford, *Scott* (1965).

D. A. Davie, *The Heyday of Sir Walter Scott* (1961).

H. J. C. Grierson (ed.), *The Letters of Scott* (12 vols.; 1932–7).

H. J. C. Grierson, *Sir Walter Scott, Bart: a New Life* (1938).

E. Johnson, *Sir Walter Scott: The Great Unknown* (2 vols.; 1970).

J. Logie Robertson (ed.), *Poetical Works* (1904).

J. G. Tait (ed.), *The Journal of Sir Walter Scott, 1825–32* (3 vols.; 1939–46).

A. Welsh, *The Hero of the Waverley Novels* (New Haven, 1963).

Portraits: oil, three-quarter length, by J. C. Gilbert: N.P.G.; oil, full-length, by W. Allan, 1832: N.P.G.; oil on panel, half-length, by E. Landseer, 1824: N.P.G.

Shaftesbury, 7th Earl of (1801–85), philanthropist and social reformer, see Cooper, Anthony Ashley, in *Lives of the Victorian Age*.

Shelburne, 1st Earl of (1737–1805), see Petty, William.

Shelley, Mary Wollstonecraft (1797–1851), novelist, and second wife of Percy Bysshe Shelley; best known as the author of *Frankenstein*.

Mary Shelley was born on 30 August 1797 in London, the only daughter of William Godwin (q.v.) and Mary Wollstonecraft. She had a difficult childhood. Her mother died not long after her birth, and when her father remarried in 1801 the hounding presence of his new wife – the former Mary Jane Clairmont –

became somewhat oppressive. Mary's stepmother had two children by a previous marriage.

Mary was a solitary and withdrawn child, and when her health began to suffer noticeably, she was sent to live with a family in Scotland. There she remained happily until she was nearly seventeen, when she was ordered home by her father. At the time, Godwin had developed a friendship with Shelley that originated in the young poet's admiration for Godwin's *Political Justice*. Shelley showed financial generosity towards Godwin after the latter's failure in a publishing venture.

Although already married, Shelley fell in love with Mary almost immediately after their first meeting in 1814. On 28 July of that year, accompanied by Mary's stepsister, Claire Clairmont, they eloped to France.

During their subsequent tour of the Continent (later written up by Mary as *History of a Six Weeks Tour*, 1817) Shelley and Mary spent some time at Lord Byron's villa in Switzerland. It was here that they met Byron's physician, Polidori. One evening the group had been reading aloud from a collection of German ghost stories, and the idea was proposed that each should attempt to write an original 'tale of horror'. Only one attempt was successful and, even in this embryonic version, Shelley realized that Mary had a talent for the genre.

Frankenstein, or The Modern Prometheus (published 1818) originated in Mary's brooding over the question of the principle of life. She was seized with the fantastic idea of life being created in a laboratory and when she told Shelley of her idea he reacted enthusiastically and encouraged her to start work on the story immediately. The original *Frankenstein* bears very little resemblance to any of the numerous film versions of our own day; it should be remembered, too, that Frankenstein was not the name of the monster created in the mind of Mary Shelley, but of the scientist who created the monster. Moreover, except for his horrible appearance – the result of his maker piecing together parts of human bodies robbed from graves and then instilling life into the grotesque creature – Mary's monster was at first rather likeable, but became the victim of human intolerance and misunderstanding.

On 30 December 1816, a few months after Shelley's wife Harriet committed suicide, Mary and Shelley were married. They were to enjoy less than six years of married life; Shelley's own death ensued in July 1822. Their life together was often hard. Shelley lost the custody of his children by Harriet and feared legal intervention in his relationship with Mary. He also discovered that he had tuberculosis, and for this as well as for other reasons, he and Mary left for Italy (1818). Mary's greatest sadness during these years was the loss of her daughter by Shelley, Clara.

Mary's other novels, though more mature than *Frankenstein*, are variable in quality and did not have the same success. They were all published after Shelley's death; among them are *Valperga* (1823), *The Last Man* (1826), and *Falkner* (1837). In *Lodore* (1835) Mary provides a barely fictionalized account of Shelley's personal difficulties with his first wife. Its main interest is in the light it sheds on some aspects of the poet's personality and emotions. She supported herself entirely from the sales of her novels until Shelley's father provided her with an allowance. This he threatened to withdraw if she persisted in her plans to publish a biography of the poet, and this seems to have deterred her. Mary did, however, edit Shelley's works, and her *Journal* and correspondence are invaluable aids to a

better understanding of the poet. She died on 21 February 1851.

H. Bloom (ed.), *Frankenstein: or the Modern Prometheus* (New York, 1965).

E. Nitchie, *Mary Shelley: Author of Frankenstein* (New Brunswick, 1953).

Muriel Spark, *Child of Light: A Reassessment of Mary Shelley* (1951).

Portraits: oil, half-length, by R. Rothwell, 1841: N.P.G.; oil, half-length, by A. Curran, 1818: N.P.G.; plaster cast of medallion, attributed to Marianne Leigh Hunt: N.P.G.

Shelley, Percy Bysshe (1792–1822), poet.

Shelley was born on 4 August 1792 at Field Place, near Horsham, Sussex, the eldest son of Timothy Shelley, a wealthy country squire and M.P. for Shoreham. He received his early education at Syon House School, Brentford, where he was sent at the age of ten. During his two years at this academy his sensitive and artistic nature made it difficult for him to adjust to the other boys; he applied himself to his studies and developed a keen interest in the classical languages. In 1804 he entered Eton, where he was to remain for six years.

According to Thomas Medwin, a cousin and schoolfellow of Shelley, the future poet was 'at this time tall for his age, slightly and delicately built, and rather narrow-chested, with a complexion fair and ruddy, a face rather long than oval'. While at Eton, Shelley developed an avid interest in science and enjoyed simple experiments in electricity and chemistry. Although never systematic in his scientific studies, he was fascinated by the potential they held for revealing the secrets of nature.

Shelley is said to have spent an unhappy six years at Eton, but his own later recollections in verse tend to throw doubt on this version of his schooling. He rebelled openly against the general fashions of the day. Although possessed of an inquiring and logical mind, Shelley lived in a mood of passion. His growing political and social ideas for reform were profoundly affected and encouraged by a chance reading of William Godwin's *Inquiry Concerning Political Justice*, which advocated the abolition of marriage and the overthrow of authority.

Shelley, as yet immature, was becoming a political idealist who believed that human perfection was a reasonable possibility, and he easily accepted Godwin's thesis that man could live in harmony with his fellows without the need for laws or formal social structures and institutions. The political content of his early work, though often naïve, renders his poetry different from others among the Romantic poets (especially Keats, q.v.) in the prominence he gave to thought over imagination. He desired not only to paint but to interpret nature. The result, in many of his longer poems, was a certain abstract philosophical flavour.

By the time Shelley entered University College, Oxford, in 1810, he had already written and published several poems. Few of them revealed the potential genius of their author. He became an intimate friend of Thomas Jefferson Hogg, a subsequent biographer. Shelley and Hogg shared similar religious views, being basically anti-Christian. Their long discussions on the subject of atheism resulted in Shelley's anonymous publication of a small pamphlet entitled *The Necessity of Atheism* (1811). Although this immature work was comparatively harmless – the product, perhaps, of an over-zealous spirit – it nevertheless resulted in Shelley's expulsion from Oxford in the same year.

The young poet moved to London, where he was introduced to a friend of one of his four sisters – Harriet Westbrook, a schoolgirl of sixteen. The youthful Shelley fell in love with her immediately. Because he himself was only nineteen, they took advantage of the more liberal Scottish law and travelled to Edinburgh, where they were married on 28 August 1811. In June 1813 their daughter Ianthe was born.

Shelley's first major poem, 'Queen Mab', was privately printed in 1813 (published in 1821). It was critical of orthodox Christianity and secular tyranny, and dealt largely with the corruption of mankind by institutions and conventional morality. The poem was hardly a masterpiece. When a pirated edition appeared a few years later, Shelley disclaimed it as immature and injurious to the cause of freedom.

In early 1814 Shelley published *A Refutation of Deism*, and in March of the same year he remarried Harriet in England, apparently so that no question over the legitimacy of their children could arise. The formality proved empty of purpose, however, since within the next month Harriet and Shelley separated, apparently by mutual consent. Harriet did not altogether share the enthusiasms and poetic compulsions of her sensitive husband.

Shelley's acquaintance with the works of William Godwin (q.v.) was by now almost a decade old. Godwin's influence on him had been profound, and in 1812 the poet had met Godwin for the first time. For his part, Godwin saw profit in the acquaintance. He was impoverished and Shelley was generous. Godwin milked the poet and frittered away the funds he got until Shelley sourly cut him off in 1818.

Shelley's meeting with Godwin, however, bore fruit that changed his life. In the summer of 1814 he met the philosopher's sixteen-year-old daughter Mary (see Shelley, Mary Wollstonecraft). He was drawn immediately to this girl, captured by her enthusiasm and intellect, and the mutual romantic attraction led, on 28 July, to an elopement to France. In the following month Mary Godwin wrote to Harriet requesting her to join them both in Switzerland. Harriet, not surprisingly, refused, and in September Shelley and Mary returned to England. On 30 November Harriet gave birth to Shelley's son. As a reconciliation seemed impossible, Shelley made financial arrangements to pay off Harriet's debts and to provide her with a fixed sum to be paid quarterly.

On 24 January 1816 Mary Godwin bore Shelley's son William. In March, while living near Windsor, Shelley published 'Alastor, or the Spirit of Solitude', a poem which greatly enhanced his reputation. In this same eventful year he and Mary went to Geneva, where they met Lord Byron. Mary's stepsister Claire Clairmont travelled with them; indeed, one purpose of the visit seems to have been to enable Claire to continue her affair with Byron, whose child she bore in January 1817. Towards the end of the year they learned that Harriet had committed suicide by drowning herself in the Serpentine, in London. Harriet's father, in a fit of grief and anger, filed suit to prohibit Shelley from having custody of Harriet's children.

Shelley and Mary were married in England on 30 December 1816, and shortly afterwards set up house in Marlow, Buckinghamshire. During this relatively tranquil period in England Mary bore him a daughter named Clara.

In 1818, Shelley having learned that he had tuberculosis, the couple went to Italy. Here the poet remained for the rest of his life and produced his greatest work. A long poem, later named *The Revolt of Islam*, was written in 1818, as were his translation of Plato's *Symposium* (which he finished in a little over a week), 'Rosalind and Helen', and 'Julian and Maddalo'. In 1819 he finished *The Cenci*, a blank-verse tragic drama on the subject of a sixteenth-century Italian patricide, Beatrice Cenci, and also the verse play *Prometheus Unbound*, which some critics consider to be his finest major work; it consists of four acts, the first and the last of which show poetic creativity of the most sublime nature. Some of his short lyric poems produced during this period are among the greatest in the English language. One of the finest is 'Ozymandias', written in 1817 and first published in 1818 by his friend Leigh Hunt (q.v.). In 1820 he wrote 'Ode to the West Wind', 'The Cloud', 'The Sensitive Plant', and 'To a Skylark'. His 'Epipsychidion', a poem on love, was influenced by a casual infatuation for Emilia Viviani, an Italian contessa whom Shelley for a time considered as his 'perfect' woman.

In 1821 Shelley responded to the *Four Ages of Poetry* of Peacock (q.v.) by writing *The Defence of Poetry*. In this prose work Shelley outlines his views of the poetic vision and the value of creative imagination.

His elegy 'Adonais', lamenting the death in 1821 of John Keats, is one of the finest examples of this genre in English, second perhaps only to Milton's 'Lycidas'. From 1821 also dates his play *Hellas*, a contemporary drama based on 'a sort of imitation of the *Persae* of Aeschylus' and sparked off by the commencement of the Greek revolt against Turkish rule.

The Shelleys' life in Italy was marred by the poet's poor health and also by the death of both Clara and William. Mary, secretly blaming Shelley for this, fell into a black melancholy, although this was somewhat relieved by the birth of their last child, Percy Florence, in 1820. In 1822 Shelley and his family moved to Lerici. In that year he wrote his last major work, 'The Triumph of Life', a fragment in which he shows how we are all deceived by the illusion that masquerades as reality.

The Shelleys' companions at Lerici were Jane and Edward Williams. Williams had long shared Shelley's love of boating, and was with him on 8 July 1822, when they set out on what was to be their last nautical adventure. While they were sailing back from Livorno to Lerici, an unexpected and particularly violent storm capsized their boat, and both were drowned. Ten days later Shelley's corpse was washed up upon the beach at Viareggio, a copy of Keats's poems in his jacket pocket. After a long delay official permission was finally granted to have the body cremated on the beach, where it had been temporarily buried. Byron, Leigh Hunt, and Edward Trelawny, a friend who was a naval officer and who was later to write his reminiscences of this period, were present at the lighting of the funeral pyre on 16 August 1822. Shelley's ashes, under Trelawny's supervision, were finally laid to rest in the city of Rome.

E. Blunden, *Shelley: A Life Story* (1946).

K. N. Cameron, *The Young Shelley: Genesis of a Radical* (New York, 1950).

Gillian Carey, *Shelley* (1975).

D. L. Clark (ed.), *Shelley's Prose: or the Trumpet of a Prophecy* (Albuquerque, 1954).

R. Ingpen and W. E. Peck (eds.), *The Complete Works of Shelley* (10 vols.; 1926–30).

F. L. Jones (ed.), *The Letters of Shelley* (2 vols.; 1964).

D. G. King-Hele, *Shelley: His Thought and Work* (1960).

G. M. Matthews (ed.), *Selected Poems and Prose* (1964).

N. I. White, *Shelley* (2 vols.; New York, 1940; rev. 1947).

L. J. Zillman (ed.), *Prometheus Unbound: a Lyrical Drama in Four Acts, with Other Poems* (Seattle, 1959).

Portraits: oil, half-length, by Amelia Curran, 1819: N.P.G.; oil, half-length, by A. Clint after Amelia Curran: N.P.G.

Sheraton, Thomas (?1751–1806), furniture designer; also author, mechanic, inventor, artist, mystic, and religious writer.

Thomas Sheraton was born in 1750 or 1751 at Stockton-on-Tees, Durham, the son of a cabinet-maker. His origins were humble and his education scanty, yet he somehow picked up the arts of drawing and geometry. He was apprenticed to a cabinet-maker, but it was as a theological writer that he first drew attention, with the publication at Stockton-on-Tees in 1782 of a pamphlet, *A Scriptural Illustration of the Doctrine of Regeneration*, to which was added 'A Letter on the Subject of Baptism'. On the title page he describes himself as 'a mechanic, without the advantage of collegiate or academical education'. He continued throughout his life as a Baptist, publishing scriptural treatises and pamphlets and preaching his faith.

Sheraton is not believed to have practised as a cabinet-maker, but in about 1790 he settled in Wardour Street, Soho, London, where, according to his trade card, he was one who 'teaches perspective, architecture, and ornaments, makes designs for cabinet-makers, sells all kinds of drawing books'.

In 1791 there appeared the important work *The Cabinet-Maker and Upholsterer's Drawing Book*. This was issued in three parts by T. Bensley, of Bolt Court, Fleet Street. The second and third editions (with improvements) appeared in 1794 and 1803. The first two parts consist of rather self-assertive lessons in perspective, architecture, and geometry, but the third part, which contains the furniture designs, is the basis of Sheraton's reputation as a furniture designer. Despite the scornful references which Sheraton makes to George Hepplewhite (q.v.) and the fact that he ignores Robert Adam (q.v.), the designs in the *Drawing Book* owe much to these two contemporary influences. The designs are well conceived, being simple and utilitarian, and they found favour with furniture-makers throughout the nineteenth century and even up to the present time. The characteristics of Sheraton's design are a rather puritanical severity which avoids compromise and prefers the straight line to the curvilinear, and a tendency to be inventive (harlequin tables, etc.). It is probable that the

subscribers to Sheraton's *Drawing Book*, many being tradesmen, exerted a restraining influence on his natural tendency to impracticality and irrelevance in the text.

The next publication was *The Cabinet Dictionary* (1803), containing an 'Explanation of all the Terms used in the Cabinet, Chair and Upholstery Branches, with Dictionary for Varnishing, Polishing, and Gilding'. It included eighty-eight copperplate engravings and numerous articles on drawing. Despite the grandiose conception, the book does not fulfil its promise. It reflects an unstable mental condition, which had by now become apparent in Sheraton. The arrangement of its terms was erratic.

At this time Sheraton was living in very poor circumstances; his tactlessness and disdain for opinions other than his own did not endear him to society or help him to commercial success. His final project, uncompleted, was the *Cabinet-Maker, Upholsterer and General Artist's Encyclopaedia*. Only one volume (A–C) was published, and this confirms Sheraton's growing eccentricity. It dealt not only with furniture but with history, botany, geography, and other subjects. The designs in it are frequently grotesque. With the increased popularity of the French 'Empire' style, Sheraton had by now abandoned his earlier principles of utility and simplicity as opposed to ornament, and produced some inferior and vulgar pieces.

Sheraton employed an assistant for this, his last project; he was Adam Black, who was later to found the publishing house Adam and Charles Black, and publish the *Encyclopaedia Britannica*. Black tells us of Sheraton's miserable way of life and says,

> This many sided worn-out encyclopaedist and preacher is an interesting character. . . . He is a scholar,

writes well, and in my opinion draws masterly – is an author, bookseller, stationer and teacher. . . . I believe his abilities and resources are his ruin in this respect – by attempting to do everything he does nothing.

Sheraton's own books indicate his character as discourteous and uncompromisingly dogmatic; such characteristics, allied to his poverty-stricken mode of life, explain his inability to attract the important patronage necessary for his commercial success.

Sheraton died on 22 October 1806 in Golden Square, London, aged fifty-five. He is believed to have died of overwork. His obituary was published in the *Gentleman's Magazine* of November 1806, and describes him as 'a well disposed man of an acute and enterprising disposition'. What was not then seen was that Sheraton, a victim of bad luck, overwork, and an angular personality, was, despite his failings, the last and probably the greatest of the eighteenth-century furniture designers.

R. Edwards and M. Jourdain, *Georgian Cabinet-Makers* (1955, 3rd ed.).

E. Fastnedge, *Sheraton Furniture* (1962).

J. Harris, *Regency Furniture Designs* (1961).

Sheridan, Richard Brinsley (1751–1816), playwright, theatre manager, and politician, known particularly for his two comedies *The Rivals* and *The School for Scandal*.

Sheridan was born in Dublin and baptized there on 4 November 1751. His chequered career started in Ireland, where he lived until the age of eight. His father, Thomas Sheridan, had achieved considerable fame as an actor, and by the time Richard was born he had become the manager of the Theatre Royal in Dublin. In spite of many conflicts with his unruly audience, Thomas managed to run the theatre successfully for several years

before a major riot broke out and it was wrecked in 1754. After this he failed to re-establish himself in Dublin and went to London, where he was joined by his wife, while Sheridan was left with his aunts. Mrs. Sheridan achieved considerable success as a writer, and a novel and two of her plays were well received in London. The Sheridans were still in financial difficulties, however, and they decided to move to France in 1764, where Mrs. Sheridan died in 1766. It was not until 1769 that Sheridan's father returned to England again.

Meanwhile, Richard Sheridan himself had come to England and had been left at Harrow. He was unhappy at school, especially in his first years there. Lord Holland commented: 'He was slighted by the masters and tormented by the boys as a poor player's son.' Sheridan said himself that he was 'a very low-spirited boy much given to crying when alone'. He learned to defend himself with his wit and, although often in trouble, used his charm to escape from punishment.

On leaving Harrow, he joined his father in London, where he was taught by a private tutor. Then in 1770 his father moved to Bath. In 1772 Elizabeth Linley asked Sheridan to help her escape from the persecution of one Captain Mathews. Miss Linley, although only eighteen when she left Bath with Sheridan, had already attracted much attention as a young singer for her musical talent and her beauty. From London they crossed to France, where Sheridan's sister claimed they were married, but more probably they were only engaged. The couple were persuaded to return to England. Captain Mathews accused Sheridan of being 'a liar and a treacherous scoundrel' and a duel was fought, in which Mathews was forced to plead for mercy and agreed to publish an apology in the Bath *Chronicle*. Mathews was then urged to re-assert his honour and a second duel was fought in which Sheridan was seriously injured.

Since both parents strongly opposed Sheridan's engagement, Elizabeth Linley returned to her family, while Sheridan was sent to Waltham Abbey in August 1772. He stayed there until the following April thoroughly occupying himself with studies. In April 1773 he entered the Middle Temple, and he was married to Miss Linley the same month. His father regarded the match as a disgrace and said so openly. The following year the couple moved into a house in Portman Square, and that autumn Sheridan announced that a play of his was about to be rehearsed at Covent Garden. Sheridan was quite unknown until the production of *The Rivals* in January 1775.

At its first performance, the play was poorly received and it had to be withdrawn, but Sheridan insisted on revising it for another performance, although such a practice was unheard of. It was cut, various passages that had been unpopular the first night were removed, and some of the cast was changed. When it was put on again eleven days later, it succeeded brilliantly and ran for fifteen nights.

In *The Rivals* Sheridan cast aside the sentimental drama of the time, and presented the characters and action with much more realism and vitality. The play abounds in life and humour and has remained one of the most popular of English comedies.

In May another play by Sheridan, *St. Patrick's Day, or the Scheming Lieutenant*, was performed at Covent Garden. He followed this success with a comic opera, *The Duenna*, for which Thomas Linley wrote the music. The opera was tremendously popular and had a record run of seventy-five nights that season.

While he was still receiving the profits from *The Duenna*, Sheridan began to

negotiate with Garrick for his share in the Theatre Royal, Drury Lane, of which Garrick was the manager. Garrick valued his share at £35,000 and Sheridan, who a year before had been penniless, had only received £2,500 for his plays and opera, of which much had disappeared. He managed to find £1,300, however, and persuaded Thomas Linley and a Dr. Ford to join him as partners, the latter providing much of the purchase money. The share was largely bought on mortgages, Sheridan optimistically counting on an income of ten per cent on the property.

In September 1776 the theatre opened under the new management. Things did not go well at first and when James Lacy, Garrick's partner, who had the other half share in the theatre, threatened to take a more active role in the management, Sheridan created a series of technical difficulties until Lacy withdrew again, leaving Sheridan in control. The theatre did not enjoy any major success until May

1777, when *The School for Scandal* was presented. The play and its exceptionally able cast received tremendous acclaim. A more polished play than *The Rivals*, it gains in brilliantly drawn wit, but loses the more open and sympathetic humour of the earlier play.

Just before the production of *The School for Scandal*, Sheridan was elected to Johnson's Literary Club. At this stage, he acquired Lacy's share of the theatre, by taking over his mortgage, and got back his original payment of £1,300 by selling his share to Linley and Ford. Sheridan thus gained a share of Drury Lane valued at £45,000 without paying out any money of his own. In 1779 his farce, *The Critic*, was presented, and two years later his final play, *Pizarro*. From this time on Sheridan gave up writing for the stage, but he continued his management of Drury Lane while he pursued a new career, in politics.

He later said that it was the happiest moment of his life when he was returned as member for Stafford in the election of 1780. In parliament he became a frequent speaker and his skill and eloquence was immediately recognized. As a Rockingham Whig, his opposition to the war in America was thought to be so effective that he was offered a large reward. In 1782 Rockingham appointed him Under-Secretary for Foreign Affairs, a position from which he resigned when Shelburne succeeded Rockingham. In 1783 he returned to office as Secretary to the Treasury in the brief coalition headed by the Duke of Portland. Meeting the Prince of Wales, Sheridan soon after became his confidant and adviser.

During the trial of Warren Hastings, Sheridan, organizer of the impeachment, made one of his greatest speeches. After speaking for over five hours, he received a 'tumult of applause' from the whole House. His reputation was now so great that, when he was to speak at the trial, seats were sold for high prices.

In 1792, while the trial was still going on, Elizabeth Sheridan died. Sheridan appeared heartbroken, although he had been notoriously unfaithful to her. Three years later he married Esther Jane Ogle, daughter of the Dean of Winchester. She was only twenty and had a lively and strong character. He seemed to be deeply in love with her for a time, although he was unfaithful later to her too.

After Pitt died in 1806, Sheridan became Treasurer of the Navy, and it was thought that he would become leader of the Whigs when Fox died in the same year, but this did not happen. In 1812 he failed to obtain re-election to parliament, apparently because he lacked funds to distribute amongst the voters.

Sheridan's financial resources had now reached a very low ebb. The Theatre Royal, Drury Lane, had been pulled down in 1791 as it was considered unsafe, and a new theatre was built at a cost of over £200,000. Sheridan rashly promised to meet many of the expenses and the extra cost of the building. The new theatre was burned down in a fire in 1809, however, making financial recovery impossible. Sheridan was briefly imprisoned for debt in 1813. In 1816, when he became too ill to leave his bed, an officer was permanently stationed in the house to fend off his many creditors. He died on 7 July 1816.

Sheridan possessed great charm and excelled as a conversationalist and orator, but in private he often suffered from severe depressions. He became a great public figure but had no truly intimate friends. The bulk of his active life had been devoted to politics and theatre management, yet though he made a name for himself in these fields, he made no lasting impression on politics and never held office for any length of time. He never wished to be regarded as a playwright, yet he is remembered today as one of the most popular writers for the stage, whose *The Rivals* and *The School for Scandal*, parodying the manners of the time, broke with the tradition of sentimental comedy established in the restoration theatre.

L. Gibbs, *Sheridan* (1947, repr. 1970).

T. Moore, *Memoirs of the Life of the Right Honourable Richard Brinsley Sheridan* (2 vols.; 1827, repr. 1971).

C. J. L. Price (ed.), *The Dramatic Works of Sheridan* (1973).

C. J. L. Price (ed.), *The School for Scandal* (1971).

R. C. Rhodes (ed.), *The Plays and Poems of Sheridan* (3 vols.; 1928, repr. 1962).

Portraits: pastel, half-length, by J. Russell, 1788: N.P.G.; oil, by G. Romney: City Art Gallery; marble bust by Thomas Kirk: National Gallery of Ireland, Dublin.

Siddons, Sarah (1755–1831), tragic actress.

Sarah Siddons was born at Brecon on 5 July 1755, the oldest of the twelve children of Roger and Sarah Kemble. Her parents ran a troupe of travelling actors, and three of her brothers, John Philip, Charles (qq.v.), and Stephen Kemble, also achieved theatrical success.

Despite her itinerant life, Sarah was strictly brought up and given education wherever possible. At fifteen her beauty brought her several suitors, but she chose William Siddons, a mediocre actor with the company, whom the Kembles at once dismissed, sending Sarah as lady's maid to the Greatheed family at Warwick.

She soon returned to her family, to the stage, and to William Siddons, whom she married at Coventry in November 1773. They acted together in the Kembles' company, subsequently joining Chamberlain and Crump. In Cheltenham in 1774 Sarah, as Belvidera in Otway's *Venice Preserved*, so impressed Lord Bruce's party that Bruce suggested to Garrick that he should see her again. He did not employ her, however, until December 1775, by which time two

children, Henry and Sally, had been born. She opened at Drury Lane as Portia and was a flop. The papers declared her 'awkward and provincial', and after a few more disastrous small parts she was dismissed just as Garrick retired.

Travelling again in the provinces, she recovered both spirits and talents, and her reputation began to grow. Acting every great part of the day, she was engaged for four seasons at Bath. Her greatest success there was Lady Macbeth, the first part that she really studied, and always her most famous role. Thomas Sheridan saw at once her 'transcendental merit' and wrote of it to his son. Though happy at Bath, her growing family – she was expecting her fifth child – led her to accept the £10 a week offered by Richard Sheridan at Drury Lane, and she returned to London.

In October 1782 she opened as Isabella in *The Fatal Marriage*. This time the audience welcomed her with rapture. She was hailed by the *Morning Post* as 'the first tragic actress now on the English stage'. This success was followed by

Euphrasia in *The Grecian Daughter*, Jane Shore, and again Belvidera. Her popularity reached extraordinary heights: the Law Society gave her a hundred guineas, her first benefit brought in £800, and she was invited to court, where the Queen appointed her 'Preceptress in English Reading to the Princesses'.

Brilliantly successful summer appearances in Dublin (1783) and Edinburgh (1784) alternated with equally brilliant winter seasons at Drury Lane. At that theatre in 1784 she did her first Shakespeare part for Sheridan, Isabella in *Measure for Measure*. But with success came the envy of others: professional jealousy led to false accusations that Sarah was greedy. Angrily she resolved to leave the stage for ever. She relented, however, and her Lady Macbeth, seen by Fox, Burke, Gibbon, and Reynolds at her first night in February 1785, has possibly never been equalled. She followed it with Desdemona and Rosalind and, as the season ended, undertook another country tour.

Winter seasons at Drury Lane continued to alternate with summer tours of the provinces until 1789, when Sarah, tired of Sheridan's growing political involvements, left the Lane for a time. Sheridan persuaded her to return to an enormous, rebuilt Drury Lane theatre. She reigned there as queen of the stage, but Sheridan's inability to pay higher wages necessitated her continued acting on exhausting provincial tours during the summer seasons to support her still-young family. Her private life, however, was saddened by the loss of her daughter Maria. She eventually made her final break with Sheridan in 1803. Still short of money, she was on a protracted Irish tour when she heard that her darling Sally, a chronic asthmatic, was ill, and by the time she returned home, Sally too

had died. Sarah never really recovered from her grief, though she continued acting, earning £50 a night under the management of her brother, John Philip Kemble.

William Siddons died at Bath in 1808 and soon afterwards Covent Garden, with all Sarah's costumes and jewels, was burnt to the ground. She worked for three seasons in the rebuilt theatre but then, at fifty-six, decided to retire. Lady Macbeth was her last part: the audience insisted that the play should end after her last scene, and she had to be led weeping from the stage. She returned once or twice for benefits, and gave occasional readings until on 8 June 1831 she died of erysipelas and gangrene. She was buried at St. Mary's, Paddington, in the presence of 5,000 mourners.

Sarah Siddons was a tall, strikingly beautiful woman with huge dark eyes and an electrifying and compelling stage presence. Her moral character was above reproach and her dignity could be frightening. Her letters, especially to Mrs. Thrale, show her to have been sensitive and intelligent, and although the 'declamatory' school of the Kembles was not to last, her fame did and still does.

Yvonne Ffrench, *Mrs. Siddons, Tragic Actress* (1954, 2nd ed.).

Kathleen Mackenzie, *The Great Sarah* (1968).

Portraits: oil, half-length, by G. Stuart, *c.*1800: N.P.G.; oil, half-length, by T. Lawrence, *c.*1797: N.P.G.; chalk, quarter-length, by J. Downman, 1787: N.P.G.; medallion by John Flaxman, Wedgwood Museum, Barlaston, Staffordshire; oil, half-length, by T. Gainsborough: National Gallery; *Mrs. Siddons as the Tragic Muse*, oil, by J. Reynolds: Huntington Library, San Marino, California.

Sidmouth, 1st Viscount (1757–1844), see Addington, Henry.

Smart, Christopher (1722–71), poet.

Christopher Smart was born on 11

April 1722 at Shipbourne in Kent, the son of Peter Smart, who came from an ancient Durham family and was at that time steward of Viscount Vane's Kentish estates. He was educated at Maidstone and later at the famous Durham School. While still a boy he presented the Duchess of Cleveland with some verses that so impressed her that she gave him a £40 pension. On the strength of this, in 1739 he went up to Pembroke College, Cambridge, and by 1745 he was not only a fellow and the college praelector in philosophy, but had also obtained other university posts. Smart was a notoriously heavy drinker, usually in company with the poet Gray, and he soon ran into debt; however, he was popular with the undergraduates, for whom he wrote his first literary work, the dramatic extravaganza *A Trip To Cambridge*. In 1747 he was confined to his college rooms by his creditors, but in 1750 gained his liberty by winning the newly instituted Seatonian Prize, for the best poem on 'the attributes of the Supreme Being'.

In 1751 there appeared the first signs of Smart's mental instability. He had a tendency to melancholy and spent a brief period in Bedlam. Soon afterwards he met John Newbery, the celebrated Grub Street publisher, who invited him to edit a satirical journal, *The Midwife, or the Old Woman's Magazine*. Writing under the pseudonym of Mary Midnight, Smart revealed an unexpected flair for publicity and an unrestrained taste for coarse buffoonery. Yet poverty and heavy drinking soon reduced him to the status of a literary hack, and he produced vast amounts of nonsense for Newbery's other magazines, including *The Lilliputian*. This did not entirely stifle Smart's more exalted talents, however, for in 1752 there appeared his *Poems on Several Occasions*; the subscribers included Voltaire and Richardson. Along with some competent Latin verse and pleasantly Swiftian squibs, the volume included *The Hop Garden*, a noble georgic on the beauties of Smart's native Kent.

In 1753, against college regulations, Smart married Anna Carnan, daughter of a Reading bookseller. The authorities eventually found out, but were mollified when Smart promised to enter for the Seatonian Prize again. But Smart had already tasted freedom, and in 1755 he resigned his fellowship. The following year he published a translation of Horace, but although the book sold well, Smart saw little of the proceeds. Soon he was in such wretched straits that he is reputed to have leased himself to the bookseller Gardener for ninety-nine years, to edit a magazine called *The Universal Visiter*. However, despite contributions by Johnson, this venture folded in 1759. Smart was now no longer able to support his family, so he sent them off to friends in Ireland.

Despite his inordinate shyness, Smart was a man with many friends; one of the closest was Garrick, who in 1759 organized a benefit performance of his favourite farce and gave the proceeds to the poverty-stricken writer. Help had come too late, however. In 1763 Smart's mind gave way again and he returned to Bedlam. Johnson visited him in his cramped cell, and concluded that there was no need for him to be locked up. While in Bedlam Smart produced several poems, including 'Rejoice in the Lamb' (or *'Jubilate Agno'*), the poem containing the famous lines to his cat. He also produced his solitary masterpiece, 'The Song to David', writing it 'partly with charcoal on the walls, or indented with a key on the panels of his cell'. The expression of a mind saturated with the language of the Bible, 'The Song to David' stands between the majesty of Milton and the mystic fervour of Blake, its occasional clumsiness and tautology transfigured by Smart's sincere religious rapture.

After his release from Bedlam, Smart wrote an oratorio libretto, *Hanna* (1764), and a verse paraphrase of *The Parables* (1768), but they came nowhere near the achievement of 'The Song to David'. When Fanny Burney met him in 1768, Smart was a pathetic figure, and she remarked that he was 'extremely grave, and still has great wildness in his manners, looks and voice'. Soon after, his creditors had him confined to the King's Bench Prison. But thanks to a subscription raised by Dr. Charles Burney and other friends, Smart's last years were made at least bearable. He died on 21 May 1771, and was buried in St. Paul's churchyard.

E. G. Ainsworth, *Smart: a Biographical and Critical Study* (Columbia, Missouri, 1943).

W. H. Bond (ed.), *Rejoice in the Lamb* (Cambridge, Mass., 1954).

N. Callan (ed.), *Collected Poems of Christopher Smart* (2 vols.; 1949).

M. Dearnley, *The Poetry of Smart* (1968).

C. Devlin, *Poor Kit Smart* (1961).

Portrait: oil, quarter-length, by unknown artist, *c.*1745: N.P.G.

Smith, Adam (1723–90), political economist and philosopher, best known for his book *The Wealth of Nations* (1776).

Adam Smith was born at Kirkcaldy, near Edinburgh, and baptized there on 5 June 1723. He was the only son of a local lawyer and customs official, but by the time that he was born his father was already dead, and he formed an unusually close attachment to his mother.

Smith received his elementary education locally and went at the early age of fourteen to Glasgow University, where he received the usual training in the classics and showed a special aptitude for mathematics and Greek philosophy. At Glasgow too he came under the influence of Dissenting teachers and got his first taste of radical opinions, reading and abstracting from the work of the philosopher David Hume (q.v.).

In 1740 the seventeen-year-old Smith won an exhibition to Balliol College, Oxford. Compared with the enlightenment of Glasgow, he found Oxford inflexibly reactionary and stultifying. The university's intolerance of advanced or radical ideas was such that, on one occasion, Smith's autographed copy of Hume's *Treatise of Human Nature*, which he had acquired while at Glasgow, was confiscated by the authorities. Smith hated Oxford, but made the best of it; it seems likely that he took his degree in 1744. Two years later he returned to Kirkcaldy, and in 1751, he was appointed Professor of Logic at Glasgow, transferring a year later to the more lucrative chair of Moral Philosophy.

In addition to teaching he took an active part in university administration and in 1758 he was elected dean of faculty. He counted as his friends aristocrats, merchants, and scientists of the stature of Joseph Black and James Watt (qq.v.). David Hume was also there, a contemporary whom Smith had met in

Edinburgh, but who long before that had ranked as Smith's most important influence. The friendship between them was lifelong, and when Hume died in 1776 Smith acted as his literary executor.

In 1759 Smith published his first work, *The Theory of Moral Sentiments*. Following Hume and others, he described the principles of 'human nature', and the stance of 'impartial spectator' necessary for making deductions concerning man's behaviour in society. Man is the victim of his passions, especially those of self-interest and self-preservation. But within him, there is an impartial reasoning intelligence approving or disapproving of what he does; rational control allows a well-ordered society to continue as a cohesive entity. And as if guided by an 'invisible hand', man will function in such a way that he will, 'without knowing it, without intending it, advance the interest of society'. With this work Smith won immediate recognition in Europe – for example, a friend of Voltaire's, living in Geneva, sent his son to Scotland for private tuition under Smith after reading the book.

As a don at Glasgow, Smith lived with his mother and his cousin, Jane Douglas, in a house provided by the college. In 1762 he was elevated to the post of Vice-Rector.

In 1761 he took his first trip to London, where he met Samuel Johnson. Around this time, too, he became acquainted with Charles Townshend (1725–67, q.v.), a politician who greatly admired him. Townshend's young stepson, Henry Scott, the 3rd Duke of Buccleuch, was in need of a tutor and Smith was offered the job of accompanying the Duke on his grand Tour. The offer was enthusiastically accepted, and in 1763 Smith resigned from his university duties.

Smith got as much out of the tour as did his young charge. In France he met many

of the prominent French *philosophes*, friends of Hume; there also he met François Quesnay and the Physiocrats; and in Geneva he met Voltaire. At Toulouse the Duke's younger brother joined the party, but shortly afterwards was murdered in a Paris street. Horrified by this sudden glimpse of the real world beyond the seminar room and the salon, Smith hastily conveyed the Duke back to England. He stayed in London until early 1767. He was made a Fellow of the Royal Society, and met Burke, Gibbon, and perhaps even Benjamin Franklin.

The Theory of Moral Sentiments was the psychological basis for Smith's subsequent work. The seeds that were to bear truly momentous fruit were nurtured by Smith in the quiet relaxed atmosphere of his home town of Kirkcaldy, where he lived in seclusion from 1767 until 1773. In the latter year he went to London, where in 1776 his master work was published.

An Inquiry into the Nature and Causes of the Wealth of Nations, to give the work its full title, is in five books. Hailed as the first classic in the field of economics, it is a natural extension of *The Theory of Moral Sentiments*, and amounts to a thesis on the historical evolution of human society, from the state of man the hunter, through the stages of nomadic existence and feudal agriculture, to the most recent phase of commercial independence. As long as nothing disturbs it, such as war or bad government, says Smith, a society will remain in this final stage and prosper, kept going by several mechanisms, notably human nature and the 'invisible hand' already analysed in *Moral Sentiments*.

The coherent model of a finely balanced society, in Smith's conception, is kept from running down by the mechanism of competition, which ensures that man's passion of self-interest does not upset the smooth running of the machine. Competition is very much the key. Aided by the profitable division of labour, competition helps to keep prices in line with production costs, and by extrapolation, with rents, wages, and profits. Interference with the element of competition – for example, by means of the granting of special privileges to merchants or the imposition of trade restrictions – throws the social machine out of balance. Thus the system must be carried on in an atmosphere of perfect liberty – what the Whigs later called '*laissez-faire*'.

The Wealth of Nations was immediately hailed as a landmark in sociophilosophical literature; Voltaire and others did not hesitate to rank Smith with Hume and Locke. The author's fine, concise, and clear literary style helped to sell the book widely on the popular market, and though it lacked the technical knowledge and analytical perception demonstrated in the work of Smith's successor, Ricardo (q.v.), it still has some value.

In 1777 Smith returned to Kirkcaldy and became a customs official like his father. Alone and ailing, he worked at revising his two books but wrote nothing new. The bulk of his private writings were destroyed during his lifetime. He asked two friends to burn 160 of his manuscripts without even looking at them. Remembrance by posterity seems to have meant nothing to him; no portraits were painted, the only likeness being Tassie's medallion. Hesitant in speech, absent-minded, and possessed of a 'vermicular' gait, Smith once said of himself: 'I am a beau in nothing but my books.' He died on 17 July 1790, and lies buried in the churchyard of Canongate, Edinburgh.

John Rae, *Life of Adam Smith* (1895, repr. 1965).
W. R. Scott, *Adam Smith as Student and Professor* (Kelley, U.S.A., 1937, repr. 1965).
Andrew Skinner (ed.), *The Wealth of Nations* (1970).

Portrait: paste medallion, quarter-length, by J. Tassie, 1787: Scottish N.P.G.; plaster cast of Tassie's medallion: N.P.G.

Smith, Sydney (1771–1845), clergyman, man of letters, and wit.

Sydney Smith was born at Woodford, Essex, on 3 June 1771, the second son of an energetic landowner. He was educated at Winchester school, where, despite his opinion that most of the work was a waste of time, he gained many academic prizes, and proceeded in 1789 to New College, Oxford, where he was awarded a fellowship two years later.

In 1794 Smith was ordained and appointed curate to Netheravon, a village on Salisbury Plain. Three years later he was asked by the local squire to accompany his son as tutor to Weimar in Germany, but the war sparked off by the French Revolution prevented this plan being carried out, and they travelled instead to Edinburgh. In 1800 Smith travelled south to Surrey to marry Catherine Amelia, a friend since childhood, but immediately after the marriage he returned to Edinburgh: the lively intellectual life of the northern city had excited his own latent talents, and he had already made many close friends there. He became tutor to the brother of his former pupil and also to another student, published a book (1800) containing six of his own sermons, and collaborated with Francis Jeffrey and Henry Brougham (qq.v.) in the founding of the *Edinburgh Review* (1802). In the twenty-five years of his connection with this influential periodical Smith wrote over eighty articles, many of them among the most lively in its history.

Having exhausted the immediate opportunities in Edinburgh, Smith moved south to London in 1803. He preached regularly at the Foundling Hospital and gave three immensely popular series of lectures on moral philosophy at the Royal Institution (1804–6). The weekly suppers at his own house were enjoyed by many young writers, lawyers, and radical politicians, and it was almost certainly because of the unashamed liberalism of his opinions and conversation that he did not gain advancement within the church. Even when a Whig ministry took office in 1806, all that could be obtained for him by his new friends Lord and Lady Holland was the living of Foston-le-Clay, a village near York. For three years Smith was able to remain in London while a curate resident in Yorkshire performed his parish duties, but after the passing of the Clergy Residence Act in 1809 he was compelled to go north. This enforced departure from London was all the more frustrating after the success of his *Letters to Peter Plymley* (1807–8), a series of witty tracts supporting Catholic emancipation and attacking Protestant bigotry. Although the letters were published anonymously the identity of the author was an open secret, and comparisons between Smith and Swift were not all in the latter's favour.

On arriving in Yorkshire Smith found that the parson's house at Foston-le-Clay had not been lived in for 150 years. With characteristic energy he designed and built a new one, had new furniture made locally, and installed a local girl as his 'butler'. (This girl, Annie Kay, was later to nurse him during his final illness.) He worked actively as a farmer, astonishing his fellow workers by the use of such accessories as a telescope, a speaking trumpet, and a newly invented scratching machine for his cows; he became a magistrate, quickly gaining a reputation for treating poachers leniently. He managed to fit in occasional visits to London and to publish a further pamphlet in support of Catholic emancipation (1826), and in 1828 he was appointed to a minor post at Bristol cathedral.

All his loyal servants as well as his family travelled south with Smith to his new living at Combe Florey in Somerset. It was generally expected that his Bristol promotion was merely the preparation to his being made a bishop, but in 1831 Smith was made nothing more than a canon-residentiary of St. Paul's Cathedral, a post that necessitated his living in London for three months of each year. Smith himself recognized that his failure to achieve higher status was owing to his 'high-spirited, honest, uncompromising' nature, but he saw no reason to change his own personality. He spoke vigorously in support of parliamentary reform at many political meetings in the West Country, and in his *Letters to Archdeacon Singleton* (1837–9) he continued to challenge the church authorities on matters of principle and conscience. All Smith's writings were justly admired for their wit, but the arguments within the style were founded on sincerely-held principles and a serious understanding of the social world. He died in London on 22 February 1845 after a protracted illness.

W. H. Auden (ed.), *Selected Writings* (1953).
Hesketh Pearson, *The Smith of Smiths* (1934).
N. C. Smith (ed.), *The Letters of Sydney Smith* (2 vols.; 1953).

Portraits: oil, three-quarter length, by H. P. Briggs: N.P.G.; medallion, J. Henning: Scottish N.P.G.

Smith, William (1769–1839), known as 'Strata Smith', geologist who was the founder of stratigraphy in Britain.

William Smith was born on 23 March 1769 at Churchill, Oxfordshire, the son of a blacksmith. When he was nearly eight years old his father died, leaving him in the care of an uncle. His early education was limited to attending the village school. A keen collector of fossils, Smith also became interested in land surveying, and by the time he was eighteen he had taught himself enough of the subject to be employed by a surveyor in Stow-on-the-Wold. He became extremely proficient in this field, and at the age of twenty-two he moved to the coal-mining regions of Somerset, and during the next eight years lived in both Stowey and High Littleton.

Smith was placed in charge of surveying the Somerset coal canal in 1793, and shortly afterwards was appointed excavating engineer on the project – a position in which he was able to observe in great detail the stratification of a wide geographical area. He discovered that the various layers of rock contained fossils that could be said to characterize each layer. Moreover, these layers must extend over considerable distances, for Smith encountered the same strata several times on his travels to examine canals and coal mines. He made his first geological map in 1794, and was encouraged by his friends to prepare detailed sketches of his findings.

Smith remained in his surveying post until his summary dismissal – the reason for which is obscure – in 1799. In that year, which saw the publication of his monograph on the *Order of the Strata and their Imbedded Organic Remains*, Smith set up as a geological engineer in the flourishing city of Bath. He stayed in Bath for twenty years, using his available financial resources on carrying out his geological mapping and exhibiting the results at local meetings, especially agricultural fairs. The depression following the Napoleonic Wars hit him hard, however: failure of a business venture reduced him to debt and in 1819 he was driven to take refuge in Yorkshire, finally settling in the seaside town of Scarborough.

The first major work Smith published was *Geological Map of England and Wales, With Part of Scotland*, issued in fifteen sheets (1815), with a scale of five miles to the inch. Throughout the next few years (1816–24) he brought out a profusion of excellent maps and studies depicting fossils characteristic of each rocky layer (*Strata Identified by Organized Fossils*), descriptive catalogues of various regions (*Stratigraphical System of Organized Fossils*), and detailed geological maps of various regions (*Geological Atlas of England and Wales*).

Thus Smith assured himself of an important place among the pioneers of English geology; he succeeded in discerning the position in geology of the science of palaeontology. Through him there began to emerge a reliable system of relative geological dating, the key being found in the fossilized flora and fauna peculiar to each stratum.

In 1831 the Geological Society of London awarded him the first Wollaston Medal and the government finally saved him from further want with the award of a life pension of £100 a year. Dublin conferred on him the degree of Doctor of Laws in 1835. Smith died at Northampton on 28 August 1839, on his way to Birmingham for a scientific conference.

L. R. Cox, *William Smith and the Birth of Stratigraphy* (1948).

C. J. Schneer (ed.), *Toward a History of Geology* (1969).

Portrait: oil, half-length, by W. Fourau, 1837: Geological Society Collection, London.

Smith, Sir William Sidney (1764–1840), naval commander; the hero of the Battle of Acre (1799).

Smith was born on 21 June 1764. He entered the navy in June 1777, and participated in actions against American and French forces under Rodney (q.v.) in American and Caribbean waters. He returned to England to go on half-pay in 1784, with post-rank.

In 1789 he visited Sweden, where he was offered and accepted employment in the Swedish navy, serving as a volunteer aide in the 1790 campaign against Russia in the Gulf of Finland. On his return to England, King George III invested him with the insignia of a Knight Grand Cross of the Order of the Sword on behalf of Gustavus III of Sweden (May 1792). He then journeyed to Constantinople, where his younger brother was Ambassador, and was there when war broke out with Revolutionary France in 1793. He decided to return to England, but *en route* for home he fell in with some stranded British sailors at Smyrna. Smith purchased a vessel and sailed with them to join Lord Hood at Toulon.

Hood readily gave him employment and in 1794 Smith was given command of the frigate *Diamond* in the North Sea and off the north coast of France in cutting-out operations. In 1796 he was taken prisoner during one such engagement, but escaped after two years.

Soon afterwards he was given command of the 80-gun *Tigre*, and in October 1798 he sailed to join St. Vincent's fleet, with an ill-defined role as joint plenipotentiary with his brother at Constantinople. The commander in chief assumed that Smith's intended function

was to conduct subordinate naval operations in the Levant, but without authority Smith hoisted the broad pennant of an independent commodore, which provoked immediate friction with Nelson, six years Smith's senior, whose own squadron was policing the Mediterranean after the Battle of the Nile.

An angry exchange of signals up and down the Mediterranean eventually reduced Smith to nominal subordination to the equally histrionically inclined Nelson. Meanwhile, Bonaparte was marching his army into Syria. Despite his lack of respect for authority Smith had the professional eye and at once saw the strategic importance of Acre, lying in the path of the French. He proceeded there with the *Tigre* and the *Theseus* (seventy-four guns) out of Nelson's squadron, going ashore in March 1799 to put some vigour into the Turkish defenders. He captured the French siege train at sea, but the French continued the siege with determination. Turkish reinforcements were in the offing, and after twelve days the French army marched away towards Egypt and ultimate surrender. The *Tigre* was involved in the naval side of subsequent operations against it, and after the capitulation at Alexandria (2 September 1801) Smith was sent back to England with dispatches.

In 1802 he was elected M.P. for Rochester, and in the following year was given command of a coastal flotilla off the Dutch coast under Keith. Promoted to rear admiral (November 1805), Smith served on several stations during the succeeding years. He distinguished himself in combined army and navy operations off the Neapolitan coast (1806); in 1807 he served in Turkish waters off Constantinople and took up a station off the Tagus; and in 1808 he was sent out to command the South America station. After a disagreement with the British minister, Lord Strangford, Smith was recalled in 1809.

Smith was promoted vice admiral on 31 July 1810, and exactly two years later went out as Pellew's second in command in the Mediterranean, an appointment which was terminated by ill-health in March 1814. In July of that year Smith ended his active career. By chance he was in Brussels in June 1815. After Waterloo (18 June) he was on hand to congratulate Wellington on his success, and subsequently travelled with the army to Paris, where Wellington invested him with the insignia of a Knight Commander of the Bath on behalf of the Regent (28 December 1815). On 19 July 1821 Smith reached admiral's rank, and his closing years were spent in Paris, where he died on 26 May 1840.

P. Mackesy, *The War in the Mediterranean, 1803–1810* (1957).

A. T. Mahan, *The Influence of Sea Power Upon the French Revolution and Empire, 1793–1812* (2 vols.; 1892).

Portraits: oil, full-length, by J. Eckstein, 1800–2: N.P.G.; statue by J. Kirk: National Maritime Museum, London.

Smollett, Tobias (1721–71), novelist.

Smollett was born at Dalquhurn, Dunbartonshire, where he was baptized on 19 March 1721. He was the second son of Archibald Smollett, a Presbyterian Whig.

In 1723 his father died, leaving the education of Tobias and his brother to their grandfather, Sir James Smollett. Tobias attended Dumbarton Grammar School and secured a place at Glasgow University, while his brother was sent into the army. But Sir James had not approved of Archibald's marriage, and when he died in 1731 his will made no provision for Tobias.

The ferocious resentment and suspiciousness that characterized both Smollett's writing and his life now began to make itself apparent. He suspected his cousins – apparently without any evidence – of defrauding him of his inheritance, and harboured resentment against the world in general and his cousins and dead grandfather in particular.

He nurtured an enthusiasm for Scottish history and composed a tragedy, *The Regicide*, based on the murder of James I of Scotland. Convinced of his genius, he abandoned his apprenticeship to a Glasgow surgeon and set off with his manuscript to seek literary fame and fortune in London.

The reality of life in London was far removed from his dreams, however. His pocket was picked in the taverns, his Scots accent was mocked, and the leading men of the theatre and of society refused to read more than the first few lines of his play. For the next twenty years he lost no opportunity of seeking revenge on the men who had refused him their patronage, notably by lampooning them in his novels and satirizing them in bad verse.

After only a few months in London, Smollett found himself, at the age of eighteen, destitute. But through the influence of a family friend he secured a position as surgeon's mate on H.M.S. *Cumberland* and set out with the British fleet to the West Indies.

Throughout 1741 the fleet was engaged in the unsuccessful siege of Cartagena, the great Spanish fortress and chief trading post of the Caribbean. Smollett has left us splendid, if somewhat exaggerated, eye-witness accounts of the miseries of the sailors and the incompetence of the commanders, both in the pages of *Roderick Random* and in a collection of *Voyages* edited by him in 1756. Eventually the siege was abandoned and the fleet withdrew to Jamaica. Here Smollett became acquainted with a number of wealthy planters, who recognized his wit and talent and were prodigal with their hospitality to young naval officers. He fell in love with the daughter and heiress of one of them, Nancy Lascelles. She followed him back to England, where Smollett discharged himself from the navy, set up as a surgeon in Downing Street, and married her. She was described as 'a fine lady, but a silly woman'. Smollett seems to have retained his affection for her to the end of his life.

At the age of twenty-six, after an interlude of writing verses such as 'The Tears of Scotland' (on the Battle of Culloden) and political satires entitled 'Advice' and 'Reproof' (all 1746), Smollett turned his attention to fiction. *Roderick Random* was published anonymously in 1748. It is an extraordinarily vivid and vital account of low life on the highways, in the taverns, brothels, and prisons, and at sea in the eighteenth century. It contains no hidden depths and the plot moves swiftly from episode to episode without much sense of purpose; the unifying theme is the hero's quarrelsomeness and his pursuit of revenge against almost everyone he meets. The story so clearly follows the course of the author's own life that, although it is fiction, one can scarcely refrain from regarding it as autobiographical. Yet the novel is funny and extremely readable, and it sold well from the moment of publication.

Encouraged by this success, Smollett journeyed to Paris, where he published *The Regicide* as 'by the author of *Roderick Random*', with the intention of intimidating his discarded patrons. However, the play again failed to find acclaim. On his return to London Smollett set about preparing his next work, but at the same time pursued his medical career. In June 1750 he was awarded an M.D. by Marischal College, Aberdeen, although there is no

evidence that he spent any length of time studying there. He revisited Paris, where much of the action of his next novel, *Peregrine Pickle* (1751), is set. Pickle is a greater scoundrel than Random, though equally engaging and quarrelsome. The rush of action is only halted by occasional digressions into vituperation and lampooning of a selection of those chosen by Smollett to be his enemies. The characterization – brilliantly grotesque, spiteful, and funny – ensures Smollett's place as one of the greatest comic novelists in the English language, at the very centre of the European picaresque tradition. He owed much to Cervantes, Rabelais, Le Sage, Defoe, and Swift, while Dickens's debt to him has often been remarked, and Sir Walter Scott freely acknowledged his influence.

Smollett, now at the age of thirty, was a successful writer, a successful surgeon, and a comparatively wealthy man. In 1752 he engaged in an exchange of scurrilous pamphlets with Fielding, and on the publication of his next work, *Ferdinand Count Fathom* (1753), he finally gave up medicine to devote himself to writing. Fathom is another great rogue; the illegitimate son of a camp follower, he adopts the title of count and proceeds to ingratiate himself with various rich and powerful families in Europe, seducing and thieving as he goes. In the manner of Defoe, Smollett has his worthless hero repent at the end of the story, but unlike Defoe and his earlier self, he appears to have made strenuous efforts to concoct a more unified plot, under the influence perhaps of Fielding's *Tom Jones*. The novel did not enjoy the success of its author's two earlier works, but influenced the later 'Gothick' school – 'Monk' Lewis and Mrs. Radcliffe (qq.v.).

Smollett may have been resentful and vindictive, but he was certainly not ungenerous. Having settled in Chelsea in

1753, he held court in grand style. In particular, he entertained impoverished authors, and also a group of London-based Scots intellectuals and medical men. In February 1756 he launched a new literary periodical, *The Critical Review*, at the same time undertaking the planning and part of the writing of a vast *History of England* and his seven-volume collection of *Voyages*. From there he went on to plan and edit an even vaster *Universal History* (1758). In 1757 he wrote a farce-cum-patriotic-extravaganza, *The Reprisal, or the Tars of Old England*, which was produced by Garrick (caricatured as Marmozet in *Roderick Random*, but now apparently forgiven). In 1755 he had edited and partly translated Cervantes's *Don Quixote*, and this inspired his least successful work of fiction, *The Adventures of Sir Lancelot Greaves*, which appeared in serial instalments in a monthly magazine (1760–2).

In 1759 he was fined and imprisoned in the Marshalsea as a result of a libel in *The Critical Review* on Admiral Sir Charles Knowles. Undeterred, he not only continued to edit that periodical, but in addition took on in 1762 the editing of another, *The Briton*. In 1763 Smollett turned his attention again to book publishing, preparing projects for a universal gazetteer and for a translation of Voltaire in thirty-eight volumes.

In April of that year, however, his only child, a daughter to whom he was devoted, died. Already suffering from the strain of overwork and general ill health, Smollett collapsed completely. Abandoning all his projects, he spent the next two years travelling in Italy and the south of France; for the rest of his life he was to suffer from rheumatism, sores and ulcers, and a lung disease (probably tuberculosis).

In 1765 he returned to England, publishing an amusing but acid-tempered account of his *Travels in France and Italy* (1766), before making a triumphant visit to Scotland, staying with his relatives and being called on by most of the eminent literary men of Edinburgh and Glasgow, including David Hume and Adam Smith.

His return to London (via Bath) in 1768 was followed by the publication a year later of *The History and Adventures of an Atom*. The atom in question is part of the person of a Japanese. Japan throughout stands for England, and under this thin disguise Smollett lashes out at all and sundry, particularly Lord Bute (Yak-strot), in a characteristically vigorous, obscene, and undiscriminating satire. But although Smollett's pen was as lively as ever, his health gave way again, and in December 1769 he left England for good, taking up residence a few miles from Livorno. Here, in spite of his failing health, he wrote the last and one of the most imaginative of his novels, *Humphry Clinker*. Cast in the form of a collection of letters, it returns to the rambling series of incidents, in place of a formal plot, with which Smollett is happiest. The portrayal of character is still acid, but the viciousness of the earlier works is less in evidence. In the person of the irascible but secretly kind-hearted Sir Matthew Bramble it is tempting to see a self-portrait of Smollett himself in his last year – the man described by David Hume as 'a coconut – rough outside, but full of human kindness within'.

Smollett did not live long enough to see the success of *Humphry Clinker*; on 17 September 1771, at the age of fifty, he died; his widow buried him at Livorno, where she herself died, friendless and destitute, some years later.

R. Alter, *Rogue's Progress: Studies in the Picaresque Novel* (1964).
J. L. Clifford (ed.), *The Adventures of Peregrine Pickle* (1964).
R. Giddings, *The Traditions of Smollett* (1967).
L. M. Knapp (ed.), *The Expedition of Humphry Clinker* (1966).

L. M. Knapp, *Tobias Smollett: Doctor of Men and Manners* (1949).

L. M. Knapp (ed.), *The Letters of Smollett* (1970).

G. Saintsbury (ed.), *The Novels of Smollett* (12 vols.; 1895).

R. D. Spector, *Tobias George Smollett* (New York, 1968).

Portrait: oil, half-length, by unknown Italian artist, *c.*1770: N.P.G.

Soane, Sir John (1753–1837), architect and founder of the Soane Museum.

Soane was born on 10 September 1753, the son of an impoverished stonemason of Reading. John Swan, as he was originally called, was educated locally and then, having changed his name to Soan, was employed as errand boy in the office of George Dance the Younger, surveyor to the City of London. Dance recognized the youth's talent and arranged for him to be transferred to the office of Henry Holland, where he gained a practical knowledge of the profession. While employed there, Soane attended the Royal Academy schools; after winning the gold medal in 1776 with a design for a triumphal arch, he was awarded the King's Travelling Studentship.

Soane left England in March 1777 and spent three years in Italy, chiefly in Rome, studying the remains of antiquity and making his own designs for public buildings. In the summer of 1780 Soane returned to England and spent several years, enjoying only moderate success as an architect, erecting country houses. The drawings for these were published under the title of *Designs in Architecture* in 1788.

In 1784 Soane made a very wealthy marriage, and used the opportunity to add the 'e' to his name. Thanks to the support of Pitt the Younger, he was appointed Architect to the Bank of England when Sir Robert Taylor died in 1788. This appointment proved to be the starting point of Soane's immensely successful career, and his work at the Bank remains the cornerstone of his fame. He was called upon to enlarge and virtually rebuild the entire structure of the Bank, which he did using by far the most original style of architecture to be seen in Europe at that time.

Other important appointments followed: in 1791 he was appointed Clerk of Works at St. James's Palace and the Houses of Parliament; in 1795 he became Architect to the Department of Woods and Forests; and in 1807 he became Clerk of Works at Chelsea Hospital. Soane was appointed Superintendent of Works to the Fraternity of Freemasons in 1813. He reached the pinnacle of his career in 1815, when he became Joint Architect to the Board of Works, with Nash and Robert Smirke, the designer of the British Museum.

At the beginning of the nineteenth century Soane executed much of his best work, including the designs for Pitzhanger Manor (1802), and for Dulwich Art Gallery and Mausoleum. In the 1820s he made designs for the New Law Courts, a Royal Palace on Constitution Hill, and his own house in Lincoln's Inn Fields. He completed his last work, the State Paper Office, in 1836.

Soane's professional appointments were accompanied by academic posts of a similar calibre. He became a Royal Academician in 1802 and in 1806 he succeeded George Dance as professor of architecture at the Academy. Soane was a lively, often controversial lecturer, who was occasionally bitter in his criticism. A particularly virulent attack against a colleague brought about the temporary suspension of his course in 1810.

Soon after he became professor, Soane, who had become a Fellow of the Society of Antiquaries in 1795, began to make a collection of antiquities, books, and works of art for the benefit of his own pupils and other students. The vastly expensive collection, including Hogarth's *Rake's Progress*, was housed in his own home at 13 Lincoln's Inn Fields, London.

In 1833, two years after receiving a knighthood, he presented this house (now the Soane Museum), with its art collection, to the nation. In the same year he resigned from all his appointments and professional engagements because of his failing eyesight.

In 1835 Soane was presented with a set of medals by the architects of England in recognition of his public services. He died on 20 January 1837, and was buried in the mausoleum that he had erected for his wife in old St. Pancras Churchyard.

Few of Soane's works remain in their original form but those that do bear witness to the architect's originality and skill. They reveal the tremendous range of sources at his command and his very personal management of space in the interior of buildings.

A. T. Bolton, *The Works of Sir John Soane* (1924).
A. T. Bolton, *The Portrait of Sir John Soane, R.A.* (1927).
J. Summerson, *Sir John Soane* (1952).

D. Stroud, *The Architecture of Sir John Soane* (1961).

Portraits: oil, half-length, by J. Jackson, 1828: N.P.G.; oil, by J. Jackson: Soane Museum, London; marble bust, by Sir F. Chantrey: Soane Museum, London.

Southey, Robert (1774–1843), poet, journalist, and man of letters; Poet Laureate 1813–43.

Robert Southey was born on 12 August 1774 at Bristol, the son of a linen-draper. He spent his earliest years chiefly in the company of his mother's half-sister, an eccentric maiden aunt who was so fond of the theatre that the poet later remarked that he saw more plays before he was seven than after he was twenty.

When he was fourteen Southey was sent to Westminster School by a maternal uncle who paid for his education. As a result of an article in the school magazine against the flogging system, Southey was expelled. By this time he had composed numerous verses, and he continued to read voraciously all the books he came across.

His uncle arranged for him to enter Balliol College, Oxford, shortly afterwards on the understanding that he would study for the church. But Southey had added the study of Gibbon to that of Rousseau, and he soon gave up all thoughts of a career to which he could not conscientiously devote himself. He did not distinguish himself at Oxford by proficiency in classical studies, but he continued to read widely in English and general literature.

After abandoning theology – he left Balliol without a degree – Southey studied medicine for a short time, but the dissecting room was too much for his nerves and he gladly forsook his intention of becoming a physician. In June 1794 he was introduced to Coleridge. He was fascinated by his eloquence and enthusiasm, and they became friends almost instantly. One of the results of their association was the formation of a new society on the principles of 'Pantisocracy' (Utopianism), and they drew up plans to establish a Utopian community on the banks of the Susquehanna. The scheme seemed workable, but eventually came to nothing.

In 1794 Southey published a volume of poems in conjunction with Robert Lovell. Lovell had married a Miss Mary Fricker, and her two sisters, Sara and Edith, soon became involved with Coleridge and Southey. Southey secretly married Edith Fricker on 14 November 1795, and just after his wedding he sailed for Lisbon with his uncle, Herbert Hill, who was chaplain of a British factory there.

During his six-month stay in Spain and Portugal, Southey underwent a great change in his political views. Having welcomed the French Revolution at its outset, he now began to hate radicalism in all its forms. This development transformed him into a staunch Tory, a state of mind for which Byron in particular was later to attack him vehemently in *Don Juan* and 'The Vision of Judgment'.

At the beginning of 1797, a generous school and college friend, Watkyn Williams Wynn, bestowed on him an allowance of £160 a year. This helped to defray the costs of supporting his family, but it was still necessary for him to supplement his income by writing reviews, translations, and the like, for various booksellers. Later that year he published a volume of minor poems, together with his *Letters Written During a Short Residence in Spain and Portugal*. A third abortive attempt at a non-literary career – this time it was the law – began in February 1798, when Southey entered Gray's Inn. Again the endeavour to break away from his dependence on writing came to nothing.

In 1803 Southey and Edith went to live at Greta Hall, Keswick, which they shared with Coleridge and his wife, Sara. When Coleridge left for Malta later that year, Southey and Edith remained behind. He was to occupy Greta Hall until his death.

When Southey and Coleridge first went to Keswick, Wordsworth was at Grasmere. The three were known as the 'Lake Poets', but they had very little in common poetically, in intensity or vision. Southey gradually amassed a huge library totalling some 14,000 volumes.

Among his forty or fifty books were *Madoc* (1805), *The Curse of Kehama* (1810), *History of Brazil* (1810–19), *A Vision of Judgment* (1821, savagely parodied in Byron's 'The Vision of Judgment'), a *Life of Nelson* (1813), *Roderick* (1814), *History of the Peninsular War* (1823–32), *Book of the Church* (1824), *Colloquies on Society* (1829), *Naval History* (1833–40), and *The Doctor* (1834–47). Southey contributed nearly 100 articles to the *Quarterly Review*, and was soon considered by many to be the most influential Tory journalist of the day.

When Sir Walter Scott declined to become Poet Laureate, the honour was offered to Southey, who accepted graciously in 1813. He did not, however, accept other proffered honours, which included the editorship of *The Times* (1817), a seat in parliament (1826), and, in 1835, a baronetcy. Southey seems at last to have committed himself fully to his writing. Coleridge once remarked of the prolific author, 'I can't think of him without seeing him either using or mending a pen.' An edition of his complete works would probably run to nearly 200 volumes.

In 1835 Sir Robert Peel arranged for Southey to be granted an annual pension of £300. In 1839, two years after the death of his first wife, Southey married Caroline Bowles. Her good nature and love of poetry made her an excellent companion

397

for the remaining years of his life, during which he was progressively failing both mentally and physically.

Children around the world who have never heard of Southey know of him indirectly through his well-known tale of 'The Three Bears', which was included in his book *The Doctor*. His contribution to English literature rests on somewhat less firm ground, for although his poetry shows sparks of genius, his visions rarely reach deeply into the implications seen by poets such as Keats and Shelley. Thackeray remarked that 'Southey's politics are obsolete and his poetry dead; but his private letters are worth piles of epics, and are sure to last among us as long as kind hearts like to sympathise with goodness and purity and upright life.' Southey died on 21 March 1843.

G. D. Carnall, *Southey and His Age: the Development of a Conservative Mind* (1960).

Kenneth Curry (ed.), *New Letters of Southey* (2 vols.; New York, 1965).

M. H. Fitzgerald (ed.), *Poems of Robert Southey* (1909).

C. W. and L. H. Houtchers (eds.), *The English Romantic Poets and Essayists: a Review of Criticism and Research* (New York, 1966, rev. ed.).

R. E. Roberts (ed.), *A Vision of Judgment* (1932).

J. Simmons, *Southey* (1945).

Portraits: pencil and chalk, full-length, by H. Edridge, 1804: N.P.G.; oil, quarter-length, by P. Vandyke, 1795: N.P.G.; pencil and water-colour, half-length, by R. Hancock, 1796: N.P.G.

Spencer, Charles (1674–1722), 3rd Earl of Sunderland; Whig statesman who, as First Lord of the Treasury (1718–21), originated the financial scheme that resulted in the crisis of the South Sea Bubble (1720).

Charles Spencer was born in 1674, the second son of Robert Spencer, 2nd Earl of Sunderland, a prominent politician. The death of his elder brother, Henry, in September 1688, made Charles Spencer heir to the peerage. In 1695 he married Arabella, daughter of Henry Cavendish, 2nd Duke of Newcastle.

In that same year Spencer entered parliament as member for Tiverton. He quickly gained a reputation for his forthrightness; his republican views aroused the hostility of the future Queen Anne. His first wife died in 1698 and in 1700 Spencer married Lady Anne Churchill, daughter of the renowned Duke of Marlborough (see Churchill, John, in *Lives of the Stuart Age*). It was through this wise union that he was fully integrated into political life, and later the dukedom of Marlborough came to the Spencers.

Succeeding to the peerage in 1702, Sunderland served as one of the commissioners for the union between England and Scotland; and in 1705 he was sent to Vienna on a diplomatic mission. As a result of the influence of the Duchess of Marlborough and Sidney Godolphin, Sunderland obtained the post of Secretary of State for the Southern Department in December 1706. But the Queen was still implacably hostile to him, and Marlborough regarded him with some suspicion. Once in office, however, he showed as few favours to his friends as to his enemies, and often differed openly from both Marlborough and Godolphin. From 1708 to 1710 he was a member of the group of five Whigs known as the Junto who dominated the government. But his imperious nature brought him many enemies, and the hostility of public opinion towards his proposed impeachment of Henry Sacheverell in 1710 gave the Queen the confidence to dismiss him in June of that year.

Sunderland had first met the future George I in 1706, and with the approaching death of Queen Anne he began to capitalize on their close association by making regular communications to the court of Hanover. But when the Elector became King in 1714, Sunderland was granted only the honorary post of Lord Lieutenant of Ireland. In August 1715 he secured a post in the cabinet as Lord Keeper of the Privy Seal; in July 1716 he obtained the sinecure of Vice-Treasurer of Ireland for life, but he still had no real authority. After a visit to Hanover, where he proceeded to intrigue against his rivals, Townshend (see Townshend, Charles, 2nd Viscount) and Sir Robert Walpole (q.v.), he became in April 1717 Secretary of State for the Northern Department.

By March 1718 Sunderland had become First Lord of the Treasury and Lord President of the Council. He concentrated his attention on home affairs while James Stanhope (q.v.) handled foreign business. Sunderland's peerage bill, designed to reduce the numbers of the House of Lords and to restrain the future power of the Prince of Wales, was defeated twice in the House of Commons (1719) as a result of Walpole's opposition.

In an effort to pay off part of the national debt Sunderland launched, in 1720, the South Sea Company, an enterprise set up as having a monopoly of trade in the Pacific. A wild outburst of speculation followed, leading to artificial inflation of stock and share prices. The South Sea Bubble soon burst, however, and the market crashed in August. Sunderland was forced by public clamour to retire, although he had not profited financially from the scheme. His colleague, Stanhope, died under the strain that resulted from the crisis and in April 1721 Sunderland was superseded by Walpole at the Treasury. Townshend became Secretary of State.

Though out of ministerial office, Sunderland continued to exercise some influence over George I, and Walpole could make very little further headway with the King. Then suddenly, on 19 April 1722, Sunderland died from an attack of pleurisy.

W. S. Churchill, *Marlborough: His Life and Times*, vols. iii and iv (1933–8).

Portraits: engraving, quarter-length, by G. Houbraken, 1746: British Museum; oil, by Sir G. Kneller: Blenheim Palace, Oxfordshire.

Spencer, John Charles (1782–1845), 3rd Earl Spencer; statesman, better known as Viscount Althorp, leader of the House of Commons during the passage of the Reform Act of 1832.

Spencer was born at Spencer House, London, on 30 May 1782, the eldest son of George John, 2nd Earl Spencer. Educated at Harrow and at Trinity College, Cambridge, he spent much of his time and money in the latter institution on hunting and racing, although he did manage to acquire some grasp of mathematics. He grew up a shy, awkward youth, who did not shine in the company of those well versed in literature or the arts. In 1804 he was elected member for Okehampton and entered parliament as one of the supporters of Pitt.

Althorp's parliamentary record up to 1830 gave no indication of what was to follow. He spent as little time as possible in the House, preferring to devote himself to country pursuits. By 1810 he had moved over towards his more natural allies – the Whigs – and he became a consistent supporter of measures for tax reduction and parliamentary reform. He always attended debates on practical topics like taxation and supported the efforts of his friend, the radical Joseph Hume, towards greater public economy. He voted for the repeal of the Test and Corporation Acts and for Catholic emancipation.

In 1830 the Whig party was reorganized under Althorp's leadership. He was the most popular Whig personality since he so perfectly embodied the Whig ideal of the liberal and enlightened country squire. Althorp, however, did not relish the responsibility and would gladly have retired at any time were it not for his zeal for the Reform Bill. Under Earl Grey he combined the office of Leader of the House of Commons with that of Chancellor of the Exchequer, but his first budget in 1831 failed dismally. Nevertheless, he continued in office even though he disliked the job and hated parliamentary life. From about August 1831 he assumed responsibility for the management of the Reform Bill in committee and acquired such a detailed knowledge of the various clauses that when he came to speak in the Commons his previous uncertainty was replaced by a new air of authority. Although neither witty nor eloquent, he managed to overcome his opponent Sir Robert Peel, and he fully justified the comment of Charles Greville that 'he became the very best leader the Commons ever had'. Althorp and Lord John Russell twice steered the Reform Bill through the Commons, and saw it eventually passed in June 1832. Persuaded to stay on as Leader against his better judgment, Althorp never recaptured that air of authority with which he had defeated Peel, and grew increasingly depressed by political conflict and the troubles in Ireland.

Althorp virtually retired with Grey in July 1834, but was prevailed upon to remain until November, when his father's death brought about his elevation to the House of Lords. Thankful to relinquish the political arena, he retired at last to his beloved country estates; in E. J. Myers's phrase, 'He came out of the fields and woods and to the fields and woods he returned.' A noted cattle breeder, Spencer became the first President, in 1838, of the Royal Agricultural Society. His last public pronouncement was in 1843, when he declared himself in favour of the repeal of the Corn Laws. He died at Wiseton Hall, Nottinghamshire, on 1 October 1845.

A. Aspinall (ed.), *Three Early Nineteenth-Century Diaries* (1952).

M. Brock, *The Great Reform Act* (1973).

Portrait: chalk, three-quarter length, by C. Turner: N.P.G.

Stanhope, Charles (1753–1816), 3rd Earl Stanhope; statesman and scientist.

Charles Stanhope was born in London on 3 August 1753, the eldest surviving son of Philip Stanhope, 2nd Earl Stanhope, himself the son of the 1st Earl, James Stanhope (q.v.). He was educated at Eton and Geneva, where he showed an early enthusiasm for both mathematics and democratic principles, and by the age of seventeen he had already invented his first mathematical instrument. In 1772 he was elected a Fellow of the Royal Society, though he was not actually admitted until he returned to England in 1775.

Stanhope married the sister of William Pitt the Younger (q.v.), Lady Hester Pitt, in 1774, and it was as a supporter of Pitt's administration that he was elected M.P. for Chipping Wycombe in 1780. In declaring that the war against the American colonies should be discontinued Stanhope was following official Whig policy, but on many other issues he showed himself to be fiercely independent: 'a savage, a republican, a royalist – I don't know what not', commented a contemporary. Between 1782 and 1786 he introduced a number of measures for parliamentary reform, including bills against bribery and corruption, for the reduction of election expenses, and for an annual register of voters.

Stanhope finally broke with Pitt over the issue of the French Revolution: as Chairman of the Revolutionary Society (formed in 1788 to celebrate the centenary of the Glorious Revolution in England) he sent several congratulatory messages to French revolutionary leaders, and in parliament he consistently advocated that

Britain should not interfere in the internal affairs of France. On being overwhelmingly defeated on this issue for the second time, Stanhope retired from politics for five years, but he resumed his seat in 1800 and immediately proposed that peace should be made with Napoleon; he also proposed extremely enlightened reforms in domestic fields such as weights and measures, coinage and currency, and education.

At his home in Chevening, Kent, Stanhope had a well-equipped laboratory, and he displayed the same originality in his scientific experiments as he did in his political career. In 1777 he constructed two calculating machines; other inventions included a monochord for tuning musical instruments, a microscope lens, and special tiles for excluding rain and snow. The Admiralty showed considerable interest in his experiments with ships powered by steam-engine propulsion in 1795, and his production of the first hand-operated printing press in 1798 was followed by his development of a stereotyping process which was later acquired by the Clarendon Press in Oxford. In 1779 he published his *Principles of Electricity*; later pamphlets, such as his reply to Edmund Burke's *Reflections on the French Revolution* of 1790, were mainly on political subjects.

All Stanhope's works bear witness to his enlightened and progressive intellect; his only known weaknesses were his inability to work with others and his failure to achieve a satisfactory relationship with his children, all of whom he disinherited. His wife, Lady Hester, died in 1780 at the age of twenty-five.

Despite the paleness of his skin, Charles Stanhope had a tall, robust body, and his speeches in the House of Lords were delivered in a powerful voice; in later life he was afflicted by dropsy. He died at Chevening on 15 December 1816.

G. P. Gooch, *Life of Charles, third Earl Stanhope* (1914).

Portraits: chalk, half-length, by O. Humphry, 1796: N.P.G.; oil, half-length, by J. Opie: N.P.G.

Stanhope, Lady Hester Lucy

(1776–1839), traveller and eccentric.

Lady Hester Stanhope was born on 12 March 1776, the eldest daughter of Charles Stanhope, 3rd Earl Stanhope (q.v.).

Her father was very much absorbed in his work, and her mother in opera and other aspects of London social life, so that Lady Hester's disorganized education did much to stimulate her own independence. Visitors to her father's home at Chevening, Kent, remarked upon her ascendancy over her sisters and in 1803 her uncle, William Pitt the Younger, asked her to become his housekeeper. She soon established herself as a forceful personality, writing many of his letters and acting as hostess at his parties.

After Pitt's death in 1806 her prospects were uncertain; for a brief period she stayed with friends in Wales and then, in 1810, with a Welsh female companion, Miss Williams, and an English physician, Charles Lewis Meryon, Lady Hester sailed from England for the Middle East. The party travelled first to Jerusalem. From here they crossed the desert to Palmyra, where they camped with Bedouin tribesmen. England by now was wholly in the past, a place to which Lady Hester was never to return.

In 1814 Lady Hester joined a community of Arab tribesmen, the Druses, on Mount Lebanon. She built her own village and totally immersed herself in eastern customs: she dressed as an Arab, practised astrology, and willingly accepted the role of prophetess in which the tribesmen cast her. Her closest retinue consisted of carefully chosen servants and a number of half-tamed animals. Stories of her eccentric way of life filtered back to Europe, and among those who came to see for themselves were Lamartine and the medical writer Robert Kinglake. Often she would compel her visitors to remain standing while she subjected them to harangues that lasted for several hours, and at least one visitor is known to have fainted before his ordeal was over.

Lady Hester's life among the Druses was no passive renunciation of western luxury, and by her intrigues against British consuls and her encouragement of the Druses to revolt against the Egyptian viceroy, Ibrahim Pasha, she caused much embarrassment in political circles. The response of even her closest companions to the recklessness of her liberality was one of alternating love and fear, so that even in old age she was unable to attain serenity.

In 1828 Miss Williams, her closest female companion, died and Dr. Meryon left the Lebanon in 1831. In 1838 Lord Palmerston stopped Lady Hester's official pension in an attempt to satisfy her many creditors, and in August of the same year she shut herself up inside her fortress with five servants and refused to see any visitors. Isolated, proud, and deserted by her former companions, Lady Hester died on 23 June 1839. A few days later the local British consul found her body unattended, her servants having fled with all her possessions except the clothes she wore.

C. L. Meryon, *Memoirs of Lady Hester Stanhope* (1845).
C. L. Meryon, *Travels of Lady Hester Stanhope* (1846).

Stanhope, James (1673–1721), 1st Earl Stanhope, soldier and Whig statesman.

James Stanhope was born in Paris in 1673, the eldest son of Alexander Stanhope and the grandson of Philip Stanhope, 1st Earl of Chesterfield. He was educated at Eton and Trinity College, Oxford, but left the university in 1688 without taking a degree. Two years later he travelled to Spain with his father, who had been appointed as British Minister there, and gained valuable early experience in diplomacy. He fought as a volunteer in Italy in 1691, and then in Flanders in 1694–5, where he distinguished himself at the siege of Namur and was awarded a commission; in 1702 he became colonel of a regiment that later became the 11th Foot Guards.

Back in England, Stanhope was elected to the House of Commons as M.P. for Newport, Isle of Wight, in 1701, and then in the following year sat for Cockermouth. He had inherited strong Whig principles from his father, and established his position in the Whig hierarchy by playing a major part in the impeachment of the Tory Henry Sacheverell (1710).

This involvement in politics did not impede Stanhope from advancing his military career during the War of the Spanish Succession. In 1702 he took part in Ormonde's expedition to Cadiz; the following year he served under Marlborough on the Meuse, and in 1705 he again distinguished himself while serving under Peterborough in the attack on Barcelona. Promoted to brigadier general, Stanhope was appointed British Minister to the court of Charles III of Spain in 1706, and in 1707 he succeeded Peterborough as commander in chief of the British forces. His bold strategies were at first extremely successful: he captured Port Mahon, won against heavy odds at the Battle of Almenar in 1710, and followed this up by capturing Saragossa. He was, however, compelled to surrender at Brihuega the following December, and he spent the next eighteen months as a prisoner of war.

The War of the Spanish Succession was ended in 1713 by the Treaty of Utrecht;

the terms included Britain's retention of Port Mahon and also Louis XIV's recognition of the Protestant succession to the British throne. Stanhope himself was instrumental in securing the succession of George I, aiding Sir Robert Walpole (q.v.) in the suppression of a minor Jacobite uprising and arranging for the impeachment of Ormonde, a Jacobite sympathizer, in June 1715. A few days after George I's arrival in England Stanhope was made Secretary of State for the Southern Department; in 1717 he was appointed First Lord of the Treasury and Chancellor of the Exchequer but, realizing his incapacity for these offices, he reverted to his former position. In domestic affairs Stanhope's ability was not equal to that of Walpole, with whom he shared the leadership of the House of Commons, but he worked hard to keep the Whig party united, and by repealing the Occasional Conformity and Schism Acts in 1718, he demonstrated his strong sympathy for religious minorities. Stanhope's services to the country were formally recognized when he was created Viscount Stanhope of Mahon in 1717 and, a year later, 1st Earl Stanhope.

His military experience on the Continent and his early experience in diplomacy made Stanhope the obvious candidate to take charge of Britain's foreign affairs, and it is in the field of international diplomacy that his greatest political achievements lie. Reversing the traditional Tory policy of alliance with France, Stanhope pursued a Whig policy of agreement with the Habsburg Emperor even though this might lead to war against France: the consequence, following the Treaty of Westminster in 1716 with the Emperor and the Dutch and also a commercial treaty with Spain, was that Britain now gained a powerful position within Europe from which her own interests could be strongly asserted.

The Triple Alliance of 1717 with France and the Dutch served to weaken foreign support for the Jacobites, and the following year Stanhope brought the Emperor Charles VI into the Quadruple Alliance in order to compel Spain to abandon her plans to recover lost territory in Italy. A brief war flared, but in the Treaty of the Hague in 1720 Spain yielded to Stanhope's terms. In northern Europe Stanhope managed to end Hanoverian influence in British affairs by including Prussia among his coalition of Baltic powers.

The financial crisis of the South Sea Bubble brought an end to Stanhope's political career: Stanhope made no personal profit out of the affair but as a leading government minister he necessarily shared in some of the public blame. The careers of many other gifted politicians were also wrecked by this crisis, and Stanhope's personal reputation for honesty and frankness was not enough to save him.

Stanhope's speeches in parliamentary debates were often impetuous. After replying vehemently to one particular attack in the House of Lords he burst a blood vessel and collapsed; he died on the following day, 5 February 1721, at his home in London.

B. Williams, *Stanhope: a study in eighteenth-century war and diplomacy* (1932).

Portraits: oil, three-quarter length, attributed to J. Van Diest, *c.*1718: N.P.G.; oil, half-length, by Kneller, 1705–10: N.P.G.

Stanhope, Philip Dormer (1694–1773), 4th Earl of Chesterfield; statesman and man of letters.

Philip Dormer Stanhope was born in London on 22 September 1694, the eldest son of Philip Stanhope, 3rd Earl of Chesterfield. His father took little interest in his education, and the strongest influence upon his formative years was

exerted by his grandmother, the Marchioness of Halifax, and his French tutor. At the age of eighteen he entered Trinity Hall, Cambridge, where he studied hard, but he left the university after only a year to travel in Europe. On the death of Queen Anne in 1714, he returned to England to be presented by his kinsman, James Stanhope (q.v.), to the new King.

George I was impressed by the young Stanhope, and in 1715 he made him Gentleman of the Bedchamber to his son and heir, the Prince of Wales. In the following year Stanhope was elected M.P. for St. Germans, Cornwall, and, despite an early controversy over his maiden speech being made while he was still under age, he soon became known for his eloquent speaking and his liberal principles. He was not afraid to incur the hostility of Sir Robert Walpole (q.v.), at that time the dominant figure in the House of Commons and a close friend of the King, and in 1725 he contemptuously rejected Walpole's offer of the Order of the Bath.

On the death of his father in 1726,

Stanhope became the 4th Earl of Chesterfield and entered the House of Lords; here he continued to win general admiration for his eloquent and witty speeches. In 1727 George II came to the throne and in the following year he offered to make Chesterfield a Privy Councillor; Walpole objected and as a compromise arrangement Chesterfield was appointed English Ambassador to The Hague. In this post Chesterfield proved himself to be an extremely able diplomat. He gained Dutch support for England's Treaty of Seville with Spain in 1728, successfully negotiated the marriage of George II's eldest daughter, Anne, to the Prince of Orange, and in 1731 took charge of the negotiations for the second Treaty of Vienna, at which England and Spain united with the Dutch to form an effective balance of power against the Habsburg dominions. In recognition of these successes, he was invested with the Order of the Garter, and in 1730 Sir Robert Walpole made him Lord High Steward.

While in the Netherlands Chesterfield became involved with a governess, Elizabeth du Bouchet, who bore him a son, Philip Stanhope, in 1732. From the age of five until his death in 1768 this child was the recipient of Chesterfield's *Letters to his Son*, his most famous literary work. These letters, written in an eloquent yet intimate style, contain Chesterfield's advice to his son, and reflect the worldly values of his contemporary society: the emphasis is on manners, deportment, and duty. In 1754 Chesterfield procured for his son a seat in parliament as M.P. for Liskeard, Cornwall. The death of this son in 1768, followed by the discovery that he had kept secret from his father a wife and two children, was to be one of the sharpest disappointments of Chesterfield's old age.

A severe illness forced him to return from the Netherlands to England in late

1732, but on his return to the House of Lords he quickly became the acknowledged leader of the opposition. His marriage in 1733 to George II's half-sister, the Countess of Walsingham, was against the King's wishes. After opposing Walpole's Excise Bill he was dismissed in 1733 from the post of Lord High Steward.

In 1741 Chesterfield spent several months in France, where he met Voltaire, Montesquieu, and many other distinguished writers, but he returned in November of that year to resume the attack on Walpole. In February 1743 Walpole finally resigned, but in a series of letters written under the pseudonym of Geffery Broadbottom, Chesterfield complained convincingly that the change had produced new men but no new policies. An unexpected result of these letters was a legacy of £20,000 from the Duchess of Marlborough, a sympathetic admirer. In 1743, despite strong opposition from George II, Chesterfield was offered the post of Viceroy of Ireland by Henry Pelham.

He took up his post in 1745 but because of further illness he was only able to remain in Ireland for a single year. His rule was both effective and enlightened: declaring that poverty and not popery was the chief enemy, he did much to encourage Irish education and local industries. When he returned to England in 1746 Chesterfield was made Secretary of State for the Northern Department, but two years later, despairing at the Duke of Newcastle's opposition to his own proposals for an immediate end to the war with France, he resigned.

The last period of Chesterfield's life was devoted to family affairs and his various literary interests. The building of Chesterfield House in South Audley Street, Mayfair, was completed in 1749. He continued to correspond with Voltaire and other French men of letters and acted as patron to the poet Henry Jones and the dramatist Colley Cibber (q.v.). In 1752 he was temporarily crippled after falling from a horse in Hyde Park. He also suffered from increasing deafness and made several visits to Bath for health reasons. Chesterfield accepted illness, social isolation and the personal disappointments of his last years with stoic strength of character. After Samuel Johnson's famous letter of 1755, a severely phrased rebuke to patrons, Chesterfield bore no malice towards him.

In 1768 came his son's death and the discovery of the boy's secret family. Despite his bitter disappointment, Chesterfield nevertheless unhesitatingly paid for the children's education and wrote amiably to the widow. As his heir he adopted a distant cousin, Philip Stanhope (1755–1815), to whom he had acted as godfather and written a further series of educative letters. The one person with whom his relationship was not entirely generous was his wife, whom he had married for political and financial reasons. But he always made certain that her material needs were satisfied and she never complained of his treatment.

Chesterfield died at Chesterfield House, London, on 24 March 1773. His will made generous provision for his heir, his servants, and Elizabeth du Bouchet, and stipulated that his own funeral should cost as little as possible within the dictates of decency.

W. Connely, *The True Chesterfield* (1939).

Bonamy Dobrée (ed.), *The Letters of Chesterfield* (6 vols.; 1932).

S. L. Gulick Jr. (ed.), *Some Unpublished Letters of Lord Chesterfield* (Berkeley, 1937).

S. Shellabarger, *Lord Chesterfield and His World* (Boston, Mass., 1951, rev. ed.).

Portraits: oil, half-length, after W. Hoare, *c.* 1742: N.P.G.; oil, half-length, by A. Ramsay, 1765: N.P.G.; oil, by Sir G. Kneller: Blickling Hall, Norfolk; oil, by W. Hoare: Trinity College, Cambridge.

Steele, Sir Richard (1672–1729), essayist, dramatist, and politician.

Richard Steele was born in Dublin and baptized there on 12 March 1672, the son of an attorney.

Both of Steele's parents having died while he was a young boy, he was put under the guardianship of an uncle who was the confidential secretary to the Duke of Ormonde (see Butler, James, 2nd Duke, in *Lives of the Stuart Age*). Through Ormonde's patronage, Steele was sent to the Charterhouse school in London, where he first met Joseph Addison (q.v.), a fellow student with whom his name was to become inseparably linked. He then went to Merton College, Oxford, but left after a short time to enlist as a cadet in the Life Guards. He eventually rose to the rank of captain in command of the Tower guard.

His first venture in prose writing was a tract entitled *The Christian Hero* (1701), in which Christian principles are held to be the true essentials of greatness. After publishing it, he was the subject of some satirical comment, for he was known for his conviviality, and his own way of life – its excesses accompanied by the usual afflictions, gout and debt – scarcely matched the high ideals set forth in the tract.

Steele next wrote several comedies of manners, which were not especially successful: *The Funeral, or Grief à-la-Mode* (1701), *The Lying Lover* (1704), and *The Tender Husband* (1705), in completing which Addison assisted him. During this period Steele continued his successful journalistic writing and in time left the army. He became a member of the Kit-Cat Club, a circle of prominent Whigs that included Addison, Congreve, Vanbrugh, and the publisher Jacob Tonson. In 1707 Steele obtained the post of gazetteer: as editor of the official government news publication he earned £300 a year. In 1705

he married a widow, Margaret Stretch, who died the following year, leaving him an income from her property. In 1707 he married Mary Scurlock (addressed as 'Dear Prue' in his many letters to her), who was also a woman of some means. None of the property or income which thus became his proved adequate to meet his natural extravagance, however, and his financial difficulties continued to the end of his life.

In 1709 Steele founded *The Tatler*. As editor he was, at first, assisted by Swift (q.v.), whose pseudonym, Isaac Bickerstaff, he borrowed. Addison shortly joined the enterprise and played a leading role in establishing its distinctive character. *The Tatler* was a mixture of essays and news items, but the political content was soon completely overshadowed by the essays, which dealt with matters of taste and conduct and so exercised a profound civilizing influence on eighteenth-century life. A total of 271 numbers appeared before publication ceased on 2 January 1711. Of these, Steele wrote about 188 numbers; Addison forty-six; and they collaborated on thirty-six. The periodical was published on Tuesdays, Thursdays, and Saturdays, in order to be in the post leaving London for the country on those days. Each issue was a folio half-sheet and, after a few free introductory issues, cost a penny. *The Tatler* was immensely popular, perhaps because its first concern was the cultivation of manners and the refinement of human life rather than the intrigue and warring of political factions.

In 1710 the Tory Harley became Chancellor of the Exchequer when the Whig government fell from power. Steele lost the gazetteership, and it may also have been Tory influence that brought about the end of *The Tatler* in 1711. In any case, scarcely two months had passed before *The Spectator* started publication with the proclaimed intention of being a non-political periodical devoted to philosophy and morality, thereby improving social life. *The Spectator* ran for 555 issues until 6 December 1712 (and then again for a short time in 1714 under Addison alone). To Addison are usually attributed 274 numbers; to Steele 240. Although from the first Addison was clearly the moving spirit behind *The Spectator* and responsible for its greater range of subject matter, to Steele belongs the credit for initiating one of the most charming features, the Club, with its representative English characters, Sir Roger de Coverley, Sir Andrew Freeport, and Captain Sentry.

Steele was the acknowledged spokesman for the Whigs in opposition in such journals as *The Guardian* (175 numbers published in 1713, fifty-one of which are contributed by Addison) and *The Englishman* (ninety-five numbers in 1713–14 and in a second series in 1715), the two most important of his political periodicals. When he collected and published his *Political Writings*, the book aroused appropriately loud protests from the Tories. In 1713 he had been elected M.P. for Stockbridge. But because of papers he had originally published in *The Guardian*, and a piece on the Hanoverian succession entitled 'The Crisis' (1714), Steele was expelled from the House of Commons for seditious writing in 1714.

His fortunes as a loyal Whig changed with the accession of George I, however, and he was appointed Justice of the Peace, Deputy Lieutenant of Middlesex, Governor of the Royal Stables, and commissioner for the forfeited estates in Scotland. In 1715 he received a knighthood, was made commissioner of Drury Lane Theatre, and was elected M.P. for Boroughbridge. In 1722 he was elected for Wendover, and he continued in politics for the rest of his active life,

sporadically giving time to the management of Drury Lane. To this period of his life belongs his most successful dramatic work, *The Conscious Lovers* (1722), a comedy in which sentimental themes are handled with characteristic liveliness. An incident that marred the final years of his literary life was a quarrel with Addison, arising in 1718 because of political differences, and remaining unresolved at the time of Addison's death in 1719.

Debt and bad health forced Steele to retire from London in 1724 to an estate in Wales belonging to his wife. Here he attempted to put his affairs in order, but in 1726 he suffered a stroke that left him partially paralysed. He died at Carmarthen on 1 September 1729. Steele was recognized in his own day as having created a new form in the periodical essays of *The Tatler*.

George A. Aitken (ed.), *The Life of Richard Steele* (2 vols.; 1889).

George A. Aitken (ed.), *The Tatler* (4 vols.; 1898–9).

R. Blanchard (ed.), *The Christian Hero* (1932).

R. Blanchard (ed.), *Correspondence of Sir Richard Steele* (1941; repr. 1968).

R. Blanchard (ed.), *The Englishman* (1955).

R. Blanchard (ed.), *Occasional Verse* (1952).

R. Blanchard (ed.), *Steele's Periodic Journalism 1714–16* (1959).

R. Blanchard (ed.), *Tracts and Pamphlets* (Baltimore, 1944).

D. F. Bond (ed.), *The Spectator* (5 vols.; 1965).

J. Loftis, *Steele at Drury Lane* (Berkeley, 1952).

J. Loftis (ed.), *The Theatre* (1962).

C. Winton, *Captain Steele: The Early Career of Richard Steele* (Baltimore, 1964).

C. Winton, *Sir Richard Steele, M.P.: The Later Career* (Baltimore, 1970).

Portraits: oil, quarter-length, by J. Richardson, 1712: N.P.G.; oil, half-length, by G. Kneller, 1711: N.P.G.; miniature, by C. Richter, c. 1720: N.P.G.; oil, by Sir G. Kneller: National Gallery of Ireland, Dublin.

Stephenson, George (1781–1848), engineer and pioneer of steam locomotives and railways.

George Stephenson was born at Wylam, near Newcastle, on 9 June 1781. At the age of fourteen Stephenson, whose early life was characterized by extreme poverty, was sent to work in the Dewley coal mines as an assistant to his father, a colliery fireman. By the time he was seventeen, his ability was such that he had been put in charge of the newly installed pumping engine at the Water Row mines. This was his first experience of a steam engine. During the next six years he worked in various collieries, always looking after stationary steam engines based on the design of James Watt (q.v.). During these years he acquired considerable manual skill, spending some of his spare time repairing clocks and watches to supplement his income. The rest of his free hours were spent at night school broadening his education.

In 1805 his wife and daughter died, and but for the need to look after his son Robert, Stephenson might well have emigrated with his sister. However, he decided to stay on in the colliery and by 1812 he had been appointed chief enginewright to all the Killingworth pits at a salary of £100 a year, which rescued him from further want. During this period he installed some forty stationary steam engines, used either for pumping out mines or as winding engines to move the mined coal in trucks both above and below ground. The rising cost of feeding pit ponies was at about this time causing some concern to mine-owners and providing them with an incentive to seek alternative means of moving the coal, not only within the colliery but also between the mines and the industrial users. Steam was an obvious possibility; the Cornish engineer, Richard Trevithick (q.v.), had as long ago as 1801 driven the first steam locomotive, and the idea of mounting a steam engine on wheels and using the power to drive the wheels had been put into practice at Gateshead in 1805, but the great weight of this first locomotive had been too much for the wooden rails that were then in use. The next development, in 1812, was a similar type of locomotive, fitted with pinion wheels engaging with iron rack rails. This arrangement was successful in carrying coal from the Middleton collieries into Leeds – albeit somewhat slowly.

The Middleton rack-and-pinion railway provided sufficient encouragement for Stephenson's employers to provide the funds to enable him to build a locomotive. His first engine, the *Blücher*, had a successful trial on 25 July 1814; it introduced flanged wheels running on iron rails as a major innovation. A year later Stephenson patented a steam blast device to increase boiler draught, and this was incorporated into his next locomotives, *My Lord* and the *Wellington*, greatly increasing their efficiency.

On the strength of these achievements, in 1815 Stephenson was invited to join the Walker Ironworks on a part-time basis, and this gave him an opportunity to perfect many of his designs and inventions. One invention of particular importance that belonged to this period was the miner's safety lamp. In 1818 he was presented with £1,000, raised by public subscription, in recognition of this work. However, Sir Humphry Davy (q.v.) and W. R. Clanny had also devised similar lamps, and considerable controversy ensued.

From this time onwards, Stephenson devoted himself entirely to the development of railways. From 1819 to 1822 he supervised an 8-mile railway for the Hetton colliery. In 1821 he was appointed chief engineer for the new Stockton-to-Darlington railway, built to enable the Auckland coalfields to compete with the pits on the river Tyne. The locomotive for this railway was built in the factory Stephenson himself founded in Newcastle in 1823 (with Edward Pease and Thomas Richardson as partners). When the line opened in September 1825, the train was drawn by Stephenson's *Locomotion*, which achieved a top speed of 16 m.p.h.

The time had now come for railways to emerge from the coal mines and their environs: Stephenson was not alone in realizing that people, as well as coal, could be moved about by steam. The first passenger-carrying railway was planned to link Manchester with Liverpool, and who better to supervise its construction than George Stephenson. The sponsors of the railway decided that the locomotive for the new line should be chosen by open competition, with a first prize of £500. Not surprisingly, Stephenson won with his *Rocket*, which covered the 12-mile trial run at Rainhill at an average speed of $13\frac{1}{2}$ m.p.h. and a top speed of 30 m.p.h. The railway opened a year later, in 1830.

In the following years, Stephenson served as chief engineer to many of the lines that made up the Midland railway system, as well as some abroad (especially

in Belgium and Spain). He was the first to advocate the liberal use of tunnels and embankments to limit gradients, and the use of malleable iron to replace cast-iron in making rails. He was, in fact, the leading figure in the nineteenth-century railway mania, though he did his best to check it and to restrict the wild financial speculations that were inevitably a part of it.

Stephenson died at his home near Chesterfield, Tapton House, on 12 August 1848. His great achievement was the transformation of a minor colliery facility into a passenger-transport system that very quickly swept the world. His son, Robert, carried on much of his work.

L. T. C. Rolt, *George and Robert Stephenson: the Railway Revolution* (1960).

Portraits: oil, half-length, by H. W. Pickersgill: N.P.G.; engraving, three-quarter length, by Charles Turner after H. P. Briggs, 1838: Science Museum.

Sterne, Laurence (1713–68), novelist, best known as the author of *Tristram Shandy*.

Laurence Sterne was born on 24 November 1713 in Clonmel, Ireland, the son of an ensign in the army, and the great-grandson of Richard Sterne (died 1683), Archbishop of York. He spent the first few years of his life on or near the various army posts to which his father was assigned, chiefly in Ireland. At the age of nine he was sent to school in Halifax, Yorkshire, where he stayed until 1731, the year of his father's death. His mother remained in Ireland, and for the next two years Sterne became accomplished in doing virtually nothing.

In July 1733 Sterne, through the help of a cousin, entered Jesus College, Cambridge. His academic life was not distinguished by any means, but he developed an avid interest in reading and became absorbed in the works of Burton, Rabelais, Montaigne, Shakespeare, Cervantes, Locke, and Swift.

He obtained his B.A. degree in 1737, and shortly afterwards took Holy Orders. For an intelligent and sensitive man without money, the clerical life provided one of the few opportunities of the day. Sterne was not ideally suited for the religious life, and even after obtaining the living of Sutton, near York, and somewhat later a prebend in the cathedral, he stated that 'books, paintings, fiddling, and shooting were my amusements'. He appears to have been an extremely likeable person, and we are told that 'in person Sterne was tall and thin, with a hectic and consumptive appearance; in conversation he was gay and witty'.

In 1741, after a courtship of two years, he married Elizabeth Lumley, a woman 'with some little fortune'. Through the influence of one of his wife's friends, he obtained the living of Stillington, Yorkshire, where he lived and worked for nearly twenty years.

His career as a writer began relatively late, for up to 1759 Sterne had published nothing except two sermons. Towards the end of the year he published his first book, *A Political Romance* (later renamed *The History of a Good Warm Watch-Coat*), which displayed no evidence of literary genius.

Sterne's wife now began showing symptoms of progressive mental illness, described at the time as 'temporary insanity'. Their marriage had not been a happy one, its only pleasant product being the birth of their daughter Lydia, whom Sterne loved dearly. Perhaps partly as an escape from his domestic problems, he had continued to work on a satirical masterpiece. It became the literary vessel into which Sterne poured all his illusions, criticisms, and ridicule; not only were science and the church his objects of satire, but also the entire range of human nature. Thus was born, late in 1759, *The Life and Opinions of Tristram Shandy, Gentleman*, the first two volumes of which were originally published in York. The following year Sterne went to London to oversee the publication of the work in its first London edition. His reputation as a wit had preceded him, and he was overwhelmed at finding himself treated as a celebrity in the literary capital of the world.

Tristram Shandy eventually reached nine volumes, the last being published in 1767. It is a strange and complex masterpiece that defies exact classification. It is certainly no novel in the usual sense; it has no plot as one would define it, for action is not its principal ingredient; and there is a total lack of logic or an orderly sequence of events. The narrator is not born until volume iv, and is largely abandoned towards the end of the book. A group of humorous characters is the vehicle for Sterne's demonstration of his lively imagination, whimsical digressions, and paradoxical humour which can be outrageous and subtle at the same time. The detours and deviations of the narrative become so convoluted that some contemporary readers considered the author to be mad; even such intelligent critics as Dr. Johnson could find no merit in it.

Sterne's life, opinions, and general philosophy are embedded, although often disguised, throughout the work. He obviously had fun writing the nine volumes, but more important, it provided him with a forum in which he could express his own attitudes and knowledge behind a light veil of teasing wit. The work achieved wide circulation and financial success.

Sterne had been suffering for some time from a consumptive disease. In 1762 he was advised to seek a warmer climate, and left with his wife and daughter on an extended trip to the south of France and Italy. He returned to England in 1764, leaving behind his wife; they had mutually agreed on a permanent though amiable separation.

As a result of several trips to the Continent, Sterne compiled *A Sentimental Journey Through France and Italy* (1768). This was a type of subjective travel book in which the personal reactions of the author to people and places became more important than the people and places themselves; and in which Smollett, among other authors, was satirized. It was to consist of four volumes, of which only two were completed.

Sterne died on 18 March 1768. His *Letters from Yorick to Eliza*, the result of a short-lived infatuation for a Mrs. Draper, was published posthumously in 1773. His only other published work is *The Sermons of Mr. Yorick*, brought out in seven volumes from 1760 to 1769 (the last three volumes being published posthumously).

W. L. Cross (ed.), *The Complete Works of Laurence Sterne* (12 vols.; New York, 1904).

L. P. Curtis (ed.), *Letters of Laurence Sterne* (1935).

D. Grant (ed.), *Selected Sermons and Letters* (1950).

L. Hartley, *Sterne in the Twentieth Century: an Essay and a Bibliography of Sternean Studies 1900–65* (1968).

Peter Quennell, *The Unsentimental Journey of Laurence Sterne* (1948).

G. D. Stout, Jr. (ed.), *A Sentimental Journey Through France and Italy, by Mr. Yorick* (Berkeley, 1967).

J. Traugott, *Tristram Shandy's World* (Berkeley, 1954).

L. Van der Hammond, *Sterne's Sermons of Mr. Yorick* (New Haven, 1948).

J. Work (ed.), *The Life and Opinions of Tristram Shandy, Gentleman* (New York, 1940).

Portraits: oil, three-quarter length, by unknown artist, *c.* 1760: N.P.G.; water-colour, full-length, by L. L. Carrogis, 1762: N.P.G.; oil, three-quarter length, by J. Reynolds, 1760: N.P.G.; oil, after Reynolds: National Gallery of Ireland, Dublin.

Stewart, Robert (1769–1822), Viscount Castlereagh and 2nd Marquis of Londonderry; statesman.

Stewart was born on 18 June 1769 in Dublin, the son of Robert Stewart, 1st Marquis of Londonderry, who came of a prominent Anglo-Irish family. He was educated privately at Armagh and then at St. John's College, Cambridge, where he distinguished himself academically. In

1790 he was elected to the Irish parliament as Whig member for County Down. There followed a brief period of service in the army during 1793 when he reached the rank of lieutenant colonel, and in 1794 he married Lady Emily Anne Hobart, youngest daughter and co-heiress of John Hobart, 2nd Earl of Buckinghamshire.

Elected to the British parliament in the same year (1794), Stewart turned Tory. In 1796 he received the courtesy title of Viscount Castlereagh, by which he is best known, and in the year following was appointed Keeper of the Irish Privy Seal.

As Acting Chief Secretary to the Viceroy of Ireland, in 1798 Castlereagh successfully took steps to quell the rebellion organized by the United Irishmen, and became firmly convinced of the need of a parliamentary union with Britain. The passage of the Act of Union through the Dublin parliament gave an early indication of Castlereagh's polished diplomacy as he managed to force the measure against strong Protestant opposition. He also favoured Catholic emancipation, which the Prime Minister,

William Pitt, was prepared to offer when union was achieved. But the bigotry of George III prevented Pitt from carrying out his promises on emancipation, and both he and Castlereagh resigned in 1801.

In 1802 Castlereagh returned to office in Addington's ministry as President of the Board of Control responsible for Indian Affairs. After Pitt's return as Prime Minister (in May 1804), he also became Secretary of State for War (July 1805). He deployed a British expeditionary force to Hanover which proved a limited success, despite Napoleon's victory at Austerlitz in December. On Pitt's death in the following month, Castlereagh left foreign and military affairs but returned to the War Department again in Portland's ministry in 1807, and was largely responsible for organizing the coalitions against Napoleon, and also for saving the Danish, Swedish, and Portuguese fleets from the French. At the outset of the Peninsular War in 1808 the government's decision to send a major expedition against Napoleon's forces there was immediate: Castlereagh entrusted command to Sir Arthur Wellesley (q.v.). But the loss in 1809 of a British expedition sent by Castlereagh against Napoleon's naval base at Antwerp provoked a scandal that gave George Canning (q.v.), Castlereagh's foremost critic, ample opportunity to discredit the War Minister's policy in the House and to engineer his removal from the cabinet. Castlereagh reacted by challenging Canning to a duel, fought on 21 September 1809 on Wimbledon Common. Canning was wounded in the thigh. Both men had already resigned and Castlereagh remained out of office for the next two and a half years.

In 1812 Castlereagh rejoined the government as Secretary of State for Foreign Affairs, and after Perceval's assassination in May he became Leader of the House of Commons. His policy, after Napoleon's defeat, was based almost entirely on the lines laid down by Pitt, aiming at the restoration of France to her old limits, the union of Belgium and Holland, the rejection of all conquests save for some essential new maritime bases, and the endeavour to parry Russian designs. England's maritime supremacy, along with her colonial possessions and prospects, had been secured before the Congress of Vienna in 1814–15, and Castlereagh had succeeded in keeping both these issues outside the discussion of a European settlement; his only desire was to preserve the peace. Castlereagh and Metternich, the Austrian Foreign Minister, dominated the negotiations, and they were able to resist the wilder territorial demands of Russia and Prussia. Security, not revenge, was what was required, and the settlement at Vienna appears as a fair embodiment of Castlereagh's principle of the 'just equilibrium'.

Castlereagh's foreign policy was misunderstood because he had neither the wish nor the ability to explain it to the country at large. Fortunately he was on intimate terms with the Prime Minister, Lord Liverpool, and also with Wellington, the greatest figure in Europe after the fall of Napoleon. No member of the Tory party could object to a policy approved by these three men. He would have been more in step with public opinion if he had made a plain declaration in favour of the spread of moderate constitutional principles. But Castlereagh tended to see public opinion rather as an obstacle to be surmounted than as a guide to his policy, and much preferred personal discussion at the highest level among men who had been associated in great events.

Castlereagh's aim was to make possible diplomacy by conference, and the periodic meetings of the contracting parties came to be known as the 'congress system'. At the congress of Aix-la-Chapelle in 1818, where France was readmitted to the concert of powers, Castlereagh was adamant in resisting Russian demands to institute a league of European powers to maintain the existing order under sanction of military force. Metternich, who was now at the height of his powers, organized a meeting at Troppau in 1820 where it was decided that the Alliance powers should act together to stamp out revolutionary movements in Europe. Castlereagh refused to treat this meeting as a full European congress, and after the congress of Laibach of 1821 (the year, incidentally, in which he succeeded his father as 2nd Marquis of Londonderry) he completely repudiated the principle of state intervention in internal affairs laid down at Troppau. The rift between Britain and the three despotic Eastern powers, Austria, Russia, and Prussia, was growing ever greater, and in the classic state paper of May 1820 Castlereagh emphasized that Britain, a parliamentary monarchy not governed by dogmatic principles, could not and would not 'act upon speculative principles of precaution'. However, the emergence in 1821 of the questions of Greek independence and the fate of the Spanish colonies brought Britain's political and commercial interest directly into the European orbit; Castlereagh decided to attend the Congress of Verona (1822) in person, and the list of instructions that he drew up for himself indicates that he had decided not to sanction forcible interference in either Greece or Spain; Britain would have to recognize any new state emerging from a successful revolution. Obviously Castlereagh was preparing, albeit reluctantly, for that break with the reactionary Eastern powers that was eventually accomplished after his death.

Castlereagh's health at this time, both physically and mentally, was beginning to suffer. Combining the offices of Foreign Secretary and Leader of the House of Commons was an arduous commitment, and exposed him to parliamentary abuse. In the late spring and early summer of 1822 Castlereagh became increasingly obsessed by dangers that seemed to be immediately pressing. In his opinion it was only his personal influence and diplomatic skill that could avert a major crisis at the forthcoming Congress of Verona. His mind was gone, and he became convinced that he was being blackmailed for alleged homosexual acts. Friends like Wellington did all they could to help him, but on 12 August 1822 in a fit of desperate depression he committed suicide with a penknife. He was buried in Westminster Abbey.

C. J. Bartlett, *Castlereagh* (1966).
H. Montgomery Hyde, *The Rise of Castlereagh* (1933).
H. Montgomery Hyde, *The Strange Death of Lord Castlereagh* (1963).
Ione Leigh, *Castlereagh* (1951).
C. Vane, Marquis of Londonderry (ed.), *Memoirs and Correspondence of Viscount Castlereagh* (12 vols.; 1848–53).
C. J. Webster, *The Foreign Policy of Castlereagh, 1812–1815* (1935.)
C. J. Webster, *The Foreign Policy of Castlereagh, 1815–1822* (1934, 2nd ed.).

Portraits: oil, half-length, by T. Lawrence, 1810: N.P.G.; pencil, half-length, by G. Dance, 1794: N.P.G.; oil, three-quarter length, by T. Lawrence, *c.*1814: Windsor Castle.

Stuart, Charles Edward Louis Philip Casimir (1720–88), see Charles Edward Louis Philip Casimir Stuart.

Stuart, James Francis Edward (1688–1766), see James Francis Edward Stuart.

Stuart, John (1713–92), 3rd Earl of Bute; statesman and favourite of George III.

John Stuart was born on 25 May 1713 in Edinburgh, the elder son of James Stuart, 2nd Earl of Bute. Educated at Eton, he succeeded as 3rd Earl on the death of his father in 1723. In 1736 he married Mary, only daughter of Edward and Lady Mary Wortley Montagu, an alliance that eventually brought him considerable wealth. In 1737 he was elected as a Scottish representative peer, taking his seat on 24 January 1738, though his attendance was occasional and he did not participate in debates. He had been appointed one of the commissioners of police for Scotland in 1737, and in 1738 was made a Knight of the Thistle.

Bute pursued his studies of botany, agriculture, and architecture on the island of Bute between 1736 and 1745, before moving to London on the outbreak of the rebellion. A chance occurrence at Egham races in 1747, when Bute was summoned to play whist with the Prince of Wales during a shower, shaped Bute's future career. He became a favourite at Leicester House and was appointed one of the gentlemen of the Prince's Bedchamber on 16 October 1750. The following year, however, the Prince died. Nevertheless, the Princess and her son maintained his preferment, despite the open contempt of the King.

Bute became the constant companion and confidant of young Prince George; the intimate relations between Bute and the Princess gave rise to much unfounded scandal, but with the accession of George III (1760), he was immediately made a member of the Privy Council and appointed Groom of the Stole and First Gentleman of the Bedchamber. He was practically the chief minister now, though his only office was in the household. King George relied upon him, calling him his 'dearest friend', and it was through Bute alone that the King's intentions were made clear.

Bute's position was clarified when in 1761 he became Secretary of State for the Northern Department. In May of that year he was re-elected as a Scottish representative peer. His main hopes were to conclude peace with France, to sever England from her connection with German politics, to break up the Whig oligarchy, and to make the King supreme over parliament. He engineered the resignation of William Pitt the Elder (q.v.) in October 1761, and when he appeared for the opening of the new parliament, he was mobbed on his way to the Guildhall. Bute's longstanding unpopularity with the people was due to the fact that he was a favourite, and a Scot; Pitt's downfall was the last straw.

Pitt's tough military policy was vindicated before the end of 1761, and in 1762 Bute was forced to declare war on Spain. He succeeded Newcastle (see Pelham-Holles, Thomas) as First Lord of the Treasury on 26 May 1762. Impatient for peace, he had been negotiating secretly with the court of Versailles for several months, and in November he entrusted the signing of the preliminary treaty to John Russell, 4th Duke of Bedford.

Doubting George Grenville's ability to defend the terms of the treaty in the face of powerful opposition in the House of Commons, Bute induced Henry Fox to desert his party and accept the leadership of the House. Employing gross bribery and intimidation – his administration probably being unsurpassed for corruption and financial incapacity – he was able to carry addresses approving the terms of the preliminary treaty through both Houses on 9 December.

The signing at Paris of the definitive treaty of peace with France and Spain on 10 February 1763 was followed by increased unpopularity for Bute. Parts of the treaty resulted in fierce objections on the grounds that they were disadvan-

tageous to Britain, and Bute was wrongly suspected of accepting French bribes. His imposition of a cider tax added to the odium, and on 9 April Bute resigned.

His suggested successor, Grenville, unwilling to act as the favourite's puppet, now insisted that Bute retire from court. Bute had advised the King to dismiss Grenville in August, but after failing in his overtures to Pitt and the Bedford grouping, he resigned the office of the Privy Purse and left the King on 28 September 1763. He kept up a correspondence with George III until 1765, when Grenville, spurred on by increased annoyance at the Earl's influence, finally obtained the King's promise that Bute 'should never directly or indirectly ... have anything to do with his business, nor give advice upon anything whatsoever'.

Apart from voting against the government on the American question and opposing the repeal of the Stamp Act in 1766, Bute withdrew from political life and into obscurity and neglect. He visited Barèges in 1768 for the sake of his health, and then travelled incognito in Italy for

415

over twelve months. Still the butt of malevolent attacks by his political opponents, and also the object of the King's ingratitude, he finally wrote to a friend: 'Few men have ever suffered more in the short space I have gone through of political warfare.' After the death of the Princess Dowager in 1772, Bute decided at last to retire from the world 'before it retires from me'. In 1780 he gave up his seat in the Lords. He died at his London home on 10 March 1792. He was buried at Rothesay on the island of Bute.

Bute's private life was happier than his public career. The father of eleven children, he was amiable and courteous among friends, though haughty and silent in public. At his palatial residence at Luton Hoo, designed for him by Robert Adam, he kept a magnificent library, a fine collection of scientific instruments, a gallery of Dutch and Flemish paintings, and a botanic garden of valuable plants. Bute was also responsible for the development of the royal estate of Kew as a botanical garden. Bute's brief hour as chief minister shows that despite his good intentions he was totally unfit to handle affairs of state.

Alice M. Coates, *Lord Bute* . . . (1975).
J. Lovat-Fraser, *John Stuart, Earl of Bute* (1912).
Sir Lewis Namier, *The Structure of Politics at the Accession of George III* (1957).
R. Pares, *George III and the Politicians* (1953).
R. Sedgwick (ed.), *Letters from George III to Lord Bute 1756–66* (1939).

Portrait: oil, full-length, by J. Reynolds, 1773 : N.P.G.

Stubbs, George (1724–1806), animal painter and etcher.

George Stubbs was born in Liverpool on 24 August 1724, the son of a tanner. His interest in anatomy and drawing became apparent when he was still a child, and his father acknowledged his need to pursue a career different from his own by allowing him to be apprenticed, at the age of fifteen, to a local engraver. However, his absolute certainty of the direction in which his talents should be developed encouraged Stubbs to recognize no other teacher but himself, and after quarrelling with his employer he left home to be a portrait painter in Leeds, and then to study and lecture on anatomy in York. His earliest surviving works are plates etched to illustrate an *Essay Towards a Complete New System of Midwifery* (1751).

In 1754 Stubbs travelled to Italy to reassure himself – in the words of a contemporary – that 'nature was and is always superior to art'. While staying briefly in North Africa on his return journey he watched a white Barbary horse stalked and then killed and devoured by a lion, an exhibition of violent natural energy that was to provide the theme for several of his most powerful paintings.

After the death of his mother in 1756 Stubbs moved to London and began to gain a reputation as an animal painter. In 1758 he rented a farmhouse in Lincolnshire, where he devoted himself for eighteen months to dissecting and drawing the carcasses of horses; after a further six years spent in making engravings from these drawings, he published the results in his *Anatomy of the Horse* (1766), an important work of reference that was praised for its skill, accuracy, and aesthetic qualities. Stubbs now received several commissions from members of the nobility, and by gaining access to private collections of animals in captivity he was able to extend his range of subject matter to include such animals as the tiger, giraffe, and rhinoceros.

In the early 1770s Stubbs painted several scenes of country life, and also experimented with enamel painting on china plaques specially made by the firm of Wedgwood. He became an Associate of the Royal Academy in 1780, but his election to full membership the following year was annulled after a dispute over certain rules of procedure.

Although his later paintings show no deterioration in his talent, Stubbs's reputation had begun to decline even before his death. A series of engravings of racehorses commissioned for *The Turf Review* in 1790 was not completed because of lack of support, and Stubbs's own grand project of *A Comparative Anatomical Exposition of the Structure of the Human Body with that of a Tiger and Common Fowl* also remained unfinished when he died at his home in Portman Square, London, on 10 July 1806. In the present century his art has been reassessed, especially his painting of horses, which he represents with unmatched feeling for both form and movement, and he has been recognized as an isolated but dedicated master of his chosen field.

W. Shaw Sparrow, *Stubbs and Ben Marshall* (1929).
B. Taylor, *George Stubbs* (1969).

Works in:
National Gallery, London.
British Museum, London.
Tate Gallery, London.
Walker Art Gallery, Liverpool.
Holburne Museum, Bath.
Provincial galleries in Glasgow, Leeds, and elsewhere.

Portraits: water-colour, half-length, by O. Humphry: N.P.G.; self-portrait, enamel on Wedgwood plaque, half-length, 1781: N.P.G.; oil, by Reginald Brunditt: Tate Gallery; pastel, by O. Humphry: Walker Art Gallery, Liverpool.

Sunderland, 3rd Earl of (1674–1722), see Spencer, Charles.

Swift, Jonathan (1667–1745), writer and cleric; one of the greatest prose satirists in the English language.

Jonathan Swift was born in Dublin on 30 November 1667, the posthumous son of Jonathan Swift, a lawyer, and the grandson of Thomas Swift, the famous ultra-Royalist Herefordshire vicar.

Swift had a disturbed childhood which appears to have given him a deep sense of insecurity. When he was a year old he was taken to live with his devoted nurse at her home in Whitehaven, Cumberland. When he was six his now impoverished mother went back to her native Leicester-shire, leaving him in Ireland in the charge of his uncle Godwin. He was sent to perhaps the best school in Ireland, Kilkenny, where Congreve was a contemporary, and in 1682 he entered Trinity College, Dublin. Swift's academic career was less disastrous than he later claimed; although he had 'little relish by nature' for study, and only received his B.A. in 1685 by the 'special grace' dispensation, this was more due to irregular attendance than to any fundamental 'dullness or insufficiency'.

The downfall of James II in 1688 caused riots at Trinity, so Swift joined his mother in Leicestershire. A practical woman, she decided that her son's lively mind needed employment; in 1689 a family friend, Sir William Temple (see *Lives of the Stuart Age*), a prominent politician under Charles II but now in retirement, took him on as secretary and amanuensis at his house in Surrey, Moor Park. His main task was preparing his employer's memoirs and correspondence for publication, so he had the chance to read widely in Moor Park's library. He also improved his academic reputation by securing an M.A. from Hart Hall, Oxford, in 1692. Most important of all, at Moor Park he met Esther Johnson, later his 'Stella'. Temple's widowed sister, Lady Giffard, lived with him, and Esther's mother was her companion. 'Stella' was only eight when Swift first met her, and he probably helped with her education.

In 1692 Swift published his first poems, a set of rather conventional Pindaric odes – his normally generous relative Dryden remarked, 'Cousin Swift, you will never be a poet.'

In 1695 the ambitious young man went back to Ireland, was ordained as a priest, and secured the living of Kilroot, near Belfast. But despite falling in love with a schoolfriend's sister, Jane Waring, Swift soon tired of a country clergyman's life. He decided to return to England to 'push his advancement', and in May 1696 again descended on the long-suffering Temple, leaving his parish in the charge of a friend.

Henceforth Swift had a close and valuable relationship with the elderly statesman and spent up to ten hours a day studying or working on Temple's papers. Esther Johnson, thirteen years Swift's junior, had by now grown into an attractive and capable young woman, 'only a little too fat', and a deep mutual affection grew up between her and Swift. It was apparently platonic, since they seldom met unchaperoned; the 'little language' of Swift's letters to 'Stella' strongly suggests that he looked to her to provide the motherly devotion he had lacked in his childhood.

But Swift also matured as a writer, turning from poetry to prose satire in the *Tale of a Tub* (written 1696–9, published 1704), which trenchantly attacks 'numerous and gross corruptions in religion and learning'. In the mock-heroic *Battle of the Books* Swift demonstrates his loyalty to Temple by ridiculing the 'modernists' Wotton and Bentley, who had attacked his employer's *Essay upon the Ancient and Modern Learning*. Swift was alarmed at attacks made on literature by pedantry, and on orthodox religion by sectarian zeal. His solidly commonsense Anglicanism led him to append a *Discourse concerning the Mechanical Operation of the Spirit*, which attacks Dissenters in such strong terms that its author's orthodoxy was later doubted.

Sir William Temple died in 1699, and with him, said Swift, 'all that was good and amiable among mankind'. Temple's family now broke with Swift, accusing him of using 'unfaithful copy' in his edition of the dead man's memoirs. His future uncertain, Swift spent a year at Dublin Castle vaguely attached to Lord Berkeley's retinue, until in 1700 he was given the livings of Laracor and three other parishes north-east of Dublin. The £230 a year stipend meant financial independence at last, which led Jane Waring to propose marriage; she was rebuffed in a cruelly sardonic letter which serves to typify Swift's ambivalent attitude towards women.

He now led a busy social life, from 1701 on dividing his time between Dublin and London, where he soon made his name with a pamphlet attacking the proposed impeachment of certain Whigs. Swift maintained that he hardly knew the difference between Whig and Tory, and that he merely wished to appeal for moderation in politics, but such prominent Whigs as Halifax and Sunderland immediately saw in him a useful ally and began to offer him preferment. *The Tale of a Tub* was at last published anonymously in 1704, but its authorship was soon guessed, and Swift became celebrated in literary circles also, earning the friendship of Addison, and the nickname 'mad parson' for his eccentric behaviour in coffee-houses. Almost despite himself, Swift was now considered the leading Whig pamphleteer.

In 1701 Swift had arranged for 'Stella' and her companion, Mrs. Dingley, to settle in Ireland. They saw a great deal of each other, the ladies even using Swift's vicarage when he was away, but never lived together; in 1704 Swift admitted that he would marry 'Stella', were his 'fortune and humour' to permit it. Nevertheless, she remained devoted to Swift until her death in 1728.

The triumph of Somers's Whigs in 1708 led to Swift's *Project for the Advancement of Religion*, which advocated firm state support for the established church. Having earlier failed to get Queen Anne's bounty extended to Ireland, Swift reopened the question with the new Whig Lord Lieutenant of Ireland, Wharton, who intimated that in return the Irish clergy must accept the intended repeal of the Test Act (which disqualified Dissenters from public office). Swift could not stomach such erosion of the Anglican church's position, and his vehement *Letter on the Sacramental Test* (1708) marks his final break with the Whigs. Dispirited and ill with vertigo, in May 1709 he retired to the tranquillity of Laracor.

The Tory victory of 1710 meant 'a new world' for Swift. The astute Harley won this dangerous writer to his side by agreeing to the grant of Queen Anne's Bounty in Ireland. Swift, though still suspicious of Tories, was sufficiently incensed at Whig ingratitude to agree in 1710 to edit the influential Tory paper *The Examiner*, in which he tirelessly advocated Harley's policy of ending the

European war and dismissing Marlborough. These turbulent times were minutely chronicled in the *Journal to Stella* (1710–13), a series of letters Swift wrote to Esther Johnson in Ireland. His notorious pamphlet, *The Conduct of the Allies* (1711), alleging that the war was being prolonged on behalf of profiteers and the Dutch, materially contributed to Marlborough's eventual fall. Even so, Swift was still sufficiently above party politics to remain a good friend of both Harley the Tory and Addison the Whig, a mobility which allowed him to help such writers as Congreve and the young Pope. By 1713 the split between Harley and Bolingbroke was endangering the Tory administration, so Swift shrewdly looked around for a lucrative church job. The best a grateful Tory party could find for him was the deanery of St. Patrick's, Dublin; Queen Anne's distaste for the 'irreligious' *Tale of a Tub* apparently denied him office in England.

In 1714 Harley fell, Queen Anne died, and the accession of George I ushered in the long Whig supremacy. Swift fled to his Dublin deanery, where for some time he lay low. However, his poem 'Cadenus and Vanessa' (1714) at least attests to a complicated private life, since it was inspired by Esther Vanhomrigh, a merchant's daughter who since 1711 had written Swift letters of increasing ardour, culminating in her following him to Ireland. Swift kept her at arm's length until her death, reputedly from unrequited love, in 1723; his diffidence was perhaps due to a supposed 'marriage' to 'Stella' in 1716, but this is now impossible to prove.

Swift soon recovered his taste for controversy, and from 1720 on issued fiery patriotic pamphlets denouncing the Whig government's oppression of Ireland, which he felt was slowly being deprived of 'law, religion, and common humanity'. In 1722 a certain ironmaster, William Wood, bribed the King's mistress, the Duchess of Kendal, to grant him the patent to mint Ireland's copper coinage. The Irish were never consulted, and in 1724 an enraged Swift wrote a series of open letters, purportedly from 'M. B. Drapier', a humble Dublin tradesman, which described Walpole's treatment of Ireland as 'the very definition of slavery'. After an unsuccessful witch hunt for 'Drapier', the government withdrew Wood's patent; all Dublin rejoiced, with ballads and bonfires.

In 1726 Swift paid a rare visit to England, to stay with Pope at Twickenham. He met Walpole to discuss Ireland's grievances, but unfortunately 'absolutely broke with him'. More important, he delivered the manuscript of *Gulliver's Travels*, which was published anonymously that autumn and became an immediate and controversial success. Beneath the sober style and concrete realism, it could equally well be a picaresque tale fit for children, a political allegory concerning Whigs and Tories, a Utopian tract, or the cynical outburst of a convinced misanthrope.

Swift's revived fame brought him to London again in 1727, when he was asked to join the anti-Walpole faction centred on the Prince of Wales. But news that Esther Johnson was seriously ill sent him hurrying back to Dublin, and he spent much of his time with her during her last weeks. On 28 January 1728, his beloved 'Stella' died. Though Swift that same night wrote the beautiful 'Character of Mrs. Johnson' in memory of her, he was too grief-stricken to attend her funeral.

Swift never again left Ireland. He became more and more embittered, denouncing his own so-called patriotism as 'perfect rage and resentment', and writing ever more grotesque satires: *A Modest Proposal* (1729) suggests that the children of the poor, being superfluous, should be used as food, and *Answer to the Craftsman* (1730) argues that Irishmen should be encouraged to join the French army, in order to facilitate the English policy of total depopulation of Ireland. He was still a staunch defender of the established church, vigorously attacking any suggestion of repealing the Test Act or modifying the tithe system. Though he was Dublin's leading citizen and very popular with the common people, he gradually became almost a recluse. Nevertheless he was a conscientious dean; he built an almshouse, and is reputed to have spent a third of his income on charity.

Swift's mind had become weakened by his lifelong vertigo (thought to be caused by Ménière's disease of the semicircular canal of the ear) and after his vehement last pamphlet *The Legion Club*, attacking the corrupt Irish parliament, he lapsed into senility. In 1739 he had a stroke, followed by softening of the brain, and in 1742 guardians were appointed to look after his affairs. Jonathan Swift died on 19 October 1745, and was buried next to his 'Stella' in St. Patrick's Cathedral, Dublin. His tragic epitaph concludes (in translation), 'where savage indignation can no more tear his heart'.

A. E. Case (ed.), *Four Essays on Gulliver's Travels* (Princeton, 1945).

H. Davis, *Jonathan Swift: Essays on His Satire and Other Studies* (1964).

H. Davis (ed.), *The Prose Works of Jonathan Swift* (14 vols.; 1939–68).

I. Ehrenpreis, *Swift: The Man, His Works and the Age* (3 vols.; 1962–   ).

A. C. Guthkelch and D. Nichol Smith (eds.), *A Tale of a Tub and the Battle of the Books* (1958, 2nd ed.).

J. Hayward (ed.), *Gulliver's Travels and Selected Writings in Prose and Verse* (1934).

M. O. Johnson, *The Sin of Wit: Jonathan Swift As a Poet* (Syracuse, 1950).

L. A. Landa (ed.), *Jonathan Swift: Gulliver's Travels and Other Writings* (Cambridge, Mass., 1960).

F. R. Leavis, 'The Irony of Swift', in *The Common Pursuit* (1952).

R. Paulson, *Theme and Structure in Swift's Tale of a Tub* (New Haven, 1960).

M. Price, *Swift's Rhetorical Art: A Study in Structure and Meaning* (New Haven, 1953).

R. Quintana, *The Mind and Art of Swift* (New York, 1953, rev. ed.).

P. Turner, *Gulliver's Travels* (1970).

H. Williams (ed.), *The Correspondence of Swift* (5 vols.; 1963–5).

H. Williams (ed.), *Journal to Stella* (2 vols.; 1948).

H. Williams (ed.), *The Poems of Jonathan Swift* (3 vols.; 1958, 2nd ed.).

K. Williams, *Jonathan Swift and the Age of Compromise* (Lawrence, Kansas, 1958).

Portraits: oil, three-quarter length, by C. Jervas, *c.*1718: N.P.G.; oil, half-length, by or after C. Jervas, 1709–10: N.P.G.; oil, by C. Jervas: National Gallery of Ireland, Dublin.

T

Tarleton, Sir Banastre (1754–1833), military commander in the War of American Independence.

Tarleton was born on 21 August 1754, the third son of a wealthy Liverpool merchant. He entered the army, by way of Oxford University, with a cornetcy in the 1st King's Dragoon Guards in April 1775. He volunteered for service in America and arrived in North Carolina in May 1776, in charge of reinforcements for Sir Henry Clinton. Enterprising and energetic as a junior officer, he soon acquired a captaincy in the 79th Regiment (1778). He was, however, a born cavalryman and was normally so employed. In 1779 Clinton designated him lieutenant colonel in charge of the 'British Legion', a mixed force of volunteer dragoons and light infantry raised in America. Tarleton distinguished himself during Clinton's three-month campaign against Charleston; on 12 May 1780 Charleston capitulated, and Clinton mentioned Tarleton in his dispatch for his work in sealing off the town's communications.

The British Legion was placed under Cornwallis, who was pursuing the Virginians under Burford escorting the Governor of Charleston towards Camden. Moving at high speed, the cavalry force came up with Burford at Waxhaws on 29 May. Although outnumbered, the Legion destroyed the Virginians without quarter; Tarleton went down when his horse was killed under him and his men, believing him dead, fought to avenge him. Thereafter he was known to the Americans as 'Bloody Tarleton'. Returning to Cornwallis, he led a cavalry charge that completed the victory at Camden on 16 August; he also led the ruthless pursuit of the beaten enemy that followed.

The same tactics of high-speed pursuit followed by a ruthless battle against superior odds were employed against General Sumpter, with the same devastating results for the Americans at Catawba Fords (18 August).

Sumpter himself escaped, only to meet Tarleton again at Blackstock Hill on 20 November. Tarleton had only a hundred dragoons and eighty-six infantrymen against Sumpter's 1,000, but nevertheless attacked and routed the Americans completely.

In 1781 Cornwallis advanced towards North Carolina. Tarleton was detached in a support operation against General Morgan, the Legion being augmented by the addition of about 1,000 men and two artillery pieces. Morgan stood at Cowpens with 900, and Tarleton attacked on 17 January 1781. Morgan, however, had prepared his trap well: the militiamen of his front line withdrew immediately, exposing the British troops to heavy fire from the flanks and rear, where Americans were concealed in the woods. Tarleton managed to rally some forty cavalrymen of the regular 17th Light Dragoons, but he lost his guns as well as 400 men, and the 7th Fusiliers lost their colours – the marks of a complete rout.

Undaunted by this defeat, Tarleton continued to render Cornwallis spirited service as his army withdrew to Wilmington in February 1781 and as it advanced north into Virginia in May. He earned unstinting praise from his commanders, and when in August Yorktown and Gloucester were occupied Tarleton was given charge of the latter post with 600 men. On 29 September the British were besieged and, although Tarleton conducted an active defence of his own position, Clinton failed to bring relief on time; on 19 October 1781 Yorktown and Gloucester were surrendered and their defenders passed into captivity.

Early in 1782 Tarleton returned to England on parole, and went on half-pay. He compiled a vainglorious history of the 1780–1 campaigns in the southern colonies, which was published in 1787. He became M.P. for Liverpool in 1790, retaining the seat until 1812, except for the years 1806–7, but he did not measure up to the duties of representing a thriving commercial community. Society provided a more promising field for his talents, and he acquired 'Perdita' Robinson, a discarded mistress of the Prince of Wales.

He was promoted to colonel on 18 November 1790 and to major general on 2 October 1794. Surprisingly, he spent the long war against France chiefly in a series of static administrative commands at home, passing to full general's rank in 1812 and baronet in 1815, and being awarded the Order of the Bath in 1820. Tarleton died on 25 January 1833, at Leintwardine, Shropshire.

J. R. Alden, *The American Revolution, 1775–1783* (1954).
P. Mackesy, *The War for America, 1775–1783* (1964).

Telford, Thomas (1757–1834), Scottish engineer; builder of the Caledonian canal and the Menai bridge.

Thomas Telford was born on 9 August 1757. He was brought up in poverty. His father died only a few months after his birth, and his mother scraped a living from occasional farm work around the village of Eskdale in Dumfriesshire. The boy gained the rudiments of an education at the parish school at Westerkirk, and as soon as he could he took a job herding cattle; at the age of fifteen he was apprenticed to a mason at Langholm, where the Duke of Buccleuch was improving his estate. Here he was given a variety of tasks, and a local lady, attracted by the boy, who was known as 'laughing Tam', gave him access to her library.

In 1780 Telford, now a journeyman mason, went to Edinburgh and worked there for two years, studying and sketching old buildings in his spare time. He then moved to London, where he obtained work on Sir William Chambers's Somerset House as a hewer. Later he obtained the job of superintending the erection of a house for the commissioner of Portsmouth docks (1784–6).

During this period he renewed an acquaintance already made with Sir W. Pulteney, a Dumfriesshire man, now member of parliament for Shrewsbury and married to the heiress of William Pulteney, Earl of Bath (q.v.), whose name he had taken. Pulteney consulted Telford on repairs to Shrewsbury castle and invited him to take charge of the work. Telford agreed, and while working on this project in 1793, he was appointed to the vacant post of Surveyor of Public Works for Shropshire. He built two bridges in this capacity, at Buildwas and Bewdley, and his success and popularity were such that a group of canal magnates asked him to become the sole engineer and architect of the Ellesmere canal, intended to link the rivers Dee, Mersey, and Severn. Telford's canal was remarkable not only for its two beautiful aqueducts high over the valleys of the Ceiriog and the Dee, but also for the innovatory use of a trough of cast-iron plates fixed into stone masonry for the canal bed, in order to obviate displacement by frost, up till then a major problem of canal maintenance.

Telford next directed his main energy toward developments in his native Scotland. He wrote an exhaustive report, presented in 1803, in which he planned the opening up of the Highlands and north of Scotland. The central feature of this plan was the building of the Caledonian canal, to provide a channel between the North Sea and the Atlantic, wide enough for warships and commercial traffic. It also involved considerable road and bridge construction. The chief roads in this part of Scotland were military ones, but they were few and inadequate. Lack of bridges further hampered communication, and the result was the virtual isolation of northern Scotland, with little commerce or industry. Telford's labour of eighteen years, aided by liberal funds granted by the government and supplied by landowners, helped change this situation. He built over 900 miles of good roads and 120 bridges. Over 3,000 men were employed each year and taught to use tools intelligently. Telford saw his responsibility as being one of social reform and economic improvement as well as engineering.

The Caledonian canal was, however, his most spectacular enterprise. It was planned on a huge scale and posed considerable engineering difficulties. Between Loch Eli and Loch Lochy, for example, in only eight miles there was a difference in water level of 90 feet. Telford surmounted this problem by constructing eight huge locks, which he called 'Neptune's staircase'. The work was begun in 1804, and in 1822 the first vessel made the journey from sea to sea.

In addition to his Scottish activities, Telford had various other undertakings on hand, including the construction of the Göta canal in Sweden, for which he received the Swedish order of knighthood – an honour not granted him in Britain.

In 1814 a parliamentary commission reported the ruinous state of the road between Glasgow and Carlisle, and Telford was given charge of sixty-nine miles of rebuilding. His roads were of more solid construction than that of the later and more popular macadam system. Telford's greatest achievement was probably the Menai suspension bridge which took ten years to build and lasted 115 years, being reconstructed in 1940. Telford used chains of wrought iron links, tested and pinned together, which were laid out full-length, towed across the strait, and hoisted into place; the deck was then suspended beneath them.

Unmoved by the railway fever sweeping the country, Telford remained faithful to canals, and designed the important Birmingham–Liverpool junction. Two more bridges, at Tewkesbury (1826) and Gloucester (1828), followed. His last work was a review of Dover harbour, requested by the Duke of Wellington. Telford, whose last years were troubled by the onset of deafness, died on 2 September 1834 in London, and was buried in Westminster Abbey.

A. Gibb, *The Story of Telford: the Rise of Civil Engineering* (1935).
L. T. C. Rolt, *Thomas Telford* (1958).

Temple, Henry John (1784–1865), 3rd Viscount Palmerston; statesman, see *Lives of the Victorian Age*.

Thompson, Sir Benjamin (1753–1814), Count von Rumford; physicist, government administrator, and founder of the Royal Institution of Great Britain.

Benjamin Thompson was born on 26 March 1753 at North Woburn, Massachusetts, the only son of Benjamin Thompson. His father died when he was less than two years old, and about three years later his mother remarried. Educated first at the village school in North Woburn, and then at Byfield and Medford, young Thompson developed an early interest in mechanics and natural philosophy.

At the age of fourteen he was apprenticed to John Appleton of Salem, who kept a large store. He spent his spare time trying to solve the problem of perpetual motion and making fireworks. He then worked for Hopestill Capen at Boston, where he also learned French and fencing and attended lectures at Harvard, picking up some knowledge of surgery and medicine. During the disputes between the American colonies and England, Thomas looked elsewhere for work, and became a schoolmaster, first at Wilmington, Massachusetts, then at Rumford (later renamed Concord) in New Hampshire.

Thompson married Sarah, the widow of Colonel Benjamin Rolfe, in 1773. They had one child, a daughter also called Sarah, who was born in 1774.

A commission was now secured for Thompson as a major in the Second Provisional Regiment; he now devoted some time to farming the land that he had acquired through his marriage. In 1775 he was imprisoned on account of his lukewarm enthusiasm for the cause of liberty; he was released shortly afterwards, though not acquitted. Realizing that America was no place for a loyalist, he then sailed for England with letters from General Gage to Lord George Sackville Germain, the Secretary of State. The latter appointed him Secretary for Georgia, and offered him a lucrative position in the colonial office. He resumed his work on gunpowder and succeeded in getting bayonets added to the carabines of the Horse Guards, for use when fighting on foot. A paper on the cohesion of bodies sent to the Royal Society led to his acquaintance with Sir Joseph Banks (q.v.) and his election in 1779 to the Society.

In September 1780 Thompson was appointed Under-Secretary for the Colonies, and subsequently lieutenant colonel of the King's American Dragoons, and returned as a soldier to America. Though involved in some skirmishing at Charleston, he had a largely uneventful military career.

On his return to England, he retired from the army on half pay and travelled abroad, meeting Gibbon while crossing the Channel and becoming acquainted with Duke Maximilian in Strasbourg. The Duke's uncle, the Elector of Bavaria, offered Thompson a position in his service. George III not only agreed to this but also, in parting with his services, bestowed on him a knighthood on 23 February 1784. Thompson then left for eleven years in Munich as Grand Chamberlain, Minister of War, and Head of Police. During this period he brought Watt's steam engine into common use, and introduced the potato as a staple food. He also improved the pay and conditions of the common soldier, solved Munich's beggar problem, and converted a large piece of waste ground into a public landscape park, the 'English Garden'. A monument was erected to him there as a token of the gratitude of the Munich citizenry, and in 1791 he was created a Count of the Holy Roman Empire under the title of von Rumford.

In the spring of 1796 Rumford went to Ireland. He introduced a number of hospital and workhouse reforms in Dublin, was elected a member of the Irish Royal Academy and Society of Arts, and received formal thanks from the grand jury and Lord Mayor of Dublin. Back in London, he made a study in improvements in foundling hospitals and continued his work in both practical and applied science. In the realm of pure science, his investigations discredited the generally held theory that heat is a liquid form of matter, and established the foundations of the modern concept that heat is a form of motion; in 1798 he published *An Experimental Enquiry Concerning the Source of the Heat which is excited by Friction*.

In 1796 Rumford presented £1,000 to the Royal Society for a gold and a silver medal to be awarded every two years for discoveries in the field of heat and light. In 1802 both medals were voted to Rumford himself. He made a similar donation to the American Academy of Arts and Science. The town of Concord also accepted a gift from Rumford, for the purpose of clothing and educating twelve poor children, with the proviso that girls too were to be eligible to receive an education.

Rumford returned to Munich in 1796. President John Adams of the United States offered him a choice of the posts of Lieutenant General and Inspector of Artillery or Superintendent of the Military Academy; Rumford courteously declined both.

Perhaps his most important achievement lay in the foundation of the Royal Institution in Albemarle Street, London. A subscription was raised and the Charter was granted in 1799. The Institution's aims were to spread the knowledge of new inventions and to teach the practical application of science. Rumford was secretary, and lived at the Institution until he left again for Bavaria in 1802.

In 1805, his first wife having died, he married Marie Anne Pierret Paulze, the widow of Lavoisier. They separated by mutual consent in mid-1809, and Rumford took an estate near Paris at Auteuil, where he lived until his death.

He died on 25 August 1814, and was buried at Auteuil. His will endowed a chair of physics at Harvard and a philosophy lectureship at the Royal Institution.

Egon Larsen, *An American in Europe: The Life of Benjamin Thompson, Count Rumford* (1953).

J. A. Thompson, *Count Rumford of Massachusetts* (1935).

Portrait: oil, quarter-length, after M. Kellerhoven: N.P.G.

Thomson, James (1700–48), poet.

James Thomson was born in September 1700 at Ednam, Roxburghshire, the fourth child of Thomas Thomson, a minister of the Scottish Church at Ednam. Two months after his son's birth, the Rev. Thomas Thomson moved to the manse at the foot of Southdean Law. James was educated locally and at Edinburgh University. In Edinburgh he joined a literary club, 'The Grotesques', and had three pieces published in the *Edinburgh Miscellany* (1720). He received a bursary from the presbytery of Jedburgh and though this was renewed for one year in 1724 he avoided entering the ministry, preferring to seek a literary career.

In 1725 Thomson travelled south to London, where in June he sought the aid of a distant kinswoman, Lady Grizel Baillie. She got him an unsalaried post, which lasted for about four months, as tutor to her grandson, Thomas Hamilton, the eldest son of Charles Hamilton, Lord Binning.

Thomson's first notable poem, 'Winter', was published in March 1726, and dedicated to Spencer Compton, Lord Wilmington, who eventually acknowledged it with twenty guineas in June. The poem was immediately successful, gaining Thomson many influential admirers. He became tutor to one of Montrose's sons, and in 1726, while he held the post, he worked at 'Summer', which was published by the bookseller John Millan early in 1727, and dedicated to Bubb Dodington. 'Spring' followed in 1728; it was published by Andrew Millar, and dedicated to the Countess of Hertford. 'Autumn' was not published separately before it appeared as part of the complete work, *The Seasons* (1730), to which Thomson added a 'Hymn' and a patriotic poem, 'Britannia'.

Thomson, in *The Seasons*, was the pioneer of a strain of descriptive and meditative poetry that grew throughout the eighteenth century, in which natural description prompted moral reflections on the human situation. This ran counter to contemporary poetic fashion, as did his use of blank verse. He voiced, with a fresh sensitivity, the early-eighteenth-century view of an ordered universe, directed by laws framed by God and discovered by Newton.

Thomson's first play, *Sophonisba*, was produced on 28 February 1730 at Drury Lane. Though a poor imitation of Otway, it was successful. That autumn, Thomson set off to tour Europe as travelling tutor and companion to Charles Richard Talbot. By late 1731 he was back at Ashdown Park, Berkshire, and though his pupil died on 27 September 1733, Talbot's father procured for Thomson a sinecure worth £300 a year.

Very contented, Thomson moved into a cottage in Richmond, where he lived for the rest of his life, taking frequent long walks to visit friends. In this happy period he worked on a cherished poem, *Liberty*; the first part was published in 1734, and another four parts followed during 1735–6. But on 14 February 1737 the elder Talbot died, and Thomson lost the sinecure. His income was now precarious despite the success of his second play, *Agamemnon* (1738). Fortunately, a new patron and devoted friend, George Lyttelton, introduced Thomson to the Prince of Wales (see Frederick Louis), who granted him £100 a year. In spite of his connection with the Prince, however,

his next play, *Edward and Eleanora*, was rejected by the newly-appointed censor. There followed in 1740 perhaps his best known poem, the ode 'Rule Britannia', which won immediate fame.

Between 1738 and 1744, Thomson revised *The Seasons*; corrected editions were published in 1744 and 1746. Lyttelton became one of the Lords of the Treasury in 1744, and obtained for Thomson the sinecure post of Surveyor General of the Leeward Islands, worth £300 a year. The following year Thomson's penultimate play, *Tancred and Sigismunda*, opened at Drury Lane on 18 March, with Garrick as Tancred. Pitt and Lyttelton took up the patronage of the play, and it was Thomson's greatest dramatic success, being performed at intervals until 1819.

Since living at Richmond, Thomson had been working on his second most important poem, *The Castle of Indolence*, a narrative poem in Spenserian stanzas and allegorical romance form, which appeared in 1748.

In August of that year, after a rapid walk, the poet took a boat and was rowed down the Thames to Kew. As a result of this expedition, he caught a severe chill; he died on 27 August 1748, and was buried in Richmond church. His last tragedy, *Coriolanus*, was presented at Covent Garden on 13 January 1749.

Lyttelton's view of his posthumous responsibilities to Thomson was exceptional. He brought out an edition of Thomson's works in 1750, and another, superbly printed and illustrated, in 1762, the King heading a list of celebrated subscribers with £100. The proceeds provided a cenotaph in Westminster Abbey.

Thomson was a man of great sensibility and good humour, and was the first to challenge the prevailing artificial poetic style. His influence was international and in his own land his sentiment of Nature was transmitted to Gray, Cowper, and ultimately Wordsworth.

R. Cohen, *The Art of Discrimination: Thomson's The Seasons and the Language of Criticism* (Los Angeles, 1964).

D. Grant, *Thomson: Poet of 'The Seasons'* (1951).

A. D. McKillop (ed.), *The Castle of Indolence* (Lawrence, Kansas, 1961).

A. D. McKillop (ed.), *The Background of Thomson's Seasons* (Minneapolis, 1942).

J. L. Robertson (ed.), *Complete Poetical Works* (1908).

O. Zippel (ed.), *The Seasons* (Berlin, 1908).

Portrait: oil, quarter-length, after J. Patoun, *c*.1746: N.P.G.

Thornhill, Sir James (1675–1734), decorative painter.

James Thornhill was born in 1675 at Melcombe Regis, Dorset. His father having dissipated the family estate, he was sent at the age of fourteen to London, where he began an apprenticeship to Thomas Highmore of the Painter-Stainers' Company. Highmore was a relative of the family; the young Thornhill took naturally to the work and began to show great talent. In 1703 he was made a freeman of the company, and within five years had secured for himself several important commissions, among which was one to decorate the Painted Hall, Lower Hall, and Vestibule of Greenwich Hospital. He worked intermittently on this from 1708 to 1727, and it is generally acclaimed as being his greatest achievement. During this period Thornhill also managed to travel abroad, studying the great contemporary artists. He returned in 1717 to complete his grisaille panels on the dome of St. Paul's Cathedral, much against the wishes of its designer, Sir Christopher Wren.

Queen Anne had favoured his work and had employed him several times in the royal palaces, his most noteworthy work being the ceiling of Her Majesty's bedroom in Hampton Court. In 1718 Thornhill was appointed History Painter to George I and, two years later, succeeded Highmore as Serjeant Painter. In the same year (1720) Thornhill became the first British painter to be honoured by a knighthood.

With his accumulated wealth Thornhill was eventually able to re-purchase the family estate in Dorset, and after his election as M.P. for Melcombe Regis, the town of his birth, he retired almost totally from the artistic world.

Thornhill's role as the only British decorative painter on a grand scale was a particularly important one since there were many respected foreign rivals then at work in England. Among these were Verrio and, later, Laguerre, whose styles strongly influenced Thornhill. The architecture of the day, with its tall and spacious rooms, certainly afforded great scope to decorative painters. This was seen to change, however, as building and decorative styles became more chaste. Thornhill's great success and status, particularly with royalty, had led him to expect the commission for the decorating of Kensington Palace. But William Kent (q.v.), whose patron was the powerful Lord Burlington, was chosen instead, and this meant a serious rebuff for Thornhill and a significant pointer to the changing taste of the English.

Thornhill encountered a signal lack of success in two other ventures also. In about 1724 he drew up a plan for a royal academy of art, but the government declined to grant the necessary funds and the scheme failed. Following this, Thornhill attempted to set up a drawing school, but this too eventually had to close. In his last years Thornhill moved back to his Dorset estate; he died there on 4 May 1734.

Besides his large-scale work on ceilings and walls, Thornhill was a very capable portrait painter. He even obtained permission to make copies of Raphael's cartoons, and he left behind him a vast quantity of drawings and sketches which reveal a spontaneity he rarely reproduced in his large-scale work. He is nowadays recognized as the greatest English history painter of the period.

Works at:
Chatsworth.
Easton Neston.
Tate Gallery.
National Portrait Gallery.
St. Mary's Parish Church, Weymouth (altarpiece).

Portrait: engraving, by J. Richardson, 1733: R.T.H.

Thrale, Mrs. Hester (1741–1821), society hostess and friend of Dr. Johnson.

Hester Salusbury was born at Bodfel, Caernarvonshire, on 27 January 1741, the only child of an irascible and neurotic rake, John Salusbury of Bach-y-graig, Flintshire, who had married his cousin Hester Salusbury Cotton.

In 1748 Hester's father went to Nova Scotia with Cornwallis, and she and her mother went to London, where she attended school at Queen Square and was taken to the theatre to see Quin and Garrick. A pampered infant prodigy, she learned Latin, logic, history, rhetoric, literature, and navigation, and became a proficient horsewoman, while her father was 'quarrelling and fighting duels' in Canada. She spent much of her time at Offley with her uncle, Sir Thomas Salusbury, and he introduced her to Henry Thrale, a rich Southwark brewer. Hester Salusbury did not like him, and nor did her newly returned father, who took her angrily back to London, but died suddenly before he could ensure that she would not marry Thrale.

To appease her mother's family, she reluctantly married Thrale in 1763; they lived at his large villa in Streatham during the summer and in a house near the brewery in Southwark during the winter. Thrale was a strict, taciturn husband who openly kept a mistress but went to church with his wife. Johnson said of him that his 'conversation does not show the minute hand, but strikes the hour very correctly'. Mrs. Thrale, forbidden to ride or to manage her household, amused herself with literature and children. She had twelve before 1778, though only four survived infancy, and was thus almost continuously pregnant throughout the first thirteen years of her famous friendship with Samuel Johnson.

Johnson was introduced to the Thrales in 1765 by Arthur Murphy, Henry Thrale's oldest friend and a rather indifferent playwright. He rapidly became one of the family, with his own rooms in both of their houses. He was not yet very famous, his table manners were revolting, and he monopolized the conversation, but Mrs. Thrale gave him cheerful home comforts and appreciated his wit, and he gave her a new and vivid interest in life. When they met he was far from well, and her shelter and care probably saved him from a breakdown. For sixteen years he lived with the Thrales, returning to his own rooms only at weekends, and holidaying with them in Brighton, France, and Wales, where Mrs. Thrale had inherited an estate.

In 1765 Mrs. Thrale wrote election addresses and went canvassing for her husband, who was elected M.P. for Southwark, retaining the seat until 1780. In 1768 she met Boswell, whom she never liked; Boswell grew to resent Johnson's loss of dignity and independence in her house, so that their ultimate rivalry and mutual dislike was intense.

In 1772 Henry Thrale became involved in two investment schemes that led to the collapse of his brewery. Despairingly he talked of suicide, but his wife set about reducing their debts, which amounted to

£130,000. Though heavily pregnant, she visited family and friends collecting loans and, by her good management, repaid all the debts within nine years. She continued to take an active part in running the business, while her husband abandoned himself to new mistresses and overeating. Their house attracted many famous people, among them Goldsmith, Burke, the Burneys, Garrick, and Reynolds, until Henry Thrale's death in 1781.

Immediately speculation began as to whether Mrs. Thrale would marry the elderly Dr. Johnson, but her heart was already set on her daughters' Italian singing teacher, Gabriel Piozzi. Though social and family pressures forced her to try to give him up, she found it impossible, and they were married in July 1784. To Johnson she had shown what Fanny Burney called 'restless petulancy'; she hurt him deeply, and cast him off. It is probable that despite himself he loved Hester Thrale, and although he told Fanny Burney 'I drive her quite out of my mind', his death in 1784 was certainly saddened, perhaps hastened, by what he saw as her betrayal.

The Piozzis went to Italy, where Mrs. Piozzi, ecstatic and victorious, joined the inane Florence Della Cruscan set and delighted in all she saw. Meanwhile she was composing her *Anecdotes* of Dr. Johnson, written in rather aggressive self-defence, which earned her critical scorn and a great deal of money.

She and Piozzi returned to England in 1787. Many old friends were irrevocably alienated, but she determinedly found new ones (notably Sarah Siddons), revived the Streatham household, and set about publishing her carefully edited letters to and from Johnson. Her next book, *Observations and Reflections made during the course of a journey through France, Italy and Germany*, Walpole found 'miserably spelt' and packed with 'ex-

cessive vulgarisms and indiscretions'.

Mrs. Piozzi was defiantly resilient and cared little about the attacks made on her. She took Piozzi off to Wales, where they lived happily until his death in 1809, and then she adopted a nephew of his, disinherited her daughters, and in 1814 retired to Bath, where she was regarded as a garrulous and rather shocking old woman. She celebrated her eightieth year with a spectacular party in January 1820. The next year she fell seriously ill, and with her daughters around her she died 'in state' at Clifton in Bristol on 2 May 1821.

Mrs. Thrale was a small perky woman of indomitable vivacity and relentless, tough egoism. Though no great writer, her amazing memory, the variety and interest of her acquaintance, and her constant indiscretions make her published recollections and innumerable letters endlessly entertaining.

Katherine Balderston (ed.), *Thraliana: the Diary of Mrs. Hester Lynch Thrale* (1951).

H. Barrows (ed.), *Observations and Reflections Made in the Course of a Journey through France, Italy and Germany* (Ann Arbor, 1967).

A. M. Broadley, *Dr. Johnson and Mrs. Thrale* (1910).

R. W. Chapman (ed.), *Letters of Samuel Johnson, with Mrs. Thrale's Genuine Letters to Him* (3 vols.; 1952).

J. L. Clifford, *Hester Lynch Piozzi (Mrs. Thrale)* (1968, rev. ed.).

S. C. Roberts (ed.), *Anecdotes of the Late Samuel Johnson* (1925).

Portrait: pencil, quarter-length, by G. Dance, 1793: N.P.G.

Tone, Theobald Wolfe (1763–98), Irish radical and patriot; a founder member of the United Irishmen.

Tone was born in Dublin on 20 June 1763, the eldest son of Peter Tone, a successful coach-maker. A very intelligent child, he was quickly moved from the socially inferior 'commercial' to the 'Latin' school and from there in 1781 he matriculated in Trinity College,

Dublin. In 1785 he impulsively began a relationship with a pretty sixteen-year-old girl named Matilda Witherington and soon eloped with her. Their subsequent marriage was happy, despite the fact that Tone was to spend much of his life away from Matilda in miserable exile for the sake of his cause.

Graduating from Trinity in 1786, Tone departed to London in the following year to study law at the Middle Temple. Tone was unsuccessful in an attempt to join the East India service, in which he had family connections; and the young Irishman went back to his legal studies. He qualified as a barrister in Dublin in 1789 and reluctantly joined the Leinster circuit.

In 1790 Tone published his first pamphlet criticizing the corrupt Castle administration of the Marquis of Buckingham, who with his Privy Council virtually ruled Ireland on behalf of the English King George III. The corrupt Irish parliament was weak and undemocratic; its legislative capability was severely limited by England, and most of its seats represented pocket boroughs in the hands of a few wealthy landowners. Into the melting pot of Ireland at this time came the teaching of such men as Tom Paine, and also the news of successful revolutions in America and France. Two key causes were espoused by the middle-class Irish intellectuals of whom Tone was one – better conditions for the poor and independence from the corrupt and suffocating rule of England.

In 1791 Tone published a pamphlet, *An Argument on behalf of the Catholics of Ireland*, telling northern Dissenters they had nothing to fear from Catholic emancipation. A month later, in October 1791, he helped to found, with his friend Thomas Russell, the radical, idealistic, non-sectarian society known as the United Irishmen. Essentially a pacifist organization, the movement gained support in the north, although few Catholics actually joined it. It soon lost its idealism and its pacifism, too, as its ranks swelled with ex-members of the Volunteer force, set up more than a decade earlier to protect Ireland during the war with America, and now led by radicals not afraid to use force to win Irish independence. The movement inevitably drifted towards anarchy. In the predominantly Catholic south, it made little headway. The Catholics, far from being supporters of revolution – most deplored what had happened in France – were finally sucked into the United Irishmen movement by reason of their hatred of the English, the only common denominator linking them with the Protestants.

An unsuccessful attempt in 1792 to outlaw the organization and incarcerate Tone and his friends was followed by infiltration of the organization by government agents and informers. Sectarian fears and distrust were stirred up, and among Protestants Catholic support was weakened when the Irish government passed a temporizing measure in

1793 granting Catholics freedom to vote. Internal strife was encouraged within the organization and finally Tone, accused of involvement with a French spy, was compelled to leave the country in 1796.

He sailed first to Philadelphia and then, with a letter of introduction from the French Ambassador there, on to Paris to seek help from the Directory. He spoke no French and had no influence in France, but was in the event well received, meeting among others the young Napoleon Bonaparte. He joined the French army, in which he attained the rank of adjutant general. Thus it was that in December 1796 he was with the French fleet of 43 sail and some 14,000 troops under the command of General Lazare Hoche, as it sailed out with the projected scheme of invading Britain. The scheme failed, however; a storm scattered the French fleet and despite protests from Hoche, the naval commander scurried back to port. A second attempt a few months later, in 1797, was made under Dutch command, but was foiled by the action of the British navy.

Although Tone pleaded with him, Napoleon, now the supreme commander of the French military forces, had no interest in expending further energy on an expedition to Ireland, and the United Irishmen were abandoned to their own devices. In 1798, without support, they took to open rebellion and were easily and cruelly overcome by the forces of the government.

The revolt induced Napoleon to grant Tone enough forces for small raids against various parts of the Irish coast. Sailing with a tiny expedition of 1,000 men, Tone left France in September 1798. Reaching Lough Swilly in County Donegal, the expedition tried to land and was captured. Tone, a military prisoner of war, was denied a civil trial and court-martialled on 10 November. In a defiant speech, parts of which he was not allowed to read, he proclaimed his undying hostility towards England and his desire to win independence for Ireland. He demanded to die in front of a firing squad but was sentenced to be hanged. Unable to face such an unmilitary and ignominious death, he attempted suicide by cutting his throat with a penknife on 12 November. But even this last gesture failed. Tone eventually died of blood poisoning on 19 November 1798.

To the English Wolfe Tone was undoubtedly a traitor, but to subsequent generations of embittered Irish nationalists he was a heroic martyr. His grave at Bowdenstown churchyard, County Kildare, has become a place of pilgrimage for republicans.

R. Hayes, *Ireland and Irishmen in the French Revolution* (1932).

F. MacDermot, *Theobald Wolfe Tone* (1939).

R. B. O'Brien (ed.), *The Autobiography of Theobald Wolfe Tone, 1763–1798* (2 vols.; 1893).

Portraits: oil, artist unknown: National Gallery of Ireland, Dublin; marble bust, by Terence Farrell: Trinity College, Dublin; engraving, by C. Hullmandel, 1827, after C. S. Tone, *c.* 1798: R.T.H.

Tooke, John Horne (1736–1812), politician and philologist.

Tooke was born John Horne on 25 June 1736 in Westminster, the third of the seven children of a fairly affluent royal poulterer. He was educated at Eton and by several private tutors. Having lost his right eye in a fight and run away at least once from his tutor because of his ignorance and dislike of grammar, he later discovered the attractions of learning, and at the age of twenty-two became senior optime at St. John's College, Cambridge. After leaving Cambridge, he entered the Middle Temple for a short while but, pressed by his father to enter the church, he acquiesced (a course he later always regretted), and was ordained, becoming curate at Brentford in 1760. However, he was too interested in other things – medicine, cards, and society – to be satisfied with the life of a rural curate, and took to acting as tutor to the sons of rich men on their grand tours. Thus in Ferney he met Voltaire, in Lyons Sterne, and in Paris Wilkes, with whom he became intimate. After returning home, he campaigned for Wilkes in the 1768 Middlesex election.

Largely to raise money to pay Wilkes's debts, Horne helped to found 'The Society for Supporting the Bill of Rights' and wrote addresses to the King on the subject. In 1771, however, he quarrelled with other members of the society and with Wilkes himself, and founded the Constitutional Society, whose political aims were broader. There followed a violent and public argument with Wilkes, as a result of which Horne lost his popularity and was burnt in effigy by a mob.

In 1771 he was granted the degree of M.A. at Cambridge, but he had lost his chance of ecclesiastical preferment and resigned his living, taking up instead philology and the law. He strenuously defended his friend William Tooke, whose land at Purley was threatened with enclosure, and this defence resulted in the withdrawal of obnoxious clauses in the Enclosure Bill – but also in mutual and lasting animosity between Horne and Charles James Fox (q.v.). Horne later, at Tooke's request, took his friend's name, but contrary to his hopes he was left nothing in his will.

The Constitutional Society now raised a subscription for 'our beloved American fellow-subjects . . . inhumanly murdered at Lexington'. For this treason, Horne was tried, convicted, fined, and imprisoned for a year. During his imprisonment he wrote a *Letter to Dunning*, deliberating over the use of prepositions, which became the basis for his later grammatical work.

On his release Horne Tooke wrote, and dedicated to William Tooke, *The Diversions of Purley*, his grammar book; and remained politically active, supporting Pitt and unsuccessfully opposing Fox in the Westminster election of 1790. His health, however, was deteriorating, and he retired to Wimbledon. He amused himself by pretending to be planning a rising in support of the French Revolution, and he was arrested and charged with high treason in 1794. He greatly enjoyed conducting his own defence, and when acquitted was described as 'the last man in England' to be open to such a suspicion.

In 1796 Horne Tooke stood again for Westminster and was defeated. But he was returned in 1801 for the pocket borough of Old Sarum. The election was, however, declared void because he was a clergyman, and he retired once more to Wimbledon, where his hospitality to Coleridge, Godwin, Paine, and others, became renowned. He died on 12 March 1812 and was buried at Ealing.

Horne Tooke was a vigorous, sturdy man whose stamina, aggression, and shrewdness could perhaps have made an excellent barrister of him, had he not been forced into the church. His philological views were advanced in their emphasis on the importance of studying Gothic and Anglo-Saxon. He had many disciples, among them Hazlitt and Charles Richardson, who called him 'the philological grammarian who alone was entitled to the name of discoverer'.

M. C. Yarborough, *John Horne Tooke* (New York, 1926).

Portrait: oil, half-length, by T. Hardy: N.P.G.

Torrington, Viscount (1663–1733), see Byng, George.

Townshend, Charles (1675–1738), 2nd Viscount Townshend; statesman responsible for British foreign policy during the periods 1714–16 and 1721–30; later known as 'Turnip' Townshend because of his agricultural interests.

Townshend was born at Raynham, Norfolk, on 18 April 1675, the son of an established Tory landowning family. His father, Horatio Townshend, 1st Viscount Townshend, was a fervent supporter of Charles II.

Charles Townshend was educated at Eton, where he formed a friendship with Robert Walpole (q.v.) that continued at King's College, Cambridge. For a brief period Townshend had been a ward of Walpole's father, and eventually they became brothers-in-law when, in 1713, Townshend married Dorothy, Walpole's sister.

Having succeeded as 2nd Viscount Townshend in 1687, Townshend took his seat in the House of Lords in 1697 and very soon switched his allegiance to the Whigs. With Walpole he supported the Whig junto who maintained the cause of religious liberty. In 1706 he was one of the negotiators of the Act of Union with Scotland, and in 1709 he was appointed plenipotentiary to England's ally Holland. In this capacity he blundered by taking an independent line and negotiating the so-called Barrier Treaty with France, which committed Britain to a restoration and extension of the Netherlands' chain of defences along its French border. This did not accord with British commercial interests, and a separate treaty was concluded with Holland in which the Hanoverian succession was guaranteed in return for a smaller commitment on the part of Britain. When Townshend returned, the House of Commons declared him an enemy of the country.

Townshend succeeded in currying favour with the Hanoverian court, however, and when George I acceded to the throne in 1714, he was appointed Secretary of State for the Northern Department. He ordered the ruthless suppression of the Jacobite rebellion in Scotland and assisted the Secretary of State for the Southern Department, James Stanhope (q.v.), in the negotiations that led to the definitive Barrier Treaty. The new Whig policy of alliance with France was due more to the work of Stanhope than to Townshend, and the latter was charged with obstructing the completion of the agreement. The Earl of Sunderland (see Spencer, Charles) intrigued with the King in order to oust Townshend, and rumour spread of a conspiracy between him and the Prince of Wales to usurp the throne. In April 1717 Townshend was dismissed, to be followed by Walpole who resigned in sympathy with his friend. For the next three years the Sunderland–Stanhope faction of the Whig party held the influence at court, while Walpole, Townshend, and their supporters provided a stern opposition.

Townshend returned to power in June 1720, when he was appointed President of the Council, and on Stanhope's death in 1721 he once again became Secretary of State for the Northern Department. Although he often embarrassed his Whig colleagues at home by advocating illiberal measures to quell public disturbances, he succeeded in recovering his prestige in the Hanoverian court and developed a friendship with the Duchess of Kendal (see Schulenburg, Countess Ehrengarde Melusina von der), the eldest and most influential of George I's mistresses. It was by means of this friendship that he was able to thwart his brilliant rival, John Carteret (q.v.), who, in trying to court the favour of the younger, but less powerful, Lady Darlington, made an enemy of the King and was dismissed in 1724. Townshend was eager to make a name for himself in European diplomacy, and he countered the Vienna alliance of 1725 between Austria and Spain with the League of Hanover (1725) which united England, France and Prussia. His enthusiasm for this policy was shared by neither Walpole nor George I. Walpole desired only that the Spanish–Austrian agreement be broken and had no time for an expensive system of alliances that seemed likely, by 1726, to bring England to war with Spain. Although accredited to Townshend, the 1729 Treaty of Seville which secured the alliance of Spain to England and France arose from Walpole's desire for peace abroad. Townshend, however, wished to conduct a campaign against the Emperor Charles VI in Germany. It was his scheme to replace the Duke of Newcastle with a more pliant personality who could be induced to support his aggressive foreign policy that brought about Townshend's defeat in the House. He lingered on another year in office before resigning in May 1730.

He then retired from public life and devoted his attention to improving his estates at Raynham. It was he who developed the four-way rotation of crops, whereby the crops grown in a particular field in a particular year are selected according to the extent to which they replenish soil with minerals depleted by the previous crops: in a four-year cycle, the natural balance of the soil is maintained without artificial aid. The series of agricultural experiments that he carried out brought him the name of 'Turnip' Townshend. He died at Raynham on 21 June 1738.

F. S. Oliver, *Endless Adventure, 1710–35* (3 vols.; 1930–5).

Portraits: oil, three-quarter length, studio of Kneller: N.P.G.; oil, full-length, by Kneller, 1704?: N.P.G.; oil, three-quarter length, after Kneller, c. 1715–20: N.P.G.; oil, attributed to C. Jervas: National Trust, Blickling Hall, Norfolk.

Townshend, Charles (1725–67), politician; Chancellor of the Exchequer (1766–7).

Townshend was born on 29 August 1725, the second son of Charles Townshend, 3rd Viscount Townshend, and the grandson of Charles Townshend (q.v.), 2nd Viscount Townshend. He was educated at Leyden University, where he knew William Dowdeswell, later his parliamentary rival, and John Wilkes (q.v.). Having entered parliament in 1747 as M.P. for Great Yarmouth, he occupied the years 1749–54 as a junior official of the Board of Trade. It was here that he first developed an interest in securing the financial independence, and hence the greater efficiency, of British administrators in the American colonies. He first made his mark in debate in May 1753 when he spoke against a proposed change in the marriage law. Townshend himself was married in August 1755 to Caroline Campbell, eldest daughter of the 2nd Duke of Argyll.

For the next decade Townshend delighted the Commons with his oratory while at the same time offending many by his unscrupulous political ambition. From 1754 until his resignation in 1755 he worked on the Board of Admiralty. When the Duke of Devonshire (see Cavendish, William) became Prime Minister in 1756, Townshend accepted the lucrative court sinecure of Treasurer of the Chamber, a position he continued to hold under William Pitt the Elder until March 1761, when he transferred his allegiance from Pitt to Bute, who offered him the post of Secretary-at-War. He was replaced in December 1762 because of his opposition to the war with Spain, and in February 1763 he accepted the post of President of the Board of Trade. Finding himself out of power again by April, he began a series of denunciations of the Grenville administration,

culminating in a speech condemning his former companion, John
Wilkes. Nevertheless in May 1765 he
took on the post of Paymaster General
and continued in it until the fall of
Rockingham's ministry in July 1766.
The failure of the ministry was in no
small part due to the arrogance displayed
by Townshend towards his fellow ministers and his refusal to defend their
policies. He was finally rewarded when
under Pitt's new administration he
became Chancellor of the Exchequer,
and in October 1766 he was admitted to
the cabinet.

Pitt's failing health, both mental and
physical, left Townshend as the strongest
and most influential personality in the
cabinet. He lost no time in exercising his
superiority. In a debate concerning the
extent of parliamentary influence in the
affairs of the East India Company
Townshend, abetted by Henry Seymour
Conway, the Secretary of State, completely overruled the solution favoured
by Pitt, safe in the knowledge that no
action would be taken against him.
Moreover, in his first budget (January
1767) Townshend was defeated in the
House when his proposal to set the land
tax at 4s. in the pound was replaced by a
measure concocted by Grenville and
Dowdeswell setting the tax at 3s. According to longstanding precedent, any
government defeated on a money bill
should immediately resign, but Pitt was
unable to control Townshend and he
continued in office, pledging himself to
devise other means of raising the extra
revenue.

Virtually every member of the House
considered the country heavily over-
taxed; hence Townshend was forced to
look further afield for revenue. He felt no
compunction in taxing the American
colonies by imposing a series of import
duties on articles like glass, paper, and

tea. Although the sum raised by this
'external taxation' would only have
amounted to £40,000, Townshend pressed on. His cabinet colleagues were now
his severest critics, for they realized the
damage that this legislation might do to
the strained relationship between England and her American colonies. Their
fears were confirmed when the news of
the taxes was received in America with
an outburst of fury; anti-importation
associations were formed, riots broke
out, and loyalist officials were removed
from office. Even though his principal
aim was really only to secure higher
incomes for the colonial governors from
a North American source of revenue,
Townshend's policy was, in the circumstances, a combination of bad timing and
heavy-handedness, which further reduced the hope of reconciliation.
Townshend died suddenly from a bowel
infection on 4 September 1767.

Sir Lewis Namier and J. Brooke, *Charles Townshend*
(1964).

Portrait: wax medallion, quarter-length, attributed
to I. Gossett: N.P.G.

Townshend, George (1724–1807), 4th
Viscount and 1st Marquis Townshend;
soldier and statesman.

George Townshend was born on 28
February 1724, the eldest son of Charles
Townshend, 3rd Viscount Townshend
(1700–64) and the elder brother of Charles
Townshend (1725–67, q.v.). After leaving St. John's College, Cambridge, he
entered the army and served under the
Duke of Cumberland (see William
Augustus) at Culloden in April 1746. The
following year he was appointed aide-de-
camp to the Duke and accompanied him
to the Netherlands, where he was present
at Lauffeld. By 1750 he had been
promoted to lieutenant colonel in the first
Regiment of Foot Guards, but retired in

the same year after differences with Cumberland.

A stern opponent of standing armies, Townshend was the author of a bill that became law in 1757 for establishing the militia system on a national basis. His talent for savage caricature and malicious sense of humour gained him a number of enemies; they were glad to see him return to the army on the retirement of Cumberland. In February 1759 he sailed for America as one of Major General James Wolfe's three brigadier generals in the expedition against French-occupied Quebec. The death of Wolfe during the battle of the Heights of Abraham in 1759 left Townshend in complete control and, despite a certain amount of indecisiveness, he managed to consolidate the British victory. Townshend returned home expecting a hero's welcome, but was disappointed to find himself the object of criticism.

In May 1763 Townshend was appointed Lieutenant General of the Ordnance and held this post until August 1767, when he was created Lord Lieutenant of Ireland. Until this date the viceroy had normally been non-resident, and the government of Ireland had been left in the hands of a small group of large landowners and borough proprietors known as the 'undertakers'. Determined to break the power of the undertakers for fear of a repetition of the situation in America, Charles Townshend engineered the appointment of his elder brother George as Lord Lieutenant in the belief that he possessed the necessary charm and skill to form an English party in the Irish Commons wholly dependent upon the crown.

Lord Townshend, however, was not blessed with a superabundance of tact, and although he threw himself energetically into the task of overcoming the undertakers, his methods left a residue of bitterness and distrust that was not conducive to good government. When he prorogued the Irish parliament, the public press abused and derided him in highly personal terms, but it was all to no avail because the suspension of the legislature had such a depressing effect on the country that in February 1771, Townshend won his majority. He failed, however, to gain any respect or popularity, and since his private life left a lot to be desired the government in England decided he was a liability and recalled him in September 1772.

Townshend returned to the post of Master General of the Ordnance, and for the remainder of his life lived quietly, holding a variety of minor administrative and courtesy posts in local government. In 1786 he was created 1st Marquis of Townshend. He died at Raynham, Norfolk, on 14 September 1807.

Trevithick, Richard (1771–1833), mechanical engineer, and one of the major contributors to the development of the steam engine. By successfully harnessing high-pressure steam he reduced the size and weight of engines, making steam locomotion possible.

Richard Trevithick was born on 13 April 1771 at Illogan in the tin-mining district of Cornwall. His father was manager of four tin mines and was responsible in 1765 for constructing a deep tunnel, and in 1775 for erecting a Newcomen engine in one of his mines. Watt's assistant, the able William Murdock, lived at near-by Redruth, and the young Trevithick grew up amid the excitement that the new inventions generated.

Trevithick's early inventive genius and his quickness of wit have become legendary. He early found an outlet for his practical imagination, and was at fourteen receiving payment for fuel-saving improvements designed for a local mine.

Trevithick obtained his first engineering job at the age of nineteen. Seven years later his father died, and he married. During the 1790s he introduced various ingenious improvements in the mechanics of mining, developing William Bull's engine, and bringing in a plunger pump, an indispensable necessity for deep mining. Watt's double-acting engine was patented in 1782 and was widely used; but this marked only the beginnings of steam development. Watt's patent expired in 1800 and a new era of high-pressure steam and steam locomotion commenced, in which Trevithick had a primary place. Watt believed 'strong steam' to be far too dangerous for practical use, but Trevithick realized that by using high-pressure steam and allowing it to expand within the cylinder, a smaller and lighter engine could be built safely without loss of power. Having constructed successful working models of stationary and locomotive high-pressure engines in 1797, he built a full-scale engine for hoisting ore. Some thirty of these were manufactured, and they were so compact that they could be transported in ordinary farm wagons. These became known as 'puffer whims' because they vented their steam into the atmosphere.

Trevithick drove the first locomotive engine up a hill in Camborne on Christmas Eve 1801, and in the following March, with his cousin Andrew Vivian, he took out a historic patent for steam engines for stationary and locomotive use. In 1803 he drove an engine through the streets of London. He constructed the first steam railway locomotive at Samuel Hombray's Penydaren Ironworks in South Wales, and on 21 February 1804 this engine won a wager for Hombray by hauling a load of ten tons of iron and seventy men along ten miles of tramway. The second locomotive was built at Gateshead in 1805, and in 1808 Trevithick demonstrated his third model, the *Catch-me-who-can*, on a circular track near the Euston Road in London. After this, however, Trevithick put aside these locomotive projects, since the brittle cast iron rails tended to snap under the weight of the engines.

In 1805 Trevithick, having turned his attention back to stationary engines, adapted his high-pressure engine to drive an iron rolling mill. A steam dredger followed in 1806, and in 1812 a threshing machine. An important development was his innovation in the design and construction of boilers, which on his plan were built as a single unit with a single internal flue (subsequently known throughout the world as the 'Cornish' type). These were used in conjunction with Trevithick's equally important pumping engines, perfected with the help of local engineers, and twice as economical as Watt's design.

Although Trevithick's inventions went quickly into widespread use, he derived little profit from his talents. By 1811 he was bankrupt, but three years later large quantities of the Trevithick engines were ordered for Peruvian silver mines, and in 1816 the inventor set sail for South America, with the idea of making his fortune. In fact he made – and lost – several fortunes and only narrowly escaped with his life in the Peruvian War of Independence, returning penniless to England in 1827, where he found ironically that others had received the benefits from his inventions. A petition to parliament on his behalf in 1828 was ignored; Trevithick died in poverty in Dartford, Kent, on 22 April 1833, and was buried in an unmarked grave.

By successfully harnessing high-pressure steam he reduced the size and weight of engines, and made steam locomotion possible, although George Stephenson is still popularly and erroneously credited with the invention of the steam locomotive.

H. W. Dickinson and A. Titley, *Richard Trevithick, the Engineer and the Man* (1934).

L. T. C. Rolt, *The Cornish Giant: The Story of Richard Trevithick, Father of the Steam Locomotive* (1960).

Tull, Jethro (1674–1741), agriculturist; inventor of the mechanical seed drill.

Jethro Tull was born at Basildon in Berkshire and baptized on 30 March 1674, the son of Jethro and Dorothy Tull. He entered St. John's College, Oxford, in 1691, and qualified as a barrister at Gray's Inn in 1699. He seems to have studied law with a view to equipping himself for political life. In the event, ill health prevented him from realizing his practical ambitions.

Almost immediately after his marriage in 1699 Tull commenced farming on land that had belonged to his father, at Howbery (near Wallingford), Oxfordshire, where (perhaps in 1701) he invented and perfected his machine drill and began experiments in his new system of sowing in drills or rows sufficiently wide apart to allow for tillage of the land between the drills by plough and hoe during almost the whole period of growth. This treatment reduced the need for leaving land fallow and, incidentally, for the use of farmyard manure.

After having farmed part of his Oxfordshire estate for nine years with considerable success, as he himself claims, Tull removed about 1709 to Mount Prosperous, a farm at Shalbourne in Wiltshire, and subsequently to Prosperous Farm, near Hungerford, Berkshire.

In April 1711 Tull was forced to travel abroad for the sake of his health. He journeyed through France and Italy, making careful observations of the methods of agriculture in those countries. On returning home in 1714 he recommenced his interrupted drill husbandry upon his Berkshire farm. To this he added improvements founded upon the knowledge gained from his travels. Foremost amongst these was the vineyard practice of pulverizing the soil between the rows of vines instead of manuring the land. A further development was the result of his growing concern as to the nature of plant nutrition. This inspired him to construct a horse hoe (a horse-drawn tillage implement for cultivation between rows) which allowed greater access of water to the plant roots. Such novel methods enabled Tull to grow wheat on the same field for thirteen years without manuring.

It was not until the last decade of his life (1731–41), that Tull published accounts of his agricultural views and experiences, and the abuse that his published work encountered caused him extreme annoyance. His troubles were complicated by difficulties with his labourers, whom he could not teach to use his instruments properly.

The Horse-hoeing Husbandry or an Essay on the Principles of Tillage and Vegetation by J.T. appeared in 1733. It was at once attacked by the Private Society of Husbandmen and Planters in their monthly publication, *The Practical Husbandman and Planter*. Tull was accused of having plagiarized from earlier authorities, and several of his theories as to the value of manure and the practice of pulverizing the earth were contested. Although he had certainly been to some extent anticipated by earlier writers, there is little doubt of Tull's originality. However, he was sensitive to these attacks and defended himself in subsequent lesser writings, mostly taking the form of notes on his longer work. *The Horse-hoeing Husbandry* ran to many subsequent editions and eventually, in 1822, it was edited, with some alterations, by William

Cobbett. Tull's ideas were more quickly accepted in France, where his work was translated between 1753 and 1757 by Duhamel du Morceau, the famous French agriculturist. Voltaire was a disciple of Tull and long cultivated his land at Ferney according to the precepts of the new husbandry. By the end of the eighteenth century Tull's ideas had been taken up by the large landowners in England, and they form the basis of modern systems of British agriculture.

Tull died at Prosperous Farm, near Hungerford, on 21 February 1741.

G. E. Fussell, *Jethro Tull, his influence on mechanized agriculture* (1973).

Turner, Joseph Mallord William
(1775–1851), painter.

Turner was born in London on 23 April 1775, the son of William Turner, a Covent Garden barber. Before he was nine years old he is known to have made sketches of scenes in London and Margate, which his father apparently sold in his shop for a shilling each. The boy was sent to school in Brentford. He gave an early indication of his financial shrewdness by agreeing to colour 140 topographical prints, at fourpence a time, for the foreman of the local distillery.

Turner's father decided that his son should become an artist, and although in an ungrateful moment Turner once said 'Dad never praised me for anything but saving a halfpenny,' his father spared no expense in ensuring that he should have a good training, sending him in 1786 to drawing lessons at the Soho Academy and later placing him with the landscape gardener Humphrey Repton. Turner also studied with Edward Malton and Edward Dayes. Finally Turner's father spent a large legacy he had received on having his son taught by Thomas Hardwick, who fortunately advised the lad to be a landscape painter.

In 1789 Turner became a student at the Royal Academy and was given the run of Joshua Reynolds's studio. From 1790 he began showing exquisite drawings of churches and country houses at the Academy's annual exhibitions. His closest friend at this time was Thomas Girtin (q.v.), and the two would go on long walks together with their sketch pads. They both belonged to a circle of young artists who met at the famous Dr. Monro's house in Adelphi to copy his Old Master drawings.

Turner's fluid topographical drawings began to be noticed, and in 1792 he was given the first of the commissions for magazine illustrations which were to make him both rich and famous. The *Copperplate Magazine* asked him to do a series on English towns, and to gather material Turner went on the first of his sketching tours, thoroughly exploring the West Country.

By 1793 he opened his own studio in Maiden Lane. For the next few years he made a comfortable living from long series of topographical and architectural drawings, which demonstrate both his ability to extend the range of the tradition in which he was working and also his growing fascination with light and the effects of the atmosphere. He also taught drawing, for anything up to a guinea a lesson.

In 1797 Turner first saw Girtin's views of York and Jedburgh, and he immediately rushed off to the Pennines to do better. What he experienced there inspired such landscapes as *Norham Castle* and *Morning on the Coniston Fells*. He was soon considered the foremost landscapist in the country and was employed by Lord Harewood and William Beckford. In 1800, at the age of twenty-four, Turner was made an associate of the Royal Academy.

Turner had difficulty in coping with his

fame. He was a small, bow-legged man with rosy cheeks and a great beak of a nose, and though he could be extremely jolly with close friends, he was so acutely aware of his lowly origins and unpolished manners that he soon gathered a reputation for surliness. He lived in surroundings of picturesque squalor and had a habit of employing housekeepers with whom he soon developed a more than professional relationship. His will makes provision for several illegitimate children.

In 1801 Turner took a house in Harley Street, moved in a new 'housekeeper', Hannah Danby, and launched into a series of spectacular Biblical paintings such as *The Fifth Plague of Egypt*. In 1802 he was made a full Royal Academician. That same year Thomas Girtin died and Turner, conscious of his debt to his boyhood friend, said, 'Had Tom Girtin lived I should have starved.' Between them they had raised watercolours to the status of an important genre.

In 1802 Turner went abroad for the first time, and was astounded by the Alps. The paintings he did during the next twenty years show that he was eagerly absorbing many such outside influences, both from natural scenery and from other painters, such as van de Velde and Claude. In 1807 Turner was prompted to emulate Claude's volume of landscape etchings, *Liber Veritatis*, by commencing his own *Liber Studiorum*, done in a mixture of mezzotint and etching.

In 1809 Turner was appointed Professor of Perspective at the Royal Academy, though his rambling lectures were often far too obscure to be of much value to the students. He was by now rich enough to design and build his own comfortable country house at Twickenham, Sandycombe Lodge. Frequent visits to northern England kept alive Turner's fascination with sunlight, mist, and rain,

and produced such oil studies as *Sun Rising Through Vapour* (1807). For many of his paintings of this period Turner adopted subjects from classical literature. In 1815 he finished his beautiful *Dido Building Carthage*, to which he became so attached that he once expressed a wish to be buried wrapped up in it.

In 1820 Turner paid his first visit to Italy, whose sunlit beauty so affected him that he stopped painting for three years in order to evolve a new and absolutely personal style, owing nothing to other painters. The first example of this was *The Bay of Baiae*, exhibited in 1823 and followed by a series of similarly poetic landscapes. At the 1827 Royal Academy exhibition his view of Cologne was hung between two paintings by Lawrence, and its brilliant colours overshadowed them. Turner generously washed his landscape down with lampblack, remarking that 'It will all wash off, and Lawrence was *so* unhappy.'

Although during this time Turner lived quietly at Sandycombe Lodge, it seems that country life was beginning to pall for him, and in 1826 he sold Sandycombe Lodge. The next year was spent in producing a hundred views of England and Wales, whose idealized colour and poetic atmosphere reflected Turner's Italian experience.

In late 1828 he set off for Rome again. English travellers in Italy remembered him as 'a good-tempered funny little elderly gentleman', speaking a mixture of bad French and worse Italian.

Turner came home in late 1829 and had not long finished *Ulysses Deriding Polyphemus* when personal tragedy struck: in September his father died, and in the following January he lost his friend Thomas Lawrence. Considerably shaken, Turner made his will, leaving his two favourite paintings, *Dido Building Carthage* and *Sun Rising Through Mist*, to the nation. Throughout most of the 1830s he produced a large number of illustrations – he visited Holland to do seascapes, France to draw river scenes, and Scotland to illustrate Scott's poems – but by the end of the decade public taste had somewhat turned away from illustrated magazines and books.

In any case, Turner's heart was elsewhere. In 1832 he had visited Venice, and that magical city became such a preoccupation with him that for fifteen years he sent at least one Venetian view to every Royal Academy exhibition. Brilliant in colour and flawless in technique, they became ever more ethereal and dreamlike. The public did not understand them, but was placated by the appearance in 1839 of perhaps Turner's most famous painting, *The Fighting Téméraire*, a rather sentimental subject suggested to the artist by a friend.

Turner's increasing eccentricity, both in his art and his behaviour, provoked some sharp comments, but the old painter usually gave as good as he got. When criticized for the black sails in *Peace – Burial at Sea*, Turner retorted, 'If I could find anything blacker than black I'd use it.' In 1842 he had himself tied for four hours to the mast of a Margate steamer in a storm, and afterwards painted his *Snow-storm*, remarking 'I did not expect to escape but felt bound to record it if I did.' Much to Turner's indignation, the painting was described as 'soapsuds and whitewash'. He was better prepared for criticism of his impressionistic *Rain, Steam, and Speed* (1844), blandly declaring 'Indistinctness is my forte.'

All this, however, was more than compensated for by the publication of John Ruskin's *Modern Painters* (1843), in which the twenty-four-year-old critic praised Turner as no living painter had ever been praised. But by 1845 Turner's failing eyesight made painting difficult

for him, and indifferent health forced him to stop his frequent visits to Europe. Nevertheless, his mind was still active and he took a great interest in the new art of photography; in 1847 Mayall took several portraits of the old painter, but these have not survived.

By this time Turner's friends had become convinced that he was leading a double life, a view confirmed by the fact that he attended the 1851 Royal Academy exhibition, but afterwards disappeared completely. A letter found in an old coat by Hannah Danby, Turner's housekeeper, gave a riverside address in Chelsea, and the old man's secret was out. Apparently he had clandestinely set up house with Sophia Booth, 'my good old Margate landlady', and was known locally as 'Puggy Booth'. His friends found him at his Chelsea cottage on 18 December 1851, just one day before his death. Turner was buried in St. Paul's Cathedral. In his will he left £140,000 to various relatives and friends; and 362 finished oil paintings and 19,000 sketches to the National Gallery. It was his stated wish that a gallery should be created in which they might be exhibited, but this has never been done.

A. J. Finberg, *The Life of J. M. W. Turner, R.A.* (1961, 2nd ed.).
L. Gowing, *Turner: Imagination and Reality* (1966).
M. Kitson, *J. M. W. Turner* (1964).
J. Lindsay, *J. M. W. Turner: A Critical Biography* (1966).
G. Reynolds, *Turner* (1969).
J. Rothenstein and M. Butlin, *Turner* (1964).

Works in:
National Gallery, London.
Victoria and Albert Museum, London.
Tate Gallery, London.
National Portrait Gallery, London.

Portraits: oil, self-portrait, half-length, *c.* 1798: Tate Gallery; chalk, half-length, by C. Turner: N.P.G.; pencil, full-length, by C. Martin: N.P.G.; pencil, by G. Dance: Royal Academy; pencil, by C. Varley: Graves Art Gallery, Sheffield; watercolour, self-portrait, half-length, 1792: N.P.G.

Turpin, Dick (1706–39), notorious highwayman.

Dick Turpin was born in September 1706 at Hempstead, Essex, the son of John Turpin, landlord of the Bell Inn. He was educated by 'one Smith, a writing master', and apprenticed to a butcher in Whitechapel. At twenty-one he married Rose Palmer, an innkeeper's daughter, and opened a butcher's shop in Waltham Abbey. When sheep stolen from Farmer Giles of Plaistow were found in his shop, he escaped the angry farmer through a window and began an overt life of crime.

Turpin joined first a gang of smugglers at Harwich and then Gregory's gang, which stole deer in Epping Forest and robbed isolated farmhouses all over Essex. Once three of the gang were caught and hanged, but Turpin again escaped through a window, and became a highwayman. He attacked travellers in the then rural areas of Wandsworth and Barnes, and then Blackheath and Twickenham – where he is said to have almost stolen the manuscript of *The Essay on Man* from Pope. In 1735 he met Tom King on the Cambridge Road and they went into partnership. Their head-quarters was a cave in Epping Forest, where Mrs. Turpin would bring them food. Turpin's only murder occurred when a keeper of the forest discovered the cave and was shot.

For some time Turpin and King terrorized travellers in Essex, until Turpin stole and decided to keep for himself a famous horse called Whitestockings. The owner of the horse, a Mr. Major of Epping, traced his mount to the Red Lion at Whitechapel, and lay in wait for Turpin with a constable. It was Tom King who walked into the ambush, but as he was being arrested he saw Turpin approaching and shouted to him to shoot the constable. Turpin fired, but the shot hit and killed his friend. He escaped with a price of £200 on his head and robbed alone until August 1737, when he went to Yorkshire and posed as John Palmer, a horse-trader. Arrested for stealing a black mare and foal, he wrote to his brother in Essex for help. His writing was recognized by Smith, his old teacher, who travelled to York and identified the horse thief as the notorious Dick Turpin. Sentenced to death, Turpin shared £3 10s. between five men to act as mourners and died bravely on 7 April 1739 at York, where his body was buried in St. George's churchyard. His 28-lb. fetters are still in York museum.

The story of Turpin's lightning ride from London on the famous mare Black Bess, which died of exhaustion on reaching York, is derived from Harrison Ainsworth's romance *Rookwood* (1834).

W

Walpole, Horace (1717–97), 4th Earl of Orford; novelist, connoisseur, and letter-writer.

Horace Walpole was born on 24 September 1717 in London, the fourth son of Robert Walpole (q.v.), 1st Earl of Orford. Horace's birth eleven years after his youngest brother and his dissimilarity to the rest of the family in looks led to the plausible suggestion that his actual father was Carr, Lord Hervey, brother of John, Lord Hervey.

Walpole spent his childhood at Sir Robert's Chelsea house. In 1727 he went to Eton where, he later frankly admitted, 'I was a blockhead.' There he befriended William Cole, the future antiquary, and Thomas Gray (q.v.), the future poet, both of whom considerably influenced his later life. In 1735 Walpole went up to King's College, Cambridge, where he proved an indifferent classics scholar. Fortunately, in 1737 Horace's father, then Prime Minister, gave him a few sinecures, including the post of Usher of the Exchequer, which brought in £1,200 a year.

In 1739 Walpole and Gray set off together on the Grand Tour. After visiting France, they stayed for fifteen months in Florence at the riverside villa of Horace Mann, the British minister. Unfortunately, Walpole became bored with culture and quarrelled with Gray, and they separated; Walpole returned to England in late 1741.

Walpole now settled in his father's house in Arlington Street, since he heartily disliked Houghton, the family's vast mansion in the windy Norfolk fens. When Sir Robert Walpole died in 1745,

he left the London house and £5,000 cash to Horace. This supported him in a leisurely literary life; he composed occasional poems and learned articles, and wrote long letters to Horace Mann and to Gray, the earliest of his many sparkling correspondences. In 1747 Walpole rented a modest house at Twickenham that had once belonged to Colley Cibber. The following year he bought it for £1,350, renamed it Strawberry Hill, and set out to turn it into 'a little Gothic castle'. To the original fabric he added a refectory, library, cloister, and round tower; he scattered battlements, pointed arches, and stained glass everywhere, and filled the rooms with books, paintings, china, metalwork, and knick-knacks. Strawberry Hill became the talking point of the fashionable world, and its owner was soon obliged to issue tickets to control would-be visitors.

In other respects Walpole's life was relatively uneventful, although in 1749 he was nearly shot in Hyde Park by James Maclaine, the 'gentle highwayman'. In 1754 he was elected M.P. for Castle Riding, but his chief interest was books, and in July 1757 he set up his own private press, the *Officina Arbuteana*, which during the next thirty years issued fine editions of such classics as Lucan's *Pharsalia* and Grammont's *Memoirs*. His own works at this time, including *Anecdotes of Painting in England* (1762–71) and *A Catalogue of Engravers* (1763), reflected his great interest in the visual arts.

Walpole's life of quiet dilettantism was temporarily disrupted by the huge popular success of his *Castle of Otranto*

(1764), a highly dramatic novel which first introduced the obligatory motifs of 'gothick' literature: an Italian background, frequent supernatural interventions, and the most purple of passions. The book's influence extended to Mrs. Radcliffe and Mary Shelley as well as to Walter Scott.

When in 1765 Walpole decided to storm Parisian high society, the brilliant Madame du Deffand, then nearly seventy and blind, developed an extraordinary infatuation for him. She wrote to him frequently until her death in 1780 and left him all her books.

Walpole again attempted the 'gothick' in 1768, with his sombre tragedy *The Mysterious Mother*, a medieval tale of incest which proved such strong meat that it was never staged. He was temporarily taken in by some of the forgeries of Thomas Chatterton (q.v.), and later felt remorse that he had failed to offer the help which might have averted Chatterton's suicide.

From the 1770s onwards Walpole published very little, though he by no means stopped writing. An interest in political personalities was in his blood, and inspired his fascinating *Memoirs of the Reign of King George the Third*, which for obvious reasons was not published until many years later. But Walpole's greatest achievement was his 3,000 letters, described by Byron as 'incomparable' and made up of an infinite variety of anecdote, epigram, wit, observation, and description. Walpole consciously designed his vast correspondence to reflect his many interests; hence it constitutes a brilliant survey of the prevailing manners and artistic taste of the eighteenth century.

Walpole succeeded to the earldom of Orford in 1791, and his last years were made happy by the devoted friendship of the accomplished Berry sisters, Agnes and Mary. After 1791, when Walpole set them up in a near-by house, Little Strawberry,

the three were inseparable. Horace Walpole died on 2 March 1797 at his town house in Berkeley Square, leaving £1,000 each to Agnes and Mary Berry.

R. W. Ketton-Cremer, *Horace Walpole* (1964, 4th edition).

W. S. Lewis *et al.* (eds.), *The Correspondence of Horace Walpole* (36 vols.; New Haven, 1937–65).

W. S. Lewis (ed.), *A Selection of the Letters of Horace Walpole* (New York, 1951).

W. S. Lewis (ed.), *The Castle of Otranto* (1964).

W. S. Lewis, *Horace Walpole* (New York, 1960).

W. H. Smith (ed.), *Walpole: Writer, Politician and Connoisseur* (New Haven, 1967).

Portraits: oil, half-length, by J. G. Eccardt, 1754: N.P.G.; pencil, half-length, by G. Dance, 1793: N.P.G.; pencil, quarter-length, by T. Lawrence: N.P.G.

Walpole, Sir Robert (1676–1745), 1st Earl of Orford; Whig statesman.

Robert Walpole was born at Houghton Hall, Norfolk, on 26 August 1676, the third son of Robert Walpole, a military colonel, and Mary Burwell, daughter of Sir Jeffrey Burwell of Roughen, Suffolk. He was educated at Great Dunham, Norfolk, and at Eton. He entered King's

College, Cambridge, in 1696, but in 1698 was forced to return to Norfolk to assist in the management of his father's estates. In 1700 his father died and he received a somewhat diminished inheritance which included the family parliamentary seat of Castle Rising. In the same year he married Catherine Shorter, daughter of a Baltic timber merchant, and made his first appearance in parliament. In 1702 he transferred to the seat for King's Lynn, which he represented in parliament – except for one short break – for forty years. A firm Whig, Walpole entered into an alliance with Charles Townshend, 2nd Viscount Townshend (q.v.), who had at one time been a ward of Walpole's father. The two had formed a childhood friendship, and now formed a political alliance that was to last for nearly thirty years.

Walpole rapidly became known as a force in the House of Commons. In 1705 he was made a member of Prince George of Denmark's council, which controlled the affairs and supplies of the navy during the War of the Spanish Succession. Walpole's administrative ability quickly became apparent, and very soon both Godolphin (see *Lives of the Stuart Age*) and the still influential Duchess of Marlborough (see Churchill, Sarah, in *Lives of the Stuart Age*) had extended their patronage to him. In 1708 Walpole became Secretary at War, and in 1710 Treasurer of the Navy. In 1711, however, he was dismissed as a result of the 1710 election, which had proved an overwhelming success for the Tories.

Walpole in opposition applied himself assiduously to his new role. By now he was a leading member of the young Whigs and was accepted socially (he was a member of the famous Kit-Cat Club). His pamphlets on Tory finance were an embarrassment to the government. In 1712 he was impeached on charges of corruption while he was Secretary at War, and actually spent some time in the Tower. He conceived a strong hatred for Robert Harley, Earl of Oxford, and Henry St. John, Viscount Bolingbroke (see *Lives of the Stuart Age*), the engineers of his disgrace.

In 1714 George I came to the throne, and the Whigs were put firmly back in power. Walpole chaired a secret committee which led to the impeachment of both Bolingbroke and Oxford on the grounds of treason. In George I's first parliament Walpole enjoyed the lucrative post of Paymaster. Townshend, now Walpole's brother-in-law, became a Secretary of State. In 1715 Walpole was promoted to the offices of First Lord of the Treasury and Chancellor of the Exchequer.

Already a division was appearing in the Whig party: Walpole and Townshend were at odds with James Stanhope (q.v.) and Sunderland (see Spencer, Charles) over British foreign policy, which Walpole felt was geared to George's Hanoverian interests rather than to British needs. In 1717 a final break came, and Walpole and Townshend resigned. Walpole threw himself into active opposition with great enthusiasm and application. In 1719 he brought about the rejection of the Peerage Bill, which had been designed to limit the royal prerogative in the creation of peers. At about this time Walpole began a lasting political alliance with Caroline of Ansbach (q.v.). However, he maintained sufficient independence to become reconciled with George I, and in 1720 he returned to office as Paymaster General of the Forces. Townshend joined him as President of the Council, although they made little impression on the combined power of Sunderland and Stanhope.

The extraordinary affair of the South Sea Bubble, however, was now coming to a head. This was a speculative scheme designed to take over the national debt by the formation of the so-called South Sea Company. Although Walpole had not advocated the scheme, he nevertheless had substantial holdings in the South Sea Company, and it appears that only the acumen of his banker, Robert Jacomb, saved him from financial ruin. Since he had not actively promoted the scheme, Walpole was not implicated in any charges of corruption or mismanagement after the South Sea Company collapsed, and was therefore in a strong position to take over the running of the government. While others suffered – Stanhope even died under the strain – Walpole used all his political skill to advance himself and Townshend and to restore confidence in the Whigs. Walpole's role in 'saving the country' from the economic consequences of the South Sea Bubble has probably been overstated, but he did provide conditions of stability, and public confidence was quickly restored. In 1721 Walpole again became First Lord of the Treasury and Chancellor of the Exchequer, offices that he continued to hold until his resignation in 1742.

Walpole's great strength lay in his intimate knowledge of the running of parliament and his familiarity with financial affairs. Foreign affairs were not his real province and he relied on Townshend, who now became Secretary of State. Walpole's dominance of parliament, the court, and the country in fact lasted only as long as he kept England at peace. When it was necessary to go to war in 1739 his influence began to weaken.

In the 1720s, however, Walpole was virtually unopposed, except by Sunderland, who died in 1722. Sunderland's successor, Carteret (q.v.), proved troublesome for a time. In 1722 Walpole disclosed a Jacobite plot implicating Francis Atterbury, Bishop of Rochester. This he exploited to its full advantage: he suspended habeas corpus; he had troops drafted into Hyde Park; he imposed a fine of £100,000 on Roman Catholics to pay for the army; and he banished Atterbury. Walpole thus used the public fear of Jacobitism to consolidate his position, practically destroying the Tory party in the process. Ministers had not enjoyed such solidarity since Tudor times.

In 1724 a scandal arose concerning 'Wood's Ha'pence' and involving the bribery of one of the King's mistresses, the Duchess of Kendal (see Schulenburg, Ehrengarde Melusina von der), by William Wood. Wood, an ironmaster, had been commissioned in 1722 to provide Ireland with a new coinage, and through this transaction the Duchess had made a profit of £10,000. Some publications by Swift (the *Drapier Letters*) stirred up a great deal of trouble in Ireland, and Carteret was also found to be involved. Walpole's manner of dealing with this was characteristic: he dismissed Carteret from office and appointed him Viceroy of Ireland, where he was responsible for subduing the unrest he had helped to foment.

Walpole was awarded a knighthood in 1725. His policies had proved popular and effective: he had subdued a Jacobite plot, restored the country's confidence after the South Sea Company came to grief, and taken major steps towards freeing trade. He regarded imports as the raw materials for British manufacture rather than as foreign threats to British trade, and introduced a system of bonded warehouses for such commodities as tea, coffee, and chocolate, a measure which was very popular with the merchants. Walpole also enjoyed the full confidence of George I.

The death of George I in 1727 was a setback in Walpole's career. Because of the animosity that had existed between the King and his son, it was not thought likely that Walpole would be able to survive as a power under George II. Yet he did survive, largely because of his old ally Queen Caroline's beneficial influence, coupled with firm promises to increase the royal civil list allowance.

In 1730 Walpole had a major disagreement with Townshend over foreign policy. Townshend resigned and Walpole was hard put to it to keep England out of continental involvements. In 1725 the Treaty of Hanover, negotiated by Townshend, had helped to strengthen the Anglo-French alliance. But difficulties were beginning to arise with Spain over trade, particularly involving Gibraltar and the West Indies. Walpole made peace, offering substantial concessions, in 1729 with the Treaty of Seville; two years later the Treaty of Vienna made a general settlement. In 1733 with the outbreak of the War of the Polish Succession Walpole had to use all his personal influence with the King to prevent England's involvement. He had secured his dominant position in parliament and in the country

with peace abroad and a concomitant low taxation. But opposition to Walpole's policy was beginning to form from a variety of sources, and a strangely assorted opposition party began to take shape. It was led by Bolingbroke (who had been pardoned in 1725) and included the remnants of a Tory party and some dissident Whigs, Jacobites, and radicals. It published its own weekly newspaper, *The Craftsman*, which attacked and lampooned Walpole regularly.

In 1733 Walpole attempted to bring in a bill to impose excise tax on wine and tobacco. This was resisted so strongly in the Commons that he was obliged to withdraw it to avoid defeat. He was successful at the 1734 parliamentary elections, although his majority was diminished. Bolingbroke gave up the fight in 1735 and retired from politics to live in France. In 1736 Walpole dealt effectively with the Porteous riots in Edinburgh, but in 1737 his position at last began to weaken. Queen Caroline, his old friend and ally, died in November, and Walpole was under pressure from a group of younger Whig leaders, such as William Pitt the Elder (q.v.). In 1737 his wife died, and in March of the following year he married his mistress Maria Skerritt, a woman of great wit and charm – only to lose her in childbirth three months later. In 1739 Walpole was finally forced to declare war on Spain. He tendered his resignation, but George II refused to accept it. Walpole's comment to Newcastle (see Pelham-Holles, Thomas) on the war is famous: 'It is your war,' he said, 'and I wish you joy of it.'

In 1741 he won the general election, but his support had waned; the opposition was increasing in strength and in February 1742 he was forced to resign after being beaten in a vote on a trivial issue that he had chosen to fight as a test of his parliamentary support. George II created him Earl of Orford and granted him an annual pension of £4,000. He remained active in retirement and retained his influence on George until his death in London, on 18 March 1745. He was buried at Houghton, Norfolk.

Walpole has been described as Britain's first Prime Minister, a term which he himself regarded as insulting. He used his influence to maintain the power and stability of the Whig party through two reigns. He was not an innovator: he worked with George I and II within the constitutional limits of his time, and at least part of the reason for the extent of his power was the lack of interest or competence of these monarchs in English parliamentary affairs. It has been said that 'He knew the strength and weakness of everybody he had to deal with.' As a skilful manipulator of parliament, he has probably never been equalled.

P. G. M. Dickson, *The Financial Revolution in England* (1967).

J. B. Owen, *The Rise of the Pelhams* (1957).

J. H. Plumb, *Sir Robert Walpole*, vol. 1, *The Making of a Statesman* (1956).

J. H. Plumb, *Sir Robert Walpole*, vol. 2, *The King's Minister* (1961).

J. H. Plumb, *The Growth of Political Stability in England, 1675–1725* (1967).

C. B. Realey, *The Early Opposition to Sir Robert Walpole, 1720–1727* (Philadelphia, 1931).

Portraits: oil, three-quarter length, studio of J. B. Van Loo, *c*.1740: N.P.G.; oil, half-length, by Kneller, 1710–15: N.P.G.; terracotta bust, by J. M. Rysbrack, *c*.1726–30: N.P.G.; oil, full-length, by J. B. Van Loo: King's College, Cambridge.

Walter, John (1739–1812), founder of *The Times* newspaper.

John Walter was born in 1739 in London, where his father was a coal merchant. For sixteen years after his father's death in 1755 Walter worked as a coal merchant, building up his father's business into a large and profitable enterprise. In 1781 he resigned from this occupation to begin a new career as an underwriter, but because of the hazards involved in the insurance of ships at war he found himself bankrupt within a year and compelled once more to find a new career.

A chance meeting with Henry Johnson, who had recently invented a new technique of printing from blocks of whole words (logotypes) rather than of separate letters, gave Walter the opportunity he needed: he bought the patents for this process from Johnson and in 1784, with the aid of a grant from his creditors, he bought premises in Printing House Square, Blackfriars, in which he set up a printing press. He printed books, 'Lloyd's List' from 1785, and the custom-house papers from 1787 to 1805. The lack of profits from his printed books prompted Walter to explore the possibilities of journalism, and on 1 January 1785 he printed the first issue of *The Daily Universal Register*, the newspaper whose title was changed in 1788 to *The Times*.

John Walter was a businessman rather than a journalist, and the early reputation of *The Times* was founded on its lengthy and accurate reporting of parliamentary debates and similar institutional affairs rather than on any journalistic innovations. Walter's several convictions for libel bear witness to the unrestricted powers of politicians and other public figures rather than to his own rashness; he was imprisoned from 1789 to 1791 for remarks about the sons of George III. After he had made sufficient money to retire to his house at Teddington in 1795 he was content to leave the management of the newspaper in the hands of his son John Walter (q.v.). He died at Teddington on 16 November 1812.

S. Morison, *The History of the Times*, vol. 1, '*The Thunderer*' *in the Making, 1785–1841* (1935).

Walter, John (1776–1847), manager of *The Times* newspaper.

Walter was born in Battersea, London,

on 23 February 1776, the second son of John Walter (1739–1812, q.v.), and educated at Merchant Taylors' School and Trinity College, Oxford, from where he was recalled by his father in 1798 to help with the management of *The Times*.

In 1803 John Walter became sole editor of *The Times* until 1810, and sole manager until his death, by which time the newspaper had a circulation larger than that of all its London rivals combined, and could justly claim to be 'the leading journal in Europe'. Walter's first great contribution to the paper's development was his maintenance of its political independence: he had determined to refuse all grants, bribes, or favours, he wrote in a leading article in 1811, because otherwise 'he should have sacrificed the right of condemning any act which he might esteem detrimental to the public welfare.' Despite government harassment, which included the deliberate delaying of dispatches from abroad and the withdrawal of certain official printing contracts, Walter maintained this policy of independence, and with the increased advertisement revenue that followed his employment of steam printing presses in 1814, his principles were strengthened by commercial prosperity.

In 1807 and 1808 Walter commissioned reports from Henry Crabb Robinson in Germany and the Peninsula, thus initiating the practice of employing foreign correspondents. His development of an elaborate communications network in Europe led to many reporting triumphs, the most spectacular of which was his publication of an account of the Battle of Trafalgar several days before the government itself had been informed. The writing of leading articles and special reports in London was conducted in an atmosphere of commitment and solidarity, almost resembling that of a pioneering secret society, and the finished articles set new standards in journalism.

After 1817 Thomas Barnes took over much of the purely editorial work of the newspaper, leaving Walter to devote himself wholly to administrative affairs and also to enjoy his new home at Bear Wood, Wokingham. Walter was M.P. for Berkshire from 1832 to 1835, and for Nottingham from 1841 until the following year, when the election was declared void. He died of cancer in London on 28 July 1847 and was succeeded as manager of *The Times* by John, his eldest son by his second marriage.

S. Morison, *The History of the Times*, vol. 1, '*The Thunderer' in the Making, 1785–1841* (1935).

Watson-Wentworth, Charles (1730–82), 2nd Marquis of Rockingham; statesman, who laid the foundations for a disciplined and reforming Whig party; Prime Minister in 1765–6 and again in 1782.

Charles Watson-Wentworth was born on 13 May 1730, the fifth and only surviving son of Thomas Watson-Wentworth, who became Marquis of Rockingham in 1746. He was educated at Westminster School and St. John's College, Cambridge. In 1750 he was created an Irish peer with the titles of Baron and Earl of Malton, in County Wicklow, and on the death of his father in the same year, he succeeded to all his honours. He took his seat in the House of Lords in 1751, and was made one of the Lords of the Bedchamber to George II. In 1752 he was made Lord-Lieutenant of the North and East Ridings of Yorkshire. Subsequent honours included fellowships of the Royal Society and the Society of Arts, and in 1755, the Order of the Garter.

Rockingham was bred in the strictest Whig principles, so that even as a boy his zeal for the house of Hanover had caused him to join the Duke of Cumberland's army during the Jacobite rising of 1745–6. He had no dealings with the Prince of

Wales nor with the party of prerogative that Bute began to organize on the accession of George III under the specious designation of 'king's friends'. Like the Duke of Devonshire, he resigned his position as a Lord of the Bedchamber shortly before the signing of the preliminaries to the Peace of Paris, and was dismissed from his various other offices.

Rockingham, a hesitant speaker, took little part in politics until March 1765, when he was induced to solicit the aid of William Pitt the Elder in organizing opposition to the arbitrary measures taken by Grenville's administration against the supporters of Wilkes. Dissatisfied with Pitt, Rockingham turned to Newcastle, who consulted him in the long struggle over the Regency Bill. During the resulting crisis, Rockingham and Pitt both received royal overtures for the formation of a coalition administration, but on Pitt's refusal of office, Rockingham accepted the Treasury; he was sworn into the Privy Council on 10 July and was re-appointed Lord-Lieutenant of the East and North Ridings of Yorkshire.

Though the ministry lasted only thirteen months, its measures included the repeal of the Stamp Act and the Cider Tax. These moves were wise but unpopular, and a law had to be passed reinforcing the British government's right to legislate in respect of the colonies. The administration also passed a new Mutiny Act and resolutions condemning general warrants (see Wilkes, John). However, a negotiation between Pitt and the court ended in Rockingham's dismissal, and Pitt, who accepted the earldom of Chatham, returned to power at the end of July 1766. Grafton (see Fitzroy, Augustus) commissioned Rockingham to form an administration as soon as parliament was prorogued on 2 July 1767, but irreconcilable divisions

among the Whigs caused the abandonment of the project. Subsequent united opposition to the Whigs was too strong, and Rockingham, disheartened, took little part in public affairs until the coming of the North ministry in 1770.

Throughout Lord North's period of government, Rockingham took an active interest in parliamentary affairs. Now aided by Chatham, he obtained a committee of the whole House on the state of the nation (2 February 1770), and supported Chatham's motion for an account of the expenditure on the civil list. He joined in the protest against the rejection of the bill to reverse the adjudications of the Commons in the matter of the Middlesex election (see Wilkes, John), but declined to follow Chatham in his attempt to force an immediate dissolution. He supported the censure of the government over its directives for the dissolution of the Massachusetts Bay assembly and for the suspension of the Virginia revenue laws, and also a motion concerning a dispute with Spain over the ownership of the Falkland Islands.

Rockingham showed himself to be liberal and tolerant. He opposed the Royal Marriage Act (1772), and in 1773 supported the measure relieving Dissenters and schoolmasters from the partial subscription to the Thirty-Nine Articles requested by the Toleration Act. In 1775 he supported Chatham's motion for the recall of troops from Boston, and in 1776 he moved an amendment to the address deprecating the continuance of the struggle, and virtually seceded from the House on its rejection.

Rockingham returned to politics with his censure of North's conciliatory bills on the conclusion of the Franco-American alliance. He declared for the immediate recognition of the colonies' independence in 1778, and remonstrated when war was declared against them in the same year. During 1780 he rejected North's overtures for a coalition and continued his criticisms of the government into 1781, deploring especially the breach in Britain's relations with Holland, occasioned by that country's commercial associations with America and France. With the war suddenly expanded – Spain was also against England – and internal political pressure becoming intolerable, North resigned in 1782.

On 27 March 1782 Rockingham returned to power at the King's request. His administration occupied the last three months of his life. With himself as First Lord of the Treasury, his ministry included Grafton (see Fitzroy, Augustus), Shelburne (see Petty, William) and Fox (q.v.), together with other prominent Rockingham Whigs. In its short life it granted legislative independence to Ireland, curtailed the power of the crown, disfranchised revenue officers, and prohibited government contractors from sitting in the Commons.

Rockingham died on 1 July 1782, and was buried in the choir of York Minster on 20 July. He left a childless wife, and his titles became extinct. Hereditary wealth and prestige hoisted him to what R. J. White called 'an elevation in the politics of his time which his own abilities scarcely could have brought him to attain'. Rockingham nevertheless created an environment in which the great Whig traditions of liberty, probity, and constitutional government were to flourish.

J. Brooke, *The Chatham Administration, 1766–8* (1956).

J. A. Cannon, *The Fox–North Coalition* (1969).

I. R. Christie, *The End of Lord North's Ministry 1780–2* (1958).

I. R. Christie, *Myth and Reality in Late Eighteenth-Century British Politics and Other Papers* (1970).

G. H. Guttridge, *The Early Career of Lord Rockingham: 1730–65* (University of California Publications in History, xliv, 1952).

G. H. Gutteridge, *English Whiggism and the American Revolution* (Berkeley and Los Angeles, 1963).

P. Langford, *The First Rockingham Administration, 1765–6* (1973).

Portraits: oil, half-length, studio of Reynolds: Mansion House, York; bust, by J. Nollekens: Birmingham City Museum and Art Gallery.

Watt, James (1736–1819), Scottish engineer and developer of the first practical steam engine.

James Watt was born at Greenock, on the River Clyde, on 19 January 1736, the son of a prosperous builder, merchant, and shipowner.

Watt, popularly but erroneously regarded as the inventor of the steam engine – an honour which rightfully belongs to Thomas Newcomen (see *Lives of the Stuart Age*) – gained his earliest technical experience as a boy in his father's workshop. His manual dexterity, combined with his sound education first at Greenock Grammar School, then in Glasgow, enabled him to find a place as an apprentice with a London maker of scientific instruments. He arrived in London in 1755, but the murky atmosphere and the hard work in the Cornhill workshop in which he was employed did not suit his delicate health, and he returned to Scotland a year later. With his father's support, he set himself up in Glasgow as an instrument maker, becoming mathematical-instrument maker to Glasgow University in 1757.

In 1764, the year of his first marriage (to his cousin, Margaret Miller), Watt was sent a classroom model of Newcomen's steam engine to repair. He had no problem in making it work, but the inefficiency of the device set him thinking about ways of improving the fundamental design. In Newcomen's engine cold water was actually injected into the cylinder in order to condense the steam; thus the cylinder itself was alternately heated and cooled. Watt perceived that this wasteful use of the steam's energy could be avoided by keeping the cylinder hot with a steam jacket and condensing the steam in a separate water-cooled condenser. He also added an air pump to the engine, and invented a means of making the engine double-acting by allowing for the introduction of steam to both sides of the piston, thereby doubling the number of working strokes.

After making a small test machine with financial help from a former schoolfriend, Joseph Black (q.v.), Watt set to work to build a working steam engine incorporating his great improvements. He went into partnership with his friend John Roebuck, but both the engine and the partnership failed. In 1767 Watt therefore travelled south to Birmingham to seek the advice of two new and influential friends, Erasmus Darwin (q.v.) and William Small. They were both favourably impressed with Watt's ideas and introduced him to Matthew Boulton (q.v.). Boulton tried unsuccessfully to buy Roebuck out of the enterprise, and it was not until 1774, after Roebuck's bankruptcy, that Boulton and Watt were able to proceed with the manufacture of the engine, even though Watt had patented his engine in 1769. Between 1767 and 1774 Watt had to earn a living by other means than manufacturing, and worked as surveyor for the Caledonian Canal, the Forth and Clyde Canal, and the harbour improvements at Glasgow, Greenock, and Ayr. In 1773 his wife, Margaret, died, leaving him to care for a family of six children. In the following year Watt took up permanent residence in Birmingham.

In 1775 Boulton obtained a prolongation of Watt's patent, and in the following years Watt perfected the engine in Boulton's Soho Engineering Works. It was not long before Watt's engine had replaced that of Newcomen as a pumping engine in mines, especially in Cornwall.

By this time Watt had been taken into partnership by Boulton, and he remained a partner in the firm of Boulton & Watt until his retirement in 1800. During this period he made many further improvements to the steam engine, including a centrifugal governor (for regulating the engine's speed), an indicator to show the pressure changes in the cylinder, a crank, and subsequently a sun-and-plant wheel assembly to convert the reciprocating motion to rotation. Although in one of his patents (1784) he described a steam locomotive and in the same year proposed a screw propeller, he never saw the immense potential of his engine fulfilled.

Apart from his work on the steam engine, Watt was responsible for a number of other inventions, including a copying-ink and a letter-copying press. After meeting Joseph Priestley (q.v.), James Keir, and others, he developed an interest in chemistry, and although we now know that it was Henry Cavendish (q.v.) who first discovered that water is a compound of what are now called oxygen and hydrogen, Watt also came to the same

453

conclusion independently, and is sometimes credited with the discovery. He
presented a paper to the Royal Society in
1783 on the composition of water, and
was elected a Fellow in 1785. In 1806 he
was made an honorary LL.D. by Glasgow
University.

A keen patron of the arts, Watt was for
many years an enthusiastic member of the
Lunar Society in Birmingham, dedicated
to the promotion of both the arts and the
sciences. In 1776 he remarried, taking one
Ann MacGregor of Glasgow as his bride.
His son James's sympathies with the
French Revolution gave him cause for
serious concern during the 1790s, but the
young man outgrew them, and later took
his father's place at Boulton & Watt.

Watt became a wealthy and revered
man. As well as the above-mentioned
honours, he was offered a baronetcy, but
modestly declined it. In 1802, during the
truce with France, he toured the
Continent. Throughout his last years
Watt maintained a lively interest in
scientific and technological matters. He
died at his home in Heathfield on 25
August 1819. The graves of Boulton and
Watt lie side by side in the cemetery of
Handsworth Parish Church. A statue of
Watt was placed in Westminster Abbey.

J. G. Crowther, *Scientists of the Industrial Revolution*
(1962).
J. Langdon Davies, *James Watt and Steam Power*
(1965).
I. B. Hart, *James Watt and the History of Steam Power*
(1961).
I. B. Hart, *James Watt, Pioneer of Mechanical Power*
(1962).
L. T. C. Rolt, *James Watt* (1962).

Portraits: oil, quarter-length, by H. Howard: N.P.G.;
oil, half-length, by C. F. von Breda, 1729: N.P.G.;
engraving, three-quarter length, by Charles
Turner, 1815, after Sir Thomas Lawrence, 1813.

Wedgwood, Josiah (1730–95), potter,
designer, and manufacturer of earthen-
ware and porcelain.

Josiah Wedgwood was born on 12 July
1730, the youngest of thirteen children of
Thomas and Mary Wedgwood. The
Wedgwood family had been resident in
Burslem, Staffordshire, since 1612, and
many of them had been potters. Josiah
received only the barest education at the
local private school; his father died before
the boy reached the age of nine, and Josiah
began work at the Burslem pottery under
his brother Thomas, where he quickly
became a skilful 'thrower'. After an attack
of smallpox in 1741 he was left extremely
weak and had to move from the throwers'
bench, going over to modelling and
studying the different clay combinations.
This was the beginning of a long career of
exhaustive experimentation and chemical
research in so far as it affected pottery.

On completion of his five-year apprenticeship, young Josiah joined the pot
works of Thomas Alders and John
Harrison at Cliffe Bank near Stoke-on-
Trent. It is reported that he improved
both quality and output, but that his
associates neither appreciated nor recom-
pensed him for his work, and he found a
more congenial partnership at Fenton
Low with Thomas Whieldon, a reputable
potter and a talented craftsman. The
period of their partnership (1754–9) was
notable for improvements in the colour,
shape, and modelling of the wares, and the
production of some of the finest work
from the Whieldon factory.

In 1759 Wedgwood parted amicably
with Whieldon to start up a business on his
own, renting part of the Ivy House Works
owned by John and Thomas Wedgwood
at Burslem. During his five years at Ivy
House, Wedgwood produced pottery
similar to that which he had developed at
Fenton, and also perfected a new green
glaze. He was a shrewd superintendent of
his business, introducing a system of
division of labour and insisting on greater
cleanliness and less waste of materials.

Business flourished, and in 1760 Wedgwood made a sizeable donation towards the establishment of a village school in Burslem. He also interested himself in transport and communication, giving evidence on the subject to a 1762 parliamentary committee, and subscribing £100 in 1765 to local roads, providently realizing the necessity of easy transit for raw materials and goods. In 1777 the canal system was improved by the opening of the Trent and Mersey Canal, which brought enormous benefit to local industry and ran through Wedgwood's own estate.

In 1765 Wedgwood was styled 'Potter to the Queen', having three years previously presented a caudle and breakfast set in improved creamware to Queen Charlotte. This recognition was well earned; Wedgwood had devoted much time to perfecting the even colour and fine texture and decoration of his creamware (from this period on, also known as Queenware). The volume of business, the new techniques, and new work methods necessitated a move in 1765 to premises at Bridge House and Works in Burslem, after which he bought some land between Burslem and Stoke-on-Trent and built on it a hall, a factory, and a workers' village, naming the place Etruria in honour of the beautiful Tuscan pottery that had recently come to light. Etruria was opened on 13 June 1769.

In 1770 the British consul in St. Petersburg approached Wedgwood with an order for a dinner service for Catherine I. Terms were negotiated, and the work, a grand commission, was delivered in 1775. It consisted of 952 pieces in all, decorated with 1,244 different scenes of great intricacy and beauty.

In 1770 Wedgwood, by now famous, opened a workshop in Cheyne Row, Chelsea, in conjunction with his partner and friend, Thomas Bentley. He produced decorated creamware, much of it in the Etruscan style, and continued to experiment widely to find other materials suitable for modelling neo-classical items. He developed in 1776 a 'fine white, artificial jasper, of exquisite beauty and delicacy; proper for cameos, portraits, and bas-reliefs'. This was soon to be seen on the market, for Wedgwood was as concerned with manufacturing and marketing as with chemical experimentation. Other newly developed materials included a new form of the traditional Staffordshire 'black basalt', and there was also a range of improved 'terra cotta' wares: the dark red *rosso antico*, the buff caneware, the green-grey drabware, the pure white stoneware, and the light red of the terra cotta itself. These were all made from local marls with the addition of 'ochreous earths' for colour. Wedgwood achieved a uniformity of form, colour, and quality in pottery formerly unknown in the field, and every article he made was perfectly adapted to its function, as well as being beautiful.

Wedgwood was elected a Fellow of the

455

Royal Society in 1783, and three years later a Fellow of the Society of Antiquaries. He married his third cousin Sarah Wedgwood, and they had seven children, of whom the eldest, Susannah, was the mother of Charles Darwin; a son, Thomas, became famous for his experiments in the field of photography; and another son, Josiah, carried on the family business.

Wedgwood had a leg amputated in 1768 (the eventual result of polio in childhood), and suffered bad health in the last five years of his life. He died at Etruria Hall on 3 January 1795, and was buried in Stoke-on-Trent churchyard. On his monument, designed by the artist Flaxman, who was employed at Etruria, is the inscription, 'He converted a rude and inconsiderable manufactory into an elegant art and an important part of the national commerce.' An amiable and conscientious man of business, he left a legacy of half a million pounds and a prospering business.

W. Burton, *Josiah Wedgwood and His Pottery* (1922).
R. E. Schofield, *The Lunary Society of Birmingham: a Social History of Provincial Science and Industry in Eighteenth Century England* (1963).
J. C. Wedgwood, *A History of the Wedgwood Family* (1909).
Julia Wedgwood, *The Personal Life of Josiah Wedgwood* (ed. C. H. Herford) (1915).

Portraits: Wedgwood medallion, quarter-length, by W. Hackwood, 1779: N.P.G.; medallion, by Joachim Smith: Manchester City Art Galleries; oil, by G. Stubbs, 1780: Wedgwood Museum, Barlaston, Staffs; creamware plaque, quarter-length, by G. Stubbs, 1780: Wedgwood Museum, Barlaston, Staffs.

Wellesley, Arthur (1769–1852), 1st Duke of Wellington; military commander and statesman.

Arthur Wellesley was born in Dublin on 1 May 1769, the fourth son of Garrett Wesley, 1st Earl of Mornington. Because of straitened family circumstances, the young Wellesley – the spelling of his name was changed in 1798 – had a varied education which included a period at Eton and some time at an academy of equitation in France. His eldest brother purchased for him an ensign's commission in the 73rd Regiment in 1787, exchanges and further purchases enabling him to pass through several regiments to lieutenant colonel's rank and the command of the 33rd Regiment in 1793. Throughout that period he remained in Ireland as aide to two successive Lords Lieutenant, and sat as member (1790–5) for Trim in the Irish parliament.

Wellesley's early career was attended by heavy debts caused by gambling and borrowing, which helped put an end to his plan for an early marriage. Action in the field, however, was not long in coming. In June 1794 he led his regiment in a force sent under Lord Moira to hold Ostend against a French advance. It merged with the retreating British army of the Duke of York in the last stages of an unsuccessful allied campaign against the French revolutionaries, and Wellesley took part in his first action at Boxtel in Holland, where the steadiness of the 33rd averted a crisis during a French attack. The retreat continued into Germany, and the demoralized remnants of the army were evacuated in March 1795. Capitalizing on this first experience of military inefficiency, the young commander resolved to give up gambling and settled down to studying the art of war.

After an abortive West Indies expedition, the 33rd was sent under Wellesley to India. He landed at Calcutta with his men in February 1797, having by then purchased his colonelcy despite continuing insolvency. In May 1798 his elder brother, the 2nd Earl of Mornington (see Wellesley, Richard Colley), arrived there as Governor General, and Arthur Wellesley enjoyed a privileged position as unofficial military adviser in the projected campaign against Tipu Sultan, ruler of Mysore. He commanded a division in the invasion of Mysore (February 1799) and afterwards was made the military governor of its capital, Seringapatam. He proved an excellent administrator, and his authority was extended over all troops in south-west India.

In 1802 Wellesley was employed in preparations for a war against the Mahratta chieftains and was gazetted a major general. In November he was given command of a division; in August 1803 he captured the Mahratta fortress of Ahmednuggur, and defeated the main Mahratta army at Assaye the following month despite being heavily outnumbered. This victory was followed by another at Argaum and the capture of Gawilghur, after which the Mahrattas yielded. Assaye brought Wellesley the Order of the Bath; prize money and emoluments enabled him to leave India (March 1805) solvent at last.

Back in England, through the patronage of Castlereagh he quickly obtained staff appointments and was made colonel of the 33rd. He also gained the confidence of William Pitt the Younger, which in turn brought the command of a brigade in a futile expedition to North Germany (1805–6). He now married Catherine Packenham, daughter of Lord Longford, and entered parliament for Rye (April 1806). Pitt's death and the fall of the ministry, however, checked his career, until Castlereagh returned to office as Secretary of War (1807). Wellesley then received the lucrative post of Chief Secretary of Ireland, exchanging his seat for Mitchell, and that later for Newport. His civil duties in Dublin were interrupted in the summer of 1807 by an independent command, a highly successful expedition to support a pre-emptive naval operation against the Danish fleet

at Copenhagen. As a result he was promoted to lieutenant general and subsequently put in charge of a force preparing for action in Venezuela.

The political need to respond to a Spanish request to assist a rising against French domination precipitated the concentration of British military effort on the Peninsula, and Wellesley's force was diverted from Venezuela to Portugal as an advance guard, landing in Mondego Bay in August. With another division brought to the area, Wellesley mustered 14,000 troops and marched to liberate Lisbon as a preliminary step. On 17 August he defeated a French army under Delaborde at Rolica, after which he advanced to Vimeiro to cover the landing of reinforcements. Here he was attacked on 21 August by the main French army, 13,000-strong under General Junot. With his own numbers increased to 17,000, Wellesley successfully defended his position, demonstrating for the first time that his combination of trained skirmishers, old-fashioned line formation and hill-crest position was, given steady troops, superior to the French shock attack with artillery-supported columns. Vimeiro was the first significant British military victory on the Continent since 1709, but it was not complete. Three generals senior to Wellesley had been appointed to the army, Dalrymple, Burrard, and Moore. Burrard arrived before the battle, wisely allowed Wellesley to conduct it, but forbade pursuit of the broken French army afterwards. The French sought an armistice and against Wellesley's wish it was granted, Dalrymple being on hand to support Burrard's decision. Under the Convention of Cintra (30 August) the French army evacuated Portugal unmolested. The government rode out the consequent political storm at home by means of an official inquiry, which exonerated the commanders, especially

Wellesley, who had returned to his secretaryship in Ireland.

In April 1809 he was charged with the task of forming a British-trained Portuguese army, with himself as commander in chief. Thus began one of the most brilliant campaigns in military history, the success of which was based upon his understanding of the importance of logistics and the ability of the Royal Navy to guarantee his supplies through Lisbon. On this he built an army with a high morale and a sound tactical method which, guided by his own optimism and attention to detail, proved the master of every French army it encountered. He himself was a tough disciplinarian but, although he is reported to have described them as 'the scum of the earth, enlisted for drink', he was respected and trusted by his troops. His disapproval of unnecessary casualties, and his realistic understanding of the demands which might reasonably be made on his soldiers, provided a striking contrast to most contemporary commanders.

He struck first at Marshal Soult's 25,000 troops in the north, making a surprise crossing of the Douro river on 12 May 1809 and bundling the French out of Oporto. Keeping them on the move by manœuvring, he cleared the country up to the border and then advanced eastwards into Spain to link up with Cuesta's Spaniards. The French concentrated 46,000 men against them under Victor, blocking the way to Madrid. Wellesley adopted a defensive stance at Talavera, and Victor was forced to retire. The victory was offset by the unreliability of the Spaniards, so that the British were obliged to fall back to the border. In September Wellesley was created Viscount Wellington of Talavera.

Appointed to restore French power in Portugal, Marshal André Masséna moved against the north-eastern border in May

1810 with 70,000 men. Wellington did not attempt to hold the frontier, retiring slowly to a strong defensive position on Busaco Ridge, which Masséna assaulted on 27 September. Trained Portuguese regiments now made up half the 51,000-strong allied army, which broke up the five strong thrusts at the ridge. Nevertheless, a French flank march compelled Wellington to withdraw again, this time to a previously prepared system of defences in front of Lisbon, the 'Lines of Torres Vedras', which Masséna could neither realistically attack nor, because of the French system of living off the land, confront for long. In March 1811 he retreated, Ney fighting a sound rearguard action against Wellington, who pressed him close until Portugal was almost cleared. Masséna attempted to relieve Almeida but was blocked by Wellington and thrown back in a fierce battle at Fuentes de Oñoro (3 and 5 May).

Before thrusting into Spain, Wellington intended to take the fortresses of Ciudad Rodrigo and Badajoz guarding the Spanish borderlands, which involved a six-month delay until a siege train could come up from Lisbon. The former fortress fell in January 1812, the latter in April, after a very costly assault, and Wellington moved forward to Salamanca with 48,000 allied soldiers. By adroit manœuvring he brought to battle Marshal Marmont, Masséna's successor (22 July), but although the allies entered Madrid in August and laid siege to Burgos in September and October, once again Wellington was unable to remain in central Spain, for the French were concentrating their superior numbers against him. He conducted a difficult retreat to winter quarters around Ciudad Rodrigo.

In May 1813 Wellington marched out with a revitalized Anglo-Portuguese army of 81,000. The French, completely misunderstanding the military situation, made a desperate retreat northwards, and were routed by Wellington at Vittoria (21 June). During the following four months, Wellington cleared the ground up to the frontier in a series of battles against Soult collectively known as the Battles of the Pyrenees, and by the capture of the fortress of San Sebastian and Pampeluna. By October 1813 the allies, including a strong Spanish contingent, were fighting on French soil. Soult endeavoured to hold his own with scratch forces but was steadily driven back. Napoleon had already abdicated (6 April) and his confinement to Elba followed in early May.

With the cessation of the war, Wellington was created a duke (3 May 1814), the principal honour of many bestowed upon him by the British and allied governments, together with more material rewards. His army was dispersed but he remained as the official ambassador in Paris, later deputizing for Castlereagh at the Congress of Vienna.

Napoleon escaped from · Elba and returned to France in March 1815, raising units of his former armies as he progressed northwards. In April, therefore, Wellington left to take command of the British and Hanoverian troops in Belgium assembling as part of the allied measures to deal with this new turn of events. The rank of field marshal was conferred upon him and the command of the Dutch-Belgian troops, giving him over 93,000 at the outset. Co-operating with him was Gebhard Blücher's Prussian army of 120,000.

The speed of the advance of Napoleon's 124,000 men, however, caught both off their guard; they had imagined themselves numerically too strong to be in danger of an attack. Wellington compounded his error by assuming that the French would drive to cut his com-

munications with the coast, and his initial orders were intended to thwart that move. He was saved from the consequences of false dispositions by his subordinates, who acted on their own initiative to preserve what Napoleon was really seeking to cut, Wellington's lateral communications with Blücher. Thus the action of Quatre Bras was fought on 16 June by regiments thrown piecemeal into action against the French Marshal Ney, ordered to seize the vital crossroads, while Napoleon drove back the Prussians at Ligny. The stand at Quatre Bras permitted Wellington to recover his position and concentrate to the rear at Mont St. Jean where, on 18 June, he was joined by Blücher as Napoleon's army completed its own destruction against the British position on the ridge of Waterloo. This, the most famous if not the most brilliant of Wellington's victories, finally destroyed the power of Napoleon and of the French First Empire.

Subsequently he accompanied Castlereagh at the allied conference at Paris and was appointed to command the joint

army of occupation that remained in France until November 1818. He then returned to England, resuming his political life in 1819 in Lord Liverpool's cabinet as Master General of Ordnance. During the social and political unrest of the ensuing period, his influence was consistently and obstinately conservative, and he served without pleasure in offices for which he was temperamentally ill-fitted, purely to avert crises. Thus in 1822 he took over Castlereagh's work at the Congress of Verona after the latter's suicide, and in January 1828 he succeeded Goderich (see Robinson, Frederick) as Prime Minister in an attempt to hold together the disintegrating ministry of the Tories. Unfortunately his aggressive, uncompromising character and his own activities served to exacerbate rather than patch up the divisions. He would not serve under Canning, who was known to favour Catholic emancipation; in 1829, however, yielding to public pressure, Wellington himself carried the act of parliament that achieved this, without renouncing his personal belief that it would ultimately produce the destruction of English rule in Ireland. When similar pressure was mounted to secure a change in parliamentary representation, he refused to repeat his previous act of compromise and resigned in 1830, making way for a Whig ministry under Grey, which was to gain the credit for the measure.

After these experiences, Wellington declined to form a ministry on the resignation of Melbourne (see Lamb, William) in November 1834, but had to take on almost all the major government offices until the return from abroad of Peel (see Lives of the Victorian Age), under whom he served as Foreign Secretary until April 1835. He supported Peel again between 1841 and 1846 as minister without office, especially during the Corn

Law crisis that brought Peel down and split the party. Wellington remained loyal, although he did not share Peel's view of the necessity for some modification of the law to secure social harmony.

In 1842, at the age of seventy-three, Wellington was appointed commander in chief of the army. He held this office until his death ten years later. His most notable military activity in his old age was the operation to preserve public order in London during the Chartist demonstrations of 1848. Generally, his reluctance to admit change was not in the best interest of the army, as the Crimean War disclosed. Nevertheless, with his withdrawal from active politics he recovered all the personal popularity he had forfeited, and ended his life as a much-revered elder statesman. He died at Walmer Castle on 14 September 1852, and was buried with full heraldic and military honours in St. Paul's Cathedral.

A. Brett-James (ed.), *Wellington at War, 1794–1815* (1961).
Sir Arthur Bryant, *The Great Duke* (1971).
M. Glover, *Wellington as Military Commander* (1968).
M. E. Howard (ed.), *Wellington Studies* (1959).
E. Longford, *Wellington: Pillar of State* (1972).
E. Longford, *Wellington: The Years of the Sword* (1969).
S. P. G. Ward, *Wellington's Headquarters ... 1809–1814* (1957).
J. Weller, *Wellington at Waterloo* (1967).
J. Weller, *Wellington in India* (1972).
J. Weller, *Wellington in the Peninsula, 1808–14* (1962).

Portraits: oil, half-length, by Francisco da Goya, 1812: Apsley House, London; oil, half-length, by Robert Home, 1804–6: N.P.G.; oil, three-quarter length, by A. D'Orsay, 1845: N.P.G.; oil, three-quarter length, by J. Jackson, *c.* 1827: N.P.G.; oil, half-length, by J. Hoppner, 1796: Stratfield Saye House, Berks.; oil, three-quarter length, by J. Hoppner, *c.* 1798: Stratfield Saye House, Berks.

Wellesley, Richard Colley (1760–1842), 2nd Earl of Mornington and Marquis Wellesley; colonial administrator.

Richard Colley Wesley was born on 20

June 1760 at Dangan Castle, the eldest son of Garrett Wesley, 1st Earl of Mornington, and the elder brother of the future Duke of Wellington.

Wellesley – this form of the surname was settled on by the family in 1798 – was educated at Eton and Christ Church, Oxford, where he attained some distinction. The death of his father in 1781 made him the 2nd Earl of Mornington, with responsibility for the family estates and debts and for the education of his five younger brothers, thus precipitating him abruptly into public life at twenty-one. He entered the Irish House of Peers, and came into the English House of Commons in 1784 as M.P. for Bere Alston, sitting subsequently (1787) for Windsor and for Old Sarum (1796). Attachment to the Younger Pitt earned him rapid advancement. He was one of the original Knights of St. Patrick upon the foundation of the Order in 1783, was made a Junior Lord of the Treasury in 1786, and was appointed to the East India Company Board of Control in 1793. In 1798 Mornington replaced Cornwallis (q.v.) as Governor General of India.

Having thoroughly familiarized himself with Indian affairs, Mornington had already reached the conclusion that the official policy of non-intervention in native matters could not continue. It presupposed a measure of political stability and the absence of French intrigue, neither of which conditions still obtained. His intention was therefore to eradicate French influence entirely from the subcontinent, and to replace native rule wherever possible by British supremacy as the most efficacious means of promoting tranquillity. His method was to be the already familiar one of the subsidiary treaty, whereby a native prince accepted Company protection – military occupation of his territory – in return for money or land. Wittingly or not,

however, the prince was ultimately relinquishing his independence.

The immediate problem was the hostility of the ruler of Mysore, Tipu Sultan, who was bolstered by the French. After preventative negotiations with other princes likely to interfere, Mornington launched British troops into Mysore in February 1799; within three months Tipu had been killed and all Mysore was subdued. A truncated Mysore state was re-established under a former Hindu dynasty, and its detached territories were divided between the Company and the client Nizam of the state to the immediate north. British influence was now paramount in southern India, and Mornington was raised in the Irish peerage as Marquis Wellesley (2 December 1799).

A disputed succession in Tanjore (now Thanjavur) in south-east India allowed the Governor General to establish Company rule in the state in October 1799; within a few months similar action followed in Surat. Wellesley then turned his attention to the Carnatic, against whose Nawab he proceeded armed with

461

alleged proof of close intrigue with Tipu. Lacking a pretext for intervention, however flimsy, and failing to browbeat two successive rulers, it took him until July 1801 to manœuvre the Carnatic into negotiated dependence. The Nawab of Oudh proved even more elusive, and utlimately it was Henry Wellesley, the Marquis's brother, who journeyed to Lucknow to persuade him to accept the Company's presence in his domain on terms similar to the Nizam's clientage.

Richard Wellesley now approached the biggest prize, the Mahratta territory in central India, where a violent struggle for power was taking place among the princes. The Peshwa of Poona, Baji Rao II, was driven out by the chiefs of Indore and Gwalior, and by the Treaty of Bassein (31 December 1802) placed himself entirely in the Company's hands in order to accomplish his restoration. The Second Mahratta War ensued, and by 1804, with the rulers of Gwalior and Berar beaten in the field and compelled to sign the treaties of Surji Arjungaon and Deogaon respectively, the Company was in control of extensive areas in the Deccan, in Gujarat, and in Cuttack. Hokar, the chief of Indore, was not subdued. He had stood aside while his fellows went down, and in April 1804 he too was attacked. The force sent against him proved too small and was driven back, and the setback convinced the authorities in London that Wellesley's forward policies (about which they already had serious doubts) were unwise. Cornwallis was therefore sent out to relieve him, and he left India on 15 August 1805.

Soon after Wellesley's return in 1806 atempts were made to fasten various charges upon him in the House of Commons. They continued until 1808, but were unsuccessful. By contrast, Pitt warmly welcomed him, along with other leading statesmen, and in 1809 he resumed his public career as ambassador extraordinary to the Spanish junta, to procure cooperation for the British army then in Portugal under his brother. In December, he succeeded Earl Bathurst as Foreign Secretary in Perceval's administration, but had no confidence in his colleagues and did not trouble to conceal it, nor did he claim competence in his particular office for himself. In January 1812 he resigned, in spite of pressure from the Prince Regent to remain. In March he became a Knight of the Garter, and in June, after the assassination of Perceval, was himself invited by the Regent to form an administration. He failed, and remained out of office until 1820, although not out of active politics.

Catholic emancipation was one of the most important political issues of the day, largely because of the possible effects in Irish constituencies. Wellesley had long favoured the move, and his appointment as Lord Lieutenant of Ireland in 1821 was not without significance as a conciliatory gesture towards the Irish. Wellesley did his best to exhibit public impartiality, with little assistance from the sectarian Irish and some opposition from his colleagues in the English government. More actively, Wellesley's tenure of office is associated with a measure of success in the suppression of illegal agitation, attempts to purge the magistracy of the more blatantly prejudiced, and a determined policy of reconciliation. In particular, he met the famine of 1822 with an organized system of relief backed by a £300,000 grant procured from the home government and a public subscription of £500,000, to which he contributed £500 from his own limited means.

In 1828, following a political crisis at home, the Duke of Wellington formed an administration. His views on the Catholic question were at variance with those of his brother, who therefore felt obliged to resign. Initiative lay with O'Connell and the Catholic Association, which within a year compelled Wellington to grant the civil equality that Wellesley had always advocated. Wellesley returned to the office of Lord Lieutenant after the Reform Act (1832), having thrown in his lot with the Whigs under Grey (q.v.). His second incumbency, characterized by the same intention to bring Catholics fully into public life, was terminated by the break-up of the Whig administration in 1834. When Melbourne resumed office in the following year, Wellesley accepted the court appointment of Lord Chamberlain, but retired after a month.

A belated recognition of his services came from the East India Company in 1837, when it became known that his financial circumstances were again under serious pressure. A grant of £20,000 was voted and placed in the hands of Company trustees for his benefit. He died on 26 September 1842, and was buried in Eton College chapel.

W. H. Hutton, *The Marquess Wellesley* (1893).
P. E. Roberts, *India Under Wellesley* (1929).

Portraits: oil, quarter-length, by J. P. Davis, *c.* 1812: N.P.G.; water-colour, head, by J. P. Davis: N.P.G.; chalk, by Sir T. Lawrence: National Gallery of Ireland, Dublin.

Wellington, 1st Duke of (1769–1852), see Wellesley, Arthur.

Wesley, Charles (1707–88), evangelist, hymn-writer, and poet; associated with his brother John Wesley (q.v.) in the founding of Methodism in England.

Charles Wesley was born on 18 December 1707, the son of Samuel Wesley and Susanna Annesley, at Epworth, Lincolnshire, and educated at Westminster School, where his eldest brother Samuel was a master. He received an excellent grounding in the classics and exhibited an inclination towards poetry,

so that when he moved on to Christ Church, Oxford, in 1726, he tended to spend much of his spare time translating Greek and Latin works into English verse.

In 1728–9 Charles Wesley, influenced mainly by his brother John, underwent a deep religious experience. He began to keep a detailed journal similar to John's diary (started in 1724), and persuaded two friends, Robert Kirkham (the brother of John's friend Sally) and William Morgan, to join him in a regimen of religious study and devotion. The society thus formed soon earned the mocking titles of the 'Methodists' and the 'Holy Club'. When John Wesley began his residence as a fellow of Lincoln College in 1729 Charles gladly handed over the leadership of the society to him, and it was under John's guiding hand that the group expanded over the next five years.

Graduating in 1730, Charles acquired his M.A. three years later, in the meantime working as a tutor. In 1735 he left Oxford with John and agreed to accompany the latter in his Georgia mission, acting as Colonel James Oglethorpe's secretary. In September 1735, before setting sail with his brother, Charles was ordained priest in the expectation of aiding John's pastoral work.

This, however, he could not do. Almost from the time of their arrival in February 1736 Charles was affected by ill health. The futility of the missionary work also affected him spiritually and, being much more emotional than his brother, he rapidly succumbed to a despairing sense of failure. After a few months Oglethorpe sent him home to England with official dispatches, a release for which he was more than thankful. He fully intended to return to Georgia with George Whitefield (q.v.), but another bout of ill health put an end to the plan and Whitefield set sail alone at the end of 1737.

John returned to England early in 1738

and Charles shared in his conversion. On Whitsunday, 21 May, Charles found himself 'at peace with God', and the singing of his celebratory hymn, commencing 'Where shall my wond'ring soul begin?', was shared by John after the Aldersgate Street meeting of 24 May.

With the launching of the Methodist movement, Charles became one of his brother's staunchest assistants. More colourful in his sermons than was his brother, he was one of Methodism's ablest and most effective preachers. Bad health tended to confine Charles Wesley's itinerant preaching to the London–Bristol axis. In 1749 he married Sarah Gwynne; their marriage was happy and Sarah bore him eight children, of whom three survived, two sons and a daughter. 1749 also marked the beginning of his virtual retirement from active involvement with Methodist preaching, brought about by the estrangement between him and John Wesley concerning his brother's love for Grace Murray. It was Charles's interference, for what he felt to be the good of the movement, that broke up this relationship and drove John into the arms of Mary Vazeille and a marriage as bereft of happiness as Charles's was full.

Taking an essentially 'armchair' role in spreading the Methodist message, Charles Wesley was no less active nor any less effective. He devoted his life to writing. Some of his work was satirical verse of some quality, but the bulk of his output is his corpus of hymns. Of the 4,600 hymns published under the joint authorship of John and Charles Wesley, Charles penned at least 4,550. He translated the gospel into song and in devotional lyrics of unparalleled beauty and quality he expressed over and over again the great saving love of God. One of his finest works, usually sung to the inspiring Welsh tune 'Hyfrydol', is 'Love divine, all loves excelling'. Another, normally sung to the

tune 'Aberystwyth', is 'Jesu, Lover of my soul'. He also wrote 'Jesus Christ is ris'n today', 'Rejoice, the Lord is King', that best known of Christmas carols 'Hark! The Herald Angels sing', and many others.

Doctrinally closer than his brother to the established Church of England, Charles deplored the separatist elements that grew apace in Methodism during the late eighteenth century. Thus he was greatly saddened when in 1784 John took it upon himself to ordain Methodist preachers for America. But although the coming of separation was evident to him, Charles did not live to see it for, predeceasing his elder brother by three years, he died in London on 29 March 1788.

F. Baker, *Charles Wesley As Revealed in His Letters* (1948).

F. Baker, *Charles Wesley's Verse* (1964).

F. Baker (ed.), *Representative Verse of Charles Wesley* (1962).

G. H. Findlay, *Christ's Standard Bearer: a Study in the Hymns of Charles Wesley* (1956).

R. N. Flew, *The Hymns of Charles Wesley: a Study of Their Structure* (1953).

T. Jackson, *Life and Correspondence of Charles Wesley* (2 vols.; 1841).

B. Manning, *The Hymns of Wesley and Watts* (1942).

E. Myers, *Singer of a Thousand Songs: a Life of Charles Wesley* (New York, 1965).

J. E. Rattenbury, *The Evangelical Doctrines of Charles Wesley's Hymns* (1941).

Wesley, John (1703–91), evangelist; the founder of Methodism.

John Wesley was born at the rectory of Epworth, Lincolnshire, on 17 June 1703. His father, the learned clergyman and poet Samuel Wesley (1662–1735), had been a Dissenter but had returned to Anglicanism, and had come to Epworth as its rector in 1695. John's mother, the former Susanna Annesley, was the daughter of a Dissenting minister. From his father, he inherited a strict orthodoxy; from his mother, who took personal charge of his early education and brought him up strictly, he gained the earnestness of the Dissenter. His elder brother Samuel, subsequently a master at Westminster School and Blundell's School in Devon, devoted himself primarily to education. On the other hand, his younger brother Charles Wesley (q.v.) was to become inextricably linked with John in the founding of Methodism.

In 1709 the Epworth rectory burned down. The six-year-old Wesley was rescued from the blazing building and the image of 'a brand plucked out of the burning' became a stock one in his later religious crusade. In 1714 he entered Charterhouse as a foundationer and six years later became a scholar at Christ Church, Oxford, graduating in 1724. In that year, influenced by his parents and by a friend, Sally Kirkham, he decided to become a clergyman. He also began to compile a meticulous record and analysis of his every action, which subsequently formed the basis of his *Journal*.

By the time Wesley received his M.A. (1727) he had been an ordained deacon for two years and a fellow of Lincoln College, Oxford, for one. He acted as his father's curate at Wroot from 1727 to 1729, and in 1728 he was ordained priest.

In 1729 the twenty-six-year-old Wesley commenced his obligatory residence at Lincoln College, where he acted as tutor and where his brother Charles was an undergraduate. Charles had persuaded two other students to join him in the formation of a society for methodical religious study and devotion. The emphasis on methodical study ('method') had already given birth to the nickname 'Methodists'; they were also known as the 'Holy Club'.

Charles was happy to hand the leadership of this society over to John and a strict regimen was instituted, including the frequent taking of communion and fasting two days a week. The society also did social work in Oxford's prisons from 1730 onwards. The society grew and in 1734 benefited greatly from the joining of George Whitefield (q.v.) but it was not to survive for long after this. In 1735 the Wesleys left on the death of their father and the society fell apart.

John went to London in that year and encountered a former Oxford colleague, John Burton, who introduced him to Colonel James Oglethorpe, the colonial governor of Georgia. Prevailed upon by these two men, Wesley undertook to go to Georgia, in order both to minister to the spiritual needs of the colonists and to carry out missionary work among the native American Indians. As he set sail for America that year, accompanied by the recently ordained Charles, John was already acutely aware of an impending personal spiritual crisis. He was to preach the gospel in America, but was far from certain that he was going about his task the right way. Why this was he could not say, and his anguish was only exacerbated by an encounter during the Atlantic crossing with a group of Moravian emigrants. Their inner peace was evident; why could he not find that peace for himself?

The Wesleys arrived in Georgia on 6 February 1736, and John must have set about his task with misgivings. The whole mission was a disaster; Charles, affected by the climate and his own sense of failure, returned home at the end of spring 1736, while John lingered on for nearly two years. His work among the Indians was fruitless, and his reputation with the colonists who constituted his flock and were mainly Low Church in their opinions was badly damaged by his naïve emotional involvement with Sophia Hopkey, niece of the chief magistrate of Savannah. Sophia eventually married a man named Williams, and Wesley's refusal to admit her to Holy Communion

led to criticism that sealed the fate of his mission. He fled back to England in December 1737.

In London early in 1738 Wesley renewed his contact with the Moravians as a result of an encounter with Peter Böhler, who answered his unexpressed question of two years earlier by telling him that all he needed was faith. A reading of Martin Luther's commentary on St. Paul's Epistle to the Galatians, in which Luther stressed the biblical doctrine of justification by grace through faith alone, confirmed this idea and Wesley was convinced. This conviction was miraculously transformed into an intense religious experience. On 24 May 1738, at a meeting in Aldersgate Street, London, Wesley heard a reading of Luther's preface to Paul's Epistle to the Romans.

About a quarter before nine [Wesley wrote later], while he was describing the change which God works in the heart through faith in Christ, I felt my heart strangely warmed. I felt I did trust in Christ, Christ alone, for salvation; and an assurance was given me that he had taken away *my* sins, even *mine*, and saved *me* from the law of sin and death.

To proclaim salvation by faith, Wesley went anywhere and everywhere, but almost immediately encountered the stuffy formality of the established Church of England. Wesley, however, had at least one method of entry into the established system, within which he desperately wanted to work. Local religious societies were already in existence and, following the practice of the Moravians – he visited in Germany in 1738 – Wesley attempted to stimulate new spiritual vigour in these societies by introducing 'bands', small groups of people of the same status and condition prepared to share their innermost secrets and accept mutual criticism.

The system worked for a year, but the religious establishment sought only to repel Wesley's Methodists. In 1739 Wesley eventually followed Whitefield's example and took his message to the unchurched masses. His first open-air sermon was preached in Bristol before 3,000 people on Sunday, 1 April. It was the first of innumerable sermons that he preached up and down the country during his long career.

A religious society in London now sought him as their leader, and as other groups sprang up in Bristol and elsewhere, they were incorporated into an expanding network of Methodist societies. The Methodist societies, held together by a set of rules laid down by Wesley in 1743, sought at the very outset not to conflict at all with the Anglican Church. Meetings were scheduled at an hour not likely to hinder attendance at regular church services. Society meetings comprised Bible Study, prayers, informal preaching, and hymn-singing. The 'band' system operated within the Methodist societies for greater intimacy in devotion, but this subsequently gave way to a less rigid 'class' system for achieving the same effect. Societies were formed into circuits served by itinerant preachers, and a general tightening-up of the system was achieved by the inauguration of the annual Methodist Conferences, the first of which was held in 1744.

Methodism spread all over Britain and Ireland and its effects were especially marked in Wales, where, however, some doctrinal disagreements with the Wesleyan line were evident during the 1740s. The Methodist emphasis on salvation by faith became entangled with a Calvinistic tenet that those who had no faith were automatically damned. As his writings show, Wesley was seriously concerned to avoid allowing this dispute to introduce discord into the movement. But Wales, affected by a more general religious revival linked to Noncon-formity, soon formed its own brand of Calvinistic Methodism.

In 1749 Wesley fell in love with a widow named Grace Murray. His brother Charles, however, interfered in the relationship for what he conceived to be the good of the movement and John, broken-hearted, consented to Grace's marriage to one of his preachers, John Bennett. Without giving himself time to get over this, the second emotional upset in his life involving a woman, he married another widow, Mary Vazeille (1751). The marriage was never a success. Mary became jealous, Wesley stayed out on his preaching trips as much as possible, and a separation was eventually effected in 1776.

A logical, reasoned speaker rather than an impassioned orator, Wesley neverthe-less scored great successes on his preaching tours. One of his last acts was to undertake himself the ordination of Methodist preachers to take his message to America.

This he had hoped could have been done within the Anglican Church. Its failure to grant his request and his consequent enforced unilateral action saddened him deeply. He had hoped that Methodism could have been accommodated within the Church of England, but in the end he probably knew it could not. A formal separation, for which many of his adherents clamoured, was, however, staved off until 1836. John Wesley died in London, a man revered throughout the country, on 2 March 1791.

F. Baker, *John Wesley and the Church of England* (1970).

V. H. H. Green, *John Wesley* (1964).

V. H. H. Green, *Young Mr. Wesley* (1961).

H. Martin (ed.), *Selections from the Journal of John Wesley* (1959).

R. C. Monk, *John Wesley: His Puritan Heritage* (1966).

A. C. Outler, *John Wesley* (1970, 2nd ed.).

M. Schmidt, *John Wesley: A Theological Biography* (2 vols.; 1962–71).

C. W. Williams, *John Wesley's Theology Today* (New York, 1960).

Portraits: oil, three-quarter length, by N. Hone, 1766: N.P.G.; oil, half-length, by W. Hamilton, 1788: N.P.G.; oil, quarter-length, after Romney, 1789: N.P.G.; medallion, artist unknown: Manchester City Art Gallery.

West, Benjamin (1738–1820), historical and portrait painter.

Benjamin West was born on 10 October 1738 at Springfield, Penn-sylvania, the tenth and youngest child of John West, a Buckinghamshire man, and Sarah Pearson, the Quaker child of a companion of William Penn.

West showed early promise. Allegedly taught to draw by a Cherokee Indian, he painted his first portrait of his sleeping infant niece when he was six. At nine, West was moved to tears by a landscape by William Williams, a Philadelphian artist. He declared his intention of becoming a painter and went at eighteen to Philadel-phia, where he painted inn-signs and portraits.

West became one of the first Americans to study art in Italy, travelling there in 1760. Befriended by the Scot Gavin Hamilton, he was shown the cities most famous for their art treasures, and in 1761 painted a portrait of Thomas Robinson (later Lord Grantham), the fame of which reached America. He stayed in Italy three years before travelling to England, intending a brief visit but staying for fifty-seven years.

West's reputation had preceded him. On his arrival he met Burke, Reynolds, Dr. Johnson (qq.v.), and other important people. He became a member of the Incorporated Society of Artists in 1765, and sent to America for his bride Elizabeth Shewell, who crossed the Atlantic with West's father. They were married in September 1765.

In 1766 West exhibited several paintings, but *Agrippina landing at Brindisium with the Ashes of Germanicus* had the greatest success. This was a commission from Robert Hay Drummond, Archbishop of York, who later tried to raise £3,000 to allow West to abandon portraiture in favour of historical painting. Failing this, Drummond introduced West to King George III, who was impressed by the Agrippina picture and suggested *The Departure of Regulus from Rome* as a subject for a commissioned picture. From this date until he was declared permanently insane, George III supported West with commissions and a salary. He chose him to paint murals at Windsor and to be one of the four planners and an original member of the Royal Academy, and in 1772 West was made Historical Painter to the King, and in 1790 Surveyor of the Royal Pictures.

In 1767 West painted his most famous picture, *The Death of Wolfe*. Reynolds and Dr. Drummond visited him in his studio to try to dissuade him from painting it in modern dress. 'The event to be com-

memorated happened in 1759,' West replied. 'The same truth which gives law to the historian should rule the painter.' When it was finished Reynolds said to Drummond, 'West has conquered. This picture will occasion a revolution in art.' West became the popular hero of 1767, and was acclaimed as 'another Raphael'.

West painted many more pictures with sacred and classical subjects and several from modern history, though he never quite repeated this success. He was also an astute collector. In 1785 he bought Titian's *Death of Actaeon* for £20 and later refused £4,000 for it. On the death of Reynolds in 1792 he was elected President of the Royal Academy, a post held almost continuously until his death. In 1805 he painted *Christ healing the sick in the Temple*, a copy of which was sold in Philadelphia to help build the Quaker hospital.

In 1814 West's wife died and his own health began to fail. He died at his house in Great Newman Street on 11 March 1820. He lay in state at the Academy and was buried at St. Paul's. He was a kindly, generous, though vain old man, always willing to help young painters, especially Americans, and happiest surrounded by his own large pictures. He painted over 400 works and was regarded as the founder of historical painting in England, although his reputation has much declined today and he has no pictures in the National Gallery.

G. Evans, *Benjamin West and the Taste of His Times* (Carbondale, Ill., 1959).

H. E. Jackson, *Benjamin West, His Life and Work* (Philadelphia, 1900).

Works:

Some of West's paintings are lost, and his work is not well represented in Great Britain. In the United States his works may be seen in the following:

Independence Hall, Philadelphia, Pa.
Wadsworth Atheneum, Hartford, Conn.
Boston Museum of Fine Art, Boston, Mass.
Pennsylvania Academy of Fine Art, Philadelphia.
Yale Gallery.

Wheatstone, Sir Charles (1802–75), scientist and inventor, see *Lives of the Victorian Age*.

Whitbread, Samuel (1758–1815), politician and advocate of reform.

Whitbread was born at Cardington, Bedfordshire, in 1758, the only son of Samuel Whitbread, a member of a prominent local Noncomformist family, and the prosperous owner of the Whitbread brewery in London. He was educated at Eton and Christ Church, Oxford, whence he was transferred to St. John's College, Cambridge, graduating in 1784. An educational tour through Europe in the company of a professional historian was followed by three years' work in the family brewery, but in 1789, the year of his marriage to the daughter of Sir Charles (later Earl) Grey (q.v.), Whitbread's political sympathies were aroused and he began to assert his own interests.

Elected as M.P. for Bedford in 1790, Whitbread made enthusiastic attacks on various aspects of government policy which quickly attracted attention. Working closely with Fox (q.v.) in matters of foreign policy, he became convinced of the need for lasting peace with France. His radical concern for the welfare of agricultural workers, who were suffering acute hardships due to the economic depression, was demonstrated in his proposal for a bill that would enable magistrates to establish minimum legal wages, but this was opposed by William Pitt the Younger (q.v.) and defeated.

In 1805 a commission of inquiry into administrative abuses at the naval department criticized the irregular conduct of its treasurer, Lord Melville. Whitbread made a powerful speech in the House of Commons detailing all the alleged abuses, and after a select committee had recommended the impeachment of Melville, Whitbread was appointed to manage it. After a three-month trial, Melville was acquitted on all charges (June 1806). Although he was criticized for mismanaging the affair, Whitbread gained a fair measure of popularity.

The most ambitious demonstration of Whitbread's concern for social welfare occurred in 1807 in his elaborate proposal for a new poor law bill. The many reforms envisaged within the terms of this bill included the establishment of a free education system, the regularization of poor relief rates throughout all the counties, and a complicated system for discrimination between the deserving and the undeserving, but although some of these proposals were later included in other bills, Whitbread lacked the knowledge and administrative skills to make his own bill practicable. In 1808, and against the advice of many of his colleagues, he moved a resolution calling for peace negotiations with France; this controversial proposal led to a major division of opinion among the Whigs, and Whitbread lost much of the support of his party.

After the destruction by fire of the Drury Lane Theatre in 1809 Whitbread involved himself energetically in the organization of its rebuilding; the theatre was eventually re-opened in 1812, and as a result of his friendship with Sheridan and his innovatory proposal that the theatre should give performances throughout the year, Whitbread's connection with it remained unbroken until his death.

From 1812 until her departure from England in 1814 Whitbread acted as the self-appointed parliamentary champion of the Princess of Wales, Caroline of Brunswick. In 1815, continuing his consistent advocacy of peace with France, he maintained that the outcome of the rivalry between Napoleon and the Bourbon dynasty for control of France was irrelevant to the essential need for the maintenance of peace, but by now his voice was virtually alone. On 6 July 1815, deeply depressed, Whitbread committed suicide in his London house in Dover Street. He was survived by his wife and four children.

Roger Fulford, *Samuel Whitbread 1764–1814: A Study in Opposition* (1967).

White, Gilbert (1720–93), naturalist; author of *The Natural History of Selborne*.

Gilbert White was born at Selborne, near Alton, Hampshire, on 18 July 1720, the eldest of eleven children. Coming from an established local family, he was educated at Basingstoke Grammar School and between 1740 and 1743 attended Oriel College, Oxford, subsequently becoming a fellow there. While at Oxford he met John Mulso, who became his lifelong friend and whose letters provide most of the information about White's early years. Like White, Mulso became a country parson and their continuous correspondence was supplemented by many reciprocal visits.

In 1743 White took his bachelor's degree, and received his M.A. in 1746. The following year he took deacon's orders and became curate to his uncle, who was rector of Swarraton and Bradley near Alresford. He travelled to Swarraton from Oxford, and then from Selborne, but by 1751, when he acted as curate in charge for the ailing vicar of Selborne, it is evident that however his work might take him abroad to neighbouring parishes, Selborne was established as his permanent home.

In 1752 White became proctor to the university and was later appointed dean. In 1763 he inherited The Wakes, the house which had been the family home since 1730 and to which he had returned during vacations and between curacies. The duties of Oxford and of his curacies kept him considerably occupied, but he found time to make a variety of changes to the garden and grounds of The Wakes, creating paths, vistas, laid walks, and melon and cucumber beds, and conducting experiments in growing plants.

White was a prodigious traveller, earning the nickname 'hussar parson' by being so frequently on horseback. He never married, and spent much time studying, closely reading Ray, Linnaeus, and Hudson. He became prominent in the Royal Society and the Society of Antiquaries. In 1777, following his papers on hirundines, he was made a Fellow of the Royal Society. He was an extremely acute observer, and though he was wrong in his suppositions about swallows' winter behaviour, he rarely erred in describing what he saw, as for instance in establishing that martins feed their young on the wing. He was responsible for the addition of the harvest mouse and the great bat to the list of British fauna, and distinguished between three kinds of warbler that look similar but have different songs.

His love and (more unusually) systematic observation of natural history began at an early age. In 1737 he was already keeping notes on bird behaviour, and began a regular journal in 1751 (published in 1795 as *The Calendar of Flora*). A special naturalists' journal was designed by his friend Daines Barrington for more rigorous daily observation, and this was kept from 1769 until thirteen days before White died, and was also published.

It was Barrington who first suggested to White that he should write a history of his parish. The idea slowly took hold: 'Out of all my journals,' White wrote,

I think I might collect matter enough and such a series of incidents as might pretty well comprehend the natural history of this district. . . . To these might be added some circumstances of the country – its most curious plants, its few antiquities – all which might be moulded together into a work. . . .

Eventually the book took shape, formed mainly out of sixty-six 'letters' to Barrington and forty-four to Thomas Pennant. Many of these were genuine epistles, somewhat edited; others were specially written for the purpose of the book. Benjamin White, Gilbert's brother, was the first publisher of *The Natural History of Selborne* (in 1788). The work was a set of lively observations and anecdotes, written without sentimentality or pretentiousness, yet full of White's feeling for the place and a geniality and appreciation of everyday life that is rarely captured. The book proved to have a remarkable and continuous appeal for general as well as specialist readers.

The intelligent geniality that was the keynote both of Gilbert White's writing and of his life prevailed until his death, which occurred on 26 June 1793.

J. Fisher (ed.), *The Natural History of Selborne* (1947).
R. Holt-White (ed.), *The Life and Letters of Gilbert White of Selborne* (2 vols.; 1901: reprinted 1970).
R. M. Lockley, *Gilbert White* (1954).
E. A. Martin, *Bibliography of Gilbert White* (1934).

Whitefield, George (1714–70), evangelist.

George Whitefield was born on 16 December 1714 in the Bell Inn, Gloucester, of which his father, Thomas Whitefield, was the proprietor. His father died when Whitefield was two, and his mother was left with the thankless task of running the inn and bringing up seven children. George left school at fifteen, ostensibly to help his mother, but he began to lead a somewhat dissolute life. A chance arose for him to re-enter grammar school, and from there he made a successful application for admission as servitor to Pembroke College, Oxford (1732).

His stay at Oxford provided Whitefield with the opportunity to develop that religious enthusiasm which, as an emotional youth, he was inclined to feel. He formed an acquaintance with Charles Wesley (q.v.), and became a leading member of the 'Holy Club'. Such was his zeal for good works and fasting that he fell ill. During this illness he experienced a revelation of God so profound that he determined to share it with others. After a brief spell in Gloucester, where he converted some of his friends and helped to form a religious society, he returned to Oxford in March 1736, and despite his youth, was accepted for ordination. On 20 June 1736 in Gloucester Cathedral he was accepted to deacon's orders.

At twenty-two, he began to earn a reputation as a preacher of great passion and in August 1737 published his first sermon. This, and later ones, proved so popular that the leaders of the Anglican Church felt obliged to denounce him in their paper the *Weekly Miscellany* as an associate of Dissenters and an avaricious charlatan.

Whitefield, however, was unabashed and decided to visit America. On 30 December 1737 he embarked for Georgia. Although his first stay lasted only four months, it did stimulate an interest in religious education which was to stay with him for the rest of his life. In order to raise more funds and obtain ordination as a priest he returned to England on 9 September 1738.

On his return Whitefield encountered much hostility and was forced to preach in the open air. The Church continued to attack him for his lack of intellectual strength and his scurrilous interpretation of the scriptures, but he still drew large crowds, and his theatrical style of preaching increased his popularity.

On 14 August 1739 Whitefield set sail again for America, and there began a life of itinerant preaching. He travelled as far north as Philadelphia and New York. His intention was to raise sufficient funds from his sermonizing to build an orphanage in Savannah, Georgia; by 1741 he had established this and christened it Bethseda. In 1741 he left again for England, and in November married Elizabeth James, a Welsh widow ten years his senior. During this spell in England he became a rigid Calvinist, finally breaking with Wesleyan Methodism.

Accompanied by his wife, Whitefield left England for America again in 1744. Until 1748 he made numerous evangelical journeys and earned a sufficient amount of money to buy himself a plantation and slaves in South Carolina, to be used as a separate source of income for his orphanage. Oddly enough, he felt slavery was justified on biblical grounds.

The remainder of Whitefield's life was spent travelling to and from America on evangelical missions. In 1769 he made his final parting from England. The following year, after a particularly hectic preaching tour of New England, his health broke and he died in Newburyport, Mass., on 29 September 1770, from an attack of asthma.

A. D. Belden, *George Whitefield, the Awakener* (1953, 2nd rev. ed.).

A. R. Buckland (ed.), *Selected Sermons of George Whitefield* (1904).

S. O. Henry, *George Whitefield: Wayfaring Witness* (New York, 1957).

I. Murray (ed.), *Journals of George Whitefield* (1962, rev. ed.).

Joseph Tracey, *Great Awakening: A History of the Revival of Religion in the Time of Edwards and Whitefield* (1969).

L. Tyerman, *Life of the Rev. George Whitefield* (2 vols.; 1876).

Portrait: oil, half-length, by J. Woolaston: N.P.G.

Wilberforce, William (1759–1833),

philanthropist, politician, and opponent of slavery.

William Wilberforce was born in Hull on 24 August 1759, the only son of a prosperous Yorkshire merchant family. He was educated first at Hull grammar school. On his father's death in 1768 he went to live with his uncle at Wimbledon where, to his mother's alarm, he became a Methodist. Hastily fetched back to Yorkshire, he went to school at Pocklington until 1776 when, Methodism eradicated, he went to St. John's College, Cambridge. On leaving, in 1780, he was elected M.P. for Hull and formed a lifelong friendship with William Pitt the Younger (q.v.), also a new M.P.

In parliament Wilberforce spoke first on matters concerning Hull, but went on to oppose the American war and was favoured by both Rockingham and Shelburne. Though he loathed the idea of party, he always supported Pitt and Shelburne whilst maintaining his independence. He patronized theatres and clubs, and lived and entertained at Wimbledon.

In 1783 he accompanied Pitt to France, where they stayed at Rheims and Paris. Returning to England, Wilberforce joined Pitt in attacking Fox's India Bill – defeated with the King's help – and supported Pitt's new government through the crisis of early 1784. Defeating his social superiors, he was elected in April for the largest constituency, Yorkshire.

Later in 1784 Wilberforce set off on a long continental tour with his family and his old Hull schoolmaster, Isaac Milner; during this occurred his profoundly important conversion. When, on his return home, he took the slave-trader-turned-evangelist Newton as his mentor, Pitt received the news kindly, and their friendship continued undiminished. Wilberforce's anxious family, fearing that a Bible-thumping Methodist was coming home to Yorkshire, were relieved when he arrived with his old virtues intact–even intensified: a friend commented, 'If this is madness, I hope he will bite us all.'

Back in London, Wilberforce founded the Proclamation Society in 1786, with the object of combating vice, and devoted himself to it with extraordinary zeal. He was supported by Hannah More, with whom he founded the Mendip schools. In 1787 Wilberforce agreed to take up in parliament the cause of abolishing slavery. Before this could happen, however, a serious disgestive illness forced him to go to Bath for a cure that could ultimately be effected only by opium, to which he became addicted. Thus it was not until 1789 that he rose to speak, with authority and eloquence, against the slave trade. A decision, however, was deferred for evidence to be gathered, delaying tactics being henceforth the major weapon of slavers. Spurred on by a moving letter from John Wesley, and despite the loss of public support occasioned by the French Revolution and the 1791 slave revolt in St. Domingue, Wilberforce worked unceasingly both in and out of parliament. When his Bill was defeated in 1791, Horace Walpole wrote with disgust that 'commerce clinked its purse'. The French War caused a painful, albeit temporary, rift between Wilberforce and Pitt, and almost killed the Abolitionist movement, whose only success was the establishment of the free colony of Sierra Leone for slaves freed in England and returned to Africa. In 1794 Wilberforce introduced another abolitionist bill, but again it was defeated.

In 1797 Wilberforce published a successful religious work entitled *A*

Practical View of the Prevailing Religious System of Professed Christians in the Higher and Middle Classes of this Country Contrasted with Real Christianity. He also became involved with a group of committed Christians soon to be known as the 'Clapham Sect'. In May of this eventful year he was married to Barbara Spooner.

The next years were filled with parliamentary business, including the annual re-introduction and defeat of the Abolition Bill, which enjoyed Pitt's constant support until his temporary fall from office in 1801. Wilberforce was instrumental in founding the *Christian Observer*, the British and Foreign Bible Society, the Church Missionary Society, and sixty-six other benevolent organizations. Eventually in 1804 his Abolition Bill was carried in the Commons, but delayed in the Lords. Pitt's death in 1806 was a great personal blow to Wilberforce; he never again had so close a political friend. However, the new administration provided so favourable a balance, particularly in the Lords, that on 25 March

1807 the Bill, after years of struggle, received the royal assent.

Thereafter Wilberforce's moral stature was unique and immense, and his fame international. He espoused many causes, always taking a strictly moral and independent view, which often amounted to obsessiveness and bigotry. After the assassination of Perceval (1812), he decided with regret that his duty to his growing children and his own falling health must force him to resign his Yorkshire seat, and sat instead for Bramber for the rest of his parliamentary career. Despite his extreme dislike of the religion, he supported Catholic emancipation on principle. Later he campaigned with vigour and success to admit missionaries to India.

Whilst Brougham's Slave Trade Felony Act of 1811 effectively enforced Britain's abolition, and Venezuela, Sweden, and Chile were also persuaded to abolish slavery, France, Spain, and Portugal were still making handsome profits from the trade. Through the African Institution, Wilberforce worked hard to achieve international abolition. By 1820 this was achieved, but only Britain properly enforced the law, and it became clear that the total emancipation of existing slaves would have to be Wilberforce's next step. Meanwhile, in the bleak aftermath of the French war, he rather surprisingly supported the Corn Laws, the 1817 suspension of Habeas Corpus, the Six Acts, and the government attacks on prominent radicals. This, and his opposition to an inquiry into Peterloo, was probably because he considered revolution such a real and disastrous threat and a menace to Christianity. This attitude was also reflected much later when towards the end of his life he referred to the 1832 Reform Act as 'being too radical'. Meanwhile, however, he supported the Factory Acts and the Chimney Sweep Bills, while opposing the savage Game Laws.

In 1820–1 Wilberforce attempted unsuccessfully to form a compromise solution in the dispute between George IV and Queen Caroline. Caroline's subsequent trial in the Lords caused him much distress.

Despite declining health, Wilberforce now stepped up his campaign against slavery. He helped the King of Haiti, ex-slave Henri Christophe, by supplying missionaries, teachers, and even ploughmen to the island, and later welcomed Christophe's widow to his house. He chose the M.P. Thomas Buxton to help and succeed him in the emancipation battle; wrote again, publicly, to the Tsar; and began work on his manifesto, published in 1823, the year in which parliamentary battle was resumed. There was an immediate West Indian outcry: Wilberforce spoke again in 1824, but collapsed with inflammation of the lungs and was unwillingly forced to retire from his seat in the Commons.

Accepting the Chiltern Hundreds, he and his family moved to Mill Hill, where he lived happily. His very poor eyesight curtailed his hitherto prolific correspondence, but his hatred of slavery and his generosity to his dependants were as great as ever. In 1831 his eldest son William went spectacularly bankrupt, and Wilberforce and his wife lived thereafter with their married clergyman sons, almost penniless but refusing countless offers of help. Wilberforce chaired another meeting of the Anti-Slavery Society in 1830 to a resounding ovation, and made his last speech at Maidstone in 1833. The emancipation of slaves was formally secured just before he died in London on 29 July 1833. He was buried in Westminster Abbey.

F. K. Brown, *Fathers of the Victorians: The Age of Wilberforce* (1961).

R. Coupland, *Wilberforce: a Narrative* (1923).

F. Joseph Klingberg, *The Anti-Slavery Movement in England* (New Haven, 1926).

A. Mackenzie-Grieve, *The Last Years of the English Slave Trade, Liverpool, 1750–1807* (1941).

R. I. Wilberforce and S. Wilberforce, *The Life of William Wilberforce* (5 vols.; 1838).

Portraits: oil, half-length, by T. Lawrence, 1828: N.P.G.; oil, quarter-length, by J. Russell, 1770: N.P.G.; marble, by Samuel Joseph: York City Art Gallery.

Wilkes, John (1727–97), radical politician and agitator.

John Wilkes was born on 17 October 1727 in St. John's Square, Clerkenwell, the second son of Israel Wilkes, a thriving malt distiller, and Sarah, daughter of John Heaton of Hoxton. He attended various schools, was tutored by a Presbyterian minister, and finally entered Leyden University in 1744. After spending two years travelling abroad, he returned to England. On 23 May 1747 he married Mary Meade, who brought him a comfortable fortune; but after a few years a separation was arranged, Wilkes retaining her Aylesbury estate and his only legitimate child, Mary (born in 1750).

Wilkes became a respected figure in Buckinghamshire – a magistrate, a colonel of the militia, and High Sheriff. In 1754 he successfully contested the seat for Berwick-on-Tweed. At no small expense he became M.P. for Aylesbury in 1757, and secured his seat at the election in March 1761, hoping to recover his fortunes by political advancement. In 1758 he became a member of the circle centred on Francis Dashwood (q.v.) that met at Medmenham Abbey, which embraced many prominent artistic and political figures. Through William Pitt the Elder and his brother-in-law Lord Temple, whose family dominated Buckinghamshire affairs, Wilkes made a certain mark. He was a poor orator, but could write well,

particularly invective, which skill he placed at the disposal of his patrons in their campaign against the Earl of Bute. In 1762 Wilkes, backed by Temple's money, founded an inflammatory political newspaper, *The North Briton*, which played upon English hatred for the Scots, and contained libellous innuendos concerning Bute and George III's mother. The anti-ministerial feeling that the campaign aroused led to Bute's retirement in April 1763. He was also partly responsible for the demise of Dashwood's private club following his malicious article which 'exposed' it.

On 23 April of that year, in No. 45 of *The North Briton*, Wilkes made a scurrilous attack upon ministerial statements in the King's speech, even insinuating that George had been induced to countenance a deliberate lie. The King and court, advised that the article was seditious libel, proceeded against Wilkes, who was eventually seized after the issue of a general warrant, since the paper bore only the printers' names. Wilkes was committed to the Tower, but following Lord Temple's application for a writ of habeas corpus, was released after a week on the grounds of parliamentary privilege.

Temple now moved to exploit the discomfiture of the ministry. With his money, Wilkes and others who had been arrested instituted actions for trespass against the Secretary of State, the Earl of Halifax, and his underlings, and as a result damages were awarded, and general warrants became illegal. However, the new Secretary of State, Lord Sandwich (see Montagu, John), a former Medmenham friend, determined to oust Wilkes from parliament and render him liable to prosecution. Accordingly when the new parliamentary session opened on 15 November 1763, Sandwich read out in the Lords the indecent *Essay on Woman* and

government failed to arrest him, and in March 1768 he was elected for Middlesex. He now surrendered himself to the King's Bench and was arrested. His outlawry was reversed by Lord Mansfield on a trivial technical point, but convictions for libel dating from 1764 were affirmed and, waiving his privilege, Wilkes submitted to sentences totalling two years in jail and fines of £1,000.

Wilkes, however, availing himself of the lax rules in the King's Bench Prison, then embarked on a campaign against the government to secure a pardon and restitution. Outside the prison, mob riots professing sympathy with his cause were almost continuous. He appealed by writ of error to the Lords, presented a petition to the Commons, and then published an inflammatory article concerning the government's use of military force against the rioters. Early in 1769 both writ and petition were dismissed, the article was voted libellous by both Houses, and Wilkes was expelled again from the Commons in February.

He was re-elected for Middlesex, but the Common annulled both this and two subsequent returns. Petitions denouncing these proceedings as unconstitutional were presented to the King and parliament, and Wilkes's cause was championed by 'Junius' (q.v.). A 'Society for the Defence of the Bill of Rights', led by Horne Tooke (q.v.), was formed early in 1769 to uphold Wilkes's cause and pay his debts; this became a political rallying point for all manner of disaffected causes. Wilkes had succeeded in turning his own misfortunes into a constitutional campaign of apparent importance.

Upon his release in 1770 he found himself a prosperous man, his liabilities of £17,000 having been discharged by the Society. He was elected an Alderman by the City of London, and had something like a private political party with funds to

its appendix containing an obscene paraphrase of the '*Veni Creator Spiritus*', which had been secured from Wilkes's private press. The Lords voted the essay a libel and a breach of privilege, while the Commons overwhelmingly voted 'No. 45' a seditious libel, subsequently resolving that the latter offence was not covered by privilege.

While recovering from a stomach wound following a duel with Samuel Martin, a friend of Bute, Wilkes left the country to visit his daughter in Paris. The medical certificate of ill-health that he dispatched to excuse his failure to appear before the House of Commons was considered unauthenticated, and he was expelled from the House on 19 January 1764. Subsequently the Lords declared him an outlaw. He settled in Paris, hoping vainly that a change of ministry would secure his reinstatement.

Having lived a wholly dissolute existence in Paris, he returned to England in December 1767, determined to stake all on his re-election, posing as a lover of liberty and a victim of injustice. The which he laid exclusive claim. For the next four years he was active in a variety of vexed issues, including the American struggle, but his reinstatement in the Commons was his real goal. In 1774 he was elected Lord Mayor and was re-elected to parliament, taking his seat for Middlesex without opposition on 2 December. The Bill of Rights Society put up a number of candidates, and Wilkes re-entered parliament with his own group of twelve M.P.s – the 'Twelve Apostles'.

Wilkes supported the programme of economic reform of the Rockingham Whigs, but since he had by now acquired a reputation for insincerity, his popularity waned, and he declined to fight the election of 1790. In the intervening years he made an attempt to bring in a bill for the redistribution of seats, opposed the American war vigorously, but con-spicuously upheld the law during the Gordon riots of June 1780. He achieved his private ambition when the resolution of 1769 against him was erased from the Commons' journals in 1782. He expressed horror at the French Revolution. He was even reconciled with George III.

Wilkes, whose charm, wit, good manners, and constancy in friendship were often remarked, died insolvent, at his house in Grosvenor Square, London, on 26 December 1797, and was buried in Grosvenor Chapel. His most important achievements are the extension of liberty to the Press and the suppression of general warrants.

J. Almon (ed.), *The Correspondence of John Wilkes* (5 vols.; 1805).
I. R. Christie, *Wilkes, Wyvill, and Reform; The Parliamentary Reform Movement in British Politics, 1760–1785* (1962).
George Nobbe, *The North Briton: A Study in Political Propaganda* (1939).
Raymond Postgate, *That Devil Wilkes* (1956, rev. ed.).
G. E. F. Rudé, *Wilkes and Liberty: A Social Study of 1763 to 1774* (1962).
C. P. Chenevix Trench, *Portrait of a Patriot: A Biography of John Wilkes* (1962).

Portraits: pencil, full-length, by R. Earlom: N.P.G.; oil, three-quarter length, by R. E. Pine: Ministry of the Environment, London; engraving, by an unknown artist after engraving by W. Hogarth, 1763: R.T.H.

Wilkie, Sir David (1785–1841), Scottish painter.

David Wilkie was born on 18 November 1785 at Cults, Fifeshire, the son of the local minister. As a child he decorated his nursery with his own cartoons and drew many portraits of the visitors to his father's manse – he later wrote of himself that he 'could draw before he could read, and paint before he could spell' – and he was encouraged in these early artistic activities by the local schools at Pittessie and Kettle. By the time he was fourteen his father had resigned himself to the fact that his son was unlikely to make a career in the church, and in November 1799 the young Wilkie was dispatched to Edinburgh with an introductory letter to the secretary of the Trustees' Academy of Design.

For five years Wilkie conscientiously studied the techniques of painting, returning to Cults in 1804 to paint his first important composition, *Pittessie Fair*, which he sold for £25. A brief and unsuccessful attempt to make a living by selling portraits in Aberdeen was fol-lowed in May 1805 by Wilkie's departure to London.

The following year Wilkie's con-fidence was confirmed by the spectacular success of his first painting to be exhibited at the Royal Academy, *The Village Politicians*. Sir George Beaumont im-mediately commissioned another work, *The Blind Fiddler*, and further commis-sions from members of the nobility followed in rapid succession. In 1811 Wilkie was elected an Associate of the Royal Academy, and two years later he became a full academician. In 1814 he travelled to Paris with his colleague Benjamin Haydon (q.v.), and in 1817 he travelled to the Netherlands. On a visit to Scotland in 1817 Wilkie painted Sir Walter Scott and his entire family in peasant costume; the popular success of his *Chelsea Pensioners Reading the Gazette of the Battle of Waterloo* in 1822 was so great that barriers had to be erected to protect the painting from its admirers.

The style of Wilkie's painting during this first phase of his career was strongly influenced by the seventeenth-century Dutch and Flemish realists, and his popularity can be explained by the direct appeal of his anecdotal subject matter; during the years 1825 to 1828, however, Wilkie was travelling constantly on the Continent, and his discovery of the works of such painters as Velasquez and Murillo had a revolutionary effect on the style of his own subsequent painting. These travels were occasioned by ill-health and personal grief at the deaths of his mother (who had been living with him in London since his father's death in 1812) and of two of his brothers. In 1825 Wilkie set out for Italy, where he spent lengthy periods at Florence, Rome, and Naples; from here he went to Switzerland, and then travelled south again to Spain before eventually returning to London in June 1828. His new paintings, often on a larger scale than his previous work and treating historical rather than commonplace subjects, were much criticized by both friends and the general public, although some twentieth-century critics have seen in them the first signs of a new romantic style and have especially praised their use of colour.

In 1830 Wilkie was appointed Painter-in-Ordinary to George IV; six years later he was knighted, and in 1837 he built for himself a large studio at Kensington. On the accession of Queen Victoria in the same year Wilkie was commissioned to paint *The First Council of Queen Victoria*.

Despite this continued prosperity, Wilkie's health continued to be delicate, and in 1840, at the age of fifty-five, he was advised again to seek the sun. He arrived in Jerusalem in February 1841, but did not stay long. On 1 June 1841, having just left Gibraltar on the final stage of his journey home, Wilkie died at sea. The most famous memorial to him is probably the painting by J. M. W. Turner (q.v.) entitled *Peace – Burial at Sea of Sir David Wilkie*.

A. Cunningham, *The Life of Sir David Wilkie* (1843).
E. Pinnington, *Sir David Wilkie and the Scots School of Painters* (1900).

Works in:
Royal Collection.
National Gallery.
National Portrait Gallery.
Tate Gallery.
Wallace Collection.
Wellington Museum.

Portraits: self-portrait, oil on panel, half-length, 1813: N.P.G.; pencil, quarter-length, by B. R. Haydon, 1816: N.P.G.; water-colour, quarter-length, by W. H. Hunt: N.P.G.; water-colour, quarter-length, by J. Jackson: N.P.G.

Wilkinson, John (1728–1808), iron-master and industrial inventor.

John Wilkinson was born in a market cart at Little Clifton, Cumberland, in 1728, the son of Isaac Wilkinson, a farmer and part-time worker at an iron furnace at Backbarrow, Lancashire. Educated in Kendal, he went to work at Barrow with his father, and together they produced and patented a laundress's box-iron. At twenty, John moved to Staffordshire, where he built the first blast furnace, the 'Bradley furnace', a crucial development introducing the use of mineral coal to replace the scarce and expensive charcoal in the smelting of iron-ore. He then returned to his father, who had moved to Bersham, Denbighshire, and they made the first plant for accurately boring cylinders. This was vital for the construction of Watt's 'Soho engine' (1755), the first example of which was, in turn, used to power the bellows at Wilkinson's new and larger works at Broseley, near Bridgnorth. Wilkinson's work soon surpassed that of all his rivals, especially in accuracy, and his boring machine was used for mortars, howitzers, and other artillery. Later innovations included a heavy water-driven hammer able to strike three hundred blows a minute, and the iron barge, first launched on the Severn in 1787. In 1779 he cast the pieces for the first iron bridge, over the Severn at Madeley, and in 1790 patented a method of making lead pipes which was to be of major importance in the construction of the Paris waterworks. He built the first large steam-engine in France, and was probably the first user of the hot-air blast in iron foundries.

Wilkinson was a rich and impressive figure locally. His first wife died at twenty-three; his second, a wealthy woman in her own right, bore him no children, and the legal claims of his three illegitimate sons to his huge fortune revealed his strange domestic arrangements. He was a High Sheriff of Denbighshire in 1799 and issued his own currency, which had a wide circulation. Though spasmodically generous, he was not popular and was ridiculed in ballads as an atheistic disciple of Tom Paine. He died at Bradley, Staffordshire, on 14 July 1808, and was buried at Castle Head, near Ulverston, in an iron coffin of his own construction.

T. S. Ashton, *Iron and Steel in the Industrial Revolution* (1951).

W. H. Chaloner, *People and Industries* (1963).

H. W. Dickinson, *John Wilkinson* (1914).

Portrait: oil, quarter-length, by L. F. Abbott: N.P.G.

William IV (1765–1837), King of Great Britain and Ireland (1830–7).

William Henry, the third son of King George III and Queen Charlotte, was born on 21 August 1765 at Buckingham House. He shared the strict and secluded family upbringing of the royal children but, to his father's concern, was too much influenced by the Prince of Wales (the future George IV). This may have been a factor in George III's decision to place Prince William in the Royal Navy. Thus, without being consulted, he was in 1799 placed as a midshipman aboard the *Prince George* (98 guns) under Robert Digby. With this ship William saw action at the Battle of Cape St. Vincent (1780). He later sailed with Digby to America, where he was fêted by New York loyalists and for a time served in Hood's squadron. He met Nelson (q.v.) when the fleet called in at Jamaica.

At the conclusion of the American war William returned to England, where his eagerness to plunge into London society prompted the King to dispatch him to Hanover, allegedly to round off his studies. He remained there until the spring of 1785, when George reluctantly allowed him home.

In 1785 William, now a lieutenant, joined the 40-gun frigate *Hebe* at Portsmouth for a cruise in British waters. At Kirkwall he encountered a jobless shipmate from the *Prince George* and bestowed upon him a pension of £40 a year for as long as he needed it – a not uncharacteristic act of spontaneous generosity which was occasionally repeated. While staying briefly at Portsmouth during the commission, he paid serious attention to the daughter of his host, Sir Henry Martin, and it was thought in the interests of everybody for him to be packed off to America again. His acquiescence was obtained by promoting him post-captain and making him commander of the 28-gun frigate *Pegasus* (1786).

His ship was directed to the West Indies station, and came under Nelson's command. He was a thoroughly competent commander, but ashore he indulged freely in fleshly pleasures, while afloat he was a martinet. The *Pegasus* returned to Plymouth in 1787 in mysterious circumstances, one suggested explanation being that she was recalled in order to disentangle the Prince from an affair with a Mrs. Wentworth in Quebec. William was bidden by the King to remain at Plymouth. After another abortive affair, this time with a local merchant's daughter, King George had William shipped out to the West Indies again, and it was only as a result of a timely bout of instability in his father that William was able to come home on the authority of his brother, the Prince of Wales.

On 16 May 1788 William was made Duke of Clarence, which in effect meant the end of his naval career, for a royal duke could not be kept in a junior command, and it was clear that he lacked the talent for a senior one. Thus, after only one more 'appearance' at sea – during the Nootka

Sound crisis of 1789 – this hearty and boorish Prince gave up the navy to establish a residence at Roehampton, and in the early summer of 1790 settled there in domestic contentment with the actress Mrs. Dorothy Jordan (q.v.). Dorothy was accepted by the royal family and society as his wife, and continued her stage career, in the intervals of which she bore him ten children, the last in 1807. The official FitzClarences were not his only children; it is said that he acknowledged paternity of a son born in Hanover, and there are suggestions of others. With Mrs. Jordan, however, he achieved emotional stability and his relations with her were, under the circumstances, above reproach for many years.

In January 1797 he was appointed Ranger of Bushey Park, a sinecure which included the use of Bushey House. Here he dabbled in Whig politics and ran up debts. He was made an admiral in 1798, but the Admiralty succeeded in finding no command for him, even in a navy expanded for the war against revolutionary France. His public life was therefore confined to speeches in the House of Lords in defence of the slave trade.

In 1811 the expense of providing for his children induced William to press his attentions upon a young heiress, Catherine Tylney-Long. Confident of success, he disembarrassed himself of Mrs. Jordan, and when Miss Tylney-Long saved herself by an engagement with the nephew of the Duke of Wellington, there was little purpose in restoring the broken union. Mrs. Jordan drove a hard bargain: maintenance for herself and her children, including those by earlier fathers, custody of the four youngest FitzClarence girls, and her carriage and house. It was not enough; her stage career collapsed, her debts increased, and she fled from her creditors to France and died in obscurity.

In 1813, at his own request, William visited the British army campaigning in the Low Countries under Sir Thomas Graham. In 1814 he escorted the returning King Louis XVIII across the Channel and, flying his admiral's flag aboard the *Impregnable*, conveyed the Emperor of Russia and the King of Prussia to England for their state visit.

The death in childbirth in 1817 of Princess Charlotte, the Prince Regent's daughter, unexpectedly endowed the Duke with some importance in the line of succession. Nearly all the other legitimate descendants of George III had now died out, and it became imperative to provide Clarence with a legal wife. His own attention was drawn towards another heiress, a Miss Wyckham of Oxfordshire, but on 13 July 1818 he married the twenty-five-year-old Princess Adelaide of Saxe-Meiningen in a double ceremony shared with Edward, Duke of Kent and Princess Victoria of Saxe-Coburg. The Duke of Clarence and his wife achieved a good measure of domestic felicity but failed to provide the crown with an heir. Finally the death in 1827 of his brother Frederick, the Duke of York, following that of George III, left the Duke of Clarence as the heir to the throne. At York's funeral Clarence was observed to be in indecently high spirits.

The death of Liverpool (see Jenkinson, Robert Banks) in the same year as York brought back George Canning (q.v.), who sought to strengthen his position in a hostile political atmosphere by making Clarence Lord High Admiral. The Duke determined to be more than just the ceremonial head of the navy – although he discharged that aspect of his duties with considerable pleasure and expensive display. His position remained unchanged when Wellington replaced the dead Canning in August 1827, except that Wellington did not need a royal buttress.

Clarence embarrassed the ministry by his enthusiastic reception of the news of the somewhat 'untoward' British naval victory over the Turks at Navarino (20 October 1827). He quarrelled with his council, particularly its senior member Sir George Cockburn, over details of naval administration. In August 1828, after receiving a royal ultimatum, the Duke resigned, but in his short tenure of real office he had forced through several genuine, if minor, reforms in the teeth of opposition from very conservative administrators.

On the death of George IV, Clarence succeeded to the throne as William IV on 26 June 1830, and the exuberance that he showed at his deceased brother's funeral became the keynote of the new reign. His hearty and disconcerting informality did much to revive the fallen popularity of the monarchy, even if it did little to attract respect. Politically, he saw his role as that of arch-conciliator between ministers and opposition, with a preference for compromises and coalitions. He was prepared to devote energy and time to business, unlike the late King, but had no larger intention than to support his ministers of the day.

In November 1830, he accepted the fall of the second Wellington ministry and the advent of Grey's Whigs with equanimity, and he was prepared to judge on its merits their pledged move to reform the House of Commons, provided that the number of members was not increased and the duration of parliaments was not shortened. At the outset, however, he suggested to Grey that the influence of the House of Commons had steadily increased, and that the long-term threat to the balance of the constitution lay in that direction. Time has not proved him wrong in that respect. He also foresaw the probability of an early clash between the two Houses over the measure itself.

Above all else, he was reluctant to sanction elections at a time of apparent social and political unrest. His hopes, therefore, rested on a moderate bill that the Tories might with honour accept.

His sense of moderation was in the event swamped by the politicians' usual ability to manufacture crises to serve the ends of personal power. But he continued to give his ministers correct constitutional support, dissolving parliament at their request in April 1831 after the bill's defeat in committee, even though this generated turbulence in the country and precipitated the confrontation with the Lords that he had feared. He then worked for compromise, and failing to find it, in the end reluctantly expressed himself willing to create enough Whig peers to swamp the Tory majority in the upper House. The threat sufficed, and on 4 June 1832 the First Reform Bill passed its third reading in the Lords. Such had been the pressure put upon his sincere instinct for political unity in preference to party manœuvres that he refused to play out the last scene devised for his ministers' personal glorification – royal support for their bill demonstrated by the royal signature. Instead, he sent commissioners to fulfil this duty on his behalf. This inaugurated a permanent constitutional custom, and resulted in his being branded in English liberal mythology, incorrectly, as an opponent of the Reform Act.

The King became disenchanted with his Whig ministers' incompetence and internal discord. Grey failed to hold them together, and Melbourne (see Lamb, William), his successor, fared no better. In November 1834 the latter informed William gloomily that the loss of Althorp to the House of Lords had robbed the ministry of its mainstay in the Commons, thus apparently confirming the King's conviction that the Whigs had lost the ability to govern. Technically, his over-prompt intimation to Melbourne that his appointment was at an end counts as a dismissal, but it was not an act of personal caprice. The sequel, however, proved extremely damaging to the principle of free exercise of the royal prerogative. The Whigs in opposition rediscovered their unity, Peel's Tory ministry found it impossible to govern against a hostile majority, and the situation was not altered by granting them a dissolution in the hope of improving their strength in the Commons. In April 1835 William at last yielded and allowed Peel to stand down, Melbourne resuming office in circumstances which were bound to be interpreted as a defeat and humiliation of the King himself. This series of events has remained a constitutional landmark: the end of the eighteenth century's view of the Prime Minister's office as dependent principally upon the monarch, and the beginning of the modern view of it as essentially derived from the party balance in the Commons.

In his remaining years, William continued to make full use of his right to be consulted on affairs of state but his main preoccupation, publicly voiced, seemed to be to live long enough to prevent his sister-in-law, the Duchess of Kent, acquiring regent's powers during the minority of her daughter, the Princess Victoria, now the heir to the throne. On 24 May 1837 Victoria came of age. On 20 June, William died.

A. Aspinall (ed.), *Mrs. Jordan and Her Family* (1951).
P. Fitzgerald, *The Life and Times of William IV* (2 vols.; 1884).
P. Ziegler, *King William IV* (1971).

Portraits: water-colour, half-length, by unknown artist: N.P.G.; pencil, half-length, by G. Hayter: N.P.G.; oil, full-length, by M. A. Shee, c. 1800: N.P.G.; oil, by G. Hayter: Walker Art Gallery, Liverpool; oil, by D. Wilkie: Apsley House, London.

William Augustus (1721–65), Duke of Cumberland; military commander in the War of the Austrian Succession and the Seven Years War, nicknamed 'Butcher Cumberland'.

William Augustus was born on 15 April 1721, the third (but second surviving) son of Caroline of Ansbach and George II, who was then Prince of Wales. In 1726 William Augustus was created Duke of Cumberland.

The young Duke was educated by Jenkyn Thomas, who found him an apt pupil. John Gay's well-known *Fables* were 'invented to amuse' him in 1725. He was his parents' favourite and they hoped he would become Lord High Admiral. He was educated for the navy, but his own preference was for the army, and he was in the end allowed to follow this inclination.

Promotion, as might be expected for a prince of the blood, was rapid. He joined the Coldstream Guards as a colonel, transferring in 1742 to the 1st Guards and becoming major general. After the Battle of Dettingen in 1743, in which he displayed great bravery and was wounded in the calf, he was made lieutenant general, and later that year he was appointed captain general of all British land forces and commander in chief of British, Hanoverian, Dutch, and Austrian troops. In 1739 he had been awarded £15,000 annual income from the civil list, and in 1742, at his majority, he took his seat in the House of Lords.

Cumberland was again commended for his bravery, and what Horace Walpole called his 'intrepidity' was remarked upon, when in trying to relieve Tournai he was defeated by Marshal Saxe at the Battle of Fontenoy in 1745. He was recalled from Flanders later that year to oppose the invasion of England by the Young Pretender, Prince Charles Edward (q.v.). He followed the Jacobite army in retreat, eventually catching up with it

after being given the slip a number of times, but he failed to cut it off as was his plan. He returned to London in January 1746, but after the defeat of General Hawley at Falkirk, went north again, and on 16 April met the Young Pretender's forces at the Battle of Culloden. Having stopped at Nairn on the previous day to celebrate his twenty-fifth birthday, Cumberland made contact with the exhausted army of Highlanders early the following morning. After an initial artillery duel, the Jacobites charged to escape the enemy's fire, but in the ensuing fighting the superior numbers and training of Cumberland's men gained the upper hand; the Jacobite right flank, whose attack had actually been effective, was soon overwhelmed, and the centre and left retreated with heavy losses. Cumberland's forces got round behind the second Jacobite line, which had meanwhile been resting, and caused great slaughter. With about 1,000 killed, the Scots broke and fled. Cumberland lost only fifty men.

For three months after his victory the Duke supervised the pursuit and the punishment of the rebels. Convinced that 'mild measures won't do', he sent foot and horse into the Highlands, burning homes and crops and shooting suspects. He spoke later of 'the good we have done' in 'a little bloodletting' being scarcely adequate; in fact, his drastic measures had dealt a fatal blow to the clan system.

On his return to London Cumberland was received with rejoicing, formally thanked by parliament for his part in Culloden, and granted an income of £25,000 in addition to his income from the civil list. Hyde Park Gate was renamed Cumberland Gate, and Handel's *Judas Maccabæus* was written in his honour, as well as a quantity of verse, including Collins's 'How Sleep the Brave'. He was given the freedom of the city of York and made Chancellor of St. Andrews University. As stories and invective began to percolate down from the north, however, the acclaim for Cumberland waned and the nickname 'Butcher' was attached to his and stuck; a number of 'anti-Butcher' jokes began to circulate with the encouragement of George II's eldest son, the Prince of Wales, who was no friend of the Duke's.

In 1747 Cumberland travelled again to Flanders to command the allies, and was defeated once again by Marshal Saxe at Lauffeld. On his return to England he was viewed with suspicion, and apart from trying to reform the army with himself as focal point, he kept to himself at Windsor, making improvements to the park and breeding horses. In 1751 the Prince of Wales died but Cumberland, much to his mortification, was not made Regent.

At the outbreak of the Seven Years War the Duke was sent to the defence of Hanover, where he was defeated by Marshal d'Estrées at the Battle of Hastenbeck in 1757. He then signed the convention of Kloster-Zeven, which disbanded much of his force. George II repudiated this convention and charged Cumberland openly with bringing 'ruin and disgrace' on himself and Britain. Cumberland resigned from his regiment and retired to Windsor. He was in very bad health: his old leg wound had developed abscesses; he was very fat, almost blind, and asthmatic; and in 1760 he suffered a stroke.

George II died in 1760, and George III was well enough disposed towards Cumberland to encourage him to take some part in politics. Cumberland was violently anti-Bute, and did much to assist Bute's fall from power in 1763.

The Duke of Cumberland died suddenly, on 31 October 1765, it is thought from a blood clot in the brain. He was buried with military honours at Westminster Abbey on 9 November. Walpole wrote of him that he had been 'proud and unforgiving, fond of war for its own sake. He despised money, fame and politics, loved gaming, women, and his own favourites, yet had not one sociable virtue.'

A. N. C. MacLachlan, *William Augustus, Duke of Cumberland* (1876).

E. Charteris, *William Augustus . . . His Early Life and Times* (1913).

E. Charteris, *William Augustus . . . and the Seven Years War* (1925).

A. and H. Tayler, *1745 and After* (1938).

John Prebble, *Culloden* (1961).

Portraits: oil, full-length, after Reynolds, c. 1758–60: N.P.G.; oil, full-length, studio of D. Morier, c. 1748–9: N.P.G.; oil, full-length, by C. Jervas, c. 1728: N.P.G.; oil, half-length, by Joshua Reynolds: Courtauld Institute, London; engraving, by W. P. Benoist after Reynolds, 1758.

Wilmington, Earl (?1673–1743), see Compton, Spencer.

Windham, William (1750–1810), statesman.

William Windham was born in London on 3 May 1750, the son of an ancient Norfolk family. His father, Colonel William Windham, was a well-educated and distinguished military man.

Having been educated at Eton, Glasgow University, and University College, Oxford, young Windham spent some time travelling in Switzerland and Italy. His easy manner in society enabled him to become acquainted with Burke and Johnson, and he became the constant companion of Johnson through the latter's declining days. It was Burke who developed his interest in political matters.

Windham's first public speech, on 28 January 1778, was in opposition to the raising of money towards the cost of the American war. In 1783 he was appointed Chief Secretary to Northington, Lord Lieutenant of Ireland in the Portland administration, but resigned the post in August of that year partly for reasons of health and partly because of his opposition to the policy of granting Irish posts to Englishmen. Elected M.P. for Norwich in April 1784, he voted steadily with the Whig opposition, although he was opposed to their espousal of the cause of parliamentary reform. He consistently adopted a liberal attitude to matters of religion, however, and in February 1791 supported a Catholic relief bill for England. With the outbreak of the French Revolution he became a committed anti-Jacobin, and in 1792–3 was one of the most ardent supporters of the government's repressive legislation. In July 1794 he was persuaded by Burke to switch his allegiance to Pitt, and he became Secretary at War with a seat in the cabinet. A great deal was achieved during his term of office, including measures to raise soldiers' pay and establish pensions. He resigned with Pitt in 1801, although he had by no means always agreed with Pitt's war policy, and felt that more could have been done in terms of military support to assist the royalists in France.

Windham strongly opposed the peace of Amiens (1802) and collaborated with Cobbett (q.v.), whom he admired, in the foundation of the *Political Register*, which later harassed the Addington administration. Transferring to the pocket borough of St. Mawes in Cornwall, he continued to oppose Addington's government after the renewal of the war (1802). He declined to join Pitt in 1804 because of the King's objection to the admission of Fox to the ministry. In Grenville's 'Ministry of All the Talents' he accepted the war and colonial office, and in April 1806 introduced a series of measures designed to improve the condition of the military forces. He was dismissed with the rest of the ministry in March 1807.

Windham was severely critical of the policies of his successor at the War Office, Castlereagh, and opposed the Copenhagen expedition of 1807, the Local Militia Bill of 1808, and the Scheldt expedition of 1810. His main concern was to support the war in Spain and Portugal, and he urged its more vigorous prosecution. He died at his house in Pall Mall on 4 June 1810 from the after-effects of an operation for the removal of a tumour from his hip.

R. W. Ketton-Cremer, *The Early Life and Diaries of William Windham* (1930).

L. Melville (ed.), *The Windham Papers: the Life and Correspondence of the Rt. Hon. William Windham, 1750–1810* (1913).

Portraits: oil, half-length, by T. Lawrence, 1803: N.P.G.; oil, half-length, by J. Reynolds, 1788: N.P.G.

Witherspoon, John (1723–94), Scottish-born Presbyterian theologian and educationist who settled in America and was one of the signatories of the Declaration of Independence.

John Witherspoon was born on 5 February 1723 in the parish of Yester near

Edinburgh, the eldest son of James Witherspoon, the local minister. Educated at Haddington grammar school and Edinburgh University, Witherspoon took his M.A. in 1739 and his divinity degree in 1743. After his ordination in April 1744, he took over the ministry at Beath, and soon established a reputation as a preacher. His fame spread even further when in June 1753 he published his gently satirical *Ecclesiastical Characteristics*. He allied himself totally with the Popular Party in the church who, despite their name, were a conservative group aiming at purity of doctrine and rigorous application of the old standards as against the more leisured and humanistic approach of the moderates. Other works followed including, in 1756, an *Essay* which clearly states the fundamentals of the Calvinist doctrine. Shortly afterwards he was so enraged by the performance of a play written by a churchman that he wrote his *Serious Enquiry into the Nature and Effects of the Stage*, and drew the conclusion that the theatre aroused violent passions incompatible with the godly life. In June 1757 he became minister of the town church at Paisley, but ran into trouble in 1762 when he published a discourse rebuking by name some young men who had blasphemed against the Lord's Supper. In consequence he was prosecuted for libel and ordered to pay damages of £150. Much sympathy was shown him, and in June 1764 the University of St. Andrews bestowed on him the honorary degree of Doctor of Divinity.

Witherspoon continued with a steady output of sermons and satires, and his obvious talents recommended him for jobs that carried greater influence and importance. Eventually he was granted the post of Principal of Princeton College, New Jersey, and in July 1768 he sailed for America.

Once there, he set about revolutionizing the College syllabus and introduced many new features, including an extension of the study of mathematics and the addition of Hebrew and French to the curriculum (1772). He lectured in history, philosophy, and divinity, and was keen to impress upon students his conviction that the purpose of an education was to fit a man for public service and develop in him a sense of community purpose and humility. Courses that inclined to speculative philosophy and the realms of pure knowledge were excluded, since Witherspoon deemed these of no use to society.

During the American War he supported the colonists, becoming an able propagandist for the cause of liberty. As a result of his sermon 'Dominion of Providence over the Passions of Men' (1776), he was chosen as a delegate to the Continental Congress in June. From this date he served in Congress, with some intermissions, until November 1782. He sat on innumerable committees, the most important of which were the Board of War and the Committee on Foreign Affairs. His great force of personality made him a powerful debater, and he expressed his views on virtually every subject from foreign policy to economic matters. He was especially opposed to the issue of paper money. Of those who signed the Declaration of Independence on 4 July 1776, Witherspoon was the only clergyman.

His later years (from 1782 onwards) were spent endeavouring to restore the College at Princeton to its pre-war status. His public life was still active, however, and in 1783 and 1789 he returned to the state legislature. From 1785 to 1789 much of his time was devoted to reorganizing the Presbyterian church along national lines. He became Moderator of the first General Assembly meeting of this body in

1789. On 30 May 1791, at the age of sixty-eight, he married for the second time. His bride, Ann Dill, many years his junior, bore him two daughters, one of whom died in infancy. For the last two years of his life he was blind. He died on his farm on 15 November 1794. Witherspoon's *Works* were published in nine volumes from 1804 to 1815.

V. L. Collins, *President Witherspoon: A Biography* (2 vols.; Princeton, 1925).

D. W. Woods, *John Witherspoon* (New York, 1906).

Woffington, Margaret (Peg)

(?1714–60), Irish actress who became one of the most striking theatrical personalities of the eighteenth century.

Born in Dublin, Peg Woffington, as she was to be known, was the elder of the two daughters of a bricklayer who died in 1720, leaving his family in debt, so that they were forced to sell watercress on the streets to survive. At ten she was employed by Madame Violante, a famous tightrope walker, to act in her children's company, where she played Polly in *The Beggar's Opera*; from there she progressed to the Smock Alley Theatre, where she played a variety of roles, including old women, Ophelia, and her most famous 'breeches' part, Sir Harry Wildair in Farquhar's *The Constant Couple*.

Coming to England in 1740, she was engaged to appear at Covent Garden, where her Irish successes were repeated and she played a leading role in every production of the season, including Silvia in Farquhar's *The Recruiting Officer*, Cherry in the same author's *The Beaux' Stratagem*, and Cordelia to Garrick's Lear. She then returned to Dublin, but was soon back in London, acting this time at Drury Lane, and living with Garrick. The lovers would pay the expenses of the establishment in alternate months, and friends were much better treated when it was Peg's turn than during the rather miserly

Garrick's month. Though Garrick went so far as to buy her a wedding ring, they never married, and eventually separated.

Despite the often violent jealousy and rivalry of other leading actresses such as Kitty Clive, Hannah Pritchard, and George Anne Bellamy, Peg kept her public enchanted at Drury Lane for many years. She was well known for her prodigious memory and versatility as well as for her beauty and talent. In 1749 she returned to Covent Garden for three years, and then took a holiday in Paris, where she met and studied with Marie Dumesnil, the great French tragedienne, who helped her to forget the rigid stylized teaching of her early admirer Colley Cibber and, by a more naturalistic style of delivery, to hide a harshness of tone which had bothered her in tragic roles.

For the next three seasons Peg appeared in Dublin where, with forty performances of four stock plays, she earned the management an unprecedented £4,000, commanding the salary of £800 for herself. Then the Smock Alley Theatre was destroyed by a mob after an unwise production of a Voltaire play had enraged the political sensibilities of the Dublin audience, and Thomas Sheridan (father of the playwright) decided against staying to manage a rebuilt theatre and travelled with Peg to London, where she was re-engaged at Covent Garden. She acted several of her most famous parts in the next three seasons, and continued to create new roles, including Angelica in Congreve's *Love for Love*. In the 1756 season, while playing Roxana to George Anne Bellamy's Statira in Nathaniel Lee's *Alexander*, 'Mrs. Woffington', it was reported, 'became so angry that she drove her rival off the stage and stabbed her, almost in sight of the audience.'

Then on 3 May 1757, whilst playing Rosalind in *As You Like It*, she collapsed and was taken off in the fifth act. She returned for the Epilogue, but screamed with terror as her voice broke and she staggered to the wings. She never acted again, and was indeed given up for dead, but she recovered and lingered on for another three years under the care and protection of Colonel Caesar, a friend of very long standing who was rumoured to have married her secretly. She carried out several charitable works in her last years, including endowing almshouses at Teddington, where she had owned a villa, and she died at Westminster on 28 March 1760. She was buried at Teddington, where a wall plaque firmly declares her to have died a spinster.

Peg Woffington was said to have been the handsomest woman ever to appear on the stage (though Horace Walpole dismissed her dark and vivacious beauty as 'rough Irish charm'). She had magnetism, wit, and a conscientious attitude to her work very rare at that time. She had countless lovers, openly preferring the company of men to women who, she said, talked of 'nothing but silks and scandals'. She was a generous, good-hearted woman who gave her mother a handsome lifelong pension and educated her sister Polly expensively in Paris, facilitating her excellent marriage to Captain Cholmondely, a nephew of Horace Walpole. On her deathbed she even asked her old rival George Anne Bellamy to visit her, and they were reconciled.

Janet Dunbar, *Peg Woffington and Her World* (1968).
J. C. Lucey, *Lovely Peggy, the Life and Times of Margaret Woffington* (1952).

Portrait: oil, half-length, by unknown artist, *c.* 1758: N.P.G.

Wolfe, James (1727–59), military commander, hero of the siege of Quebec.

James Wolfe was born on 2 January 1727 at Westerham, Kent, the elder son of Lieutenant-Colonel (later General) Edward Wolfe. His earlier years were marred by ill-health, but he was nevertheless determined to be a soldier and obtained by his father's influence a commission in the Marines (1741) and an appointment as ensign in the 12th Foot (1742). With this regiment he served in the Low Countries (1742–6) and enjoyed the experience, his enthusiasm elevating him to the position of acting adjutant. In that capacity he was actively engaged in the Battle of Dettingen (27 June 1743), where his energy was noted by the Duke of Cumberland (see William Augustus) and commended to King George II, who was himself present on the field. Wolfe was accordingly confirmed in his appointment and promoted lieutenant.

The army withdrew to Flanders for the winter, and Wolfe was given a captaincy in the 4th Regiment, Barrell's. After being made a brigade major in June 1745 he went back to Britain with Cumberland to quell the second Jacobite rebellion, being made aide-de-camp to General Hawley. Thus he was present when Hawley's badly-handled force was mauled by the clansmen at Falkirk (17 January 1746), and also at Culloden (16 April), where his general commanded the cavalry on the government left flank. Barrell's Regiment remained in Scotland, but at the end of the year Wolfe returned to Flanders in Cumberland's entourage. He was wounded at the Battle of Lauffeld (2 July 1747) and was formally thanked by the Duke for his gallantry.

With the conclusion of the War of the Austrian Succession in 1748, Wolfe resumed regimental duty, being promoted major and appointed to the 20th Regiment, commanded by Sackville (q.v.) (1749), then in the Scottish garrison. In the prolonged absence of the commanding officer, Wolfe discharged that office and was officially promoted lieutenant colonel in the following year. He remained with the 20th in its various stations in Britain until 1757 and made a lasting impression upon it by his serious concern for its efficiency and the welfare of its men, a characteristic so rare among contemporary commanders as to attract attention. His youth, however, prevented him from receiving further advancement even when the Seven Years War began in 1756.

Eventually he was offered the post of quartermaster general in Ireland (March 1757), but before he could take it up he was given a more active appointment – quartermaster general and chief of staff to an expedition designed to attack Roche-fort (July). Wolfe drew up the plan of attack but his superiors lacked the resolution to carry it out successfully, for which they had later to face an inquiry. But Wolfe received his long-awaited promotion to colonel (October 1757), followed quickly by further promotion to brigadier's rank and an assignment to another expedition. Major-General Amherst (q.v.) was in command, together with Admiral Boscawen (q.v.), and their objective was the capture of Louisbourg, which would give an entrance to the St. Lawrence river and Canada itself.

Wolfe had some share in the plan of attack, but was not responsible for the landing across well-defended beaches. Nevertheless he personally led the men ashore, and his energetic direction was equally valuable in the siege which followed. The town capitulated on 27 July, and despite Wolfe's urging, Amherst allowed the campaign season to close without making a move towards Quebec. Wolfe therefore returned on leave to England, where he was at once offered the command of the projected attack at Quebec and promoted major general.

He sailed once more in February 1759, but because of shortage of official funds and the dilatoriness of colleagues, he did not get his force of 9,000 clear of

Louisbourg until June. The next month saw his troops established in camps around the Quebec basin while he grappled with the problems of assaulting a city built on heights – the famous Heights of Abraham – the guns of which commanded the river, where prevailing westerly winds and adverse tidal conditions severely handicapped free movement. His attempt in July to establish a bridgehead below the city was a costly failure: the defenders were too active and were not intimidated by the bombardment of the city, which continued throughout August. A bout of fever compelled Wolfe to leave operations to his brigadiers for a time, but by 30 August he had recovered, and the wind had shifted in his favour.

Wolfe perceived that his real object must be to destroy the French army under the Marquis de Montcalm, and thereby gain the city. His purpose was therefore to lure the enemy to give battle in the open, a purpose hampered by the need to get the fleet away from the river before the onset of winter.

489

During the nights of 5 and 6 September troops were transferred by ship up the river, forcing Montcalm to detach some of his own troops in anticipation of a possible landing above Quebec. Wolfe was now poised to strike downstream at a moment and point of his own choosing. Personal reconnaissance disclosed a practicable way up the steep cliff two miles above the city. During the early hours of 13 September the troops were ferried down in boats and scaled the slopes of the Heights of Abraham in the darkness, Wolfe among them and an assault group of picked light-infantrymen leading the way. A firm lodgment having been obtained, the main body of the army was brought across the river, and by 9.30 a.m. Wolfe's 800-strong force was drawn up on the plain facing Quebec. With his defences turned, Montcalm was compelled to concentrate against him at once to save the city, and advanced with a hastily-assembled line of 3,500 men. It broke under the musket-fire from the well-ordered British army, losing about one-third of its number in casualties. Montcalm himself was mortally wounded. Wolfe was also hit, living barely long enough to hear of his victory, and command passed to one of his brigadiers, Townshend, who failed to exploit the initial success. Consequently, the broken French regiments escaped and Quebec was not surrendered until 18 September. Nevertheless the action had been decisive in opening Canada to British conquest. Wolfe's body was taken back to England and buried in Greenwich.

A. Doughty and G. W. Parmelee, *The Siege of Quebec and the Battle of the Plains of Abraham* (6 vols.; 1901).

R. Reilly, *The Rest to Fortune: the Life of Major-General James Wolfe* (1960).

R. Reilly, *Wolfe of Quebec* (1973).

C. P. Stacey, *Quebec, 1759: the Siege and the Battle* (Toronto, 1959).

Portraits: *The Death of Wolfe*, oil, by Benjamin West, 1771: Kensington Palace; oil, by Sir Thomas Gainsborough: Manchester City Art Gallery; sketch, quarter-length, by G. Townshend: McCord Museum, Montreal; oil, half-length, attributed to J. S. C. Schaak: N.P.G.; bronze and plaster casts of bust by J. Witton, c. 1759: N.P.G.

Wollaston, William Hyde (1766–1828), physician and natural scientist.

Born at East Dereham, Norfolk, on 6 August 1766, Wollaston was educated at Charterhouse and then at Gonville and Caius College, Cambridge, where he was made a senior fellow in 1787. On gaining his medical degree in 1789 he commenced work as a physician in Huntingdon, later moving to Bury St. Edmunds. In March 1795 he became a Fellow of the Royal College of Physicians, and two years later moved his practice to London. Although successful in his job, he was a sensitive man who allowed himself to become rather personally involved with the problems of his patients and this, combined with a growing devotion to his research in physics, chemistry, and botany, led him to retire from his practice in 1800.

In 1801 Wollaston began a series of experiments. Within five years he had discovered a process whereby pure platinum could be made malleable for chemical research and manufacture. This discovery he kept secret until the last years of his life, and it earned him £30,000 in all. It enabled him to spend the rest of his life in original research and he made great advances in every field he studied. While researching into platinum he discovered the elements palladium and rhodium in crude platinum, and amongst his other important discoveries were the isolation of the amino-acid cystine, the development of a goniometer for measuring crystal angles, and the noting of the dark (Fraunhofer) lines in the solar spectrum. He was one of the first to accept Dalton's atomic theory of 1807, and he predicted the need to develop a three-dimensional concept of the relative arrangement of

work the mineral wollastonite was named after him. He died in London on 22 December 1828.

E. Ferguson, *Journal of Chemical Education* (1941). D. Macdonald, *A History of Platinum* (1960).

Portrait: pencil, three-quarter length, by J. Jackson, *c.* 1827: N.P.G.

Wollstonecraft, Mary (1759–97), writer and feminist.

Mary Wollstonecraft was born on 27 April 1759 into a prosperous Spitalfields family. She was the second of the five children of a restless, feckless father, Edward John Wollstonecraft, and his Irish wife, Elizabeth Dixon. Her childhood was spent in following her father's fortunes all round England, not returning to the London suburb of Walworth until she was eighteen. Her formal education had been sporadic and scanty, but the family had stayed long enough in Beverley for her to make a close friend of Jane Arden, the first recipient of her vivid, intense letters. She had also been befriended by a childless Hoxton couple, Mr. and Mrs. Clare, who lent her books, encouraged her to study, and introduced her to Fanny Blood, a girl to whom Mary soon became very devoted.

In 1778 Mary took a job as paid companion to a Mrs. Dawson, a formidable widow who divided her time between Bath and Windsor. In 1782 she was recalled to her home to nurse her dying mother, after which her father rapidly remarried and left for Wales. Mary subsequently had to live with the Bloods until she was again recalled to nurse her sister Eliza, who was suffering a breakdown after the birth of her child. Mary decided to rescue her sister from her unhappy marriage, and took her to Hackney, where they lived under assumed names. Eliza's baby died and her marriage was wrecked, for which she later blamed

elementary atoms. In the field of optics, he provided microscopists with the camera lucida and the Wollaston doublet, and he developed concavo-convex lenses for the purposes of oculists.

He was elected a Fellow of the Royal Society in 1793, and became its secretary in 1804, serving until 1816. He enjoyed most of all the company of his fellow scientists and was a great friend and confidant of Sir Humphry Davy (q.v.). In later years the certainty and deliberation with which he tackled scientific problems seemed to denote an aura of infallibility and this earned him the nickname 'Pope Wollaston'. He was appointed to work on several royal commissions, including the one that opposed the adoption of the decimal system of weights and measures (1819), and the imperial gallon measure adopted by parliament in 1824 stemmed from one of his proposals. On learning, in 1827, that he was dying of a brain tumour he took steps to ensure that his previously unrecorded work was gathered together, and much of this was published posthumously. As a token of respect for his

Mary. Meanwhile, however, they decided to start a school with Fanny at Islington, but this failed when no pupils could be found. Her third sister, Everina, joined them and they moved to Newington Green, where their school was more successful and where Mary began her interest in radical politics.

In January 1785 Fanny left for Lisbon to marry Hugh Skeys, a businessman she had known for some years. Mary languished at Newington for a time, before deciding that her place was in Lisbon with Fanny, who was already pregnant and far from well. In November Mary arrived to find Fanny in labour and dying of consumption. The baby died also, and in their great grief Mary and Skeys were drawn together and became lifelong friends.

Returning to England in 1786, Mary resolved to send Fanny Blood's parents to their son George in Ireland. The £10 needed for this was an advance from the publisher Joseph Johnson, later to become her kindest benefactor, on her first book *Thoughts on the Education of Daughters*. Influenced as much by the Dissenters as by Rousseau, this book inveighs equally against the evils of cosmetics and of learning by rote. Most impressively it sets out the pitiful position of women with no means of support save the career of teacher or governess, but it slips into religious platitudes about the benefits of adversity.

Mary now took a job as governess to the children of Viscount Kingsborough in Ireland. Unfortunately, mutual jealousy and Mary's proud resentment of her inferior position led to friction with Caroline, Lady Kingsborough, who dismissed her after a year. Out of work and in need of money, Mary was rescued by Johnson, her publisher, for whom she proceeded to work on the *Analytical Review*, brainchild of Thomas Christie and the first magazine to consist almost entirely of book reviews. She also wrote *Original Stories*, about the poverty and suffering around her – the second edition of this work was illustrated by William Blake – and she did translations for Johnson from the French and the German. In 1788, too, her first novel *Mary* was published, a largely autobiographical work containing biting satire of the Kingsboroughs.

While working for Johnson, Mary conceived a grand but unrequited passion for his friend, the artist and writer Henry Fuseli (q.v.). Rebuffed, she was forced to find an outlet elsewhere. Her opportunity was the French Revolution, which she and her Dissenting friends hailed rapturously. Burke's *Reflections on the Revolution in France* (1790) cleverly and convincingly condemned the revolutionary movement. In zealous fury, Mary immediately wrote an inspired, if somewhat ill-planned answer to Burke, *A Vindication of the Rights of Man*. It was popular and brought her fame.

In 1791 Mary met William Godwin (q.v.) for the first time. In January 1792 she published *A Vindication of the Rights of Woman*, in which she argued that women are human before they are sexual and deserve and demand economic independence. She favoured co-educational day schools, serious sex education, and the revision of women's legal position.

In December 1792 Mary decided to visit Paris alone, and there she became part of a small clique of English Dissenters. In 1793, with the outbreak of the Anglo-French war, most Revolutionary sympathizers found their way to Paris, Godwin sending them his newly-published *Political Justice* to support them, though the street riots and the Reign of Terror just beginning were scarcely the freedom of which they dreamed. Food became scarce and foreigners aroused suspicion and were prevented from leaving France. In April Mary took up with Gilbert Imlay, an American army captain and a mediocre writer, and fell passionately in love with him. Scorning marriage, she had a rapturous affair with Imlay at Neuilly but, finding herself pregnant, she returned to Paris, where she escaped arrest only because Imlay had registered her as his wife at the American Embassy. Soon, however, he went to Le Havre, leaving her in Paris to her pregnancy and her new book, *A Historical and Moral View of the French Revolution*. In January 1794, in financial straits, she joined him at Le Havre, where their daughter Fanny was born on 14 May and where they lived on for another three months until Gilbert abandoned her, departing to London.

Mary came to Imlay in London in 1795, but he now had a new mistress. Although he was exercising the freedom she had always admired, she found her position very hard to bear and attempted suicide with an overdose of laudanum. Imlay now persuaded her to go to Scandinavia on business for him, and she complied, sailing with Fanny from Hull in June 1795. She returned to find him living with yet another woman. Again she tried suicide, by jumping from Putney Bridge. Unconscious, she was rescued by two watermen and won a little grudging sympathy from Imlay, who, however, soon left her for the last time and returned to Paris. Recovering her stamina, she set to work and published a travel book of her letters from Scandinavia, which won much praise. At last she forgot Imlay and returned to her old life.

In April 1796 Mary again met Godwin, now at the height of his fame. She moved into a theatrical circle that included Mrs. Siddons and John Philip Kemble (qq.v.) and began work on another novel, never to be finished, called *Maria, or the Wrongs of Woman*, a series of case histories containing an outspoken assertion that women had sexual feelings and rights.

In July 1796 Mary became Godwin's mistress. They quarrelled and were reconciled often, until Mary's panic on discovering her second pregnancy forced Godwin to abandon his principles, and he married her on 29 March 1797 at St. Pancras. They still bickered, but by August had reached a state of happy domesticity, and on 30 August their daughter Mary was born. But infection set in, causing septicaemia and general blood poisoning, and on 10 September 1797, twelve days after the birth, she died. She was buried at St. Pancras, where Godwin's stone still stands, but her body was subsequently moved to Bournemouth.

Mary's daughter Fanny, rejected by her aunts and finding life with Godwin and his new family intolerable, committed suicide at the age of twenty-two; her second daughter, Mary, married the poet Shelley (see Shelley, Mary). Godwin published his *Memoir* of his wife in 1798. Mary Wollstonecraft was a courageous visionary who endured opposition, ridicule, and humiliation to speak up for the justice for women that she believed in, but her ideas were widely regarded as a bogy of revolution and atheism for more than a century.

E. V. Lucas (ed.), *Original Stories from Real Life* (1906).

Clair Tomlin, *The Life and Death of Mary Wollstonecraft* (1974).

R. M. Wardle (ed.), *Godwin and Mary: Letters of William Godwin and Mary Wollstonecraft* (Lawrence, Kansas, 1866).

R. M. Wardle, *Mary Wollstonecraft* (Lawrence, Kansas, 1952).

Portrait: oil, half-length, by J. Opie: N.P.G.

Wordsworth, William (1770–1850), Romantic poet.

William Wordsworth was born at Cockermouth in Cumberland on 7 April 1770, the second son of John

Wordsworth, an attorney. His mother died in 1778, and his father died in 1783. William, his three brothers, and his sister, Dorothy, were placed under the reluctant guardianship of two uncles, and William lived in Penrith in the house of his grandparents. In contrast to the uneasy atmosphere of his new home, Wordsworth greatly enjoyed his schooldays at Hawkshead grammar school, which he attended as a boarder. Under the tutorship of William Taylor he supplemented his knowledge of Shakespeare and Milton by a wide reading of contemporary poetry. In 1787 he entered St. John's College, Cambridge. The sudden change of environment from familiar countryside to the busy confusion of the university was more than the young Wordsworth was able to adapt to, and it was in a mood of nostalgia that he began to write his first poem to be published, 'An Evening Walk'. A walking tour with a friend through France, Italy, and Switzerland in the long vacation of 1790 furnished material for 'Descriptive Sketches'. Both these poems, published in 1793, are written in the established conventions of eighteenth-century verse but contain passages that indicate Wordsworth's later revolt against this style.

Wordsworth gained a B.A. degree in January 1791. In the following winter he travelled in France, and met Annette Vallon, the daughter of a surgeon in Blois, who in December 1792 gave birth to his illegitimate daughter, Caroline. He also came under the influence of Michael Beaupuy, a young officer stationed in Blois, who introduced him to the doctrine of republicanism. His return to England in late 1792 (necessitated by his uncles' demands and by his own lack of money) was undertaken with deep regret.

For a short period Wordsworth was attracted to the ideas of William Godwin (q.v.), whose *Political Justice* (1793) advocated the virtues of dispassionate reason and severe emotional restraint. With neither home nor means of livelihood, and with his affections irreconcilably divided between England and France, Wordsworth endured the unhappiest period of his life, until a legacy in January 1795 enabled him to join with Dorothy in establishing a home at Racedown in Dorset. There he became acquainted with Samuel Taylor Coleridge (q.v.). In 1797 Wordsworth and his sister moved to a house at Alfoxden, in the Quantock Hills overlooking the Bristol Channel, in order to be nearer to Coleridge's own house at Nether Stowey. There the two poets collaborated on a book of poems published anonymously in September 1798 as *Lyrical Ballads*, which included the well-known 'Lines written above Tintern Abbey'.

The first edition carried only a brief advertisement by Wordsworth to explain the attempt to discover how far ordinary spoken language 'is adapted to the purposes of poetic pleasure'. The second, enlarged edition of January 1801 contained Wordsworth's famous Preface which is widely recognized as a manifesto for the romantic movement in general: in place of 'the gaudiness and inane phraseology' of declining eighteenth-century conventions, there was now to be offered a description of the common incidents of life 'in a selection of language really used by men', as based upon the simple but dignified concept of the poet as 'a man speaking to men'.

In September 1798, on the eve of the publication of *Lyrical Ballads*, the Wordsworths travelled with Coleridge to Germany. Later parting from Coleridge they spent the winter of 1798–9 at Goslar. The series of poems known as the 'Lucy' poems, written at Goslar, represent the most extreme development of Wordsworth's use of simple language to suggest deep emotion. He also began writing his greatest poem, *The Prelude*. Planned as a series of separate books, it is an autobiographical account of 'the growth of a poet's mind', sustained throughout by Wordsworth's psychological insight and powerful memory, and celebrating the universal harmony between the life of man and the processes of nature. The poem was not finished until 1805, and not published until 1850, after Wordsworth's death.

On his return to England Wordsworth spent the late summer of 1799 at the farm of his friends the Hutchinsons by the River Tees, and renewed his childhood friendship with Mary Hutchinson. In December he moved into Dove Cottage at Grasmere in the Lake District; two years later (after a brief and dramatic visit to Calais to see Annette Vallon and his child), Wordsworth married Mary Hutchinson, and with Coleridge now living at near-by Greta Hall, the Lake community was complete. He now identified completely with the character and people of the Lake District; and the characters in 'Michael', 'Resolution and Independence', and many other poems, are all representative of the sturdy farmers and workers amongst whom Wordsworth lived, and his feelings for these characters derived from his belief that it is such ordinary, uneducated people whose lives reflect most purely the rhythms of nature.

He toured Scotland in 1801, visited Calais in 1802, and toured Scotland again in 1803, where he became the friend of Walter Scott. In 1807 he published the ode to 'Duty' and 'Ode on the Intimations of Immortality from Recollections of Early Childhood', in which he was already reflecting on the decline of his creative impetus: 'the visionary gleam' was gone, leaving the comfort only of 'the philosophic mind'. Set against the steady growth of his reputation were the private distresses caused by quarrels with Coleridge and by the deaths of friends; the drowning of his favourite brother John in 1805 caused him especial grief. In 1808 Wordsworth moved from Dove Cottage to a larger house at Allanbank; in 1813 he accepted the sinecure post of distributor of stamps for Westmorland, with an annual salary of £400, and moved to Rydal Mount, where he remained until his death. In 1843 he was made Poet Laureate.

Wordsworth's way of life came to be that of an Anglican and a Tory: he found comfort in regular church attendance, and because of his fear of the encroaching interests of industry and commerce he gave sincere support to the preservation of the existing social order. Throughout these years he continued to write poetry, but despite the excellence of some few of his later sonnets he was, in the eyes of the second generation of Romantic poets, a lost leader. He died aged eighty on 23 April 1850.

E. C. Batho, *The Later Wordsworth* (1933).
R. L. Brett and A. R. Jones (ed.), *Lyrical Ballads* (1963).

E. de Selincourt (ed.), *The Early Letters of William and Dorothy Wordsworth, 1787–1805* (1935; rev. by C. L. Shaver, 1967).

E. de Selincourt (ed.), *The Letters of William and Dorothy Wordsworth: The Middle Years* (2 vols.; 1937; rev. by M. Moorman and A. G. Hill, 1968).

E. de Selincourt (ed.), *The Letters of William and Dorothy Wordsworth: The Later Years* (3 vols.; 1939).

E. de Selincourt (ed.), *The Prelude* (1933; rev. by H. Darbishire, 1959; 2nd ed. corrected by S. Gill, 1970).

E. de Selincourt and H. Darbishire (eds.), *The Poetical Works of William Wordsworth* (5 vols.; 1940–9).

J. Jones, *The Egotistical Sublime: A History of Wordsworth's Imagination* (1954).

F. D. McConnell, *The Confessional Imagination* [a study of the *Prelude*] (1974).

M. C. Moorman, *William Wordsworth: A Biography* (2 vols.; 1957–65).

W. J. B. Owen (ed.), *Preface to Lyrical Ballads* (Copenhagen, 1957).

D. D. Perkins, *Wordsworth and the Poetry of Sincerity* (Cambridge, Mass., 1964).

S. Prickett, *Coleridge and Wordsworth: The Poetry of Growth* (1970).

C. Salvesen, *The Landscape of Memory: a Study of Wordsworth's Poetry* (1965).

F. M. Todd, *Politics and the Poet: A Study of Wordsworth* (1957).

Portraits: oil, full-length, by H. W. Pickersgill: St. John's College, Cambridge; pencil and chalk, half-length, by R. Hancock, 1798: N.P.G.; oil, three-quarter length, by B. R. Haydon, 1842: N.P.G.; oil on panel, quarter-length, by W. Boxall, 1831: N.P.G.; sketch, quarter-length, by H. Edridge: Dove Cottage, Grasmere.

Wright, Joseph (1734–97), painter.

Joseph Wright was born on 3 September 1734 in Derby, the youngest son of an attorney. His twin interests in art and mechanics first developed while he was attending Derby Grammar School, where as well as making sketches of the local assize court, he constructed models of spinning wheels, guns, and theatres. In 1751 he was sent to London to study painting under Thomas Hudson (also the teacher of Sir Joshua Reynolds); he returned to Derby in 1753, went back to Hudson for a brief period in 1756, and finally settled in Derby in 1758. Wright exhibited several portraits of members of the local hunt in Derby town hall, and in some other portraits that he painted by candle light he was already experimenting with effects of light and shade.

In 1765 Wright held his first London exhibition at the Society of Artists. Over half of the thirty-one pictures that Wright painted in the next eight years were of candle-lit or firelit scenes, and paintings such as *The Experiment with the Air Pump* (1768) had an important influence in their departure from traditional subject matter. In 1773, in company with his newly-married wife, Ann Swift, he travelled to Italy. There he made so many sketches of the frescoes by Michelangelo in the Sistine Chapel that his health suffered from overwork. Also in Italy Wright witnessed the eruption of Vesuvius, a violent and dramatic spectacle that he was to recreate during the next four years in eighteen separate pictures.

On his return to England in 1775, Wright settled briefly in Bath, where he hoped to succeed Gainsborough as the leading painter of society portraits. His own domestic style of portraiture was very different from that of Gainsborough and Reynolds, however, and because the fashion was not in his favour he moved back to Derby after only two years. From 1778 to 1782 he exhibited annually at the Royal Academy, most of his paintings during these years being of Italian scenes. In 1781 he was elected an associate of the Academy, and three years later a full academician, but he declined the latter honour because of his increasing anger at the way his pictures were being hung. A private exhibition of his paintings was held at a friend's house in Covent Garden in 1785, and after a further complaint against the Academy in 1794 – when his pictures were left on the floor and damaged by passing feet – it was too late for the breach between Wright and the Academy to be healed.

Wright's health had been consistently poor since he had exhausted himself by too much work during his visit to Italy; after a further deterioration he died in Derby on 29 August 1797. Among his closest friends were such prominent figures as Josiah Wedgwood (q.v.) and the physician, botanist, and poet Erasmus Darwin. But because of his modesty and deep attachment to the countryside of Derbyshire Wright always retained the admiration of his local community. His paintings, whose most original aspects have much in common with the new ideas of the Romantic movement, are characterized above all by qualities of integrity and poetic realism.

W. Bemrose, *The Life and Works of Joseph Wright* (1885).
B. Nicolson, *Joseph Wright of Derby* (1968).

Works in:
Art Gallery, Derby.

Portrait: self-portrait, oil, quarter-length: N.P.G.

Wyatt, James (1746–1813), architect.

James Wyatt was born on 3 August 1746 at Burton Constable, Staffordshire, the sixth of the seven sons of Benjamin Wyatt, farmer, timber-merchant, architect, and builder. He was sent to a local school, and his skill in drawing was noticed by Lord Bagot, Ambassador to the Pope, who took the fourteen-year-old boy with him to Rome, where he stayed four years and caused amazement by, among other exploits, risking a 300-foot fall to make scale drawings of the dome of St. Peter's. He moved to Venice for a further two years, where he studied architectural painting under Viscentini, and returned to London in 1766.

In 1770 Wyatt was elected an Associate of the Royal Academy and began work on converting the Oxford Street Pantheon into a theatre. Said to have been inspired by Santa Sophia at Constantinople, it was burnt down in 1792, but it was such a success in its short life that Wyatt's popularity was assured. Soon after this Wyatt was invited to become court architect to the Empress Catherine of Russia, but was paid £1,200 by a group of noblemen to stay in England. He built many Graeco-Italian mansions – notably Heaton House, near Manchester – remarkable for their interior comfort, and in 1776 he was appointed surveyor of Westminster Abbey.

Wyatt's style became gradually more Gothic. His first 'modern' Gothic design was Lee Priory near Canterbury, and he went on to make restorations at Salisbury, Lichfield, Durham, and Hereford Cathedrals, which were severely criticized by medievalists. In 1795 he built the sensationally extravagant Fonthill Abbey, and in 1796 the Royal Military College at Woolwich. In the same year he succeeded Chambers as Surveyor-General to the Board of Works; this led to appointments at the House of Lords and by George III at Windsor Castle. He worked hard and exhibited many designs at the Academy, becoming a full academician in 1785 and temporary president in 1805.

Among his other commissions, Wyatt added wings to Chiswick House, built a 'strange, castellated palace' at Kew, designed the front of White's Club in St. James's Street, built Ashridge Castle, Hertfordshire, and designed mausoleums at Cobham and Brocklesby.

As Wyatt was travelling from Bath to London on 4 September 1813, his carriage was overturned near Marlborough. He was killed instantly. He was buried at Westminster Abbey on 28 September, leaving a widow and four sons.

A stylistic weathercock, Wyatt had

technique, taste, and inventiveness, but he was an irresponsible architect, often letting his clients down, and his work was often shoddy and facile. Indeed the Great Tower at Fonthill collapsed only twenty-five years after its erection. He was even accused of plagiarism by the Adam brothers, and it was only at the very end of his life that his genius for severe and fastidious domestic architecture began to emerge. His elaborate Gothic work may be said to have bridged the gap between the rococo Gothic of the mid eighteenth century and the serious medievalism of the early nineteenth century.

A. Dale, *James Wyatt, Architect, 1746–1813* (1956, 2nd ed.).

Portrait: bronze bust, by J. C. F. Rossi: N.P.G.

Wyndham, Sir William (1687–1740), 3rd baronet; politician, and Jacobite sympathizer.

William Wyndham was born in 1687 at Orchard-Wyndham, Somerset, the only son of Sir Edward Wyndham, 2nd baronet. Educated at Eton and Christ Church, Oxford, Wyndham became M.P. for Somerset in 1710, a few months before the fall of the Whig government. The autumn election brought his party, the Tories, into office, and through court influence he joined the new administration. Promoted to Secretary at War in 1712, he was appointed Chancellor of the Exchequer in 1713. Before the end of the year Bolingbroke (see St. John, Henry, in *Lives of the Stuart Age*) and Wyndham were in the ascendant, but when the new parliament met in February 1714 the Tory majority was paralysed by its division into Hanoverian and Jacobite, and Wyndham's official career ended when, in the midst of party intrigues, Queen Anne died.

Two events, however, had already revealed Wyndham's political purpose. It was Bolingbroke's deliberate policy to secure absolute control of the executive pending the death of the Queen, and to this end Wyndham argued in favour of the Whig Steele's expulsion from the Commons. Wyndham was also sponsor of the Schism Act (1714). Ostensibly in defence of the Church, this closed the schools of the Dissenters, but the real motive was political, for Wyndham and his party had resolved to support the High Church and the Jacobites.

After the 1715 election Wyndham began his leadership of the opposition by objecting to the terms of the King's proclamation; only Walpole's tact saved him from the Tower. He was formally censured after a long debate during which he left with the whole of his party behind him. He contributed little in the ensuing debates on the impeachment of the Tory leaders, as he was plotting a rising in the west in favour of the Stuarts. He was arrested on 21 September 1715 at Orchard-Wyndham after the outbreak of the rebellion, escaped with a price of £1,000 on his head, and then surrendered on the advice of his father-in-law, the Duke of Somerset, upon which he was committed to the Tower. Somerset withdrew from the cabinet when Townshend persisted in Wyndham's arrest, resigning his office in a fury, since George I had promised him that Wyndham would not be arrested. Wyndham, liberated on bail in July 1716, never having been tried, was much blamed for raising the rebellion in Somerset and then running away from his responsibilities.

Committed to the Jacobite cause, Bolingbroke had fled to France in spring 1715, and now Wyndham as his mouthpiece was labouring assiduously in England for the reinstatement of the High Church and its principles. Wyndham's

Jacobite sympathies, however, gave rise to the suspicion with which the impotent Tory party was long viewed. Bolingbroke wrote of his disgust with James, urging Wyndham to abandon the Jacobites; then in 1717 he followed this with his famous apology. By 1726 Bolingbroke was at Twickenham, while in parliament Wyndham, under Bolingbroke's instructions, was co-operating with Pulteney (q.v.) in the Commons to attack Walpole's policies.

In 1728 the formation of an organized opposition, with Wyndham leading the Tory wing, and Bolingbroke in the background, gave Walpole considerable trouble. In one particularly caustic speech Wyndham attacked Walpole during the discussion of the Septennial Act (1734). Walpole replied, attacking Bolingbroke violently, so that the latter's dream of a Tory–Whig opposition led by himself through Wyndham was now doomed. The 1735 election renewed the Whig majority; Bolingbroke again left England, and Wyndham now led the opposition with diminished vigour.

In his last years Wyndham supported the Prince of Wales in the quarrel over his allowance, and opposed a convention with Spain. He died on 17 June 1740 at Wells, following a hunting accident.

Portrait: oil, full-length, by J. Richardson, 1713–14: N.P.G.

Young, Edward (1683–1765), poet.

Edward Young was born at Upham, near Winchester, where he was baptized on 3 July 1683. He was the son of Edward Young, then the local rector, but later Dean of Salisbury and a royal chaplain.

Young was educated at Winchester College, and in 1702 he became a commoner at New College, Oxford, moving later to Corpus Christi College. In 1705 Young's father died, and in 1708 Archbishop Tenison, out of respect for the late Dean Young's memory, gave his son an All Souls law fellowship. This may not have been entirely deserved; Pope maintained that Young was 'a foolish youth, the sport of peers and poets'.

In 1711 Young's friend Thomas Tickell introduced him to Addison (q.v.) and his literary set. Always an ambitious man, Young now realized that he could earn preferment with his pen. Accordingly, he launched upon a series of unashamedly flattering verse epistles addressed to the famous and influential, especially such important Tories as Lord Lansdowne; however, he took due care not to upset the Whigs either, and both Addison and Steele (q.v.) printed pieces by him. Fortunately, Young had enough self-respect to suppress these works later.

Young's tireless place-seeking paid dividends in 1715 when he accepted a pension of £200 from Philip, Duke of Wharton. In 1719 Young's play *Busiris* was produced at Drury Lane and was deemed a great success, running for nine nights. In 1721 Young stood unsuccessfully as parliamentary candidate for Cirencester, and his disappointment was increased by the cool reception given to his tragedy *The Revenge*, a bombastic reworking of *Othello*. Lord Wharton had become dilatory in paying Young's pension, and in 1725 Wharton left England for good, leaving his protégé to fend for himself.

That same year the undismayed Young began publishing *The Universal Passion*, a series of satires which, though uneven and sometimes obscure, in many respects anticipated Pope's satirical verse by their brilliance and wit. Not only did Young earn a reputed £3,000 from these poems, but by dedicating each one to a famous public figure, he made a lot of useful friends also, including Bubb Dodington, and Walpole who in 1726 paid him a £200 pension. Young did not shrink from flattering even the highest, and in 1728 dedicated an ode to the newly-crowned George II.

For all this, preferment did not come, and Young turned his attention to the Church. He quickly took orders, and in late 1728 was fortunate enough to be appointed a royal chaplain. Eager to study theology, he sought the advice of Pope, who recommended Thomas Aquinas. Young then retired to 'an obscure place in the suburbs' to read Aquinas's complete works; Pope called six months later, to find Young on the brink of 'a derangement' brought on by his studies.

In 1730 Young was at last given a comfortable living, Welwyn, worth £300 a year, and the following May he married Lady Elizabeth Lee. He proved a conscientious pastor, endowing a charity school and building a new steeple, but had practically ceased writing. In 1736, however, his stepdaughter died during a family trip to France, and in 1741 his wife died also.

Long brooding on these personal tragedies drove Young to write *Night Thoughts on Life, Death and Immortality*, which was published in 1742. Though a laboured and gloomy work, littered with such epigrams as 'Procrastination is the thief of time', and containing some of the worst rhymes in English literature, *Night Thoughts* nevertheless showed sparks of genius, and was a great and enduring popular success, if not an artistic one.

Content with his new-found reputation as a religious poet, and despairing of his latest patron, the unreliable Prince of Wales, Young retired to his Welwyn home, ruled over by the redoubtable Miss Caroline Hallows, his housekeeper. In 1753 he dug out his play *The Brothers*, written decades earlier, and gave the proceeds of its Drury Lane production to the Society for the Propagation of the Gospel. His lively epistle on 'Original Composition', published in 1759, greatly impressed Diderot and the German poets of Klopstock's school. Young's ode 'Resignation', written in 1762 to console Admiral Boscawen's widow, typifies the most poignant strain in his writing, his profound sense of disappointment with life. Edward Young died on 5 April 1765 at Welwyn.

J. Nichols (ed.), *Complete Works of Edward Young* (2 vols.; 1854).

H. Pettit (ed.), *Correspondence of Edward Young* (1970).

H. C. Shelley, *The Life and Letters of Young* (1914).

C. V. Wickler, *Edward Young and the Fear of Death* (Albuquerque, 1952).

Young, Thomas (1773–1829), physicist, physician, and Egyptologist.

Born on 13 June 1773 at Milverton, Somerset, Young was the youngest of ten children. Educated mainly at home, he displayed prodigious and precocious talent in languages, ancient literature, and mathematics. He spent part of his teens as a private tutor to Hudson Gurney, a gentleman from Youngsbury, Hertfordshire. At the age of nineteen, however, he decided to study medicine, entering St. Bartholomew's Hospital, London, in 1792. While a student there he submitted a paper to the Royal Society on the muscle fibres of the eye, which so impressed the Society that he was elected a Fellow (1794). Shortly afterwards Young moved to Scotland to continue his medical studies at the University of Edinburgh, but in 1795 he went to Göttingen, and in the following year obtained his first M.D.

On his return to England Young entered Emmanuel College, Cambridge, as a fellow commoner (1797), but he did not qualify for his second M.D. until 1808. His uncle, Dr. Richard Brocklesby, had died in 1797, the year that Young entered Cambridge. His will provided his nephew with a modest fortune, permitting him to pursue less scientific interests with relative financial freedom.

In 1800 Young began his medical practice in London. During the next three years he submitted papers to the Royal Society on his theories of light and colour. These included some of his most startling discoveries, including the concept of the interference of light. His discovery of this phenomenon, by passing light through a pair of very narrow slits – 'Young's Slits' – was crucial to the final establishment of the wave theory of light. Another area of investigation was the elasticity of materials subjected to strain. The result of this work was the well-known ratio bearing his name – Young's modulus.

Young held the post of Professor of Natural Philosophy at the Royal Institution from 1801 to 1803, during which time he delivered a series of nearly 100 lectures (published in 1807). He resigned this position subsequently because he felt it conflicted with his medical practice. For similar professional reasons most of his non-medical papers were published anonymously.

In June 1804 Young had married Eliza Maxwell. Earlier the same year he submitted a paper to the Royal Society on his theory of capillary attraction and the 'cohesion of fluids'. During the next few years he wrote extensively for the *Encyclopaedia Britannica*, providing them with seventeen scientific articles and forty-six biographies.

He also wrote the entry on Egypt, and in many respects it is Young, and not the French scholar Champollion, who deserves the title 'Father of modern Egyptology'. His *Encyclopaedia Britannica* article, which appeared in 1824, reflects a long-standing interest in the subject, and the first authoritative and popular English essay on it. The Rosetta Stone, the key to the entire discipline of Egyptology as we now know it, came to Britain in 1801. Young brought what amounted to a touch of genius to its deciphering – genius which paved the way for the unveiling of several mysteries concerning Ancient Egyptian. By 1814 he had translated the demotic text; he was to spend the next few years working on the hieroglyphic scripts.

Young was appointed Secretary to the Board of Longitude and placed in charge of the Nautical Almanac in 1818. He died on 10 May 1829.

Thomas Young was a man of extraordinarily wide accomplishments, and during his career he wrote papers on a great variety of subjects. He was the first to show that tiny muscles in the eye change the shape and curvature of the crystalline lens, permitting visual focus at different distances. He was the first to suggest that colour vision is possible because of three distinct types of nerve ending in the retina, responding respectively to red, green, and violet light. He described astigmatism. He wrote on the haemadynamic functions of the heart and arteries, and (in 1813) published *An Introduction to Medical Literature, Including a System of Practical Nosology*. The breadth of his interests undoubtedly entitles him to a place among the greatest polymaths; as one of his biographers, in summing up Young's contributions to physical science, has stated: 'His works are noted for their highly philosophical spirit, and in particular by the constancy with which they keep in view the distinction between *beings* and *actions*; a distinction too often lost sight of in crude theories of physics.'

G. Peacock, *Life of Thomas Young* (1885).
R. W. Pohl, 'Discovery of Interference by Thomas Young', *American Journal of Physics*, 28 (1960).
H. B. Williams, *Thomas Young* (1930).
Alexander Wood, *Thomas Young* (1954).

Young Pretender, The (1720–88), see Charles Edward Louis Philip Casimir Stuart.

Z

Zoffany, Zoffanji, or Zaffanii, Johann or John (1734–1810), German-born painter.

Johann Zoffany was born in Frankfurt-am-Main in 1734, the son of the architect to the Prince of Tours. His ancestry may have been partly Hungarian.

Zoffany studied for a short time at Ratisbon under Martin Speer, but at the age of thirteen he ran away to Rome, remaining in Italy for twelve years. After a brief return to Germany, he came to England in about 1760.

An Italian well-wisher rescued Zoffany from the extreme poverty of his early months in London by finding him employment with Stephen Rimbault, an eminent clockmaker; a few months later Zoffany himself found work as assistant to a drapery painter, Benjamin West, a job in which his own artistic talents could be more usefully employed. In the course of time he became friendly with David Garrick (q.v.) through whom he became established as a professional artist, and by 1762 he had gained membership of the Society of Artists. His success was based on his many paintings of theatrical scenes, a genre pioneered by William Hogarth but fully developed by Zoffany in such pictures as *The Clandestine Marriage* and *Garrick in The Farmer's Return*. Garrick himself proved an influential patron, fully aware of the publicity he could exploit from these paintings, and in 1769 Zoffany was elected to membership of the Royal Academy.

The fashion for theatrical scenes declined around 1770, but having gained an introduction to the royal family Zoffany had continued success with portraits and domestic scenes. A plan to accompany Sir Joseph Banks on Captain Cook's second voyage of exploration fell through because of a dispute over inadequate accommodation, and in 1772 Zoffany travelled instead to Italy with a commission from Queen Charlotte to paint the *Tribuna of the Uffizi Gallery, Florence*; from here he continued to Vienna, where he painted several portraits of the imperial family and was created a baron of the Austrian empire by the Empress Maria Theresa. Other honours gained by Zoffany on this tour included membership of the academies of Bologna, Tuscany, and Parma.

On his return to England Zoffany continued his successful and prolific career as a painter of portraits and lively domestic

scenes in the style of Hogarth. He was fortunate in that his own talents coincided with contemporary fashion, and though his paintings have little original artistic merit, they remain valuable to the historian as accurate records of costume and manners. In 1783 Zoffany travelled to India, where he stayed for lengthy periods at Calcutta and Lucknow and painted several portraits of the local gentry and Indian hunting scenes. He returned to England in 1790. *Charles Towneley Among His Marbles* is perhaps the most notable of his later works, but by now his ability was waning and despite his continued work he could produce little to enhance his reputation. Zoffany, now a wealthy man, lived out his final years in considerable comfort, and died at Strand-on-the-Green in Middlesex on 11 November 1810.

Lady V. Manners and G. C. Williamson, *John Zoffany, R.A.: his Life and Works* (1920).

O. Millar, *Zoffany and His Tribuna* (1967).

E. K. Waterhouse, *Painting in Britain 1530–1790* (1962).

Works in:
National Gallery.
National Portrait Gallery.
Tate Gallery.
Royal Collection.
The Garrick Club, London.

Portraits: self-portrait, oil, half-length, 1761: N.P.G.; self-portrait, pencil, quarter-length: N.P.G.

INDEX

References in **bold type** indicate a main entry

CLASSIFIED INDEX